HORACE: ODES

BOOK 1

A COMMENTARY ON
HORACE : ODES
BOOK 1

BY

R. G. M. NISBET

*Fellow of Corpus Christi College
Oxford*

AND

MARGARET HUBBARD

*Fellow of St. Anne's College
Oxford*

OXFORD
AT THE CLARENDON PRESS

Oxford University Press, Ely House, London W. 1

GLASGOW NEW YORK TORONTO MELBOURNE WELLINGTON
CAPE TOWN IBADAN NAIROBI DAR ES SALAAM LUSAKA ADDIS ABABA
DELHI BOMBAY CALCUTTA MADRAS KARACHI LAHORE DACCA
KUALA LUMPUR SINGAPORE HONG KONG TOKYO

ISBN 0 19 814439 3

First Published 1970
Reprinted (with corrections) 1975

Printed in Great Britain
at the University Press, Oxford
by Vivian Ridler
Printer to the University

PREFACE

THE *Odes* of Horace, in spite of all their popularity, are unusually liable to misinterpretation. The standard commentaries, though they often explain the meaning of the words, tend to be less illuminating on the wider issues. The obvious exception is Heinze's revision of Kiessling, but even that is short in scale, as well as being now forty years old. The modern interest in literary history finds expression, for the most part, in articles and general studies. It becomes all the more necessary, and all the more difficult, to write new commentaries.

We are greatly indebted to our predecessors; here it will be enough to single out Lambinus, Bentley, Mitscherlich, Peerlkamp, Orelli–Hirschfelder, Keller and Holder, Lucian Müller, Kiessling–Heinze. We tried to read as much periodical literature as we could, but like others before us were defeated by its bulk. Many recent articles on Horace are strangely implausible; these are usually left unrefuted. Others, though deserving or innocuous, could find no mention in a book already overloaded. Sometimes, it may be assumed, a theory is ignored because we never heard of it. To our regret we could take no account of work that appeared after July 1968.

Horace has suffered from undiscriminating praise even more than other ancient writers. This seems the wrong attitude towards so astringent a poet, and we have occasionally suggested that some odes may be better than others. Our irreverence will be regarded by some as Philistinism; we can only say that if we had not regarded Horace as a great poet we could not have borne to write about him. But though we have waged war on the Panglosses of classical studies, we do not expect to please the literary critics either. We do not rule out the possibility of serious literary criticism on a Latin poet, but we had neither the confidence nor the time to take on the job ourselves.

We have cited a large number of parallel passages, many of which we believe to be new. It is easy to misunderstand this procedure: classical scholars must seem a strange breed of pedants who refuse to admit that life is short unless they can find ten parallels to prove it. In fact we are trying to show how a very literary poet takes over themes conventional in various genres and adapts them to his new idiom. We also believe that many problems, both large and small, can be illuminated by the collection of evidence, and that without such evidence the most ingenious theorizing is often misdirected. We hope that our stores may be found serviceable by commentators on other works of ancient literature.

It would have been pointless to undertake any original work on the manuscripts, even if we had thought ourselves competent to do so; such an enterprise would naturally involve Horace's poems as a whole and not just a single book. In any case further research, while it would increase our understanding of early medieval scholarship, would probably make no difference to our decisions on what Horace wrote. The manuscripts divide into two groups, whose composition shifts from book to book and crux to crux; the significant divergences are presumably ancient, and not to be settled by constructing *stemmata*, weighing scholiasts, or triumphantly citing the lost Blandinianus. We have not even printed an existing text, though a commentary without the poems may seem a trifle austere; but it was represented to us that many people would prefer to consult the notes in a separate volume. We have included a brief account of the ancient commentators, to help the reader to find his bearings. But we are conscious that progress in this area must depend on detailed work, which we have not done, on scholia in general.

We owe much to the help of our friends. We should not have begun at all but for the insistence of Professor Sir Roger Mynors; we are grateful for his encouragement and support. Mr. A. F. Wells was originally a partner in our enterprise, *anima qualem non candidiorem terra tulit*; we should like our book to be thought of as a tribute to his memory. Mr. D. A. Russell read the whole of the completed commentary, Mr. J. Griffin a considerable part; both made valuable suggestions, and removed regrettable mistakes. Dr. S. Weinstock helped us generously on some aspects of Roman religion. Mr. F. A. Lepper kindly offered to read the proofs: his corrections are not confined to misprints. At a late stage Professor R. G. Austin and Professor Hugh Lloyd-Jones suggested further improvements;

we only wish we had consulted them earlier. We are indebted in various ways to Dr. E. K. Borthwick, Mr. E. L. Bowie, Mrs. M. Griffin, Dr. A. Joseph, Mrs. A. Lonsdale, Miss G. M. Matthews, Mr. O. Murray, Mrs. E. Patterson, and Mr. L. P. Wilkinson. We have also benefited from discussions with many pupils, both graduates and undergraduates. Nor have we forgotten the Delegates of the Press, who accepted our book, or the officials who saw it through.

One debt remains to be acknowledged. Like many of our generation we owe to Eduard Fraenkel our whole approach to ancient literature, and in particular to Horace. He has always taken a sympathetic interest in our work, and lent us his books freely; if we have shown him nothing of what we have written, it is because we wish to remain as independent as we can. He will often find us guilty of plagiarism, sometimes of recalcitrance. We must trust to his magnanimity to forgive us for both.

M. H.

R. G. M. N.

Oxford
December 1968

CONTENTS

INTRODUCTION

1. THE *ODES* AND THEIR LITERARY FORM

T H E *Odes* of Horace are too familiar to be easily understood. They have been the most important single influence on European lyric verse, not only the proclaimed models of a Ronsard or a Herrick, but the unacknowledged source of many poetic themes. But there are important differences between the ancient and modern ways of writing poetry, and since the Romantic movement the gap has been widened by ideological disagreement, disconcerting even when recognized. The present sketch is an attempt to suggest some of the more distinctive qualities of the Horatian ode. Yet it is dangerous to generalize about a hundred self-contained and remarkably varied entities: the ideas of poets cannot be summarized without consideration of context and occasion. The unit of discussion must remain the individual ode, and an account of each will be found in the commentary. The most that can be done here is to provide signposts and cross-references.

One of the most striking characteristics of a classical poet is his awareness of his literary pedigree. In Greece the categories of poetry were sharply divided according to function, and each had its own conventions of dialect, metre. and style. The scholarly Alexandrians naturally cultivated the traditional manners, while the Romans from the start tried to reproduce the forms of the Greeks. Yet the nature of this imitation can easily be misrepresented. The poet obeys the *lex operis*, the rules of the genre; to do otherwise would be a breach of literary decorum (an obsolete concept in the twentieth century). In particular he imitates familiar passages of illustrious predecessors: thus Horace borrows from Alcaeus to proclaim that he is writing lyric, and Persius borrows from Horace to proclaim that he is writing satire. Such allusions are not displays of private erudition, but acknowledgements of a shared culture; associations and contrasts are suggested to the reader's mind without waste of words. But one must establish one's independence as well as one's allegiance, and the Roman poets rightly claimed originality even while they flaunted their borrowings (1. 26. 10 n.). They speak mainly of the technical difficulty of transferring alien metres and standards of finish to their intractable language, but in fact they achieved much more. Though the subject-matter of poetry was traditional, that did not limit the poet's freedom, but rather let him concentrate on what mattered. He saw it as his business to express the old truisms in a modern, Roman setting and an original, personal idiom.

Horace claimed that his odes were modelled on Alcaeus (1. 1. 34, 1. 26. 11, 1. 32. 5, *epist.* 1. 19. 29), and his admirers have always been ready to believe him (*epist.* 2. 2. 99 'discedo Alcaeus puncto illius'). As one would expect from ancient literary theorizing, the most conspicuous aspects of the borrowing concern technique rather than attitude of mind. Apart from other metrical imitations (as in the Greater Asclepiad), Horace uses the Alcaic stanza in over a third of his lyric poems, though by his greater use of long words and long syllables (p. xl) he produces a weightier impression. He operates within the same categories as Alcaeus and uses many of the same commonplaces; the vigorous rhetoric and masculine incisiveness of the best political odes must also have seemed reminiscent of his model. Even so, the poems that at first sight look most Alcaic turn out to be quite original (1. 9, 1. 10, 1. 14; cf. also p. 58); elsewhere the borrowing is confined to a 'motto' in the same metre as the source (1. 18. 1, 1. 37. 1, 3. 12. 1). The differences between the two poets are in fact more illuminating than the resemblances. Alcaeus's verses, even if less spontaneous than they pretend, at least reflect the loves and hates of a forthright aristocrat; they were capable of being sung on social occasions, whether a symposium or a religious festival; they were straightforward in theme and diction, and could be appreciated by ordinary men. Horace, on the other hand, is an unpolitical poet composing for a reading public; the situations which he describes are imaginary, or at any rate stylized; his literary sophistication is remote from the simplicities of archaic Greek lyric. The Roman poets, like those who write about them, attached too much significance to the 'inventor of the genre', by which they meant the first poet in a particular manner whose writings had survived. Horace's debt to Alcaeus is like Virgil's to Hesiod, a matter not so much of intellectual standpoint as of contrived reminiscence.

The influence of other monodic Greek poets may be dismissed more briefly. Horace uses the Sapphic stanza repeatedly, but this means little: so also had Alcaeus. He once speaks of Sappho herself with unaccustomed warmth (4. 9. 10 ff.); this is simply the trick of style, frequent for instance in Longinus, by which one imitates the writer one is talking about (so 4. 2. 5 ff. on Pindar). Horace's cool and worldly realism has little in common with the enthusiasms of post-Romantic scholarship; like the shades in the underworld (2. 13. 30 ff.) he rightly found Alcaeus more interesting. Sappho's taste for the intense and the beautiful lay behind a different poetical tradition, that of the neoterics and love-elegists, but when Horace writes in this manner his purpose is usually derisive (1. 13). He must have felt a greater affinity with the unobtrusive elegance of Anacreon: he catches his spirit admirably in 1. 23 ('vitas inuleo'), and the symposium in 1. 27 starts with a dressed-up allusion ('pugnare Thracum est'). He also owes something to the rustic hedonism of the *Anacreontea* (cf. 1. 17), yet the triviality of these poems, and to a lesser extent of Anacreon himself, is remote from the seriousness and complexity of the *Odes*.

The influence of choral lyric must also be considered. Horace professes conventional admiration for the 'graves Camenae' of Stesichorus (4. 9. 8), but his imitation of the famous palinodes is more incidental than is usually realized (1. 16). He borrows the theme of a narrative poem from Bacchylides, together with much of the manner, but introduces some modern notes (1. 15). An occasional aphorism comes from Simonides (3. 2. 14, 3. 2. 25 f.); for a less certain imitation cf. 1. 28. The influence of Pindar is much more important.[1] Horace claims that it is dangerous to imitate Pindar (4. 2. 1 ff., *epist.* 1. 3. 10), but in the tradition of rhetoric his protestations of reluctance are themselves an acceptance of the challenge. He begins 1. 12 with a motto from the Second Olympian ('quem virum aut heroa . . .?'), and ends 1. 8 with a reminiscence from the Third Nemean; the poet's power to confer immortality is another Pindaric theme (4. 8, 4. 9). There are other less obvious forms of borrowing: though Horace's metres are Alcaic and Sapphic, his structural complexity owes more to choral lyric. Thus he imitates Pindar's roundabout introductions (1. 1, 1. 7), his rolling periods (4. 2. 5 ff. on the river, 4. 4. 1 ff. on the eagle), his rambling developments (3. 11. 17 ff., wrongly excised), his heroic speeches, sometimes loosely attached (1. 7. 25 ff., 3. 3. 18 ff., 4. 4. 50 ff.),[2] his portentous maxims paratactically introduced (4. 4. 29 ff. on heredity), his abrupt admonitions, his wide sweep and veering transitions, even his naïve digressions (4. 4. 18 ff. on the weapons of the Vindelici). Above all 3. 4 ('descende caelo') reproduces some very Pindaric ideas (Fraenkel 276 ff.); here we have the same consciousness of the poet's exalted status, the same association of poetical and political harmony, the same myth of the giants to symbolize the forces of mindlessness. Yet one must not exaggerate: even here the clipped rhetoric is very un-Pindaric.

Horace nowhere expresses a debt to the Hellenistic poets: from the formal point of view he is writing in a different category (which is what matters when acknowledgements are paid), and in spirit he reacts against the sentimentality of much Greek epigram and Roman

---

[1] Cf. especially Campbell 203 ff. (for such abbreviated references see the bibliography).

[2] R. Helm, *Philologus* 90, 1935, 368 ff. (who also points out the original elements in Horace's speeches).

elegy. Yet he was a modern man, whose devotion to archaic poetry cannot be taken too literally; he could not remain indifferent, even if he had wished, to the dominating trends of the past three centuries.[1] His convivial odes owe as much to epigram as to Alcaeus; the love interest is almost entirely Hellenistic; the political odes are indebted in general outline to Alexandrian court-poetry. The spring poems derive from Leonidas (1. 4, 4. 7, 4. 12), the hymn to Venus from Posidippus (1. 30); other odes have affinities with dedicatory epigram (1. 5, 3. 22, 3. 26). Horace's obsession with death argues no exceptional morbidity, his doubt on an after-life no unusual scepticism; these are the commonplaces of the *Anthology*. Of course he is more elaborate and more personal than his models: the Archytas ode (1. 28) plays with motifs from sepulchral epigram without being itself such a poem, the encounter with the wolf (1. 22) has parallels in Greek, but gives a greater air of immediacy. Horace's relation to Callimachus deserves especial attention (Wilkinson 118 ff.); from him he derives the *recusatio* (1. 6, 2. 12, 4. 2, 4. 15), something of the *propempticon* (1. 3), as well as other occasional topics (1. 7. 6, 1. 31. 8, 4. 3. 1 f.). In particular Horace owes more than is recognized to the Callimachean manner. The Μοῦσα λεπταλέη achieved her effects not by lushness of sentiment or beauty of language, but by discrimination, incisiveness, and the piquant juxtaposition of the poetical and the colloquial (Newman 313 f.). If we look at the essentials of style as well as the accidents of metre and mythology, Horace no less than Propertius is a Roman Callimachus.

One of the most important differences between Greek and Roman poetry is that the latter was influenced by a long and serious prose literature. There had been an important sententious element in early Greek elegy and lyric, but Horace's admonitions to enjoy the day are strengthened by hints at the teaching of Epicurus (1. 11. 3, 1. 11. 8, 3. 29. 43 ff.),[2] while his apophthegms on the good man recall Stoic dogma (1. 22. 1, 3. 3. 1). The poet's humanity and rationalism are less original than some Horatians suppose. Rather they reflect the enlightenment of Hellenistic moral philosophy: the wise man makes conscious efforts to achieve ἀταραξία of mind, he foresees trouble before it comes (2. 10. 14 ff.), and achieves happiness by the limitation rather than the fulfilment of desire (2. 2. 9 ff.). The *epicedion* on Quintilius (1. 24) draws from prose literature on consolation; 'quid dedicatum . . . ?' (1. 31) develops commonplaces on the objects of prayer; 'o matre pulchra' (1. 16) is a skit on treatises *de ira*. The popular διατριβή, whose influence on the *Satires* is familiar, also affected the *Odes*:[3] Horace's denunciation of human enterprise

[1] See especially Pasquali, Reitzenstein, Newman.
[2] N. W. De Witt, *CPh* 34, 1939, 127 ff.   [3] W. Kroll, *WS* 37, 1915, 223 ff.

can be paralleled in the Hermetic Corpus (1. 3), and when he compares the love of money with dropsy (2. 2. 14 ff.) the metaphor is
closer to Epictetus than Alcaeus. Yet no less than Cicero and Seneca,
Horace enlivens his platitudes with contemporary Roman details.
The pointlessness of avarice is exemplified by *latifundia* and luxury
building (2. 15. 1 ff., 3. 1. 33 ff.), cares flit like Cupids round the
gilded ceilings (2. 16. 11 f.), and when death comes it deprives a man
of his park-land and his Caecuban (2. 3. 17 ff., 2. 14. 21 ff.).

Other forms of prose writing also play a part. In his longest ode on
Augustus (1. 12) Horace alludes to Hellenistic theories on kingship;
in the Lalage poem (1. 22) he toys with the technicalities of geography; in 'intactis opulentior' (3. 24) he uses the clichés of ethno-
graphy. By the Augustan period the rhetorical theorists not only
drew on the poets but also influenced them, and Horace must have
studied treatises on how to write a *propempticon* (1. 3) or an *epicedion*
(1. 24). The political odes in particular should be related to the topics
of panegyric[1] as expounded by Menander Rhetor (pp. 377 ff. Sp.),
and exemplified in Cicero, Pliny, and the *panegyrici Latini*. Thus the
ruler is conventionally compared with the sun or other heavenly
bodies (1. 12. 47 n., 4. 5. 6 f.); his domains extend to the ends of
the earth (3. 3. 53 ff., 4. 14. 45 ff., 4. 15. 14 ff., *paneg. Lat.* 2. 2. 1,
2. 31. 1, 10. 10. 1); his enemies are no longer feared (4. 5. 25 ff. etc.,
Menander 377); he brings peace on sea and land (4. 5. 17 ff., *BMI*
894, Menander 377); he protects morals (3. 24. 28 f., 4. 5. 21 ff.,
carm. saec. 17 ff., Cic. *Marc.* 23, Menander 376); he can be appreciated
properly only after his death (3. 24. 30 ff., Cic. *Marc.* 29, *paneg. Lat.*
3. 31. 1).

It will be convenient now to look at the *Odes* from a different viewpoint, that of category. Convivial poems make an obvious sub-
division which goes back to Alcaeus's συμποτικά, but in his choice of
occasion Horace owes more to Hellenistic epigram. Thus his ode
may take the form of an invitation (1. 20, 4. 12), or describe prepara-
tions for a party (3. 19, 4. 11). It may celebrate a home-coming
(1. 36), a festival (3. 28), a birthday (4. 11), or a national event (3. 14).
The usual appurtenances of the symposium are included, scent,
rose-petals, celery-garlands, flute-girls; these of course were Roman
institutions as well as Greek, but their repeated mention in such
poems owes much to the convention of the genre. The wine introduces an Italian element into the traditional Greek framework, and
is carefully chosen to suit the occasion: Caecuban implies grandeur,
Sabinum simplicity, and even the date may have particular associations (1. 20. 3 f., 3. 8. 12, 3. 21. 1). The setting is usually unspecified,
though Mount Soracte is once mentioned to give local colour (1. 9. 2);

[1] Cf. Doblhofer, together with the review in *CR* N.S. 19, 1969.

if the sea is hinted at, the feature is presumably derived from Greek lyric (1. 9. 10, 1. 11. 5). The male participants are real with a few exceptions (1. 9. 8 Thaliarchus, 1. 27. 10 f. the brother of Opuntian Megylla, 1. 36. 14 Bassus). The girls are fictitious and sometimes romanticized: it cannot be supposed that Horace readily joined in songs on Diana or the green hair of the Nereids (3. 28. 9 ff.). The convivial poems as a whole are a skilful blend of the Roman and the Greek, the actual and the fanciful. The augur Murena appears in the same poem as the beautiful Telephus and the jealous Lycus (3. 19), just as Virgil's Gallus drifts through a pastoral setting (*ecl.* 10), or Tibullus's idealized Delia picks apples for the real Messalla (1. 5. 31 f.). To point this out is not to criticize; such a treatment is much more evocative than a representational description of the mundane details of a particular symposium (p. 118). Yet in spite of all his subtle art, Horace has been treated both in the ancient and modern world simply as the light-hearted writer of occasional verse. It is not surprising that he was resentful (*epist.* 1. 19. 10 f.).

About a quarter of Horace's odes may be classed as ἐρωτικά. The modern reader is apt to draw unfavourable comparisons with Catullus and Propertius, but they were intending something very different. Horace is not concerned with his own emotions; exceptions are embarrassing, however explicable in the context (1. 13. 5 ff., 4. 1. 33 ff.). The lady's beauties are mentioned only in the most general terms (1. 19. 5 ff.), and where any particulars are given the poet claims to be unsusceptible (2. 4. 21 ff.). Horace has rather the satirist's eye for social comedy, for the credulous trust of the inexperienced boy (1. 5. 5 ff.), the assumed reluctance of the flirtatious girl (1. 9. 21 ff.), the rapacity of the predatory woman (3. 20), the chain of incompatible and unrequited loves (1. 33). The rituals are as stylized as in operetta; we find the *comissatio* and the serenade (1. 25. 1 ff., 3. 7. 29 ff., 3. 10), lovers' perjuries (2. 8. 1 ff.) and quarrels (3. 9), the *militia amoris* (3. 26. 2), the rival (1. 33. 3). The blonde and musical girls owe more to the conventions of erotic writing than to the realities of *Venus parabilis*. Even the young men have exotic Greek names (Calais, Enipeus, Gyges, Hebrus, Sybaris, Telephus), though sometimes they are to be found in familiar surroundings, riding in the Park, swimming in the Tiber, or even hunting the boar (1. 8. 5 ff., 3. 7. 25 ff., 3. 12. 7 ff.). One poem is addressed to a boy (4. 10), and homosexual affairs are alluded to in a few other passages, but these should not be over-literally interpreted (1. 4. 19 n.). Occasionally Horace imitates the more pungent side of Hellenistic literature, derived by epigram from comedy and mime: Lydia whines in a gusty alley (1. 25. 9 ff.), and Lyce turns into an ugly and drunken hag (4. 13). Really serious notes, as opposed to this factitious realism, are rather rare, though Horace once praises the felicity of a stable union in the manner of the best elegiac poetry (1. 13. 17 ff.). More normally he assumes a detached, ironic pose, which as far as love-poetry is concerned seems very original. Sometimes he scoffs at the absurdities of Roman elegy: thus he consoles Tibullus because his lady has preferred a younger man (1. 33), urges Valgius to forget his lost Mystes and sing of Augustus's victories instead (2. 9), or himself lies in the wind and the snow, just like Asclepiades, expostulating absurdly with his mistress (3. 10. 13 ff.). Similarly he treats his own middle age with urbane amusement (2. 4. 22 ff.). He is a successful veteran who has hung up his crowbars and retired from the competition (1. 5, 3. 26); he is not always going to lie all night on doorsteps (3. 10. 19 f.); if Neaera cannot come, his messenger is not to trouble (3. 14. 23 ff.).

Another traditional category adopted by Horace is the hymn. Here he is faced with a difficulty of procedure. A direct imitation of the archaic Greek poets would be pointless now that their religious environment had disappeared; even in his hymn to Mercury (1. 10) Horace is rhetorical and allusive, and thinking of literature rather than cult. On the other hand the *carmina* of a genuine Roman religion were too crude and unliterary for a poet's purposes. Horace only once wrote a hymn that could actually be sung, the *Carmen Saeculare*, but even here he broke away from real ceremonial language. Other hymns are a fusion of the old and the new, of ritual formulas and literary references, with a modern setting to give point and relevance. Thus the poem to Diana and Apollo (1. 21) combines allusions to Delos and Algidus, and ends with a prayer for people and *Princeps*; the more complex ode to Fortuna (1. 35) addresses a real Latin goddess, but develops a variety of illustration impossible in cult, and ends with a very un-hymn-like outburst on the miseries of civil war. Elsewhere the literary element is even more predominant: 1. 30 simply develops a motif of Posidippus, while 3. 18 and 3. 22, though they profess to be more personal, move equally at the level of epigram. The fact is that the genre was too formal and constricting for Horace's special talents. It is no accident that the best specimen of all is a parody addressed to a wine-jar (3. 21).

The political odes are much more original: Hellenistic court-poetry provided a general outline rather than specific models. Yet the spontaneity of these poems is often exaggerated; as has been seen, they drew heavily on the conventions of prose panegyric, and social pressures reinforced the constraints of literary form. It is evident that Maecenas subsidized Horace primarily for political reasons: he was not simply looking for short-term gains (coins and buildings reached a wider audience than poetry), but to the regime's reputation

in future ages. Horace in turn wrote political odes praising his benefactors; it is not a coincidence that the other Augustan poets did
the same, except for Ovid, who died at Tomi. There is no point
in questioning Horace's sincerity: *fides* to Maecenas required co-
operation, there was no sane alternative to the regime, and everybody likes to participate in important causes. On the other hand it is
absurd to talk as if he were a judicious observer, whose opinions
of men and measures deserve the historian's respect: the test of
independence must always remain 'Was he in any position to say
the opposite?' Horace is admired for his supposed loyalty to the
Republican cause (2. 7) and his manly praise of the defeated Cato
(1. 12. 35f., 2. 1. 24); but a frank avowal of past opposition and an
ostentatious truculence on dead issues are easy and familiar forms
of flattery. When Horace glorifies Octavian as Caesar's avenger
(1. 2. 44) or reminds Pompeius of the disasters under Brutus (2. 7.
1f., 11f.), he completely renounces the causes of his youth. Some
scholars even think that Horace gave advice to the regime, as if the
opinions of poets could ever be of the slightest consequence in Roman
society. On the contrary he reflects with tactful precision the successive phases of Augustan ideology. He treats Cleopatra with exactly
the right mixture of virulence and magnanimity (1. 37), he provides
support for moral legislation (3. 6, 3. 24, 4. 5) and the rebuilding of
temples (3. 6. 1 ff.), he pours scorn on the prisoners of Carrhae, not
yet retrieved after twenty-five years in captivity (3. 5. 5 ff.). So too
with the poems on Augustus. The triumphant Octavian, recently
returned from Alexandria, is celebrated by the extravagant mythology of 1. 2. The constitutional *Princeps* is praised as Jupiter's vicegerent in a poem combining elements from Republican history and
Hellenistic political philosophy (1. 12). Finally we have serene and
sentimental reverence for a securely established institution (4. 5):
children resemble their parents thanks to a salutary social legislation, the ox perambulates the fields oblivious of confiscation and proscription, and the contented rustic pours libations to the *numen* of
his benefactor.

These considerations are generally thought of no importance to the
poetry. On the contrary they are fundamental. The virtues of irony
and sense, that distinguish Horace from most poets, desert him in
the political odes; this astute and realistic man, who had lived
through such remarkable events, cannot comment on them with
intelligence. Only once, in addressing the historian Pollio, does he
look at the situation historically, and then he is magnificent:
'ludumque Fortunae gravisque / principum amicitias et arma / nondum expiatis uncta cruoribus' (2. 1. 3 ff.). When he imagines
Octavian as a Mercury incarnate (1. 2. 41 ff.), or visualizes him drink-

ing nectar among the gods (3. 3. 11 f.), apologists talk of conventional poetic symbols, but these symbols allow no sensible interpretation. The trouble is that the subject-matter of politics does not adapt itself to poetry. The actual mechanism is technical or unedifying (*carm. saec.* 18 f. 'decreta super iugandis / feminis') while the larger achievements are not specific enough to make a direct appeal to the imagination. Horace saw the difficulties no less than his brother poets: his panegyrics on Augustus only reach their goal circuitously (1. 2, 1. 12), and by and large he avoids a direct description of victories (as in 4. 14). His approach is usually more subtle; for instance, by means of the Hellenistic *recusatio* he praises the regime without abandoning his habitual *persona*. Even the so-called 'Roman Odes' (3. 1–6) are less persistently political than is sometimes supposed; often they are rather a development of moral commonplace in aspects relevant to the national situation. Many of the most successful political allusions are merged in essentially private poems. Horace contrasts Maecenas's heavy responsibilities with his own care-free life (3. 29. 25 ff.); at the dedication of Apollo's temple he prays for personal health (1. 31); he gives a concrete and convincing reason for celebrating Augustus's return from Spain (3. 14. 14 ff. 'ego nec tumultum / nec mori per vim metuam tenente / Caesare terras').

Many of Horace's odes do not fit into any of the recognized subcategories of ancient poetry. This is partly to be explained by the deliberate contamination of two types of poem. In the Hellenistic period, when literature was no longer directly related to social occasion, the distinctions between the genres had been partially blurred. Horace carries the process much further (Kroll 209, 241). Thus 1. 3 begins as a *propempticon*, but turns into a diatribe against inventiveness. 1. 4 begins with a spring epigram and ends with a scene at a symposium. 1. 16 combines elements from palinode and philosophical treatise. 2. 13 begins with a humorous skit on the curse-poem and ends with a κατάβασις to the underworld. 3. 11 begins as a hymn to Mercury and the lyre, and ends as a mythological narrative on Hypermestra. 3. 14 begins as a panegyric on Augustus and ends with a private revel. 3. 27 begins as a *propempticon* to Galatea and ends with a mythological narrative on Europa. Ancient poets conventionally lamented that everything had already been said, but by such a mixture of themes Horace was able to give new life to the old forms.

But though many odes cannot be assigned to a single category, topics recur in different types of poem. For instance, Horace sometimes speaks grandly of his own vocation: he describes himself as a *vates* (1. 1. 35) or a priest of the Muses (3. 1. 3), he uses the Hellenistic imagery of the grove (1. 1. 30), the spring, and the garland

(1. 26. 6 f.), more surprisingly he shouts *Euhoe* and declares himself inspired by Bacchus (2. 19, 3. 25). Such passages form an interesting link between Pindar and the German Romantics, but Horace's enthusiasm is purely literary; he surely had a less exalted view of his own spiritual state than that sometimes attributed to him. He is much more convincing when he aspires to fame for himself (1. 1, 1. 32, 2. 20, 3. 30) or for his patrons (4. 8, 4. 9); here he uses Greek themes that still make sense in his own day, and in ours. His poems on poetry are most appealing when he breaks away from his models and adds an individual touch, when he compares himself with a Matine bee rather than a swan (4. 2. 25 ff.), or innocently boasts of his success with the *carmen saeculare* (4. 3. 13 ff.), or stands in front of the statue of Apollo Citharoedus and prays that his creative power may not fail (1. 31. 20).

The countryside is another of Horace's recurring themes (Troxler-Keller). One does not expect sharp, Tennysonian detail in the scene-painting of ancient poets; the hurrying brook and shady tree belong to the conventional *amoenus locus*.[1] As with the rest of the Romans, Horace's taste is for the pleasant rather than the picturesque, and he cares more for the orchards at Tibur than the waterfall (1. 7. 13 f., 4. 3. 10). His landscapes are a background to human activity or inactivity (1. 17. 17 ff.): the pine and poplar embrace that the poet may enjoy the shade (2. 3. 9 ff.), and one of the attractions of the *fons Bandusiae* is that he himself is writing about it (3. 13. 13 ff.). The moral superiority of the countryside is another hackneyed theme (Vischer); Horace's rustics live simply but abundantly, gather wood for their mothers (3. 6. 39 ff.), and sleep at nights (3. 1. 21 f.). Yet the picture is not all idyllic: the billy-goat smells (1. 17. 7), the plough-man kicks the hard ground (3. 18. 15 f.), and when the peasant is evicted his children are convincingly dirty (2. 18. 28). All this might suggest that Horace's treatment of the countryside is nothing but a cento of varied commonplaces. In fact he is nowhere more original. The Hellenistic epigrammatist might write nostalgically about the country, but he preferred his own metropolis. The middle-class Roman poets, on the other hand, not only came from Italy, but also went back: their natural affections were reinforced by the pride of ownership and the need to collect the rent. Horace seems to be the first European poet who persistently connects the charm of the country with a specific and recognizable locality. The villages of his childhood and the place-names of the Digentia valley are given significance because he himself happened to write about them (1. 17, 3. 4. 14 ff.). The Romans owed least to the Greeks in the more

[1] G. Schönbeck, *Der Locus Amoenus von Homer bis Horaz*, Diss. Heidelberg, 1962.

personal genres, satire, love-poetry, letter-writing. In the same way Horace's Sabine farm introduces a new way of thinking to European literature.

Friendship also plays an unusual part in Horace's poetry, and the *Odes* foreshadow some of the attitudes displayed most brilliantly in the *Epistles*. Hellenistic philosophers and poets had taken the subject seriously, and Horace imitates their fulsome compliments: Virgil is half his soul (1. 3. 8), and another part is reserved for Maecenas (2. 17. 5). But the urbane and humorous poem of friendship is a product of the Roman governing class, whose members were self-confident enough to indulge the idiosyncrasies of personality, and well enough known for their concerns to be of interest to the narrow circle of poetry-readers. Horace, like Catullus before him, transfers to verse some of the attitudes of Cicero's correspondence, tactful sympathy, friendly banter, a delight in the attributes that mark a friend off from other men. Tibullus and Valgius are laughed at for their absurd elegiac verses (1. 33, 2. 9), Varius is jokingly described as a swan of Homeric song (1. 6. 2), and even Virgil is not immune from the teasing associated with the invitation-poem (4. 12). The studious Iccius is mocked for his military ambitions (1. 29), just like Cicero's friend Trebatius, while Lamia, the magnate of Formiae, is linked with Lamus and the local Laestrygones (3. 17). Yet Horace's 'friends', unlike most of Cicero's, may often have been comparative strangers. One cannot suppose that the poet was at all intimate with Plancus and Agrippa; the recipients of Pindaric admonitions would surely have resented such familiarities in prose (2. 2 Sallustius Crispus, 2. 10 Licinius Murena); some odes have the appearance of having been commissioned (1. 36 Numida, 4. 8 Censorinus, 4. 9 Lollius). Yet even with his grander acquaintances Horace is always eager to introduce personal touches. Plancus is associated with Tibur (1. 7), Varus perhaps with a poem by Catullus (1. 18). Pollio is praised for his writings (2. 1. 1 ff.), Torquatus for his eloquence and lineage (4. 7. 23). Above all, Maecenas is reminded of his regal ancestry (1. 1. 1, 3. 29. 1), his interest in astrology (2. 17. 17 ff.), and the river of his native Arezzo (1. 20. 5 n.).

Horace's relationship with his patron may cause misunderstanding in an age when patronage survives only in its less acknowledgeable forms. Maecenas was a man of unusual discrimination, as far as other people's work was concerned, and he fostered poets for his own glory as well as Augustus's. Horace owed him not only his beloved Sabinum, but the resources that enabled him to write. That was a satisfactory basis for friendship, especially where both parties were tactful and astute: Maecenas was a manager of men, particularly literary men, and Horace, like his hero Aristippus, knew how to handle kings (*epist*. 1. 17. 13 ff.). But modern scholars tend to take too literally Horace's courteous protests of affection. One cannot detect in the relationship any of the equality required by essayists on *amicitia*; when Maecenas sends for Horace he comes (2. 20. 6), or at least makes excuses for not coming (*epist*. 1. 7. 1 ff.). It is note-worthy that after 20 B.C. Horace mentions his patron only once, though warmly (p. xxxviii); Maecenas was now in political eclipse, and Horace had found other backers.

But it is easy to talk too much about subject-matter: what makes a poet is the more intangible quality of style. Here Horace was triumphant, but his methods were unfashionable. He used words that tended to be avoided as prosaic not only by the epic poets, but to a lesser extent even in the *Eclogues, Georgics*, and the elegists (Axelson 98 ff.). Some of these words are metrically inconvenient in dactylic verse, but the phenomenon goes much further; Axelson's list includes *atqui, attinet, cena, comis, condicio, delecto, idoneus, nequam, norma, ordino, pecunia, peritus, pernicies, plerumque, praesidium, recreo, stultitia, vestimentum*. Of course it may be difficult to catch the exact nuance of a particular word at the time when Horace was writing: too little late Republican poetry has survived, the *Aeneid* was only 'published' after most of the *Odes*, and the vocabulary of Silver Age epic largely depended on the *Aeneid*. Even so, it is a plausible view that Horace affected a drier diction than contemporaries more subject to neoteric influences; this would cohere well with the poet's realism in other respects. It need hardly be added that it is not a criticism to call Horace prosaic: more, perhaps, than any other Augustan poet he writes in Latin.

Horace's style is down-to-earth in other ways besides vocabulary. A poet's use of adjectives deserves particular scrutiny: Horace's tend to be functional or conventional, without the picturesqueness of Catullus or his Augustan heirs. By and large he avoids alliteration, onomatopoeia, and haunting vowel-sounds: he does not evoke more than he says. His metaphors are sparse and trite, and even his similes may be cautiously expressed (4. 14. 20 f.). Of course, no ancient lyric poet could simply reproduce the language of prose, and Horace gave distinction to his style with his Greek syntax (1. 1. 8 n., 1. 22. 1 n.), ἀπὸ κοινοῦ constructions, and the ellipse of unnecessary terms (1. 7. 10 n.); sometimes he evolves ingenious verbal complexes (1. 5. 13 ff., 1. 9. 21 ff.), and occasionally ventures a mannered hyper-baton (1. 23. 12, 1. 35. 5 n.). Yet the incidence of such phenomena can easily be exaggerated; in general his word-order is more straight-forward than that of his contemporary poets. He achieves his effects largely by metrical virtuosity: the words click into place with seem-ing inevitability, and no rubble is needed to fill the cracks.

The structure of classical poems tends to be neglected by modern readers, who are more sensitive to surface beautification than to harmony of design. The Horatian ode is planned as a unity; the poet has an architect's eye for over-all coherence; it would be difficult to subtract a section without disrupting the whole. The rigid metrical framework helps to impose a symmetry that has seldom been aimed at in English lyric since the seventeenth century. Sometimes the ode is divided into more or less equal blocks (1. 2, 1. 12); sentence balances sentence, and stanza stanza (1. 1, 3. 9); the end of the poem may come back full circle to the beginning (1. 1, 1. 16, 1. 22). The structure is reinforced by anaphora (1. 10. 9 n.), 'polyptoton' (1. 2. 25 ff.), or the judicious placing of contrasting words. Yet Horace is not always formal and predictable: variation is itself a rhetorical ideal. The skilful use of enjambement breaks up the pattern of the metre, or several stanzas are included in a reverberating period (1. 37. 12 ff., 4. 4. 1 ff.). As in his satires, Horace may approach the core of his thought circuitously, and as if by accident; sometimes he uses the device of the 'priamel' (1. 1, 1. 7), sometimes other forms of introduction (3. 11, 3. 27). A poem may suddenly change direction in the middle (1. 4, 1. 28), or gently glide to a different topic (1. 17, 2. 13, 3. 14). Sometimes it gathers momentum towards the close (1. 4, 1. 18, 1. 35), sometimes fades away in a quiet cadence (2. 1, 3. 3, 3. 5, 4. 2). The unity sought by Horace, as by Pindar, was based on formal structure rather than on subject-matter. When they talked of weaving garlands of flowers the image suggests alike the variety of the components and the harmony of the composition.

The arrangement of the odes within the book also deserves attention, though in fact it is much less important. The Alexandrian editors of Greek *lyrici* had given some attention to such trivialities, and they were followed by the Roman poets (Kroll 225 ff.). The first ode in a book is naturally addressed to a person of eminence (1. 1 Maecenas, 2. 1 Pollio, 4. 1 Paullus Maximus). The closing poems are also carefully chosen: 1. 38 is a quiet declaration of simplicity, 2. 20 and 3. 30 are grandiloquent claims to lasting renown; 2. 20 is addressed to Maecenas, and 4. 15 to Augustus. The second and penultimate places may also be important: 1. 2 and 1. 37 deal with high political matters; 3. 29 is addressed to Maecenas, before the epilogue to the collection, 4. 2 to Iullus Antonius, 4. 14 to Augustus. Even the central position may be significant; 1. 20 and 3. 16 are both addressed to Maecenas, while 4. 8 (to Censorinus) is written in the Asclepiad metre of 1. 1 and 3. 30. The opening poems of Book I contain addresses direct or indirect to famous men (1 Maecenas, 2 Octavian, 3 Virgil, 4 Sestius, 6 Agrippa, 7 Plancus); moralizing odes are prominent in the second book; relatively few odes in the third book are addressed to real individuals. Sometimes poems of similar content are juxtaposed (1. 34 and 1. 35 on Fortuna, 3. 1–6 on national themes, 4. 8 and 4. 9 on the immortality bestowed by the poet, 4. 14 and 4. 15 on Augustus); but an ode can never derive its meaning simply from its position (see on 1. 15 and 1. 38). More often *variatiò* is the dominating principle. Thus in the first nine poems of Book I Horace parades nine different metres, and a tenth is added at 1. 11; only two other metres are used in the first three books (2. 18 and 3. 12). In the first eleven poems of Book II Alcaics and Sapphics are found alternately, and indeed all the odd-numbered poems of this book are in Alcaics. Apart from the 'Roman Odes' (3. 1–6) the same metre is seldom used twice in succession; exceptions are found only at 1. 16–17, 1. 26–7, 1. 34–5, 2. 13–15, 2. 19–20, 3. 24–5, 4. 14–15. One may also sometimes observe a contrast of the private and political (as at 1. 36–8), the slight and grandiloquent (thus the 'Roman Odes' are followed by relatively trivial poems). Yet it is only too easy to imagine some subtle principle either of similarity or difference in every juxtaposition, not to mention more complicated sequences and cycles. Most of these suggestions seem completely fanciful, and equally ingenious reasons could be adduced to justify any arrangement.

Quite apart from style and structure Horace's odes have other characteristics alien to the manner of much modern poetry.[1] He normally professes to be talking *in propria persona*; the only obvious exception is 1. 28 (Archytas).[2] And he talks at somebody, usually a real or imaginary friend, sometimes a god or Muse, occasionally even an inanimate object (1. 3, 1. 14, 1. 32, 2. 13, 3. 11, 3. 13, 3. 21). Like his Greek predecessors he often starts from a shared occasion, the coming of spring (1. 4) or the view of a mountain (1. 9). He does not meditate or introspect, but exhorts, questions, invites, consoles, prays, and orders. The moralizing is public, in the ancient manner, being directed at the improvement of others rather than the poet. Occasionally things happen while the poem is going on: we overhear a conversation at a drinking-party (1. 27. 10 ff.), or a busy merchant suddenly passes an unburied corpse (1. 28. 23). Even the narrative poems include a dramatic element: in 1. 15 Nereus utters prophecies to Paris, in 3. 11 (Hypermestra) and 3. 27 (Europa) there are introductory allocutions as well as closing speeches. Admittedly the story of the thunder (1. 34) is addressed to nobody in particular, but that is an exception that calls attention to the rule. In the social and

---

[1] R. Heinze, *Neue Jahrb.* 51, 1923, 153 ff. (= *Vom Geist des Römertums*, ed. 3, 1960, pp. 172 ff.).

[2] 3. 12 is naturally taken as an address to Neobule rather than a soliloquy by her (as in Alcaeus 10).

political poems it is naturally less easy to invent an interlocutor
(2. 15, 2. 18, 3. 1–3, 3. 5, 3. 24). Yet even here Horace provides
prayers (1. 2. 30 ff., 1. 12. 49 ff.) and speeches (3. 3. 18 ff., 4. 4. 50 ff.),
celebrates national events by calling for a party (1. 37, 3. 14), and
if no friend is forthcoming he addresses his readers as if they were a
public meeting (3. 6. 2 *Romane*, 3. 14. 1 o *plebs*).

As Horace's odes profess to be directed at somebody, they naturally
use the techniques of rhetoric (*RE* 8. 2384). Urgent questions are
common: 'do you hear?' to one Lydia, and repeated 'why's?' to
another (3. 10. 5, 1. 8. 1 ff.), 'what boy?' to Pyrrha (1. 5. 1), 'quae
caret ora cruore nostro?' to Pollio (2. 1. 36). Exclamations also
create an illusion of spontaneity (1. 24. 5 f., 1. 35. 33 f.). The common
experience of humanity is crystallized in *sententiae* that aim at
novelty of expression rather than of thought. Dogmatic assertions
are given plausibility by conventional *exempla* from mythology or
nature. Fertile variations on a single theme produce not only ampli-
tude but an illusion of cogency (2. 10. 1 ff., 3. 4. 65 ff., 4. 4. 29 ff.).[1]
Tact and humour, no less than in Cicero, subserve the needs of λόγος
πρὸς τὸν ἀκροατήν. Arguments are set in syllogistic form, sometimes
with suppressed premisses (3. 5. 31 ff.). Horace is particularly influenced by the already growing art of declamation: the clipped
soliloquies of the Europa ode read like something out of the elder
Seneca (3. 27. 34 ff.). This perhaps explains Horace's taste for point
and epigram, which has no full counterpart in Greek poetry, but
rather foreshadows the manner of the Silver Age.

Yet the *Odes* cannot be treated simply as a formal exercise in the
manipulation of words, metres, topics, and figures. They also have
a tone of voice. Horace's urbanity has some analogies in the gentle-
manly conversation of Plato or Cicero, but it is not easy to parallel
in verse. Except in some of his political poems he writes within his
strength (cf. *serm.* 1. 10. 13 f. 'parcentis viribus atque / extenuantis
eas consulto'). Apart from the obvious instances of banter and
εἰρωνεία a dry humour pervades the whole. Horace fluctuates from
the grandiose to the off-hand no less than in his epistles (cf. 4. 1. 12
'si torrere iecur quaeris idoneum'). His manner is quite inimitable
and was never successfully copied by any Roman, still less by the
translators, who are unable to distinguish him from Martial. The
austerities of Milton's sonnets perhaps come nearest, but they fall
short in subtlety and charm.

It is traditional to approach Horace through the medium of biography. The poet's personality seems sympathetic to scholars of very
different type, and all identify him with themselves; to the English
he is a tolerant clubman, to the Germans a person with earnest views

[1] Cf. D. A. Russell, *G & R* 14, 1967, 140 f.

about poetry and politics. There are dangers in this approach, and the purpose of this commentary is largely to point out the common store on which Horace drew. At times he seems simply to be an actor wearing different masks. The truculent satirist becomes the urbane epistolographer, not so much because of a mellowing in his own temperament, but because truculence and urbanity suited the respective genres. So too in the *Odes*, the genial hedonist, the humane moralist, the modest country-dweller, the flattering panegyrist, all utter the clichés appropriate to their role. Horace, who was supposed to be the most accessible of the ancients, begins to seem enigmatic and elusive.

Such a conclusion would not necessarily ruin the poetry. The touchstone used to be 'sincerity', a misleading word: it suggests that the poet who does not speak the whole truth is in some way bogus. Yet even the Romantics rearranged the facts of experience; still more the ancient poets, with their convention of self-effacement. The literary tradition suggested commonplaces and an appropriate stylistic level. The artefact mattered more than the humdrum details of the artist's life. Personal confessions would have lacked the dignity of high poetry as well as the public intelligibility which literature required. Nobody supposes that the dramatist must himself experience all the emotions he describes. In the ancient world other poets, even love-poets like Propertius, were given licence to invent.

But the biographical critic need not utterly despair: something may still be detected of Horace the man.[1] It will not be found in the trivial occurrences he purports to describe, neither in flirtations with Lydia nor the drinking-party with Thaliarchus, nor yet in the episode of the thunder or the adventure with the wolf. The manner of the *Odes* is much more illuminating than the matter. The poet makes us feel his presence not only by his selection of material but by the way he handles it. Horace could never have written like Propertius, nor Propertius like Horace. The *Epistles* and *Odes* belong to very different genres, yet throughout we are aware of a consistent attitude, humane, realistic, and ironic. It is hard to believe that these qualities do not represent facets of Horace's own character. We still know more of him than of other ancient poets. By bringing to lyric something of the self-expression, however stylized, that he had borrowed from Lucilius in the *Satires*, Horace began a fruitful development in European literature.

[1] Cf. N. Rudd, 'The Style and the Man' (*Phoenix* 18, 1964, 216 ff.).

2. THE CHRONOLOGICAL SETTING OF *ODES* I–III

§ 1. *Horace's early life.*[1] Q. Horatius Flaccus was born on 8 December
65 B.C. (*epist.* 1. 20. 26 ff., Suet. *vita*), five years after Virgil, two years
before Augustus. His birthplace was the Apulian colonia of Venusia
(*serm.* 2. 1. 35); he sometimes refers with affection to the scenes of
his childhood (*serm.* 1. 5. 77, *carm.* 1. 28. 26 f.), Mons Vultur or the
river Aufidus (*carm.* 3. 4. 9 ff., 3. 30. 10), but by the time he wrote his
poetry his roots were elsewhere. He suffered socially and perhaps
psychologically from the taint of servile origin, though he himself
was born free (*serm.* 1. 6. 6, 1. 6. 45 f.). His father was a *coactor* by
occupation (*serm.* 1. 6. 86), an unsavoury trade that involved money-
lending; though he started poor he acquired a small estate and
enough money to educate Horace, first under the learned Orbilius at
Rome (*serm.* 1. 6. 71 ff., *epist.* 2. 1. 70 f.), then at Athens with the
sons of noblemen (*epist.* 2. 2. 43 ff.).

Horace was still at Athens on the Ides of March 44 B.C., and shared
the enthusiasm of aristocrats and philosophers for the Republican
cause. He served under Brutus in Asia and then in 42 B.C. in the
terrible campaign of Philippi (*serm.* 1. 6. 48, *epist.* 2. 2. 46 ff., *carm.*
2. 7. 9 ff., 3. 4. 26). His rank of *tribunus militum* was an impressive
achievement for a young man of 22 without social advantages, and
a proof of both force and tact. After the rout he returned to Rome
and won his pardon, though he lost his father's property (*epist.* 2.
2. 50 f.). He became a *scriba quaestorius* in the *aerarium*; this was
a responsible civil-service post, but by Roman standards no doubt
marked a descent from what he had earlier achieved. As a consequence of his first poems he was introduced to Maecenas by Virgil
and Varius about 38 B.C. (*serm.* 1. 6. 54 ff., 2. 6. 40 ff.). He dedicated
to his patron two books of satires, issued about 35 and 30, and one
book of epodes (about 30, though some poems are considerably
earlier). He was rewarded with an attractive property in the Digentia
valley beyond Tibur (*serm.* 2. 6). He may have served against Sextus
Pompeius in 36 (cf. 3. 4. 28), perhaps also against Antony in 31.[2]
Such an assumption would explain a strange phrase in the ode to
Septimius (2. 6. 7 f. 'sit modus lasso maris et viarum / militiaeque');
it would also make sense of *epist.* 1. 20. 23 'me primis urbis belli
placuisse domique' (the view that this is a loyal reference to the
tyrannicides is much less likely).

---

[1] Suetonius, *de poetis*, ed. A. Rostagni, 1944, pp. 107 ff., *RE* 8. 2337 ff.,
Fraenkel 1 ff.

[2] Cf. *epod.* 1. 1 ff., E. Wistrand, *Horace's ninth Epode*, 1958. On the other
hand we agree with Fraenkel (71 ff.) that *nauseam* at *epod.* 9. 35 does not refer
to sea-sickness at Actium.

§ 2. *Odes up to 30 B.C.*[1] In 31 B.C. Octavian defeated Antony at
Actium; the campaign is celebrated in the first and ninth epodes.
In August 30 he captured Alexandria (p. 409); *carm.* 1. 37 was written some time afterwards. Yet it would be rash to assume that the
epodes were finished before the odes were begun:[2] 1. 37 does not
read like a first attempt at Alcaics. It is true that the *Odes* contain
no historical allusions that can be assigned with certainty to before
30 B.C.; but the explanation may simply be that the earliest poems
of the collection were mainly non-political.

Where historical allusions are ambiguous or non-existent, metrical
statistics may be invoked. There is reason for thinking that date
played a larger part in the arrangement of *Odes* I–III than scholars
generally assume, i.e. that the first book for the most part is earlier
than the second, and the second than the third. The evidence comes
from three phenomena in the Alcaic stanza (see below, pp. xl ff.).
(i) In the first three lines the percentage of short initial syllables is
7·2 in Book I, 3·1 in Book II, 2·0 in Book III, o in Book IV. (ii) The percentage of type B fourth lines ('torquibus exiguis renidet') is 35·0
in Book I, 22·1 in Book II, 17·8 in Book III, 13·2 in Book IV. (iii) The
percentage of type B third lines ('fatalis incestusque iudex') is 5·0
in Book I, 5·8 in Book II, 24·6 in Book III, 30·2 in Book IV. Where
individual poems are analysed the variations are also striking,
though here one must allow for the statistical dangers of small
numbers. The following are the only Alcaic poems with two or more
type B third lines: 2. 1 (2 out of 10); 3. 1 (2 out of 12); 3. 3 (4 out of
18); 3. 4 (9 out of 20); 3. 5 (3 out of 14); 3. 6 (4 out of 12); 3. 29 (6 out
of 16); 4. 4 (4 out of 19); 4. 9 (4 out of 13); 4. 14 (4 out of 13); 4. 15 (4
out of 8). As 3. 4–6 seem to belong about 28 or 27, the figures suggest
that some of the odes must be significantly earlier.

The Alcaic ode to the Fortuna of Antium (1. 35) is a case in point.
It has 3 short syllables in the first position (10 per cent of possible
places);[3] it has 4 type B fourth lines (40 per cent); there are no type
B third lines (out of 10 chances). Therefore there is some difficulty
in the view that the poem was written as late as 3. 4–6,[4] and we are
tempted to suggest that the historical evidence is at least compatible
with a date about 35. Horace envisages a campaign against Britain

---

[1] For the chronology of the *Odes* see especially C. Franke, *Fasti Horatiani*,
1839, Wickham 19 ff.

[2] Cf. A. Kappelmacher, *WS* 43, 1922–3, 44 ff.

[3] This is pointed out by J. D. P. Bolton, who assigns the poem to the
preliminaries of Actium (*CQ* N.S. 17, 1967, 451 ff.); we do not agree with his
conclusion (below, p. 387), but owe much to him for reopening the question.

[4] However, 1. 31 (28 B.C.), a poem of half the length, has 2 short syllables in
the first position, 1 type B fourth line, and no type B third lines (out of 5
chances).

(29 f.); this is usually associated with the plans of 27 and 26 (below, § 4), but already in 34 Octavian had set out for Gaul with the supposed intention of undertaking such an expedition (Dio 49. 38. 2). The ode also predicts wars against the Arabs (line 40), and in the neighbourhood of the Indian Ocean (30 ff. 'et iuvenum recens / examen Eois timendum / partibus Oceanoque rubro'); this is usually connected with the campaign of Aelius Gallus, which should perhaps be placed as early as 26–25 (§ 10). Yet Horace's grandiose ambitions, extending from the Indian Ocean to the Massagetae, suggest a general Eastern campaign; it might be relevant that in 35 B.C. Octavian sent Antony 2,000 men, who were only a fraction of the two legions promised (Plut. *Ant.* 35. 4, 53. 2, Dio 49. 33. 4). The Fortuna of Antium may have played a part in the naval war of 36 B.C. against Sextus Pompeius (1. 35. 6 n.); and Horace's denunciation of civil strife would suit the aftermath of that campaign (admittedly *epod.* 7, which may belong to the same period, is far more pessimistic in tone).

Other odes may well have been written between 35 and 30, perhaps for instance some of the imitations of Alcaeus; it may be significant that these are concentrated in the first book (except for the metrical tour de force 3. 12). 1. 9 (Soracte) begins with an extended adaptation of Alcaeus; it may belong to the same time as the similar thirteenth Epode (1. 11 also shows a kindred spirit). 1. 18 begins with a motto from Alcaeus; an early date perhaps suits its dedication to Varus, who is probably the consul of 39 and recipient of the sixth Eclogue. 1. 37 (Cleopatra), another poem with an Alcaic motto, is also fairly early (30 B.C.). 1. 14 (the Ship of State) is more of a problem; it could be placed as early as 34 B.C., though other arguments might suggest a date about 29 (pp. 180 f.). The first book contains borrowings from several Greek lyric poets, and some of these should perhaps also be placed before 30 B.C. One may mention the imitations of Bacchylides (1. 15, a narrative poem with reminiscences of the *Epodes*, cf. pp. 192 f.), of Stesichorus (1. 16, with allusions to libellous *iambi*), of Anacreon (1. 23 and 1. 27, the former with metrical abnormalities). Horace's accident with the tree perhaps belongs to 33 B.C. (below, p. 244); this would provide a *terminus post quem* for 1. 20, 2. 13, 2. 17. Some scholars assume that 3. 8 belongs to the first anniversary of the episode, and reach a number of consequential conclusions, but that view depends on a mistranslation (p. 244).

On the other hand inclusion in the first book is by no means a guarantee of earliness. 1. 1 may well belong to the same time as the corresponding epilogue 3. 30 (so perhaps 2. 20). 1. 12 may be dated on political grounds to about 24 (§ 12), well after the 'Roman Odes' of the third book. The death of Quintilius, mourned in 1. 24, is assigned by Jerome to 23 B.C. (though this may well be an illegitimate inference from the date of the completed collection). 1. 26 has been thought early on the grounds of a single metrical oddity (11 'hunc Lesbio sacrare plectro'), yet an allusion to Tiridates suggests a date about 26 (§ 7). 1. 29 with its prediction of the Arabian war seems to belong about the same time (§ 10). Even epodic metre is not a proof of earliness; 1. 7, it is true, may be assigned to 32 or soon after (p. 91), but 1. 4 was written for the consul of 23 (unless it was an old poem turned to new account in the completed collection).

§ 3. *29–27 B.C.* In the summer of 29 Octavian returned from the East and celebrated his triumphs. Soon afterwards he insincerely pretended to contemplate abdication, and this is a possible context for 1. 14 on the Ship of State (see also § 2 and p. 181). In 28 B.C. he restored the temples (*res gest.* 20. 4, Dio 53. 2. 4); this is the most natural place for 3. 6[1] (which refers to the rebuilding in the future tense) and for 1. 31 (which is occasioned by the dedication of Apollo's Palatine temple in October 28). Octavian's first attempt at moral legislation should be assigned to the same year (cf. 3. 6. 17 ff.), when he was still present in the city; this suggests a date soon afterwards for 3. 24 ('intactis opulentior'), which refers to the failure of that legislation. In January 27 Octavian resigned his extraordinary powers, but retained the consulship together with proconsular *imperium* over Spain, Gaul, and Syria; 1. 2 probably refers to the floods of this month, though it reflects the foreboding of the past few years (pp. 17 ff.). At the same time he assumed the name 'Augustus', which is found in 3. 3 and 3. 5; the latter poem seems to belong to 27 as the conquest of Britain is still contemplated. It is natural to assign 3. 4 to the same period, though one cannot attach too much importance to 37 f. ('militia simul / fessas cohortis abdidit oppidis'); Horace may be influenced by the demobilization of 29/8, but he expresses himself in an entirely general way. Nothing very useful can be said about the other 'Roman Odes'; even if they were planned as a cycle, which is uncertain, their composition could still have extended over several years.

§ 4. *Britain.* In 27 B.C. Augustus set out for Gaul, part of his new *provincia* in the West. It was generally believed both in this and the following year that he was contemplating an invasion of Britain; for these and similar plans cf. 1. 35. 30 n. This has been thought a possible context for 1. 21, where Apollo is invited to banish pestilence to Britain, but the reference need not be so specific. Many scholars

---

[1] Cf. also 13 f. 'paene occupatam seditionibus / delevit urbem Dacus et Aethiops'. These lines would have been inappropriate a few years later.

assign 1. 35 to the same period; for another possibility see above, § 2. At some stage the British chieftains sent embassies to Augustus (Str. 4. 5. 3); this process may have begun in 27/6, as after that time there are no more poetic demands for conquest.[1] Aponius in his commentary on the *Song of Songs* professes to quote Livy:[2] 'Caesar Augustus in spectaculis populo Romano nuntiat, regressus a Britannia, totum orbem terrarum Romano imperio pacis abundantia subditum.' There is some muddle here, but perhaps a substratum of truth; if so, a suitable context for Augustus's announcement is his return from Spain in 24 B.C.

§ 5. *Spain*. Augustus entered on his eighth consulship (26 B.C.) at Tarraco in Spain (Suet. *Aug.* 26. 3); soon he was detained by a major war. The time had come for a settlement with the Cantabri and Astures, who occupied the long and inaccessible range near the north coast. They were under arms in January 29 B.C., when Janus's temple was closed: possibly one should assign to this period 2. 6. 2 'Cantabrum indoctum iuga ferre nostra' (for other evidence on this poem see § 1 *ad fin.*). Soon afterwards they were temporarily subdued by Statilius Taurus (Dio 51. 20. 5); at 3. 4. 34, in a poem that apparently was written about 28/7 (§ 3), Horace makes a topical allusion to the Cantabrian Concani (*RE* 4. 798). The plots of Cantabrian and Scyth are mentioned together at 2. 11. 1, but this poem might belong anywhere between 29 and 25.

In 26 B.C.[3] Augustus commanded in person against the Cantabri with a drive from Segisama (west of Burgos) to the north coast; later he fell seriously ill and wintered at Tarraco. In 25 the Astures were defeated by the legates Antistius and Carisius. This is the natural context for 3. 8. 21 f. 'servit Hispanae vetus hostis orae / Cantaber sera domitus catena'; some assign the poem to early in the decade, but in the turmoil after Actium a Spanish victory would have seemed less significant (see also §§ 7, 9). The temple of Janus was closed (Dio 53. 26. 5), and in 24 Augustus returned to Rome after his long absence; his entry to the city is celebrated by 3. 14 ('Herculis ritu'). The Cantabri rebelled again in 24 and 22 (Dio 53. 29. 1, 54. 5. 1); on the former occasion the Roman commander was Horace's friend L. Aelius Lamia (below, p. 301). They were finally subjugated by Agrippa in 20 (Dio 54. 11. 2–5, cf. *epist.* 1. 12. 26).

---

[1] Cf. P. A. Brunt, *JRS* 53, 1963, 173 f.

[2] T. E. Mommsen, *AJP* 75, 1954, 175 ff., more sceptically H. D. Meyer, *Historia* 10, 1961, 110 ff.

[3] For this and the following campaigns cf. D. Magie, *CPh* 15, 1920, 323 ff., R. Syme, *AJPh* 55, 1934, 293 ff., W. Schmitthenner, *Historia* 11, 1962, 54 ff.

§ 6. *The Alps.* In 25 B.C. Terentius Varro was sent by Augustus against the Salassi, an Alpine tribe living in the Val D'Aosta to the south of the Great St. Bernard Pass; he sold 36,000 of them into slavery and established the colony of Augusta Praetoria, the modern Aosta (Str. 4. 6. 7, Dio 53. 25. 3–5). Dio records that in honour of this and other victories Augustus was given a triumphal arch in the Alps, presumably the one still standing at Aosta (53. 26. 5, *RE* 7 A. 1. 404). This monument seems to be mentioned by Horace at 2. 9. 18 ff. (the ode to Valgius) 'nova / cantemus Augusti tropaea / Caesaris'.[1]

§ 7. *Parthia.* Crassus's army was overwhelmed at Carrhae in 53 B.C.; the recovery of the prisoners, and more important the standards, became a major preoccupation of Roman statesmanship. Antony's general Decidius Saxa was defeated by Pacorus in 41 B.C., and the Parthians temporarily overran Syria, Cilicia, and the inland cities of Asia. Antony himself suffered heavy losses when invading Parthia in 36; cf. 3. 6. 9 f. 'iam bis Monaeses et Pacori manus / non auspicatos contudit impetus'. The Roman poets replied with spirit. Horace himself envisages a large-scale expedition to the Persian Gulf (1. 35. 30 ff., above, § 2), foresees new Roman victories (1. 2. 51, 3. 3. 43 f.), and looks for the addition of Parthia to the empire (3. 5. 4). All this surely reflects official policy (Brunt, cited above, § 4); similarly the Regulus ode (27 B.C.), with its condemnation of Crassus's army (3. 5. 5 f.), cannot be dissociated from Augustus's failure to retrieve the prisoners.

The Romans were helped by internal dissidence in Parthia. Tiridates revolted against Phraates IV about the time of the Actium campaign, and on his defeat was allowed to settle in Syria (Dio 51. 18. 2–3). Later, about 26, he started a second rebellion, apparently in conjunction with Phraates's son, but at the approach of a Scythian army fled with the young prince to Augustus in Spain (Justin 42. 5. 6). The occurrence of two separate rebellions is supported by *res gest.* 32. 1. 'ad me supplices confugerunt reges Parthorum Tiridates et postea Phrates regis Phratis filius' (see Mommsen's note). The second rebellion is confirmed by Parthian sources: in 26 B.C. Tiridates struck a coin with the legend Φιλορώμαιος, and about August 25 Phraates overstruck a tetradrachm of Tiridates, a standard declaration of victory.[2]

Horace's reference to Tiridates should probably be linked with

---

[1] Cf. J. Gow, *CR* 9, 1895, 303 f.

[2] For these events see W. W. Tarn, *Mélanges Glotz*, 1932, 2. 831 ff., N. C. Debevoise, *A political History of Parthia*, 1938, p. 137, K.-H. Ziegler, *Die Beziehungen zwischen Rom und dem Partherreich*, 1964, pp. 45 ff.

the second of these two rebellions. The poet claims to be uninterested in the worries of Tiridates (1. 26. 5 f.), but in the aftermath of Actium that would not be a natural preoccupation. In 3. 8 ('Martiis caelebs') Horace alludes to civil dissension in Parthia (19 f.); this would seem unimportant in 30, and a date in 25 suits the references to the Cantabri (§ 5) and the Scythians (§ 9). In the same context Horace tells Maecenas 'mitte civilis super urbe curas' (3. 8. 17); this has been thought to suit the period after Actium, when Maecenas was left in charge of the city (Dio 51. 3. 5). Yet though the fact is nowhere stated, it is likely enough that he was again left in charge during Augustus's absence in the West (27–24). This is also the right context for 3. 29. 27 f. (the great ode to Maecenas) 'quid Seres et regnata Cyro / Bactra parent Tanaisque discors'; this would have been an absurd remark in 30 B.C. when Octavian was still in the East. Other allusions are less easily dated: 2. 2. 17 (on the restoration of Phraates) probably refers to the events of 25; 1. 34. 14 ff. could belong to the same period, though the reference to the loss of crowns may be entirely general.

During this period the Romans kept up the pressure. There is a hint of intervention in Armenia (2. 9. 20 'rigidum Niphaten'), and an advance to the Euphrates (2. 9. 21 'Medumque flumen gentibus additum', Prop. 2. 10. 13 f. 'iam negat Euphrates equitem post terga tueri / Parthorum'); a date about 25 is suggested for 2. 9 in § 6, and this is supported by a reference in Propertius's poem to the Arabian campaign (§ 10). Soon after Horace is found predicting triumphs over Parthia (1. 12. 35 f.). The climax came in 20 B.C., too late for the collection of odes: Crassus's standards and the surviving prisoners were restored, a Roman nominee was put on the throne of Armenia, and the Parthian king's sons were taken as hostages.[1]

§ 8. *Dacians.* The Dacians aroused Roman fears about the time of Actium; cf. *serm.* 2. 6. 53 'numquid de Dacis audisti?', *carm.* 3. 6. 13 ff., 1. 35. 9 n. In 29/8 M. Licinius Crassus waged a vigorous campaign against the Dacians, Bastarnae, and Moesi,[2] for which he triumphed in 27. Many scholars see an allusion to this war in 3. 8. 18 'occidit Daci Cotisonis agmen'; yet Crassus's campaigns are described in considerable detail by Dio (51. 23–6) without any mention of this chieftain. On other grounds it seems desirable to place 3. 8 about 25 (§§ 5, 7, 9), and Cotiso may have been defeated shortly before that date. Horace is still talking about the Dacians in 2. 20. 17 f. 'qui dissimulat metum / Marsae cohortis Dacus'; this epilogue-poem was presumably written fairly late in the collection.

---

[1] L. R. Taylor, *JRS* 26, 1936, 161 ff.
[2] Dio 51. 23–6, *RE* 13. 272 ff., A. Mócsy, *Historia* 15, 1966, 511 ff.

The problem remained with Rome for many years afterwards (*res gest.* 30. 2, Suet. *Aug.* 21. 1, Dio 54. 36. 2).

§ 9. *Scythians.* This term covers many races, and we need not assume that Horace's geographical knowledge was more precise than our own. The most significant event in our period is the embassy to Augustus (*res gest.* 31. 2 'nostram amicitiam appetiverunt per legatos Bastarnae Scythaeque et Sarmatarum qui sunt citra flumen Tanaim et ultra reges' with Mommsen's note, Suet. *Aug.* 21. 3, Flor. *epit.* 2. 34); Orosius states that this embassy reached Augustus at Tarraco (6. 21. 19), presumably therefore about 25 B.C. (§ 5). This is the context for 3. 8. 23 f. 'iam Scythae laxo meditantur arcu / cedere campis'; as has been seen (§§ 5, 7), the references to Spain and Parthia in the same poem also suit 25 B.C. Cf. also 2. 9. 23 f. 'intraque praescriptum Gelonos / exiguis equitare campis' (see § 6 for another allusion to 25 B.C. in the same poem), *carm. saec.* 55 'iam Scythae responsa petunt', 4. 14. 42 f., 4. 15. 24. Horace's other references to the Scythians have less precision: nobody will take him seriously when he talks of an expedition against the Massagetae, east of the Caspian (1. 35. 40 n.). Sometimes the Scythians are associated with the Parthians as a potential threat (1. 19. 10, 3. 29. 28, 4. 5. 25), once with the Cantabrians (2. 11. 1). By a different convention they are held up to our admiration as paragons of primitive virtue (3. 24. 9 ff.).

§ 10. *Arabs and Indians.* In 1. 35. 40 Horace talks of fighting not only Massagetae but Arabs (cf. § 2); here there is probably no specific expedition in the poet's mind. On the other hand the ode to Iccius (1. 29) refers to a real campaign, that of Aelius Gallus. This is generally assigned to 24 B.C. (cf. Dio 53. 2. 9), but may really belong to 26 and 25.[1] In that case Horace's poem could have been written as early as 27.

The Indians on more than one occasion sent envoys to Augustus (*res gest.* 31. 1 with Mommsen's note, Suet. *Aug.* 21. 3); one such mission saw him at Tarraco in Spain (Oros. 6. 21. 19), i.e. about 25 B.C. A date hereabouts is appropriate for Prop. 2. 10. 15 f. (the projected conquest of Indians and Arabs), 1. 12. 55 f. ('sive subiectos Orientis orae / Seras et Indos'). For further references to Indians and Chinese see 1. 12. 56 n.

§ 11. *The Odes and contemporary literature.* The decade of the *Odes* was one of the most remarkable in the history of European literature. The *Georgics* were finished about 29, and Horace is indebted to the first book for some of the ideas of 1. 2 (pp. 16 f.). Varius was still

---

[1] S. Jameson, *JRS* 58, 1968, 71 ff.

Rome's leading poet in the grand manner; his *Thyestes*, produced in 29, is alluded to in 1. 6 (p. 81). Virgil was working on the *Aeneid* between 26 and his death in 19; the first book seems to contain an imitation of 1. 7 (p. 107), which was written some years previously (p. 91). The sixth book was completed after the death of Marcellus in the autumn of 23 B.C.; it was influenced by 1. 12, where he is still alive (§ 12).

Horace mocks the plaintive elegies of Tibullus (1. 33), whose first book contains allusions to Messalla's eastern expedition (probably 30 B.C.) and his Aquitanian triumph (27). In another poem he teases the elegist C. Valgius Rufus (2. 9); an allusion to Augustus's *tropaea* suggests a date about 25 (§ 6). Propertius was less congenial (*epist.* 2. 2. 99 ff.), but provides some links,[1] especially in his second book. Thus Prop. 2. 31 refers to the opening of Apollo's *porticus*, presumably in 28 (cf. *carm.* 1. 31); Prop. 2. 7 refers to the repeal of Augustus's marriage legislation, perhaps about 27 (cf. *carm.* 3. 24); Prop. 2. 10 refers to the Arabian expedition, perhaps about 25 (cf. *carm.* 1. 29). On the other hand Propertius's third book is to be dated later than the 'publication' of the *Odes*; 3. 18 is an *epicedion* on Marcellus, who died in 23 B.C.

Two great prose works were being composed about the same time. When Horace wrote 2. 1, Pollio had already begun his history;[2] the ode's denunciation of naval battles could refer to the events either of 36 or 31, but the metre better suits the latter date (§ 2). Livy finished his first five books before 25, and perhaps even earlier.[3] The words of the preface 'nec vitia nostra nec remedia pati possumus' must reflect the failure of Augustus's first attempt at moral legislation (above, § 3). Livy and Horace were part of the same movement; both alike idealized the Augustan present and the Republican past.

§ 12. *Date of 'publication'*. The first three books of the *Odes* seem to have been issued together, though the fact is nowhere explicitly stated. In *epist.* 1. 13, when Horace sends his poems to Augustus, he speaks of books in the plural (*volumina, libellis, librorum*). The first poem of the first book and the last of the third balance each other in metre and theme. Poems in the third book were not necessarily written later than those in the first; thus 1. 12 can hardly have been written before 25 B.C., when Marcellus was married to Julia, while 3. 6 predicts the restoration of the temples, which took place in 28 B.C.

[1] D. Flach, *Das literarische Verhältnis von Horaz und Properz*, 1967.

[2] Cf. J. André, *La Vie et l'œuvre d'Asinius Pollion*, 1949, pp. 44 ff.

[3] 1. 19. 3, 4. 20. 7; cf. R. Syme, *HSPh* 64, 1959, 42 ff., R. M. Ogilvie's commentary, p. 2.

The crucial argument for the dating of the collection concerns the status of Sestius, the recipient of 1. 4. This poem occupies a very prominent place in the book, immediately after odes to Maecenas, Octavian, and Virgil, and before odes to Agrippa (1. 6) and Plancus (1. 7). Sestius became consul suffect not earlier than the end of June 23 B.C.[1] It seems likely that Horace has adopted the conventional practice of honouring a consul during his term of office.[2] This argument could not be pressed if we had no other pointers to dating; but as all the other evidence suggests a date round about 23, the prominent position of 1. 4 may be given decisive weight.

1. 12 is often thought relevant to the date of 'publication'. This poem refers to the glory of Marcellus (46 n.); though the conqueror of Syracuse is meant, he would hardly have been mentioned so conspicuously, and without a hint of sorrow, after the death of the young Marcellus. This took place in the autumn of 23 B.C., certainly after the beginning of August (Plin. *nat.* 19. 24), probably after the *ludi Romani* in September (Prop. 3. 18. 19 f. *magnis ludis, RE* 3. 2767). But though this argument is relevant to the dating of this particular poem, it has no bearing on the dating of the collection as a whole. There is no reason why the tactful reference to old Marcellus should have been cancelled after young Marcellus's death.

The misfortunes of Licinius Murena seem more relevant to our problem. Horace gives a friendly warning to a certain Licinius against over-confidence (2. 10). It is reasonable to identify this person with the Licinius Murena of whom Dio says ἀκρατῷ καὶ κατακορεῖ τῇ παρρησίᾳ πρὸς πάντας ὁμοίως ἐχρῶτο (54. 3. 4); as the brother of Maecenas's wife Terentia (54. 3. 5) he moved in the same circles as the poet. Licinius Murena spoke indiscreetly at the trial of Primus for *maiestas* (assigned by Dio to 22 B.C.), was accused of complicity in the ensuing conspiracy of Caepio, and was put to death (Dio 54. 3. 1–5). This was a major scandal, which affected the political position of Maecenas; it is unlikely that Horace would have issued his poem afterwards, even as a testimony to his own prophetic insight. Likewise he would surely have deleted 2. 2. 5–8, an inorganic stanza on Proculeius's regard for his brothers, among whom Licinius Murena was included (Dio 54. 3. 5). These arguments suggest that the collection was given to the world before the denunciation of Caepio.

The position is admittedly complicated by the notorious entry in the *Capitoline Fasti* for 23: 'A. T[erentius . . . Var]ro Murena . . . . . . est. in e(ius) l(ocum) f(actus) e(st) [Cn. Calpurn]ius Cn. f. Cn. n. Pis[o.' Dio's Licinius Murena is called Varro Murena by other sources, and his sister was named Terentia; therefore the Murena of

---

[1] *Fasti Feriarum Latinarum* ap. *inscr. Ital.* 13. 1, pp. 150 f., 514.

[2] Cf. R. Syme, *Tacitus*, 1958, 2. 672.

the *Fasti* may be identical with Horace's Licinius. Perhaps the consul of 23 was forced to resign office early in the year,[1] consoled by an ode soon afterwards, and done to death in 22 after graver indiscretions.[2] Or perhaps the Murena of the *Fasti* died before entering office, and was a different person from the Licinius of Horace and Dio;[3] this hypothesis would not affect our dating of the *Odes*. Alternatively[4] some have supposed that Licinius Murena was dismissed and killed in 23, and that Dio has mistaken the year and ignored the high office of the victim. But the Horatian evidence argues against any view that leaves too short an interval between Murena's dismissal and his death. The collection seems to have been issued in the latter half of 23; otherwise the prominence of Sestius is hard to explain. At that time Murena cannot have been consul, but was not dead or irretrievably ruined; otherwise Horace would have shown an untypical lack of tact. The difficulty would be avoided if Murena's downfall were put in two stages, with the *Odes* coming between.

§ 13. *Horace's later life.* For the sake of completeness Horace's later career may be briefly summarized. He seems to have been disappointed with the reception of *Odes* 1–3; he speaks, not without humour, of his failure to canvass the literary coteries (*epist.* 1. 19. 35 ff.), and many years later refers in Callimachean vein to the jealousy of his critics (4. 3. 16 'et iam dente minus mordeor invido'). His next book was *Epistles* 1, issued in 21 or perhaps rather 20 B.C. (*epist.* 1. 20. 27 f., 1. 12. 26 ff.); the move to a different genre was to be expected in any event, and there is no need to explain it by disappointment. The *Carmen Saeculare* (17 B.C.) gave Horace the public recognition which he craved (4. 3. 13 ff., 4. 6. 41 ff.), but again there is nothing to prove that it was this that gave him the impulse to return to lyric poetry. The fourth book of *Odes*, though it contains only 15 poems, may have been written over a period of years; the last datable allusion is 13 B.C. Meanwhile Horace continued his hexameter writings with epistles to Florus (2. 2) and to Augustus himself (2. 1); the former perhaps belongs to 20 or 19 B.C., the latter perhaps about 13. The date of the *Epistula ad Pisones* (*Ars Poetica*) is far from certain, but it should probably be put towards the end of the poet's life. Horace's later work shows certain general tendencies: he has a new awareness of his own distinction and his power to confer

---

[1] His successor Piso was already in office by July, and possibly much earlier (*Fasti Feriarum Latinarum*).

[2] R. Hanslik, *RhM* 96, 1953, 282 ff. We also owe much to discussion with Mr. E. L. Bowie.

[3] K. M. Atkinson, *Historia* 9, 1960, 440 ff., M. Swan, *HSPh* 71, 1966, 235 ff.

[4] Cf. D. Stockton, *Historia* 14, 1965, 18 ff.

immortality on others; he retains an effortless command of technique alike in hexameters and lyrics; at the same time there is some loss in intimacy and originality compared with the earlier odes and epistles. After 20 B.C. Maecenas is mentioned only once (*carm.* 4. 11. 19 f.), but in his will he urged Augustus to remember Horace as himself (Suet. *vita*). His death in 8 B.C. was soon followed by Horace's own, a coincidence comforting alike to astrologers (*carm.* 2. 17) and Romantic critics.[1]

3. THE METRES OF THE *ODES*[2]

§ 1. *Asclepiad-based systems*

Horace uses Asclepiads either continuously (κατὰ στίχον) or in combination with Glyconics and Pherecrateans. The components are as follows:

Asclepiad — — — ∪ ∪ — / — ∪ ∪ — ∪ ⏓
(Maecenas atavis edite regibus)[3]

Greater Asclepiad — — — ∪ ∪ — / — ∪ ∪ — / — ∪ ∪ — ∪ ⏓
(nullam, Vare, sacra vite prius severis arborem)

Glyconic — — — ∪ ∪ — ∪ ⏓
(cui flavam religas comam)

Pherecratean — — — ∪ ∪ — ⏓
(grato, Pyrrha, sub antro)

The systems used by Horace are as follows:

(*a*) *First Asclepiad*[4] (1. 1; 3. 30; 4. 8). This metre consists simply of a series of Asclepiad lines written κατὰ στίχον. It is used similarly by Alcaeus (34b, 112, 117b, 349A–353).

(*b*) *Second Asclepiad* (1. 6, 15, 24, 33; 2. 12; 3. 10, 16; 4. 5, 12). Three

---

[1] W. Wili, *Horaz*, 1948, p. 374 'die Seele erfüllte ein Gesetz, dessen Gültigkeit dem Verstand entzogen bleibt'.

[2] See Bo 3. 29 ff.; E. Burck's appendix to the 12th edition of Kiessling–Heinze, pp. 606 ff.; F. Cupaiuolo, *Lettura di Orazio lirico*, 1967, pp. 137 ff.; R. Heinze, *Die lyrischen Verse des Horaz* (= *Vom Geist des Römertums*, ed. 3, 1960, pp. 227 ff.); Klingner 314 ff.

[3] See further L. J. Richardson, *AJPh* 22, 1901, 283 ff., H. Sadej, *Eos* 45. 1, 1951, 109 ff., A. R. Bellinger, *YClS* 15, 1957, 103 ff.

[4] The names are not worth memorizing, but as different terminologies are found a comparative table may be useful:

Klingner (adopted here)	1	2	3	4	5
Wickham, Raven (*Latin Metre*)	1	4	5	3	2
Page	1	3	4	2	5

Asclepiads are followed by a Glyconic. This stanza is also found in Alcaeus (5, 67).

(*c*) *Third Asclepiad* (1. 5, 14, 21, 23; 3. 7, 13; 4. 13). Two Asclepiads are followed by a Pherecratean and a Glyconic.

(*d*) *Fourth Asclepiad* (1. 3, 13, 19, 36; 3. 9, 15, 19, 24, 25, 28; 4. 1, 3). The stanza consists of two distichs, each made up of a Glyconic followed by an Asclepiad.

(*e*) *Fifth Asclepiad* (1. 11, 18; 4. 10). The system consists of a series of greater Asclepiads written κατὰ στίχον. It was used by Alcaeus (39a, 44, 50, 115a, 296b, 340–9), Callimachus (fr. 400), Theocritus (28, 30), and Catullus (30).

(i) In the Greek poets Asclepiads, Glyconics, and Pherecrateans begin with the so-called 'Aeolic base' of two common syllables, i.e. with either a spondee or a trochee or an iambus or a pyrrhich (◡ ◡). Horace always begins with a spondee, with one apparent exception: at 1. 15. 36 the Glyconic runs 'ignis Iliacas domos' (see n. ad loc.).

(ii) In Alcaeus Asclepiads usually have a word-break after the sixth or seventh syllable, though the fragments show exceptions. The Horatian Asclepiad has a word-break after the sixth syllable; the only exceptions are at 2. 12. 25 'dum flagrantia detorquet ad oscula' (where the prefix *de* is perhaps regarded as almost detachable), and 4. 8. 17 'non incendia Carthaginis impiae' (where interpolation has been suspected). Horace twice has irrational lengthening at this position (1. 13. 6 'certa sede manēt umor et in genas', 3. 16. 26 'quam si quidquid arāt impiger Apulus'). Similarly the greater Asclepiad normally has word-breaks after the sixth and tenth syllables; the only exception is at 1. 18. 16 'arcanique Fides prodiga perlucidior vitro' (where *per-* may be regarded as detachable).

In the case of Asclepiads it is misleading to describe these breaks as *caesurae*. The sixth syllable is quite often a monosyllabic linking conjunction (*et, aut, nec, seu, quos*), and there is sometimes a strong pause after the fifth syllable (1. 6. 17 'nos convivia, nos proelia virginum', 3. 13. 10 'nescit tangere, tu frigus amabile', 3. 25. 14 'mirari libet. o Naiadum potens', 4. 5. 33 'te multa prece, te prosequitur mero'). Similarly in the greater Asclepiad the tenth syllable may be a linking conjunction (1. 18. 2 'circa mite solum Tiburis et moenia Catili', 1. 18. 5 'quis post vina gravem militiam aut pauperiem crepat?').[1]

---

[1] Such phenomena occur at the *caesurae* of the Alcaic and Sapphic hendecasyllables, but in the Alcaics they are only half as common as in the Asclepiad line, and in the Sapphics very rare indeed. The difference of treatment suggests that Horace thought of the lesser Asclepiad line as made up of two separate cola − − − ◡ ◡ − and − ◡ ◡ − ◡ −, whereas he treated the Sapphic and Alcaic hendecasyllables rather as units with *caesurae*.

(iii) In all these systems hiatus between the lines is rare, particularly after short vowels. For instances of the latter cf. 1. 3. 24 f. 'non tangenda rates transiliunt vada. / audax omnia perpeti', 1. 11. 7 f. 'fugerit invida / aetas', 1. 36. 16 f. (where the text has been doubted; see n. ad loc.), 3. 24. 61 f. 'indignoque pecuniam / heredi properet'. Between the Pherecratean and Glyconic (i.e. in the Third Asclepiad stanza) the only instances of hiatus are at 1. 23. 3 f. 'vano / aurarum', 1. 23. 7 f. 'lacertae / et'. Moreover if one posits synaphea between the lines the Pherecratean always ends with a long syllable (as at 1. 14. 3 f. 'nonne vides ut / nudum remigio latus').

The Glyconic and Asclepiad are also closely linked (i.e. in the Fourth Asclepiad stanza); there is actually synaloepha between them at 4. 1. 35 f. 'decoro / inter'. If one posits synaphea between the lines the Glyconic usually ends with a long syllable; of 20 exceptions (out of 164 places) 6 occur in 1. 3 (e.g. 'pater / obstrictis').[1] The Asclepiad in this stanza seldom ends with an open short vowel; out of 14 exceptions 9 occur in 1. 3 (e.g. 'lucida sidera').

Lines sometimes end with a connective or other weak word (1. 3. 19 f. 'qui vidit mare turbidum et / infamis scopulos', 38 f. 'neque / per nostrum patimur scelus', 1. 19. 13 f. 'hic vivum mihi caespitem, hic / verbenas', 1. 21. 14 f. 'pestemque a populo et principe Caesare in / Persas atque Britannos', 4. 13. 6 'ille virentis et / doctae psallere Chiae').

§ 2. *The Alcaic stanza* (1. 9, 16, 17, 26, 27, 29, 31, 34, 35, 37; 2. 1, 3, 5, 7, 9, 11, 13, 14, 15, 17, 19, 20; 3. 1–6, 17, 21, 23, 26, 29; 4. 4, 9, 14, 15)

Two Alcaic hendecasyllables are followed by an enneasyllable and a decasyllable:

$$\underset{\smile}{-}-\cup--/-\cup\cup-\cup\underset{\smile}{-}$$
$$\underset{\smile}{-}-\cup--/-\cup\cup-\cup\underset{\smile}{-}$$
$$\underset{\smile}{-}-\cup----\cup-\underset{\smile}{-}$$
$$-\cup\cup-\cup\cup-\cup-\underset{\smile}{-}$$

(i) In Alcaeus the first syllable in the first three lines may be short. In Horace it is normally long, but is short thirteen times in Book 1 (1. 9. 1, 16. 9, 17. 7, 27. 17, 27. 22, 29. 7, 31. 9, 31. 17, 35. 15, 35. 37, 35. 38, 37. 15, 37. 22), eight times in Book 2 (2. 1. 6, 3. 3, 7. 22, 9. 5, 14. 6, 17. 3, 19. 22, 20. 11), and seven times in Book 3 (3. 1. 2, 1. 26, 3. 34, 3. 71, 4. 78, 5. 22, 29. 11). In Alcaeus the fifth syllable in the first three lines may be short, but in Horace it is invariably long; at

---

[1] For this and the following point see J. P. Postgate, *CQ* 16, 1922, 29 ff.

3. 5. 17 'si non periret immiserabilis', we have an irrational lengthening rather than a short syllable; cf. §§ 1 (ii), 2 (v), 3 (ii).

(ii) In the first two lines there is normally a word-break after the fifth syllable; there are exceptions to this rule at 1. 16. 21 'hostile aratrum exercitus insolens', 1. 37. 5 'antehac nefas depromere Caecubum', 1. 37. 14 'mentemque lymphatam Mareotico', 2. 17. 21 'utrumque nostrum incredibili modo', 4. 14. 7 'spectandus in certamine Martio' (at 1. 37. 5 the prefix may be regarded as separable, at 1. 16. 21 and 2. 17. 21 the irregularity is mitigated by the preceding elision). At rather more than a dozen places the word-break comes after a monosyllabic conjunction or similar word (e.g. *et* with elision before it 2. 13. 2, 3. 3. 49, 3. 4. 1, 3. 5. 10, 3. 6. 22, *an* 2. 3. 22, *ex* 3. 2. 6, *se* 3. 5. 33, *te* 3. 21. 10, 4. 14. 33, *o* 4. 4. 37, *non* 4. 4. 73, 4. 14. 41, *qui* 4. 14. 45); this list neglects cases like 1. 9. 2 'Soracte, nec iam sustineant onus' and 1. 9. 18 'morosa, nunc et Campus et areae', where the presence of a second monosyllable makes some difference. There is quite frequent elision over the word-break of a short vowel or of a syllable ending in *-m* (e.g. 3. 3. 41 'insultet armentum et catulos ferae'), of a long vowel only at 1. 34. 10 'quo Styx et invisi horrida Taenari', 3. 2. 5 'vitamque sub divo et trepidis agat', 3. 3. 33 'Marti redonabo. illum ego lucidas'.

(iii) Hiatus is rare at the end of any line, but is found at all of them; there is hiatus after a short syllable only at 1. 16. 27, 1. 17. 13, 2. 13. 7, and after *-m* only at 1. 31. 14, 2. 5. 9, 2. 13. 11. There is synaloepha between the third and fourth lines at 2. 3. 27 f. 'aeternum / exsilium' and 3. 29. 35 f. 'Etruscum / in mare'.

The first line sometimes ends with a connective or other weak word; cf. 1. 19. 13 f. 'quid sit futurum cras fuge quaerere et / . . .', 2. 15. 5, 3. 1. 25, 3. 26. 9, 3. 29. 49, 4. 9. 1. The second and third lines are usually more separate; yet see 3. 1. 38 f. 'neque / decedit', 3. 29. 46 f. 'neque / diffinget', 4. 4. 18 '— quibus / . . .'. The third and fourth lines are closely linked by the occurrence at the end of the third of *et* (8 times, always with elision before it), *in* (1. 35. 39, also with elision before it), and *nec* (2. 7. 19).

(iv) Horace normally distributes the words in the third line of the Alcaic according to certain favoured patterns. It will be convenient to arrange these possibilities (somewhat over-schematically) according to the number of syllables in the last word or word-group; the only instances not covered by the main heads are 1. 26. 11 'hunc Lesbio sacrare plectro',[1] 2. 7. 19 'depone sub lauru mea, nec' and 2. 3. 27 'sors exitura et nos in aeternum'.

---

[1] This line is unique in having a word-break after the fourth syllable; in Alcaeus this is found only with elision (208a. 8, cf. Hor. 2. 3. 27) or where a monosyllable precedes (326. 7 λαῖφος δὲ πὰν ζάδηλον ἤδη, 76. 12).

A. TRISYLLABIC

(*a*) preceded by a trisyllable:

> pignusque dereptum lacertis
> lenesque sub noctem susurri
> ad arma cessantes ad arma

(*b*) preceded by longer words:

> silvae laborantes geluque
> non erubescendis adurit (rare)

B. DISYLLABIC (when preceded by a word longer than a disyllable)

> fatalis incestusque iudex
> ludo fatigatumque somno

C. QUADRISYLLABIC[1]

(*a*) monosyllable plus trisyllable:

> stetere causae cur perirent

(*b*) quadrisyllable proper:

> nodo coerces viperino

double disyllable:

> pronos relabi posse rivos

(The oddity of this last is sometimes mitigated by anaphora at the beginning of the next line; cf. 1. 16. 3 f. 'sive flamma / sive mari', 1. 26. 7, 2. 13. 27, 2. 14. 11, 2. 19. 7. For exceptions to this tendency see 1. 29. 11, 2. 1. 11, 2. 19. 11.)

The distribution of these types in the different books of the *Odes* is as follows (percentage figures in brackets):

Book		I		II		III		IV		Total
A	(*a*)	32	(53·3)	36	(41·9)	59	(50)	21	(39·6)	148
	(*b*)	8	(13·3)	23	(26·7)	21	(17·8)	10	(18·9)	62
B		3	(5)	5	(5·8)	29	(24·6)	16	(30·2)	53
C	(*a*)	12	(20)	13	(15·1)	9	(7·6)	6	(11·3)	40
	(*b*)	4	(6·7)	7	(8·1)	0		0		11
Others		1	(1·7)	2	(2·3)	0		0		3
		60		86		118		53		317

The most interesting feature in this list is the startling increase of type B (disyllabic ending) in the third and fourth books, as well as the disappearance of C (*b*) (double disyllabic ending). These facts

---

[1] This break is only admitted by Alcaeus if the fifth syllable is short (except with elision at 326. 3).

may have some bearing on the date of composition (p. xxviii). One may also note the comparative rarity of A (*b*) in Book I and its sudden increase in Book II; this again suggests that when Horace arranged his first three books the date of composition may have played a bigger part than is generally supposed.

(v) In the last line of the Alcaic stanza there is usually a word-break after the fourth syllable. There is irrational lengthening at this place at 2. 13. 16 'caeca timēt aliunde fata'.

The following figures again show a changing pattern from book to book. The only line not covered by the main heads is 3. 5. 56 'aut Lacedaemonium Tarentum'.

A. Main word-break after the first trochee:

> Caesar ab Italia volantem
> vitis Achaemeniumque costum

B. Main word-break after the first dactyl:

> torquibus exiguis renidet
> liquimus? unde manum iuventus
> Antiochum Hannibalemque dirum

C. Main word-break after the choriamb:

> sensit iners timuitque mortem
> Hesperiae mala luctuosae
> missilibus melior sagittis

D. Main word-break after the second trochee (usually in conjunction with other breaks):

> o Thaliarche, merum diota

Book	I		II		III		IV		Total
A	2	(3·3)	4	(4·7)	3	(2·5)	4	(7·5)	13
B	21	(35)	19	(22·1)	21	(17·8)	7	(13·2)	68
C[1]	33	(55)	61	(70·9)	92	(78)	41	(77·3)	227
D	4	(6·7)	2	(2·3)	1[2]	(0·8)	1	(1·9)	8
Others	0		0		1	(0·8)	0		1
	60		86		118		53		317

[1] The choriamb is followed by a pyrrhich word (e.g. 'concutitur. valet ima summis') in the following number of cases:

> Book I   II   III   IV
> 5 (8·3)   7 (8·1)   24 (20·3) 11 (20·8)

[2] 3. 5. 12 'incolumi Iove et urbe Roma', where the elision and the following monosyllable make a difference.

§ 3. (a) *The Sapphic stanza* (1. 2, 10, 12, 20, 22, 25, 30, 32, 38; 2. 2, 4, 6, 8, 10, 16; 3. 8, 11, 14, 18, 20, 22, 27; 4. 2, 6, 11; *carm. saec.*)

Three Sapphic hendecasyllables are followed by an adonius:

$$- \cup - - - \cup \cup - \cup - \underline{\cup}$$
$$- \cup - - - \cup \cup - \cup - \underline{\cup}$$
$$- \cup - - - \cup \cup - \cup - \underline{\cup}$$
$$- \cup \cup - \underline{\cup}$$

(i) In Sappho and Alcaeus the fourth syllable of the hendeca-syllable may be short;[1] so also in the Hellenistic hymn to Rome by Melinno (Stob. 3. 7. 12) and in Catullus. In Horace it is always long.

(ii) In Books I–III there is normally a word-break after the fifth syllable of the hendecasyllable; this occurs in five-eighths of the instances in Alcaeus, less often in Sappho. Elision is rare at this place (short vowel 2. 4. 10, 2. 16. 26, 3. 27. 10, *-um* 4. 11. 27). There is an irrational long at the word-break at 2. 6. 14 'angulus ridēt, ubi non Hymetto'. There is a break after *et* (preceded by an elision) at 1. 32. 13, 2. 2. 21, 3. 8. 14, and without elision at 3. 11. 50 'dum favet nox et Venus, i secundo'.

A break after the sixth syllable[2] occurs a few times in Books I and II (three in the hymn to Mercury 1. 10, one in the hymn to Venus 1. 30, one in the hymnal first line of 1. 12, and also at 1. 25. 11, 2. 6. 11). There is no example in Book III, even in the three hymns (3. 11, 3. 18, 3. 22). In the *Carmen saeculare* and in Book IV this break is quite common.

(iii) There is synaloepha between hendecasyllables at 2. 2. 18, 2. 16. 34, 4. 2. 22, and perhaps 3. 27. 10. Lines end with *et* at 2. 6. 1, 2. 6. 2, 2. 16. 37, 3. 8. 26, 3. 11. 5, 3. 27. 22, 3. 27. 29, 3. 27. 46, and with *qui* at *carm. saec.* 9.

The adonius is still more closely linked with the last hendeca-syllable. For synaloepha see 4. 2. 23, *carm. saec.* 47; for weak words at the end of the hendecasyllable see 3. 8. 3, 3. 8. 27 (?), 4. 6. 11; for a word shared between the lines see 1. 2. 19 'u-/xorius', 1. 25. 11 'inter-/lunia', 2. 16. 7 've-/nale' (this last feature is found in Sappho, but not in Alcaeus; cf. Page, op. cit., p. 318).

On the other hand hiatus is found 10 times between hendeca-syllables, 4 times between hendecasyllable and adonius. Normally it occurs after a long vowel; for instances after *-m* cf. 1. 2. 47, 1. 22. 15, 3. 27. 33, and perhaps 3. 27. 10.

(b) *Greater Sapphic* (1. 8)

$$- \cup \cup - \cup - -$$
$$- \cup - - - \cup \cup - / - \cup \cup - \cup - -$$

---

[1] For this and other points see Page, *Sappho and Alcaeus*, pp. 318, 324.
[2] D. W. Prakken, *CPh* 49, 1954, 102 ff.

An Aristophaneus is followed by a greater Sapphic line, which is like a Sapphic hendecasyllable with a choriamb added after the fourth syllable. The second half of the greater Sapphic is identical with the Aristophaneus. Horace has a break after the fifth and the eighth syllables. The metre is not found in the fragments of Sappho and Alcaeus.

§ 4. *Epodic metres*

(a) *First Archilochian* (or *Alcmanian*) (1. 7, 1. 28; cf. *epod.* 12, anon. *GLP* 91)

A dactylic hexameter is followed by a dactylic tetrameter:

$$- \underline{\cup}\underline{\cup} - \underline{\cup}\underline{\cup} - \underline{\cup}\underline{\cup} - \underline{\cup}\underline{\cup} - \underline{\cup}\underline{\cup} - \underline{\cup}$$
$$- \underline{\cup}\underline{\cup} - \underline{\cup}\underline{\cup} - \underline{\cup}\underline{\cup} - \underline{\cup}$$

In general the hexameter follows the pattern of the heroic hexameter. Elisions are infrequent (1. 7. 5 'unum opus', 1. 7. 13 'Anio ac', 1. 28. 18 'exitio est', 1. 28. 19 'senum ac', *epod.* 12. 9 'neque illi'). The line normally ends in a disyllable or trisyllable; exceptions are 1. 7. 1 'aut Mitylenen', 1. 28. 15 'una manet nox', 1. 28. 21 'comes Orionis', *epod.* 12. 23 'conviva, magis quem'.

In the tetrameter there are a number of quadrisyllabic or double-disyllabic endings, and *epod.* 12. 6 ends with a single monosyllable ('ubi lateat sus'). For a weak ending cf. 1. 7. 6 'celebrare et'. For hiatus in the middle of the line cf. 1. 28. 24 'capiti inhumato'.

(b) *Second Archilochian* (4. 7)

A dactylic hexameter is followed by a dactylic hemiepes:

$$- \underline{\cup}\underline{\cup} - \underline{\cup}\underline{\cup} - \underline{\cup}\underline{\cup} - \underline{\cup}\underline{\cup} - \underline{\cup}\underline{\cup} - -$$
$$- \cup\cup - \cup\cup\underline{\cup}$$

There is no hiatus between lines, but a short vowel ends 22. There is only one elision (15 'neque enim').

(c) *Third Archilochian* (1. 4; cf. Archil. 112–16, Simon. *anth. P.* 13. 26, Palladius, *anth. Lat.* 628, Prud. *perist.* 12)

A greater Archilochian line is followed by an iambic trimeter catalectic. The greater Archilochian is an asynartete combination of a dactylic tetrameter and an ithyphallic; it is found also in Call. *epig.* 39, 40, Theoc. *epig.* 20, 21, and several times in the Anthology (13. 8 Theodoridas, 13. 27 Phalaecus, 13. 28 attributed to Bacchylides or Simonides).

$$- \underline{\cup}\underline{\cup} - \underline{\cup}\underline{\cup} - \underline{\cup}\underline{\cup} - \cup\cup \, / - \cup - \cup - -$$
$$\underline{\cup} - \cup - - \, / - \cup - \cup - -$$

In Horace the diaeresis after the tetrameter is constant, and the last foot of the tetrameter is always a pure dactyl. The trimeter has the normal caesura after the fifth syllable; its first syllable is short only at 2. There is hiatus after a long vowel at the end of 9. Elision does not occur at all.

(d) Hipponactean (2. 18)

A trochaic dimeter catalectic (lecythion) is followed by an iambic trimeter catalectic:

$$-\cup-\cup-\cup\underset{\smile}{\,}$$
$$\underset{\smile}{\,}-\cup-\underset{\smile}{\,}\,/-\cup-\cup--$$

The first syllable of the trimeter is long only at 6 and 34, the fifth short only at 2, 14, 38, 40; the fourth syllable is resolved in 34. There is one hiatus after the dimeter (5), and three after the trimeter (8, 18, 30); the dimeter ends in a short vowel at 17 and 21.

§ 5. Ionics (3. 12)

This poem is made up of 40 continuously linked ionic metra $(\cup\cup--)$. The only constant pause occurs after every 10th metron.[1]

Alcaeus 10, from which this poem takes its motto, seems to offer a 4-line stanza, the first line of which is a tetrameter, and the last perhaps a trimeter. Other ionic fragments of Sappho and Alcaeus are preserved only in single lines or parts of lines (Sappho 135, Alcaeus 380, 387, 393, 397).

Note on stanzas[2]

Horace's odes are normally written in multiples of 4 lines. The only exception is 4. 8 (34 lines), where interpolation has been suspected (partly on other grounds).

Many of the odes (such as those in Sapphics and Alcaics) are visibly written in 4-line stanzas, normally with a sense-pause at the end of the stanza. Exceptions occur at 58 places out of 280 in Alcaics, 8 places out of 179 in Sapphics.

In other metres the basic unit is of 2 lines, though there too 4-line sense-groups are often found (1. 4, 1. 8, 1. 13, 1. 19, 4. 7). But in other odes (1. 7, 1. 28, 2. 18) little is gained by thinking of units larger than the distich.

The poems written κατὰ στίχον show diverse treatment. 1. 1 breaks into 4-line sense-groups, but for the most part the divisions come, not after 4, 8, etc., but after 6, 10, etc.; it has the appearance of being eight 4-line stanzas framed by two distichs. The other such poems have nothing but the number of lines to suggest stanza form.

---

[1] See also J. P. Postgate, CQ 18, 1924, 46 ff.

[2] For further details see K. Büchner, Horaz, 1962, pp. 52 ff.

4. THE ANCIENT COMMENTATORS

The surviving commentaries of Porphyrio and pseudo-Acro are the inadequate representatives of a long tradition. We hear of writings on Horace by Claranus (Porph. *serm.* 2. 3. 83, *RE* 3. 2627) and Modestus (ps.-Acro, second *vita*, *RE* 2. 2294) ; these scholars are mentioned together by Martial (10. 21. 1 f.), and were presumably his contemporaries. Q. Terentius Scaurus, the principal grammarian of Hadrian's age, also commented on Horace (Porph. *serm.* 2. 5. 92, *RE* 5 A. 674 f., Schanz–Hosius 3³. 158) ; Charisius twice cites his 'commentarii in artem poeticam lib. X' (*gramm.* 1. 202. 26 = 263. 11 B., 210. 19 = 272. 27 B.), by which he probably means the tenth book of a commentary on all Horace. Later in the second century the learned Helenius Acro wrote his lost commentary (*RE* 7. 2840) ; it was used by Porphyrio (*serm.* 1. 8. 25), and is described by another writer as 'omnibus melius' (ps.-Acro, second *vita*). It is certainly plausible that some of these commentaries were better than anything that we now possess; this is suggested not so much by the superior quality of the Virgilian scholia (for he was always a special case) as by the uneven standard of Porphyrio himself. In particular one may note the thoroughness of his prosopographical notes[1] on the *Satires* (cf. for instance 1. 7. 19, 1. 8. 39, 2. 2. 50, 2. 3. 239) ; some of these notes refer to unnamed earlier scholars 'qui de personis Horatianis scripserunt' (*serm.* 1. 3. 21, 1. 3. 90).

Of the two extant commentaries that of Pomponius Porphyrio[2] is earlier and better. His date is disputed. He quotes Suetonius, Terentius Scaurus, and the real Acro (who seems to have flourished after Gellius) ; therefore he cannot have lived earlier than the end of the second century. He is quoted by the fourth century Charisius (*gramm.* 1. 220. 27 = 285. 12 B.), in a section *de adverbio* derived from Julius Romanus (*RE* 10. 788 f.). Romanus in turn quotes one Marcius Salutaris, whom he describes as *vir perfectissimus* (*gramm.* 1. 229 = 297. 8 B.) ; a person of this name was *procurator Augustorum* in A.D. 246 (*RE* 14. 1590 f.), but the identification cannot be guaranteed. It may be significant that Porphyrio still speaks of Parthians, though their empire fell to the Persian Sassanids in A.D. 226; cf. 1. 27. 5 'gladius Parthicus' (ps.-Acro 'gladius Persarum'), 2. 12. 21 'Achaemenis rex Parthorum fuit' (ps.-Acro 'nomen regis Persarum').[3] All the same, this material might be tralatician and so

[1] See A. Kiessling, *Index schol. Greifsw.*, 1880.
[2] See O. Keller, *Symbola Philologorum Bonnensium*, 1864–7, pp. 491 ff., Schanz–Hosius 3³. 167 f., *RE* 21. 2412 ff. Text by A. Holder, 1894.
[3] As the reference in each case is to ancient objects or persons, *Persarum* is in fact more accurate.

does not provide complete proof of a third-century date. It may also be noted that Porphyrio never refers to Juvenal and only twice to Lucan, while he shows a mild partiality to early Latin, notably Lucilius;[1] however, this pattern is found not only in Romanus but in Charisius as a whole, and so is compatible even with a fourth-century date. One thing at any rate is certain, though it does not take us very far: Porphyrio writes as if pagan cults were still flourishing (*carm.* 1. 5. 12–13, 1. 36. 1–2, 3. 11. 6, *serm.* 1. 3. 10–11).

If we can trust his claims to autopsy, Porphyrio had been in Rome (*carm.* 3. 11. 6); but he gives the impression of writing for an audience outside Italy (*carm.* 1. 23. 6–7 'sic denique et a rusticis hodieque in Italia appellantur', 1. 36. 1–2, 3. 23. 15–16). He uses Greek words freely and familiarly (*serm.* 2. 7, *epist.* 2. 1. 128, *carm.* 1. 16. 17, *ars* 42), yet shows no signs of belonging to Greece. Some scholars assign him to Africa, which would be appropriate for a man of literary and rhetorical tastes alike in the third and fourth centuries. Keller claims to detect some actual knowledge of Africa; his best instance is *epist.* 2. 2. 181 (on *Gaetulo murice*) 'significat purpuram Girbitanam'. Porphyrio's language contains some vulgarisms, but attempts to find specifically African features are as always misguided.

In its original form, as the note on *serm.* 1. 9. 52 shows, Porphyrio's work was designed to accompany a punctuated text. It is however preserved as a separate commentary in two early manuscripts, the Vaticanus (9th century) and the Monacensis (10th century); it is therefore accessible to us in a form not corrupted by medieval accretions. But our extant version has suffered abbreviation, as one can see from the note on *carm.* 1. 2. 15 'monumentum non sepulchrum tantum dicitur, sed omnia, quidquid memoriam testatur. *regis* ergo Numae Pompilii significat'; to be intelligible, this note needs to be supplemented by the information we have in ps.-Acro 'regiam dixit *monumenta regis*. locus enim est in quo Numa Pompilius habitavit ⟨ad⟩ Vestae habens regiam'. Some of the commentary's defects may be attributed to this cause.

Porphyrio has good moments. But for him we should not be aware that 1. 15 is derived from Bacchylides. He knows not only that Alcaeus wrote a hymn to Mercury, but that he described the theft

---

[1] On the *Odes* he cites no Greek poet but Homer, though the commentary on the *ars* cites Callimachus, that on the *Epistles* Theognis. Of his Latin parallels a large number are Virgilian, and most of the rest come from Republican or early Augustan authors (the Twelve Tables, Plautus, Ennius, Pacuvius, Terence, Lucilius, Titinius, Varro, Cicero, Lucretius, Catullus, Sallust, Livy, Pollio). There are very occasional references to Ovid, and in the commentary on the *Satires* frequent citation of Persius; otherwise Imperial literature is totally ignored.

of Apollo's quiver (1. 10). His comments on the supposed division of 1. 7 are not only sensible but well-informed: 'hanc oden quidam putant aliam esse, sed eadem est; nam et hic ad Plancum loquitur, in cuius honore et in superiore parte Tibur laudavit. Plancus enim inde fuit oriundus.' He knows the meaning of *tergeminis honoribus* better than modern commentators (*carm.* 1. 1. 8 n.), and he sees that Horace is suggesting that Varius has Homeric qualities (1. 6. 13 n.). Some of his comments even show signs of a tentative literary criticism (1. 2. 9 n., 1. 9. 21 n.).

On the other hand his deficiencies are conspicuous, especially in the *Odes*. Unlike pseudo-Acro he gives no information on metre. He fails to record fundamental Greek influences, Alcaeus on 1. 9, 1. 14, 1. 18, 1. 37, Stesichorus on 1. 16, Anacreon on 1. 23; it is fair to assume that other important allusions have been totally lost. He makes little mention of Hellenistic poetry, and displays no interest in such literary categories as the *propempticon* and *paraclausithyron*. His use even of Latin literature is inadequate; he misses the imitations of the *Georgics* in 1. 2, and he does not explain that Varius wrote a *Thyestes* (1. 6. 8). He has no detailed knowledge of the historical background: thus he associates 1. 2 with the assassination of Julius Caesar, and makes even worse blunders on 1. 14 ('in hac ode ad Marcum Brutum loquitur, qui apud Filippos Macedoniae urbem ab Augusto fusus videbatur rursus ⟨se⟩ instruere ad pugnam'). He often fails to provide cross-references to reappearances of a proper name (1. 22 Fuscus, 1. 24 Quintilius, 1. 29 Iccius). Even on points of Latinity he sometimes introduces strange confusions: cf. 1. 1. 5 'ambiguum utrum nobilis deos an nobilis palma', 1. 4. 10 (he considers the possibility that *terrae solutae* may refer to untilled land), 1. 6. 2 'ut si diceret *Homericis auspiciis* ac per hoc *Homerica sublimitate*', 1. 21. 14 'numquid *principe* et ad populum referemus, ut sit a populo principe . . .?'. It may be remarked finally that he is of far less importance for textual criticism than is sometimes supposed; where two ancient variants are available his support for one of them adds nothing to our information, and his *lemmata*, which are sometimes quoted with respect, have no ancient authority.[1]

The scholia of the so-called pseudo-Acro,[2] unlike those of Porphyrio, survive not in separate manuscripts but in the margins of texts of Horace. They comprise a shifting agglomeration of material from a variety of sources; as far as the *Odes* are concerned, the least contaminated authority is the tenth-century Paris manuscript 7900 A. They refer twice by name to the real Acro (*carm.* 4. 9. 37

[1] O. Keller, *Epilegomena zu Horaz*, 1879, pp. 796 f.
[2] O. Keller, loc. cit. (p. xlvii above), pp. 499 ff., Schanz–Hosius 3³. 166 f., *RE* 7. 2841 ff. Text by Keller, 2 vols., 1902 and 1904.

and *vita*), and frequently take over material from Porphyrio. The nucleus of the compilation seems to have been formed in the early fifth century A.D.; see *carm.* 2. 11. 1 (on the Scythians) 'gens septentrionalis, post Hunnorum dicta', 4. 15. 22 (the Getae are called *Gothi*), *serm.* 1. 9. 76 'sic Servius magister exposuit'. There are allusions to pagan rites as a thing of the past (*carm.* 1. 36. 1, 2. 16. 14, 3. 11. 5); this suggests a date after 394, when sacrifices were stopped. One may also note the distribution of pseudo-Acro's *testimonia*; in their striking partiality for Juvenal and Lucan and their comparative playing down of early Latin (at least by Porphyrio's standards) they show the pattern of the sixth-century Priscian rather than the fourth-century Charisius and Diomedes (see the index to Keil's *Grammatici Latini*). The collection of scholia was continually added to; cf. *serm.* 1. 5. 97 'ut dixit grammaticus Theotistus' (Theoctistus taught Priscian at Constantinople towards the end of the fifth century; cf. *RE* 5 A. 1704 f.), *carm.* 3. 29. 4 (a reference to the seventh-century Isidore). Finally there were medieval accretions, as was natural in a text preserved in such a way. The name Acro is not attached to the collection before perhaps the fifteenth century.

The pseudo-Acro scholia are much fuller than Porphyrio's commentary, and occasionally they have something pertinent to offer that is not found in the earlier work. Thus they refer to Varius's *Thyestes* at *carm.* 1. 6. 8, and to Stesichorus's palinode at *carm.* 1. 16. 1.[1] They cite priestly lore at *carm.* 1. 12. 19, 1. 12. 59. They show knowledge of Pupius at *epist.* 1. 1. 67, of Titinius at *epist.* 1. 13. 14, of Caecilius at *ars* 238. Moreover they are preceded by a metrical preface and include a metrical analysis of individual poems.

On the other hand most of the extra material is extremely elementary; it largely consists of superfluous paraphrases and notes for schoolboys on grammar and mythology. The abundant poetical parallels are often irrelevant: for instance, at 1. 5. 14 allusion is made to Juv. 14. 301 f. 'naufragus assem / dum rogat et picta se tempestate tuetur'. There is even less than in Porphyrio on Horace's Greek models; at *carm.* 1. 15 the reference to Bacchylides has disappeared. Difficulties are often ignored: there is no consideration of the bearing of the question *quis Martem . . . ?* in 1. 6, no note on *quinta parte* at 1. 13. 16 or on *divides* at 1. 15. 15 (which Porphyrio at least attempts to explain, though unsuccessfully). When alternative solutions are offered, they sometimes betray a most unscholarly doubt: cf. 1. 1. 34 '*Lesboum* propter Alcaeum et Sappho, quos in Lesbo insula natos

---

[1] They have here some information that could not be inferred from the ode or from *epode* 17, namely that Stesichorus composed his palinode *responso Apollinis*. This assertion might of course be false, but should not be ignored by Stesichorus's editors; cf. *oraculo admonitum* in Porph. *epod.* 17. 42.

esse constat, aut ab eo Lesbio qui primus fuit lyricus scriptor, aut a
Periandro rege Lesbi cui primum Mercurius lyram ostendit', *ars* 136
'cyclicus poeta est, qui ordinem variare nescit, vel qui carmina sua
circumfert quasi circumforaneus; aut nomen proprium est Cyclicus
et significat Antimachum poetam'. There is a lack of common sense
in interpreting even the simplest passages: cf. *carm.* 1. 3. 9 (on *aes
triplex*) 'verbum ab usurariis tractum posuit, quorum avaritia spe
lucri vel commercii inventum navigium sit', 1. 5. 5 'simplicem munditiis dicit animo factiosam', 1. 12. 29 'laus stellae a tempore; nam
verno tempore nascitur quo et nives resolvuntur', 1. 13. 9 'ordo est:
seu immodicae rixae turparunt tibi candidos umeros mero'. Sometimes the errors seem simply due to a misunderstanding of Porphyrio
or other scholarly sources: contrast, for example, Porph. *carm.* 1. 1.
34 'barbiton organi genus est in modum lyrae' with pseudo-Acro ad
loc. 'lyra maior organi sono similis'.

A third body of notes is sometimes mentioned even in nineteenth-
century editions; this is ascribed to the so-called 'Commentator
Cruquianus'.[1] It was first printed by Cruquius in his edition of 1611,
the notes of the Commentator on each poem preceding those of
Cruquius himself. In fact the Commentator is a ghost figure born
from Cruquius's despair of attributing to particular authorities the
notes that he found in manuscripts and editions and from his refusal
to believe that comments of this quality should be assigned to
honoured names like those of Acro and Porphyrio; this is plain from
his own preface. The 'commentary' itself is an amalgam of margi-
nalia, 'Acronian' and later, of material drawn from printed editions
of Porphyrio and pseudo-Acro, and of notes in Renaissance editions,
notably that of Lambinus. It does not provide any ancient material
to which we have no other access.

5. ABBREVIATIONS, ETC.

(A) EDITIONS OF THE ODES

We have included only the editions which we have found most useful.
For fuller lists cf. Schanz–Hosius 2. 152, and especially Lenchantin–
Bo (cited below), vol. 1, pp. xlv ff.

Lambinus, D.: Lyons, 1561. His contributions are mainly incorporated
in later commentaries.

Bentley, R.: Cambridge, 1711; ed. 3, Amsterdam, 1728 (reprinted 1869).
Select *adversaria*, still requiring the closest attention.

---

[1] See Keller, *Pseudacron*, vol. 2, pp. x ff., J. Endt, *Studien zum Commentator
Cruquianus*, 1906. For the text see Cruquius's own edition.

Mitscherlich, C. G.: vol. 1, Leipzig, 1800. Offers some useful parallels neglected by later commentators.

Ritter, F.: Leipzig, 1856. A few good things.

Peerlkamp, P. Hofman: ed. 2, Amsterdam, 1862. Interesting but perverse.

Keller, O.: *Epilegomena zu Horaz*, Leipzig, 1879. Detailed discussions of textual issues, often trivial.

Schütz, H.: vol. 1, ed. 3, Berlin, 1881. A good school-book.

Dillenburger, G.: ed. 7, Bonn, 1881. Short, but better than most of its kind.

Orelli, J. C., revised by J. G. Baiter and W. Hirschfelder: vol. 1, ed. 4, Berlin, 1886. An indispensable commentary, alike the repository and the source of much tralatician lore.

Kiessling, A.: vol. 1, ed. 2, Berlin, 1890. Less full than Heinze's revision (see below), but not always inferior.

Page, T. E.: London, 1895. A useful school-book, but less attractive than the same editor's *Virgil*.

Gow, J.: Cambridge, 1896. An elementary commentary by a good scholar.

Wickham, E. C.: vol. 1, ed. 3, Oxford, 1896. The best English commentary, but still short on literary history.

Keller, O. and Holder, A.: vol. 1, ed. 2, Leipzig, 1899. No commentary, but valuable lists of parallels.

Müller, Lucian: 2 vols., St. Petersburg and Leipzig, 1900. Original and ingenious.

Shorey, P. and Laing, G. J.: ed. 2, Chicago, 1910 (reprinted Pittsburgh, 1960). Fresh parallels, many from English poets.

Wickham, E. C., revised by Garrod, H. W.: ed. 2, Oxford, 1912. Text only; the short *apparatus* gives the main lines adequately.

Plessis, F.: Paris, 1924 (reprinted Hildesheim, 1966). Not comparable with Lejay's *Satires*.

Villeneuve, F.: Paris, 1927. Text (Budé) and translation only.

Heinze, R.: vol. 1, Berlin, 1930 (ed. 7 of Kiessling). Brief and not always clear, but has far wider horizons than any other commentary. The tenth edition, 1960, has a valuable bibliographical appendix by E. Burck.

Campbell, A. Y.: ed. 1, London, 1945; ed. 2, Liverpool, 1953. *Adversaria*, usually absurd, but sometimes revealing difficulties.

Tescari, O.: ed. 3, Turin, 1948. The best Italian commentary.

Lenchantin de Gubernatis, M., revised by Bo, D.: 3 vols., Turin, 1957–60. Bibliographies in first volume, grammatical and metrical indexes in third.

Klingner, F.: ed. 3, Leipzig, 1959. Text only; the most up-to-date, but relies too much on *stemmata*.

Turolla, E.: Turin, 1963. No commentary, but full bibliography on each poem.

(B) OTHER BOOKS CITED

This is not a bibliography, but simply a list of the abbreviated titles used in the commentary; such references as 'André 123' may be elucidated here. We have not included periodicals, for which we follow the system of *L'Année philologique*. A select bibliography is prefixed to the commentary on every ode; the expressions 'op. cit.' and 'loc. cit.' normally point to those bibliographies, not to this list. For further bibliographical information see Schanz–Hosius 2. 127 ff.; the editions cited above by Heinze–Burck, Lenchantin–Bo, Turolla; K. Büchner, *JAW* 267, 1939; *Der kleine Pauly* 2. 1224; and above all, *L'Année philologique*.

ALL	*Archiv für lateinische Lexikographie und Grammatik*, ed. E. Wölfflin, Leipzig, 1884–1909.
André	J. André, *Études sur les termes de couleur dans la langue latine*, Paris, 1949.
Appel	G. Appel, *De Romanorum precationibus*, Giessen, 1909 (*Religionsgeschichtliche Versuche und Vorarbeiten*, Bd. 7, Heft 2).
Axelson	B. Axelson, *Unpoetische Wörter, ein Beitrag zur Kenntnis der lateinischen Dichtersprache*, Lund, 1945.
Baumeister	A. Baumeister, *Denkmäler des klassischen Altertums zur Erläuterung des Lebens der Griechen und Römer in Religion, Kunst und Sitte*, Munich and Leipzig, 1885–9.
Bell	A. J. Bell, *The Latin Dual and Poetic Diction*, London, 1923.
Blümner	H. Blümner, *Römische Privataltertümer*, Munich, 1911.
Blümner, *Technologie*	H. Blümner, *Technologie und Terminologie der Gewerbe und Künste bei Griechen und Römern*, Leipzig, 1875–87 (vol. 1, ed. 2, 1912).
BMI	*The Collection of Ancient Greek Inscriptions in the British Museum*, Oxford, 1874–1916.
Boucher	J.-P. Boucher, *Études sur Properce: problèmes d'inspiration et d'art*, Paris, 1965.
Bowra	C. M. Bowra, *Greek Lyric Poetry*, ed. 2, Oxford, 1961.

Broughton, *MRR* T. R. S. Broughton, *The Magistrates of the Roman Republic*, New York, 1951–2.

Bruchmann C. F. H. Bruchmann, *Epitheta Deorum quae apud poetas Graecos leguntur*, Leipzig, 1893 (supplement in Roscher, vol. 7).

CAH *The Cambridge Ancient History*, Cambridge, 1923– .

Campbell A. Y. Campbell, *Horace*, London, 1924.

Carter J. B. Carter, *Epitheta Deorum quae apud poetas Latinos leguntur*, Leipzig, 1902 (supplement in Roscher, vol. 7).

CGL *Corpus Glossariorum Latinorum*, ed. G. Goetz, Leipzig, 1888–1923.

CIL *Corpus Inscriptionum Latinarum*, Berlin, 1863–.

Commager S. Commager, *The Odes of Horace: A Critical Study*, New Haven and London, 1962.

Cook, *Zeus* A. B. Cook, *Zeus: a Study in Ancient Religion*, Cambridge, 1914–40.

corp. paroem. gr. *Corpus paroemiographorum Graecorum*, ed. E. L. Leutsch and F. G. Schneidewin, Göttingen, 1839–51 (reprinted Hildesheim, 1958).

Cumont F. Cumont, *Recherches sur le symbolisme funéraire des Romains*, Paris, 1942.

Curtius E. R. Curtius, *European Literature and the Latin Middle Ages*, translated by Willard R. Trask, London, 1953.

Denniston J. D. Denniston, *The Greek Particles*, ed. 2, Oxford, 1954.

Diels–Kranz *Die Fragmente der Vorsokratiker*, ed. H. Diels and W. Kranz, ed. 7, Berlin, 1954.

Doblhofer E. Doblhofer, *Die Augustuspanegyrik des Horaz in formalhistorischer Sicht*, Heidelberg, 1966.

Dodds E. R. Dodds, *The Greeks and the Irrational*, Berkeley and Los Angeles, 1951.

D.–S. C. Daremberg and E. Saglio, *Dictionnaire des antiquités grecques et romaines d'après les textes et les monuments*, Paris, 1877–1919.

Farnell L. R. Farnell, *The Cults of the Greek States*, Oxford, 1896–1909.

FGrH *Die Fragmente der griechischen Historiker*, ed. F. Jacoby, Berlin–Leiden, 1923– .

Fraenkel E. Fraenkel, *Horace*, Oxford, 1957.

Fraenkel, *Kl. Beitr.*	E. Fraenkel, *Kleine Beiträge zur klassischen Philologie*, Rome, 1964.
Fraenkel, *Plautinisches im Plautus*	E. Fraenkel, *Plautinisches im Plautus*, Berlin, 1922 (cf. *Elementi plautini in Plauto*, translated by F. Munari, Florence, 1960).
Gatz	B. Gatz, *Weltalter, goldene Zeit und sinnverwandte Vorstellungen*, Hildesheim, 1967.
GLP	*Greek Literary Papyri*, vol. 1, ed. D. L. Page, London and Cambridge, Mass. (Loeb), 1942.
Gow–Page	*The Greek Anthology: Hellenistic Epigrams*, ed. A. S. F. Gow and D. L. Page, Cambridge, 1965.
Gow–Page, *Philip*	*The Greek Anthology: The Garland of Philip and some contemporary epigrams*, ed. A. S. F. Gow and D. L. Page, Cambridge, 1968.
Grassmann	V. Grassmann, *Die erotischen Epoden des Horaz*, Munich, 1966.
Gruppe	O. Gruppe, *Griechische Mythologie und Religionsgeschichte*, Munich, 1906.
Hand	F. Hand, *Tursellinus seu de particulis Latinis commentarii*, Leipzig, 1829–45.
Head	B. V. Head, *Historia Numorum: A Manual of Greek Numismatics*, ed. 2, Oxford, 1911.
H.–Sz.	J. B. Hofmann, *Lateinische Syntax und Stilistik*, neubearbeitet von Anton Szantyr, Munich, 1965.
IG	*Inscriptiones Graecae*, ed. maior, Berlin, 1873–1939.
IG²	*Inscriptiones Graecae*, ed. minor, Berlin, 1913– .
IGRR	*Inscriptiones Graecae ad res Romanas pertinentes*, ed. R. Cagnat, etc., Paris, 1911–27.
ILS	H. Dessau, *Inscriptiones Latinae Selectae*, Berlin, 1892–1916.
inscr. Ital.	*Inscriptiones Italiae*, Rome, 1931– .
Kaibel, *EG*	G. Kaibel, *Epigrammata Graeca ex lapidibus conlecta*, Berlin, 1878 (reprinted Hildesheim, 1965).
Kambylis	A. Kambylis, *Die Dichterweihe und ihre Symbolik*, Heidelberg, 1965.
Kern	O. Kern, *Orphicorum Fragmenta*, Berlin, 1922.
K.–G.	R. Kühner and B. Gerth, *Ausführliche Grammatik der griechischen Sprache: Satzlehre*, ed. 3, Hanover, 1904 (reprinted 1955).

Kroll	W. Kroll, *Studien zum Verständnis der römischen Literatur*, Stuttgart, 1924 (reprinted Darmstadt, 1964).
K.–S.	R. Kühner and C. Stegmann, *Ausführliche Grammatik der lateinischen Sprache: Satzlehre*, ed. 3, revised by A. Thierfelder, Darmstadt, 1955.
La Penna	A. La Penna, *Orazio e l'ideologia del principato*, Turin, 1963.
Latte	K. Latte, *Römische Religionsgeschichte*, Munich, 1960.
Lattimore	R. Lattimore, *Themes in Greek and Latin Epitaphs*, Urbana, 1962 (= *Illinois Studies in Language and Literature* 28, 1942, 1–2).
Lejay, *Satires*	P. Lejay, *Œuvres d'Horace: Satires*, Paris, 1911 (reprinted Hildesheim, 1966).
Lilja	S. Lilja, *The Roman Elegists' Attitude to Women*, Helsinki, 1965.
Löfstedt, *Late Latin*	E. Löfstedt, *Late Latin*, Oslo, 1959.
Löfstedt, *Peregrinatio*	E. Löfstedt, *Philologischer Kommentar zur Peregrinatio Aetheriae*, Uppsala, 1911.
Löfstedt, *Syntactica*	E. Löfstedt, *Syntactica: Studien und Beiträge zur historischen Syntax des Lateins*, Lund, vol. 1, ed. 2, 1956; vol. 2, 1933.
Mattingly	H. Mattingly, *Coins of the Roman Empire in the British Museum*, vol. 1 *Augustus to Vitellius*, London, 1923 (reprinted 1965).
Nettleship, *Latin Lexicography*	H. Nettleship, *Contributions to Latin Lexicography*, Oxford, 1889.
Neue–Wagener	F. Neue and C. Wagener, *Formenlehre der lateinischen Sprache*, ed. 3, Berlin, 1892–1905.
Newman	J. K. Newman, *Augustus and the New Poetry*, Brussels, 1967 (Collection Latomus, vol. lxxxviii).
Norden, *Aen.* 6	E. Norden, *P. Vergilius Maro: Aeneis, Buch VI*, ed. 3, Berlin, 1926 (reprinted Stuttgart, 1957).
Norden, *Agnostos Theos*	E. Norden, *Agnostos Theos: Untersuchungen zur Formengeschichte religiöser Rede*, Berlin, 1913 (reprinted Stuttgart, 1956).
OED	*A New English Dictionary on Historical Principles*, Oxford, 1888–1933.
OGIS	W. Dittenberger, *Orientis Graeci inscriptiones selectae*, Leipzig, 1903–5.

Otto	A. Otto, *Die Sprichwörter und sprichwörtlichen Redensarten der Römer*, Leipzig, 1890 (reprinted Hildesheim, 1962).
Ox. pap.	*The Oxyrhynchus Papyri*, London, 1898– .
Page, *Sappho and Alcaeus*	Denys Page, *Sappho and Alcaeus*, Oxford, 1955.
Pape–Benseler	W. Pape and G. F. Benseler, *Wörterbuch der griechischen Eigennamen*, Brunswick, ed. 3, 1911 (reprinted Graz, 1959).
pap. Brit. Mus.	H. J. M. Milne, *Catalogue of the Literary Papyri in the British Museum*, London, 1927.
pap. Gr. mag.	*Papyri Graecae magicae: die griechischen Zauberpapyri*, ed. K. Preisendanz, Leipzig, 1928–31.
Pasquali	G. Pasquali, *Orazio lirico*, Florence, 1920 (reprinted, 1964).
Pearson	A. C. Pearson, *The Fragments of Sophocles*, Cambridge, 1917.
Peek, *GV*	W. Peek, *Griechische Vers-Inschriften I*, Berlin, 1955.
PIR	*Prosopographia Imperii Romani*, ed. 1, Berlin, 1897–8.
PIR²	*Prosopographia Imperii Romani*, ed. 2, Berlin and Leipzig, 1933– .
PMG	*Poetae Melici Graeci*, ed. D. L. Page, Oxford, 1962.
Powell	J. U. Powell, *Collectanea Alexandrina*, Oxford, 1925.
RE	*Real-Encyclopädie der classischen Altertumswissenschaft*, Stuttgart, 1893– .
R. Reitzenstein, *Aufsätze*	R. Reitzenstein, *Aufsätze zu Horaz*, Darmstadt, 1963.
RLAC	*Reallexikon für Antike und Christentum*, Stuttgart, 1950– .
Rohde, *Roman³*	E. Rohde, *Der griechische Roman und seine Vorläufer*, ed. 3, Leipzig, 1914 (reprinted Hildesheim, 1960).
Roscher	W. H. Roscher, *Ausführliches Lexikon der griechischen und römischen Mythologie*, Leipzig, 1884–1937 (reprinted Hildesheim, 1965–).
Schanz–Hosius	M. Schanz and C. Hosius, *Geschichte der römischen Literatur*, Munich, vol. 2, ed. 4, 1927; vol. 3, ed. 3, 1922.

Schwyzer	E. Schwyzer, *Griechische Grammatik*, Munich, 1939–53.
SEG	*Supplementum Epigraphicum Graecum*, ed. J. J. E. Hondius and A. G. Woodhead, Leiden, 1923– .
Shackleton Bailey, *Propertiana*	D. R. Shackleton Bailey, *Propertiana*, Cambridge, 1956.
SIG³	W. Dittenberger, *Sylloge Inscriptionum Graecarum*, ed. 3, Leipzig, 1915–24.
Sommer	F. Sommer, *Handbuch der lateinischen Laut- und Formenlehre*, ed. 3, Heidelberg, 1914.
Syme, *Roman Revolution*	R. Syme, *The Roman Revolution*, Oxford, 1939.
Thes.l.L.	*Thesaurus linguae Latinae*, Leipzig, 1900– .
Troxler-Keller	I. Troxler-Keller, *Die Dichterlandschaft des Horaz*, Heidelberg, 1964.
Vischer	R. Vischer, *Das einfache Leben*, Göttingen, 1965.
Volkmann	R. Volkmann, *Die Rhetorik der Griechen und Römer in systematischer Übersicht*, ed. 2, Leipzig, 1885 (reprinted Hildesheim, 1963).
Wackernagel, *Kleine Schriften*	J. Wackernagel, *Kleine Schriften*, Göttingen, 1953.
Wackernagel, *Vorlesungen*	J. Wackernagel, *Vorlesungen über Syntax*, ed. 2, Basle, 1926–8.
Wagenvoort	H. Wagenvoort, *Studies in Roman Literature, Culture and Religion*, Leiden, 1956.
D. West	David West, *Reading Horace*, Edinburgh, 1967.
Wilamowitz, *Hellenistische Dichtung*	U. von Wilamowitz-Moellendorff, *Hellenistische Dichtung in der Zeit des Kallimachos*, ed. 2, Berlin, 1924 (reprinted, 1962).
Wilkinson	L. P. Wilkinson, *Horace and his Lyric Poetry*, ed. 2, Cambridge, 1951.
Wissowa	G. Wissowa, *Religion und Kultus der Römer*, ed. 2, Munich, 1912.

References to Latin texts follow the system of the index to the *Thesaurus*. Greek references can be elucidated, where necessary, from Liddell and Scott.

1. MAECENAS ATAVIS

[G. Carlsson, *Eranos* 44, 1946, 404 ff.; Fraenkel 230 ff.; La Penna 203 ff.; H. Musurillo, *TAPhA* 93, 1962, 230 ff.; D. Norberg, *Uppsala Universitets Årsskrift* 1945, 6.]

1–10. *Some men, Maecenas, find happiness in an Olympic victory, some in political success or extensive land-owning.* 11–18. *In spite of every hardship the farmer will never become a sea-captain or the sea-captain a farmer.* 19–28. *Some choose a lazy life, some manly activities like war or sport.* 29–36. *The poet's ivy and the Muses' favour bring me my felicity; if you include me among the classical lyric poets my head will hit the stars.*

The first poem of an ancient collection naturally had a particular significance. It often contained an element of dedication, appropriately deferential, to a prominent friend (just like a prose preface); thus our ode is addressed to Maecenas (so *epod. 1, serm. 1. 1, epist. 1. 1,* Prop. 2. 1), Dionysius Chalcus's opening elegy to one Theodorus (fr. 1), the first epigram in Meleager's *Garland* to Diocles (*anth. P.* 4. 1), Catullus 1 to Cornelius Nepos, the first poem in both books of Tibullus to Messalla. The main point of the ode is the poet's desire to be included by Maecenas in the canon of classics (35 n.); Catullus in his dedication expresses similar though more limited aims (1. 10 'plus uno maneat perenne saeclo'), and Horace himself in the parallel ode at the end of the collection, which is also written in stichic Asclepiads, confidently proclaims that his aspirations have now been fulfilled (3. 30). But in an opening poem it might have seemed immodest to acknowledge such ambitions too abruptly; instead Horace goes a long way round with a description of other men's varied occupations. These occupations are followed with a single-mindedness that seems incomprehensible to the outsider; by pointing out that men's drives differ in this way Horace provides an apology for his own devotion to poetry (cf. *serm.* 2. 1. 27 f. 'quot capitum vivunt, totidem studiorum / milia: me pedibus delectat claudere verba', Prop. 3. 9. 7 ff.). Yet unlike poetry these other occupations are described mostly in critical terms; thus Horace suggests that his own way of life is not only justifiable but superior.

The diversity of men's pleasures and pursuits was in fact an old literary topic. The prototype appears as early as Solon (1. 43 ff.):

σπεύδει δ' ἄλλοθεν ἄλλος· ὁ μὲν κατὰ πόντον ἀλᾶται
ἐν νηυσίν, χρῄζων οἴκαδε κέρδος ἄγειν

ἰχθυόεντ', ἀνέμοισι φορεύμενος ἀργαλέοισιν,
φειδωλὴν ψυχῆς οὐδεμίαν θέμενος·
ἄλλος γῆν τέμνων πολυδένδρεον, εἰς ἐνιαυτὸν
λατρεύει, τοῖσιν καμπύλ' ἄροτρα μέλει·
ἄλλος Ἀθηναίης τε καὶ Ἡφαίστου πολυτέχνεω
ἔργα δαεὶς χειροῖν ξυλλέγεται βίοτον,
ἄλλος Ὀλυμπιάδων Μουσέων πάρα δῶρα διδαχθεὶς
ἱμερτῆς σοφίης μέτρον ἐπιστάμενος.

A fragment of Pindar (221) seems particularly relevant to our poem:
ἀελλοπόδων μέν τιν' εὐφραίνοισιν ἵππων | τιμαὶ καὶ στέφανοι, | τοὺς δ' ἐν
πολυχρύσοις θαλάμοις βιοτά· | τέρπεται δὲ καί τις ἐπ' οἶδμ' ἄλιον | ναὶ
θοᾷ †διαστείβων. Bacchylides refers in turn to poets, soothsayers,
pleasure-seekers, and farmers (10. 38 ff.): μυρίαι δ' ἀνδρῶν ἐπισταμαι
πέλονται· | ἢ γὰρ σοφὸς ἢ Χαρίτων τιμὰν λελογχὼς | ἐλπίδι χρυσέᾳ
τέθαλεν | ἤ τινα θευπροπίαν εἰδώς· ἕτερος δ' ἐπὶ παισὶ | ποικίλον τόξον
τιταίνει· | οἱ δ' ἐπ' ἔργοισίν τε καὶ ἀμφὶ βοῶν ἀγέλαις | θυμὸν αὔξουσιν.
It is also worth remembering that Euripides in the *Antiope* drew
a contrast between the active life typified by the huntsman Zethus and
the indolent life of the poet Amphion (fr. 184 ff.).

Horace is also influenced by the Greek philosophers who compare
philosophy favourably with other occupations. Thus Plato had
already noted three sorts of life, φιλότιμος, φιλοκερδής, and φιλόσοφος
(*rep.* 581 c, Arist. *eth. Nic.* 1095^b17 ff. with the note in Gauthier–
Jolif, cf. La Penna 203 ff.). A passage of Libanius suggests that such
themes were also exploited in the rhetorical schools: ὁ μὲν ἐρᾷ τοῦ
δύνασθαι λέγειν, καὶ τἆλλ' αὐτῷ μικρά· τῷ δὲ τὸ κρατεῖν ἐν μάχαις μέγα,
καὶ τῶν ἄλλων οὐδεὶς λόγος· ὁ μὲν ἐπιθυμεῖ τῶν ἐκ γῆς καρπῶν καὶ
φρίττει τὴν θάλατταν· τῷ δὲ τὸ πλεῖν ἥδιον τοῦ περὶ τὴν γῆν ταλαιπωρεῖν·
ἕτερος ἥττων χρημάτων καὶ τὰ λοιπὰ γέλως· τῷ δὲ μία σπουδὴ στέφανον
ἐξ Ὀλυμπίας λαβεῖν, καὶ πᾶς αὐτῷ χρυσός, εἰ πρὸς τὸν κότινον ἐξετάζοιτο,
φαῦλος (*decl.* 30. 31 = 6. 635 f.). For further instances cf. *serm.* 1. 1.
4 ff., *epist.* 1. 1. 77 ff. (a sardonic parody of the commonplace), Virg.
georg. 2. 503 ff., La Penna, loc. cit., Musurillo, loc. cit. (who quotes
Egyptian and Jewish instances), R. Joly, *Le Thème philosophique
des genres de vie dans l'antiquité classique*, 1956.

Not only the content but also the form of our ode is traditional.
The real subject of the poem is Horace's devotion to poetry, but it only
comes as the climax to a long list of other people's preferences. This
kind of pattern can be seen in a memorable fragment of Sappho (16):

οἱ μὲν ἱππήων στρότον οἱ δὲ πέσδων
οἱ δὲ νάων φαῖσ' ἐπὶ γᾶν μέλαιναν
ἔμμεναι κάλλιστον, ἔγω δὲ κῆν' ὅτ-
τω τις ἔραται.

See also Pind. *N*. 8. 37 ff. χρυσὸν εὔχονται, πεδίον δ' ἕτεροι / ἀπέραντον, ἐγὼ δ' ἀστοῖς ἁδὼν καὶ χθονὶ γυῖα καλύψαι. So Eur. fr. 659. 1 ff. ἔρωτες ἡμῖν εἰσι παντοῖοι βίου· / ὁ μὲν γὰρ εὐγένειαν ἱμείρει λαβεῖν, / τῷ δ' οὐχὶ τούτου φροντίς, ἀλλὰ χρημάτων / πολλῶν κεκλῆσθαι βούλεται πάτωρ δόμοις. / . . . ἐγὼ δὲ τούτων οὐδενὸς χρῄζω τυχεῖν, / δόξαν δὲ βουλοίμην ἂν εὐκλείας ἔχειν, Shakespeare, *sonnet* 91 'Some glory in their birth, some in their skill, Some in their wealth, some in their body's force; Some in their garments, though newfangled ill; Some in their hawks and hounds, some in their horse . . . But these particulars are not my measure'. German scholars have given the name 'priamel' to this stylistic device; the word simply means 'preamble'. See further 1. 7. 1 ff., F. Dornseiff, *Die archaische Mythenerzählung*, 1933, pp. 3 f., 78 ff., W. A. A. van Otterlo, *Mnemosyne*, ser. 3, 8, 1940, 145 ff., Fraenkel on Aesch. *Ag.* 899 ff., U. Schmid, *Die Priamel der Werte im griechischen von Homer bis Paulus*, 1964, C. M. Bowra, *Pindar*, 1964, pp. 199 ff.

But though the theme and the arrangement are Greek, Horace has skilfully adapted them to his own purposes. The Olympic victor, it is true, belongs to the traditional topic, but thereafter the actors are Roman (*Quiritium* marks the change of scene): we meet in turn the successful politician, the big landowner, the smallholder laboriously cultivating his mountain soil, and the sea-captain dreaming of a very Italian *oppidum*. The φιλήδονος is addicted to nothing more licentious than the countryside, much like Horace himself; the treatment both of the soldier and the *chasseur* is given local colouring. Only at the end, when Horace speaks of his devotion to poetry, is the Greek note emphasized: nymphs and satyrs, Euterpe and Polyhymnia, the foreign words *Lesboum* and *barbiton*. Yet even here one might easily miss the tone of *lyricis vatibus*: *lyricis* is still a Greek word, but *vatibus* is redolent of old Latium (for the juxtaposition cf. 1. 32. 3 f. 'age dic Latinum, / barbite, carmen', 4. 3. 23 'Romanae fidicen lyrae'). Horace's overture is very simple in structure and metre, but it does not lack unpretentious artistry.

Metre: First Asclepiad.

1. **atavis** . . . **regibus**: Maecenas was descended, perhaps on his mother's side, from the Cilnii of Arretium (Arezzo) in northern Etruria. The family had already achieved unpopularity in the fourth century B.C. (Liv. 10. 3. 2); it may well have belonged to the *lucumones* who ruled Etruria (Serv. *Aen.* 8. 475). Horace's patron is actually called 'Cilnius Maecenas' by Tacitus (*ann.* 6. 11. 3); but it appears from the tombstones of his freedmen that *Maecenas* was his gentile name (*ILS* 7848, *PIR* M 30). Cicero knew of an *eques* called

C. Maecenas, one of the *robora populi Romani* who resisted Livius
Drusus (*Clu.* 153). He would have been surprised by the extravagances of the Augustan poets; cf. 3. 29. 1, *serm.* 1. 6. 1 f., Prop. 3. 9. 1
'Maecenas eques Etrusco de sanguine regum', *eleg. in Maec.* 13.
Augustus himself was less impressed; cf. *epist.* fr. 32 M. 'vale mi
ebenum Medulliae, ebur ex Etruria, lasar Arretinum, . . . Tiberinum
margaritum, Cilniorum smaragde'. See further K. J. Reckford,
TAPhA 90, 1959, 195 ff., J.-M. André, *Mécène, essai de biographie
spirituelle*, 1967.

edite: grandiloquent, like *atavis* and *o*; cf. Virg. *Aen.* 8. 136 f.
'Electram maximus Atlas / edidit', Ven. Fort. *carm.* 9. 1. 5 (to the
Merovingian Chilperic) 'inclite rex armis et regibus edite celsis',
Thes.l.L. 5. 2. 84. 32.

2. praesidium: an unpoetical word; it is found only once in Virgil,
and is not used at all by Catullus, Tibullus, Propertius, Ovid in the
Metamorphoses, Lucan, Valerius Flaccus, Silius (Axelson 98). It
describes, for instance, the protection a man gives his wife and
family; cf. the moving words of Lucretius 'non poteris factis florenti-
bus esse tuisque / praesidium' (3. 897 f.). In the semi-feudal society of
ancient Rome, with its complicated network of personal obligations,
men likewise looked for succour to their powerful friends; cf. 2. 1. 13,
2. 17. 3 f., *epist.* 1. 1. 103, Cic. *de orat.* 1. 184 'praesidium clientibus . . .
porrigentem', *laus Pis.* 243 ff. 'o decus in totum merito venerabilis
aevum / Pierii tutela chori, quo praeside tuti / non umquam vates
inopi timuere senectae', Juv. 7. 22 f. 'si qua aliunde putas rerum
spectanda tuarum / praesidia', J. Hellegouarc'h, *Le Vocabulaire
latin des relations et des partis politiques sous la république*, 1963,
pp. 172 f. In return the unimportant man lavished on his patron,
without consciousness of sycophancy, the loyalty which the modern
world concedes only to institutions.

dulce decus: acquaintance with the great is a distinction (*epist.* 1.
17. 35), and the Romans never thought of pretending otherwise; cf.
2. 17. 4, Virg. *georg.* 2. 40 f. 'o decus, o famae merito pars maxima
nostrae / Maecenas', Prop. 2. 1. 74. *decus* and *praesidium* seem to
have made a conventional pair; cf. Lucr. 2. 643 'praesidioque parent
decorique parentibus esse', Prud. *apoth.* 393 f. (on Christ) 'o nomen
praedulce mihi, lux et decus et spes / praesidiumque meum', *Thes.l.L.*
5. 1. 247. 70 ff. *dulce* ('dear') is naturally used of family and friends,
and here adds a warmer note; cf. 1. 36. 7, *serm.* 1. 9. 4, *epist.* 1. 7. 12
(so γλυκύτατος and ἥδιστος in Greek). For the collocation with *decus*
cf. Macr. *somn.* 1. 1. 1 'Eustachi fili, vitae mihi dulcedo pariter et
gloria', Ven. Fort. *carm.* 11. 5. 1, [Alcuin], *conflictus veris et hiemis*
'salve, dulce decus, cuculus, per saecula salve'.

3. **sunt quos . . .**: the glory of an Olympic victory was a regular feature in the 'catalogue of occupations'; cf. Pindar and Libanius cited above (p. 2). One may compare also a story about Pythagoras, going back to Heraclides Ponticus (Cic. *Tusc.* 5. 8–9); cf. Diog. Laert. 8. 8 καὶ τὸν βίον ἐοικέναι πανηγύρει· ὡς οὖν εἰς ταύτην οἱ μὲν ἀγωνιούμενοι, οἱ δὲ κατ᾽ ἐμπορίαν, οἱ δέ γε βέλτιστοι ἔρχονται θεαταί, οὕτως ἐν τῷ βίῳ οἱ μὲν ἀνδραποδώδεις, ἔφη, φύονται δόξης καὶ πλεονεξίας θηραταί, οἱ δὲ φιλόσοφοι τῆς ἀληθείας, Iamblichus, *vit. Pyth.* 58.

For references to such victories in Augustan poetry cf. 4. 3. 3 ff., Virg. *georg.* 3. 49 f., Prop. 3. 9. 17. Boucher (35) suggests that Maecenas himself sought distinction in the chariot race; he points out that the passages cited from Virgil and Propertius, as well as our own, are addressed to him. But in view of the conventional nature of the theme it seems pointless to look for any topical allusion.

The Olympic games had in fact lost much of their former glory at the time when Horace was writing (*RE* 18. 1. 39, E. N. Gardiner, *Olympia*, 1925, pp. 158 ff.). It is true that Tiberius won the chariot race at some date before A.D. 4 (*SIG³* 782), and Germanicus in A.D. 17 (*SIG³* 792); but Julius Africanus says that on the latter occasion the race had been πάλαι κωλυθείς. Even if this statement is formally disproved by the first of the two inscriptions cited above (cf. also Ov. *trist.* 4. 10. 95 f.), it goes some way to suggest that at the date of our ode Olympic chariot races were not important.

curriculo: probably ἅρματι, 'with their chariots'; cf. Pind. *P.* 1. 32 f. Πυθιάδος δ᾽ ἐν δρόμῳ κάρυξ ἀνέειπέ νιν ἀγγέλλων Ἱέρωνος ὑπὲρ καλλινίκου | ἅρμασι, 6. 17 f. εὔδοξον ἅρματι νίκαν | Κρισαίαις ἐνὶ πτύχαις ἀπαγγελεῖ. Some interpret 'in the race'; cf. ἐν δρόμῳ (cited above). But the Pindaric usage requires a place-name or some other specification; and on grounds of Latinity one would sooner, on this theory, expect *Olympico* (Heinze).

pulverem . . . collegisse: not 'to become dusty' but 'to raise a dust'; cf. *serm.* 1. 4. 31 'fertur uti pulvis collectus turbine', Virg. *georg.* 1. 324 'collectae ex alto nubes'. Dust was an obvious hardship to southern athletes (1. 8. 4 n.), and in the chariot race made a conventional topic; cf. Simon. 516, Bacch. 5. 44, Soph. *El.* 714 f., Ov. *met.* 7. 542, Stat. *silv.* 5. 2. 25 f. The tense of *collegisse* is alleged to imply that there was more joy in the victory than in the race; yet the perfect infinitive is often used in a timeless sense with verbs like *iuvat*, and perhaps so here.

4. **meta . . . evitata**: the charioteer tried to round the turning-post as close as possible without touching (cf. Hom. *Il.* 23. 338 ff., Soph. *El.* 743 ff., Theoc. 24. 119 f.). The phrase probably provides a second subject for *iuvat*. For the change from the impersonal to the personal

construction Bentley compared 4. 1. 29 ff. 'me nec femina nec puer /
iam nec spes animi credula mutui / nec certare iuvat mero', Juv. 11.
201 f. Some editors take *meta* . . . *evitata* with *evehit*; but though
a successful turn was half the battle, it should not be equated with
the palm of victory.

fervidis: ancient wheels, which had iron rims, must have become
intensely hot in a race; cf. Ov. *ars* 3. 396 'metaque ferventi circum-
eunda rota', Virg. *Aen.* 11. 195.

5. palmaque: a symbol of victory derived ultimately from the East.
It is not mentioned as a prize in Pindar, but is well attested in the
fourth century; perhaps it first appeared at the Delian games (revived in 426). It is recorded in Rome as early as 293 B.C.; cf. Liv. 10.
47. 3 'palmaeque tum primum translato e Graeco more victoribus
datae'. Cf. further Paus. 8. 48. 2 οἱ δὲ ἀγῶνες φοίνικος ἔχουσιν οἱ πολλοὶ
στέφανον· ἐς δὲ τὴν δεξιάν ἐστι καὶ πανταχοῦ τῷ νικῶντι ἐστιθέμενος
φοῖνιξ, Plut. *quaest. conv.* 723 f., V. Hehn, *Kulturpflanzen und Haustiere*, 1911, pp. 274 ff., *RE* 20. 401 ff., F. B. Tarbell, *CPh* 3, 1908,
264 ff.

nobilis: ἀρίγνωτος; the palm attracts attention alike to itself and
the victor. For the latter cf. Sen. *Thy.* 409 f. 'celebrata iuveni stadia
per quae nobilis / palmam paterno non semel curru tuli'; Seneca has
remembered Horace's phrase, but *suo more* gives it rather a different
application.

6. terrarum dominos: the Olympic victor seems like one of the lords
of earth; cf. Ov. *Pont.* 2. 8. 26 'terrarum dominum quem sua cura
facit' (Augustus), Luc. 8. 208 f. 'terrarum dominos et sceptra Eoa
tenentes / exul habet comites', Mart. 1. 4. 2 'terrarum dominum pone
supercilium' (to Domitian). Some argue that Horace is referring to
literal princes, such as competed in the Olympic games in Pindar's
time. Yet the predicative position of the phrase suggests that the
exaltation of the victors is purely a consequence of their victory; cf.
4. 2. 17 f. 'quos Elea domum reducit / palma caelestes' (a very
significant parallel).

Many editors think that *dominos* is in apposition to *deos* (for the
word-order cf. 1. 3. 2). They compare Ov. *Pont.* 1. 9. 35 f. 'nam tua
non alio coluit penetralia ritu / terrarum dominos quam colis ipse
deos', 2. 2. 12 '(nec nos) in rerum dominos movimus arma deos'; but
in the first of these passages *deos* refers to Augustus, and in the second
rerum dominos proves nothing about *terrarum dominos*. There is
little point here in attaching the compliment to the gods; it would
be a very circuitous way of saying that the victor feels like a lord
of earth.

O. Skutsch argues in favour of the last interpretation that Horace tends to avoid rhyme in the *Odes* except between words syntactically related (*BICS* 11, 1964, 73 ff.). He cites the following figures for Horace's use of rhyme in the sixth and twelfth syllables of the lesser Asclepiad: 39 'attributive', 3 'parallel', and 7 'unrelated'. The 7 certain instances of 'unrelated' rhyme all involve *-um* (1. 36. 12, 4. 1. 28, 4. 5. 3) or *-us*; these syllables seldom occur where related words rhyme. Skutsch reaches similar conclusions for Sapphics and Alcaics. His paper is interesting and important, but where the numbers are relatively small one cannot exclude the possibility of exceptions. Each case must still be decided on its own merits.

evehit ad deos: for the hyperbole cf. 4. 2. 17 f. (quoted in previous note), Pind. *I*. 2. 28 f. ἵν' ἀθανάτοις Αἰνησιδάμου / παῖδες ἐν τιμαῖς ἔμιχθεν, Lucian, *Anachars*. 10 ὁρᾷς . . . τὸν . . . νικήσαντα αὐτῶν ἰσόθεον νομιζόμενον.

7. hunc: understand *iuvat*, in spite of the intervening *evehit*. Because of this difficulty Bentley proposed *evehere* (cf. 1. 12. 26 f. 'superare pugnis / nobilem'); but this makes *nobilis* less precise. Some put a stop after *nobilis*; of these Müller takes *terrarum dominos* with *deos* (which makes the phrase far too emphatic), while others more interestingly interpret of the Romans as opposed to the Greeks (so M. L. Earle, *CR* 16, 1902, 398 ff.; cf. Plut. *Tib. Gracch.* 9. 4 κύριοι τῆς οἰκουμένης εἶναι λεγόμενοι, μίαν δὲ βῶλον ἰδίαν οὐκ ἔχοντες). But a pause after an odd line would be unique in this poem (though in 3. 30 there is a pause after the fifth line); the theory leaves *evehit ad deos* without a satisfactory subject; and *terrarum dominos* is peculiarly suited to the Olympic victor.

mobilium . . . Quiritium: the grandiloquence of the noun is satiric; Horace is hinting at the drawbacks of other men's pursuits. *mobilium* must be right against *nobilium*; cf. Dem. 19. 136 ὁ μὲν δῆμός ἐστιν ἀσταθμητότατον πρᾶγμα τῶν πάντων καὶ ἀσυνθετώτατον, ὥσπερ ἐν θαλάττῃ κῦμ' ἀκατάστατον ὡς ἂν τύχῃ κινούμενον, Sen. *Herc. f.* 169 ff., Stat. *silv.* 2. 2. 123, Otto 378.

8. tergeminis . . . honoribus: Porphyrio rightly understands of reiterated applause. This explanation has been unjustly neglected, probably because *honoribus* is unusual of a tribute offered (as opposed to received); yet cf. 1. 26. 9 f. 'nil sine te mei / prosunt honores', with parallels there cited. Convincing parallels can also be offered for *tergeminis*; cf. 2. 17. 25 f. 'populus frequens / laetum theatris ter crepuit sonum', Virg. *georg.* 2. 508 ff. 'hunc plausus hiantem / per cuneos geminatus enim plebisque patrumque / corripuit' (the whole passage has affinities with our poem), Mart. 3. 46. 8 'at tibi tergeminum mugiet ille sophos', *anth. Lat.* 804. 8 'plausus ter geminante manu'. Moreover, this interpretation suits *certat*; cf. Luc. 7. 9 ff. 'nam

E

Pompeiani visus sibi sede theatri / innumeram effigiem Romanae
cernere plebis / attollique suum laetis ad sidera nomen / vocibus et
plausu cuneos certare sonantes'.

Modern editors interpret 'triple magistracies', presumably the
aedileship, praetorship, and consulship. Here again parallels can be
offered for *tergeminis*, mostly referring to the repetition of the same
magistracy; cf. Prop. 4. 11. 65 'vidimus et fratrem sellam geminasse
curulem', Liv. 39. 39. 9 'invidiam geminati honoris' (the praetorship
as well as the aedileship), Curt. 6. 5. 22 'geminato honore', Plin.
paneg. 92. 1 'nec continuatus tantum sed geminatus est honor', Tac.
ann. 1. 3. 1 'M. Agrippam . . . geminatis consulatibus extulit', Prosp.
chron. 1. 484. 1375 'vir gemini consulatus'. On the other hand it is
hard to see why Horace should talk of successive victories; these are
a sign of the crowd's consistency, not of its fickleness. An even greater
difficulty lies in *certat*: unless the people go round canvassing (and
nothing here suggests it) the effort of one voter cannot be greater
than that of any other.

   tollere: the infinitive was used more freely in early Latin than in
formal classical prose. This tendency, already present in the language,
was exaggerated by the poets, and above all by Horace. Greek
influences played a part; so also the desire for a diction that should
be brief, distinctive, and metrically tractable. See further K.–S. 1.
680 ff., H.–Sz. 344 ff., Wickham 1. 406 ff., G. Kirsten, *De infinitivi
atque accusativi cum infinitivo apud Horatium usu*, 1938.

9. illum: presumably a big landowner; cf. 3. 16. 25 ff. 'contemptae
dominus splendidior rei / quam si quidquid arat impiger Apulus /
occultare meis dicerer horreis, / magnas inter opes inops', *epist.* 2. 2.
177 f. 'quid vici prosunt aut horrea? quidve Calabris / saltibus adiecti
Lucani?', Sen. *epist.* 2. 6 'quid enim refert quantum illi in arca, quantum in horreis iaceat, quantum pascat aut feneret?'

   A. Y. Campbell interestingly suggests that Horace is referring to
a grain-importer; this interpretation would provide an instance of
the φιλοχρήματος to balance the politically ambitious φιλότιμος. The
wealth of the middleman is well illustrated by Cic. *fin.* 2. 84 (on the
supposed utility of friendship): 'num igitur utiliorem tibi hunc
Triarium putas esse posse quam si tua sint Puteolis granaria?'
Yet the closest parallel to our passage refers to Apulia (3. 16. 26,
cited above); and south Italy suggests *latifundia* rather than large-
scale exports to Roman granaries.

10. quicquid . . .: humorous hyperbole. Cf. 3. 16. 26 f., *serm.* 2. 3. 87
'frumenti quantum metit Africa', Sen. *Thy.* 356 f., Stat. *silv.* 3. 3.
90 f., Otto 8. Grain is a bulky commodity and Africa was proverbially
fertile.

verritur: after threshing on the open-air *area* (Varro, *rust.* 1. 51–2, Colum. 2. 19–20) the grain was swept into baskets; cf. Ov. *fast.* 2. 523 'nam modo verrebant nigras pro farre favillas', Stat., loc. cit.

11. **gaudentem . . .**: a sympathetic sketch, drawn without satire; cf. *epod.* 2. 3 'paterna rura bobus exercet suis', Claud. *carm. min.* 20. 1 (the old man of Verona) 'felix qui propriis aevum transegit in arvis'.
   findere: cf. Solon 1. 47 ἄλλος γῆν τέμνων, Ap. Rhod. 1. 628 πυροφόρους τε διατμήξασθαι ἀρούρας, Lygd. 3. 12.
   sarculo: the *sarculum* was a hoe, with a blade set at an angle to a pole (Blümner 566, D.–S. 4. 1075). It was used, among other things, as a substitute for the plough on rocky soil (Plin. *nat.* 18. 178 'montanae gentes sarculis arant'); for further details see K. D. White, *Agricultural Implements of the Roman World*, 1967, pp. 43 ff., Mayor on Juv. 15. 166. For the hardship involved in such operations cf. Cato, *or. fr.* 128 'ego iam a principio in parsimonia atque in duritia atque industria omnem adulescentiam meam abstinui agro colendo, saxis Sabinis, silicibus repastinandis atque conserendis', A. Maiuri, *Passeggiate in Magna Grecia*, 1963, pp. 206 f.

12. **Attalicis**: a Greek poet might have mentioned Croesus; the Roman alludes instead to the Hellenistic Attalids, whose magnificence is still revealed by the ruins óf Pergamum. Plautus had already introduced Attalus I of Pergamum (who cannot have been in his Greek original) as a symbol of Asiatic wealth; cf. *Persa* 339, Fraenkel, *Plautinisches im Plautus*, p. 17. Horace must have thought particularly of Attalus III (cf. 2. 18. 5), who in 133 B.C. left his kingdom to the Romans. His luxury was no doubt exaggerated at a time when the Romans were acquiring expensive tastes; he was particularly associated with cloth of gold (Prop. 3. 18. 19).
   condicionibus: 'terms', 'offers'; cf. *epist.* 1. 1. 51 'cui sit condicio dulcis sine pulvere palmae', Cic. *ad Q.fr.* 1. 1. 8. The Attalids were ready to move populations (Str. 13. 1. 70), but there is no evidence that compensation was offered.

13. **demoveas**: 'dislodge'; the word suits the shifting of a firmly-rooted object. The variant *dimoveas* should not be accepted in classical Latin in this sense.
   Cypria: the specific adjective adds colour. Cyprus was famous for its woods and its shipbuilding (*RE* 12. 70); cf. especially Amm. 14. 8. 14 'tanta autem tamque multiplici fertilitate abundat rerum omnium eadem Cyprus, ut nullius externi indigens adminiculi, indigenis viribus, a fundamento ipso carinae ad supremos usque carbasos, aedificet onerariam navem, omnibusque armamentis instructam mari committat'.

14. Myrtoum: the sea between the Peloponnese and the Cyclades (*RE* 16. 1169 f.). The name was used particularly in the Roman period, by geographers as well as poets. All seas are stormy in Horace, but the area of the Cyclades is especially notorious (1. 14. 20).

nauta: not an able-bodied seaman but a merchant-adventurer (cf. 1. 28. 23). For the terrors of the sea cf. 1. 3. 9 ff.; for the conventional contrast between sailor and farmer cf. *anth. P.* 7. 265. 1, 7. 532, 7. 586, 7. 636, 7. 650, Prop. 3. 7. 43, Libanius 8. 349 ff., Nicolaus, *progymn.* 1. 349, 365 f. Walz, H. Kier, *De laudibus vitae rusticae*, 1933, pp. 47 ff., K. F. Smith on Tib. 1. 9. 7–10.

secet: cf. Hom. *Od.* 3. 174 f. ἠνώγει πέλαγος μέσον εἰς Εὔβοιαν / τέμνειν, Sen. *Phaedr.* 88, below, 1. 7. 32 n. The contrast with *findere* is probably deliberate: cutting the sea is easier than cleaving the land.

15. Icariis: in the eastern Aegean, where Icarus fell, between Samos and Myconus (Plin. *nat.* 4. 51). The picture is Homeric; cf. *Il.* 2. 144 ff. κινήθη δ' ἀγορὴ φὴ κύματα μακρὰ θαλάσσης / πόντου Ἰκαρίοιο τὰ μέν τ' Εὖρος τε Νότος τε / ὤρορ'.

16. mercator: the trader was more useful than most people in the ancient world, but the poets are critical (1. 31. 11 ff., 3. 24. 35 ff., *serm.* 1. 4. 29 ff., *epist.* 1. 1. 45 ff., K. F. Smith on Tib. 1. 3. 39–40). Such remarks are derived from popular philosophy, and can be traced back to Plato and Aristotle; they reflect the prejudices of the Greek city state, where foreign trade was in the hands of metics (J. Hasebroek, *Staat und Handel im alten Griechenland*, 1928, pp. 21 ff.). Cicero's attitude is illuminating: 'mercatura autem, si tenuis est, sordida putanda est; sin magna et copiosa, multa undique apportans multisque sine vanitate impertiens, non est admodum vituperanda, atque etiam si satiata quaestu vel contenta potius, ut saepe ex alto in portum, ex ipso portu se in agros possessionesque contulit, videtur iure optimo posse laudari' (*off.* 1. 151).

otium: contrasted with the *negotium* of the *mercator* (or *negotiator*); cf. 2. 16. 1, *serm.* 1. 1. 29 ff. 'perfidus hic caupo, miles nautaeque per omne / audaces mare qui currunt, hac mente laborem / sese ferre, senes ut in otia tuta recedant, / aiunt', Plaut. *trin.* 838 'apage a me sis, dehinc iam certumst otio dare me; sati' partum habeo', Julianus, *anth. P.* 7. 586. 3 f. εἴη μοι γαίης ὀλίγος βίος· ἐκ δὲ θαλάσσης / ἄλλοισιν μελέτω κέρδος ἀελλομάχον.

17. laudat: μεμψιμοιρία (discontent with one's lot) was a favourite topic of moralists; cf. *serm.* 1. 1. 4 ff. ' "o fortunati mercatores" gravis annis / miles ait, multo iam fractus membra labore; / contra mercator navim iactantibus Austris / "militia est potior . . ."; / agricolam laudat iuris legumque peritus . . .', ps.-Hippocr. *epist.* 17

(9. 368 Littré) δυσαρεστεύονται πᾶσι καὶ πάλιν τοῖσιν αὐτέοισιν ἐμπελά-
ζονται, ἀρνησάμεναι πλόον πλέουσι, γεωργίην ἀπειπάμενοι αὖθις γεωρ-
γεῦσιν . . ., Max. Tyr. 15. 1 b καὶ ἴδοις ἂν τὸν μὲν γεωργικὸν μακαρίζοντα
τοὺς ἀστικοὺς ὡς συνόντας βίῳ χαρίεντι καὶ ἀνθηρῷ, τοὺς δ᾽ ἀπὸ τῶν
ἐκκλησιῶν καὶ τῶν δικαστηρίων καὶ τοὺς πάνυ ἐν αὑτοῖς εὐδοκίμους
ὀδυρομένους τὰ αὑτῶν καὶ εὐχομένους ἐπὶ σκαπάνῃ βιῶναι καὶ γηδίῳ
σμικρῷ, Lejay, Satires, pp. 7 f., N. Rudd, The Satires of Horace, 1966,
pp. 20 ff.

rura: combined with oppidi, without paradox; cf. Luc. 1. 419
'rura Nemetis', Sil. 4. 227 'nebulosi rura Casini', 8. 431 'scopulosae
rura Numanae'. Even today Italian countrymen live in communities
more than their English counterparts, and commute long distances
to their work in farm-carts. There is therefore no merit in Acidalius's
tuta.

mox reficit rates: Horace seems to be recalling Eur. fr. 793 μακάριος
ὅστις εὐτυχῶν οἴκοι μένει· / ἐν γῇ δ᾽ ὁ φόρτος, καὶ πάλιν ναυτίλλεται
(cited by Rudd, loc. cit.).

20. solido: i.e. integro; cf. Sen. epist. 83. 3 'hodiernus dies solidus est,
nemo ex illo quicquam mihi eripuit; totus inter stratum lectionemque
divisus est'. For similar expressions cf. 2. 7. 6 f. 'cum quo morantem
saepe diem mero / fregi', Varro, rust. 1. 2. 5 'aestivo die, si non
diffinderem meo insiticio somno meridie, vivere non possum', Plin.
epist. 3. 1. 9 'sumit aliquid de nocte et aestate', 9. 40. 2 'multumque
de nocte vel ante vel post diem sumitur'. See also Mayor on Juv.
1. 49.

21. arbuto: the arbutus is shady and associated with lonely places;
cf. Prop. 1. 2. 11 'surgat et in solis formosius arbutus antris'.

22. stratus: the indolence will seem to some peculiarly Horatian; cf.
2. 3. 6 ff., 2. 7. 18 ff., 2. 11. 13 ff., epod. 2. 23 ff., epist. 1. 14. 35. In fact
the scene is sanctioned by poetical convention as well as the needs of
a hot climate; cf. Hes. op. 588 ff. ἀλλὰ τότ᾽ ἤδη / εἴη πετραίη τε σκιὴ
καὶ βίβλινος οἶνος, Theoc. 1. 15 ff. (with Gow's note), Anyte, anth. P.
9. 313, Mosch. 5. 11 f. αὐτὰρ ἐμοὶ γλυκὺς ὕπνος ὑπὸ πλατάνῳ βαθυφύλλῳ /
καὶ παγᾶς φιλέοιμι τὸν ἐγγύθεν ἦχον ἀκούειν, Lucr. 2. 29 ff., Opp. hal.
1. 20 ff.

lene: 'gently-murmuring'; there is a contrast with the blare in the
next sentence.

sacrae: springs were regarded as sacred, as was natural in thirsty
southern lands; cf. h. Merc. 263 ἱερῶν ἀπὸ πηγέων, Pl. Crit. 111 d,
Frontin. aq. 1. 4 'fontium memoria cum sanctitate adhuc exstat et
colitur', Serv. Aen. 7. 84 'nullus enim fons non sacer', ILS 3887 'fonti
sanctissimo sacrum', Mayor on Juv. 3. 13. So rivers in general; cf.

West on Hes. *th.* 788, H. Fugier, *Recherches sur l'expression du sacré dans la langue latine*, 1963, pp. 77 f.

23. lituo: cf. Luc. 1. 237 'stridor lituum clangorque tubarum'. The *lituus* was a curved bugle (*RE* 13. 804 f.) with a shrill note (Enn. *ann.* 530 'lituus sonitus effudit acutos') ; ps.-Acro says that it was used by the cavalry. Such instruments were particularly associated with the attack; cf. Ov. *fast.* 3. 216, Tac. *ann.* 1. 68. 3, less heroically Juv. 14. 199 f. 'trepidum solvunt tibi cornua ventrem / cum lituis audita'.

24. matribus detestata: cf. *epod.* 16. 8 'parentibusque abominatus Hannibal', Catull. 64. 348 f. 'illius egregias virtutes claraque facta / saepe fatebuntur gnatorum in funere matres', Virg. *Aen.* 8. 556, 11. 215, Stat. *Theb.* 3. 377, Sil. 3. 73.

25. manet: *pernoctat*; cf. Cic. *Mil.* 46 'dixit . . . Clodium illo die in Albano mansurum fuisse' (so *mansio* means 'lodging'). The soldier and the huntsman belong to the same type; the stop before *manet* is a semicolon rather than a period. *venatio* was a pursuit much favoured by the Roman upper classes; cf. *epist.* 1. 18. 49 f. 'Romanis sollemne viris opus, utile famae / vitaeque et membris', Plb. 32. 15 Schw. (= 31. 29. 5 ff. Hultsch), Sall. *Cat.* 4. 1 'agrum colundo aut venando, servilibus officiis'. The ancient *venator* was not always a noisy enthusiast clattering about the countryside but sometimes a patient stalker, ready to lie all night in a thicket to secure his prey.

sub Iove frigido: cf. 1. 22. 19 n. For stalking in cold weather cf. 1. 37. 18 n., *serm.* 2. 3. 234 f., Cic. *Tusc.* 2. 40 'pernoctant venatores in nive', Liv. 5. 6. 3 'venandi studium ac voluptas homines per nives ac pruinas in montes silvasque rapit'.

27. tenerae: young and soft. For the old quarrel between love and sport cf. *epod.* 2. 37 f. 'quis non malarum quas amor curas habet / haec inter obliviscitur?', Ar. *Lys.* 785 ff., Parthen. *erot.* 10. 1, Prop. 2. 19. 17 f. 'iam nunc me sacra Dianae / suscipere et Veneris ponere vota iuvat', Ov. *rem.* 199 f. 'vel tu venandi studium cole; saepe recessit / turpiter a Phoebi victa sorore Venus'.

28. seu rupit . . . : pig-sticking was a favourite Roman blood sport; cf. J. Aymard, *Les Chasses romaines*, 1951, pp. 297 ff. Nets were used to rope off an area of the *saltus*, and the victim was driven towards them (*epod.* 2. 31 f., Xen. *cyn.* 10. 19). The *plaga* (ἐνόδιον) was relatively short (12 to 30 feet) and was used to block gaps between bushes; cf. *RE* 9. 588 ff., D.-S. 4. 850 ff., Blümner 518 f., Enk on Grattius 24 ff. Yet sometimes a beast got away; cf. Ov. *ars* 1. 392 'non bene de laxis cassibus exit aper', Sen. *Phaedr.* 75 f. 'retia vinctas tenuere feras, / nulli laqueum rupere pedes'.

teretes: 'fine' (ps.-Acro 'de tereti fune ait factas'). For this rare meaning cf. Sen. *Phaedr.* 45^b 'alius teretes properet laqueos', Plin. *nat.* 11. 80 'tam tereti filo et tam aequali deducit stamine'; Pliny is talking of the spider's web, which he compares in the same context to a hunting-net. The cord of hunting-nets was exceptionally fine; cf. Plin. *nat.* 19. 11 'vidimusque iam tantae tenuitatis, ut anulum hominis cum epidromis transirent, uno portante multitudinem qua saltus cingeretur. nec id maxime mirum, sed singula earum stamina centeno quinquageno filo constare' (see also Aymard, op. cit., pp. 207 ff., D. B. Hull, *Hounds and Hunting in Ancient Greece*, 1964, pp. 10 ff.). For another view cf. A. Treloar, *CR* N.S. 13, 1963, 17.

Marsus: the Abruzzi, like other parts of Italy, was thickly wooded in antiquity (1. 22. 14 n.); it must have provided boars with acorns as well as hide-outs.

29. me: the emphatic pronoun naturally comes at the end of the priamel; cf. 1. 7. 10, Tib. 1. 1. 5.

doctarum: a hard word to translate; 'learned' is too heavy, and 'cultured' too pretentious. The early Greeks thought of the poet as σοφός, that is to say trained in an art; cf. Solon 1. 51 f. (above, p. 2). In Pindar, however, the word implies genius rather than technical know-how; cf. *O*. 9. 28 f. ἀγαθοὶ δὲ καὶ σοφοὶ κατὰ δαίμον' ἄνδρες / ἐγένοντ', C. M. Bowra, *Pindar*, 1964, pp. 1 ff., H. Maehler, *Die Auffassung des Dichterberufs im frühen Griechentum bis zur Zeit Pindars*, 1963, pp. 94 ff. The Alexandrians, with their consciousness of a poetic tradition, likewise emphasized σοφία. In Rome *doctrina* was similarly associated with poetry, and not only by the neoterics: Cicero describes as *homines doctissimi* Alcaeus, Anacreon, and Ibycus (*Tusc.* 4. 71). The adjective is particularly common in verse, and is applied impartially to the poet, the poet's lady, and the Muses themselves (*Thes.l.L.* 5. 1. 1757. 2 ff., Kroll 37).

hederae: the poetical plural is metrically necessary (cf. Löfstedt, *Syntactica*, 1². 45). For the wearing of ivy by poets cf. Plin. *nat.* 16. 147 'alicui (hederae) et semen nigrum, alii crocatum, cuius coronis poetae utuntur', Serv. auct. *ecl.* 8. 12 'hedera autem ideo coronantur poetae quoniam poetas saepe vino plurimo manifestum est uti . . . et haec herba nimium frigida est et vini calorem temperat', Mayor on Juv. 7. 29. As the ivy belonged to Bacchus it suited the lighter genres; cf. Prop. 4. 1. 61 f. 'Ennius hirsuta cingat sua dicta corona; / mi folia ex hedera porrige, Bacche, tua', Prud. *cath.* 3. 26 ff. So Horace's claim is more modest than his request for bay in the parallel poem at the end of the collection (3. 30. 16).

30. dis miscent superis: *miscent* means 'set among'; cf. 4. 5. 34 f. 'et Laribus tuum / miscet numen', Pind. *I*. 2. 29 ἔμιχθεν (above, 6 n.).

gelidum nemus: for such 'green retreats' cf. *epist.* 2. 2. 77 'scriptorum chorus omnis amat nemus et fugit urbis', Tac. *dial.* 9. 6 'adice quod poetis . . . relinquenda conversatio amicorum et iucunditas urbis, deserenda cetera officia, utque ipsi dicunt in nemora et lucos, id est in solitudinem secedendum est' (see Peterson's and Gudeman's parallels), Plin. *epist.* 1. 6. 2, 9. 10. 2, Juv. 7. 56 ff. 'hunc qualem nequeo monstrare et sentio tantum / anxietate carens animus facit, omnis acerbi / impatiens, cupidus silvarum . . .', E. M. W. Tillyard, *Some Mythical Elements in English Literature*, 1961, pp. 72 ff. Quintilian, practical as always, takes a more balanced view: 'non tamen protinus audiendi qui credunt aptissima in hoc nemora silvasque . . . namque illa quae ipsa delectant necesse est avocent ab intentione operis destinati' (*inst.* 10. 3. 22–3).

Of course the 'sacred wood' also has a symbolical element, standing for something rare and inaccessible in poetry. The image is borrowed from Alexandria by the Roman poets; cf. 3. 4. 6 ff., 3. 25. 13, Prop. 3. 1. 1 f. 'Callimachi Manes et Coi sacra Philitae, / in vestrum quaeso me sinite ire nemus', Ov. *am.* 3. 1. 1 ff., Kambylis 103 f., Troxler-Keller 40 ff., 94 ff., Boucher 216 f.

31. Nympharumque . . . : nymphs and satyrs belonged to the thiasos of Dionysus and as such were fit company for a poet; so more humorously *epist.* 1. 19. 3 f. 'ut male sanos / adscripsit Liber Satyris Faunisque poetas'.

32. secernunt populo: on the surface Horace is referring to the peace of the countryside; cf. *ars* 298 'secreta petit loca, balnea vitat', Auson. 417. 90 f. (of his native Bordeaux) 'me iuga Burdigalae, trino me flumina coetu / secernunt turbis popularibus' (for the philosopher's retreat from the crowd see A.-J. Festugière, *Personal Religion among the Greeks*, 1954, pp. 53 ff.). But partly he is echoing Callimachus's rejection of popular tastes and values; cf. 3. 1. 1 'odi profanum vulgus et arceo', Call. *ep.* 28. 4 σικχαίνω πάντα τὰ δημόσια, Catull. 95. 10 'at populus tumido gaudeat Antimacho', Ov. *am.* 1. 15. 35 'vilia miretur vulgus', [Virg.] *catal.* 9. 64 'pingui nil mihi cum populo'.

si . . . : the conditional clause expresses cautiously a hope for continuing inspiration; the understatement is continued in *neque cohibet* and *refugit tendere*. For the same blend of modesty and confidence cf. Pind. *O.* 9. 26 f. εἰ σύν τινι μοιριδίῳ παλάμᾳ / ἐξαίρετον Χαρίτων νέμομαι κᾶπον, Virg. *georg.* 4. 6 f. 'at tenuis non gloria si quem / numina laeva sinunt auditque vocatus Apollo'.

33. Euterpe: for the Muses in Horace cf. 1. 24. 3 n. They are appropriately mentioned in a dedication poem; cf. Meleager, *anth. P.* 4.

1. 1 *Μοῦσα φίλα, τίνι τάνδε φέρεις πάγκαρπον ἀοιδάν;*, Catull. 1. 9
'patrona virgo'.

35. quodsi . . .: this must introduce a climax. A. Y.
Campbell com-
plains 'To join the company of the gods in heaven is surely if anything a still greater privilege than to grow in stature until one makes
physical contact with the firmament'. But *dis miscent superis* conveys a fairly familiar idea (like *evehit ad deos* in 6 above); to ancient
feeling the fantastic hyperbole of the last stanza is much more
extravagant.

lyricis: the nine poets of the Greek canon; there were no Latin
lyrici before Horace. Cf. Cic. *orat.* 183 'qui λυρικοί a Graecis nominantur', Sen. *epist.* 49. 5 'negat Cicero, si duplicetur sibi aetas, habi-
turum se tempus quo legat lyricos', R. Pfeiffer, *History of Classical
Scholarship*, 1968, pp. 182 f.

vatibus: this word was originally applied to seers who delivered
their prophecies in verse (cf. Varro, *ling.* 7. 36). In early Latin *vates*
were given a bad name; cf. Enn. *ann.* 214 'versibus quos olim fauni
vatesque canebant', *scaen.* 319 'superstitiosi vates impudentesque
harioli' (so also Hor. *epist.* 2. 1. 26, Auson. 70. 8, 394. 38). The word
was ennobled in the Augustan period to describe the poet in his
inspired aspect; cf. Virg. *ecl.* 9. 33 ff. 'me quoque dicunt / vatem
pastores . . .', Hor. *epod.* 17. 44, *carm.* 1. 31. 2, *epist.* 2. 1. 119 f. See
further 1. 31. 2 n., Gudeman on Tac. *dial.* 9. 3, M. Runes, *Festschrift
für P. Kretschmer*, 1926, pp. 202 ff., H. Dahlmann, *Philologus* 97, 1948,
337 ff. (who thinks that the usage 'poet' is derived from Varro's misunderstanding of Enn. *ann.* 214), E. Bickel, *RhM* 94, 1951, 257 ff.,
Newman 99 ff.

inseres: cf. 4. 3. 13 ff. 'Romae principis urbium / dignatur suboles
inter amabilis / vatum ponere me choros', Prop. 2. 34. 94 'hos inter si
me ponere Fama volet', Ov. *ars* 3. 339 'forsitan et nostrum nomen
miscebitur istis', *epig. Bobiensia* 57. 1 ff. 'si Pergamenis digna cani-
mus paginis, / teque adprobante, columen urbis, Attice, / nihil
Latinos demoror librarios / quin inter orsa vetera nostra sint quoque'.
Horace's *inseres* represents the Greek ἐγκρίνειν, 'to include in the
canon' (οἱ ἐγκριθέντες, the *classici*); cf. R. Pfeiffer, op. cit. (above on
lyricis), p. 206. The future is better than the variant *inseris*: Horace's
odes are more dramatic than the average English lyric (p. xxiv), and
here he pretends that Maecenas has still to read the collection.

36. feriam sidera: a proverbial phrase. Cf. *com. adesp.* 531 K. οὕτως
ἀράσσει τῇ κεφαλῇ τὸν οὐρανόν, Aristaenetus 1. 11 καὶ τὸ λεγόμενον δὴ
τοῦτο ἐδόκει τῇ κεφαλῇ ψαύειν τοῦ οὐρανοῦ, Ov. *met.* 7. 60 f., *Pont.* 2. 5.
57, Sen. *Thy.* 885 f., Otto 63, U. Dönnges, *Aevum* 31, 1957, 47 ff.,
Pease on Virg. *Aen.* 4. 177, Ben Jonson, *Sejanus* 5. 1. 8 f. 'And at

each step I feel my advanced head Knock out a star in heaven'. Horace's contemporary critics might have quoted Apelles's judgement on Protogenes (Ael. *var. hist.* 12. 41): ἀπολείπεταί γε μὴν τῆς χειρουργίας ἡ χάρις, ἧς ὁ ἀνὴρ εἰ τύχοι, ὁ πόνος αὐτοῦ τοῦ οὐρανοῦ ψαύσει.

2. IAM SATIS TERRIS

[K. Barwick, *Philologus* 90, 1935, 257 ff.; Commager 176 ff. and *AJPh* 80, 1959, 37 ff.; J. Elmore, *CPh* 26, 1931, 258 ff.; Fraenkel 242 ff.; C. Gallavotti, *PP* 4, 1949, 217 ff.; M. E. Hirst, *CQ* 32, 1938, 7 ff.; L. MacKay, *AJPh* 83, 1962, 168 ff.; D. Norberg, *Eranos* 44, 1946, 398 ff.; L. R. Taylor, *The Divinity of the Roman Emperor*, 1931.]

1–12. *God has sent enough ill-omened weather. We began to be afraid that the age of the Flood might return.* 13–24. *We have seen the avenging Tiber make for the Temple of Vesta; our descendants will hear that we fought each other instead of the Parthians.* 25–40. *To which of the gods will the people and Vestals turn for succour? Who will expiate our sin? Come and save us, Apollo, or Venus, or Mars.* 41–52. *Or perhaps Mercury is already here on earth in the guise of a young man, condescending to be known as Caesar's avenger. May you live long amongst us, and take vengeance on the Parthians—Caesar.*

This poem owes some of its inspiration to the First Georgic (Fraenkel 243 ff.). In the opening stanza Jupiter wields the thunderbolt with flashing right hand; the image and the words are derived from Virgil's section on weather-signs (2 n.). Horace describes disturbing omens, lightning on the Capitol and floods threatening Vesta; here he is imitating Virgil's account of the portents that attended Caesar's assassination (1. 466 ff.; for particular echoes see below on 13 *vidimus* and 21 *audiet*). Horace appeals in turn to a number of possible protectors, ending with Octavian; the 'Reihengebet' in Virgil's exordium (1. 5 ff.) had also ended with Octavian. Horace expresses doubt about which god will save Rome (29 ff.), and imagines Octavian in the guise of Mercury; Virgil had expressed doubt about where Octavian would rule after his death and imagines him in the guise of a sea-god (1. 24 ff., especially 29 'an deus immensi venias maris'). But above all Horace is indebted to the great prayer at the end of the First Georgic (498 ff.):

> di patrii, Indigetes, et Romule Vestaque mater,
> quae Tuscum Tiberim et Romana Palatia servas,
> hunc saltem everso iuvenem succurrere saeclo
> ne prohibete. satis iam pridem sanguine nostro

Laomedonteae luimus periuria Troiae;
iam pridem nobis caeli te regia, Caesar,
invidet, atque hominum queritur curare triumphos,
quippe ubi fas versum atque nefas . . .

Horace shows the same feeling of weariness (1 *iam satis*), and the same consciousness of national guilt (29 *scelus*); he also records a somewhat similar supplication to Vesta (28). Like Virgil he looks for a saviour, whom he first describes as *iuvenis* (41) and only later as *Caesar* (52). Like Virgil, he too alludes to Octavian's terrestrial triumphs (49), and prays that he will remain on earth in spite of its wickedness (45 ff.).

Horace's debt to Virgil is so pervasive that it has led to a serious misunderstanding. Already Porphyrio assumed that because Virgil's portents referred to 44 B.C., Horace's must do the same. This is quite impossible. The prodigies of 44 were much more serious than Horace's snow and hail, and on the earlier occasion nothing is said (except by Porphyrio) about Tiber floods. *iam satis* must refer to recent bad weather, not to events which took place long before Horace started writing lyrics; and the Tiber floods must be associated with this recent bad weather (13 n.). Yet commentators persist in putting Julius Caesar at the centre of the poem. The flooding Tiber is said to be avenging the dictator's death; in fact the reference is mythological (17 n.). The *scelus* of line 29 is thought to be the assassination; in fact it is the sin of civil strife in general. Horace does indeed describe the Princeps as *Caesaris ultor* (44), but that is a comment about Octavian, not about Julius, who had now been dead for several wars.

There is no doubt whatever that Horace's panegyric was written after Actium. The mood of war-weariness would be quite unseemly before the crisis had passed. This general impression is confirmed by a simple objective fact: Octavian is regarded as responsible for the Parthian problem (51), and that was Antony's business until his death in 30. In view of the resemblances cited above, the poem must have been written later than the *Georgics*; nobody can believe that at scattered places in the First Book Virgil chose to imitate and improve on a single ode of Horace. The *Georgics* allude to the conquest of Egypt in 30 and the reorganization of the East in 30–29 (3. 26 ff., Dio 51. 18. 1); the triumph of August 29 is in the air, but the poet seems unaware of its triple character (3. 33 'bisque triumphatas utroque ab litore gentes'). This suits the tradition that Virgil read the completed work to Octavian at Atella on his return from the East in the summer of 29 (Donat. *vit.* 91 ff.).

Yet the precise date of Horace's ode is difficult to determine. Some attribute the opening storm to the winter of 30–29 (thus Norberg, Elmore); the extravagance of Alexandrian ruler-cult was then at its

most influential, and Octavian personally commanded a large army
in the East which might have been used against Parthia. On the
other hand a date so early hardly gives Horace and his readers
enough time to absorb the First Georgic (though the piecemeal
character of ancient 'publication' makes this argument less decisive
than at first sight appears). Others more plausibly assign the poem
to the winter of 29–28 (thus Heinze). Octavian has now returned from
the East, and held his triumphs (to which there seems to be a specific
allusion in line 49). He has insincerely threatened to surrender office,
and men are in doubt about the future (cf. Suet. *Aug.* 28. 1 'de red-
denda re publica bis cogitavit, primum post oppressum statim
Antonium', below, p. 181). He still wears the magnificence of an
Eastern conqueror, and has not yet become the moderate leader of
a supposedly constitutional government; this again suits the grandiloquent claims of Horace's ode.

Others again assign the poem to the winter of 28–27 (thus Gallavotti, MacKay). The Tiber flooded the city on 16–17 January 27, the
night after Octavian was given the name Augustus, and three nights
after he laid down his extraordinary powers: cf. Dio 53. 20. 1
Αὔγουστος μὲν δὴ ὁ Καῖσαρ ὥσπερ εἶπον ἐπωνομάσθη, καὶ αὐτῷ σημεῖον
οὐ σμικρὸν εὐθὺς τότε τῆς νυκτὸς ἐπεγένετο· ὁ γὰρ Τίβερις πελαγίσας
πᾶσαν τὴν ἐν τοῖς πεδίοις Ῥώμην κατέλαβεν ὥστε πλεῖσθαι, καὶ ἀπ'
αὐτοῦ οἱ μάντεις ὅτι τε ἐπὶ μέγα αὐξήσοι καὶ ὅτι πᾶσαν τὴν πόλιν ὑπο-
χειρίαν ἕξοι προέγνωσαν. This is the first flood big enough to be
recorded by Dio after 54 B.C.; he mentions others in 23 and 22 B.C.
and A.D. 5 and 15. There no doubt were more floods of which we hear
nothing, but even if one makes allowance for the exaggerations of
poetry, Horace seems to be talking of something out of the ordinary
(cf. 5 f.). Fraenkel argues against this dating that Horace could not
celebrate the new constitution of 27 with a reference to ill-omened
weather. His arguments have force, but perhaps they are less than
conclusive. A poet may compress a series of events, and even distort
their order; though the ode begins in gloomy talk of a collapsing
empire (which at any date after 30 is unrealistic), it proceeds to
tentative optimism, and concludes with a confident appeal; in short
it does not describe the attitudes of a moment but summarizes the
fears and hopes of several years. It is true that the extravagant
presentation of Octavian is incompatible with a restored republic;
yet Horace is writing a poem and not a legal document, he ends with
a reference to the constitutional appellation of *princeps* (50), and in
any case it may be doubted whether January 27 marked such a conspicuous break to contemporaries as it does to historians (the name
'Augustus', after all, was not very moderate). Other arguments can indeed be used against 27: no mention is made of the name 'Augustus',

though there are hints at 'Quirinus', which was previously being canvassed (46 ff.); 'Caesaris ultor' (44) becomes less topical after the dedication in August 29 of the temple of Divus Julius; and when Augustus went abroad in the summer of 27 he did not turn against Parthia, as Horace prayed, but proceeded to Gaul and then Spain (Dio 53. 22. 5). Yet when all is said and done, there are some attractions in 27: here we have a major flood which was inevitably linked with Augustus, and which by a little ingenuity could be made to represent the end of the old order and not the beginning of the new.

No matter what the date, Horace's eulogies of the Princeps are astonishing, and demand some explanation. It was one of the tritest truisms of classical Greek moralists that men are not gods, though a Harmodius or a Brasidas might be allowed the cult of a hero after his death. But even before the conquest of the East, Philip of Macedon was given some divine honours (Taylor, op. cit., pp. 12 f.). The decisive change came with Alexander, who took over the superhuman asso-ciations of the defeated kings of Egypt and Persia. The Ptolemies and Seleucids continued to expect and receive the treatment of *praesentes dei*; and even provincial and local magnates were honoured with cults, in life and in death, by Greeks as well as barbarians. See further C. Habicht, *Gottmenschentum und griechische Städte*, 1956.

The Romans were not immune from such institutions. Republican proconsuls accepted with gratification the traditional appurtenances of benefactors; for a list of known instances cf. G. W. Bowersock, *Augustus and the Greek World*, 1965, pp. 150 f. But Roman ruler-cult was started effectively by the megalomania of Julius Caesar. He acquired a statue in the temple of Quirinus with an inscription 'Deo Invicto'. A packed senate voted him a festival on his birthday, sacrifices for his safety, a temple with Clementia, and a priesthood (Taylor, op. cit., pp. 65 ff.). At this juncture, not surprisingly, he was assassinated. Yet his supporters, undeterred, offered him sacrifices in the Forum, and after the appearance of a strange comet at the games in his honour, he was formally deified on the first day of 42.

Octavian learned caution, if not moderation, from the experience of Julius; for details of his honours see Taylor, op. cit., pp. 270 ff., *RE* Suppl. 4. 821 f. He was treated as a god throughout the East, but insisted that in provincial, as opposed to municipal, cults he should share his shrine with the goddess Roma (Suet. *Aug.* 52). Roman citi-zens in these parts, in the earlier stages of his reign, had to be con-tent with shrines to Divus Julius and Roma (Dio 51. 20. 6). In the West Augustus was not a *praesens deus*; yet he was a god's son and a future god, he was intimately linked with the cults of Divus Julius and Venus Genetrix, and ceremonies in honour of his Genius

increased conspicuously in the latter part of his reign. Scholars are
far too ready to make excuses. They attribute the extravagances of
the poets entirely to literary convention, as if they could be detached
from what was going on in the real world; or they suggest a pardon-
able excess of zeal in a war-weary generation and, most incredible
of all, praise Augustus's moderation in not taking even more. Of
course by 30 B.C. all sane men would have welcomed any solution
that offered stability. One might go further and concede what some
would deny, that the more sensible cause won at Actium. Yet the
fact remains that Augustan ideology made straight thinking on
political matters impossible. It also led almost inevitably to the
greater excesses of the following century.

   Of course it is not disputed that there is a large element of literary
convention in Horace's poem; obviously he allows himself a licence
in an ode that would have been impossible in a prosaic epistle. Here
we are handicapped by our ignorance of Hellenistic court poetry.
The panegyrics of Ptolemy II by Callimachus (*hymn* 1) and by
Theocritus (17) have little in common with Horace's lively and
topical ode. But there must have been many other political panegyrics of which we know nothing, and not only in Alexandria.
Hermocles (?) wrote for Demetrius Poliorcetes (Athen. 253 d = 173 f.
Powell), Simonides of Magnesia for Antiochus, and Musaeus of
Ephesus for the Attalids. Roman statesmen were given similar
honours, though our evidence is again scanty; a few lines are preserved of a paean in honour of Flamininus (p. 253), while Crinagoras
of Mitylene wrote fairly innocuous epigrams in praise of Augustus
(Gow–Page, *Philip* 2. 210 ff.). Perhaps equally significant is Melinno's
poem to Rome, which may belong to the second century B.C.
(C. M. Bowra, *JRS* 47, 1957, 21 ff.); though the subject-matter has
nothing in common with Horace's ode, it is interesting to observe
that a Greek at that date could write Sapphics on a political subject.
There must have been much more of this type of literature that is
now completely lost to us. Yet Horace's poem is so much directed to
an actual historical situation that we cannot look for a lost Hellenistic prototype to explain its difficulties and excesses.

   Horace's ode has conspicuous merits. It is both very original and
very lively, from the wandering river to the winged saviour; one may
contrast the tedious catalogues of 1. 12. Yet the subject-matter of
a poem cannot be disregarded, whatever the literary critics say; and
Horace's appeal to Octavian is an offence against the Horatian
qualities of moderation and rationality (one may contrast such admirable political poems as 2. 1 to Pollio, and Marvell's *Horatian Ode*).
Even within the terms of Augustan poetry Horace shows none of the
imagination of the First Georgic. Virgil sees Caesar's assassination

as part of vast cosmic processes; Horace's portents are just exceptionally bad weather. Virgil uses the myth of Laomedon with
Aeschylean impressiveness to suggest an inescapable burden of in-
herited guilt; Horace paints frivolous Alexandrian miniatures, Pyrrha
agape at a passing flock of seals, Ilia whining to her uxorious river-
husband. Virgil's prayer for a saviour is indeed excessive, but it is
harmonized with the traditional pieties of a genuine Roman religion;
Horace conjures up a bizarre amalgam of Greek levity and Oriental
superstition, a winged Mercury who resignedly accepts incarnation in
order to wreak vengeance on the poet's old comrades-in-arms. He
must be given credit for welcoming the end of civil strife (not that his
ideas had the novelty imagined by some moderns), but then he proceeds to advocate further wars on the Eastern frontier. Here again
as elsewhere (p. 409) Virgil shows a more sensitive mind and a wider
vision (*georg.* 1. 505 ff.):

> tot bella per orbem,
> tam multae scelerum facies; non ullus aratro
> dignus honos; squalent abductis arva colonis,
> et curvae rigidum falces conflantur in ensem . . .

Metre: Sapphic.

1. **satis:** as in many languages 'enough' is a euphemism for 'more
than enough'; it expresses not satisfaction but exhaustion (Fraenkel
243 and on Aesch. *Ag.* 1659). One may further suggest that *satis* had
a place in the language of prayer; cf. Virg. *georg.* 1. 501 f. (above,
p. 16), Apul. *met.* 6. 28. 3 (to Fortuna) 'sat tibi miseris istis cruciatibus
meis litatum est', 11. 2. 4 (to Isis) 'sit satis laborum, sit satis pericu-
lorum'. See also Aesch. *Ag.* 511.

nivis: snow falls at Rome only about one or two days a year. Perhaps if persistent it might seem something of a portent; cf. Solon
10. 1 ff. ἐκ νεφέλης πέλεται χιόνος μένος ἠδὲ χαλάζης, / βροντὴ δ' ἐκ
λαμπρᾶς γίγνεται ἀστεροπῆς. / ἀνδρῶν δ' ἐκ μεγάλων πόλις ὄλλυται.

dirae: the word suggests a sinister omen; cf. Virg. *georg.* 1. 488
'diri . . . cometae', Prop. 3. 13. 53 f. 'diras . . . nives', Germ. fr. 4. 81
'dirae . . . grandinis', 4. 115, *Thes.l.L.* 5. 1. 1272. 17 ff., Milton, *P.L.* 2.
588 f. 'beat with perpetual storms Of whirlwind and dire hail'.

2. **rubente:** red from the flame of the thunder-bolt; cf. Pind. *O.* 9. 6
Δία τε φοινικοστερόπαν, 10. 80 f. καὶ πυρπάλαμον βέλος ὀρσικτύπου Διός,
Milton, *P.L.* 2. 173 f. 'Should intermitted vengeance arm again His
red right hand to plague us'. Horace is imitating Virg. *georg.* 1.
328 f. 'ipse pater media nimborum in nocte corusca / fulmina molitur
dextra' (Fraenkel 244).

3. arces: not the seven hills of Rome (as at Virg. *georg.* 2. 535) but the Mons Capitolinus (cf. Sil. 4. 288, 12. 741). Strictly speaking, the Arx stood on the northern summit, the Temple of Jupiter on the southern; but here *arces* refers primarily to the latter (cf. Ov. *met.* 15. 866 'quique tenes altus Tarpeias Iuppiter arces', *fast.* 1. 79).

Ancient temples were tall buildings without lightning-conductors; they were often struck, to the alarm of the devout and the derision of the irreligious. Cf. Cic. *div.* 1. 19 = *carm.* fr. 11. 36 ff. T. (prodigies of 65 B.C.) 'nam pater altitonans stellanti nixus Olympo / ipse suos quondam tumulos ac templa petivit / et Capitolinis iniecit sedibus ignis' (Pease cites many parallels), Lucr. 2. 1101 f., 6. 417 f., Ov. *am.* 3. 3. 35 'Iuppiter ipse suos lucos iaculatur et arces' (alluding to the Capitol), Ar. *nub.* 401 ἀλλὰ τὸν αὑτοῦ γε νεὼν βάλλει καὶ Σούνιον ἄκρον Ἀθηνέων, Lact. *inst.* 3. 17. 9 ff., below, 1. 12. 59 n.

5. gentis: the word refers to foreign peoples, whether inside or outside the Roman empire. This is a well-established usage, even in classical Latin; cf. 1. 35. 10, Löfstedt, *Syntactica* 2. 464 ff., *Late Latin*, 1959, pp. 74 f. Later the word was used by Christians for the Gentiles (τὰ ἔθνη).

ne rediret saeculum: cf. 4. 2. 39 f. 'quamvis redeant in aurum / tempora priscum', Virg. *ecl.* 4. 5 f. 'magnus ab integro saeclorum nascitur ordo, / iam redit et Virgo, redeunt Saturnia regna'. Horace seems to be thinking of the doctrine of the 'magnus annus', particularly favoured by the Stoics; according to this, when the heavenly bodies returned to the position where they started, all history repeated itself (Pease on Cic. *nat. deor.* 2. 51, M. Pohlenz, *Die Stoa*, 1949, 1. 78 ff., 2. 44, Gatz 24 ff.). Each cycle ended either with fire (ἐκπύρωσις) or flood (κατακλυσμός); for the latter cf. Pl. *Tim.* 22 c, Arist. *meteor.* 352ᵃ28 ff., Chrysippus 2. 186. 25 f. von A., 2. 337. 29 ff., Cic. *rep.* 6. 23, Pease on Cic. *div.* 1. 111 and *nat. deor.* 2. 118, Sen. *nat.* 3. 27. For a Jewish belief in a flood at the end of the world cf. P. Volz, *Jüdische Eschatologie*, 1903, p. 105. Of course Pyrrha's flood belonged originally to a different and inconsistent range of ideas; but Phaethon and Deucalion were sometimes linked with ἐκπύρωσις and κατακλυσμός (Roscher 3. 2189 f.).

6. Pyrrhae: she and her husband Deucalion survived the Flood in an ark, built on the advice of her father-in-law Prometheus; cf. especially Ov. *met.* 1. 262 ff., Apollod. 1. 7. 2, Claud. 15. 43 'Pyrrhae saecula sensi', *RE* 24. 77 f. For flood legends from many countries see H. Usener, *Die Sintfluthsagen*, 1899, J. G. Frazer, *Folk-lore in the Old Testament* 1, 1918, 104–361, H. Gressmann, *Das Gilgamesch-Epos*, 1911, pp. 213 ff., P. Schnabel, *Berossos und die babylonisch-hellenistische Literatur*, 1923, pp. 264 ff., *RLAC* 3. 788 ff.

7. pecus: i.e. seals. The picture of the seal-herd is suggested ulti-mately by Hom. *Od.* 4. 411 ff. (on Proteus) φώκας μέν τοι πρῶτον ἀριθμήσει καὶ ἔπεισιν. / αὐτὰρ ἐπὴν πάσας πεμπάσσεται ἠδὲ ἴδηται, / λέξεται ἐν μέσσῃσι νομεὺς ὣς πώεσι μήλων. Archilochus and some of his imitators talk of the pasture of dolphins (below, 9 n.). Cf. also Liv. Andr. *trag.* 5 'lascivum Nerei simum pecus' (dolphins), Pacuv. *trag.* 408 'Nerei repandirostrum incurvicervicum pecus', Virg. *georg.* 4. 393 f. 'immania cuius / armenta et turpis pascit sub gurgite phocas'.

8. visere montis: Proteus conducted his seals to the mountains like a drover taking his cattle along the *calles* to their distant upland *saltus*. For this system of animal husbandry cf. *epod.* 1. 27 f., Soph. *OT* 1133 ff., Varro, *rust.* 2. 2. 9, A. J. Toynbee, *Hannibal's Legacy*, 1965, 2. 286 ff., 570 ff. (on 'nomadic pastoral economy').

9. piscium . . .: this topic starts as a proverbial impossibility (ἀδύνα-τον). Cf. Archil. 74. 7 ff. μηδ' ἐὰν δελφῖσι θῆρες ἀνταμείψωνται νομόν / ἐνάλιον καί σφιν θαλάσσης ἠχέεντα κύματα / φίλτερ' ἠπείρου γένηται, τοῖσι δ' ὑλήειν ὄρος, Hdt. 5. 92 a. 1 ἦ δὴ ὅ τε οὐρανὸς ἔνερθε ἔσται τῆς γῆς καὶ ἡ γῆ μετέωρος ὑπὲρ τοῦ οὐρανοῦ, καὶ ἄνθρωποι νομὸν ἐν θαλάσσῃ ἕξουσι καὶ ἰχθύες τὸν πρότερον ἄνθρωποι, ὅτε γε ὑμεῖς, ὦ Λακεδαιμόνιοι, ἰσοκρατίας καταλύοντες τυραννίδας ἐς τὰς πόλις κατάγειν παρασκευάζεσθε, Virg. *ecl.* 1. 59 f. 'ante leves ergo pascentur in aethere cervi / et freta destituent nudos in litore piscis', Hor. *epod.* 16. 34, *ars* 30, Prop. 2. 3. 5 f., Rufinus, *anth. P.* 5. 19. 5 f. βοσκήσει δελφῖνας ὁ δενδροκόμης Ἐρύμανθος / καὶ πολιὸν πόντου κῦμα θοὰς ἐλάφους, Nemes. *ecl.* 1. 75, Claud. 1. 169 f., 18. 355.

In our poem Horace describes his flood not as a quaint impossi-bility but as something that has actually happened. For this compare Lycophron 83 ff. φηγὸν δὲ καὶ δρύκαρπα καὶ γλυκὺν βότρυν / φάλλαι τε καὶ δελφῖνες αἵ τ' ἐπ' ἀρσένων / φέρβοντο φῶκαι λέκτρα θουρῶσαι βροτῶν, Ov. *met.* 1. 299 ff., Nonnus 6. 263 ff., Ennod. *carm.* 1. 5. 37. One suspects a lost Hellenistic source of a descriptive character, influenced only in part by Archilochus, and influencing in turn Lycophron, Horace, Ovid, and Nonnus.

Porphyrio provides an interesting note on our passage: 'leviter in re tam atroci et piscium et palumborum meminit, nisi quod hi excessus lyricis concessi sunt'. This recalls Seneca's comment on Ovid's flood, 'non est res satis sobria lascivire devorato orbe ter-rarum . . . magnifice haec, si non curaverit quid oves et lupi faciant' (*nat.* 3. 27. 14). The criticism is more deserved by Horace than by Ovid; such descriptions are a frivolous way of describing chaos, and do not suit a political poem.

genus: cf. Lucr. 1. 162 'squamigerum genus', Virg. *georg.* 3. 243 'genus aequoreum', *Thes.l.L.* 6. 2. 1893. 69 ff. So in Greek φῦλα, ἔθνεα,

F

γένος, γενεή, in English 'the finny tribe', 'the tabby kind'; see further
G. Tillotson, *Essays and Studies* 25, 1940, 77 ff. (= *Essays in Criticism
and Research,* 1942, pp. 82 ff.).

haesit ulmo: cf. Ov. *met.* 1. 296 'hic summa piscem deprendit in
ulmo'. The fish are caught as in a net; cf. Plaut. *rud.* 984 'ubi demisi
retem atque hamum, quidquid haesit extraho', Juv. 4. 41.

10. columbis: Bentley points out that *columbae* in the strict sense
rarely settle on trees; he considers *palumbis* (a variant in Porphyrio),
which is the proper word for wood-pigeons. Yet cf. Suet. *Aug.* 94. 11
'(palma) frequentaretur . . . columbarum nidis, quamvis id avium
genus duram et asperam frondem maxime vitet'.

13. vidimus: co-ordinate with *misit* and *terruit* (a point obscured by
some commentators); the clause refers to a recent event. The appeal
to experience is a familiar rhetorical device, and *videre* is often used
of unpleasant experiences (so ἐπιδεῖν, 'live to see'). Cf. 3. 5. 21, Enn.
scaen. 97 'haec omnia vidi inflammari', Cic. *poet. fr.* 11. 15 T. 'vidisti
et claro tremulos ardore cometas', Virg. *georg.* 1. 471 f. 'quotiens
Cyclopum effervere in agros / vidimus undantem ruptis fornacibus
Aetnam' (Horace's immediate model), *Aen.* 2. 498 ff., Prop. 4. 2. 53,
Octavia 231 f.

The Tiber, like many Italian rivers, is liable to sudden flooding:
its basin is large in relation to its size, it has important tributaries
flowing over impermeable soil, and the Apennines are exposed to
sustained bursts of torrential rain. Serious inundations are repeatedly
recorded by Livy and Dio, and after the floods of A.D. 15 special com-
missioners were appointed by the senate (Tac. *ann.* 1. 76). In later
times important floods took place in 856, 1476, 1530 (described vividly
by Benvenuto Cellini), 1557 (reaching the site of the Piazza di
Spagna), 1598 (eight hundred deaths), 1660, 1870 (boats in the Corso),
1898. For a photograph of the flooded Forum see R. Lanciani, *The
Destruction of Ancient Rome,* 1899, p. 140; cf. also E. T. Merrill, *CR*
15, 1901, 129 'I have myself seen the Tiber more than once back up
the ancient sewer-system to within a very few feet of the Temple of
Vesta'. The trouble only stopped when the river was enclosed in
embankments during the present century. For details see Strother
A. Smith, *The Tiber and its Tributaries,* 1877.

In so superstitious a city the flooding of the Tiber was naturally
regarded as a supernatural visitation. See Plin. *nat.* 3. 55 'quin immo
vates intellegitur potius ac monitor, auctu semper religiosus verius
quam saevus', Cic. *ad Q. fr.* 3. 7. 1 (humorously connecting the floods
of 54 with the acquittal of Gabinius), Tac. *ann.* 1. 76. 2 (Asinius
Gallus wants to consult the Sibylline books). In 1530 an inscription
was affixed to the convent of the Minerva: 'huc Tiber ascendit,

iamque obruta tota fuisset / Roma, nisi huc celerem Virgo tulisset opem'. And in 1598 Castaglio wrote a poem to Cardinal Aldobrandini explaining the flood as a punishment for the sins of the people (Smith, op. cit., p. 78).

flavum: a conventional euphemism, perhaps from Ennius; cf. 1. 8. 8, 2. 3. 18, Virg. *Aen.* 7. 31 'multa flavus harena', Bömer on Ov. *fast.* 6. 228, G. Lugli, *Fontes ad topographiam veteris urbis Romae pertinentes* 2, 1953, p. 26, André 129. More extravagantly 'caeruleus Thybris' (Virg. *Aen.* 8. 64).

14. litore Etrusco: the right (western) bank of the Tiber; for *litus* of a river-bank cf. Cic. *inv.* 2. 97, Virg. *Aen.* 8. 83, Shackleton Bailey, *Propertiana*, p. 69. Just beyond the Isola Tiberina the river, which has been flowing to the south-east, changes its course to the south-west; about this point the flood flowed north-east to the Forum. Horace pictures the water as deflected by the salient on the west bank.

Porphyrio explains *litus* as the shore of the *mare Tyrrhenum* at the mouth of the Tiber (cf. *epod.* 16. 40 'Etrusca praeter et volate litora', *carm. saec.* 37 f. 'Iliaeque / litus Etruscum tenuere turmae'). The Nile floods were attributed by some to winds blowing at the mouth; cf. Thales A 16 Diels (cf. Sen. *nat.* 4. 2. 22), Hdt. 2. 20. 2, Lucr. 6. 715 ff. Dio is prepared to consider such an explanation for the Tiber floods in 54 B.C.: εἴτε καὶ σφοδροῦ πνεύματος ἐκ τῆς θαλάσσης τὴν ἐκροὴν αὐτοῦ ἀνακόψαντος (39. 61. 1). Seneca mentions that the same hypothesis was invoked to explain floods generally: 'si crebrioribus ventis ostium caeditur et reverberatus fluctu amnis resistit qui crescere videtur quia non effunditur' (*nat.* 3. 26. 2). Some floods are certainly caused by the pile-up of water at a river-mouth; but such an explanation is false for the Tiber, where there is no tide, and no broadening estuary to catch the sea (Smith, op. cit., pp. 98 ff.). Yet we are dealing here not with facts but opinions, and the theory is attested in Rome in more recent times; Smith, p. 94, quotes a sixteenth-century poem 'at si forte graves aspirat ab aequore flatus / egressum nostris impedit Auster aquis'.

Many editors follow this explanation in our passage, but the first theory seems preferable. *vidimus* has more point if the phenomenon was seen and not simply inferred. The violent *retortis* also suits the first explanation (cf. Stat. *silv.* 2. 6. 64 f. 'seu Thybridis impetus altas / in dextrum torsisset aquas'); if Horace were describing pressure at the river-mouth one would sooner expect *repulsis* or *reiectis*. Finally, on the first theory *litore* is instrumental ('by the bank'), which is vigorous and natural; on the second theory it seems to be either local ('on the shore') or separative ('from the shore'), neither of which suits *retortis* so well.

15. monumenta regis: the round temple of Vesta in the Forum, the Atrium Vestae, and the Regia; *templa* is not distinct from *monumenta*, but more specific. The buildings were attributed to Numa; cf. Ov. *fast.* 6. 259 'regis opus placidi', 6. 263 f. with Bömer's note. The temple housed the sacred fire and the precious Palladium; so the threat of flooding might seem a sinister omen.

17. Iliae: Rhea Silvia, the mother of Romulus and Remus (*RE* 1 A. 341 ff., Bömer on Ov. *fast.* 2. 383). After the birth of her children she was thrown into the Tiber; Ennius related the episode (Porph. ad loc.; cf. *ann.* 35 ff.). According to the usual story Ilia was married to the Anio; cf. Porph. 'antea enim Anieni matrimonio iuncta est; atque hic (Horace) loquitur quasi Tiberi potius nupserit', ps.-Acro 'sepulta ad ripam Anienis fluvii dicitur, qui in Tiberim cadit, et quia abundans aquis Anio cineres Iliae in Tiberim deduxit, dicta est Ilia Tiberi nupsisse . . . alii dicunt quod ista Ilia Anieni nupserit; nam multi hoc sentiunt poetae. sed Horatius, ut Tiberi det causas irascendi, Tiberis magis dixit uxorem', Serv. *Aen.* 1. 273 'tum ut quidam dicunt Iliam sibi Anien fecit uxorem, ut alii inter quos Horatius Tiberis'. It is sometimes suggested that marriage with the Tiber goes back to Ennius, but that view is hardly compatible with the above scholia; one may note in particular Acro's embarrassed attempt to reconcile Horace with the traditional story about the Anio (for which see Ov. *am.* 3. 6. 45 ff.). Horace's account is followed implicitly by Stat. *silv.* 2. 1. 99 f., and explicitly by Claud. 1. 224 f., Sidon. *carm.* 5. 28.

 nimium querenti: what is Ilia complaining about so excessively? The answer escapes most commentators; yet at the most literal level it can only be 'because she was thrown into the river'. She was drowned because she broke her Vestal vows; so she might reasonably encourage the river to flood the Temple of Vesta.

 Of course there is more than one meaning in all this; the floods are linked with the snow and hail, which are a sign of divine displeasure at civil wars. Strictly speaking such an allusion is incompatible with the mythological reference to Ilia; but poets sometimes employ inconsistent forms of motivation simultaneously (cf. the human and supernatural elements in epic). One finds the same ambiguity in Virg. *georg.* 1. 502 'Laomedonteae luimus periuria Troiae'; the poet uses Laomedon's perjury as a symbol for more recent guilt. Horace himself elsewhere links the mythological and the historical: 'sic est: acerba fata Romanos agunt / scelusque fraternae necis / ut immerentis fluxit in terram Remi / sacer nepotibus cruor' (*epod.* 7. 17 ff.).

 Porphyrio says that Ilia is lamenting the assassination of Julius Caesar, and most modern interpreters accept this explanation (not

Hirst or Commager). Yet to say no more, *nimium* would be intolerably offensive to Caesar's avenger and heir. As *pontifex maximus*, it is true, Julius Caesar was in charge of the Vestals (Ov. *fast.* 3. 699 f. 'meus fuit ille sacerdos; / sacrilegae telis me petiere manus'); yet it is hard to see why Ilia should wish the destruction of the temple with which her priest was associated. It is also true that Ilia and Caesar were in a sense 'related', as both were supposed to be descended from Aeneas; but the connection is not played up in the mythology of the age, and there is no suggestion that Caesar was directly descended from Ilia (Romulus died childless).

18. iactat ultorem: Horace treats the legend in a lively Alexandrian way in terms of everyday married life. Tiberis plays the part of a big strong river, and tells his querulous wife that he will show them (all this would be quite unsuitable if a reference to the assassination were intended). For the dative cf. Ov. *epist.* 12. 175 f. 'dum te iactare maritae / quaeris', Liv. 39. 43. 2 'iactantem sese scorto', Juv. 1. 62 'lacernatae cum se iactaret amicae'. Yet here *ultorem* makes some difference.

vagus: a common epithet of rivers (1. 34. 9 n.), here applied with special force to a river in flood. Cf. Sen. *Med.* 586, Luc. 9. 752, Plin. *paneg.* 30. 4, Claud. 15. 41, Prud. *ham.* 243, Ven. Fort. *carm.* 3. 12. 9.

19. labitur ripa: elsewhere such expressions mean that a river is flowing within its banks (*epod.* 2. 25, Lucr. 2. 362 'summis labentia ripis'). Here the phrase rather signifies 'takes the left bank as its course'; the strangely gentle *labitur* is properly used of the normal flow of rivers. Presumably *ripa* means the whole area on the left bank, like the Rive Gauche in Paris; cf. Cic. *rep.* 2. 10 '(Romulus) urbem perennis amnis . . . posuit in ripa'.

non probante: litotes for *improbante*. At first sight the remark seems inconsistent with Jove's thunderbolt in the first stanza and the talk of expiation in 29 f. Porphyrio comments 'quod Iuppiter terreri populum iusserit, non perire'. Yet it is possible that Horace has not noticed a minor incoherence.

uxorius: cf. Virg. *Aen.* 4. 266 f. 'pulchramque uxorius urbem / exstruis'. The word may be less prosaic than 'uxorious', but the picture of the doting Tiber remains frivolous. The run-over between the third and fourth lines (above, p. xliv) suggests a river out of control.

21. audiet . . .: Porphyrio comments 'ἀσυνδέτως transiit', and the drift equally perplexes modern editors. They do not observe the connection between *vidimus* and *audiet*; for this common contrast cf. Pind. *P.* 1. 26 τέρας μὲν θαυμάσιον προσιδέσθαι, θαῦμα δὲ καὶ

παρεόντων ἀκοῦσαι. Here Horace compares the vivid personal experience of the immediate sufferers with the detached astonishment
of a future generation; he no doubt remembers Virg. *georg.* 1. 493 ff.
'scilicet et tempus veniet cum finibus illis / agricola incurvo terram
molitus aratro / exesa inveniet scabra robigine pila, / aut gravibus
rastris galeas pulsabit inanis / grandiaque effossis mirabitur ossa
sepulcris'. The present experience is told in terms of thunderstorms
and floods, not explicitly interpreted; in turning to future generations Horace for the first time states the objective truth, that citizens fought citizens. But the evil that men do lives after them: the
civil war may be only a tale, but its effects will survive in the depopulation of Italy, here alluded to with Horatian economy.

   cives: the word is edged; Horace is saying briefly and euphemistic-
ally that the war was a civil one. Cf. Cic. *Att.* 14. 19. 1 'castris civilibus',
Prop. 2. 1. 27 'civilia busta Philippos', P. Jal, *La Guerre civile à Rome*,
1963, pp. 64 ff.

   acuisse ferrum: cf. Virg. *Aen.* 8. 386, Ov. *met.* 15. 776 'en acui
sceleratos cernitis enses?', Aesch. *Ag.* 1262 θήγουσα φωτὶ φάσγανον.

22. Persae: a more grandiose name for the Parthians, whose empire
included the territory of the Persians; cf. 51 'Medos', 1. 21. 15, 3. 5. 4.
Horace is remembering the defeat of Crassus (53 B.C.), the Parthian
occupation of Syria and Cilicia (41–39), and Antony's disastrous
retreat from Phraaspa (36). For the theme cf. 1. 35. 38 ff., *epod.* 7. 5 ff.
'non ut superbas invidae Karthaginis / Romanus arces ureret, /
intactus aut Britannus ut descenderet / Sacra catenatus via', Luc.
1. 10 ff. 'cumque superba foret Babylon spolianda tropaeis / Ausoniis
umbraque erraret Crassus inulta / bella geri placuit nullos habitura
triumphos?'

   melius perirent: 'it would be better that the Parthians perished'.
As so often, the adverb carries the weight of the sentence; cf. Virg.
ecl. 9. 67 'carmina tum melius, cum venerit ipse, canemus', Prop.
3. 11. 37, Ov. *epist.* 6. 93, with Palmer's note.

24. iuventus: young men of military age. For the depopulation of
Italy cf. Varro, *de vita pop. Rom.* 115 Riposati (= Non. 501 M.) 'ipsa
Italiae oppida sunt vastata quae prius fuerunt hominum referta',
Sen. *dial.* 9. 2. 13, Luc. 1. 27, 7. 398 f. 'crimen civile videmus / tot
vacuas urbes'.

25. quem . . . .: note the rhetorical 'tricolon'. The three interrogative
pronouns are each in a different case ('polyptoton'), and the subject
is also varied.

   divum: probably the archaic genitive plural; cf. 4. 6. 22 'divum
pater', Aesch. *Th.* 93 f. τίς ἄρα ῥύσεται, τίς ἄρ' ἐπαρκέσει / θεῶν ἢ

θεᾶν;, Plaut. *capt.* 863 'quoi deorum (sacruficem)?', *Thes.l.L.* 5. 1.
1653. 54 ff. For the accusative cf. 1. 12. 3 'quem deum?', Cic. *Marc.* 23.

ruentis: *ruina*, which applies literally to the collapse of a building,
is often used metaphorically of the breakdown of orderly government. Cf. 1. 37. 7, 2. 1. 32, *epod.* 16. 2, *carm. arv.* 2 'neve lue rue,
Marmar, sins incurrere in pleoris' (cf. E. Norden, *Aus altrömischen
Priesterbüchern*, 1939, pp. 127 f.), Cic. *Vat.* 21 'quod invitus facio ut
recorder ruinas rei publicae', Luc. 5. 200 f.

26. fatigent: the word stresses the persistence of the suppliant and
not the impatience of the deity. Cf. Lucr. 4. 1239 'nequiquam divum
numen sortisque fatigant', Shackleton Bailey, *Propertiana*, p. 138,
Thes.l.L. 6. 348. 71 ff., Milton, *P.L.* 11. 310 'To weary him with my
assiduous cries'.

27. virgines: the Vestal Virgins prayed for the public safety; cf. Cic.
Font. 48 (of a Vestal) 'cuius preces si di aspernarentur, haec salva
esse non possent', Symm. *rel.* 3. 11 'saluti publicae dicata virginitas',
Prud. *c. Symm.* 2. 1104. For solemn invocations of Vesta cf. Cic. *dom.*
144, Ov. *fast.* 4. 828, Vell. 2. 131. 1 'Iuppiter Capitoline . . . et Gradive
Mars perpetuorumque custos Vesta ignium, . . . custodite servate
protegite hunc statum'.

minus: an idiomatic understatement for *non*; cf. *epod.* 5. 61. For
audire of prayers cf. Appel 119, K. Ziegler, *De precationum apud
Graecos formis quaestiones selectae*, 1905, pp. 59 ff.

29. scelus: the guilt of civil war; cf. 1. 35. 33, Virg. *ecl.* 4. 13 'si qua
manent sceleris vestigia nostri', Luc. 1. 2. Some refer to the death of
Caesar; but there is nothing in the text to encourage so particular an
explanation. The guilt will be 'expiated' by fighting foreign enemies;
cf. below, 51 n., Tac. *ann.* 1. 49. 5 'truces etiam tum animos cupido
involat eundi in hostem, piaculum furoris'.

30. tandem: cf. Soph. *El.* 411, *Phil.* 1041, Sen. *Herc. f.* 277 f. 'adsis
sospes et remees precor / tandemque venias victor ad victam
domum'.

venias: a regular feature of the κλητικὸς ὕμνος (the god's presence
was essential). Cf. Sappho 1. 5. ἀλλὰ τυίδ' ἔλθ', Soph. *OT* 167, Ar. *Ach.*
665, *eq.* 559, *Lys.* 1298, *Thesm.* 319, *apoc.* 22. 20 ἔρχου Κύριε 'Ιησοῦ. So
in Christian hymns 'veni creator spiritus', 'veni veni Emmanuel'.

31. nube: to be taken with *amictus*; cf. Hom. *Il.* 5. 186 νεφέλη εἰλυμένος
ὤμους, 15. 308 (of Apollo) εἰμένος ὤμοιιν νεφέλην, *apoc.* 10. 1 καὶ εἶδον
ἄλλον ἄγγελον ἰσχυρὸν καταβαίνοντα ἐκ τοῦ οὐρανοῦ, περιβεβλημένον
νεφέλην. *candentis* makes an artistic contrast with *nube*; for white
shoulders cf. 1. 13. 9 f., 2. 5. 18, Hom. *Od.* 11. 128 ἀνὰ φαιδίμῳ ὤμῳ.

The ancients did not admire sunburn, and marble statuary reinforced their image of the god.

32. augur: a very Roman version of μάντις; so *carm. saec.* 61 'augur ... Phoebus', Cic. *div.* 1. 87 'Calchantem augurem scribit Homerus longe optumum', Virg. *Aen.* 4. 376, Val. Fl. 1. 234, Stat. *Theb.* 1. 495, *Thes.l.L.* 2. 1367. 27 ff.

Apollo: the Julian *gens* sacrificed to Vediovis (*ILS* 2988), who was identified with Apollo (Gell. 5. 12. 12); as early as 431 B.C. Cn. Julius dedicated a temple to Apollo (Liv. 4. 29. 7). Octavian used the tripod of Apollo in coins of 37 B.C., he started the Palatine temple soon after (Vell. 2. 81. 3), he was said by his admirers to be Apollo's son (Suet. *Aug.* 94. 4, Dio 45. 1. 2), and by his enemies to dress up as the god (Suet. *Aug.* 70). Apollo suited the ideals of enlightenment and civilization for which he professed to stand; and after the battle of Actium, which conveniently took place near two shrines of Apollo (at Actium and Leucas), the myth gained in authority. See further Taylor, op. cit., pp. 118 ff., H. Boas, *Aeneas' arrival in Latium*, 1938, pp. 130 ff., J. Gagé, *Apollon romain*, 1955, pp. 499 ff., Bömer on Ov. *fast.* 4. 951.

33. mavis: not 'prefer' but 'wish rather'. It would be natural to say 'shall I invoke Apollo or Venus?'; here the decision is left to the gods themselves. For prayers to a series of gods cf. Aesch. *Th.* 109 ff., Varro, *rust.* 1. 1. 5–6, Virg. *georg.* 1. 5 ff., Sen. *Ag.* 310 ff., *ILS* 5035, Fraenkel, *Kl. Beitr.* 1. 355 ff. (= *Philologus* 86, 1931, 3 ff.), Norden, op. cit. [above, 25 *ruentis*], pp. 148 f.

Erycina: Erice, formerly S. Giuliano, is an isolated mountain of 2,500 ft. on the west coast of Sicily. On the summit was an ancient cult-centre of Venus, no doubt Phoenician in origin (Theoc. 15. 101, Bömer on Ov. *fast.* 4. 872, Head 138 f.). It came into the Roman orbit with the accession of Segesta in 263, and played an important part in the Romanization of Sicily; in 215 the cult was brought to Rome, and a temple dedicated on the Capitoline (R. Schilling, *La Religion romaine de Vénus*, 1954, pp. 233 ff.). In Horace's day the famous prostitutes of the Sicilian temple had disappeared, but the cult still flourished merrily: cf. Diod. Sic. 4. 83. 6 οἱ μὲν γὰρ καταντῶντες εἰς τὴν νῆσον ὕπατοι καὶ στρατηγοὶ καὶ πάντες οἱ μετά τινος ἐξουσίας ἐπιδημοῦντες, ἐπειδὰν εἰς τὸν Ἔρυκα παραβάλωσι, μεγαλοπρεπέσι θυσίαις καὶ τιμαῖς κοσμοῦσι τὸ τέμενος, καὶ τὸ σκυθρωπὸν τῆς ἐξουσίας ἀποθέμενοι μεταβάλλουσιν εἰς παιδιὰς καὶ γυναικῶν ὁμιλίας μετὰ πολλῆς ἱλαρότητος. Soon afterwards, on the night of Christ's birth according to later legend, the ancient building collapsed; however, Tiberius restored it with appropriate piety (Tac. *ann.* 4. 43. 6 'suscepit curam libens ut consanguineus').

Venus is mentioned here as the ancestress of the Roman race (Bömer on Ov. *fast.* 1. 717), and in particular of the Julian house (ibid. 4. 20). The Julii connected themselves with the city of Ilium, and the name Iulus was at some stage given to Ascanius, son of Aeneas and grandson of Venus. Venus Genetrix appears on the coins of Sex. Julius Caesar about 125 B.C. (E. A. Sydenham, *The Coinage of the Roman Republic*, 1952, no. 476) and of L. Julius Caesar about 94 (Sydenham, op. cit., no. 593; note the two Cupids); the latter performed services for Ilium (*ILS* 8770). C. Julius Caesar was already boasting of his divine ancestry in 68 B.C.; cf. Suet. *Jul.* 6. 1 'amitae meae Iuliae maternum genus ab regibus ortum, paternum cum diis immortalibus coniunctum est', Vell. 2. 41. 1. Contemporaries were rather amused; cf. Cic. ap. Suet. *Jul.* 49. 3 'floremque aetatis a Venere orti in Bithynia contaminatum', Cael. ap. Cic. *epist.* 8. 15. 2 'Venere prognatus'. The myth became really important during the dictatorship, as is shown alike by the coinage (Schilling, op. cit., pl. xxx), and the great temple of Venus Genetrix. Though the relationship was less emphasized under the puritanical Augustus, the whole theme of the *Aeneid* shows that it was not forgotten (for coins cf. Schilling, pl. xxxi).

ridens: Horace adds a Homeric epithet to the familiar cult-title; cf. Hom. *Il.* 3. 424 φιλομμειδής, *h.Ven.* 49 ἡδὺ γελοιήσασα φιλομμειδὴς Ἀφροδίτη.

34. quam: for relative clauses in prayers cf. 1. 10. 2 n. For Venus's retinue cf. 1. 19. 1 n., 1. 30. 5 n.; here one may refer to the putti portrayed in the temple of Venus Genetrix (E. Nash, *Pictorial Dictionary of Ancient Rome* 1, 1961, pp. 424 ff.).

Iocus: the word can refer not just to amusing remarks but to enjoyable behaviour, especially in love; cf. 1. 33. 12, *epist.* 1. 6. 65 f., 2. 2. 56, Catull. 8. 6. For the personification of *iocus* cf. Plaut. *Bacch.* 114 ff. 'quis istic habet? /—Amor Voluptas Venus Venustas Gaudium / Iocus Ludus Sermo Suavisaviatio. /—quid tibi commercist cum dis damnosissimis?', epigram on Plautus 2 f. (p. 32 Morel) 'scaena est deserta, dein Risus Ludus Iocusque / et Numeri innumeri simul omnes conlacrimarunt', Stat. *silv.* 1. 6. 6, Philostr. *imag.* 1. 25. 3 (of Dionysus) τὸν Γέλωτά τε ἄγει καὶ τὸν Κῶμον, ἰλαρωτάτω καὶ ξυμποτικωτάτω δαίμονε, Milton, *L'Allegro* 25 f. 'Haste thee, Nymph, and bring with thee Jest, and youthful Jollity'. A Greek vase shows Paidia pushing Himeros on a swing (Roscher 3. 1252, *RE* 18. 2. 2386 f.).

circum volat: cf. Sappho 22. 11 f. σε δηὖτε πόθος . . . / ἀμφιπόταται, Catull. 68. 133 'quam circumcursans hinc illinc saepe Cupido', Q. Smyrn. 5. 71.

36. respicis: the *vox propria*; cf. Plaut. *Bacch.* 638a 'deus respiciet

nos aliquis', Ter. *Phorm.* 817, Cic. *Att.* 7. 1. 2, Aesch. *Th.* 106 f. (hymn
to Ares) ὦ χρυσοπήληξ δαῖμον, ἔπιδ' ἔπιδε πόλιν, evang. *Luc.* 1. 68
εὐλογητὸς ὁ Θεὸς τοῦ Ἰσραήλ, ὅτι ἐπεσκέψατο καὶ ἐποίησεν λύτρωσιν
τῷ λαῷ αὐτοῦ, K. Ziegler, op. cit. [above, 27 n.], pp. 73 f.
    auctor: Mars, the father of Romulus. He had a special connection
with the Julian house, and appears sometimes on its coins; cf. *SIG³*
760 (a dedication by the cities of Asia to Julius Caesar) τὸν ἀπὸ Ἄρεως
καὶ Ἀφροδείτης θεὸν ἐπιφανῆ καὶ κοινὸν τοῦ ἀνθρωπίνου βίου σωτῆρα.
The temple to Mars Ultor, dedicated in 2 B.C., contained statues to
Venus Genetrix, Mars Ultor, and Divus Iulius; for a possible imitation, found on a relief from Carthage, cf. Taylor, op. cit., p. 203.
    In our passage *auctor* is nominative rather than vocative, and is
correlative with *nepotes*. Cf. Seneca's elaboration (*Ag.* 404 ff.), 'generis
nostri, Iuppiter, auctor, / cape dona libens / abavusque tuam non
degenerem / respice prolem' (*abavus* there corresponds to *auctor*
here). For the word *auctor* cf. also Virg. *Aen.* 4. 365, Rut. Nam. 1. 67
'auctores generis Venerem Martemque fatemur'.

37. satiate: Ares was conventionally insatiable; cf. Hom. *Il.* 5. 388
ἇτος πολέμοιο, Hes. sc. 346 ἀκόρητος ἀϋτῆς. For the idea in Roman
prayers cf. *carm. arv.* 3 'satur fu fere Mars', Sen. *Ag.* 519 ff. 'quisquis
es nondum malis / satiate tantis caelitum, tandem tuum / numen
serena', Petron. 121. 119 f., Norden, op. cit. [25 *ruentis*], pp. 134 f.,
146 f. The meaning of our passage is not 'now that you are sated,
come', but 'be sated and come'; cf. Soph. *Ai.* 695 f. ὦ Πὰν Πὰν
ἁλίπλαγκτε . . . φάνηθ' ('come over the sea and appear to us'), Tib.
1. 7. 53 (to Osiris) 'sic venias hodierne' (with K. F. Smith's note),
K.-S. 1. 255 f., Löfstedt, *Syntactica* 1². 103 ff., H.-Sz. 25 f.

38. quem iuvat: the relative clause makes a piquant contrast with line
34. The motif here is common in descriptions of gods, both in hymns
and elsewhere. Cf. *h. Hom.* 11. 2 f. (Pallas Athene) ᾗ σὺν Ἄρηι μέλει
πολεμήια ἔργα / περθόμεναί τε πόληες αὐτή τε πτόλεμοί τε, Ar. *eq.* 551 ff.,
Call. *h.* 5. 44, Sil. 9. 554 f. (of Mars) 'quamquam lituique tubaeque /
voleneraque et sanguis et clamor et arma iuvarent', Val. Fl. 3. 84 f.
    leves: smooth with repeated polishing over the years; cf. 2. 7. 21,
Virg. *Aen.* 7. 626 'pars levis clipeos et spicula lucida tergent'.

39. Marsi: the emendation of Tanaquil Faber for *Mauri* of the
manuscripts and scholiasts; it is defended by Bentley with great virtuosity. The Marsi provided the stalwart rustics who were the back-
bone of the Roman infantry; cf. 2. 20. 17 f., 3. 5. 9, Enn. *ann.* 276
'Marsa manus, Peligna cohors, Vestina virum vis', Cic. *Vat.* 36, Virg.
georg. 2. 167 'genus acre virum, Marsos pubemque Sabellam . . .',
Str. 5. 4. 2, App. *civ.* 1. 46. 203 ἔθνος πολεμικώτατον . . . οὔτε κατὰ

Μάρσων οὔτε ἄνευ Μάρσων γενέσθαι θρίαμβον. As the name was connected with Mars (originally a rustic deity), it is strikingly appropriate here. *cruentum* is not 'blood-stained', but 'bloodthirsty' (its
only natural meaning when combined with *hostem*). *voltus* suggests
not aggression but defiance; cf. Sall. *Cat.* 61. 4 'ferociamque animi,
quam habuerat vivos, in voltu retinens'.

The objection to *Mauri* is not, as Faber supposed, that they were
unwarlike; see Virg. *Aen.* 4. 40 'Gaetulae urbes, genus insuperabile
bello', Calp. *ecl.* 4. 40 'trucibus . . . Mauris'. It is much more important that the Moors were particularly associated with cavalry. It is
no defence to argue that they had some foot-soldiers (Sall. *Jug.* 59.
3), for these were not typical; and it is implausibly artificial to
explain *peditis* as 'dismounted'. *cruentum* is also strange: the enemy
of a savage Moor cannot appropriately be called 'bloodthirsty', and
if the enemy is blood-stained (i.e. losing) the point of *acer vultus* is
weakened. Above all, it is not clear why Mars should rejoice in the
exploits of barbarians against a Roman *hostis*.

Wodrig proposed 'acer et Maurum peditis cruenti / vultus in
hostem'; this conjecture was approved by Housman in lectures
(Mr. Wilkinson reports). *peditis* implies that the Moor was on horse-
back, and this is appropriate. Yet too much attention is perhaps
concentrated on the enemy; the nationality of the *pedes* is not stated,
and he is given a less conspicuous place in the sentence.

Palmer proposed 'acer et Mauri peditem cruenti / vultus in hostem'; the Moor is now properly called 'bloodthirsty'. Yet some of
the difficulty of the transmitted reading remains: Mars should not
take pleasure in Moors, and *hostem* should not suggest Romans.
Moreover, Palmer's word-order is unattractive.

41. mutata . . . figura: μεταμορφωθείς, *transfiguratus* (which only
occurs later). Cf. *ciris* 56 'alia perhibent mutatam membra figura',
Calp. *ecl.* 4. 142 ff. (an imitation of our passage) 'tu quoque mutata
seu Iuppiter ipse figura, / Caesar, ades, seu quis superum sub imagine
falsa / mortalique lates (es enim deus): hunc precor orbem, / hos
precor aeternos populos rege; sit tibi caeli / vilis amor, coeptamque,
pater, ne desere pacem', Claud. *carm. min.* 27. 54, *Thes.l.L.* 6. 1. 723.
69 ff.

iuvenem: Octavian was born in 63, and technically men from 17 to
45 were *iuvenes*. It is more relevant that he was portrayed in the
guise of a heroic young Alexander, as in the Capitoline statue. Cf.
serm. 2. 5. 62, Virg. *ecl.* 1. 43 'hic illum vidi iuvenem', *georg.* 1. 500
(above, p. 16).

42. ales: Horace is referring to the wings on the *talaria* and cap of
Mercury. There is an artistic contrast with *in terris*.

imitaris: 'you assume the guise of'; cf. Ov. *met.* 11. 613 f. 'hunc circa passim varias imitantia formas / somnia vana iacent'. At first sight *si imitaris* seems co-ordinate with *sive mavis* and to be part of the protasis to *venias*. But that in the strict sense is impossible; Mercury cannot be invited to descend from heaven if he is already on earth. In fact the construction has begun to loosen; this *sive* clause is to be taken not so much with *venias* as with the following *redeas* (for instances of somewhat similar inconcinnity cf. E. Wistrand, *Horace's Ninth Epode*, 1958, pp. 47 f.). The change of direction is not due to negligence but deliberately contrived; Horace subtly begins to suggest that the hoped-for saviour has already arrived.

43. filius Maiae: some regard *filius* as a nominative form used as a vocative (Wackernagel, *Kleine Schriften* 2. 984). In fact it is probably an ordinary nominative (like 36 *auctor*); cf. *serm.* 1. 6. 38 'tune, Syri Damae aut Dionysi filius, audes', *Thes.l.L.* 6. 1. 752. 75 f.

Horace's identification of Mercury and Octavian is a matter for surprise, which needs a note of some length. One alleged parallel is a stucco ceiling fragment of the Augustan period from a house found in the grounds of the Villa Farnesina; it is now to be seen in the Museo Nazionale Romano. This shows a possible representation of Augustus carrying Mercury's emblem, the *caduceus* (O. Brendel, *MDAI(R)* 50, 1935, 231 ff. and Tafel 26). Fraenkel thinks that it may have been stimulated by our passage (248 n. 1); but Horace was never a popular poet like Virgil, and it seems unlikely that he influenced works of art in this way. An ancient gem formerly in the Marlborough collection also displays, together with a *caduceus*, a head with a possible resemblance to Augustus (A. Furtwängler, *Die antiken Gemmen*, 1900, 2. 184, Taf. 38. 30, K. Lehmann-Hartleben, *MDAI(R)* 42, 1927, 173 f.). A Mercury on an altar from Bologna has been alleged to bear the features of Augustus, but in this case the evidence is completely unsatisfactory (cf. Lehmann-Hartleben, loc. cit., 163 ff., K. Scott, *MDAI(R)* 50, 1935, 225 ff.).

There is also some numismatic evidence, whose relevance is likewise uncertain. An imperial denarius, minted in the East, shows Mercury sitting naked on a rock; it bears the inscription 'Caesar divi f.' which implies a date of before 29 B.C. (Mattingly 1, p. cxxiii and no. 596, J. Chittenden, *Num. Chron.* 6 ser. vol. 5, 1945, 41 ff. and pl. ix). For bronze coins portraying Hermes cf. Chittenden, pp. 46 f., M. Grant, *From Imperium to Auctoritas*, 1946, pp. 225 f. For further details on Mercury–Octavian see P. Riewald, *De imperatorum Romanorum cum certis dis et comparatione et aequatione*, Halis Saxonum, 1912, pp. 268 ff., K. Scott, *Hermes* 63, 1928, 15 ff. (valuable in getting rid of false identifications), E. Bickel, *BJ* 133, 1928, 13 ff.

The antecedents of our passage lie in Hellenistic ruler-cult. Alexander dressed up as Hermes (Ephippus ap. Athen. 537 e), and Ptolemy III appears on a gem wearing Hermes's *petasus* (Furtwängler, op. cit., 2. 158, Taf. 32. 24). The famous Rosetta stone (196 B.C.), deciphered by Champollion, compares Ptolemy V (Epiphanes) to the Egyptian Hermes (*OGIS* 90. 19 and 26 f.). Hellenistic rulers frequently gave themselves the names of specific gods (Arsinoe Aphrodite etc.). Among the Romans Julius Caesar adopted the title of Jupiter Julius shortly before his death (Dio 44. 6. 4); Antony played the part of Dionysus, Sextus Pompeius of Neptune, Octavian himself of Apollo (Suet. *Aug.* 70. 1). The *cena* δωδεκάθεος cannot be dismissed as a frivolous charade; Octavian was much more serious than his enemies allowed. And later members of the imperial house were called after various gods (Wissowa 93 f.).

Yet our passage seems unusually theological in tone. The normal Hellenistic σωτήρ might be a god in heaven, or a man become a god, or even a new god on earth; but here he is one of the old gods become a man. This saviour is to make good the Roman sin (*expiandi*), and his sojourn on earth involves, if not suffering, at least an element of condescension (43 *patiens* n.). One does not wish to press analogies too far, but it would be equally wrong to ignore clear resemblances. Nobody will suppose that Horace was directly acquainted with the writings of theologians and mystics, but it is hard to deny that his language bears some resemblance to certain eastern inscriptions in honour of Augustus (see below). And in spite of all the important differences of emphasis it is not a mere coincidence that the area and age that produced these inscriptions also produced, under strong Jewish influence, Christian theology. See further R. Reitzenstein, *Poimandres*, 1904, pp. 174 ff., A. D. Nock in *Essays on the Trinity and the Incarnation*, ed. A. E. J. Rawlinson, 1928, pp. 51 ff.

Here it will suffice to quote a few documents. In the year 9 B.C. the province of Asia passed a decree to celebrate Augustus's birthday: ἐπε[ιδὴ ἡ θείως] διατάξασα τὸν βίον ἡμῶν πρόνοια . . . τὸ τελἠότατον τῷ βίῳ διεκόσμη[σεν ἀγαθὸν] ἐνενκαμένη τὸν Σεβαστόν, ὃν εἰς εὐεργεσίαν ἀνθρώ[πων] ἐπλήρωσεν ἀρετῆς, ⟨ὥ⟩σπερ ἡμεῖν καὶ τοῖς μεθ᾽ ἡ[μᾶς σωτῆρα χαρισαμένη] τὸν παύσαντα μὲν πόλεμον, κοσμήσοντα [δὲ εἰρήνην,] . . . ἦρξεν δὲ τῷ κόσμῳ τῶν δι᾽ αὐτὸν εὐαγγελί[ων ἡ γενέθλιος ἡμέ]ρα τοῦ θεοῦ . . . (*OGIS* 458). An inscription from Halicarnassus is equally extravagant: ἐ]πεὶ ἡ αἰώνιος καὶ ἀθάνατος τοῦ παντὸς φύσις τὸ [μέγ]ιστον ἀγαθὸν πρὸς ὑπερβαλλούσας εὐεργεσίας ἀνθρ[ώ]ποις ἐχαρίσατο, Καίσαρα τὸν Σεβαστὸν ἐνεν[κ]αμένη [τ]ὸ[ν] τῷ καθ᾽ ἡμᾶς εὐδαίμονι βίῳ πατέρα μὲν τῆς [ἑαυ]τοῦ πατ[ρ]ίδος θεᾶς Ῥώμης, Δία δὲ πατρῷον καὶ σωτῆρα τοῦ κο[ιν]οῦ τῶν ἀνθρώπων γένους . . . (*IBM* iv. 1 no. 894). One should compare with these inscriptions and with our poem several sentences from the Hermetic Corpus (which though compiled much later contains earlier ideas) ; cf. fr. xxiii. 62 (God is speaking) ἑτέρα γὰρ ἐν ὑμῖν τις ἤδη τῆς ἐμῆς ἀπόρροια φύσεως (cf. the second inscription) ὃς δὴ καὶ ὅσιος ἔσται τῶν πραττομένων ἐπόπτης, καὶ ζώντων μὲν κριτὴς ἀμεθόδευτος, φρικτὸς δ' οὐ μόνον, ἀλλὰ καὶ τιμωρὸς τῶν ὑπὸ γῆν τύραννος. And again, ibid. 64 (Isis speaking) ὁ μόναρχος θεὸς ὁ τῶν συμπάντων κοσμοποιητὴς καὶ τεχνίτης †τι† τὸν μέγιστόν σου πρὸς ὀλίγον ἐχαρίσατο (compare the second inscription) πατέρα "Οσιριν καὶ τὴν μεγίστην θεὰν "Ισιν, ἵνα τῷ πάντων δεομένῳ κόσμῳ βοηθοὶ γένωνται. And again, ibid. 69 ταῦτα πάντα ποιήσαντες, ὦ τέκνον, "Οσιρίς τε κἀγώ, τὸν κόσμον πληρέστατον ἰδόντες ἀπῃτούμεθα λοιπὸν ὑπὸ τῶν τὸν οὐρανὸν κατοικούντων. This way of talking has affinities with lines 45 ff. of our poem, and also with *Georgics* 1. 503 f. (above, p. 17).

What then emerges from this tangled story? The identification of Mercury and Octavian is not a pretty fancy of the poet's, but was derived from something that was going on in the real world. This range of ideas belongs to the East, and Horace's words show blurred traces of the eastern belief in a divine saviour. The idea could have come to Rome at any time after Caesar's dictatorship, yet it might be relevant that Octavian had recently conquered an Antony–Osiris in Egypt.

patiens: for the Grecizing construction cf. *epist.* 1. 16. 30 'cum pateris sapiens emendatusque vocari', Housman on Manil. 2. 694. The word is suitable to suggest the condescension of a superior being who consents to life on earth: cf. Eur. *Alc.* 1 f. ὦ δώματ' Ἀδμήτει', ἐν οἷς ἔτλην ἐγὼ / θῆσσαν τράπεζαν αἰνέσαι θεός περ ὤν. Horace may even be reflecting some Eastern religious doctrine; cf. *Philipp.* 2. 6–8 Χριστῷ 'Ιησοῦ ὃς ἐν μορφῇ Θεοῦ ὑπάρχων οὐχ ἁρπαγμὸν ἡγήσατο τὸ εἶναι ἴσα Θεῷ, ἀλλ' ἑαυτὸν ἐκένωσεν μορφὴν δούλου λαβών. ἐν ὁμοιώματι ἀνθρώπων γενόμενος, καὶ σχήματι εὑρεθεὶς ὡς ἄνθρωπος ἐταπείνωσεν ἑαυτόν (cf. *Oxford Dictionary of the Christian Church* s.v. 'Kenotic Theories').

44. Caesaris ultor: Octavian rose to power as the avenger of his adopted father Julius Caesar; it is important to remember that the process had only recently ended with the executions after Actium (Vell. 2. 87. 3). Cf. *res gest.* 2 'qui parentem meum interfecerunt, eos in exilium expuli, iudiciis legitimis ultus eorum facinus et postea bellum inferentis rei publicae vici bis acie', Ov. *fast.* 3. 709 f. 'hoc opus, haec pietas, haec prima elementa fuerunt / Caesaris, ulcisci iusta per arma patrem', Claud. 28. 116 ff. 'pavit Iuleos inviso sanguine manes / Augustus, sed falsa pii praeconia sumpsit / in luctum patriae civili strage parentans'. In our passage Horace effectively renounces his Republican past; it is impossible to suppose, as some scholars do, that they contain any hint of criticism. On the other hand it is true that Horace sees the act of vengeance as a disagreeable burden; now that it is complete he hopes that Octavian will turn his attention to the Parthians (51 *inultos*).

45. serus: cf. Prop. 3. 11. 50, Ov. *met.* 15. 868 ff. 'tarda sit illa dies et nostro serior aevo / qua caput augustum quem temperat orbe relicto / accedat caelo', *trist.* 2. 57, 5. 2. 52, 5. 5. 61, 5. 11. 25 f., *eleg. in Maec.* 2. 27, Vell. 2. 131. 2 (on Tiberius) 'eique functo longissima statione mortali destinate successores quam serissimos', Thallus, *anth. P.* 6. 235. 6 εὐχομένοις ἡμῖν πουλὺ μένοις ἐπ' ἔτος, Sen. *dial.* 11. 12. 5 (on Claudius) 'sera et nepotibus demum nostris dies nota sit qua illum gens sua caelo asserat', Luc. 1. 45 ff. (on Nero), Sil. 3. 626 f. (on Domitian), Stat. *silv.* 4. 2. 22, *Theb.* 1. 30 f., Mart. 8. 39. 5, 13. 4. 1, Lessing (on Frederick I of Prussia) 'Von Himmel bist du, Herr, zu uns herabgestiegen, Kehr spät, kehr spät zurück'.

The theme must have belonged to conventional panegyric; cf. Menander rhet. 3. 377. 28 f. Sp. ἐπὶ τούτοις εὐχὴν ἐρεῖς αἰτῶν παρὰ θεοῦ εἰς μήκιστον χρόνον προελθεῖν τὴν βασιλείαν, Doblhofer 53 f. One would like to know the terms of official prayers for the Princeps (*res gest.* 9. 1 'vota pro valetudine mea suscipi per consules et sacerdotes quinto quoque anno senatus decrevit', L. W. Daly, *TAPhA* 81, 1950, 164 ff.). It is perhaps worth remembering that the Princeps was often ill, for instance in 27 (*fast. fer. Lat.* '[imp. Caesar vale]tudin. inpeditus fuit'). Yet the topic presumably went back to Hellenistic ruler-cult; it may have been influenced by the thought that saviours are not given much time in which to complete their work (above, p. 36 πρὸς ὀλίγον, ἀπητούμεθα; see also Plutarch in next note ταχέως).

in caelum redeas: from the fifth century some people had believed that the soul was from heaven and would return there after death (A.-J. Festugière, *La Révélation d'Hermès Trismégiste* 3, 1953, pp. 27 ff.). Naturally such theories suit ruler-cult; cf. Plut. *fort. Alex.* 330 d εἰ δὲ μὴ ταχέως ὁ δεῦρο καταπέμψας τὴν Ἀλεξάνδρου ψυχὴν ἀνεκαλέσατο δαίμων. Even Cicero says of *principes civitatis* 'hinc profecti huc revertuntur' (*rep.* 6. 13). So (of Augustus) Manil. 1. 799 f.: 'descendit caelo caelumque replebit, / quod reget, Augustus', Vell. 2. 123. 2 'animum caelestem caelo reddidit'.

46. laetus: the epithet suggests the gracious pleasure of a visiting deity; cf. Virg. *Aen.* 1. 415 f. 'sedesque revisit / laeta suas'. *intersis* is used naturally of a *praesens deus*; cf. *ars* 191 'nec deus intersit', Liv. 1. 21. 1 'cum interesse rebus humanis caeleste numen videretur'.

populo Quirini: so Ov. *fast.* 1. 69, *met.* 15. 572, 15. 756, Sidon. *epist.* 9. 16. 3. 21. The name is a grander equivalent for 'Remi nepotes,

(Catull. 58. 5), or 'turba Quirini' (Ov. *met.* 14. 607) or 'turba Remi' (Juv. 10. 73 with Mayor's note); it may be influenced by the official phrase 'populus Romanus Quiritium'. The Sabine god Quirinus was identified with Romulus already before Ennius (Bömer on Ov. *fast.* 2. 475, Ogilvie on Liv. 1. 16, Pease on Cic. *nat. deor.* 2. 62, *RE* 1 A. 1098 f.); the name was especially used in connection with Romulus's ascension (*ILS* 64 'receptusque in deorum numerum Quirinus appellatus est'). It is also relevant that Quirinus was one of the names which Octavian considered adopting (Serv. *georg.* 3. 27, *Aen.* 1. 292, K. Scott, *TAPhA* 56, 1925, 82 ff., A. Alföldi, *MH* 8, 1951, 212 ff.).

47. vitiis: Horace pictures Octavian as leaving the earth in disgust, like Astraea (Iustitia) in the old legend; cf. Arat. *phaen.* 133 f. καὶ τότε μισήσασα Δίκη κείνων γένος ἀνδρῶν / ἔπταθ᾽ ὑπουρανίη. vitiis refers primarily to the guilt of the civil wars. Considering that Octavian's own ambition was partly responsible for these wars, the stanza seems particularly outrageous. But commentators betray no sign of shock or surprise.

iniquum: again a religious word; as applied to gods it is a euphemism for *iratus* (*Thes.l.L.* 7. 1. 1640. 43 ff.).

48. ocior aura: Romulus, according to one account, was snatched away by the wind; cf. Liv. 1. 16. 2 'sublimem raptum procella', Luc. 1. 197 'rapti secreta Quirini'. For similar disappearances cf. Hom. *Od.* 4. 727 νῦν αὖ παῖδ᾽ ἀγαπητὸν ἀνηρείψαντο θύελλαι, 20. 66, *h.Ven.* 208, Pl. *Phaedr.* 229 c (on Oreithyia) καὶ οὕτω δὴ τελευτήσασαν λεχθῆναι ὑπὸ τοῦ Βορέου ἀνάρπαστον γεγονέναι, Ov. *met.* 2. 506 f., *carm. epig.* 1535 B. 1 f. 'aurae etulere parvolum . . . accessit astris', Nonnus 19. 7, Cumont 111, 128 ff.

49. hic magnos . . . : Horace is imitating Virg. *georg.* 1. 503 f. (above, p. 17). In August 29 B.C. Octavian celebrated three triumphs, Dalmatian, Actian, and Alexandrian. But Horace, unlike Virgil, is writing after this event, and may also be looking forward to a Parthian triumph.

50. ames: cf. Stat. *silv.* 1. 1. 105 f. 'certus ames terras et quae tibi templa dicamus / ipse colas, nec te caeli iuvet aula'. ames is to be taken both with *triumphos* and *dici* (cf. 1. 1. 19 ff.). For *ames dici* cf. Eur. fr. 912. 2 f. Ζεὺς εἴτ᾽ Ἀΐδης / ὀνομαζόμενος στέργεις.

pater: Augustus was officially given the title *pater patriae* in 2 B.C. (*res gest.* 35. 1 etc.). Yet even before that the title of *pater* or *parens* had been in general use; cf. Ov. *fast.* 2. 127 ff. 'sancte pater patriae, tibi plebs tibi curia nomen / hoc dedit, hoc dedimus nos tibi nomen eques; / res tamen ante dedit', Dio 55. 10. 10 καὶ ἡ ἐπωνυμία ἡ τοῦ

πατρὸς ἀκριβῶς ἐδόθη· πρότερον γὰρ ἄλλως ἄνευ ψηφίσματος ἐπεφημίζετο.
Coins of between 19 and 16 B.C. read 'S.P.Q.R. parenti conservatori
suo' (Bömer on Ov. loc. cit.). Augustus himself made a bitter joke
about his grandiose title: 'duas habere se filias delicatas, quas necesse
haberet ferre, rem publicam et Iuliam' (Macr. *sat.* 2. 5. 4).

The title 'parens patriae' should be associated particularly with
Augustus's wish to be regarded as a second founder of the city. It
had been given before him to Julius Caesar (Suet. *Jul.* 76. 1, 85, Dio
44. 4. 4, *ILS* 71, 72). Rome numbered among her previous parents
Romulus (Enn. *ann.* 113, Liv. 1. 16. 6), Camillus (Liv. 5. 49. 7),
Fabius Cunctator (Plin. *nat.* 22. 10), Marius (Cic. *Rab. perd.* 27); and
the title was first bestowed formally on Cicero in 63 (*Pis.* 6). Juvenal
points out the difference from the imperial convention: 'sed Roma
parentem / Roma patrem patriae Ciceronem libera dixit' (8. 243 f.).

princeps: in the late Republic the leading consulars were unofficially
known as *principes civitatis*. The name admirably suited Augustus's
pretence that he was simply a leader among equals; cf. *res gest.* 13,
30. 1, 32. 3, Tac. *ann.* 1. 1. 3 'cuncta discordiis civilibus fessa nomine
principis sub imperium accepit'. For the use of the title by the Augustan poets cf. 1. 21. 14, 4. 14. 6, *epist.* 2. 1. 256, Prop. 4. 6. 46, Ov. *fast.*
2. 141 f. 'vis tibi grata fuit; florent sub Caesare leges; / tu domini
nomen, principis ille tenet', *RE* 22. 2058. Our passage seems to be the
first appearance of the name with reference to Octavian. Its occurrence here might be used as an argument for dating the poem after
the 'restoration of the republic' in January 27. Yet it would be an
unreliable one; in the *res gestae* Augustus talks of himself as *princeps*
in 29 B.C. (chapter 13) or even 35–34 (chapter 30); cf. *RE* 22. 2070 f.

For the alliteration cf. Manil. 1. 7 'tu, Caesar, patriae princepsque
paterque'. For further details about *princeps* cf. A. Gwosdz, *Der
Begriff des römischen Princeps*, Diss. Breslau, 1933, Syme, *Roman
Revolution*, pp. 311 f., J. Béranger, *Recherches sur l'aspect idéologique
du Principat*, 1953, pp. 31 ff., *RE* 22. 1998 ff.

51. neu sinas: a regular formula in prayers; cf. *carm. arv.* 2 'neve lue
rue Marmar sins incurrere in pleores', Plaut. *Bacch.* 173 ff. (to
Apollo) 'veneroque te / ne Nicobulum me sinas nostrum senem /
prius convenire . . .', Petron. 112. 7, Tac. *hist.* 4. 58. 8, Norden, op. cit.
[25 *ruentis*], pp. 130 f. *neu* is only used in classical Latin prose when
preceded by a negative (K.–S. 1. 193); however, it is sometimes used
in prayer-style when preceded by a positive (Norden, loc. cit.).

Medos: the poets repeatedly threaten expeditions against Parthia;
cf. 1. 2. 22 n., 1. 12. 53 ff., 1. 29. 4, 2. 13. 18, 3. 5. 4, Prop. 2. 10. 13 f.,
3. 4. 6, 3. 12. 3. In this they surely reflect official policy. Augustus
was less pacific than is sometimes supposed (above, p. xxxii)

equitare: 'to prance, career'; cf. 2. 9. 24. For the dangerous Parthian cavalry cf. 1. 19. 11 n.

inultos: there seems to be deliberate contrast with 44 'Caesaris ultor'. The task of avenging Caesar has at last been completed; now Rome can turn her energies against the Parthians (cf. 29 n., 1. 35. 38 ff.).

52. te duce: for the ablative absolute referring to the subject of the sentence cf. K.–S. 1. 788. The word *duce* could be used, at least in poetry, in any military context (cf. 1. 7. 27 'Teucro duce'), but it particularly suits Octavian who enjoyed this semi-official title (E. Knierim, *Die Bezeichnung 'dux'*, Diss. Giessen, 1939, Syme, *Roman Revolution*, pp. 311 f., Béranger, op. cit., pp. 48 ff.). It was a convenient way of describing Octavian's status in the War of Actium (*res gest.* 25. 2), but its use here has no bearing whatever on the date of the poem; cf. *epist.* 1. 18. 56 (20 B.C.) 'sub duce qui templis Parthorum signa refigit', *carm.* 4. 5. 5 (13 B.C.) 'dux bone'.

Caesar: first Horace has described Mercury with hints of Octavian; only in the last word does he explicitly state to whom he is referring. Of course the poem is not addressed to Octavian in the normal sense of the word.

3. SIC TE DIVA POTENS CYPRI

[J. P. Elder, *AJPh* 73, 1952, 140 ff.; G. L. Hendrickson, *CJ* 3, 1907–8, 100 ff.; F. Jäger, *Das antike Propemptikon und das 17. Gedicht des Paulinus von Nola*, Rosenheim, 1913; Pasquali 260 ff.; K. Quinn, *Latin Explorations*, 1963, pp. 239 ff.]

1–8. Preserve Virgil on his voyage to Attica, O ship. 9–24. The first sailor was unnaturally fearless. God did not intend us to cross the seas. 25–40. Man's reckless daring leads him to ruin. Prometheus stole fire, Daedalus flew through the air, Hercules broke into Hades; we are like Giants assailing Heaven and provoking divine vengeance.

This ode is addressed, though not directly, to Virgil, already by far the most important poet of the day. It occupies a prominent place in the collection, immediately after the dedication to Maecenas and the panegyric on Octavian. Its professed occasion is a voyage by Virgil to Greece, certainly not the fatal journey of 19 B.C., which came too late for our poem. Virgil was an old friend who had brought Horace to Maecenas's notice about 38 (*serm.* 1. 6. 54 f.), and showed discriminating approval of his poetry (*serm.* 1. 10. 81). In turn Horace wrote for Virgil an *epicedion* on Quintilius (*carm.* 1. 24) and probably an amusing invitation-poem (4. 12). He speaks in the

warmest terms of his brother-poet; cf. 1. 3. 8, *serm.* 1. 5. 41 f. Of
course one cannot test the strength of the intimacy; the differences of
background and temperament were considerable. It is perhaps worth
observing, though the point need have no special significance, that
the *Aeneid* was entrusted not to the eminently efficient Horace, but
to two old Epicurean friends, Varius and Tucca.

Journeys in the ancient world were serious occasions. Absences
were long, communications uncertain, and the sea strange and
unpredictable. Hence the occasion for a 'sending-off' poem, or
propempticon, as it was called. Elements of the genre are already
found in early Greek lyric and elegy. See Sappho 5. 1 f. Κύπρι καὶ]
Νηρήιδες ἀβλάβη[ν μοι / τὸν κασί]γνητον δ[ό]τε τυίδ᾽ ἴκεσθαι, 94. 7 f.
χαίροισ᾽ ἔρχεο κἄμεθεν / μέμναισ᾽, οἶσθα γὰρ ὥς σε πεδήπομεν (cf. 3. 27.
14 'et memor nostri Galatea vivas', Juv. 3. 318, Paul. Nol. *carm.* 17.
9), Theogn. 692 καί σε Ποσειδάων χάρμα φίλοις ἀγάγοι, perhaps
Alcaeus 286 a and Pind. *O.* 6. 103 f. We are also told that Simonides
mingled tears with his poetry Ἱέρωνα πέμπων ἐκ Σικελίας (Himer.
or. 31. 2).

The genre was taken up by the Hellenistic poets. Athenaeus
quotes from a *propempticon* which he ascribes with some hesitation
to Erinna (fr. 1): πομπίλε ναύταισιν πέμπων πλόον εὔπλοον, ἰχθύ, /
πομπεύσαις πρύμναθεν ἐμὰν ἀδεῖαν ἑταίραν. More important for Horace
was a poem by Callimachus of which the first two lines survive
(fr. 400):

> ἁ ναῦς ἃ τὸ μόνον φέγγος ἐμὶν τὸ γλυκὺ τᾶς ζόας
> ἅρπαξας, ποτί τε Ζανὸς ἱκνεῦμαι λιμενοσκόπω . . .

This fragment has in common with our ode an Asclepiad metre, an
address to a ship, a reference to a protecting deity, and a strong
protestation of friendship; if more had been preserved no doubt
other influences on the genre would be apparent. Theocritus in the
Thalysia also includes snatches of the motif (7. 52 ff.): ἔσσεται Ἀγεά-
νακτι καλὸς πλόος εἰς Μιτυλήναν, / . . . χἀλκυόνες στορεσεῦντι τὰ κύματα
τάν τε θάλασσαν / τόν τε νότον τόν τ᾽ εὖρον. An epigram by Meleager
was influenced by Callimachus, and in turn influenced Horace (8 n.).
Parthenius wrote a *propempticon* of which nothing survives, unless
indeed one should attribute to it the line Γλαύκῳ καὶ Νηρῆι καὶ
εἰναλίῳ Μελικέρτῃ imitated by Virgil at *georg.* 1. 437. This poem may
lie behind Cinna's *propempticon* in honour of the young Pollio (Morel,
pp. 87 f.). It seems that Cinna preceded Horace and Statius in
including a reference to St. Elmo's fire (2 n.), and other elements
may be conjectured from their presence in later poets (see below).
Horace himself in his tenth epode wrote a *propempticon* in reverse,
wishing nothing but harm for Maevius (4 n.). The Galatea ode (3. 27)

also begins nominally in the form of a *propempticon*; the reference to
the Adriatic and Iapyx (19 f.), as in our poem, suggests a common
source in Cinna.

It is possible, though by no means certain, that the poem of
Gallus alluded to in Virgil's tenth eclogue and imitated by Propertius
(1. 8) was a *propempticon*. However that may be, Propertius's own
poem is a blend of the traditional *propempticon* with love-elegy; it
includes warnings of the terrors of the sea (5 'tune audire potes
vesani murmura ponti?') and prayers for a safe voyage:

> sed quocumque modo de me, periura, mereris,
> sit Galatea tuae non aliena viae:
> ut te, felici praevecta Ceraunia remo,
> accipiat placidis Oricus aequoribus (17 ff.).

Ovid also wrote a love-*propempticon* (*am.* 2. 11) with conventional
elements, some of which may go back to Cinna or even to Callimachus: he includes the folly of shipbuilding (1 ff., cf. Hor. 1. 3.
9 ff.), the dangers of Ceraunia (19), probably from Cinna (cf. Hor.
1. 3. 20 n., Prop. 1. 8. 19), prayers to the Dioscuri (29, cf. Hor. 1. 3. 2)
and to Galatea (34, cf. Prop. 1. 8. 18), the 'praecipites Noti' (52, cf.
Hor. 1. 3. 12 ff.). For a more formal specimen of the genre one may
turn to Statius's facile effusion in honour of Maecius Celer (*silv.* 3. 2);
in it he elaborates and sometimes adapts themes and phrases from
Horace's more compressed lyric. Like Horace he appeals to the gods
of the sea, in particular the Dioscuri (2 n.) and Aeolus (4 n.); he
describes Maecius as part of his soul (8 n.), and uses the commercial
metaphor of the *depositum* (5 n.); he bewails the folly of the first
navigators (22 n.), and compares man's audacity with that of the
giants (38 n.). No doubt minor versifiers kept the *propempticon* alive;
at any rate in the fourth century Paulinus of Nola wrote 85 Sapphic
stanzas to commemorate the departure of his friend Nicetas. The
good bishop goes protected not by the Dioscuri but by the Cross
of the mast: 'victor antemna crucis ibis undis / tutus et austris'
(*carm.* 17. 107 f.). As a result he can face the monsters of the deep
(presumably another traditional motif) with more equanimity than
Virgil (117 ff.): 'audient Amen tremefacta cete / et sacerdotem domino
canentem / laeta lascivo procul admeabunt / monstra natatu'. For
the *propempticon* see further F. Jäger, op. cit., K. Quinn, op. cit.,
K.-E. Henriksson, *Griechische Büchertitel in der römischen Literatur*,
Helsinki, 1956, pp. 35 f.

Throughout the Hellenistic period prose *propempticon* must also
have been a regular form of literary exercise. A few flowery compositions of Himerius have survived (10, 12, 31, 36), but they throw
no light on our poem. A chapter in Menander, the rhetorical writer

of the third century A.D., is more illuminating (3. 395 ff. Sp.). He comments on the ἦθος ἐρωτικόν of such poems; this would be impossible for Horace, but the vestiges appear in the phrase 'animae dimidium meae' (8 n.). The writer should include a reproach (396. 4 ff.): σχετλιάσει πρὸς τὴν τύχην ἢ πρὸς τοὺς ἔρωτας, ὅτι μὴ συγχωροῦσι θεσμὸν φιλίας διαμένειν βέβαιον. Most of the topics suggested by Menander are irrelevant to our poem: the common education of the two friends, the familiar scenes of Athens, and much panegyric of a sentimental sort. The conclusion is important to our poem more for its differences than its resemblances (399. 1 ff.): ἐὰν δὲ διὰ θαλάττης ἀνάγηται, ἐκεῖ σοι μνήμη θαλαττίων ἔσται δαιμόνων, Αἰγυπτίου Πρωτέως, Ἀνθηδονίου Γλαύκου, Νηρέως, προπεμπόντων τε καὶ συνθεόντων τῇ νηί . . . ἡ δὲ ναῦς θείτω θεοῖς ἐναλίγκιον ἄνδρα φέρουσα, ἕως ἂν προσαγάγῃς αὐτὸν τοῖς λιμέσι τῷ λόγῳ, καταστρέψεις δὲ εἰς εὐχὴν τὸν λόγον αἰτῶν αὐτῷ παρὰ τῶν θεῶν τὰ κάλλιστα.

Horace ends with none of the prayers enjoined by Menander. Nor like other writers of *propemptica* does he look forward to the drink and talk that will greet the wanderer's return (Ov. *am.* 2. 11. 49, Stat. *silv.* 3. 2. 133 ff.). Instead he turns to the folly of navigation and human inventiveness in general; only references to the Adriatic (15) and Acroceraunia (20) remind us that he is still thinking of a voyage to Greece. Presumably curses on the inventor of ships belong to the traditional σχετλιασμός enjoined by Menander (and natural also in epigrams on death at sea), but Horace carries his protests far beyond the normal limits; his remarks are not calculated in the least to console or flatter Virgil. In fact the poem should be regarded as a conflation of two quite different types, the *propempticon* proper, and the diatribe on inventiveness.

The folly of navigation is a theme already found in Hesiod, who comments on the absence of ships in the state of the just (*op.* 236 f.). The topic was elaborated by Hellenistic and Roman poets; cf. Arat. *phaen.* 110 f., Lucr. 5. 1004 ff., Virg. *ecl.* 4. 31 f., Hor. *epod.* 16. 57, Prop. 3. 7, Tib. 1. 3. 35 ff. The miseries and dangers of seafaring, which were very real in the ancient world, were conventionally exaggerated (cf. *RE* 2 A. 413, Mayor on Juv. 12. 58). Moralists argued that men sailed for reasons of avarice; the gods intended us to be land animals, and navigation is an inversion of the laws of nature (21 n.). Some of these themes are combined in an epigram by Antiphilus of Byzantium (*anth. P.* 9. 29):

Τόλμα, νεῶν ἀρχηγὲ (σὺ γὰρ δρόμον ηὕραο πόντου,
καὶ ψυχὰς ἀνδρῶν κέρδεσιν ἠρέθισας),
οἷον ἐτεκτήνω δόλιον ξύλον, οἷον ἐνῆκας
ἀνθρώποις θανάτῳ κέρδος ἐλεγχόμενον.

ἦν ὄντως μερόπων χρύσεον γένος, εἴ γ᾽ ἀπὸ χέρσου
τηλόθεν ὡς Ἀίδης πόντος ἀπεβλέπετο.

The rhetoricians vied with the poets, and Nicolaus reiterates some of
the trite topics of a ψόγος ναυτιλίας (1. 347 ff. Walz): τὴν πονηρίαν τῇ
μεταβολῇ τῶν χωρίων παιδεύεται . . . δύο περιπίπτει τοῖς ἐσχάτοις
ὀνείδεσι, θράσει καὶ δέει . . . κατεπιορκεῖ τῶν θεῶν ἐρῶσα τοῦ κέρδους,
αἰτεῖ δὲ θεοὺς σωθῆναι σπουδάζουσα. For further details see K. F.
Smith on Tibullus 1. 3. 37–40, A. Oltramare, Les Origines de la diatribe
romaine, Geneva, 1926 (see index s.v. navigation), A. O. Lovejoy and
G. Boas, Primitivism and Related Ideas in Antiquity, 1935.

Horace goes still further and turns to an attack on human inventiveness in general. The ancients by no means lacked appreciation
of such enterprise; cf. Aesch. Pr. 459 ff., Soph. Ant. 332 ff., Lucr. 5.
1241 ff., Cic. nat. deor. 2. 150 ff., off. 2. 13 ff., Virg. georg. 1. 129 ff. Yet
poets and moralists regularly stressed the other point of view, not
necessarily with any overwhelming conviction. Prometheus was too
often the symbol not for man's conquest of nature, but for impious
defiance of the gods (W. Headlam, CQ 28, 1934, 63 ff.). Particularly
significant for our poem is a passage in the Corpus Hermeticum where
Momus criticizes Hermes for encouraging man's audacity (fr. xxiii.
45–6): τολμηρὰς ἐκτενοῦσι χεῖρας καὶ μέχρι θαλάσσης, καὶ τὰς αὐτοφυεῖς
ὕλας τέμνοντες μέχρι καὶ τῶν πέραν διαπορθμεύσουσιν ἀλλήλους . . . τὰ
μέχρις ἄνω διώξουσι, παρατηρῆσαι βουλόμενοι τίς οὐρανοῦ καθέστηκε
κίνησις . . . εἶτα οὐ καὶ μέχρις οὐρανοῦ περίεργον ὁπλισθήσονται τόλμαν
οὗτοι; Momus begins, as in our poem, with the audacity of seafaring;
he then proceeds to an attack on scientific curiosity (Horace treats
this in a more mythological way by the stories of Prometheus and
Daedalus); finally both writers end up with an assault on heaven,
described in terms of a literal battle (which must stand for spiritual
impiety). There must have been much of this way of talking in
Hellenistic ethical disquisitions; cf. Max. Tyr. 36. 2 b, Nemesius 40.
533 a Migne τίς δ᾽ ἂν ἐξειπεῖν δύναιτο τὰ τούτου τοῦ ζῴου πλεονεκτήματα;
πελάγη διαβαίνει, οὐρανὸν ἐμβατεύει τῇ θεωρίᾳ, ἀστέρων κίνησιν καὶ
διαστήματα καὶ μέτρα κατανοεῖ, γῆν καρποῦται καὶ θάλασσαν, θηρίων καὶ
κητῶν καταφρονεῖ, πᾶσαν ἐπιστήμην καὶ τέχνην καὶ μέθοδον κατορθοῖ.
See further R. Reitzenstein, SHAW 8, 1917, 10. Abh., pp. 76 f.,
A. S. Ferguson in W. Scott, Hermetica, vol. 4, 1936, pp. 455 ff., J. P.
Elder, loc. cit., p. 144 n. 11, Lovejoy–Boas, op. cit.

Horace's ode is an accomplished piece of versification, but little
more. The poet may protest his affection for Virgil, but he shows
none of his usual tact and charm; there is not a hint of Virgil's
poetry, and it is wrong to argue, as some do, that the ode's sombre
and religious tone is directed specifically towards the recipient. The

second part of the poem is equally unsatisfactory; one expects a Horatian ode to veer widely, but here the trite and unseasonable moralizing seems out of place in a poem of friendship. The diatribe against enterprise has none of the universal validity which we expect from Horatian commonplaces, and though no more foolish than the conventional praises of poverty, it sounds particularly unconvincing to modern ears. Nor is the flatness of the thought redeemed by any special excellence in the writing. The poem is probably none the worse for lacking the ἁβρότης and χάρις which Menander Rhetor enjoins: Horace had no taste for the picturesque sea-scapes and cavorting Nereids of Hellenistic poetry. It matters more that we miss the Horatian virtues of brevity and incisiveness (cf. 12 ff.). The poem may have been written early, when Horace was still trying to surmount the technical difficulties of writing Latin lyrics; a voyage to Greece was a considerable enterprise, and there may well have been a long interval between this expedition and Virgil's last journey in 19.

Metre: Fourth Asclepiad.

1. sic . . .: 'so may Venus guide you, deliver Virgil safe'; that is to say 'as you hope for Venus's guidance . . .'. In English this idiom is more familiar in assertions ('So help me God, I did not steal the money'; cf. *OED* 'so' B 19). In Greek and Latin it is also common in petitions; cf. Milton, *Lycidas* 18 ff. 'Hence with denial vain and coy excuse: So may some gentle Muse With lucky words favour my destined urn'. See further J. E. Church, *TAPhA* 36, 1905, lv ff., H.–Sz. 331, Appel 152.

Our passage is unusual in one respect. Normally the boon proposed in the *sic* clause is a *quid pro quo* which is to operate on the fulfilment of the speaker's own request; according to this pattern Horace might have written 'so may all your voyages prosper, keep Virgil safe'. But in our passage he only mentions the voyage which is itself a prerequisite for Virgil's safe arrival. It is unlikely that this simple point escaped Horace's notice. Even his bargaining concessions are designed to promote Virgil's safety.

diva: it was traditional in a *propempticon* to invoke the gods of the sea. Aphrodite counted as one of these gods (1. 5. 16 n.), and was worshipped as 'Euploia' at Cnidus (Paus. 1. 1. 3). For her power to guide ships cf. Solon 7. 3 f. αὐτὰρ ἐμὲ ξὺν νηὶ θοῇ κλεινῆς ἀπὸ νήσου / ἀσκηθῆ πέμποι Κύπρις ἰοστέφανος, Anyte, *anth. P.* 9. 144. 1 ff., Lucian, *amor.* 11, Rut. Nam. 1. 156.

potens Cypri: cf. *h.Ven.* 292 χαῖρε θεὰ Κύπροιο ἐυκτιμένης μεδέουσα, 1. 30. 1 n. The genitive is often used in religious contexts; cf. 1. 5. 15 n., 1. 6. 10, 3. 25. 14, *carm. saec.* 1, Virg. *Aen.* 1. 80, Ov. *am.* 3. 10.

35 'diva potens frugum', Manil. 2. 60, Stat. *silv.* 3. 4. 19 f., *ILS* 3061
'Iovi o.m. Tempestatium divinarum potenti'.

2. fratres Helenae: for protection by the Dioscuri cf. 1. 12. 27 n.
lucida sidera: Horace is referring to 'St. Elmo's fire'. This is a dull
blue glare ('point discharge' or 'corona discharge') that appears on
the masts and rigging of ships, and was even observed by Sir J. J.
Thomson on the pinnacles of King's College Chapel (Cook, cited
below). It was associated with the Dioscuri, and regarded as a pro-
pitious omen during a storm. The name 'Elmo' has been variously
explained as a corruption of 'Erasmus' and a sobriquet of S. Pedro
González; cf. K. Jaisle, *Die Dioskuren als Retter zur See*, Tübingen,
1907, pp. 64 ff., *Oxford Dictionary of the Christian Church*, p. 447.

Commentators assume without argument that Horace is talking
about St. Elmo's fire, though his words by themselves could refer
simply to a constellation in the sky. But though their reasoning is
inadequate their conclusion is correct. The reader can assume that
St. Elmo's fire is meant because this was a regular feature of the
propempticon. It must already have appeared in Cinna; cf. fr. 2
'lucida cum fulgent summi carchesia mali' (note especially *lucida*).
Statius's treatment may be regarded not simply as an elaboration of
Horace but as a reflection of traditional motifs: 'proferte benigna /
sidera et antemnae gemino considite cornu, / Oebalii fratres; vobis
pontusque polusque / luceat; Iliacae longe nimbosa sororis / astra
fugate, precor, totoque excludite caelo' (*silv.* 3. 2. 8 ff.). Statius is
alluding to the legend that the single illumination of Helen was
dangerous to shipping (Pliny and Cook, cited below). So when
Horace calls the Dioscuri the 'fratres Helenae' he may be drawing on
a source which referred explicitly to the menace of Helen's star.

For other allusions to St. Elmo's fire cf. Alcaeus 34(a). 7 ff. ῥήα δ'
ἀνθρώποις θανάτω ῥύεσθε / ζακρυόεντος / εὐσδύγων θρῴσκοντες .. ἄκρα
νάων / πήλοθεν λάμπροι, Xenophanes A 39 Diels–Kranz τοὺς ἐπὶ τῶν
πλοίων φαινομένους οἷον ἀστέρας, οὓς καὶ Διοσκούρους καλοῦσί τινες,
νεφέλια εἶναι κατὰ τὴν ποιὰν κίνησιν παραλάμποντα, Sen. *nat.* 1. 1. 13
'in magna tempestate apparere, quasi stellae solent velo insidentes;
adiuvari se tunc periclitantes aestimant Pollucis et Castoris numine',
Plin. *nat.* 2. 101, Lucian, *navig.* 9 ἔφασκεν ὁ ναύκληρος ... τινα λαμπρὸν
ἀστέρα Διοσκούρων τὸν ἕτερον ἐπικαθίσαι τῷ καρχησίῳ καὶ κατευθῦναι
τὴν ναῦν, Shakespeare, *The Tempest* I. ii. 96 ff. (Ariel speaks) 'Now on
the beak, Now in the waist, the deck, in every cabin I flamed
amazement: sometimes I'ld divide, And burn in many places; on the
topmast, The yards, and bowsprit, would I flame distinctly, Then
meet, and join', Marvell, *First Anniversary* 269 f. 'While baleful
Tritons to the shipwreck guide And corposants along the tacklings

slide', Macaulay, *Battle of the Lake Regillus* 40. 15 f. 'If once the Great Twin Brethren Sit shining on the sails'. For further details see Cook, *Zeus* 1. 771 ff., T. H. Martin, *RA* 13, 1866, 168 ff., 14, 1866, 260 ff., J. P. Mahaffy, *RAL* 6, 1897, 93, Pease on Cic. *div.* 1. 75, 2. 77 and p. 597, P. F. Mottelay, *Bibliographical History of Electricity and Magnetism*, 1922, pp. 23 f. For technical discussions cf. J. A. Chalmers, *Report on Progress in Physics* 17, 1954, 109 ff. and *Atmospheric Electricity*, 1957, pp. 156 ff., L. B. Loeb, *Electrical Coronas*, 1965 (who provides a coloured photograph as his frontispiece).

3. ventorum . . . pater: in traditional Greek mythology Aeolus is the master of the winds, not their father. So *pater* seems to be used in the sense of *paterfamilias*; cf. *serm.* 2. 8. 7 'cenae pater' (= *dominus convivii*), Stat. *silv.* 3. 2. 42 (see next note), Juv. 13. 81 'pater Aegaei Neptune'.

4. obstrictis aliis: an epic phrase; cf. Hom. *Od.* 5. 383 ff. ἦ τοι τῶν ἄλλων ἀνέμων κατέδησε κελεύθους / . . . ὦρσε δ᾽ ἐπὶ κραιπνὸν Βορέην, 10. 20 (on Aeolus) ἔνθα δὲ βυκτάων ἀνέμων κατέδησε κέλευθα, Call. *h.* 3. 230, Virg. *Aen.* 1. 52 ff. 'vasto rex Aeolus antro / luctantes ventos tempestatesque sonoras / imperio premit ac vinclis et carcere frenat'.

It seems to have been a conventional prayer in the *propempticon*, perhaps deriving ultimately from Cinna, that only the west wind should blow. Cf. Ov. *am.* 2. 11. 41 'ipsa roges, Zephyri veniant in lintea soli', Stat. *silv.* 3. 2. 42 ff. 'et pater Aeolio frangit qui carcere ventos / . . . artius obiecto Borean Eurumque Notumque / monte premat; soli Zephyro sit copia caeli'. In Horace's epode on Maevius the situation is reversed; Auster, Eurus, and Aquilo blow together, but there is not a word about Zephyrus (*epod.* 10. 3 ff.).

Iapyga: Iapygia was the 'heel' of Italy, and Iapyx the WNW. wind that blew ships from Brindisi to Greece. Cf. 3. 27. 19 f. 'albus . . . Iapyx', Virg. *Aen.* 8. 709 f. (Cleopatra after Actium) 'illam inter caedes pallentem morte futura / fecerat Ignipotens undis et Iapyge ferri', Serv. ad loc. 'vento qui de Apulia flans optime ad Orientem ducit', Gell. 2. 22 (a discussion of this and similar names), *RE* 8 A. 2299 f.

5. creditum: imitated by Stat. *silv.* 3. 2. 5 f. 'grande tuo rarumque damus, Neptune, profundo / depositum'; cf. also 1. 24. 11, Val. Fl. 2. 292 'talin possum te credere puppi?', Dioscorides, *anth. P.* 12. 171. 1 f. τὸν καλόν, ὡς ἔλαβες, κομίσαις πάλι πρός με θεωρὸν / Εὐφραγόρην, ἀνέμων πρηΰτατε Ζέφυρε. One is meant to think of a valuable object deposited with a friend for safe keeping; cf. Juv. 13. 15 f. 'sacrum tibi quod non reddat amicus / depositum' (with Mayor's note), Plin. *epist.* 10. 96. 7 '(the Christians swore) ne depositum adpellati abnegarent'.

6. finibus Atticis: Porphyrio comments 'ambiguum utrum *debes finibus Atticis* an *finibus Atticis reddas*'. The second explanation is the right one; the dative to be understood with *debes* is not *finibus* but *mihi*. Besides, on the first interpretation the sentence straggles.

8. animae dimidium meae: the lineage of this and kindred phrases makes an interesting chapter of literary history. Perhaps its origin is to be found in Aristophanes's speech in Plato's *Symposium* (189 c– 193 d); yet see 205 d καὶ λέγεται μέν γέ τις, ἔφη, λόγος, ὡς οἳ ἂν τὸ ἥμισυ ἑαυτῶν ζητῶσιν, οὗτοι ἐρῶσιν (cf. Empedocles B 63). The idea was developed by Callimachus in an influential epigram (41. 1 f.): ἥμισύ μευ ψυχῆς ἔτι τὸ πνέον, ἥμισυ δ᾽ οὐκ οἶδ᾽ / εἴτ᾽ Ἔρος εἴτ᾽ Ἀίδης ἥρπασε, πλὴν ἀφανές (cf. Gow–Page 2. 158, Gow on Theoc. 29. 5). Callimachus was imitated by Meleager, *anth. P.* 12. 52. 1 f. οὔριος ἐμπνεύσας ναύταις Νότος, ὦ δυσέρωτες, / ἥμισύ μευ ψυχᾶς ἅρπασεν Ἀνδράγαθον. Horace conflates Callimachus's Asclepiads (above, p. 41) with Meleager, but he gives up the sentimentality of the Hellen- istic *propempticon* for a note of sober friendship (cf. 2. 17. 5 'te meae . . . partem animae'). Here he may be influenced by a less erotic range of expressions; cf. Eur. *Or.* 1045 f. ὦ φίλτατ᾽, ὦ ποθεινὸν ἥδιστόν τ᾽ ἔχων / τῆς σῆς ἀδελφῆς ὄνομα καὶ ψυχὴν μίαν, Arist. *eth. Nic.* 1168ᵇ6 f. καὶ αἱ παροιμίαι δὲ πᾶσαι ὁμογνωμονοῦσιν, οἷον τὸ "μία ψυχή", Otto 25 f. For the similar idea that a friend is an *alter idem*, cf. Arist. *eth. Nic.* 1166ᵃ31, Diog. Laert. 7. 23, Cic. *Lael.* 80, F. Lossmann, *Hermes Einzelschrift* 17, 1962, 33 ff., F. A. Steinmetz, *Die Freund- schaftslehre des Panaitios*, 1967, pp. 138 ff.

Later Latin writers imitate Horace freely; cf. Ov. *trist.* 1. 2. 44, 4. 10. 32 with de Jonge's note, Pers. 5. 22 f. Statius ingeniously com- bines a reference to our passage and to 2. 17. 5: 'animae partem super aequora nostrae / maiorem transferre parat' (*silv.* 3. 2. 7 f.). For later developments cf. Rut. Nam. 1. 426 with Helm's note, Aug. *conf.* 4. 6. 11, ps.-Sen. *anth. Lat.* 445. 9, Ven. Fort. *carm.* 6. 10. 48, Shake- speare, *sonnet* 39. 2 'When thou art all the better part of me', 74. 8, Milton, *P.L.* 4. 487 f. 'Part of my soul I seek thee, and thee claim My other half', 5. 95 'Best image of myself and dearer half'. Finally comes the Victorian vulgarism 'my better half', which can be traced back to Sidney, *Arcadia* 3. 280 (*OED* s.v. 'better', 3 c).

9. robur et aes triplex: in early poetry a metal heart was a mark of toughness, insensitivity, or cruelty; cf. Hom. *Il.* 2. 489 f. οὐδ᾽ εἴ μοι δέκα μὲν γλῶσσαι, δέκα δὲ στόματ᾽ εἶεν, / φωνὴ δ᾽ ἄρρηκτος, χάλκεον δέ μοι ἦτορ ἐνείη, 24. 205 σιδήρειόν νύ τοι ἦτορ (of Priam going to Achilles), Hes. *th.* 764 f. τοῦ δὲ σιδηρέη μὲν κραδίη, χάλκεον δέ οἱ ἦτορ / νηλεὲς ἐν στήθεσσιν (see West's note), Pind. fr. 123. 4 f. ὃς μὴ πόθῳ κυμαίνεται, ἐξ ἀδάμαντος / ἢ σιδάρου κεχάλκευται μέλαιναν καρδίαν (for further material cf. B. A. van Groningen, *Pindare au Banquet*, 1960, p. 56, Otto 4, 134, R. Hildebrandt, *Philologus* 70, 1911, 52 ff., Pease on Virg. *Aen.* 4. 366). For wood cf. Cic. *Lucull.* 100 'non enim est e saxo sculptus aut e robore dolatus' with Reid's note, *Lael.* 48 with Seyffert–Müller, pp. 331 ff., Ach. Tat. 5. 22. 5 ὁ δὲ σιδηροῦς τις ἢ ξύλινος ἤ τι τῶν ἀναισθήτων ἦν ἄρα πρὸς τὰς δεήσεις τὰς ἐμάς, Hildebrandt, loc. cit., pp. 55 f., 61, West on Hes. *th.* 35. In view of these parallels Horace may be suggesting insensitivity as well as fearlessness; cf. especially Tib. 1. 1. 63 f. 'flebis; non tua sunt duro praecordia ferro / vincta, nec in tenero stat tibi corde silex'.

Horace was imitated by Herrick, *Hesperides* 106. 75 f. 'A heart thrice wall'd with Oke, and Brasse, that man Had, first, durst plow the Ocean'. The expression 'heart of oak', on the other hand, refers primarily to the hard centre of the oak-tree; cf. anon. (1760) 'Heart of oak are our ships, Heart of oak are our men', *OED* 'heart' 19 b. But often the meaning of 'heart' is misunderstood, perhaps under the influence of such passages as our own; cf. Tennyson, *Buonaparte*, 'He thought to quell the stubborn hearts of oak'.

10. truci: cf. Catull. 4. 9 'trucemve Ponticum sinum'. In Horace the word is pointedly placed next to *fragilem*. Paulinus's imitation is less terse (*carm.* 24. 27 f.): 'Narbone solvit per trucem ponti viam / fragili carinae credulus'.

12. primus: the first ship was traditionally Jason's Argo, though there were conflicting claims (Pease on Cic. *nat. deor.* 2. 89). For disparaging remarks on the inventor of ships cf. Prop. 1. 17. 13 f. 'a pereat quicumque rates et vela paravit / primus et invito gurgite fecit iter', Ov. *am.* 2. 11. 1 f. 'prima malas docuit mirantibus aequoris undis / Peliaco pinus vertice caesa manus', Sen. *Med.* 301 f. (modelled on our passage) 'audax nimium qui freta primus / rate tam fragili perfida rupit', Plin. *nat.* 19. 6 (on the inventor of linen sails) 'nulla exsecratio sufficit contra inventorem . . . cui satis non fuit hominem in terra mori, nisi periret et insepultus', Val. Fl. 1. 648 f., Stat. *silv.* 3. 2. 61 ff. 'quis rude et abscissum miseris animantibus aequor / fecit iter, solidaeque pios telluris alumnos / expulit in fluctus pelagoque immisit hianti / audax ingenii?' (*abscissum, immisit*, and *audax* are influenced by Horace), Ach. 1. 64 f., Opp. *hal.* 1. 354 ὦ πόποι, ὃς πρώτιστος ὄχους ἁλὸς εὕρατο νῆας, Claud. *rapt. Pros.* praef. 1 ff., especially 9 'praeceps audacia'. Some of these passages refer specifically to the Argo; the topic was no doubt encouraged by Eur. *Med.* 1 ff. on the disasters that followed from the Argo's voyage.

It was a widespread conviction in antiquity that all arts and artefacts must have been invented by somebody. Already in Aeschylus, Prometheus appears as the inventor of writing and arithmetic, yokes and ships, and the popular basis of such attitudes emerges from many colloquial allusions in comedy and elegy. In particular, imprecations on an inventor were a common theme; cf., for instance, Aquilius, *com.* 1 f. 'ut illum di perdant primus qui horas repperit / quique adeo primus statuit hic solarium'. Philosophers attempted to put the discussion on a more scientific basis: Aristotle, Theophrastus, and others wrote περὶ εὑρημάτων (Clem. Alex. *strom.* 1. 16. 77. 1), and Posidonius revealed some interest in the problem (cf. Sen. *epist.* 90. 7). See further Plin. *nat.* 7. 191 ff., F. Leo, *Plautinische Forschungen*, ed. 2, 1912, pp. 152 ff., M. Kremmer, *De catalogis Heurematum*, 1890, A. Kleingünther, *Philologus* Suppl. 26. 1, 1933, K. Thraede, *RhM* 105, 1962, 158 ff. and *RLAC* 5. 1191 ff., Pease on Cic. *nat. deor.* 1. 38 and 3. 45; a list of references in the Augustan poets is supplied by Boucher 419.

nec timuit: cf. Arist. *eth. Nic.* 1115ᵇ26 ff. εἴη δ᾽ ἄν τις μαινόμενος ἢ ἀνάλγητος εἰ μηδὲν φοβοῖτο, μήτε σεισμὸν μήτε κύματα, καθάπερ φασὶ τοὺς Κελτούς.

praecipitem Africum: in the Mediterranean the καταιγίς, or swooping squall, was a constant danger (*RE* 8 A. 2305). See, for instance, Hom. *Il.* 2. 148 λάβρος ἐπαιγίζων, Leonidas, *anth. P.* 7. 273. 1 αἰπήεσσα καταιγίς, Virg. *georg.* 2. 310 f., 4. 29 'praeceps . . . Eurus', Ov. *am.* 2. 11. 52 (his *propempticon*) 'nec te praecipites extimuisse Notos', *epist.* 10. 30, *met.* 2. 185, 11. 481. Perhaps it might be suggested that *praeceps* refers to a wind in Juv. 1. 149 f. 'omne in praecipiti vitium stetit: utere velis, / totos pande sinus'.

13. decertantem . . .: 'the most forbidding feature of the Mediterranean is the frequency of its winter gales, which change direction rapidly and create incalculable cross-seas in confined waters' (M. Cary and E. H. Warmington, *The Ancient Explorers*, 1929, c. 2 § 1). Hence the frequent allusions in the poets to the battle of the winds; cf. Hom. *Il.* 16. 765 ὡς δ᾽ Εὖρός τε Νότος τ᾽ ἐριδαίνετον ἀλλήλοιιν, *Od.* 5. 295 f., Aesch. *Pr.* 1085 ff., Enn. *ann.* 443 ff., Pacuv. *trag.* 415, Virg. *georg.* 1. 318, *Aen.* 1. 84 ff., 10. 356 ff., Prop. 3. 15. 32, Ov. *met.* 11. 490, Sen. *Ag.* 474 ff., Sil. 12. 617 f., Pope, ΠΕΡΙ ΒΑΘΟΥΣ, *or, Of the Art of Sinking in Poetry*, 1727, c. 15 'Take Eurus, Zephyr, Auster and Boreas, and cast them together in one verse . . . Brew your tempest well in your head, before you set it a-blowing'. Aristotle takes a more sensible view (*meteor.* 364ᵃ27 ff.): οὕτω δὲ τεταγμένων τῶν ἀνέμων δῆλον ὅτι ἅμα πνεῖν τοὺς μὲν ἐναντίους οὐχ οἷόν τε (κατὰ διάμετρον γάρ· ἅτερος οὖν παύσεται ἀποβιασθείς), τοὺς δὲ μὴ οὕτως κειμένους πρὸς ἀλλήλους οὐδὲν κωλύει (cf. Sen. *nat.* 5. 16. 2). See further *RE* 8 A. 2241 f., and for literary storms 1. 14. 3 n.

14. Hyadas: a cluster of stars in the constellation Taurus. Their

morning setting (November) and evening rising (late October) were
supposed to indicate rain; their name was rightly or wrongly connected with ὕειν (though the Roman word *Suculae* suggests a derivation from ὗς, 'a pig'). See especially Pancrates, *anth. P.* 7. 653. 1 f.
ὤλεσεν Αἰγαίου διὰ κύματος ἄγριος ἀρθεὶς / λὶψ Ἐπιηρείδην Ὕάσι
δυομέναις, Tiro ap. Gell. 13. 9. 4 'et cum oriuntur et cum occidunt
tempestates pluvias largosque imbres cient', Virg. *Aen.* 1. 744 and
3. 516 'pluviasque Hyadas', Ov. *fast.* 5. 165, Tennyson, *Ulysses* 10 f.
'Thro' scudding drifts the rainy Hyades Vext the dim sea'. See further
W. Smith's *Dictionary of Antiquities* 1. 219, 232 (a very clear summary of the evidence on risings and settings of constellations), *RE* 6.
2430, 8. 2615 ff., Pease on Cic. *nat. deor.* 2. 111.

15. arbiter: cf. 2. 17. 19 f. 'tyrannus / Hesperiae Capricornus undae',
3. 3. 4 f. 'Auster / dux inquieti turbidus Hadriae', Petron. 114. 3
'Italici litoris aquilo possessor'; on the same lines the French *mistral*
is the 'master-wind' (*magistralis*). The storms of the Adriatic were
and are notorious (*RE* 1. 418).

16. tollere seu ponere: cf. Hom. *Od.* 10. 21 f. (on Aeolus) κεῖνον γὰρ
ταμίην ἀνέμων ποίησε Κρονίων, / ἠμὲν παυέμεναι ἠδ' ὀρνύμεν ὅν κ'
ἐθέλῃσιν, *Aen.* 1. 66 'et mulcere dedit fluctus et tollere vento'. The
winds are sometimes said in ancient poetry to still the sea; cf. Soph.
Ai. 674 f. δεινῶν τ' ἄημα πνευμάτων ἐκοίμισε / στένοντα πόντον, Virg.
ecl. 2. 26 'cum placidum ventis staret mare', *Aen.* 3. 69 f., 5. 763.

17. quem mortis timuit gradum: presumably this simply refers to the
approach of death; cf. below, 33, Luc. 2. 100 'quantoque gradu mors
saeva cucurrit', Stat. *silv.* 5. 1. 75 'venitque gradu fortuna benigno'.
Yet these expressions are fairly vivid; Lucan in particular suggests
μακρὰ βίβας. In Horace, on the other hand, the general form of the
phrase blurs the picture.

Ps.-Acro seems to interpret 'degree of death' ('ac si diceret genus
mortis'). Some consideration has to be given to this explanation, as
on this sort of point a scholiast's knowledge of the language may be
of value. One would have to assume that different deaths are of
different 'degrees' according to their unpleasantness; yet the notion
is not easy to illustrate. There is an apparent but misleading parallel
at Auson. 159. 7 f. 'quae Numa cognatis sollemnia dedicat umbris /
ut gradus aut mortis postulat aut generis'; in fact he must be
referring to the rank of the dead man. Some editors explain 'aditum
ad mortem', but this is impossible.

18. siccis oculis: cf. Aesch. *Th.* 696 ξηροῖς ἀκλαύτοις ὄμμασιν, Prop.
1. 17. 11 'siccis . . . ocellis'; Bentley adds further parallels. Ancient
southerners showed their emotions much more freely than modern

Englishmen (Elizabethans were different). In particular they were readier to scream during a storm; cf. *epod.* 10. 17 'et illa non virilis eiulatio', Lucian, *peregr.* 43 ἐκώκυε μετὰ τῶν γυναικῶν, Synes. *epist.* 4 p. 641 Hercher ἀνδρῶν οἰμωγή, γυναικῶν ὀλολυγή. Even today voyagers in the Aegean can recount surprising behaviour.

Bentley proposed *rectis oculis.* He argued that tears are not natural in the face of danger: it is therefore absurd to emphasize the bravery of the man who remains dry-eyed. But tears were a conventional property in a variety of literary situations, notably in epic (Schol. B on *Il.* 1. 349, Pease on Virg. *Aen.* 4. 449) and history (Kroll 342 n. 25). Fear is given elsewhere as a cause of weeping; cf. Hom. *Il.* 13. 88 f. τοὺς οἵ γ' εἰσορόωντες ὑπ' ὀφρύσι δάκρυα λεῖβον· / οὐ γὰρ ἔφαν φεύξεσθαι ὑπὲκ κακοῦ, Caes. *Gall.* 1. 39. 4 (some of Caesar's soldiers on hearing of the valour of the Germans) 'neque vultum fingere neque interdum lacrimas tenere poterant'. In particular there are other instances of weeping at sea; cf. Simon. 543. 5 (Danae adrift) οὐκ ἀδιάντοισι παρειαῖς, Ov. *met.* 11. 539 'non tenet hic lacrimas', Phaedr. 4. 18. 4, Val. Fl. 1. 633, Ennod. *carm.* 1. 5. 44 (modelled on our passage) 'nec siccis oculis respexi marmoris iras', Shakespeare, *3 Henry VI* v. iv. 7 f. 'like a fearful lad With tearful eyes add water to the sea'.

monstra natantia: cf. 3. 27. 26 f. 'scatentem / beluis pontum', 4. 14. 47 f., Albinov. *carm.* 5 ff., Val. Fl. 5. 481 f., Tac. *ann.* 2. 24. 6 'monstra maris, ambiguas hominum et beluarum formas, visa sive ex metu credita', Milton, *Lycidas* 157 f. 'Where thou perhaps under the whelming tide Visit'st the bottom of the monstrous world'. See further Plin. *nat.* 9. 2 ff., Mayor on Juv. 14. 283, K. Shepard, *The Fish-Tailed Monster in Greek and Etruscan Art*, New York, 1940, A. Lesky, *Thalatta*, 1947, pp. 138 ff., Bühler on Moschus, *Europa* 115–24.

19. vidit: 'endured to see'; cf. Virg. *Aen.* 3. 431 f. 'informem vasto vidisse sub antro / Scyllam', Shackleton Bailey, *Propertiana*, p. 3, Aesch. *Pers.* 100 ff. ἔμαθον . . . ἐσορᾶν πόντιον ἄλσος.

turbidum: cf. 3. 3. 5 'dux inquieti turbidus Hadriae', Lucr. 5. 1000 f. 'turbida ponti / aequora', Ov. *epist.* 18. 7 f., 18. 172, *trist.* 1. 11. 34, Sen. *Herc. O.* 456, Avien. *Arat.* 656, 850, 1458, 1761. The variant *turgidum* is a less conventional adjective, though cf. Hom. *Il.* 23. 230 (of the Thracian sea) οἴδματι θυίων, Hes. *th.* 109, 131, Arat. *phaen.* 909 οἰδαίνουσα θάλασσα (before a storm), Sacerd. *gramm.* 6. 533. 17 'lapides mare turgidum eluens', Avien. *Arat.* 307 'glauci vada turgida ponti', Prud. *perist.* 5. 475 f. 'quae turgidum quondam mare / gradiente Christo straverat'. Either word is tolerable, but *turbidum* describes a present danger more forcibly; *turgidum* rather refers to the swell before a storm. Moreover, *turbidum* can be paralleled much more convincingly from important Latin poets. Champions of *turgidum* regard it as more interesting and less trite; but in cases of this kind 'facilior lectio potior' is the wisest maxim.

20. infamis: cf. Liv. 21. 31. 8 'infames frigoribus Alpes', Sen. *epist.* 14. 8, Stat. *Theb.* 3. 121, *Thes.l.L.* 7. 1. 1340. 44 ff. Of course Acroceraunia was not yet notorious at the time of the first voyage, but Horace is looking at the situation from Virgil's point of view. For the mannered word-order cf. Ov. *epist.* 4. 171 'montanaque numina Panes', *met.* 2. 616 'temeraria tela sagittas', Norden on Virg. *Aen.* 6. 7, Housman on Manil. 2. 23, H.–Sz. 409.

Acroceraunia: the Ceraunian range (Maj'e Çikës) in N. Epirus (S. Albania) reaches a height of 5,300 feet within two miles of the sea; as it is situated at the place where the Adriatic is narrowest it is a notable landmark to travellers from Brindisi. Some modern authorities state that Acroceraunia (as opposed to Ceraunia) was the name of the promontory to the north (Glossa, Linguetta, Gjuhëzës), rising to 2,800 feet at the southern entrance to the gulf of Valona. This is very doubtful; the *acropolis* is the top part of a city, not the far end, and Acrocorinthus the top part of Corinth. A more decisive argument comes from Plin. *nat.* 4. 4 'in Epiri ora castellum in Acrocerauniis Chimera'; this refers to the modern Himarë, which is situated well south of the promontory.

The mountains derived their name from their frequent thunderstorms; cf. Serv. *Aen.* 3. 506 'Ceraunia sunt montes Epiri a crebris fulminibus propter altitudinem nominati: unde Horatius expressius dixit Acroceraunia propter altitudinem et fulminum iactus', Virg. *georg.* 1. 332 f. 'aut alta Ceraunia telo / deicit', Macaulay 'And the great Thunder cape has donned His veil of inky gloom'. The area was dangerous to shipping; cf. Caes. *civ.* 3. 6. 3, Ov. *rem.* 738, *RE* 11. 268 f. Octavian lost some ships there after Actium (Suet. *Aug.* 17. 3). Ceraunia may well have figured in Cinna's *propempticon* (above, p. 41); his poem referred to Corcyra (cf. fr. 5), which is only a little to the south.

21. abscidit: 'In vain did Nature's wise command / Divide the waters from the land' (Dryden). 'abscidit . . . oceano . . . terras' probably means 'divided land from ocean', not 'separated the lands with the ocean'. The former interpretation involves a more exact use of *abscindere*; and as the reader reaches *oceano* before *terras* he naturally understands the ablative as separative. There is strong support for this view in Ovid's account of the creation (*met.* 1. 22): 'nam caelo terras et terris abscidit undas' (note the plural *terras*, as in Horace). See also Statius's imitation of our passage (*silv.* 3. 2. 61 f.): 'quis rude et abscissum miseris animantibus aequor / fecit iter?'; by the dative *animantibus* Statius suggests more explicitly than Horace

that the sea is out of bounds; both writers presumably remembered
Arat. *phaen.* 110 χαλεπὴ δ' ἀπέκειτο θάλασσα (of the Golden Age). Cf.
further Sil. 11. 455 '(canebat) deus ut liquidi discisset stagna pro-
fundi'. On the other side it must be admitted that *abscidit* is used
with an accusative plural of the separation of two lands; cf. Val. Fl.
2. 616 ff. 'has etiam terras . . . Neptunia quondam / cuspis et adversi
longus labor abscidit aevi', Claud. *rapt. Pros.* 1. 144 f. 'rupit confinia
Nereus / victor et abscissos interluit aequore montes'. *abscidit* is also
used with an accusative and ablative of the separation of one land
from another (Virg. *Aen.* 3. 417 f. 'venit medio vi pontus et undis /
Hesperium Siculo latus abscidit').

Horace is alluding, not altogether seriously, to a doctrine of the
early Greek philosophers, who described the creation of cosmos out
of chaos by the separation of the elements; cf. W. Spoerri, *Spät-
hellenistische Berichte über Welt, Kultur und Götter*, 1959, pp. 107 ff.,
G. S. Kirk and J. E. Raven, *The Presocratic Philosophers*, 1962,
pp. 32 ff., F. Lämmli, *Vom Chaos zum Kosmos*, 1962. The theme was
taken up by the poets; cf. Ap. Rhod. 1. 496 ff. ἤειδεν δ' ὡς γαῖα καὶ
οὐρανὸς ἠδὲ θάλασσα, / τὸ πρὶν ἔτ' ἀλλήλοισι μιῇ συναρηρότα μορφῇ, /
νείκεος ἐξ ὀλοοῖο διέκριθεν ἀμφὶς ἕκαστα, Virg. *ecl.* 6. 35 f. 'tum durare
solum et discludere Nerea ponto / coeperit', Bömer on Ov. *fast.* 5. 11.
It is particularly relevant that Seneca alludes to the topic in a
diatribe against navigation which contains other reminiscences of
our poem (12 n.); cf. *Med.* 335 ff. 'bene *dissaepti* foedera mundi /
traxit in unum Thessala pinus / iussitque pati verbera pontum /
partemque metus fieri nostri / mare *sepositum*'. Horace and Seneca
are simply elaborating the theme that sailing is a violation of the
laws of nature; cf. Colum. 1 praef. 8 'an bellum perosis maris et
negotiationis alea sit optabilior ut rupto naturae foedere terrestre
animal homo ventorum et maris obiectus irae fluctibus pendeat?'

22. prudens: the word suggests the wise foresight of divine providence; cf. 3. 29. 29.

dissociabili: 'incompatible'; cf. Tac. *Agr.* 3. 1 'res olim dissociabilis
miscuerit principatum et libertatem' (the prefix negatives as in
dissimilis). The sea in a literal physical sense 'cannot be mixed';
Horace goes further than Ov. *met.* 1. 25 'dissociata locis concordi
pace ligavit' (this line occurs in the creation myth which has already
provided a parallel for *abscidit*). Also, from the moral point of view,
the sea is a thing that men should have nothing to do with; Horace
may be thinking of such Greek adjectives as ἀκοινώνητος or ἀνεπί-
μικτος. Cf. also Albinov. *carm.* fr. 21 f. 'aliena quid aequora remis /
et sacras violamus aquas?', Ambr. *Hel.* 71 'cur separatioris elementi
profunda rimaris?'

Many editors interpret *dissociabili* as active in sense, with the meaning 'separating'; *Oceano* would then be instrumental ablative. One may compare Lucr. 5. 203 'et mare quod late terrarum distinet oras', Stat. *silv.* 1. 3. 32 f. 'sic dissociata profundo / Bruttia Sicanium circumspicit ora Pelorum', Rut. Nam. 1. 330 'tamquam longinquo dissociata mari', Arnold, *Marguerite* (in a passage evidently modelled on our own) 'A god, a god their severance ruled, And bade betwixt their bounds to be The unplumbed, salt, estranging sea'. The poets sometimes use adjectives in *-bilis* in an active sense (see Munro on Lucr. 1. 11)'; in particular one may compare 2. 14. 6 f. 'illacrimabilem / Plutona'. Yet in a passage where there is real ambiguity one naturally expects the passive, especially as *dissociabilis, insociabilis*, and *sociabilis* always seem to be passive elsewhere.

24. non tangenda: the phrase suggests sacrilege; cf. 1. 35. 35, *epist.* 1. 3. 16. *transiliunt* suits a skimming boat, but also implies audacity; cf. Juv. 14. 278 f. 'nec Carpathium Gaetulaque tantum / aequora transiliet'. Shallows (*vada*) are particularly dangerous.

25. audax: *audacia* (τόλμα) is an impious self-assertion; cf. E. R. Dodds, *Pagan and Christian in an Age of Anxiety*, 1963, pp. 24 ff.

omnia perpeti: to put up with anything was not in the ancient world a virtue; cf. 3. 24. 42 f. 'pauperies . . . iubet / quidvis et facere et pati'. For other instances of the phrase *omnia perpeti* see Shackleton Bailey, *Propertiana*, p. 291 (on 2. 26. 35).

26. per vetitum nefas: for *ruere per nefas* cf. Luc. 5. 312 f. 'ipse per omne / fasque nefasque rues?', *Octavia* 787, Prud. *perist.* 10. 515, *cath.* 11. 93, Mar. Victor, *aleth.* 3. 22 ff. For *vetitum* cf. Ov. *am.* 3. 4. 17, Claud. 20. 52, Orient. *comm.* 2. 49 'in vetitum ruimus cupimusque negata'.

27. Iapeti genus: Prometheus; the reference is one of several Hesiodic touches in the poem (see next note). For the grandiloquent *genus* (= 'scion') cf. *serm.* 1. 6. 12 'Laevinum Valeri genus', Catull. 61. 2 'Uraniae genus', Eur. *Cycl.* 104 Σισύφου γένος. From the Renaissance Iapetus was identified with the son of Noah; cf. Ben Jonson, *Underwoods*, 1641, *An Ode to himselfe* 27 ff. 'with *Japhets* line, aspire *Sols* Chariot for new fire, To give the world againe', Milton, *P.L.* 4. 616 f. For similarities between the two figures cf. West on Hes. *th.* 134.

28. ignem . . .: Prometheus stole fire from heaven; cf. Hes. *op.* 50 ff. (Ζεὺς) κρύψε δὲ πῦρ· τὸ μὲν αὖτις ἐὺς πάις Ἰαπέτοιο / ἔκλεψ' ἀνθρώποισι Διὸς πάρα μητιόεντος / ἐν κοίλῳ νάρθηκι λαθὼν Δία τερπικέραυνον, *th.* 565 ff., Aesch. *Pr.* 7 f., 109 ff., West on Hes. *th.* 507–616.

fraude mala: the expression is similar to *dolo malo* but is not itself

H

a legal technicality. Cf. Plaut. *truc.* 298, Stat. *silv.* 3. 1. 32, Plin. *epist.* 7. 4. 6 (verse), Apul. *met.* 10. 27. 3.

29. post ignem . . .: as a consequence of Prometheus's theft of fire (note the emphatic repetition of *ignem*) Zeus sent Pandora to Epimetheus with a jar full of diseases. Cf. Hes. *op.* 102 f. νοῦσοι δ᾽ ἀνθρώποισιν ἐφ᾽ ἡμέρῃ, αἱ δ᾽ ἐπὶ νυκτὶ / αὐτόματοι φοιτῶσι κακὰ θνητοῖσι φέρουσαι, Serv. *ecl.* 6. 42 'ob quam causam irati dii duo mala immiserunt terris, mulieres (v.l. macies) et morbos, sicut et Sappho et Hesiodus memorant. quod tangit etiam Horatius dicens "post ignem aetheria . . ." ', Shelley, *Prom.* 2. 4. 49 ff. 'For on the race of man First famine, and then toil, and then disease, Strife, wounds, and ghastly death unseen before, Fell'. For a Cynic rationalization of the myth cf. Dio Chrys. 6. 25 τὸν μῦθον λέγειν ὡς τὸν Προμηθέα κολάζοι ὁ Ζεὺς διὰ τὴν εὕρεσιν καὶ μετάδοσιν τοῦ πυρός, ὡς ἀρχὴν τοῦτο καὶ ἀφορμὴν τοῖς ἀνθρώποις μαλακίας καὶ τρυφῆς.

Pandora is surprisingly little mentioned in classical literature; her 'box' was really a huge jar or πίθος, mistranslated by Erasmus in his *Adagia* as *pyxis*. Cf. J. E. Harrison, *JHS* 20, 1900, 99 ff., D. and E. Panofsky, *Pandora's Box*, 1956, pp. 14 ff.

aetheria domo: a grandiloquent expression; cf. the passages cited in 1. 28. 5 n.

31. incubuit: ἐνέσκηψεν; cf. Lucr. 6. 1143 '(mortifer aestus) incubuit tandem populo Pandionis omni', Lact. *inst.* 2. 1. 9 'si morborum pestifera vis incubuit', Pallad. 4. 15. 1, Macr. *sat.* 7. 5. 10.

cohors: diseases are to be counted in battalions; cf. Aesch. *supp.* 684 νούσων . . . ἑσμός, Sen. *epist.* 95. 23 'innumerabiles esse morbos non miraberis: cocos numera', Plin. *nat.* 7. 172 'morborum vero tam infinita est multitudo', Dio Chrys. 6. 23 (citing Diogenes) νοσημάτων γέμοντας ἃ μηδὲ ὀνομάσαι ῥᾴδιον, Juv. 10. 218 ff. 'circumsilit agmine facto / morborum omne genus, quorum si nomina quaeras, / promptius expediam quot amaverit Oppia moechos, / quot Themison aegros autumno occiderit uno'. Horace is imitated by Gray, *Ode on a Distant Prospect of Eton College* 81 ff. 'A griesly troop are seen, The painful family of Death'.

32. semotique prius: these words belong together. Before Pandora men died only of old age; cf. Hes. *op.* 91 f. νόσφιν ἄτερ τε κακῶν καὶ ἄτερ χαλεποῖο πόνοιο / νούσων τ᾽ ἀργαλέων αἵ τ᾽ ἀνδράσι κῆρας ἔδωκαν.

necessitas leti: cf. Hom. *Il.* 16. 836 ἦμαρ ἀναγκαῖον, Eur. *Hipp.* 1388 Ἅιδου μέλαινα νύκτερός τ᾽ ἀνάγκα.

33. corripuit gradum: 'quickened her pace'; cf. Stat. *Theb.* 2. 142 f.

34. vacuum: cf. Pind. *O.* 1. 6 ἐρήμας δι' αἰθέρος, 13. 88, Virg. *georg.* 3. 109 'aera per vacuum ferri'.

Daedalus: no doubt criticism of Daedalus was conventional in the diatribe; cf. Sen. *epist.* 90. 14 'quomodo, oro te, convenit, ut et Diogenen mireris et Daedalum?'

36. perrupit: the long final vowel is an archaism. It is attested in Plautus and Terence in the third person perfect active, and -*eit* in some archaizing inscriptions (Sommer 576 f., A. Ernout, *Morphologie historique du latin*, 1945, pp. 336 f.). Horace allows himself this and similar licences when the syllable is supported by the beat of the verse, sometimes also by a pause in the middle of the line (p.′xxxix). For similar phenomena in his hexameters see *serm.* 1. 4. 82, 1. 5. 90, 2. 1. 82, 2. 2. 47; for other poets see Nettleship's appendix to Coning-ton's Virgil (vol. 3, pp. 469 f.), Norden on Virg. *Aen.* 6, pp. 450 ff., Austin on *Aen.* 4. 64.

Acheronta: not simply the river, but the abode of the dead. The usage is common in Hellenistic poetry (Gow–Page 2. 119), and became rooted in Latin at an early stage; cf. Fraenkel, *Plautinisches im Plautus*, pp. 179 f.

Herculeus labor: the expression is reminiscent of the Homeric βίην Ἡρακληείην (*Od.* 11. 601); for this type of locution cf. K.–S. 1. 242. Of course Horace is referring specifically to the labours of Hercules, the last of which was the theft of Cerberus from the under-world. The same phrase is used in different ways by Sen. *Herc. f.* 1316, *Herc. O.* 1455, Sil. 1. 369.

37. nil mortalibus ardui est: *ardui* is more forceful than the variant *arduum* ('there is no such thing as difficulty' as against 'nothing is difficult'). Horace is presumably reflecting a Greek commonplace: cf. Opp. *hal.* 5. 2 f. ὡς οὐδὲν μερόπεσσιν ἀμήχανον, οὐκ ἐνὶ γαίῃ / μητρὶ καμεῖν, οὐ κόλπον ἀν' εὐρώεντα θαλάσσης. He is imitated in turn by *itin. Alex.* 34 'probat nihil ita mortalibus arduum cui non viam per-facile sapientia straverit'.

38. caelum: the climax of impiety; Horace is no longer thinking of Daedalus but of the giants (Hom. *Od.* 11. 315 f.). So more explicitly Statius's imitation (*silv.* 3. 2. 64 ff.): 'nec enim temeraria virtus / illa magis summae gelidum quae Pelion Ossae / iunxit anhelantemque iugis bis pressit Olympum'. Cf. also Pind. *P.* 10. 27 ὁ χάλκεος οὐρανὸς οὔ ποτ' ἀμβατὸς αὐτῷ, *I.* 7. 44, Rhianus 1. 15 Powell ἠέ τιν' ἀτραπιτὸν τεκμαίρεται Οὔλυμπόνδε, Min. Fel. 5. 6 'caelum ipsum et ipsa sidera audaci cupiditate transcendimus'. Add Alcman 1.16.

stultitia: this word is avoided by the major Latin poets. Apart from Horace, it is found only in Lucretius (once) and Ovid (twice).

Horace uses it at 4. 12. 27 and often in the *Satires* and *Epistles*; here it suits the διατριβή style. See Axelson 100.

40. iracunda . . . fulmina: cf. Pind. *N*. 6. 53 ἔγχεος ζακότοιο (of Zeus), Prop. 2. 16. 52 'nec sic de nihilo fulminis ira cadit', Juv. 13. 226 'iratus cadat in terras et vindicet (iudicet *codd.*) ignis' (with Mayor's note). Dryden translates finely: 'We reach at Jove's Imperial Crown, And pull the unwilling thunder down.'

4. SOLVITVR ACRIS HIEMS

[W. Barr, *CR* n.s. 12, 1962, 5 ff.; C. Becker, *Das Spätwerk des Horaz*, 1963, pp. 147 ff.; E. Defourny, *LEC* 14, 1946, 174 ff.; Fraenkel 419 ff.; Pasquali 714 ff.; K. Quinn, *Latin Explorations*, 1963, pp. 14 ff.]

1–4. *The Zephyr has ended the winter, and activity is beginning again on sea and land.* 5–8. *Venus dances with the nymphs and Graces, while her husband is busy in his forge.* 9–12. *It is time to put on a garland and sacrifice to Faunus.* 13–20. *Death comes to all: remember, Sestius, not to hope far ahead. At any moment death may overcome you, and then you will no longer delight in the symposium or the love of the boy Lycidas, soon to become a young man.*

The coming of spring is a natural subject for poetry, which draws on universal human experience; cf. *Song of Solomon* 2. 11 f. 'For, lo, the winter is past, the rain is over and gone; The flowers appear on the earth; the time of the singing of birds is come, and the voice of the turtle is heard in our land'. Yet, Augustan poetry being what it is, one looks for Greek literary antecedents to Horace's ode. Our poem may be influenced in the first place by a poem of Alcaeus (286), which survives in tantalizing scraps; cf. Page, *Sappho and Alcaeus*, pp. 289 ff., W. Barner, *Neue Alkaios-Papyri aus Oxyrhynchos*, Hildesheim, 1967, pp. 3 ff. In successive lines one reads πολυανθέμω (presumably applied to spring), κρύερος πάγος (there is a marginal comment τὰ τοῦ χειμῶνος διαλύεται, which suggests Horace's *solvitur*), ὑπὰ Τάρταρον (the point is uncertain; an allusion to death's imminence could hardly come in so early), [ἐπ]ὶ νῶτ' ἔχει (the sea's back is meant, as is shown by the note ἀντὶ τοῦ γαλήνη ἐστὶ κατὰ τὴν θάλασσαν). It seems quite likely that Horace has drawn his opening, as so often, from Alcaeus; but the development of his theme depends on very different sources.

The most important of these, so far as the first part of the poem is concerned, was an influential and familiar epigram by Leonidas of

Tarentum, which was quoted several times by Cicero in the civil war
(*anth. P.* 10. 1):

Ὁ πλόος ὡραῖος· καὶ γὰρ λαλαγεῦσα χελιδὼν
ἤδη μέμβλωκεν, χὠ χαρίεις Ζέφυρος·
λειμῶνες δ' ἀνθεῦσι, σεσίγηκεν δὲ θάλασσα
κύμασι καὶ τρηχεῖ πνεύματι βρασσομένη.
ἀγκύρας ἀνέλοιο, καὶ ἐκλύσαιο γύαια,
ναυτίλε, καὶ πλώοις πᾶσαν ἐφεὶς ὀθόνην.
ταῦθ' ὁ Πρίηπος ἐγὼν ἐπιτέλλομαι ὁ λιμενίτας,
ὤνθρωφ', ὡς πλώοις πᾶσαν ἐπ' ἐμπορίην.

Leonidas's epigram was imitated in several others in the tenth book
of the Palatine Anthology (2, 4, 5, 6, 14, 15, 16); most of the poems are
later than Horace, but no doubt continue an established tradition.
Elements common to the group are the swallow (cf. Hor. *carm.* 4. 12.
5 ff.), the Zephyr, flowers, the calm sea, the opening of the navigation
season, an allusion to Priapus; the word ἤδη recurs in several poems
(5 n.), and sometimes a reference to the miseries of the past winter
(3 n.). Some of the above features are also found in a hexameter
poem by Meleager (*anth. P.* 9. 363). The motifs of the spring poem
were taken over in Latin by Catullus (46. 1 ff. 'iam ver egelidos
refert tepores, / iam caeli furor aequinoctialis / iucundis Zephyri
silescit auris'), by Horace himself in 4. 7 and 4. 12 (in the latter case
conflated with an invitation poem), and by Ovid in several passages
(Bömer on *fast.* 1. 151); one may refer especially to a moving elegy
from Tomi (*trist.* 3. 12), whose opening words ('frigora iam Zephyri
minuunt') re-echo Horace 4. 7. 9.

Against his scenes from the countryside Horace sets another more
imaginative miniature, reminding us of the contrasted world of
field and castle in medieval books of hours. The dance of Venus and
the Graces is derived from early Greek hexameter poetry (5 n.); but
as a similar dance of the Graces occurs in the companion poem 4. 7
one may suspect a more immediate source in a Hellenistic epigram.
Yet Venus is often associated with spring, notably in the proem of
Lucretius's first book; this includes a mention of Favonius, flowers,
and a calm sea. Even more relevant to our poem is 5. 737 ff.:

> it ver et Venus et Veneris praenuntius ante
> pennatus graditur, Zephyri vestigia propter
> Flora quibus mater praespargens ante viai
> cuncta coloribus egregiis et odoribus implet.

The third stanza with its rustic sacrifice to Faunus shows a considerable slackening of tension, and might be thought less impressive
than the rest of the poem; yet it has the function of lulling the senses

before the onslaught of 13. It should further be observed that all the eight poems on spring in the tenth book of the Anthology end with a mention of Priapus, in his capacity as a god of navigation (1. 7, 2. 7, 4. 7, 5. 7, 6. 7, 14. 9, 15. 7, 16. 11). It looks as if in Horace's ode Faunus, though he has no connection with navigation, in some way represents Priapus; both gods were connected with the fertility of the animal kingdom. It seems significant that Horace offers Faunus a sacrifice of either a lamb or a kid, according to taste; similar alternatives are offered to Priapus in two of the above-mentioned epigrams (11 n.).

In line 13 Death kicks at the door with thrilling suddenness. We must ask ourselves what led Horace to this unexpected line of thought. The romantic biographer will too readily assume that the poet is describing a unique experience intensely felt on a particular spring day and revealing a personal preoccupation with human mortality. The literary critic will point to the poetical effectiveness of the theme, and with his usual indifference to facts will inquire no further. Others look for hidden allusions whose elucidation will explain all: thus Mr. W. Barr has ingeniously observed that the Parentalia, or festival of the dead, immediately followed the sacrifice to Faunus in his urban temple (below, on 11 *Fauno*).

The most promising line of approach (if Horace's practice elsewhere is a reliable guide) is surely a further investigation of the ode's literary antecedents. It is true that Horace in this place seems unusually independent; but something may be learnt from the later poem 'Diffugere nives' (4. 7), which probably draws on similar sources (it is less likely to be a restatement of a theme invented by the poet himself). There too the return of spring leads to meditations on mortality, but the sequence of thought is much more explicit than in our ode. First of all the procession of the seasons reminds the poet of the flight of time (4. 7. 9 'frigora mitescunt Zephyris, ver proterit aestas'); New Year's Day and other anniversaries may bring us similar reflections, but the coming of spring in a northern climate is too treacherous to be noticed quite so sharply. Secondly Horace introduces a false antithesis between the changing and renewing phases of inanimate nature and the decay of individual human life: 'damna tamen celeres reparant caelestia lunae: / nos ubi decidimus . . .' (4. 7. 13 f.). This point had previously been made by Catullus (5. 4 ff. 'soles occidere et redire possunt; / nobis cum semel occidit brevis lux, / nox est perpetua una dormienda'). One may compare further the significant parallel from the *Epitaphium Bionis* 99 ff. αἰαῖ ταὶ μαλάχαι μέν, ἐπὰν κατὰ κᾶπον ὄλωνται, / ἠδὲ τὰ χλωρὰ σέλινα τό τ' εὐθαλὲς οὖλον ἄνηθον / ὕστερον αὖ ζώοντι καὶ εἰς ἔτος ἄλλο φύοντι· / ἄμμες δ' οἱ μεγάλοι καὶ καρτεροί, οἱ σοφοὶ ἄνδρες, / ὁππότε πρᾶτα θάνωμες, ἀνάκοοι ἐν χθονὶ κοίλᾳ / εὕδομες εὖ μάλα μακρὸν ἀτέρμονα νήγρετον ὕπνον. It looks as if this line of thought had wider currency in Hellenistic poetry than our surviving fragments would immediately suggest; though Horace's thought has no precise parallels in Greek, one can hardly regard it as uniquely original (unlike all the other maxims in his poetry).

In the last three lines the poem veers again, this time to the febrile pleasures of the symposium. Here Horace introduces other more familiar commonplaces: in the manner of much Greek poetry, from Alcaeus to the Anthology, he contrasts the brevity of human love and gaiety with the meagre and shadowy existence of the dead (18 n.). He illustrates the lapse of the years by remarking that Lycidas will soon be loved by women instead of by men. The theme is found in the Anthology (cf. Phanias, *anth. P.* 12. 31. 3 f. ἤδη γὰρ καὶ μηρὸς ὑπὸ τρίχα καὶ γένυς ἥβᾳ / καὶ Πόθος εἰς ἑτέρην λοιπὸν ἄγει μανίην) ; its Greek origin would be apparent even if no parallel existed. The emphasis on the flight of time is reinforced by the movement of the poem; after a light but fairly end-stopped opening it now gathers momentum, with frequent enjambements and a long final sentence.

The ode is often compared with 4. 7, as is natural with two poems so similar in subject and pattern of development (cf. Becker, Fraenkel, Quinn, loc. cit.). Both describe the disappearance of winter, the coming of the zephyr, the changing seasons (1 vice), and the dance of the nymphs and Graces. But the earlier poem has greater liveliness of illustration (winches pulling dry keels, dances hand in hand under a looming moon). It also includes more striking contrasts; the activity of spring is opposed to the sluggishness of winter, the gaiety of Venus to the heavy industriousness of her husband. Moreover, it shows a much subtler ambivalence of feeling; 4. 7 maintains a uniformly melancholy note throughout, but our poem combines simultaneously an intense awareness of the joys of spring and the horrors of the underworld, the eternity of death and the brevity of happiness. This ambivalence of feeling is reinforced by the metre, which is much more interesting than that of the later poem: the ecstatic long lines are even livelier than hexameters, but are pulled up by the slow catalectic iambics, whose closing cadence yet re-echoes that of the long lines. Above all Horace has shown here as perhaps nowhere else his full power to fuse elements of totally different provenance, the Hellenistic spring epigram, scenes from early Greek mythology, Roman feeling for Faunus and the Manes, and a hectic scene from a Greek symposium at the end. Though for an understanding of his methods an analysis of his sources is essential, that should not blind us to the fact that the poet has combined these ideas in his own consciousness and made them uniquely his own.

Metre: Third Archilochian.

1. solvitur: Horace describes the annual miracle when winter suddenly dissolves. *solvitur* suggests the melting of the snow, the
softening of the ground, the release of mind and body from the
numbness of winter. The word may represent something in Alcaeus
(above, p. 58); it is echoed below by *solutae* (10 n.). Cf. Luc. 1. 17
'bruma rigens ac nescia vere remitti', Isid. *nat.* 37. 4 '(Favonius)
hiemis rigorem gratissima vice relaxat, flores producit'.

acris: 'biting'; cf. Enn. *ann.* 424, Lucr. 6. 373, 3. 20 'nix acri con-
creta pruina', 1. 9. 4 n.

vice: 'succession'. Here the genitive describes the new arrival,
Favonius and the spring; normally it refers to what is altered by
a change. For the use of an adjective with *vice* cf. 1. 28. 32, *epod.* 13.
7 f. 'deus haec fortasse benigna / reducet in sedem vice', Prop. 1. 13.
10 *miseras, culex* 226 *vanas*, Luc. 9. 998 f. 'grata vice moenia red-
dent / Ausonidae Phrygibus', Auson. 418. 19 'tenui vice vocis', Drac.
laud. dei 3. 58 *immites*. One may admire the astringency of Horace's
diction; unlike some Anthology poets he is not tempted to sentimentality, even by the advent of spring.

Favoni: the Zephyr is conventionally associated with spring; cf.
4. 7. 9, 4. 12. 1, Leonidas, *anth. P.* 10. 1. 2 (above, p. 59) together with
its imitations, Cic. *Verr.* 5. 27 '(veris) initium iste non a Favonio
neque ab aliquo astro notabat', Plin. *nat.* 18. 337 'hic ver inchoat
aperitque terras tenui frigore saluber, hic vites putandi frugesque
curandi, arbores serendi, poma inserendi, oleas tractandi ius dabit
adflatuque nutricium exercebit', Milton, *To Mr. Lawrence* 6 ff. 'till
Favonius reinspire The frozen earth, and clothe in fresh attire The
lily and rose'.

The wind began to blow, according to Pliny, on the 8th of February (*nat.* 2. 122); see also Ov. *fast.* 2. 148 (5 Feb.), Colum. 11. 2. 15
(7 Feb.). These dates all seem to be over-precise.

2. trahuntque: the renewal of navigation was one of the themes of
Leonidas's spring poem (above, p. 59), as well as of his imitators in
the tenth book of the Anthology. Particularly relevant for our ode is
Paul. Sil. *anth. P.* 10. 15. 1 ff. ἤδη μὲν ζεφύροισι μεμυκότα κόλπον
ἀνοίγει / εἴαρος εὐλείμων θελξινόοιο χάρις· / ἄρτι δὲ δουρατέοισιν ἐπω-
λίσθησε κυλίνδροις / ὁλκὰς ἀπ᾽ ἠιόνων ἐς βύθον ἑλκομένη. There is presumably a common Hellenistic source behind Horace and Paulus.

We find it hard to imagine the effect of winter on transport in
the ancient world. There was of course some winter sailing; but the
captain had to be hardy or desperate, and the ship well-found. The
date of the opening of the navigation season was commonly put in

early March (cf. Veg. *mil.* 4. 29 'ex die igitur tertio Idus Novembres usque ad diem sextum Idus Martias maria clauduntur') or even later (cf. *Fasti Praenestini, inscr. Ital.* 13. 2. 17 (under April) 'maria . . . aperiuntur'). Yet sometimes it was earlier; cf. 3. 7. 1 f. '(Gygen) tibi candidi / primo restituent vere Favonii', 4. 12. 1 f., Plin. *nat.* 2. 122 (above, 1 *Favoni*). See further E. de Saint-Denis, *REL* 25, 1947, 196 ff.

siccas . . . carinas: *carina* is often used in poetry for a ship, but here the word has point: even the keels are dry. Horace uses his ornaments economically in this poem, but very effectively. In the tideless Mediterranean ships were drawn up a few feet to keep them clear of winter storms; cf. Min. Fel. 3. 5 (describing the shore at Ostia) 'cum ad id loci ventum est ubi subductae naviculae substratis roboribus in terrena labe suspensae quiescebant, pueros videmus certatim gestientes testarum in mare iaculationibus ludere'.

machinae: ships were manœuvred onto a sled and kept upright with blocks. The sleds were either fitted with wheels or laid above rollers or boards, and were moved sometimes by a compound pulley, sometimes by a winch; see the description and illustrations in A. G. Drachmann, *The Mechanical Technology of Greek and Roman Antiquity*, 1963, pp. 95 ff. The use of such *machinae* in hauling ships up is mentioned in Vitr. 10. 2. 10 'in plano etiam eadem ratione et temperatis funibus et trochleis subductiones navium efficiuntur' (cf. also Liv. 25. 11. 18). The machines are called ὁλκοί in Thuc. 3. 15. 1, χαμουλκοί in Poll. 7. 191, *chamulci* in Amm. 17. 4. 14, χελῶναι in Hero, *mech.* 3. 1.

3. neque . . .: writers on this poem are tempted to comment on Horace's subtlety in introducing a contrasting counter-scene. They do not point out that the *neque iam* motif belonged to the tradition; cf. 4. 12. 3 f. 'iam nec prata rigent nec fluvii strepunt / hiberna nive turgidi', Antip. Sid. *anth. P.* 10. 2. 1 f. ἀκμαῖος ῥοθίη νηὶ δρόμος, οὐδὲ θάλασσα / πορφύρει τρομερῇ φρικὶ χαρασσομένη, Ov. *trist.* 3. 12. 29 f. 'nec mare concrescit glacie nec, ut ante, per Histrum / stridula Sauromates plaustra bubulcus agit', Agathias, *anth. P.* 10. 14. 3 f. οὐκέτι δὲ σπιλάδεσσι περικλασθεῖσα θάλασσα / ἔμπαλιν ἀντωπὸς πρὸς βάθος εἰσάγεται. However, the subject-matter of Horace's counter-scenes finds no parallel in the Anthology poems.

stabulis: *stabula* might be open-air enclosures to protect flocks and herds from wild beasts; but the ancients also built roofed stables for the winter (cf. D.–S. 4. 1448).

arator: not just equivalent to 'farmer'; ploughing was done in the spring (Ov. *fast.* 1. 159). Virgil puts it soon after the arrival of the Zephyr (*georg.* 1. 43 f.), Pliny mentions the time between Favonius

and the equinox for some soils (*nat.* 18. 242), Varro a time after the
equinox (*rust.* 1. 30). Obviously the exact date varied according to
circumstances; for a more precise statement cf. Colum. 2. 4. 3
'uliginosi campi proscindi debent post Id. mensis Aprilis . . .', 9
'colles pinguis soli . . . mense Martio, si vero tepor caeli siccitasque
regionis suadebit, Februario statim proscindendi sunt'.

igni: cf. Virg. *georg.* 1. 299 'hiems ignava colono'. Hesiod gives
a vivid picture of farmers sitting round the forge in the winter (*op.*
493 f.) : πὰρ δ' ἴθι χάλκειον θῶκον καὶ ἐπαλέα λέσχην | ὥρῃ χειμερίῃ.

4. canis albicant: *canus* and its compounds are often reinforced by
other words signifying whiteness; cf. Virg. *georg.* 2. 71 f. 'ornusque
incanuit albo | flore piri', Tib. 1. 10. 43 'liceatque caput candescere
canis', *priap.* 76. 1 f. 'meumque canis | cum barba caput albicet
capillis', André 67.

For *albicant* cf. Varro, *Men.* 75 'ubi rivus . . . offensus aliquo
a scopulo lapidoso albicatur', Catull. 63. 87 'at ubi umida albicantis
loca litoris adiit', *carm. epig.* 1522. 8 'dente aper albicanti'. Yet in
spite of these occurrences in poetry the word has a colloquial and
rustic flavour; the only pagan prose writers who use it are Columella
and the elder Pliny, with whom it is a favourite.

5. iam: for the repeated *iam* cf. the spring poems 4. 12. 1 ff., Catull.
46. 1 ff., and ἤδη . . . ἤδη in *anth. P.* 10. 5 and 16.

choros: cf. 4. 7. 5 f. 'Gratia cum Nymphis geminisque sororibus
audet | ducere nuda choros', Hom. *Od.* 18. 193 f. ἐυστέφανος Κυθέρεια |
. . . εὖτ' ἂν ἴῃ Χαρίτων χορὸν ἱμερόεντα, *h.Ap.* 194 ff. αὐτὰρ ἐυπλόκαμοι
Χάριτες καὶ εὔφρονες ῟Ωραι | Ἁρμονίη θ' ῞Ηβη τε Διὸς θυγάτηρ τ'
Ἀφροδίτη | ὀρχεῦντ' ἀλλήλων ἐπὶ καρπῷ χεῖρας ἔχουσαι, *Cypria* fr. 5.

imminente luna: night is a favourite time of the nymphs as of the
fairies; cf. Ap. Rhod. 1. 1223 f. μέλε γάρ σφισι πάσαις | ὅσσαι κεῖν'
ἐρατὸν νύμφαι ῥίον ἀμφενέμοντο | ῎Αρτεμιν ἐννυχίῃσιν ἀεὶ μέλπεσθαι
ἀοιδαῖς, 1. 1231 f. πρὸς γάρ οἱ διχόμηνις ἀπ' αἰθέρος αὐγάζουσα | βάλλε
σεληναίη, Theoc. 13. 44 Νύμφαι ἀκοίμητοι, Stat. *silv.* 1. 1. 94 f. 'sub
nocte silenti, | cum superis terrena placent', Milton, *P.L.* 1. 781 ff.
'Or faery elves, Whose midnight revels, by a forest side Or fountain, some belated peasant sees, Or dreams he sees, while overhead
the Moon Sits arbitress, and nearer to the Earth Wheels her pale
course'.

6. Gratiae: their number varied in different cults, but they were
normally three; cf. Hes. *th.* 907 ff. τρεῖς δέ οἱ (Διὶ) Εὐρυνόμη Χάριτας
τέκε καλλιπαρῄους, | . . . Ἀγλαΐην τε καὶ Εὐφροσύνην Θαλίην τ' ἐρατεινήν,
Pind. *O.* 14. 13 ff. They were associated with the delights of spring by
Stesichorus (212): τοιάδε χρὴ Χαρίτων δαμώματα καλλικόμων | ὑμνεῖν

Φρύγιον μέλος ἐξευρόντας ἀβρῶς / ἦρος ἐπερχομένου (imitated by Ar. *pax* 796 ff.). Pausanias (9. 35) gives much interesting information about their cults and their representation by poets and artists in ancient times.

Here, as in 4. 7, the Graces dance with the Nymphs, an image less potent in later times than the dance of the three Graces alone. In art and in philosophy the union of this trinity of shifting figures was for centuries subject to much allegorizing interpretation; cf. E. Wind, *Pagan Mysteries in the Renaissance*, 1958, ch. ii. Horace's picture, as well as Lucretius's, powerfully contributed to the formal structure of Botticelli's *Primavera* (cf. Wind, op. cit., ch. vii).

decentes: a rather austere word for 'lovely'; cf. εὐπρεπεῖς.

7. quatiunt: dancing in the ancient world, as still in Eastern Europe, was not effete gliding, but vigorous and noisy exercise. Cf. 3. 18. 15 f. 'gaudet invisam pepulisse fossor / ter pede terram', Hom. *Il.* 18. 571 f. τοὶ δὲ ῥήσσοντες ἁμαρτῇ / μολπῇ τ' ἰυγμῷ τε ποσὶ σκαίροντες ἕποντο (*h.Ap.* 516), *Od.* 8. 264, Ap. Rhod. 1. 539, Call. *h.* 4. 306, Enn. *ann.* 1 'Musae quae pedibus magnum pulsatis Olympum', Catull. 61. 14, Lucr. 5. 1402. Horace's dance may seem too obstreperous for the Graces (cf. Schol. Townl. on Hom. *Il.* 18. 571); yet cf. Hes. *th.* 70 (on the Muses visiting Zeus) ἐρατὸς δὲ ποδῶν ὕπο δοῦπος ὀρώρει.

dum . . .: Venus can frolic gaily while her lame and ponderous husband is superintending his thunderbolt factory. There was an exceptional demand for his product in the springtime; cf. Lucr. 6. 357 ff. 'autumnoque magis . . . concutitur domus undique totaque tellus, / et cum tempora se veris florentia pandunt', Plin. *nat.* 2. 136.

gravis: the word vaguely suggests heavy industry. The workshop was not itself heavy, but the apparatus was, and the work (cf. ps.-Acro 'pro operis labore'), and the workmen (who cannot skip with the Graces).

Cyclopum: the Cyclopes as smiths of the lightning appear in Hes. *th.* 139 ff. Κύκλωπας ὑπέρβιον ἦτορ ἔχοντας, / Βρόντην τε Στερόπην τε καὶ Ἄργην ὀβριμόθυμον, / οἳ Ζηνὶ βροντήν τ' ἔδοσαν τεῦξάν τε κεραυνόν, Ap. Rhod. 1. 730 f. We first meet them as Hephaestus's servants in Call. *h.* 3. 46 ff. αὖθι δὲ Κύκλωπας μετεκίαθε· τοὺς μὲν ἔτετμε / νήσῳ ἐνὶ Λιπάρῃ . . . ἐπ' ἄκμοσιν Ἡφαίστοιο / ἑσταότας περὶ μύδρον. Their workshops are sometimes placed on Hiera in the Lipari islands, sometimes on Etna, sometimes on Lemnos; cf. Pfeiffer on Call. fr. 115. 11, Pease on Cic. *nat. deor.* 3. 55, Bömer on Ov. *fast.* 4. 287, *RE* 8. 322 f. For a picture of the Cyclopes at work see Roscher 1. 2070.

8. ardens: as the god of fire; for less extreme but more vivid expressions cf. Suidas 2. 164 αἰθαλόεις θεός· ὁ Ἥφαιστος, ὡς χαλκεύς, Lucian, *sacr.* 6 Ἥφαιστον . . . πυρίτην ἐν καπνῷ τὸ πᾶν βιοῦντα καὶ σπινθήρων

ἀναπλέων οἷα δὴ καμινευτήν. Horace's phrase was imitated by Stat.
Theb. 10. 100 f., *silv.* 3. 1. 132, Claud. *carm. min.* 46. 3 f., Prud. *perist.*
2. 404.

visit: the word has none of the prosaic associations of the English
'visit', but is naturally used of the movements of a god; cf. 3. 28. 15,
Virg. *Aen.* 4. 144 'Delum maternam visit Apollo'. It also suits inspec-
tions or 'visitations'; cf. Liv. 40. 2. 7 f. '(Marcius) ad res Graeciae
Macedoniaeque visendas missus erat . . . Asiae regibus ac Rhodiis
responsum est, legatos ad eas res visendas senatum missurum'. For
similar journeys by Hephaestus in Greek poetry cf. Hom. *Od.* 8. 273
βῆ δ᾽ ἴμεν ἐς χαλκεῶνα, 283, 294, Ap. Rhod. 3. 41 ἀλλ᾽ ὁ μὲν ἐς χαλκεῶνα
καὶ ἄκμονα ἦρι βέβηκεν. The variant *urit* would mean 'burns down'
and could not refer to firing the furnaces; it does not deserve the
slightest consideration.

officinas: a prosaic word, here effective; cf. Cic. *nat. deor.* 3. 55
'(Vulcanus) qui Lemni fabricae traditur praefuisse', Virg. *Aen.* 8. 418
'Cyclopum . . . caminis'. A volcanic mountain glowing at night sug-
gests a gigantic iron-foundry.

9. nitidum: λιπαρόν. The word suggests unguents for the hair, which,
together with garlands, were regular concomitants of a festivity. Cf.
2. 7. 7 f. 'nitentis / malobathro Syrio capillos', *epist.* 1. 14. 32, Tib.
1. 7. 51 'illius et nitido stillent unguenta capillo', Ov. *epist.* 21. 166
'spissaque de nitidis tergit amoma comis', Strato, *anth. P.* 11. 19. 3 f.
καὶ στεφάνοις κεφαλὰς πυκασώμεθα, καὶ μυρίσωμεν / αὑτούς, *RE* 1 A.
1854 ff.

10. flore . . .: in Mediterranean countries flowers are associated with
spring and not with summer; cf. Plin. *nat.* 21. 64 f. 'florum prima ver
nuntiantium viola alba—tepidioribus vero locis etiam hieme emi-
cat—post ea quae ion appellatur et purpurea, proxime flammeum,
quod phlox vocatur . . .'.

solutae: the word echoes 1 *solvitur*; cf. Virg. *georg.* 1. 44 'Zephyro
putris se glaeba resolvit', 2. 330 f. 'Zephyrique tepentibus auris /
laxant arva sinus', Lygd. 5. 4 'cum se purpureo vere remittit humus'.

11. Fauno: see below, 1. 17. 1 n. W. Barr, loc. cit., points out an
interesting juxtaposition in the Roman calendar. On the 13th or the
Ides of February a sacrifice to Faunus took place in his temple on
the Insula Tiberina (*Fasti Esquil., inscr. Ital.* 13. 2. 32, Ov. *fast.* 2.
193 f.). At the sixth hour of the same day began the festival of the
dead, the *dies parentales*, which culminated in the Feralia on the
18th; cf. Ioh. Lyd. *de mensibus* 4. 29 Εἰδοῖς Φεβρουαρίοις· ἀπὸ ταύτης
τῆς ἡμέρας ἀπὸ ὥρας ἕκτης διὰ τὰς τῶν κατοιχομένων χοὰς τὰ ἱερὰ
κατησφαλίζοντο (quoted by Barr, p. 10). Therefore, when death

knocks so unexpectedly at the door, the sequence of thought may be justified by the facts of the Roman calendar.

This is a most ingenious theory. It is no argument against it to say that the evidence is obscure to us, for an educated Roman would know the dates of important festivals. One may further agree that the early lines of the ode point on the whole to February (against Plessis, who sees a progression from February to April, and Defourny, who puts the poem entirely in April). Yet, as Barr himself points out (p. 9), we only know the date of Faunus's urban festival; it is not at all clear that sacrifice *in umbrosis lucis* would take place on the same day. It is an even more serious objection that the companion poem 4. 7 proceeds from spring to thoughts of mortality without any help from the calendar (above, p. 60). It also seems probable that Faunus is playing the part of Priapus in Horace's models (ibid.) These circumstances do not rule out the possibility that Horace is adding to the spring topics an ingenious connection of his own; but they make it distinctly less likely.

immolare: properly 'to sprinkle with *mola salsa*' before sacrificing. The word came to mean 'to sacrifice', normally with the accusative that its etymology would lead one to expect; the Tabula of the Arval Brothers presents a regular alternation between, for example, *immolare taurum* and *bove aurato vovemus esse futurum*. The ablative seems intended to give an archaistic flavour; cf. Cic. *leg.* 2. 29 'quibus hostiis immolandum quoique deo', Liv. 41. 14. 7 'immolantibus Iovi singulis bubus', 42. 30. 8, Macr. *sat.* 3. 10. 3 (from Ateius Capito) 'Iovi tauro verre ariete immolari non licet', *Thes.l.L.* 7. 1. 489. 54 ff. It is an extension of the use of the instrumental with *facere*, 'to perform a sacrifice'; cf. *Thes.l.L.* 6. 1. 97. 37 ff., K.–S. 1. 384 f., H.–Sz. 121.

12. agna sive . . . haedo: for alternative sacrifices cf. Antip. *anth. P.* 9. 72. 3 f. (Heracles) ἕνα . . . κτίλον ἢ παχὺν ἄρνα / αἰτεῖ, Agathias, ibid. 10. 14. 9 f. μοῦνον ἐνορμίταο παραὶ βωμοῖσι Πριήπου / ἢ σκάρον ἢ βῶκας φλέξον ἐρευθομένους, Theaetetus, ibid. 10. 16. 11 ff. The sacrifice of a female animal to a male god is ritually wrong from a Roman point of view; so Horace may be imitating a lost Greek epigram. Yet for similar inaccuracies cf. Ov. *fast.* 2. 361 'cornipedi Fauno caesa de more capella', 4. 650 ff. (with Bömer's note).

13. pallida: used of *Mors* also at Sen. *Herc. f.* 555, Hier. *in Os.* 6. 54; cf. also Virg. *georg.* 1. 277, Tib. 1. 10. 38, Pease on Virg. *Aen.* 4. 26, 4. 644.

Mors: the personification is Greek; cf. the opening scene of the *Alcestis*, where Thanatos comes to fetch his victim. For Latin instances cf. 3. 2. 14, *serm.* 2. 1. 58, Sen. *Herc. f.* 555, *Oed.* 164, *Tro.* 1171, Lattimore 153 f., Cumont 477 ff.

aequo: for the *communis locus* on the impartiality of death cf. 1. 28. 16 n. The quality of Death is here applied to Death's foot; so 1. 37. 1, 3. 25. 11, 3. 1. 17 f., 3. 2. 16, 1. 17. 26 n.

pulsat: for the same figure cf. Ov. *epist.* 21. 46 'Persephone nostras pulsat acerba fores'. Here Death expresses her impatience by kicking; cf. Call. *h.* 2. 3 τὰ θύρετρα καλῷ ποδὶ Φοῖβος ἀράσσει, Ter. *eun.* 284 f.

pede: the alliteration expresses the barrage of kicks. *pede* also echoes a very different use of the word in 7.

pauperum: cf. 2. 3. 21 ff., 2. 14. 11 f. 'sive reges / sive inopes erimus coloni', 2. 18. 32 ff. 'aequa tellus / pauperi recluditur / regumque pueris', Pind. *N.* 7. 19 f. ἀφνεὸς πενιχρός τε θανάτου πέρας / ἅμα νέονται, Kaibel, *EG* 459. 7 f. πάντων δέ, φίλε, τέλος θάνατος καὶ βύθος, / πλούτου πενίης, ἀλόγων τε καὶ ἀνδρῶν, Peek, *GV* 1185. 7 f., Seb. Brant, *Narrenschiff* 85. 41 f. 'der dot mit glichem füß zerschütt / der kunig säl und hirten hüt', Malherbe, *Poésies* 6. 90. 77 ff. 'Le pauvre en sa cabane, où le chaume le couvre, Est sujet à ses lois; Et la garde qui veille aux barrières du Louvre N'en défend point nos rois'.

tabernas: the wooden shacks of the poor. The word is prosaic, and contrasts with the romantic *turres* ('castles').

14. regum: to the passages quoted above add 4. 7. 15 'quo dives Tullus et Ancus', Peek, *GV* 2035. 17 f. (= Kaibel, *EG* 502. 17 f.) ἧς δ' ἔλαχέν τις / μοίρης ταύτην ἐκτελέσει· καὶ γὰρ βασιλῆες, 301. 9 τέτλαθι· καὶ γὰρ ἄνακτες ἀμειδήτῳ ποτὲ πένθει / κύρσαντες τοίης ἄλγος ἔχουσ' ὀδύνης, Lucr. 3. 1025 f. 'inde diu multi reges rerumque potentes / occiderunt', *carm. epig.* 970. 14 'haec eadem et magneis regibus acciderunt', 1068 'hoc etiam multis regibus ⟨h⟩ora tulit'. These passages argue decisively against the view that *regum* is colloquial for 'great men', such as Sestius himself.

beate: less vulgar than 'rich'; the word suggests felicity as well as prosperity (cf. *epod.* 9. 4). *o* is emotional.

Sesti: L. Sestius, son of P. Sestius, tribune in 57 B.C.; we first meet him as a *praetextatus* appearing for pathetic effect at his father's trial in 56 (Cic. *Sest.* 144 'video hunc praetextatum eius filium oculis lacrimantibus me intuentem'). He joined the liberators in 44, served as Brutus's proquaestor in Macedonia, was proscribed and finally pardoned; he maintained an intransigent regard for the memory of Brutus, which, we are told, earned the respect of Augustus (App. *civ.* 4. 51. 223). When, in the middle of 23 B.C., Augustus resigned his consulship, he appointed Sestius as suffect because of his republican sentiments (cf. Dio 53. 32. 4, p. xxxvi).

The long postponement of the vocative is unusual; yet cf. 1. 7. 19, 2. 1. 14, 2. 12. 11. Here the delay need cause no surprise, as the poem is in no way about Sestius.

15. summa brevis: the tone is dry; cf. 4. 7. 17 f. 'quis scit an adiciant hodiernae crastina summae / tempora di superi?' For commonplaces on *vita brevis* cf. Otto 375. Yet here the adjective does not go with *vita* but with *summa*; cf. Ov. *trist.* 5. 7. 7 'sum miser: haec brevis est nostrorum summa malorum'.

incohare: 'to begin what will not be completed'. Horace's expression rightly impressed Seneca: cf. *epist.* 101. 4 'quam stultum est aetatem disponere ne crastini quidem dominum! o quanta dementia est spes longas inchoantium!', 13. 16.

longam: 'distant' in the sense that it takes a long time to fulfil; cf. 1. 11. 7, Tac. *ann.* 13. 37. 6 'spe longinqua et sera', *trag. adesp.* 127. 9 f. μακρὰς ἀφαιρούμενος ἐλπίδας / θνατῶν πολύμοχθος Ἅιδας, Macedonius, *anth. P.* 10. 70. 4 δολιχαῖς δ' ἐλπίσι παιζόμενος (in a context on mortality).

16. iam: with the future, 'soon'. In a warning context, as here, it suggests 'all too soon', in a reassuring one 'quite soon' (2. 5. 10).

premet: the verb goes most closely with *nox*; cf. Virg. *Aen.* 6. 827 'nocte premuntur', Ov. *epist.* 10. 112 (so also of the darkness of oblivion *carm.* 4. 9. 26 ff. 'omnes illacrimabiles / urgentur ignotique longa / nocte'). Yet it is not inappropriate with *manes*; the *di inferi* were oppressive. For the use of *premet* with *domus* cf. Pind. fr. 207 Ταρτάρου πυθμὴν πιέζει σ' ἀφανὴς / σφυρηλάτοις ἀνάγκαις.

nox: for night as an image of death cf. Hom. *Il.* 5. 659 τὸν δὲ κατ' ὀφθαλμῶν ἐρεβεννὴ νὺξ ἐκάλυψεν, 13. 425, 580, 14. 439, 22. 466, *Od.* 20. 351, Asclepiades, *anth. P.* 12. 50. 8 (on 18 below), Peek, *GV* 1765. 1 (= Kaibel, *EG* 312. 1) νὺξ μὲν ἐμὸν κατέχει ζωῆς φάος ὑπνοδοτείρη. Latin examples are very numerous. Cf. the use of *lux* and φάος for life (Lattimore 161 ff.).

fabulaeque manes: it is generally assumed that *fabulae* is nominative in apposition to *manes* and adjectival in sense; cf. *carm. epig.* 1504. 10 'fabulas Manes ubi rex coercet'. Yet apart from this evident imitation it is difficult to find a completely satisfactory parallel. In Greek ὄλεθρος is sometimes found in apposition (Ar. *Lys.* 325, Dem. 18. 127); but this colloquialism seems a special case. In Latin invective we find 'Phalarim grammaticum' (Cic. *Pis.* 73) and 'mulio consul' (Juv. 8. 148); but these have an epigrammatic point that is lacking in *fabulae manes*. The adjectival use of *anus* in high poetry (Catull. 68. 46, 78. 10) is probably based on that of γέρων. See further Wackernagel, *Vorlesungen* 2. 53 ff., who includes our passage as an instance of 'Adjektivierung'.

Editors in general are reluctant to consider the possibility that *fabulae* is genitive ('the shades of story'); yet Bentley thought it might well be so. For the collective use of *fabula* he cited the obvious

imitation by Prudentius, c. *Symm.* 1. 191 f. 'quos fabula Manes /
nobilitat'. For other possible instances of *fabula* in a collective sense
cf. *Thes.l.L.* 6. 1. 27. 43 ff.; unfortunately none of these is as decisive
as might be wished. However, if it is granted that *fabula* may be
collective, the genitive can be regarded with more tolerance, though
it is admittedly no better paralleled than the strange nominative.

In any case, whether nominative or genitive, *fabulae* probably
suggests only that in the underworld one will be oppressed by the
shades famed in legend. Some editors cite Persius's phrase 'cinis et
manes et fabula fies' (5. 152); but though Persius was certainly
influenced by Horace's expression, he seems to be making a different
point, that the dead survive only as a subject of conversation on the
lips of men. Still less should one compare passages that imply that
the shades are only an old wives' tale (cf. Call. *ep.* 13. 3 f. *Ὦ Χαρίδα,
τί τὰ νέρθε; Πολὺ σκότος. Αἱ δ' ἄνοδοι τί; / Ψεῦδος. Ὁ δὲ Πλούτων;
Μῦθος. Ἀπωλόμεθα,* Sen. *Tro.* 405 f. 'rumores vacui verbaque inania / et
par sollicito fabula somnio', *dial.* 6. 19. 4). Horace cannot lament the
horrors of the underworld and in the same breath deny their reality.

manes: the *manes* were the collective spirits of the dead; by the
time of this poem one also finds references to the *manes* of an individual (*ILS* 880). But they were also beings who held the right of life
and death, and who had to be appeased; cf. Virg. *georg.* 4. 489
'scirent si ignoscere manes', *carm. epig.* 542. 1 'manes si saperent,
miseram me abducerent coniugem', 1034. 3 'me potius manes rapuis-
sent', Lattimore 93 ff. Horace's *manes* seem to carry this kind of
association; they are not just companions in misfortune, in which
case *premet* would suggest nothing worse than overcrowding, but the
unsympathetic and oppressive *di inferi*.

17. domus exilis Plutonia: the *domus Plutonia* is the δῶμ' Ἀίδαο.
exilis means 'meagre'; cf. *epist.* 1. 6. 45 'exilis domus est ubi non . . .
multa supersunt'. The house of Pluto is not well equipped, and its
inhabitants lead the opposite of a full life. *exilis* might also hint at the
ghostly, insubstantial character of the underworld (cf. ἀμένηνα
κάρηνα). It cannot mean 'narrow' in the literal sense; *exilis* is not the
same as *angustus*.

The adjective *Plutonia* is more grandiose than the genitive
Plutonis; cf. Löfstedt, *Syntactica* 1². 107 ff., K.–G. 1. 261 ff., Austin
on Virg. *Aen.* 2. 543. For the qualification of a noun by two adjectives when one is a proper name cf. *epist.* 2. 1. 157 f. 'horridus . . .
numerus Saturnius', Virg. *Aen.* 10. 408 f. 'horrida . . . acies Volcania'.

mearis: *meare* is archaic, and much used by Lucretius. Here it
keeps up the grandiose epic note; cf. 4. 7. 14 f. 'nos ubi decidimus, /
quo pater Aeneas, quo dives Tullus et Ancus'.

4. SOLVITVR ACRIS HIEMS 71

18. nec . . .: with another sudden turn Horace moves from the shadowy after-life to the warmth and sensuality of the symposium. For similar themes in Greek cf. Alcaeus 38 (to Melanippus), Theogn. 973 ff. οὐδεὶς ἀνθρώπων, ὃν πρῶτ' ἐπὶ γαῖα καλύψῃ / εἶς τ' Ἔρεβος καταβῇ, δώματα Περσεφόνης, / τέρπεται οὔτε λύρης οὔτ' αὐλητῆρος ἀκούων / οὔτε Διωνύσου δῶρ' ἐσαειράμενος, 1007 ff., Asclepiades, *anth. P.* 5.85 φείδῃ παρθενίης· καὶ τί πλέον; οὐ γὰρ ἐς Ἄιδην / ἐλθοῦσ' εὑρήσεις τὸν φιλέοντα, κόρη. / ἐν ζῴοισι τὰ τερπνὰ τὰ Κύπριδος· ἐν δ' Ἀχέροντι / ὀστέα καὶ σποδιή, παρθένε, κεισόμεθα, 12. 50. 7 f. πίνωμεν, δυσέρως· μετά τοι χρόνον οὐκέτι πουλύν, / σχέτλιε, τὴν μακρὰν νύκτ' ἀναπαυσόμεθα, anon. *PMG* 1009 ἔπειτα κείσεται βαθυδένδρῳ / ἐν χθονὶ συμποσίων τε καὶ λυρᾶν ἄμοιρος / ἰαχᾶς τε παντέρπεος αὐλῶν, Strato, *anth. P.* 11. 19 καὶ πίε νῦν καὶ ἔρα, Δαμόκρατες· οὐ γὰρ ἐς αἰεὶ / πίομεθ', οὐδ' αἰεὶ παισὶ συνεσσόμεθα.

regna vini: the presidency of the feast, here decided by the fall of dice; cf. 2. 7. 25 f., Plaut. *asin.* 904. The president might also be elected (Xen. *an.* 6. 1. 30), appointed (Plaut. *Stich.* 702), or, outrageously, self-appointed (Pl. *symp.* 213 e). Plut. *quaest. conv.* 620 a gives an interesting account of the duties of the συμποσίαρχος. Cf. also Lucian, *sat.* 4.

talis: 'knuckle-bones', ἀστράγαλοι, dice with four sides and two rounded ends, as distinct from *tesserae*, κύβοι, with six sides (Gow–Page 2. 60). The best throw was the *iactus Venerius*, when all four dice showed a different number (Lucian, *am.* 16); the worst was 'the dog', κυνωπός, when all four dice showed the number one (Poll. 9. 99). Real knucklebones might be used, though *tali* were often artificial; many bronze ones have been found, and ivory ones are mentioned by Prop. 2. 24. 13, golden by Justin 38. 9. 9. The game is still played in South Italy; for illustrations cf. G. Rohlfs, *Antikes Knöchelspiel im einstigen Großgriechenland*, Tübingen, 1963.

19. Lycidan: for the name cf. Bion fr. 9. 10, Virg. *ecl.* 7. 67. The homosexual implication has no bearing on Sestius's actual behaviour, but is a conventional motif derived from Greek erotic poetry. Even Q. Catulus, *cos.* 102 B.C. and conqueror of the Cimbri, implausibly claimed (imitating Callimachus) that his soul had taken refuge with Theotimus (fr. 1 Morel). For further discussion see G. Williams, *JRS* 52, 1962, 39 ff. Yet literary convention would not be enough to explain Horace's language here if the Romans had condemned homosexuality as firmly as some other societies. In fact the practice was widespread (Cic. *Cael.* 6–9, *RE* 11. 905 f.), and at least where slave boys were concerned seems to have provoked little censure; note the grounds of Horace's disapproval in *epist.* 1. 18. 74 ff. and see the odd boast of C. Gracchus, *or.* fr. 27 'biennium fui in provincia;

I

si ulla meretrix domum meam introivit aut cuiusquam servulus propter me sollicitatus est, omnium nationum postremissimum nequissimumque existimatote. cum a servis eorum tam caste me habuerim, inde poteritis considerare quomodo me putetis cum liberis vestris vixisse'.

quo calet . . .: cf. Pind. *P.* 10. 58 f. θαητὸν ἐν ἅλιξι θησέμεν ἐν καὶ παλαιτέροις / νέαισί τε παρθένοισι μέλημα, Theogn. 1319 f. ὦ παῖ, / . . . σὸν δ᾿ εἶδος πᾶσι νέοισι μέλει, Chariton 1. 1. 10 ἐφίλει γὰρ αὐτὸν ἡ νεολαία. For the causal ablative cf. Prop. 2. 3. 33 'hac ego nunc mirer si flagret nostra iuventus?', H.–Sz. 133.

20. tepebunt: less strong than *calet*; cf. Stat. *silv.* 1. 2. 139 f. (on the remarriage of the widow Violentilla) 'ipsam iam cedere sensi / inque vicem tepuisse viro'.

5. QVIS MVLTA GRACILIS

[R. Storrs, *Ad Pyrrham*, 1959; T. Zielinski, *Philologus* 60, 1901, 2.]

1–5. What slim boy presses you, Pyrrha, on a bed of roses? 5–12. Though he now believes you trustworthy, he will be astonished at the coming squall. 12–16. I have survived shipwreck and as the dedicatory tablet shows have hung up my wet clothes to Venus.

The farewell to love was an overworked topic of Greek erotic poetry. The theme is already to be found in Mimnermus, and it was developed sentimentally or realistically in the *Anacreontea* and the Anthology. Sometimes a successful rival is introduced as the object of the poet's jealousy; cf. Meleager, *anth. P.* 5. 160. 1 f. Δημὼ λευκοπάρειε, σὲ μέν τις ἔχων ὑπόχρωτα / τέρπεται, ἁ δ᾿ ἐν ἐμοὶ νῦν στενάχει κραδία, below, 1. 33. 3 n. But occasionally even the epigrammatists show a more philosophic attitude; thus Philodemus, *anth. P.* 5. 112. 5 f. καὶ παίζειν ὅτε καιρός, ἐπαίξαμεν· ἡνίκα καιρὸς / οὐκέτι, λωιτέρης φροντίδος ἁψόμεθα. This urbane outlook is particularly characteristic of Horace (so also 3. 10, 3. 14, 3. 26).

There are also other traditional elements in the poem, though here again Horace handles the commonplaces in a fresh way. Women had been compared to the sea since at least Semonides of Amorgos (7. 37 ff.): ὥσπερ θάλασσα πολλάκις μὲν ἀτρεμὴς / ἕστηκ᾿ ἀπήμων χάρμα ναύτῃσιν μέγα / θέρεος ἐν ὥρῃ, πολλάκις δὲ μαίνεται / βαρυκτύποισι κύμασιν φορευμένη. Many Greek epigrammatists had played with the double function of Aphrodite, who was a goddess of the sea as well as of love (16 n.). The ode also has some affinities with the dedicatory epigram, which was often written for purely epideictic purposes (cf. Book VI of the Palatine Anthology). One may note in particular a poem by Leonidas of Tarentum, which professes to be written under a picture recording an escape from a lion (*anth. P.* 6. 221. 9 f.). The retirement from love was also a theme of Greek dedicatory epigram; for an instance referring to a woman cf. Pl. *anth. P.* 6. 1 (Lais hangs up her mirror), and there were presumably other similar poems applied to men. These have left traces alike on our poem, on 3. 26 (Horace hangs up the tools of his trade), perhaps also on Prop. 3. 24. 19 f. (Propertius on breaking with Cynthia dedicates himself to Mens Bona).

Yet the literary character of our poem often seems to be misunderstood. Classical scholars are inveterate sentimentalists, and Pyrrha encourages them to colourful scene-painting or romantic biography. Thus Mackail: 'The *antrum* is an arbour or grotto . . . over which, in an Italian spring, the roses (real roses, not ramblers) spurt and foam . . . Such was the picture flashed for half a minute on Horace's eye as he passed it, perhaps in Maecenas' gardens on the Esquiline' (*CR* 35, 1921, 5). But there was surely a scarcity of agreeable grots in Roman public parks. The bed of roses is a stage property of the Greek novel (1 n.), where the time and the place and the loved one regularly come together. And Pyrrha herself is the wayward beauty of fiction, totally unlike the compliant *scorta* of Horace's own temporary affairs. Of course it is true that the poem suits Horace's character or at any rate his *persona*, as it would not suit Catullus or Propertius. But to extract from the ode facts about his way of life is simply to ignore the literary and social customs of antiquity.

The manner of the poem is perfectly attuned to its matter. The structure is flawless; one may note in particular the word-order of the first line and last stanza, and the way that the pattern of the sentences cuts across the pattern of the metre. The diction is prosaic (*munditiis, amabilis, vestimenta*), but precise and economical. The sheer ingenuity of the poem is remarkable; the metaphor that began with *aequora, aurae, intemptata nites* reaches a triumphant conclusion in the last stanza and the last word (16 n.). The Pyrrha ode is not sentimental, heart-felt, or particularly pretty. It may be admired for rarer virtues, which have eluded the myriad translators, wit, urbanity, and astringent charm.

Metre: Third Asclepiad.

1. **gracilis:** the word refers objectively to the slight figure of an adolescent boy. In some contexts it is clearly abusive; cf. *serm.* 1. 5.

69 'gracili sic tamque pusillo'. On the other hand there need be no derogatory implication; Ovid says of himself 'graciles, non sunt sine viribus artus' (*am.* 2. 10. 23). In girls *gracilitas* was much admired; cf. Ov. *ars* 2. 660 (on the need to make the best of the loved one's deficiencies) 'sit gracilis, macie quae male viva suast', Ter. *eun.* 313 ff. 'haud simili' virgost virginum nostrarum quas matres student / demissis umeris esse, vincto pectore ut gracilae sient; / siquaest habitior paullo pugilem esse aiunt, deducunt cibum: / . . . itaque ergo amantur', Lucil. 296.

rosa: for the collective singular cf. Cic. *Tusc.* 3. 43 'sertis redimiri iubebis et rosa?', K.–S. 1. 68, 70. But here Pyrrha and her friend are not wearing garlands (as some imagine), but lying on the petals (as *multa* shows). The bed of roses comes from Greek erotic writings; cf. [Lucian], *asin.* 7 τῶν δὲ στρωμάτων ῥόδα πολλὰ κατεπέπαστο, τὰ μὲν οὕτω γυμνὰ καθ᾽ ἑαυτά, τὰ δὲ λελυμένα, τὰ δὲ στεφάνοις συμπεπλεγμένα, Philostr. *epist.* 20(32), 54(28) εἰ κἀμὲ φεύγεις, ἀλλ᾽ ὑπόδεξαι κἂν τὰ ῥόδα ἀντ᾽ ἐμοῦ. καί σου δέομαι μὴ στεφανοῦσθαι μόνον ἀλλὰ καὶ κοιμηθῆναι ἐπ᾽ αὐτῶν. To lie on roses was the height of hedonism; cf. Ael. *var. hist.* 9. 24 (on Smindyrides of Sybaris) φύλλοις ῥόδων γοῦν ἐπαναπεσὼν καὶ κοιμηθεὶς ἐπ᾽ αὐτῶν ἐξανέστη λέγων φλυκταίνας ἐκ τῆς εὐνῆς ἔχειν, Cic. *fin.* 2. 65 '(Regulum) beatiorem fuisse quam potantem in rosa Thorium', *Tusc.* 5. 73, *eleg. in Maecen.* 1. 93 f. 'sic est: victor amet, victor potiatur in umbra, / victor odorata dormiat inque rosa', Sen. *epist.* 36. 9.

2. perfusus: the prefix marks the thoroughness of the treatment. In ancient as in modern Italy young men in love paid inordinate attention to their hair. Cf. Prop. 2. 4. 5 'nequiquam perfusa meis unguenta capillis', Ov. *ars* 3. 443, Aristaenetus 1. 27 ἔοικέ μοι καὶ περὶ καλὴν ἀσχολεῖσθαι τὴν κόμην· ἐπεὶ καὶ τοῦτό γε τοῦ ἔρωτος ἴδιον καὶ μάλα μέντοι καλόν, τὸ σφόδρα πείθειν τοὺς ἐρῶντας ἐπιμελῶς ἄγαν διακοσμεῖσθαι.

urget: 'presses', tactfully inexplicit, but the lovers are not merely talking. Cf. Prop. 4. 3. 12 'cum rudis urgenti bracchia victa dedi'; more crudely Pompon. *Atell.* 99 'nescioquis molam quasi asinus urget uxorem tuam'.

3. Pyrrha: the Greek name is found alike in legend and in inscriptions (*RE* 24. 77 ff., Pape–Benseler 1290). It was probably favoured by hetaerae, and is the title of a play by Diphilus. It also appears in the Greek Anthology: when Pyrrha passed by, the studious poet exclaimed ἔργα τί μοι παρέχεις, ὦ γέρον Ἡσίοδε; (Marc. Argent. 9. 161).

The name suggests a girl with reddish-yellow or auburn hair; cf. Paul. Fest. 28 L. (= 31M.) 'burrum dicebant antiqui quod nunc dicimus rufum; unde rustici burram appellant buculam quae rostrum habet rufum', below, 4 n. Such colours, being unusual among Mediterranean peoples, were much admired; cf. Pease on Virg. *Aen.* 4. 590, 698, André 326 f. The deficiencies of nature were sometimes made good by art, or even by purchase; cf. Cato, *orig.* 114 'mulieres nostrae capillum cinere unguitabant ut rutilus esset', Ov. *am.* 1. 14. 45 'nunc tibi captivos mittet Germania crines', Lucian, *am.* 40, Tert. *cult. fem.* 2. 6. 1 with Oehler's note, Blümner 276.

antro: caves are commoner in Italy than in England, yet the scene belongs to pastoral (Theoc. 3. 6, Virg. *ecl.* 9. 41 f.) or novelette rather than to real life. Orelli's note has more relevance to nineteenth-century than to Augustan social history: 'sic solent etiamnunc Itali beatiores, praecipue ad lacum Larium, in antris vel a natura cavatis vel arte factis vini apothecas habere in iisque potare atque amoribus frui'.

4. cui: 'to please whom?' Cf. *epod.* 12. 22, Theoc. 14. 38, [Tib.] 3. 12. 3, Ov. *epist.* 15. 77, Paul. Sil. *anth. P.* 5. 228. 1 f. (below, 1. 6. 18 n.). The dative seems to be parodied by Ar. *Thesm.* 401 ff. κᾶν ἐκβάλῃ / σκεῦός τι κατὰ τὴν οἰκίαν πλανωμένη, / ἀνὴρ ἐρωτᾷ "τῷ κατέαγεν ἡ χύτρα; / οὐκ ἔσθ' ὅπως οὐ τῷ Κορινθίῳ ξένῳ."

flavam: the colour of honey (Lucr. 1. 938), ripe corn (Virg. *ecl.* 4. 28), gold (*Aen.* 1. 592), and sand (*Aen.* 7. 31). Here the word is meant to suggest Pyrrha's own name. According to Hyginus, Achilles at Scyros was called Pyrrha 'quoniam capillis flavis fuit et Graece rufum πυρρόν dicitur' (*fab.* 96. 1). Cf. also Luc. 10. 129 ff. 'pars tam flavos gerit altera crines / ut nullis Caesar Rheni se dicat in arvis / tam rutilas vidisse comas', Philostr. *epist.* 21(38) οὖσά τις ξανθὴ ῥόδα ζητεῖς . . . τί δὲ τὴν κεφαλὴν στεφανοῖς πυρί;, Gow on Theoc. 8. 3.

religas: in simple style; cf. 2. 11. 24, Ov. *ars* 3. 143.

5. simplex munditiis: *simplex* shows the simplicity of Pyrrha's 'toilette'; cf. Prop. 4. 8. 40 (of a castanet-girl) 'munda sine arte'. At the same time it suggests the opposite of *duplex animi*. One foolishly expects that Pyrrha's innocent appearance will be matched by her behaviour.

mundus means 'clean' and hence 'spick-and-span', 'tasteful'. But it suggests simplicity as well as taste; that is to say, *munditiis* does not make an oxymoron with *simplex* but points in the same direction. Cf. 3. 29. 14, Cic. *off.* 1. 130 'adhibenda praeterea munditia est non odiosa neque exquisita nimis', Ulp. *dig.* 34. 2. 25. 10 'sicut et mulier potest esse munda, non tamen ornata'.

munditia is in fact often used of feminine grooming. Cf. Plaut. *Poen.* 191 f. 'oculos volo / meos delectare munditiis meretriciis', *Pseud.* 173 f. 'vos quae in munditiis mollitiis deliciisque aetatulam agitis / viris cum summis, inclutae amicae', Lucr. 4. 1280 ff. (an ugly woman can win love without divine intervention) 'nam facit ipsa suis interdum femina factis / morigerisque modis et munde corpore culto / ut facile insuescat te secum degere vitam', Ov. *ars* 3. 133 f. 'munditiis capimur: non sint sine lege capilli; / admotae formam dantque negantque manus'.

In the present context an adequate English translation seems impossible. 'Daintiness' suggests a doll-like fragility. 'Chic' and 'elegance' are too sophisticated; in ancient as in modern Rome *munditiæ* could be achieved on limited resources. 'Neatness' does not give the right impression of spotless taste (and Milton's 'plain in thy neatness' is much too puritanical). None of these words suggests so clearly as *munditiis* that Pyrrha's appearance is due to careful, though unobtrusive, grooming.

fidem: it seems best to understand *mutatam*; cf. Plaut. *mil.* 983 f. 'sed ne istanc amittam et haec mutet fidem / vide modo' (the soldier may let one girl go and find the other disloyal). In lovers' language *fides* is the fidelity of either partner or the relationship of trust between them (cf. 1. 33. 4, 3. 7. 4). For the word-order cf. 3. 5. 7 'pro curia inversique mores', *serm.* 1. 3. 129 f. 'ut quamvis tacet Hermogenes cantor tamen atque / optimus est modulator'.

Others, less plausibly, take *fides* alone and interpret as *perfidia*. Cf. 1. 18. 16 'arcanique Fides prodiga' (but that is an oxymoron), Cic. *Sex. Rosc.* 119 'fidem magistri cognostis', Liv. 6. 27. 3, *Thes.l.L.* 6. 1. 676. 38 ff.

6. deos: cf. Prop. 1. 1. 8 'cum tamen adversos cogor habere deos'.

7. nigris . . . ventis: cf. *epod.* 10. 5 'niger . . . Eurus', Hom. *Il.* 12. 375 ἐρεμνῇ λαίλαπι, Catull. 68. 63, Virg. *georg.* 3. 278, André 54. *nigris* in our passage, when juxtaposed with *aequora*, suggests that the clouds darken the sea. For similar scene-painting cf. Hom. *Il.* 7. 63 f. οἵη δὲ Ζεφύροιο ἐχεύατο πόντον ἔπι φρὶξ / ὀρνυμένοιο νέον, μελάνει δέ τε πόντος ὑπ' αὐτῆς, Virg. *Aen.* 3. 285 'et glacialis hiems aquilonibus asperat undas', Tennyson, *Lady of Shalott* 11 f. 'Little breezes dusk and shiver Through the wave that runs for ever'.

8. emirabitur: the word may well be a coinage of Horace's (cf. ἀποθαυμάζειν, ἐκθαυμάζειν); it is only used occasionally thereafter. Long prosaic compounds help to build the monumental masonry of a Horatian line (cf. 1. 9. 11 *deproeliantes*, 2. 7. 24 *deproperare*, 2. 14. 11 *enaviganda*, 3. 5. 54 *diiudicata*, 3. 17. 3 *denominatos*).

Bentley objected that *quotiens* is inconsistent with *insolens*; he therefore suggested *ut mirabitur*, so that *quotiens* should apply only to *flebit*. But the pause after *flebit* is unusual; moreover, it is unlikely that Horace would refer in the first clause to the boy's *many* disappointments, and in the second to his surprise at the *earliest* of these disappointments. One might try to circumvent Bentley's difficulty by saying that the boy is disappointed many times, and never gets used to his unkind treatment; but such a subjective use of *insolens* does not seem natural. It is better to argue that *insolens* refers to the present time ('unaccustomed as he now is'), and not to the future time of the boy's surprise; cf. 1. 8. 4 n., *epod.* 7. 7 f.

insolens: contrast Prop. 1. 4. 4 'assueto . . . servitio', 1. 18. 25 f. 'omnia consuevi timidus perferre superbae / iussa', 2. 3. 47 ff.

9. credulus: cf. Prop. 2. 25. 21 f. 'tu quoque qui pleno fastus adsumis amore, / credule, nulla diu femina pondus habet', Ov. *epist.* 6. 21, Sen. *Phaedr.* 634.

aurea: a lover's word, here perhaps particularly appropriate because of Pyrrha's golden hair. Cf. Hom. *Il.* 3. 64 χρυσέης Ἀφροδίτης, Ar. *Ach.* 1200 φιλήσατόν με μαλθακῶς ὦ χρυσίω (cf. *vesp.* 1341, *Lys.* 930), Philodemus, *anth. P.* 5. 123. 3 αὔγαζε χρυσέην Καλλίστιον, anon. ibid. 5. 201. 2, Plaut. *asin.* 691, Prop. 4. 7. 85 'hic Tiburtina iacet aurea Cynthia terra', Ov. *am.* 1. 2. 42, 2. 18. 36, *rem.* 39, *priap.* 83. 40, Aristaenetus 1. 1 χρυσοῦς Ἔρως, André 156.

10. vacuam: 'untenanted', 'disengaged'; cf. Ov. *epist.* 20. 149 'elige de vacuis quam non sibi vindicet alter', Quint. *decl.* 376 p. 417 'vacuis indicere nuptias, non occupatis', Tac. *ann.* 11. 12. 2 'nam in C. Silium . . . ita exarserat ut Iuniam Silanam . . . matrimonio eius exturbaret vacuoque adultero poteretur'. The word has almost a legal sense (which *fruitur* also bears): Pyrrha is now *sine possessore*, but the young man has no more than the temporary *usus fructus*.

11. aurae fallacis: cf. Prop. 2. 12. 8 'nostraque non ullis permanet aura locis' (with Shackleton Bailey's note), 2. 25. 27 'mendaces ludunt flatus in amore secundi', Ov. *am.* 2. 9. 33 'incerta Cupidinis aura'. *aurae* seems to be in tension with 13 *aurea*; cf. Virg. *Aen.* 6. 204 'auri . . . aura'.

12. miseri: the omission of the copula is common in such sententious exclamations; cf. Pl. (?) ap. Diog. Laert. 3. 31 ἆ δειλοὶ νεότητος ἀπαντήσαντες ἐκείνης / πρωτοπλόου (of a courtesan), Tib. 2. 1. 79 'a miseri quos hic graviter deus urget', below, 1. 13. 17 n.

13. intemptata: ἀπείρατος; the word suits both the girl and the sea. Cf. 3. 4. 30 f., Virg. *ecl.* 4. 32 'temptare Thetin ratibus', Sen. *suas.* 1. 2 'humanae intemptatum experientiae pelagus', Lucian, *Tox.* 3 τὸν Πόντον ἀπείρατον ἔτι τοῖς Ἕλλησιν ὄντα, Ambr. *hex.* 3. 3. 15.

nites: the word suits a beautiful girl; cf. 1. 19. 5 'Glycerae nitor', Hom. *Il.* 3. 392 κάλλεΐ τε στίλβων. Yet it also suggests the treacherous

glitter of a shining sea; cf. Lucr. 5. 1004 f. 'nec poterat quemquam
placidi pellacia ponti / subdola pellicere in fraudem ridentibus undis', Plut. *Caes.* 4. 4 ὥσπερ θαλάττης τὰ διαγελῶντα (of Caesar's attractive but treacherous policy). For the use of the image in erotic
contexts cf. Meleager, *anth. P.* 5. 156 ἁ φίλερως χαροποῖς Ἀσκληπιὰς
οἷα γαλήνης / ὄμμασι συμπείθει πάντας ἐρωτοπλοεῖν, anon. ibid. 12. 156.
3 f. καὶ ποτὲ μὲν φαίνεις πολὺν ὑετόν, ἄλλοτε δ' αὖτε / εὔδιος, ἁβρὰ γελῶν
δ' ὄμμασιν ἐκκέχυσαι, Alciphron 1. 11. 2 (= 3. 1. 2) καὶ μειδιᾷ τῆς
θαλάττης γαληνιώσης χαριέστερον . . .

me: emphatic and self-satisfied; Horace is not *miser* but *ter felix*.

tabula: it was a common practice to commemorate an escape from
danger by affixing a tablet to a temple wall. In an illiterate age the
plaque often told its story by means of a picture. Cf. Porph. ad loc.
'videmus autem hodieque pingere in tabulis quosdam casus quos in
mari passi sint, atque in fanis marinorum deorum ponere', *serm.* 2. 1.
32 ff. 'quo fit ut omnis / votiva pateat veluti descripta tabella / vita
senis', Tib. 1. 3. 27 f., Juv. 12. 27 f. 'et quam votiva testantur fana
tabella / plurima: pictores quis nescit ab Iside pasci?', Headlam on
Herodas 4. 19, Pease on Cic. *nat. deor.* 3. 89, Bömer on Ov. *fast.* 3. 268,
Spenser, *F.Q.* 3. 4. 10 'Then when I shall my selfe in safety see,
A table for eternall moniment Of thy great grace, and my great
ieopardee, Great *Neptune*, I avow to hallow unto thee'. When the
number of such tablets was cited as a proof of the care of the gods for
men, Diagoras the atheist was not at a loss for an answer: ' "ita
fit", inquit, "illi enim nusquam picti sunt qui naufragia fecerunt in
marique perierunt" ' (Cic. *nat. deor.*, loc. cit.).

Such tablets are still produced in Catholic countries. Those celebrating escape from fatal accident vividly document the transition
from horse to motor transport. They have become regrettably rarer
with the increase of manufactured silver hearts. Yet in Bavaria one
can see home-made pictures portraying the return of a soldier from
Russian captivity. See further Samuel Butler, *Ex Voto*, chapter 11.

14. uvida . . . vestimenta: rescued sailors sometimes dedicated their
clothes *ex voto* to the gods. Cf. Virg. *Aen.* 12. 768 f. 'servati ex undis
ubi figere dona solebant / Laurenti divo (i.e. Fauno) et votas suspen-
dere vestes', Diodorus, *anth. P.* 6. 245. 3 ff. εὔξατο κῆρα φυγών,
Βοιώτιε, σοί με, Κάβειρε / δέσποτα, χειμερίης ἄνθεμα ναυτιλίης, / ἀρτήσειν
ἁγίοις τόδε λώπιον ἐν προπυλαίοις. Porphyrio in our passage speaks as
if the custom were current in his day: 'sunt etiam qui vestem quoque
ibi suspendant dis eam consecrantes'.

15. potenti: to be taken with *maris* ('that has power over the sea');
cf. 1. 3. 1 n. As a piece of Latin *maris . . . deae* could mean 'the goddess
of the sea'; cf. Ov. *met.* 2. 531 'di maris adnuerant', *epist.* 19. 145

'deo pelagi', Milton's translation of our ode, 'the stern god of sea'. But the more intricate word-order binds the sentence with a subtlety more characteristic of our poem.

16. deae: the manuscripts and Porphyrio and a quotation by Eutyches all read *deo*; yet Neptune has nothing to do with the metaphorical sea of love. *deae* is an emendation by Zielinski, loc. cit. It refers, of course, to Venus, who was born from the foam; cf. 3. 26. 4 ff. (also describing a dedication) 'barbiton hic paries habebit / laevum marinae qui Veneris latus / custodit', Pease on Cic. *nat. deor.* 3. 59, Bömer on Ov. *fast.* 4. 131.

The double function of Aphrodite provided a subject for the wit of Greek epigrammatists. See anon. *anth. P.* 5. 11 εἰ τοὺς ἐν πελάγει σώζεις, Κύπρι, κἀμὲ τὸν ἐν γᾷ / ναυαγόν, φιλίη, σῶσον ἀπολλύμενον, Gaetulicus, ibid. 5. 17. 3 ff. αὔριον Ἰονίου γὰρ ἐπὶ πλατὺ κῦμα περήσω, / σπεύδων ἡμετέρης κόλπον ἐς Εἰδοθέης. / οὔριος ἀλλ' ἐπίλαμψον ἐμῷ καὶ ἔρωτι καὶ ἱστῷ, / δέσποτι καὶ θαλάμων, Κύπρι, καὶ ἠιόνων, Antip. (Thess.?) ibid. 9. 143 λιτός τοι δόμος οὗτος, ἐπεὶ παρὰ κύματι πηγῷ / ἵδρυμαι νοτερῆς δεσπότις ἠιόνος, / ἀλλὰ φίλος· πόντῳ γὰρ ἐπὶ πλατὺ δειμαίνοντι / χαίρω, καὶ ναύταις εἰς ἐμὲ σωζομένοις· / ἱλάσκευ τὴν Κύπριν· ἐγὼ δέ σοι ἢ ἐν ἔρωτι / οὔριος, ἢ χαροπῷ πνεύσομαι ἐν πελάγει, Philodemus, ibid. 10. 21. 5 ff. Κύπρι, τὸν ἡσύχιόν με, τὸν οὐδένι κοῦφα λαλεῦντα, / τὸν σέο πορφυρέῳ κλυζόμενον πελάγει, / Κύπρι φιλορμίστειρα, φιλόργιε, σῶζέ με, Κύπρι, / Ναιακοὺς ἤδη, δεσπότι, πρὸς λιμένας. For other references to the sea of love cf. Meleager, *anth. P.* 5. 190, 12. 157, 12. 167, Macedonius, ibid. 5. 235, Alciphron 1. 21 (= 18). 3, Fulg. *myth.* 40 'hanc (Venerem) etiam in mari natantem pingunt, quod omnis libido rerum patiatur naufragia, unde et Porfyrius in epigrammate ait "nudus egens Veneris naufragus in pelago"', Pasquali 499 f., Enk on Prop. 2. 14. 29.

It is argued against *deae* that Venus did not rule the waves, whereas Neptune did (cf. Pind. *O.* 6. 103 ποντόμεδον, Plaut. *trin.* 820 *salsipotenti*). Yet cf. Musaeus 249 f. ἀγνώσσεις ὅτι Κύπρις ἀπόσπορός ἐστι θαλάσσης; / καὶ κρατέει πόντοιο καὶ ἡμετέρων ὀδυνάων, Ov. *epist.* 16. 23 ff. (on Venus) 'illa dedit faciles auras ventosque secundos: / in mare nimirum ius habet orta mari. / perstet [*praestat*? cf. 15. 213, *met.* 11. 748] et ut pelagi, sic pectoris adiuvet aestum, / deferat in portus et mea vota suos'. For dedications to the maritime Venus cf. *ILS* 3179 'Veneri Pelagiae', *Inscr. Ant. Orae Septentrion. Ponti Euxini* 2. 25 Ποσιδῶνι σωσινέῳ καὶ Ἀφροδίτῃ ναυαρχίδι, Athen. 676 a–c.

It may also be argued against *deae* that a man in Horace's position should not be on good terms with the goddess of love. He is not here making the normal dedication on retirement (as in 3. 26); he seems rather to be giving a thank-offering for rescue, apparently in

fulfilment of a vow. Elsewhere when Venus saves the ἐρωτοπλοοῦντα
she brings him to the κόλπος of the beloved : here (it is argued) she is
an unfriendly deity from whom Horace has had a lucky escape. Yet
this argument also fails: it is not in itself unreasonable to make
a dedication to a dangerous power which shows mercy, and the
ironic twist to the more common motif is agreeably Horatian.

deae has been rejected by editors with the not altogether reassuring
exception of A. Y. Campbell. It was described by Housman in lectures as superficial. Clearly there is some risk in adopting it, especially
when one knows that the vast majority of readers will greatly prefer
to follow the manuscripts. Yet *deae* rounds off the ode perfectly with
a continuation of the maritime metaphor which Horace has exploited
so ingeniously. At the same time it provides a link with a common
theme in Hellenistic epigram. One would like to believe that this
stroke of wit could have occurred to Horace as well as to Zielinski.

6. SCRIBERIS VARIO

[Fraenkel 233 f.; Housman, *J. Phil.* 17, 1888, 303 ff.; W. Wimmel, *Kallimachos
in Rom, Hermes Einzelschriften*, Heft 16, 1960.]

1–12. *Varius will write of your military and naval exploits. I cannot
handle such matters, Agrippa, any more than the conventional themes
of epic and tragedy.* 13–20. *Who would be the man to recount worthily
the deeds of Diomede? I write* συμποτικά *and* ἐρωτικά, *and even there
I am not serious.*

M. Vipsanius Agrippa was born in 64 B.C., a year after Horace,
a year before Augustus. In 44 B.C. he was studying with the young
Octavius at Apollonia, and he became a foundation member of the
victorious party. He was its greatest general, and admiral (cf. 3
navibus); he took part in the war against Perusia in 40, defeated
the Aquitani in 38, Sextus Pompeius in 36 in naval battles at Mylae
and Naulochus, Antony in 31 at Actium, the Cantabrians in 19.
He was consul in 37, 28, 27, and held the *tribunicia potestas* from
18; even in the twenties he was unquestionably the second man
in Rome. His third wife was Julia, the emperor's unsatisfactory
daughter. He was an engineer of vision who built harbours (Portus
Iulius), aqueducts, roads, and the Pantheon; Horace's reference to
mortalia facta (*ars* 68) should perhaps be read in the light of his death
in 12 B.C. Agrippa's authoritative features are preserved on coins and
on the wrongly-named 'Ara Pacis'. See further M. Reinhold, *M.
Agrippa*, 1933, Syme, *Roman Revolution*, passim, *RE* 9 A. 1226 ff.

L. Varius Rufus was much more Horace's sort of person. He was praised by Virgil already in the *Eclogues* (9. 35 f. 'nam neque adhuc Vario videor nec dicere Cinna / digna, sed argutos inter strepere anser olores'); for his connection with the Epicurean set at Herculaneum see p. 279. By 35 B.C. he was Rome's leading epic poet (*serm.* 1. 10. 43 f. 'forte epos acer / ut nemo Varius ducit'). He was an early protégé of Maecenas, to whom he introduced Horace (*serm.* 1. 6. 55); he admired Horace's poetry (*serm.* 1. 10. 81), and became a valued friend (*serm.* 1. 5. 41 f.). His tragedy *Thyestes* was compared by Quintilian with the best Greek plays (10. 1. 98; cf. Tac. *dial.* 12. 6); a *didascalia* gives 29 B.C. as the date (Schanz–Hosius 2. 162 f.), and this provides a *terminus post quem* for our ode (8 n.). Varius's mysterious poem *de morte* contained a criticism of Antony ('leges fixit pretio atque refixit') which was imitated by Virgil to describe a category of the damned (*Aen.* 6. 621 f.). More relevant for our ode is the *Panegyricus Augusti* (cf. *epist.* 2. 1. 247); according to Porphyrio Horace quoted it in the *Epistles* (1. 16. 27 ff.), though the rhythm of the lines tells strongly against this view. After Virgil's death in 19 B.C. Varius and Tucca prepared the *Aeneid* for publication; and in the *Ars Poetica* Horace still mentions Varius and Virgil as the leading poets of his day (54 f.). See further *RE* 8 A. 410 ff., Housman, *CQ* 11, 1917, 42 ff., E. Bickel, *SO* 28, 1950, 17 ff., H. Bardon, *La Littérature latine inconnue* 2, 1956, 28 ff.; for the scanty fragments see W. Morel, *Fragmenta Poetarum Latinorum*, 1963, pp. 100 f.; for an ingenious but implausible identification of Varius with the Lynceus of Prop. 2. 34 cf. J.-P. Boucher, *REA* 60, 1958, 307 ff.

In this poem Horace politely declines to write about Agrippa, and recommends Varius instead. A professed inability to handle pompous themes may be quite an old literary motif; cf. *Anacreontea* 23. 1 ff. θέλω λέγειν Ἀτρείδας, / θέλω δὲ Κάδμον ᾄδειν· / ἁ βάρβιτος δὲ χορδαῖς / ἔρωτα μοῦνον ἠχεῖ. But more important for our purposes are some of the pronouncements of Callimachus, particularly in the prologue to the second edition of the *Aetia*. Here the ageing poet in his dry authoritative way declares his beliefs about literature (fr. 1. 17 ff.):

> ἔλλετε Βασκανίης ὀλοὸν γένος· αὖθι δὲ τέχνῃ
> κρίνετε, μὴ σχοίνῳ Περσίδι τὴν σοφίην·
> μηδ' ἀπ' ἐμεῦ διφᾶτε μέγα ψοφέουσαν ἀοιδὴν
> τίκτεσθαι· βροντᾶν οὐκ ἐμόν, ἀλλὰ Διός.
> καὶ γὰρ ὅτε πρώτιστον ἐμοῖς ἐπὶ δέλτον ἔθηκα
> γούνασιν, Ἀπόλλων εἶπεν ὅ μοι Λύκιος·
> . . . ἀοιδέ, τὸ μὲν θύος ὅττι πάχιστον
> θρέψαι, τὴν Μοῦσαν δ' ὠγαθὲ λεπταλέην.

In a series of memorable metaphors Callimachus rejects the main

road for the by-path, the donkey's bray for the cicada's chirp, the
trite and over-fluent for the original and highly-worked.

Callimachus's ideals were imported to Rome by Parthenius and the
neoterics (cf. Catullus 95 on Cinna's *Zmyrna*). Virgil translated and
transmuted the splendid lines from the *Aetia* (*ecl.* 6. 3 ff.):

> cum canerem reges et proelia, Cynthius aurem
> vellit et admonuit: 'pastorem, Tityre, pingues
> pascere oportet oves, deductum dicere carmen'.

But the Roman poets used the *recusatio* not simply as a manifesto in
favour of the short poem. They sometimes found it an elegant
device to brush off importunate patrons, avid for commemoration in
the grander genres. A diffident reluctance to praise might prove the
least exhausting form of flattery, and was recommended by the
preceptors of panegyric (12 n.). For further material on the *recusatio*
see Wimmel, op. cit.

Propertius was naturally fertile in Callimachean excuses (2. 1.
17 ff.):

> quod mihi si tantum, Maecenas, fata dedissent
> ut possem heroas ducere in arma manus,
> non ego Titanas canerem, non Ossan Olympo
> impositam, ut caeli Pelion esset iter . . .
> bellaque resque tui memorarem Caesaris, et tu
> Caesare sub magno cura secunda fores. . . .
> nos contra angusto versantis proelia lecto:
> qua pote quisque, in ea conterat arte diem.

In 3. 3 the venturesome poet tries to drink at the spring of Ennius,
but is deterred by Apollo; in 3. 9 he gracefully defends himself by
using as a model Maecenas's own ostentatious humility. For Ovid
the need for excuse was less real, but he still plays ingenious variations on the conventional motif (*am.* 1. 1. 1 ff.): 'arma gravi numero
violentaque bella parabam / edere, materia conveniente modis. /
par erat inferior versus; risisse Cupido / dicitur, atque unum sur-
ripuisse pedem.'

The Hellenistic convention was particularly suited to Horace's
ironic muse. Already in the *Satires*, when the jurist Trebatius advises
him to write on political themes, the poet is ready with an evasion
(2. 1. 12 ff.):

> cupidum, pater optime, vires
> deficiunt: neque enim quivis horrentia pilis
> agmina, nec fracta pereuntis cuspide Gallos
> aut labentis equo describat vulnera Parthi.

In the first collection of *Odes* Maecenas is diverted with urbane
charm (2. 12), and later the same strategy is used directly against

Augustus himself: after praising the panegyrics by Virgil and Varius Horace goes on (*epist.* 2. 1. 250 ff.):

> nec sermones ego mallem
> repentis per humum quam res componere gestas . . .
> si quantum cuperem possem quoque; sed neque parvum
> carmen maiestas recipit tua, nec meus audet
> rem temptare pudor quam vires ferre recusent.

In the fourth book of the *Odes* Horace suggests a more suitable poet, Iullus Antonius (4. 2. 33 f. 'concines maiore poeta plectro / Caesarem'). And in the last ode of all he reverts to a direct imitation of Callimachus (4. 15. 1 ff.): 'Phoebus volentem proelia me loqui / victas et urbes increpuit lyra / ne parva Tyrrhenum per aequor / vela darem . . .'.

Our poem should not be taken more seriously than Horace intended. He may have admired Agrippa as a tremendous public figure, but relations between the grim general and the aesthetic circle of Maecenas can hardly have been close. Horace is just as much concerned to flatter and to tease his old friend Varius, the swan of Maeonian song. In his affectation of humility he is simply trifling; he shows elsewhere a juster knowledge of his own worth. This elegant *jeu d'esprit* does not aspire to the heights of poetry, but it must have amused and gratified, if not Agrippa, at any rate Varius.

Metre: Second Asclepiad.

1. **scriberis:** the future indicates ironic confidence ('Varius will write'), not contemptuous indifference ('Varius can write'); cf. 1. 7. 1 n. The verb is rather prosaic and suits historical epic; cf. *epist.* 1. 3. 7 'quis sibi res gestas Augusti scribere sumit?', 1. 2. 1 'Troiani belli scriptorem', Enn. *ann.* 213 'scripsere alii rem'. For an English imitation cf. Milton, *Sonnet* 3 (to Mr. Henry Lawes) 7 f. 'To after age thou shalt be writ the man That with smooth air couldst humour best our tongue'.

Vario: ablative of agent (see below on 2 *alite*). In the *recusatio* the poet sometimes suggests an alternative panegyrist in a higher style; cf. 2. 12. 9 f. (Maecenas will write prose history), 4. 2. 33 f. (Iullus Antonius will write Pindaric odes), Virg. *ecl.* 6. 6 f. 'namque super tibi erunt qui dicere laudes, / Vare, tuas cupiant et tristia condere bella', *paneg. in Mess.* 179 f. 'est tibi qui possit magnis se accingere rebus / Valgius: aeterno propior non alter Homero', Prop. 2. 34. 61 f. 'Actia Vergilium (iuvet) custodis litora Phoebi, / Caesaris et fortes dicere posse rates', Val. Fl. 1. 12 'versam proles tua pandet Idumen' (on Vespasian and Domitian).

fortis et hostium victor: the brevity, worthy of an archaic *elogium*, suits a *vir fortis* like Agrippa; cf. *serm.* 2. 1. 16 'iustum poteras et dicere fortem', *epist.* 1. 9. 13 'fortem crede bonumque'. For the Graecizing construction with *scriberis* cf. Antip. Sid. *anth. P.* 7. 424. 9 ἱππαστὴρ δ' ὅδε κῆμος ἀείσεται οὐ πολύμυθον, Headlam on Herodas 4. 47.

2. Maeonii: After epitomizing the field-marshal with trenchant austerity, Horace portrays the poet with flowery exuberance. Homer was the son of Maeon according to a tradition that went back to Hellanicus (*FGrH* 4 F 5, *RE* 8. 2192); Maeonia was the Homeric name for Lydia, and Homer by some accounts came from Smyrna. *Maeonides* is a piece of Hellenistic poetic diction (cf. Antip. Sid. *anth. P.* 7. 2. 2); it is used freely by the Latin poets, but this is the first attested instance (cf. also 4. 9. 5 f. 'Maeonius . . . Homerus'). A few years later it was Virgil who was being compared with Homer; cf. Prop. 2. 34. 66 'nescioquid maius nascitur Iliade', *catal.* 15. 2, *laus Pis.* 232 'Maeoniumque senem Romano provocat ore'.

alite: cf. *carm. Bob.* 5. 3 'Iunius Ausoniae notus testudinis ales' (this tells strongly against Atterbury's conjecture *aemulo*). Horace is alluding to the swan, which was believed to be a musical bird. Hence poets are often described as swans; cf. 2. 20. 1 ff., 4. 2. 25, Virg. *ecl.* 9. 36 (above, p. 81) also of Varius, Ben Jonson of Shakespeare 'Sweet Swan of Avon'. For many Greek parallels cf. D'Arcy Thompson, *Glossary of Greek Birds*, 1936, pp. 182 f.

alite is the reading of the manuscripts and scholia (including Porphyrio). The construction is 'ablative of agent without *a*'. The decisive parallel is Sil. 13. 409 'cetera quae poscis maiori vate canentur'; cf. also Ov. *met.* 7. 49 f. 'perque Pelasgas / servatrix urbes matrum celebrabere turba'. Elsewhere the ablative of agent refers to a quasi-instrument, i.e. something more inanimate than a poet; cf. *epist.* 1. 1. 94 'curatus inaequali tonsore', Juv. 1. 13 'adsiduo ruptae lectore columnae', K.–S. 1. 380, H.–Sz. 122. Some in our passage interpret as ablative absolute, but the word-order would be impossible, to say no more.

Passerat proposed *aliti*, thus taking *Vario* as a dative of agent. Servius twice quotes *scriberis Vario* as a parallel to datives of agent (*georg.* 3. 6 'cui non dictus Hylas puer', *Aen.* 1. 440 'neque cernitur ulli'). This dative is relatively uncommon unless when combined with a perfect participle or gerundive, yet it is found (Cic. *inv.* 1. 86 'illa nobis alio tempore . . . explicabuntur', Virg. *Aen.* loc. cit., H.–Sz. 96 f.). Cf. especially *epist.* 1. 19. 2 f. 'nulla placere diu nec vivere carmina possunt / quae scribuntur aquae potoribus'; this is presumably dative in view of *serm.* 1. 10. 16 'illi scripta quibus comoedia prisca viris est'. Passerat's proposal is interesting, particularly in view of the quotations from Servius, yet the parallel from Silius argues against change. It should also be noted that *aliti* produces a rhyme with *Maeonii* which by Skutsch's canon raises doubts (cf. 1. 1. 6 n.).

3. quam . . . cumque: editors speak of an anacoluthon, but *quicumque* does not require an antecedent any more than English 'whatever' (Prop. 1. 21. 9, Housman, *J. Phil.* 21, 1893, 184). *gesserit* of course is future-perfect.

navibus aut equis: a poetical variation for *terra marique* (κατὰ γῆν καὶ κατὰ θάλατταν); for this phrase cf. A. Momigliano, *JRS* 32, 1942, 62 ff., E. Kemmer, *Die polare Ausdrucksweise in der griechischen Literatur*, Würzburg, 1903, pp. 166 ff. Horace conflates it with the other military polarism 'with horse and foot' (ἵππῳ καὶ πεζῷ, equis virisque); cf. Doblhofer 36. For similar eulogies cf. Pind. *P.* 2. 65 f. τὰ μὲν ἐν ἱπποσόαισιν ἄνδρεσσι μαρνάμενον, / τὰ δ' ἐν πεζομάχοισι, Virg. *Aen.* 6. 880 f.

5. nos: contrasted with *Vario*; such antitheses occur elsewhere in *recusationes* (2. 12. 13, Prop. 1. 7. 5, Ov. *am.* 2. 18. 3, etc.). The plural of authorship is not pompous, but (if anything) more urbane than *ego*; cf. E. Hancock, *CQ* 19, 1925, 45 ff., W. S. Maguinness, *CQ* 35, 1941, 127 ff., H.–Sz. 19 f. For the ironic pretence of incapacity cf. *serm.* 2. 1. 12 f., *epist.* 2. 1. 257 (see pp. 82 f.), Prop. 3. 9. 4 f. 'non sunt apta meae grandia vela rati. / turpe est quod nequeas capiti committere pondus', Ov. *trist.* 2. 333 f. 'at si me iubeas domitos Iovis igne Gigantas / dicere, conantem debilitabit opus'.

nec gravem . . .: Horace briefly gives the arguments of the *Iliad* and *Odyssey*. For such summaries cf. *epist.* 1. 2. 6 ff., Prop. 3. 12. 23 ff., *paneg. in Mess.* 52 ff., *priap.* 68. 18 ff. 'nobilis hinc mota nempe incipit Ilias ira, / . . . altera materia est error fallentis Ulixei'.

6. stomachum: 'bad temper'; the word is prosaic. Horace is deliberately playing down the μῆνις of Achilles; cf. Charis. *gramm.* 1. 271 (= 357 Barwick) 'tapinosis est rei magnae humilis expositio ut apud Horatium Flaccum *Pelidae stomachum cedere nescii*' (so Diom. *gramm.* 1. 450. 27 ff.). *gravem* is likewise mild compared with Homer's οὐλομένην.

cedere nescii: cf. *epod.* 17. 14 'pervicacis ad pedes Achillei', *ars* 121 'impiger iracundus inexorabilis acer'. For the infinitive cf. 4. 6. 18, Virg. *Aen.* 12. 527.

7. duplicis: 'double-dealing' (cf. 'duplicity'), the opposite of *simplex*. Cf. Eur. *Tro.* 286 (of Odysseus) διπτύχῳ γλώσσᾳ, *Rhes.* 395 κοὐ διπλοῦς πέφυκ' ἀνήρ, [Dion. Hal.] *rhet.* 11. 5, p. 379. 3, Ov. *am.* 1. 12. 27 (to writing tablets) 'ergo ego vos rebus duplices pro nomine sensi'. Here

the word is a pejorative translation of Hom. *Od.* 1. 1 πολύτροπον
(which the scholiast contrasts with ἁπλοῦς, and Livius Andronicus,
fr. 1 renders by *versutum*). Elsewhere the more Stoic aspects of
Odysseus are exaggerated; cf. *epod.* 17. 16 *laboriosi* (cf. πολύτλας),
epist. 1. 2. 19 *providus*, *epist.* 1. 7. 40 *patientis*. For these varied dis-
tortions of the Homeric characterization cf. F. Buffière, *Les Mythes
d'Homère et la pensée grecque*, 1956, pp. 365 ff., W. B. Stanford, *The
Ulysses Theme*, 1963.

8. saevam Pelopis domum: the rejection of conventional mythology
goes back to Callimachus (fr. 1. 5 ἥρωας); cf. also 2. 12. 5 ff., Prop. 1.
7. 1 ff., 2. 1. 19 ff., Opp. *cyn.* 1. 28 μὴ γένος ἡρώων εἴπῃς, μὴ ναυτίλον
Ἄργω. But here the sorrows of Pelops' line have a special point:
Horace is alluding to the famous *Thyestes* of Varius (above, p. 81).

9. tenues: Horace modestly suggests that he is an unimportant person, like Cicero's *tenuiores cives*; cf. 4. 2. 31 f. 'operosa parvus /
carmina fingo'. The word also implies the plain style in literature
('tenue genus'), which Horace claimed as his own; cf. 2. 16. 38
'spiritum Graiae tenuem Camenae', 3. 3. 72 'magna modis tenuare
parvis', *epist.* 2. 1. 225. The theme goes back to Callimachus with his
ideal of the Μοῦσα λεπταλέη (above, p. 81, *ep.* 27. 3); contrast *serm.*
2. 6. 14 f. 'pingue pecus domino facias et cetera praeter / ingenium'.
See further M. Puelma Piwonka, *Lucilius und Kallimachos*, 1949,
pp. 153 ff., E. Reitzenstein, *Festschrift R. Reitzenstein*, 1931, pp. 25 ff.,
F. Wehrli, *MH* 1, 1944, 72, H. J. Mette, *MH* 18, 1961, 136 ff., R.
Pfeiffer, op. cit. [p. 15], p. 137, J-M. Jacques, *REA* 62, 1960, 57 ff.
    grandia: cf. Ov. *am.* 2. 18. 3 f. '(while you write epic) nos, Macer,
ignava Veneris cessamus in umbra / et tener ausuros grandia frangit
Amor'. The word suggests grandeur of style as well as theme (cf.
'grande genus orationis'); it is pointedly juxtaposed with *tenues*.
    pudor: cf. *epist.* 2. 1. 259 (above, p. 83).

10. imbellisque lyrae: cf. 1. 15. 15, Prop. 4. 6. 32 'carmen inerme
lyrae', 4. 6. 36, Ov. *am.* 3. 15. 19, Pl. *leg.* 815 d τῆς ἀπολέμου μούσης
(of non-military dancing), *Anacreontea* 2. 1 f. δότε μοι λύρην Ὁμήρου /
φονίης ἄνευθε χορδῆς. For the anti-militarism of the Roman elegists cf.
Boucher 20 f. For the genitive with *potens* cf. 1. 3. 1 n., *ars* 407
'Musa lyrae sollers'.
    Musa: for the Muse as counsellor cf. 2. 12. 13, Prop. 3. 3. 39 ff. In
Callimachus the part is taken by Apollo (above, p. 81), and so in
many of his Roman imitators (4. 15. 1, Virg. *ecl.* 6. 3, Prop. 3. 3. 13,
4. 1. 133 f., Ov. *ars* 2. 493, Nemes. *cyn.* 5 ff.). Elsewhere the good
advice is given by Quirinus (*serm.* 1. 10. 32), Horus (Prop. 4. 1. 71),
Artemis (Opp. *cyn.* 1. 24). See further Wimmel, op. cit., pp. 135 ff.

11. egregii: the word is relatively uncommon in poetry, but recalls the austere commendations of a historian; it is applied elsewhere by Horace both to Augustus (3. 25. 4) and Regulus (3. 5. 48).

Caesaris: the *recusatio* is designed for Augustus as well as Agrippa; for equal tact cf. 2. 12. 9 f. 'tuque pedestribus / dices historiis proelia Caesaris', *serm.* 2. 1. 11 'Caesaris invicti res dicere'. Horace does not directly address a poem to the Princeps till *epist.* 2. 1, *carm.* 4. 14, 4. 15. For the other point of view cf. Suet. *Aug.* 89. 3 'componi tamen aliquid de se nisi et serio et a praestantissimis offendebatur'.

12. culpa . . . ingeni: cf. *epist.* 2. 1. 235 ff. 'sed veluti tractata notam labemque remittunt / atramenta, fere scriptores carmine foedo / splendida facta linunt', Prop. 2. 1. 41 f. 'nec mea conveniunt duro praecordia versu / Caesaris in Phrygios condere nomen avos', Ov. *trist.* 2. 335 ff. 'divitis ingenii est immania Caesaris acta / condere, materia ne superetur opus. / et tamen ausus eram. sed detractare videbar, / quodque nefas, damno viribus esse tuis'. Such affectations of humility were recommended by the rhetoricians (cf. *rhet. Her.* 3. 11 'vereri nos ut illius facta verbis consequi possimus; . . . ipsa facta omnium laudatorum eloquentiam anteire') ; they become particularly abject in late antiquity and the Middle Ages. See further Curtius 83 ff., 411 ff., L. Arbusow, *Colores Rhetorici*[2], 1963, pp. 105 f., T. Janson, *Latin Prose Prefaces*, 1964, pp. 124 f., Doblhofer 35 f. For *deterere* cf. Auson. *Mos.* 390.

13. quis . . . : the suggested reply is perhaps 'only another Homer' (this formulation is suggested to us by Mr. Russell). But Horace is tactfully implying that Varius might be a suitable candidate; on any other interpretation the structure of the poem is very obscure (*quis* balances 17 *nos* just as 1 *Vario* balances 5 *nos*). Moreover, it was a conventional part of the *recusatio* to propose other more suitable writers (1 n.), and it is likely enough in itself that this theme is maintained. On the other hand the hint is put very delicately with a vague question; Horace is leaving Varius room for escape.

Peerlkamp argued that the only reasonable reply is *nemo*, and accordingly deleted the last two stanzas as an absurd interpolation; this makes the whole poem intolerably lame. Meineke and Lehrs deleted the fourth stanza; this at least leaves the poem coherent, but the lines sound Horatian, and no reason for interpolation can be suggested. Housman, loc. cit., placed the fourth stanza after the first, reading *qui* for *quis*; but the resulting relative clause is rambling, one would expect *et* for *aut*, and after *gesserit* the disparate *scripserit* is awkward.

Fraenkel suggests that the rhetorical question could admit the answer 'no ordinary poet and certainly not I'; he thinks that after

K

the initial stanza Horace 'is far less concerned with what Varius might be able or unable to achieve than with what he, Horace, feels absolutely unable to undertake' (p. 234). Even this gives the wrong emphasis: the poem falls apart if a broad hint at Varius is not intended here. Perhaps one should meet the difficulty by arguing that 'quis digne scripserit?' does not elicit such a bleak negative as the conventional formula 'quis scripserit?'. The phrase almost means 'who would be the right man to write about?'

tunica . . . adamantina: when Diomede wounds Ares (16 n.) Homer says ὁ δ' ἔβραχε χάλκεος Ἄρης (*Il.* 5. 859; cf. 704, 866). Enyalios is χαλκοθώραξ at Soph. *Ai.* 179 (perhaps Pind. fr. 169. 12). 'Adamant' is a poetical word for any hard metal, later used for steel or diamond; it is not mentioned in Homer, but appears first in Hesiod. For a *tunica* of metal cf. Varro, *ling.* 5. 116 'ex anulis ferrea tunica'.

14. pulvere . . . nigrum: cf. 1. 15. 20, 2. 1. 22, Val. Fl. 1. 13 (of Titus) 'Solymo nigrantem pulvere fratrem'. Again the touch is un-Homeric.

15. Merionen: in the *Iliad* Meriones is the squire of Idomeneus, the Cretan leader (Roscher 2. 2836 ff., *RE* 15. 1031 ff.). He is mentioned only briefly in the *aristeia* of Diomede (5. 59 Μηριόνης δὲ Φέρεκλον ἐνήρατο); in the Doloneia he wishes to accompany Diomede on his raid (10. 229), but Odysseus is preferred. Yet in 1. 15. 26 ff. he appears in close association with Diomede; and in our passage he is introduced between brazen Mars and Diomede, who would naturally go together. Horace seems to have been influenced by some poet other than Homer; it is significant that the scholiast on *Il.* 2. 96 mentions a Meriones as a herald of Diomede; cf. also Eur. *IA* 199 ff. Διομήδεά θ' ἡδοναῖς δίσκου κεχαρημένον, | παρὰ δὲ Μηριόνην, Ἄρεος | ὄζον, θαῦμα βροτοῖσιν.

But even if Diomede and Meriones appeared together in one of the Cyclic poems, one would still want to know why Horace mentions this non-Homeric association not once (which would be explicable) but twice. Perhaps some contemporary work of literature suggested the story to the poet's mind. Nothing can be proved, but the possibility must be considered that Varius was contemplating a *Diomedeia* (Iullus Antonius later wrote one in twelve books; cf. ps.-Acro on 4. 2. 33). That would also account for *Maeonii* (2).

16. Tydiden: Diomede, son of Tydeus, wounded Aphrodite (Hom. *Il.* 5. 335 ff.) and finally Ares himself (855 ff.); he was prompted and assisted by Athene (828 τοίη τοι ἐγὼν ἐπιτάρροθός εἰμι). Ares finally complains αὐτὰρ ἔπειτ' αὐτῷ μοι ἐπέσσυτο δαίμονι ἶσος (884); however, in our passage *superis parem* means 'a match for the gods'.

17. nos . . . : heroic warfare is contrasted with the warfare of love;

cf. *Anacreontea* 26 A σὺ μὲν λέγεις τὰ Θήβης, / ὁ δ᾽ αὖ Φρυγῶν αὐτάς· / ἐγὼ δ᾽ ἐμὰς ἁλώσεις. / οὐχ ἵππος ὤλεσέν με, / οὐ πεζός, οὐχὶ νῆες· / στρατὸς δὲ καινὸς ἄλλος / ἀπ᾽ ὀμμάτων με βάλλων, Ov. *am.* 2. 18. 1 ff. 'carmen ad iratum dum tu perducis Achillem, / . . . nos, Macer, ignava Veneris cessamus in umbra / . . . resque domi gestas et mea bella cano'.

proelia: for erotic *proelia* cf. Tib. 1. 3. 63 f., Prop. 2. 1. 45, 3. 5. 2, Ov. *am.* 1. 9. 45, Mart. 10. 38. 6, Apul. *met.* 5. 21. 5, Aristaenetus 1. 10 *sub fin.* For the *militia amoris* in general cf. Brandt on Ov. *am.* 1. 9, A. Spies, *Militat omnis amans*, Diss. Tübingen, 1930.

18. sectis: for female scratchings cf. Theoc. 27. 19 χεῖλος ἀμύξω, Meleager, *anth. P.* 5. 157 τρηχὺς ὄνυξ ὑπ᾽ Ἔρωτος ἀνέτραφες Ἡλιοδώρας· / ταύτης γὰρ δύνει κνίσμα καὶ ἐς κραδίην, Prop. 3. 8. 6 'et mea formosis unguibus ora nota', 4. 8. 57, Ov. *am.* 1. 7. 64, *ars* 2. 452, Sil. 15. 761 f., Mart. 11. 84. 15, Ach. Tat. 2. 22. 2 ἀμύσσεις τοῖς ὄνυξι καὶ **δάκνεις** τοῖς ὀδοῦσι. ταὐτὰ γὰρ οὐ ποιεῖ μαχομένη γυνή;, Claud. 14. 5 ff. 'ne cessa, iuvenis, comminus adgredi, / impacata licet saeviat unguibus. / non quisquam fruitur veris odoribus, / Hyblaeos latebris nec spoliat favos, / si fronti caveat, si timeat rubos; / armat spina rosas, mella tegunt apes', *carm. min.* 25. 135 f., W. H. Alexander, *Univ. Calif. Publ. Phil.* 13, 1944–50, 178 'Have none of our classicists ever seen a domestic fight in Italy? Nothing is barred, certainly not finger-nails'.

In our passage commentators from Porphyrio suggest that cut nails mean a sham fight (contrast *epod.* 5. 47 f. where Canidia has an *inresectum pollicem*); yet this view does not suit *acrium*. But *sectis* can be defended if we assume that the girls' nails were sharpened to a point (thus ps.-Acro). Even dandified men in antiquity may have pointed their nails; cf. Paul. Sil. *anth. P.* 5. 228. 1 f. εἰπὲ τίνι πλέξεις ἔτι βόστρυχον, ἢ τίνι χεῖρας / φαιδρυνέεις, ὀνύχων ἀμφιτεμὼν ἀκίδα;

Bentley interestingly proposed *strictis* 'with drawn nails' (against a *testimonium* as well as the manuscripts). He compared Ov. *am.* 1. 6. 14 'non timeo strictas in mea fata manus', Stat. *Theb.* 3. 535 (of eagles) 'strictis unguibus instant'. These parallels are unsatisfactory: *strictas manus* refers to armed hands, and eagles, unlike girls, have retractable claws. Yet *strictis unguibus* might be defended as a joke; cf. Petron. 96. 3 'stricto [acutoque] articulo'.

An important but ambiguous clue is provided by Firmicus Maternus in his account of the Rape of Proserpine (*err.* 7. 2): 'nec †reservati ungues contra amatorem rusticum aliquid profuerunt, nec clamor atque ululatus adiuvit nec ceterarum strepitus puellarum'. Here Haupt's *resecati* has been generally accepted (for the form cf. Apul. *met.* 1. 13. 6 *praesecata*). Firmicus may be drawing a contrast between the delicately-nurtured Proserpine and her rustic lover; perhaps he wrongly assumed that Horace's *secti ungues* were ineffective weapons.

19. vacui: 'heart-whole', 'fancy-free'; cf. Prop. 1. 10. 30 'qui numquam vacuo pectore liber erit', Ov. *am.* 1. 1. 26 'uror et in vacuo pectore regnat amor', *rem.* 752, Agathias, *anth. P.* 5. 278. 1 f. αὐτή μοι Κυθέρεια καὶ ἱμεροέντες Ἔρωτες / τήξουσιν κενεὴν ἐχθόμενοι κραδίην. *vacuus* can also mean 'carefree' in a more general sense (Sall. *Jug.* 52. 6), and so goes well with *cantamus*.

sive . . .: 'or if I am on fire, a trifler as usual'. *sive = vel si* (K.–S. 2. 437, H.–Sz. 670); *leves* is co-ordinate with *vacui* in terms of grammar, though not of sense. When Horace says that he is on fire, he means that he is writing personal love-poetry; *leves* suits both the fickle lover (Catull. 61. 97) and the light poet. For the ironic pretence of triviality cf. 2. 1. 40 'leviore plectro', 3. 3. 69 'iocosae . . . lyrae'.

7. LAVDABVNT ALII

[F. R. Bliss, *TAPhA* 91, 1960, 30 ff.; J. P. Elder, *CPh* 48, 1953, 1 ff.; C. F. Kumaniecki, *Eos* 42, 1947, 5 ff.; Pasquali 722 ff.; J. Stroux, *Philologus* 90, 1935, 317 ff.; J. Vaio, *CPh* 61, 1966, 168 ff.]

1–14. *Others will praise the celebrated cities of Asia and Greece, but I love none of them so much as Tibur.* 15–21. *Drown your sorrows in wine, Plancus, whether on military service or in your home at Tibur, to which you will return.* 21–32. *Teucer, when exiled from his home, addressed his sorrowing friends at a symposium and urged them not to despair.*

This is the fifth ode of the book concerned with a prominent political figure, here L. Munatius Plancus, *cos.* 42 B.C. He is said by Porphyrio to have come from Tibur, and a republican inscription shows a Munatius holding office there (*ILS* 6231). Plancus was Caesar's legate in Gaul in 54 and in the civil war (Caes. *Gall.* 5. 24. 3, *civ.* 1. 40. 5, *bell. Afr.* 4). Later he was one of the *praefecti urbi* of 46–45 (Dio 43. 28. 2, 43. 48. 1 ff.). He was then governor of Transalpine Gaul (44–43), where he founded Lugdunum (Lyons) and also Raurica (near Basle). Our best first-hand information about him is in the vivid series of letters that he exchanged with Cicero between Caesar's murder and his own compact with M. Antonius in August 43 (Cic. *epist.* 10. 1–24); on the whole transaction see Syme, *Roman*

Revolution, c. 13. Nothing in Plancus's career belies the general opinion cited by Cicero, *epist.* 10. 3. 3 'scis profecto . . . fuisse quoddam tempus cum homines existimarent te nimis servire temporibus'. The name of his brother (or cousin) stood third on the list of people proscribed by his new associates (App. *civ.* 4. 12. 46) ; on 29 Dec. 43 Plancus and M. Lepidus (whose brother was first on the list) triumphed together, and the troops sang 'de germanis, non de Gallis, duo triumphant consules' (Vell. 2. 67. 4).

Plancus was consul with Lepidus in 42, and in 41, after halfhearted support of L. Antonius at Perusia, he left Italy to join M. Antonius. In the next ten years he was a marshal (in Asia and Syria) and a courtier of Antonius. Legend made him the umpire when Cleopatra drank the pearl (Plin. *nat.* 9. 121), and he won more notoriety by wearing a sea-god's tail in a charade (Vell. 2. 83. 2 'cum caeruleatus et nudus caputque redimitus arundine et caudam trahens, genibus innixus Glaucum saltasset in convivio').

In 32 B.C. he deserted Antonius for Octavian, 'not' says Velleius (2. 83. 1), 'through any conviction that he was choosing the right, nor from any love of the republic or of Caesar, . . . but because treachery was a disease with him ('sed morbo proditor')'. In 27 he proposed the name Augustus for Octavian ; by this time he was probably the senior consular, except for the disgraced Lepidus. In 22 B.C. he held the censorship with Paullus Aemilius Lepidus, the son of the triumvir's proscribed brother and husband of Propertius's Cornelia. The regal mausoleum that Plancus built at Caieta (called locally the Torre d'Orlando) summarizes his successful career (*ILS* 886) : 'L. Munatius L. f. L. n. L. pron. Plancus cos. cens. imp. iter. vii vir epulon. triump. ex Raetis, aedem Saturni fecit de manibIs, agros divisit in Italia Beneventi, in Gallia colonias deduxit Lugudunum et Rauricam.'

It is not clear where Horace's poem belongs in this distinguished life. Kumaniecki, loc. cit., suggests 40–35, when Plancus was driven from Asia by Labienus and took refuge in the Greek islands ; R. Hanslik, *PhW* 58, 1938, 670 ff., prefers the command in Syria in 35. A date before 35 would be very early for an ode, and when Plancus was serving with Antonius in the East he was probably unknown to Horace. The time of the Actium campaign must be considered ; our poem implies that Plancus was still on service (20 *castra*), and Horace may even have been out in Greece in 31 (above, p. xxvii). The difficulty is that Plancus returned to Rome in 32 (Dio 50. 3. 3), and it is unlikely that he was given another command. Perhaps the ode was written soon after his return, and tactfully puts in the future what has already happened. The similarities with *epode* 13 also support a date before 30 B.C.

The first part of the poem (1–14) deals with Tibur, the hill resort 20 miles east of Rome; it is relevant because Plancus came from there, and indeed was the town's greatest living son. Horace's approach is very circuitous; the first 11 lines deal not with Tibur but with famous Greek cities which the poet, and by inference Plancus, think less attractive (10 f.). We need not, and indeed should not, suppose that Plancus has been travelling round these cities; there are too many of them for that, and they are mentioned not as garrison towns or administrative centres but as places famous in Greek poetry. Horace is simply using the conventional device of the 'priamel' (above, pp. 2 f.); and he is using it here because it is characteristic of Pindar and Bacchylides, who knew how to honour famous men. Horace is also thinking of the eulogies of countries and cities popular with poets of the Hellenistic age, with their strong interest in local themes. One may note especially the Ἀχαικά, Ἠλιακά, and Θεσσαλικά of Rhianus (Powell 12 ff.; cf. also 5 n.); such poems seem to have been diffuse and anti-Callimachean (cf. K. Ziegler, *Das hellenistische Epos*, ed. 2, 1966, p. 19, R. Pfeiffer, *History of Classical Scholarship*, 1968, pp. 144, 148 f.).

Such eulogies also belong to encomiastic rhetoric; the rhetor Menander (3. 344 ff. Sp.) gives lengthy recipes for them. Cf. also Quint. *inst.* 3. 7. 26 'laudantur autem urbes similiter atque homines', Plin. *epist.* 3. 21. 3 'fuit moris antiqui eos qui vel singulorum laudes vel urbium scripserant aut honoribus aut pecunia ornare', E. Kienzle, *Der Lobpreis von Städten und Ländern in der älteren griechischen Dichtung*, Diss. Basel, 1936, F. Wilhelm, *RhM* 77, 1928, 396 ff., Volkmann 334 f. It seems to have been a feature in these encomia to disparage famous beauty spots in contrast to one's favourite site; cf. especially Greg. Nyss. *epist.* 20. 2 ff. P. πολλὰ γὰρ ἐγὼ καὶ παρὰ πολλοῖς ἤδη τεθεαμένος, πολλὰ δὲ καὶ διὰ τῆς τῶν λόγων ὑπογραφῆς ἐν τοῖς διηγήμασι τῶν ἀρχαίων κατανοήσας, λῆρον ἡγοῦμαι τὰ πάντα ὅσα τε εἶδον καὶ ὅσα ἤκουσα συγκρίσει τῶν τῇδε καλῶν. οὐδὲν ἐκεῖνος ὁ Ἑλικών· μῦθος τῶν μακάρων αἱ νῆσοι· μικρόν τι χρῆμα τὸ πέδον τὸ Σικυώνιον· κόμπος τις ἄλλως ποιητικὸς τὰ κατὰ τὸν Πηνειὸν διηγήματα, ὅν φασι πλουσίῳ τῷ ῥείθρῳ τὰς ἐκ πλαγίων ὄχθας ὑπερχεόμενον τὰ πολυύμνητα πεδία (P, τέμπη F) τοῖς Θετταλοῖς ἀπεργάζεσθαι. τί γὰρ τοιοῦτόν ἐστιν παρ' ἑκάστῳ τῶν εἰρημένων, οἷον ἡμῖν ἡ Οὐάνωτα τοῖς οἰκείοις ἐπεδείξατο κάλλεσιν;

The second and central section of the poem (15–21) advises Plancus to enjoy life in time of trouble. We must not suppose (as some suggest) that Plancus had written to the poet apprising him of a melancholy mood. Horace could have no intimate acquaintance with a *princeps civitatis* who had held appointments in the East for many years; he is rather following the Pindaric tradition that a poet may address sententious admonition to his betters. In supposing Plancus to be *tristis*, Horace takes for granted the conventional pretence of men of affairs that they dislike office and long for retirement. The images of the *paraenesis* are of course derived from Greek lyric; wine symbolizes enjoyment of the present, and the changing weather suggests hope for the future (15 n.).

In the last section of the poem (21–32), the *paraenesis* is reinforced by a mythological *exemplum*, somewhat loosely attached. We find the same technique in *epode* 13, where the exhortation to drink is supported by Chiron's advice to Achilles before his departure for Troy. This pattern must have been borrowed from Greek lyric poetry (cf. Wilamowitz, *Sappho und Simonides*, 1913, p. 306 n. 1); Fraenkel pertinently compares the brief myth and the direct speech at the end of the Fourth Olympian (p. 66). The story of Teucer, however, as opposed to the framework in which it is set, seems to derive from Greek and Roman tragedy (21 n., 25 n.). We should not look for too close a parallel between Teucer and Plancus; Teucer's exile justifies no inferences about the reason for Plancus's *tristitia*. For the parallel to hold, it is sufficient that both Teucer and Plancus have *curae*, and that Teucer drowned his cares in wine, as Plancus is urged to do.

The structure of Horace's poem is subtle and complex. The first and second sections are joined by the thought of Tibur, though the connection of Plancus with Tibur is not made explicit until the end of the second section. The myth of the third section is also relevant to the *paraenesis* of the second, and the connection is reinforced verbally by the repetition of *tristitiam* (18) and *tristis* (24). Plancus is not to worry wherever he may be (19 ff.), just as Teucer advises in the myth and more explicitly in Pacuvius's famous play (25 n.). On the other hand, there is no direct connection between the first and third sections of the ode. This puzzles moderns, who expect a lyric poem to deal with a single subject. But the apparent lack of unity is not due to inexperience or inattention; Horace is simply imitating the wide sweep and deliberately casual transitions of the Pindaric encomium.

Attempts to find a tighter order in the poem have led to some confusions. Porphyrio specifically rejects an ancient theory that divided the ode into two after line 14 (an absurd interpretation that is also represented by many manuscripts). W. Riedel, *PhW* 62, 1942, 575, pointed out that the Gallaeci in north-west Spain claimed descent from Teucer (Justin 44. 3. 2 f.); he suggested that Plancus was fighting this tribe in the wars of 27–25 B.C. But it is unlikely that our poem is so late; the information would be as obscure to Horace as it is to us; there is no evidence that Plancus fought the Gallaeci, and if he had, a compliment to their ancestor would be ill-timed.

J. P. Elder, loc. cit., thinks that the unifying theme of the poem is that one should not tie one's happiness to any one place; yet the clear drift of the first section is not (as he supposes) 'tastes differ about the relative merits of places' but rather 'Tibur is the place for me'. That is to say, instead of emphasizing the unimportance of one's geographical situation, Horace does precisely the opposite. Perhaps the strangest of all attempts to impose a unity is that of Kumaniecki, loc. cit.: Teucer was unjustly accused of doing his brother to death, and Kumaniecki takes the poet to be condoling with Plancus on people's unpleasantness about the proscription business.

The poem suffers rather from comparison with *epode* 13, but it has considerable merits of its own, which are hard to analyse. At first sight the catalogue of Greek cities seems rambling and frigid (so Pasquali 728); but Horace's method has the poetic purpose of suggesting contemptuous dismissal. Of course this technique would only be possible in the looser epodic style, which allows the poet to write with more loquacity than the sometimes congested alcaics. The praise of Tibur is completed in a few allusive strokes, but is all the better for that reason; Horace perhaps shows more boldness than we realize in comparing a local and familiar scene with the famous splendours of Tempe. But the poem owes most to the myth of Teucer; here Horace has recaptured the simplicity and force of archaic Greek poetry, and related it with remarkable ingenuity to a contemporary situation. We must not think of Plancus simply as he appears to the cynical scrutiny of the Roman historian. The poet and panegyrist may be allowed to take at his own valuation a senior statesman, field-marshal, and founder of cities, who thanks to Hercules ἡγεμών and his own fortune had survived many wars and other vicissitudes, and now after a prolonged absence might soon expect to return to the familiar falls of Anio and grove of Tiburnus.

Metre: First Archilochian.

1. laudabunt alii . . .: for the use of the priamel in encomia cf. Timocreon 727 ἀλλ' εἰ τύ γε Παυσανίαν ἢ καὶ τύ γε Ξάνθιππον αἰνεῖς, / ἢ τύ γε Λευτυχίδαν, ἐγὼ δ' Ἀριστείδαν ἐπαινέω / ἄνδρ' ἱερᾶν ἀπ' Ἀθανᾶν / ἐλθεῖν ἕνα λῷστον, Daniel, *Sonnets to Delia* 55. 1 'Let others sing of Knights and Palladines', *The British Grenadiers*, 'Some talk of Alexander And some of Hercules'. In the present passage there is also a hint of *recusatio* (pp. 81 ff.); Horace suggests that inflated and hackneyed themes are not for him. This suits the future *laudabunt* (cf. 1. 6. 1 'scriberis', Virg. *ecl.* 6. 6 f. 'super tibi erunt qui dicere laudes, / Vare, tuas cupiant'), as well as the Callimachean tone of *carmine perpetuo* (6 n.).

Other writers also contrast the peace of familiar and charming surroundings with the splendours of the Greek world. One may compare
Prop. 3. 22, where Tullus, who has been living in Asia for some years,
is reminded of the beauties of Italy (including the Anio). For more or
less similar developments cf. Mart. 4. 55. 4 ff. 'Argivas generatus
inter urbes / Thebas carmine cantet aut Mycenas, / aut claram
Rhodon aut libidinosae / Ledaeas Lacedaemonos palaestras: / nos
Celtis genitos et ex Hiberis / nostrae nomina duriora terrae / grato
non pudeat referre versu', Plin. *epist.* 8. 20. 2, Dio Chrys. 44. 6 οὐ δὴ
θαυμαστόν, εἰ ἐγὼ πατρίδα τοιαύτην οὕτω σφόδρα ἠγάπηκα ὥστε οὔτ᾽
ἂν Ἀθήνας οὔτε Ἄργος οὔτε Λακεδαίμονα, . . . εἱλόμην ἂν εἶναί μοι
πατρίδας πρὸ ταύτης, Greg. Nyss., above, p. 92.

For the tense cf. 1. 20. 10, 3. 23. 12 f. 'victima pontificum securis /
cervice tinguet', Virg. *Aen.* 6. 847 'excudent alii spirantia mollius
aera', H.–Sz. 311. The future is sometimes called 'concessive' or
'permissive'; however, 'may celebrate' would be a misleading translation, as we need a statement of fact to balance 5 *sunt quibus*. 'Will
celebrate' is perfectly idiomatic English.

claram: on the surface this means simply 'famous'; cf. Catull. 4. 8
'Rhodumque nobilem'. Yet the word also means 'sunny', and is so
interpreted by Porphyrio here ('propterea claram quod soli sit op-
posita dicit'); it is significant that Martial, in his imitation, gives the
epithet to Rhodes rather than to equally famous cities (4. 55. 6 cited
above). Rhodes was known for its cult of Helios and for its brilliant
climate; cf. Pind. *O.* 7, Manil. 4. 765 'tumque domus vere solis, cui
tota sacrata est', Luc. 8. 247 f. 'claram . . . sole Rhodon', Plin. *nat.* 2.
153 'Rhodi et Syracusis nunquam tanta nubila obduci ut non aliqua
hora sol cernatur', Antiphilus, *anth. P.* 9. 178, *The Times*, 11 Dec.
1964, 'Rhodes has become today a major tourist centre in the
Aegean, and with good reason. The island is so blessed by sunshine
that local farmers had to invoke divine providence in mid-November
for some rain to save their thirsty crops'.

Rhodon . . .: in the fourth and third centuries Rhodes had been
the Venice of antiquity, but it was now little more than a pleasant
retreat for rhetoricians and distressed gentlemen (e.g. Tiberius). For
its splendours cf. Str. 14. 2. 5 οὐκ ἔχομεν εἰπεῖν ἑτέραν ἀλλ᾽ οὐδὲ πάρισον,
μή τί γε κρείττω ταύτης τῆς πόλεως.

For Mytilene cf. Cic. *leg. agr.* 2. 40 'urbs et natura ac situ et di-
scriptione aedificiorum in primis nobilis'. For Ephesus cf. Antip. Sid.
anth. P. 9. 58, 9. 790, especially 3 f. θοῶν βασίλειαν Ἰώνων / τὰν δορὶ
καὶ Μούσαις αἰπυτάταν Ἔφεσον, Prop. 3. 22. 15, Str. 14. 1. 24 ἡ δὲ πόλις
τῇ πρὸς τὰ ἄλλα εὐκαιρίᾳ τῶν τόπων αὔξεται καθ᾽ ἑκάστην ἡμέραν,
ἐμπόριον οὖσα μέγιστον τῶν κατὰ τὴν Ἀσίαν τὴν ἐντὸς τοῦ Ταύρου. The
city was particularly famous for its Artemision; cf. *act. apost.* 19.

27 f. κινδυνεύει . . . τὸ τῆς μεγάλης θεᾶς Ἀρτέμιδος ἱερὸν εἰς οὐθὲν
λογισθῆναι, μέλλειν τε καὶ καθαιρεῖσθαι τῆς μεγαλειότητος αὐτῆς, ἣν ὅλη
ἡ Ἀσία καὶ ἡ οἰκουμένη σέβεται. ἀκούσαντες δὲ καὶ γενόμενοι πλήρεις
θυμοῦ ἔκραζον λέγοντες· Μεγάλη ἡ Ἄρτεμις Ἐφεσίων, Pease on Cic. nat.
deor. 2. 69.

The cities of Asia were still flourishing, and were natural stopping
places in a Roman gentleman's grand tour of the East; cf. epist. 1.
11. 1 ff., 17, Catull. 46. 6 'ad claras Asiae volemus urbes', Prop. 1. 6.
13 f. 'an mihi sit tanti doctas cognoscere Athenas / atque Asiae
veteres cernere divitias?', 3. 22. 1 ff., Ov. trist. 1. 2. 77 f. 'nec peto,
quas quondam petii studiosus, Athenas, / oppida non Asiae, non
loca visa prius', Pont. 2. 10. 21, Plut. Cato min. 12. 2 βουληθεὶς . . .
πλανηθῆναι καθ᾽ ἱστορίαν τῆς Ἀσίας, G. M. Bowersock, Augustus and
the Greek World, 1965, pp. 76 ff.

2. bimarisve: Corinth had two harbours; cf. Pind. O. 13. 40 ἀμφιάλοισι
Ποτειδᾶνος τεθμοῖσιν, Eur. Tr. 1097 f. δίπορον κορυφὰν / *Ἴσθμιον, Cic.
leg. agr. 2. 87, Str. 8. 6. 20. bimaris is first attested here; it is applied
to Corinth six times by Ovid, and later by Sidonius, Prudentius, and
others (Thes.l.L. 2. 1990. 11 ff.).

Corinthi moenia: the ruins of old Corinth, which had been destroyed by Mummius in 146 B.C. Corinth had lately received a Julian
military colony, and was to become again a great city, worthy of
a Pauline epistle. But the tourist's pleasure was especially derived
from the contemplation of the ruins of the older city; cf. Antip. Sid.
anth. P. 9. 151. 1 ff. ποῦ τὸ περίβλεπτον κάλλος σέο, Δωρὶ Κόρινθε; / ποῦ
στεφάναι πύργων, ποῦ τὰ πάλαι κτέανα . . .;, Serv. Sulp. Cic. epist. 4. 5. 4
'post me erat Aegina, ante me Megara, dextra Piraeus, sinistra
Corinthus, quae oppida quodam tempore florentissima fuerunt, nunc
prostrata et diruta ante oculos iacent', Str. 8. 6. 21 (describing what
he saw after the foundation of the Julian colony) συμπεριείληπτο δὲ
τῷ περιβόλῳ τούτῳ καὶ τὸ ὄρος αὐτὸ ὁ Ἀκροκόρινθος ᾗ δυνατὸν ἦν τειχι-
σμὸν δέξασθαι, καὶ ἡμῖν ἀναβαίνουσιν ἦν δῆλα τὰ ἐρείπια τῆς σχοινίας,
Paus. 2. 2. 6 λόγου δὲ ἄξια ἐν τῇ πόλει τὰ μὲν λειπόμενα ἔτι τῶν ἀρχαίων
ἐστιν, 9 n.

3. Apolline . . . insignis: to be taken with Tempe as well as with
Delphos; hence the change from vel to aut. For the ancient associa-
tion of Apollo with Tempe cf. 1. 21. 9, Call. fr. 194. 34 ff. οἱ Δωριῆς δὲ
Τεμπόθεν με τέμνουσιν / ὀρέων ἀπ᾽ ἄκρων καὶ φέρουσιν ἐς Δελφούς, / ἐπὴν
τὰ τὠπόλλωνος ἴρ᾽ ἀγινῆται, Aristonous 17 (Powell 163) ἁγνισθεὶς ἐνὶ
Τέμπεσιν, Plut. quaest. gr. 293 c, defect. orac. 421 c, Ael. var. hist. 3. 1,
IG 9. 2. 1034 Ἀπλουνι Τεμπείτᾳ, RE 5 A. 478 f.

4. Tempe: the valley where the Peneus flows between Ossa and

Olympus was deservedly celebrated; cf. Eur. *Tr.* 214, Theoc. 1. 67
Πηνείω καλὰ τέμπεα, Ael. *var. hist.* 3. 1 (perhaps from Theopompus;
note the resemblance to the scholion on Theoc. loc. cit.), *RE* 5 A.
473 ff. The Romans share the enthusiasm of their predecessors; cf.
Catull. 64. 285 f., Ov. *met.* 1. 568 ff. Even the elder Pliny grows lyrical
(*nat.* 4. 31 'ultra visum hominis attollentibus se dextra laevaque
leniter convexis iugis intus valle luco viridante. hac labitur Penius,
vitreus calculo, amoenus circa ripas gramine, canorus avium con-
centu') ; neither this nor most other descriptions indicate autopsy, in
spite of the military road that the Romans built through the pass.
For Tempe as a theme of conventional praise cf. Synes. *Dion* 3 p. 39 c
ἔστω παράδειγμα ἡ τῶν Τεμπῶν φράσις καὶ ὁ Μέμνων. The name was
used generally for any wooded valley (cf. Cic. *Att.* 4. 15. 5, Virg.
georg. 2. 469, Ov. *am.* 1. 1. 15, *fast.* 4. 477) ; so in the eleventh-century
Fulco of Beauvais, prologue to *vita S. Blandini* 15 'dum fontes,
saltus, dum Thessala Tempe reviso' (cf. Curtius 198 ff.).

5. sunt quibus . . .: cf. the poem of Euphorion called Μοψοπία ἢ
Ἄτακτα. Suidas seems to explain the latter title by the statement
ἔχει γὰρ συμμιγεῖς ἱστορίας. He derives the former from an archaic
name of Attica, commenting ὁ λόγος τοῦ ποιήματος ἀποτείνεται εἰς τὴν
Ἀττικήν (cf. 28 Powell). For poetic praise of the olive cf. especially
Soph. *OC* 694 ff., Call. fr. 194.

  intactae: 'virginis', ἀθίκτου; cf. Catull. 62. 45, Virg. *Aen.* 1. 345,
Prop. 2. 6. 21, Headlam on Herodas 1. 55.

6. carmine perpetuo: a *carmen perpetuum* is a continuous long poem;
cf. Cic. *epist.* 5. 12. 2 'perpetuis . . . historiis' (as opposed to mono-
graphs), Varro, *Men.* 398 'poesis est perpetuum argumentum e
rhythmis, ut Ilias Homeri et annalis Enni', Ov. *met.* 1. 4 'ad mea
perpetuum deducite tempora carmen'. So in Greek Call. fr. 1. 1 ff.
Τελχῖνες ἐπιτρύζουσιν . . . εἵνεκεν οὐχ ἓν ἄεισμα διηνεκὲς . . . ἐν πολλαῖς
ἤνυσα χιλιάσιν. In our passage (after *unum*) *perpetuo* sounds a derisory
note, as if the encomia went on for ever; this implication is also
present in Callimachus.

7. undique decerptam: 'that has been plucked from anywhere and
everywhere'; for this sense of *undique* cf. 1. 16. 14 n. Horace no
doubt remembers Lucretius's statement of his own originality (1.
928 ff.): 'iuvatque novos decerpere flores / insignemque meo capiti
petere inde coronam / unde prius nulli velarint tempora Musae'.
undique decerptam in our passage may be contrasted with Lucretius's
novos (or with *integra prata* in Manil. 2. 53). The phrase suggests that
the works of Greek poets are themselves the place where the picking
is done; cf. Cic. *Sest.* 119 'non sum tam ignarus, iudices, causarum,

non tam insolens in dicendo ut omni ex genere orationem aucuper et
omnis undique flosculos carpam atque delibem'. Some think that
undique means 'from every quarter of Attic soil' or 'from every
source in Attic legend'. But the word cannot properly have such
a limited meaning (nothing corresponds 'to the 'Attic'), and Horace
is emphasizing the triteness rather than the completeness of the
poetical treatment given to Athenian institutions.

Some interpret 'to put on their own brows the crown they pluck
from every other poet's'. Yet Lucretius's *decerpere* and Cicero's
undique tell against this explanation. Moreover, one plucks leaves
from trees, not from other people's brows; the latter interpretation
demands a more violent word like *dereptam*.

Wickham gives two explanations which he wrongly regards as one :
'plucked on every hand' and 'plucked by everyone, i.e. by any poet,
however feeble'. The first is much the same as the one adopted
above, though it does not suggest indiscriminateness quite enough.
For the other compare the use of *unde* for *a quo*; cf. *serm.* 1. 6. 12 f.
'Laevinum, Valeri genus, unde Superbus / Tarquinius regno pulsus
fugit'. But there *unde* has a mock-heroic note, which in our passage
is inappropriate.

Erasmus ingeniously proposed *undique decerptae frondi* 'to prefer
the olive to foliage plucked from any other tree'. This has the merit
of giving *praeponere* its normal meaning of 'to prefer'; the sense 'to
put on the front of', demanded by other interpretations, is unparalleled (though see below for similar locutions). Yet the conjecture
dissociates our passage from the convincing parallels cited from
Lucretius and Cicero.

praeponere: the preposition implies ostentation as in *prae se ferre*
or *praeferre*; cf. Tert. *cor.* 7. 4 'Hercules nunc populum capite prae-
fert, nunc oleastrum, nunc apium' (a passage perhaps derived from
Callimachus; cf. Pfeiffer on fr. inc. 804). Bentley cites in its support
Prop. 4. 2. 46 'impositus fronti', Sen. *Med.* 70 'praecingens roseo
tempora vinculo', Val. Fl. 3. 436 'comis praetexere frondes'.

olivam: for the image of the poet's crown cf. Kambylis 173 ff. It
may be of ivy (1. 1. 29, Prop. 2. 5. 26, Virg. *ecl.* 7. 25) or of bay (3. 30.
16) ; Ovid's Muse wears a myrtle crown (*am.* 1. 1. 29) because her subject is Venus, Horace one of vine leaves in honour of Bacchus (3. 25.
20). Here the crown is of olive because it concerns Attica.

8. plurimus: 'many a one'. The singular presents no difficulty; cf.
Val. Fl. 6. 223 f. 'cui plurima silva / pervigilat materna soror', Juv.
3. 232 'plurimus hic aeger moritur vigilando'. The absence of a noun
is much stranger; yet cf. Luc. 3. 707 f. 'multus sua vulnera puppi /
adfixit moriens'.

Some take *plurimus* to mean 'copious' (reading *in honore* with Oudendorp). But though *multus* and πολύς are used in this sense (cf. Pease on Cic. *nat. deor.* 2. 119), *plurimus* and πλεῖστος are not. Moreover, in the stereotyped patterns of the priamel (1 n.), *plurimus* must mean 'many a one'; cf. 1. 1. 19 ff. 'est qui . . .; multos . . .', *epist.* 1. 1. 77 ff. 'sunt qui . . .; multis . . .', Sen. *dial.* 10. 2. 1 f. 'alium . . ., alium . . ., quosdam . . ., sunt quos . . ., multos . . .', Boeth. *cons.* 3. 2 'alii . . .; alii . . .; sunt qui . . .; at quibus . . .; plurimi . . .'. There is no answer to this argument.

in Iunonis honorem: cf. Quint. *inst.* 1. 1. 6 'Hortensiae Q. filiae oratio . . . legitur non tantum in sexus honorem' (so *inst.* 11. 2. 12), Prop. 4. 6. 13 'Caesaris in nomen ducuntur carmina'.

Iunonis: cf. Hom. *Il.* 4. 51 ff. (Hera speaks) ἦ τοι ἐμοὶ τρεῖς μὲν πολὺ φίλταταί εἰσι πόληες, / Ἄργος τε Σπάρτη τε καὶ εὐρυάγυια Μυκήνη, Pind. *N.* 10. 2 Ἄργος Ἥρας δῶμα θεοπρεπὲς ὑμνεῖτε. Two of Homer's three cities are mentioned in 9, the third, slightly detached from them, in 10. For the Heraeum at Argos cf. Pease on Cic. *nat. deor.* 1. 82.

9. aptum . . . equis: ἱππόβοτον (Hom. *Il.* 2. 287 and often elsewhere), ἱπποτρόφον (Pind. *N.* 10. 41). The expression is used with more propriety in *epist.* 1. 7. 41 'non est aptus equis Ithace locus'. According to Str. 8. 8. 1 the horses of the Argolid were still good (cf. Virg. *georg.* 3. 121, Gratt. 502).

dicet: the manuscripts are evenly divided between future and present; the future is preferable because it is different from the last tense (*sunt* in 5) and absolves us from identifying the panegyrists of Argos. Nevertheless, for an Argive poet cf. Paus. 1. 13. 8.

Argos: though Alpheius of Mytilene, a poet of the Augustan age, laments the eclipse of Argos (*anth. P.* 9. 104), the city seems not to have suffered unduly from Roman rule; cf. Str. 8. 6. 18 καὶ νῦν συνέστηκεν ἡ πόλις δευτερεύουσα τῇ τάξει μετὰ τὴν Σπάρτην. Many of the extant remains belong to the Roman period.

The Greek form of the name is suited to a lyric poem. In his satires and epistles Horace uses the Latin form *Argi* (so also Virgil). Cf. Varro, *ling.* 9. 89 'itaque dicimus *hic Argus* cum hominem dicimus, cum oppidum graecanice *hoc Argos*, cum latine *Argi*'.

ditis . . .: πολύχρυσος, cf. Hom. *Il.* 7. 180 and elsewhere, Soph. *El.* 9. The total disappearance of the city of gold is a commonplace in the poets of the Anthology (9. 28, 101, 102, 103); cf. also Str. 8. 6. 10, Lucian, *Charon* 23 Μυκήνας δὲ καὶ Κλεωνὰς αἰσχύνομαι δεῖξαί σοι . . . πλὴν ἀλλὰ πάλαι μὲν ἦσαν εὐδαίμονες, νῦν δὲ τεθνᾶσι καὶ αὗται.

10. me nec . . .: the distribution of the illustrative proper names reveals an interesting aspect of Horace's technique. From the prosaic standpoint one might have expected him to say 'Let others

tell of Argos, Mycenae, Sparta, and Larissa; I prefer Tibur to all of
them'. Instead we find 'Let others tell of Argos and Mycenae; I prefer Tibur to Sparta and Larissa'. So also 1. 9. 9 ff. 'When the gods
have stilled the waves, the woods are no longer shaken', 1. 14. 14 n.,
1. 19. 16 n., 1. 20. 9 n., 1. 31. 9 ff. 'Others may drink expensive wines;
I eat olives and mallows', 4. 8. 1 ff. 'I wish I could give plate, bronze
statues, and tripods to all my friends; you would have a marble
statue or a painting'.

patiens: καρτερική; cf. Arist. *pol.* 1269ᵇ19 f. ὅλην γὰρ τὴν πόλιν ὁ
νομοθέτης εἶναι βουλόμενος καρτερικήν, Nepos, *Alc.* 11. 4 'Lacedae-
monios, quorum moribus summa virtus in patientia ponebatur'.
The discipline was incongruously elaborated in an age that did not
need it; in Horace's time and later boys were flogged to death at the
altar of Artemis Orthia, a practice that suggested useful reflections
to the philosophic tourist. Cf. Cic. *Tusc.* 2. 34, 5. 77, Plut. *inst. Lac.*
239 d, *Lyc.* 18. 1, Paus. 3. 14. 10, 3. 16. 10, Liban. *or.* 1. 23, R. M.
Dawkins, *Artemis Orthia, JHS* Supplement, 1929, s.v. καρτερίας ἀγών,
especially the discussion on pp. 404 f.

11. Larisae: the principal town of Thessaly, situated in the fertile
plain of Pelasgiotis (Str. 9. 5. 19). Though not mentioned in Homer,
it was a great city from early times, and in Horace's day still kept its
prosperity; cf. Str. 9. 5. 3 τῶν δὲ πόλεων ὀλίγαι σώζουσι τὸ πάτριον
ἀξίωμα, μάλιστα δὲ Λάρισα.

percussit: ἐξέπληξεν, cf. Virg. *georg.* 2. 476 '(Musarum) sacra fero
ingenti percussus amore', *Aen.* 9. 197 'magno laudum percussus
amore'. The metaphor is reinforced by the mention of a weapon in
Lucr. 1. 922 f. 'acri / percussit thyrso laudis spes magna meum cor'.

opimae: cf. Hom. *Il.* 2. 841 Λάρισαν ἐριβώλακα (though that passage refers to the Asiatic Larisa, near Cyme). Both the Asiatic and
the Thessalian cities were assigned a legendary king called Piasos,
who had a daughter called Larisa (cf. Suidas 1. 67 s.v. ἀθέμιστα, *RE*
20. 1185); it seems possible that Piasos means 'fat' or 'fertile' (cf.
Roscher 3. 2493). Thus both cities are connected with fertility not
merely by the facts of geography but by literary association.

12. domus Albuneae resonantis: Albunea was the Sibyl of Tibur and
had a cult there. Cf. Lact. *inst.* 1. 6. 12 (citing Varro) 'Tiburtem
nomine Albuneam, quae Tiburi colatur ut dea iuxta ripas amnis
Anienis, cuius in gurgite simulacrum eius inventum esse dicitur
tenens in manu librum', Tib. 2. 5. 69 f. 'quasque Aniena sacras
Tiburs per flumina sortes / portarit sicco pertuleritque sinu', *CIL* 14.
4262. Virgil seems to be thinking of Tibur when he refers to an oracle
at Albunea (*Aen.* 7. 82 ff. 'lucosque sub alta / consulit Albunea,
nemorum quae maxima sacro / fonte sonat saevamque exhalat

opaca mephitim', *RE* 6 A. 833 f.); for another site see R. L. Dunbabin, *CR* 47, 1933, 56 n. 2, B. Tilly, *JRS* 24, 1934, 25 ff., H. Boas,
Aeneas' Arrival in Latium, 1938, pp. 195 ff., M. Guarducci, *Albunea*,
in *Studi in honore di Gino Funaioli*, 1955, pp. 120 ff.

The *domus* of Albunea has been explained in two different ways.
L. Müller plausibly referred to the 'Grotta di Nettuno', the dark
gulf into which the Anio used to fall. Statius speaks of *antra* near the
Anio fall (*silv.* 1. 3. 70), and these would be a suitable home for
Albunea. For the use of *domus* cf. Hes. *th.* 777 f. (of Styx) with
West's note, Virg. *Aen.* 1. 166 ff., Prop. 1. 20. 33 f., Philippus, *anth. P.*
6. 203. 5 ff. Others less plausibly identify the *domus* with one of the
two small temples perched on the edge of the Anio gorge, just above
the point at which the cascade used to fall (see the map in *RE* 6
A. 837).

resonantis: one can speak of a transferred epithet; yet the adjective is more poetical with *Albuneae* than it would be with *domus*.
The gorge under the waterfall might seem to resound with the voice
of the Sibyl.

13. praeceps: 'cascading'; cf. Stat. *silv.* 1. 5. 25. The Villa Gregoriana
where the Anio falls is a beauty-spot familiar to modern tourists.
Yet the dryness of Horace's description need not surprise us. To the
ancients Tivoli was connected with cool air and pleasant orchards;
the water added to the freshness of the place, but the romantic
spectacle as such attracted little comment. Statius is more interested
in the Anio after it had been diverted into the water-works of his
friend Vopiscus (*silv.* 1. 3); even today Italians put a higher price on
the artificial charms of the Villa d'Este than on the natural ones of
the Villa Gregoriana. See further Troxler-Keller 76, 134 ff.

Tiburni: the foundation of Tibur was attributed either to Catillus
(1. 18. 2 n.) or to three brothers, Tiburnus (Tiburtus in Virg. *Aen.* 7.
671), Coras, and Catillus. The legends were sometimes accommodated
by the assumption of two Catilli, the three brothers then becoming
the sons of Catillus I. The *lucus* implies a hero-cult of Tiburnus and
presumably contained the holm-oaks mentioned by Pliny (*nat.* 16.
237). Its situation is not certain; Weinstock's map in *RE* puts it on
the spur above the cascade. In Suetonius's time the guides pointed
out Horace's *domus* (a town rather than a country house) 'circa
Tiburni luculum' (*vit. Hor.* v. 65 f. Rostagni); see further *epist.* 1. 8.
12, *carm.* 4. 2. 30, 4. 3. 10, Dunbabin, loc. cit. [12 n.].

uda mobilibus pomaria rivis: the apple orchards in the valley
below the cascade, watered by irrigation channels. The *rivi* are
mobiles because the water can be directed now into one channel, now
into another. This is the interpretation of Dacier, citing Mart. 12.

31. 2 'riguae ductile flumen aquae'; for inscriptions regulating the irrigation system at Tibur cf. M. P. Nilsson, *Eranos* 43, 1945, 301 ff. The *Thesaurus l.L.* (8. 1198. 45 ff.) interprets 'swiftly moving' and cites Claud. *rapt. Pros.* 2. 103 f. 'fontes / roscida mobilibus lambebant gramina rivis', Cypr. Gall. *num.* 79 'mobilibus delibans pocula rivis'; these two late authors may be remembering Horace, but that does not guarantee that they interpreted him aright.

The orchards are mentioned also in Colum. 10. 138, Sil. 4. 224 f., Stat. *silv.* 1. 3. 81 f., Symm. *epist.* 7. 18. 3, 7. 19. The Anio itself is called *pomifer* in the MSS. of Prop. 4. 7. 81 and Ov. *am.* 3. 6. 46 (but cf. G. P. Goold, *HSPh* 69, 1965, 51 f.). However, the Epicurean Catius thought the apples of Tibur overrated (*serm.* 2. 4. 70). For *udus* as a conventional epithet of Tibur cf. Troxler-Keller 134 f.

15. albus: 'clearing' (cf. 3. 27. 19, Call. fr. 228. 51 νότος αἴθριος, Virg. *georg.* 1. 460 'claro . . . Aquilone'). The epithet is emphatic and pointed; the south wind is often associated with rain, but even it sometimes blows clear. In particular Horace is suggesting the technical term λευκόνοτος (the clearing south wind that blew especially in early January); cf. Arist. *meteor.* 362ª14 ff., *probl.* 942ª34 ff., Theophr. *de ventis* 11; the name distinguished it from the rain-bringing νότοι of winter, for which cf. Hdt. 2. 25. 2, *RE* 12. 2284 ff.

deterget: 'wipes away'; the verb is not at this period common in poetry. For its conjunction with *nubila* cf. Claud. 28. 539 f. '(aer) solis radiis detersa removit / nubila', Symm. *epist.* 2. 83 'nubem invidiae . . . abstergeat'. The word suggests the wiping away of tears (cf. *Thes.l.L.* 5. 1. 796. 55 ff., 61 ff., Rufinus, *anth. P.* 5. 43. 5 ἐκμάξαι, μὴ κλαῖε, τέκνον).

16. parturit: cf. Lucr. 6. 259 'fulminibus gravidam tempestatem atque procellis', 440, Manil. 1. 853 'gravidas . . . nubes', 2. 75, *Orph. h.* 82. 3 f. (to the South Wind) ἔλθοις . . . ὄμβροιο γενάρχα· / τοῦτο γὰρ ἐκ Διός ἐστι σέθεν γέρας ἠερόφοιτον, / ὀμβροτόκους νεφέλας ἐξ ἠέρος εἰς χθόνα πέμπειν.

17. perpetuo . . .: Plancus is urged to imitate the *albus Notus* and clear away his troubles. Similarly, in 2. 9. 1 ff. Valgius's perpetual tears are compared, to their disadvantage, with the rains, which sometimes give over.

The manuscripts are divided between *perpetuo* and *perpetuos*; with *sic* following, corruption either way would have been very easy. *perpetuo* gives a better formal parallel to *saepe* and to the *semper* of 2. 9. 1. It is also more precise (and this is the crucial point). *parturit imbres perpetuos* would mean 'is on the point of giving birth to perpetual rain' (*parturit* does not mean *parit*, a fact sometimes

obscured by the translation 'breeds'). But it is the present heaviness
of the clouds that is relevant, not the duration of the future storm.

sapiens: the adjective conceals the command 'be sensible'; cf.
1. 11. 6 n.

finire . . . : 'to set a limit to', for the time being, not necessarily for
ever; cf. 3. 4. 37 ff. 'vos Caesarem altum, militia simul / fessas
cohortis abdidit oppidis, / finire quaerentem labores / Pierio re-
creatis antro'.

19. molli: 'mellow'; cf. Virg. *georg.* 1. 341, Juv. 1. 69, Hor. *carm.* 3. 21.
8 'languidiora vina', 3. 29. 2 'lene merum'. μαλακός ('mild') is used of
wine in Arist. *probl.* 873^b34.

seu . . . tenent seu . . . tenebit: 'whether the camp holds you as
now or, as in future, your home at Tibur'; the disjunction implies
that Plancus is now on a campaign (cf. p. 91) and promises a home-
coming. Attempts to get rid of *tenebit* (e.g. L. Müller's *latebris* or P.
Maas's *recepit*) make much worse sense; they imply that Horace
does not know whether Plancus is at home or abroad.

fulgentia signis: the Roman army made a glittering show; cf. Liv.
33. 10. 2 'omnia circa iuga signis atque armis fulgere', Luc. 1. 244
'notae fulsere aquilae Romanaque signa', Tac. *hist.* 3. 82. 2. The
eagles were normally of silver; cf. Cic. *Cat.* 1. 24, App. *civ.* 4. 101. 425,
and especially Plin. *nat.* 33. 58 (of the colour of silver) 'ideo militaribus signis familiarior quoniam longius fulget'.

The phrase gives a decorative particularity to the commonplace
opposition between *castra* and *umbra*, which is often used, as here, to
contrast the active with the inactive life; cf. Cic. *Mur.* 30 'cedat . . .
stilus gladio, umbra soli', *Brut.* 37, *leg.* 3. 14, Juv. 7. 173, Sen. *contr.* 3.
pr. 13, 1. 32. 1 *vacui* n.

21. tui: cf. Juv. 3. 319 'tuo . . . Aquino'. Plancus came from Tibur
(above, p. 90).

Teucer . . . : the pattern of the ending (a myth and a speech
illustrating a maxim) is clearly derived from Greek lyric (below,
24 n.). However, the immediate source for Teucer's speech is much
less clear. Stroux, loc. cit., pointed out some apparent resemblances
in Jason's speech in Val. Fl. 1. 241 ff. Jason, like Teucer, exhorts his
companions on the day before departure ('o socii, . . . ite viri mecum'),
reminds them of a god's support, and urges them to enjoy what time
remains ('hanc vero, socii, venientem litore laeti / dulcibus alloquiis
ludoque educite noctem'). This latter passage has obvious affinities
with Chiron's speech in Horace's thirteenth epode (cf. 17 f. 'illic
omne malum vino cantuque levato / deformis aegrimoniae dulcibus
alloquiis'). But that does not justify us in positing a common source
for the speeches of Chiron, Teucer, and Jason. Chiron's speech seems

L

to be connected with a papyrus fragment plausibly attributed to Bacchylides (*Ox. pap.* 23. 2364, pointed out by Fraenkel 66); and there is no obvious place for Teucer's kind of exhortation in that context. Our myth may be modelled on a totally different poem from Greek choral lyric of which we know nothing; or more probably Horace himself inserted in a lyric framework elements of quite different provenance (see below). As for Jason's speech, Valerius Flaccus may simply have combined two Horatian passages with certain general resemblances.

Certainly a Roman reader would associate Teucer's speech not with lyric (in spite of the setting) nor with epic (in spite of the diction), but primarily with tragedy. Sophocles had described how Teucer was banished from the Attic Salamis because he returned from Troy without his brother Aias; see *Ai.* 1008 ff., and especially the fragments of the *Teucer* (Pearson 2. 214 ff.). Pacuvius produced a Roman version of this play; and in it, as in Horace's version, Teucer showed readiness to accept whatever fortune might bring (25 n.).

22. fugeret: with *Salamina* the word suggests 'was going into exile from', ἔφευγεν; cf. Virg. *ecl.* 1. 4.

uda: 'flown with wine', a loftier substitute for the comic and prosaic *madidus*; cf. 4. 5. 39, *serm.* 2. 6. 69 f. 'seu quis . . . modicis (poculis) uvescit', Mart. 5. 84. 5.

Lyaeo: the wine-god stands for the wine itself; cf. Lucr. 2. 656 f. 'Bacchi nomine abuti / mavult quam laticis proprium proferre vocamen'. The figure is as old as Homer; cf. *Il.* 2. 426 σπλάγχνα δ' ἄρ' ἀμπείραντες ὑπείρεχον Ἡφαίστοιο with Leaf's note, Wackernagel, *Vorlesungen* 2. 62.

The name *Lyaeus* means 'the loosener' (from care); cf. *epod.* 9. 37 f. 'curam metumque . . . dulci Lyaeo solvere', Plut. *adul. et amic.* 68 d ἀντιταττόμενον τῷ Λυαίῳ θεῷ καὶ λύοντι τὸ τῶν δυσφόρων σχοίνιον μεριμνᾶν κατὰ Πίνδαρον (fr. 248), Dodds 76 f., 1. 18. 4 n. Here *Lyaeo* seems to be in tension with *vinxisse*; cf. Prop. 3. 5. 21 'multo mentem vincire Lyaeo', Boucher 243 f.

23. populea: the crown of white poplar is found in several cults, notably that of Sabazius or Dionysus (cf. Dem. 18. 260, Gruppe 2. 1532 n. 4); but it was particularly associated with Hercules. Cf. Theoc. 2. 121 κρατὶ δ' ἔχων λεύκαν, Ἡρακλέος ἱερὸν ἔρνος, schol. ad loc. ⟨Ἐρατοσθένης ἐν πρώτῳ⟩ Ὀλυμπιονικῶν φησὶ τὸν Ἡρακλέα κατελθόντα εἰς Ἅιδου εὑρεῖν παρὰ τῷ Ἀχέροντι φυομένην τὴν λεύκην καὶ αὐτῇ ἀναστέψασθαι ἣν Ὅμηρος ἀχερωΐδα καλεῖ, Pfeiffer on Call. fr. inc. 804 (add Serv. *Aen.* 5. 134, Paus. 5. 14. 2, Gruppe 1. 146). For Latin instances cf. Virg. *ecl.* 7. 61, *georg.* 2. 66, *Aen.* 8. 276, Ov. *epist.* 9. 64, Phaedr. 3. 17. 4, Tert. *cor.* 7. 4 (cited on 7 above).

Teucer is perhaps given a poplar crown because he is going on a dangerous journey. Hercules was *vagus* (3. 3. 9), ἡγεμών (Xen. *anab.* 6. 2. 15), the patron of adventurers and explorers (*anab.* 4. 8. 25 ἀποθῦσαι τῷ Διὶ τῷ σωτῆρι καὶ τῷ ʿΗρακλεῖ ἡγεμόσυνα). It is also just possible that Horace is tying up his myth with the rest of the poem. There was a very important cult of Hercules at Tibur (*RE* 6 A. 827 ff.), and it is highly probable that a local magnate like Plancus held a priesthood. Perhaps on ceremonial occasions in his native town he appeared, like Teucer, bedecked with poplar. It may be objected that such circumstances would not be known to the generality of Horace's readers, but they need have been no more obscure than the joke about Trebatius (*serm.* 2. 1. 8); that passage can only be fully savoured if we realize that Trebatius was a swimmer (Cic. *epist.* 7. 10. 2).

The form *populeus* may have been coined by Ennius (*ann.* 577) as a metrically convenient equivalent for *populneus*; *populnus* once seems to perform the same function (Plaut. *Cas.* 384).

fertur: the word is not sceptical, but simply claims that the story is traditional; cf. 1. 16. 13 (Prometheus), 3. 5. 41 (Regulus), 3. 21. 11 *narratur* (the elder Cato), *epod.* 14. 9 *dicunt* (Anacreon). Such appeals to tradition are already found in Sappho (166) and in Pindar (*O.* 6. 29, 7. 54, 9. 49, and elsewhere), and the learned poets of Alexandria similarly disclaim invention, even of eccentric details; cf. Call. fr. 612 ἀμάρτυρον οὐδὲν ἀείδω, h. 3. 210 f. καὶ δέ σέ φασι / καλὴν Ἀντίκλειαν ἴσον φαέεσσι φιλῆσαι, 5. 56, 6. 52, Euphorion fr. 40 Powell πορφυρέη ὑάκινθε, σὲ μὲν μία φῆμις ἀοιδῶν / ʿΡοιτείης ἀμάθοισι δεδουπότος Αἰακίδαο / εἴαρος ἀντέλλειν γεγραμμένα κωκύουσαν, Norden on *Aen.* 6. 14, Fordyce on Catull. 64. 1, Newman 46, R. Pfeiffer, *History of Classical Scholarship*, 1968, pp. 125 f.

24. adfatus: Teucer's words are spoken at a symposium on the day before sailing. *adfatus* is thus present in tense, as deponent participles often are (cf. K.–S. 1. 759 f.). For the technique of ending a myth with a speech cf. R. Führer, *Formproblem-Untersuchungen zu den Reden in der frühgriechischen Lyrik*, 1967, p. 77, above, p. 93.

25. quo nos cumque feret . . .: Teucer's readiness to make a home-land anywhere is treated as an *exemplum* by Cicero, who is probably quoting Pacuvius's play; cf. *Tusc.* 5. 108 'itaque ad omnem rationem Teucri vox accommodari potest: "patria est ubicumque est bene" (*trag. inc.* 92)'. The same passage is also cited by Sen. *rem. fort.* 8. 2, ps.-Sen. *mor.* 43. The topic is an old Greek one; cf. Democritus fr. 247 ἀνδρὶ σοφῷ πᾶσα γῆ βατή· ψυχῆς γὰρ ἀγαθῆς πατρὶς ὁ ξύμπας κόσμος, Eur. fr. 777, 1047. 2 ἅπασα δὲ χθὼν ἀνδρὶ γενναίῳ πατρίς, *trag. adesp.* 318 (perhaps from Sophocles's *Teucer*) τῷ γὰρ καλῶς πράσσοντι πᾶσα γῆ

πατρίς with Nauck's note, Pearson 2. 216, Ar. *Plut.* 1151 πατρὶς γάρ
ἐστι πᾶσ' ἵν' ἂν πράττῃ τις εὖ, Otto 268, Pease on Cic. *nat. deor.* 1. 121,
Bömer on Ov. *fast.* 1. 493. This line of argument was particularly
used in philosophical consolations against the deprivations of exile;
cf. Sen. *dial.* 12. 8, Plut. *exil.* 600 e ff., Muson. fr. 9 p. 42 Hense, E. T.
Silk, *YClS* 13, 1952, 148 f.

   melior: 'kinder'; cf. Ov. *rem.* 761 'me certe Sappho meliorem fecit
amicae', *Thes.l.L.* 2. 2087. 28 ff. Cicero quotes a harsh speech of
Telamon's (Pacuv. *trag.* 327 ff.): 'segregare abs te ausu's aut sine illo
Salamina ingredi? / neque paternum aspectum es veritus, quom
aetate exacta indigem / liberum lacerasti orbasti extinxti, neque
fratris necis / neque eius gnati parvi, qui tibi in tutelam est tradi-
tus?'; cf. also 342/3 'te repudio nec recipio: naturam abdico: i
facesse', Paus. 1. 28. 11 (where Telamon is said to have accused
Teucer of actual complicity in Aias's death).

26. ibimus: Bentley, without comment, puts a full stop after this
word in his second edition of 1713. This has the advantage of making
the pathetic *o socii* begin a sentence; it is also nearer to the closely
parallel passage in Virgil (*Aen.* 1. 197, cited on 30 below). But it is
doubtful whether Horace's readers would have known that they
were to stop at this point; there is not another strong pause in the
middle of the tetrameter.

   o socii: both words are heroic; cf. *epist.* 1. 2. 21 'dum sibi, dum
sociis reditum parat' (translating Hom. *Od.* 1. 5 ἀρνύμενος ἥν τε
ψυχὴν καὶ νόστον ἑταίρων), Lucil. 1323, Prop. 3. 7. 41, 3. 21. 11, Luc. 3.
716, 6. 164, Sil. 2. 44.

27. Teucro: Teucer's speech is full of appropriate μεγαλοψυχία. This
is heightened by his grandiloquent use of his own name; cf. Landgraf
on Cic. *S. Rosc.* 32, Gudeman on Tac. *dial.* 3. 3, Headlam on Herodas
1. 76, H.–Sz. 412. One can add Soph. *OT* 7 f. αὐτὸς ὧδ' ἐλήλυθα, / ὁ
πᾶσι κλεινὸς Οἰδίπους καλούμενος, Virg. *Aen.* 11. 440 ff. 'vobis animam
hanc soceroque Latino / Turnus ego, haud ulli veterum virtute
secundus, / devovi', 2. 79.

   Teucro duce et auspice Teucro: the heroics are set in very Roman
terms; the technical equivalent would be *ductu auspiciisque Teucri*
(cf. inscr. ap. Plin. *nat.* 3. 136 'quod eius ductu auspiciisque gentes
Alpinae omnes . . . sub imperium p. R. sunt redactae', Ogilvie on
Liv. 3. 1. 4, M. A. Levi, *RIL* 71, 1938, 101 ff.). It is true that though
things were done 'under the auspices' of a Roman general, he himself was not, in the historical period, called an *auspex*; but Horace is
looking back to an heroic age when the general literally took the
omens. The variation on the technical phrase is quite in Horace's
manner; cf. 2. 4. 24 'claudere lustrum' (for *condere*), 3. 5. 42 'capitis

minor' (= *capite deminutus*), 4. 2. 42 'publicum ludum' (for the plural), 4. 14. 1 'quae cura patrum quaeve Quiritium' (for *senatus populive Romani*).

The variant *Teucri* is well attested and ancient. Ps.-Acro explains 'auspice: fautore vel suasore' and 'auspice Teucri: Apollinem dicit cuius responsum vel promissa sequebatur'; he thus took the phrase to mean 'under the guidance of Teucer and of Teucer's protecting god'. For *auspex* applied to gods cf. *epist.* 1. 3. 13, Virg. *Aen.* 3. 19 f., 4. 45, Stat. *silv.* 2. 2. 39, 3. 5. 74. But it is hard to separate *duce* and *auspice*, which naturally make a pair.

Some editors punctuate after *auspice* and take *Teucri* or *Teucro* with the following sentence. But no ancient author could hope to be understood if, in an age without punctuation, he stopped a sentence at the end of the fifth foot and then postponed his *enim* until the third place. Those who adopt this interpretation dislike the presence of *Teucro* twice in one sentence; but the naïve braggadocio suits Horace's picture of Teucer's self-confidence.

28. certus: Apollo is both unerring and truthful, νημερτής and ἀψευδής. For his oracle cf. Eur. *Hel.* 148 ff.

29. ambiguam: Teucer's Salamis in Cyprus 'disputed the name' with its parent city; contrast Sen. *Tro.* 844 'Aiacis Salamina veram' (Scaliger, *veri* codd.). *ambiguam* reinforces *nova*; both imply a new Salamis. It is also in tension with *certus*; but the contrast is purely formal, and has nothing to do with the precise meaning of *ambiguam* in this context. Some editors, not appreciating this, see an allusion to the traditional ambiguity of oracles; but after saying that Apollo was *certus*, Teucer could not undermine the confidence of his men by suggesting that he spoke in riddles.

30. peioraque passi: a conflation of Hom. *Od.* 12. 208 ὦ φίλοι, οὐ γάρ πώ τι κακῶν ἀδαήμονές εἰμεν and 20. 18 τετλάθι δή, κραδίη· καὶ κύντερον ἄλλο ποτ' ἔτλης (a familiar line in ethical teaching; cf. Pl. *rep.* 390 d). See also *serm.* 2. 5. 21, Virg. *Aen.* 1. 197 f. (in a context imitating the first Homeric passage) 'o socii, neque enim ignari sumus ante malorum, / o passi graviora, dabit deus his quoque finem'. This may be one of the rare places where Horace has influenced Virgil, unless both are indebted to an earlier poet, perhaps Naevius; cf. Serv. auct. *Aen.* 1. 198 'et totus hic locus de Naevio belli Punici libro translatus est'.

32. cras . . . : cf. Hom. *Od.* 12. 23 ff. ἀλλ' ἄγετ' ἐσθίετε βρώμην καὶ πίνετε οἶνον / αὖθι πανημέριοι· ἅμα δ' ἠοῖ φαινομένηφι / πλεύσεσθ', 293.

iterabimus: Teucer had come from Troy to Salamis and now had to set sail again. Horace is alluding to the rustic meaning 'to plough a second time'; cf. Cic. *de orat.* 2. 131 'agro non semel arato sed iterato', Varro, *rust.* 1. 29. 2 'terram cum primum arant, proscindere appellant . . .; cum iteratur, offringere vocant', Colum. 2. 4. 4, Serv. auct. *georg.* 1. 97. It is very significant that Catullus uses *proscindere* of the first ship (64. 12). Ploughing words are often applied to sailing; cf. τέμνειν (Hom. *Od.* 3. 175), ἀροῦν (Aesch. *supp.* 1007), ἀρότας (Call. fr. 572), *arare* (Virg. *Aen.* 2. 780, etc.), *sulcare* (Virg. *Aen.* 5. 158, etc.). For a different application of the metaphor cf. Hes. *th.* 440 with West's note.

8. LYDIA DIC

1–3. Why, Lydia, are you making Sybaris die of love? 3–12. Why does he keep away from the Campus Martius with its manly sports? 13–16. Why does he skulk in hiding like Achilles before the Trojan War?

It was generally recognized in the ancient world that love and athletics are incompatible pursuits. The sententious slave in Plautus's *Bacchides* contrasts the old and new behaviour of the young (428 ff.):

> ibi cursu luctando hasta disco pugilatu pila
> saliendo sese exercebant magis quam scorto aut saviis:
> ibi suam aetatem extendebant, non in latebrosis locis.

So also the moralizing historian: 'magisque in decoris armis et militaribus equis quam in scortis atque conviviis lubidinem habebant' (Sall. *Cat.* 7. 4). Indeed, a sudden aversion to exercise could be regarded as a symptom of love (Plaut. *most.* 149 ff.):

> cor dolet quom scio ut nunc sum atque ut fui,
> quo neque industrior de iuventute erat
> ⟨quisquam nec clarior⟩ arte gymnastica:
> disco hastis pila cursu armis equo
> victitabam volup.

The topic was treated more sentimentally in the novel; cf. Chariton 1. 1. 9–10 (Chaereas in love with Callirhoe) τῷ δὲ ηὔξετο τὸ κακὸν ὥστε μηδὲ ἐπὶ τὰς συνήθεις προιέναι διατριβάς. ἐπόθει δὲ τὸ γυμνάσιον Χαιρέαν καὶ ὥσπερ ἔρημον ἦν. ἐφίλει γὰρ αὐτὸν ἡ νεολαία. From diverse Hellenistic sources the commonplace flowed to Roman elegy; cf. Prop. 2. 16. 33 f. 'tot iam abiere dies cum me nec cura theatri / nec tetigit Campi nec mea mensa iuvat'.

Horace, like Propertius, sets the Greek situation in the mundane surroundings of the Campus Martius. He gives the athletic exercises a healthy national flavour (cf. Cic. *off.* 1. 104 'suppeditant autem et

Campus noster et studia venandi honesta exempla ludendi'). His treatment particularly suits his own period, when Augustus instituted *collegia iuvenum* as a Romanized equivalent of the Greek *ephebia*. This youth movement concentrated on military skills, and above all on riding. See Dio 52. 26. 1 (a speech attributed to Maecenas) ἐπί τε τοὺς ἵππους καὶ ἐπὶ τὰ ὅπλα τρέπωνται, E. Norden, *Neue Jahrb.* 7, 1901, 263. 1 (= *Kleine Schriften*, 1966, p. 373 n. 41), M. Della Corte, *Iuventus*, 1924, pp. 5 ff., L. R. Taylor, *JRS* 14, 1924, 158 ff., H. I. Marrou, *Histoire de l'éducation dans l'antiquité*, ed. 6, 1965, pp. 431 ff. and 609.

But in spite of this realistic element in Horace's poem some incongruity remains. In Greece the athlete was idealized by poets and sculptors, and the gymnasium was an institution at the heart of the community's social life. Riding in the Campus Martius was less significant, and Horace did not belong to the riding set. In Greece the palaestra was associated with homosexuality; thus Philostratus complains to an imaginary youth who neglects his beauty (*epist.* 27 [39]) οὐχ ἵππον ἀναβαίνεις, οὐκ ἐς παλαίστραν ἀπαντᾷς, οὐχ ἡλίῳ δίδως ἑαυτόν (cf. also Rufinus, *anth. P.* 5. 19. 1 f. οὐκέτι παιδομανὴς ὡς πρίν ποτε, νῦν δὲ καλοῦμαι / θηλυμανής, καὶ νῦν δίσκος ἐμοὶ κρόταλον). In Rome there was no such convention; the young man in love with a girl had less reason to avoid Campus and Tiber, but might rather disport himself before her (8 n., Tib. 1. 4. 11 f.). But these inconsistencies do not matter; a charming blend of the Greek and the Roman, the fanciful and the actual, is a characteristic feature of Horace's *Odes*. Hellenistic sentimentality and Augustan militarism might seem not to mix, but in this poem Horace does not take either of them too seriously.

In the last stanza Horace's accusations become a little more specific; he suggests that Sybaris has disappeared because Lydia is hiding him. This is brought out by the myth of Achilles at Scyros: when Achilles lay hid in the *gynaeceum* he was the lover of Deidamia. In the same spirit Catullus asks his friend Camerius where he is skulking (55. 1 f.): 'oramus si forte non molestum est / demonstres ubi sint tuae latebrae' (*tenebrae* codd.). And he forms the same suspicion as Horace (15 ff.): 'dic nobis ubi sis futurus, ede / audacter, committe crede luci. / num te lacteolae tenent puellae?'

The ode is one of the best of Horace's ἐρωτικά. As he does not profess to describe his own experiences he can assume the detached, amused pose that suits him so well. The rapid cross-examination of Lydia suggests a real situation, even while the reader knows that such a situation is impossible. No words are wasted; the alliteration adds to the impact (3–4, 8, 16); Horace writes with a verve more typical of Catullus than of himself. The poem owes much of its success to its gay and catchy metre (cf. p. xliv). One seems to hear galloping hooves on the riding-track, the rush of the javelin over-shooting the mark, the clattering charge on the Lycian spearsmen.

Metre: Greater Sapphic.

1. Lydia: the exotic name suggests luxury and voluptuousness (cf. Xenophanes 3. 1 ἁβροσύνας δὲ μαθόντες ἀνωφελέας παρὰ Λυδῶν). Valerius Cato, the scholar and poet who helped to launch the neoteric movement, wrote a *Lydia*; Horace himself used the name elsewhere (1. 13, 1. 25, 3. 9), as did an anonymous versifier in the Virgilian Appendix. Heinze sees in our passage a possible allusion to the Lydian princess Omphale, to whom Hercules was enslaved; cf. Soph. *Tr.* 432 ἡ Λυδία, Prop. 3. 11. 17 f. 'Omphale . . . Lydia Gygaeo tincta puella lacu', Ov. *fast.* 2. 356, Stat. *Theb.* 10. 646, Tert. *pall.* 4. 3 'tantum Lydiae clanculariae licuit ut Hercules in Omphale et Omphale in Hercule prostitueretur'. Yet after Valerius Cato had popularized the name it is not certain that such a reference would be detected.

2. te deos oro: the variant *hoc deos vere* is supported by more and 'better' manuscripts, by ps.-Acro, and by the bulk of the *testimonia*; for the details, which are of no practical importance, see Keller and Holder. *hoc deos oro* is also attested, apparently a conflation of the two other readings. The first two of these variants presumably go back to the ancient world; therefore there is no point in counting authorities or even weighing them. Only sense and idiom can show what Horace wrote.

On these counts *te deos oro* is clearly superior. For similar phrases in Horace cf. *serm.* 1. 7. 33 f. 'per magnos Brute deos te / oro', *epist.* 1. 7. 94 f. Moreover, the position of *te*, tucked away between *omnes* and *deos*, is idiomatic; cf. Plaut. *capt.* 977 'per tuom te genium obse-cro', Ter. *Andr.* 538, 834, Virg. *Aen.* 12. 56 ff. 'Turne, per has ego te lacrimas . . . / unum oro', K.–S. 1. 584 f., 2. 593, Wackernagel, *Kleine Schriften* 1. 28 f. A combination of *per deos* with *dic* (without *oro*) is not wrong; cf. Cael. ap. Cic. *epist.* 8. 14. 4 'curre per deos atque homines', F. Vollmer, *Hermes* 45, 1910, 470 ff. Yet *vere* is pointless in a question such as ours, to which no answer can conceivably be given; contrast Hom. *Od.* 11. 140 ff. ἀλλ᾽ ἄγε μοι τόδε εἰπὲ καὶ ἀτρεκέως κατά-λεξον / . . . εἰπέ, ἄναξ, πῶς κέν με ἀναγνοίη τὸν ἐόντα;, W. S. Gilbert, *Patience* 'Prithee, pretty maiden—prithee, tell me true . . . Have you e'er a lover a-dangling after you?'

The blame for the corruption rests with the ancient metricians (H. W. Garrod, *CR* 35, 1921, 102 f.). Caesius Bassus (the friend and literary executor of Persius) first of all quotes the line in the correct form 'te deos oro Sybarin cur properes amando' (*gramm*. 6. 270. 4 ff.). But then he goes on to say that according to the practice of Alcaeus the line should have begun with a choriamb; to illustrate this point he modifies Horace's line to read 'hoc dea vere Sybarin cur properes amando' ($- \cup \cup - - \cup \cup - - \cup \cup - \cup - -$). He explains that Horace substituted a spondee for an iambus in the first choriamb, and to show what he means he repeats his own invented line with the least possible change 'hoc deos vere Sybarin'. But through the clumsiness of his expression he implies that this is what Horace actually wrote. For a similar account cf. Atilius Fortunatianus, *gramm*. 6. 300. 19 ff.

Sybarin: the name belongs to the imaginary world of Hellenistic epigram or romance (cf. 1. 13. 1 Telephus, 1. 17. 25 Cyrus, 2. 5. 20 Gyges). Here one thinks of the inhabitants of the sixth-century city who yawned on rose-petals in the relaxing atmosphere of the Tarentine gulf. Athenaeus supplies an agreeable anthology of fictions about their sybaritic behaviour: piped wine, anti-noise by-laws, patent rights for cooks, and tax-relief for the eel-mongers (518 c–521 d). It may also be relevant that erotic novelettes called Συβαριτικά were current in Horace's world; cf. Ov. *trist*. 2. 417 'nec qui composuit nuper Sybaritica fugit', S. Trenkner, *The Greek Novella in the Classical Period*, 1958, pp. 175 f.

amando refers to Sybaris's love rather than Lydia's. The gerund does not necessarily refer to an action of the subject of the sentence; cf. Cic. *Pis*. 43 'M. Regulus quem Carthaginienses . . . vigilando necaverunt', Virg. *georg*. 3. 215 'uritque videndo', J. Lebreton, *Études sur la langue et la grammaire de Cicéron*, 1901, p. 394.

3. perdere: 'to make die of love'; see Ov. *am*. 2. 18. 10 'quae me perdunt oscula mille dedit', Philodemus, *anth. P*. 12. 173. 1 Δημώ με κτείνει καὶ Θέρμιον (cf. the commoner use of *perire* and *perdite amare*).

4. oderit: 'avoids' rather than 'loathes' (1. 38. 1 n.).

Campum: the Campus Martius (1. 9. 18 n.). Strabo gives an enthusiastic picture of its use for riding and recreation (5. 3. 8): τὸ μέγεθος τοῦ πεδίου θαυμαστὸν ἅμα καὶ τὰς ἁρματοδρομίας καὶ τὴν ἄλλην ἱππασίαν ἀκώλυτον παρέχον τῷ τοσούτῳ πλήθει τῶν σφαίρᾳ καὶ κρίκῳ καὶ παλαίστρᾳ γυμναζομένων. Most of the time the Romans were pent up in narrow alleys and overcrowded squares; here they took the sun (cf. *ars* 162 'gaudet equis canibusque et aprici gramine Campi').

patiens: 'though hitherto . . .'; for this use of the adjective cf. Liv. 25. 34. 7 'dux cautus et providens Scipio . . . temerarium capit consilium', Friedrich on Catull. 66. 28. There is therefore no need for Bentley's *impatiens*. Horace makes a similar point in urging his young friend Lollius to go hunting: 'praesertim cum valeas et / vel cursu superare canem vel viribus aprum / possis; adde virilia quod speciosius arma / non est qui tractet' (*epist.* 1. 18. 50 ff.).

pulveris atque solis: cf. *trag. inc.* 206 ff. 'nihil horum similest apud Lacaenas virgines, / quibus magis palaestra Eurota sol pulvis labor / militia studio est quam fertilitas barbara', Cic. *leg.* 3. 14, Sen. *epist.* 80. 3, Tac. *hist.* 2. 99. 1, Symm. *or.* 1. 1, Veg. *mil.* 1. 3, Milton, *Areopagitica* 'I cannot praise a fugitive and cloistered virtue, unexercised and unbreathed, that never sallies out and sees her adversary, but slinks out of the race where that immortal garland is to be run for, not without dust and heat' (οὐκ ἀκονιτί).

Sunburn was a sign of manliness. Cf. Eur. *Ba.* 457 ff. λευκὴν δὲ χροιὰν ἐκ παρασκευῆς ἔχεις, / οὐχ ἡλίου βολαῖσιν, ἀλλ' ὑπὸ σκιᾶς, / τὴν Ἀφροδίτην καλλονῇ θηρώμενος, Pl. *rep.* 556 d, Ov. *ars* 1. 513 'fuscentur corpora Campo'.

5. cur neque . . .: Horace may be referring to two separate activities, first military formation-riding, secondly a solo rodeo stunt. *militaris* is probably accusative plural rather than nominative singular. The word is normally an adjective in classical Latin; exceptions seem to refer to military men as a class or type. Yet it could be argued in favour of the other view that it is unnatural to qualify *aequalis* with an adjective.

6. equitat: the indicative here is much less well attested than the subjunctive, and below at *temperat* it has negligible support. Yet the structure of the poem is improved if the indirect questions end in the first stanza; then follow two stanzas (without a break in the middle) containing a series of direct questions and mentioning specific sports; another self-contained stanza rounds the poem off. After the subjunctives of the first stanza a copyist might accidentally continue in the same mood.

For riding in the Campus Martius cf. 3. 7. 25 f., 3. 12. 8, Str. loc. cit. [4 n.], Stat. *silv.* 5. 2. 113 ff. Such exercises were patriotic as well as invigorating; cf. Suet. *Aug.* 83 'exercitationes campestres equorum et armorum statim post civilia bella omisit', *Tib.* 13. 1 'equi quoque et armorum solitas exercitationes omisit'. So Marius, to show that he was still fit for a command, ὁσημέραι κατέβαινεν εἰς τὸ Πεδίον καὶ μετὰ τῶν νεανίσκων γυμναζόμενος ἐπεδείκνυε τὸ σῶμα κοῦφον μὲν ὅπλοις, ἔποχον δὲ ταῖς ἱππασίαις (Plut. *Mar.* 34. 3). See further Plut. *Coriol.* 2, Blümner 329.

Gallica . . . ora: i.e. *ora equorum Gallicorum*. For Gallic horses cf. Str. 4. 4. 2 καὶ ἔστι 'Ρωμαίοις τῆς ἱππείας ἀρίστη παρὰ τούτων.

lupatis: *lupi* (λύκοι or ἐχῖνοι) were spikes in the mouthpiece of a bit used to hurt the horse's tongue and palate. Cf. Serv. *georg.* 3. 208 '*duris parere lupatis*: frenis asperrimis. dicta autem lupata a lupinis dentibus, qui inaequales sunt, unde etiam eorum morsus vehementer obest', Ov. *trist.* 4. 6. 4, Prud. *psych.* 191, Call. fr. 488 Ἀτράκιον δήπειτα λυκοσπάδα πῶλον ἐλαύνει (with Pfeiffer's note). The ancients' methods were undeniably cruel, and probably not very efficient. Dio Chrysostom tells how Apelles had difficulty in recapturing the colour of a horse's foam οἷον ἂν γένοιτο μιγέντος αἵματος καὶ ὑγροῦ κατὰ συνεχῆ μῖξιν, διώκοντος μὲν τοῦ ἄσθματος τὸ ὑγρὸν τῶν στομάτων, ἀφρίζον τῇ κοπῇ τοῦ πνεύματος, αἷμα δὲ ἐπιρραινούσης τῷ ἀφρῷ τῆς ἐκ τοῦ χαλινοῦ ὕβρεως. In despair he threw his sponge at the picture, and by this piece of action-painting produced the desired polychromatic effect (63. 5, cf. Plut. *fort.* 99 b). For details about ancient bits see J. K. Anderson, *Ancient Greek Horsemanship*, 1961, pp. 40 ff., C! L. des Noettes, *L'Attelage et le cheval de selle à travers les âges* 2, 1931, pl. 62, 248, Fraenkel on Aesch. *Ag.* 1067.

8. Tiberim: Ostia Lido was too far from Rome in the ancient world, and even the most gilded young men had to be content with the yellow Tiber. See 3. 7. 27 f. 'nec quisquam citus aeque / Tusco denatat alveo', 3. 12. 7, Cic. *Cael.* 36 'habes hortos ad Tiberim ac diligenter eo loco paratos quo omnis iuventus natandi causa venit', Sen. *dial.* 10. 12. 6. The jurist Trebatius was an accomplished swimmer (Cic. *epist.* 7. 10. 2, cf. Hor. *serm.* 2. 1. 7 f.), and Horace himself, at least in his dreams, emulated the exploits of his sixth-century namesake (*carm.* 4. 1. 40). Yet even swimming could be regarded as part of military training; cf. Plut. *Cato mai.* 20. 4 οὐ μόνον ἀκοντίζειν οὐδ' ὁπλομαχεῖν οὐδ' ἱππεύειν διδάσκων τὸν υἱόν, ἀλλὰ καὶ τῇ χειρὶ πὺξ παίειν καὶ καῦμα καὶ ψῦχος ἀνέχεσθαι καὶ τὰ δινώδη καὶ τραχύνοντα τοῦ ποταμοῦ διανηχόμενον ἀποβιάζεσθαι, Veg. *mil.* 1. 10 'et ignorantia (natandi) non solum ab hoste sed etiam ab ipsis aquis discrimen incurrit; ideoque Romani veteres, quos tot bella et continuata pericula ad omnem rei militaris erudiverant artem, Campum Martium vicinum Tiberi delegerunt, in quo iuventus post exercitium armorum sudorem pulveremque dilueret ac lassitudinem cursus natandi labore deponeret'. For many interesting details about ancient swimming see *RE* Suppl. 5. 847 ff.

One would expect the plunge in the Tiber to come after the other activities; cf. Ov. *trist.* 3. 12. 19 ff. 'usus equi nunc est, levibus nunc luditur armis, / nunc pila, nunc celeri vertitur orbe trochus; / nunc ubi perfusa est oleo labente iuventus, / defessos artus Virgine tingit aqua', Veg. loc. cit. The time-table of Horace's sports shows signs of poetic licence.

tangere: the verb suggests the timidity of a bather afraid to get his feet wet.

olivum: the word symbolizes athletics; cf. Catull. 63. 64 'ego gymnasi fui flos, ego eram decus olei', Gow on Theoc. 4. 7. Oil was used by athletes of every sort, and above all by wrestlers (*RE* 17. 2463).

9. **sanguine viperino**: for similar locutions cf. *epist*. 1. 17. 30 f. 'alter Mileti textam cane peius et angui / vitabit chlamydem', Theophr. *char*. 1. 7 φυλάττεσθαι μᾶλλον δεῖ ἢ τοὺς ἔχεις, Otto 25. The ancients not unnaturally regarded snake's blood as poisonous; cf. *epod*. 3. 6 f. 'num viperinus his cruor / incoctus herbis me fefellit?', Plin. *nat*. 11. 279 'Scythae sagittas tingunt viperina sanie et humano sanguine; inremediabile id scelus: mortem ilico adfert levi tactu'.

10. **livida . . . armis**: cf. Sidon. *carm*. 7. 242 f. 'rutilis etiam nunc livida cristis / ora gerens'. Horace is referring to chafing by the *lorica*; cf. Prop. 4. 3. 23 'dic mihi num teneros urit lorica lacertos?' Heinze suggests that the *arma* are the *rudes*, or blunt wooden sticks used in sword-training (*RE* 1 A. 1179 f., D.–S. 4. 897 f.). But the parallel from Propertius seems to argue against this interpretation.

11. **disco**: the discus was a solid disc of metal, or in earlier times a stone. Surviving specimens vary from 3 to 15 lb. in weight; the remarkable long-jumper Phayllus (who could jump 55 ft.) threw one 95 ft. The sport could be dangerous, as Hyacinthus found to his cost (cf. Mart. 14. 164); more sedentary people, like Horace or Trimalchio, preferred the hoop or ball. Something at least of the technique of throwing is illustrated by the varying copies of Myron's Discobolos; there are detailed discussions by J. Jüthner, *Über antike Turngeräthe*, Wien, 1896, pp. 18 ff., E. N. Gardiner, *JHS* 27, 1907, 1 ff. and *Athletics of the Ancient World*, 1930, pp. 154 ff.

12. **trans finem**: cf. Hom. *Od*. 8. 192 f. ὁ δ' ὑπέρπτατο σήματα πάντων / ῥίμφα θέων ἀπὸ χειρός.

expedito: perhaps 'cleared', or more accurately 'sped through all intervening obstacles'; cf. 4. 4. 75 f. '(Claudiae manus quas) curae sagaces / expediunt per acuta belli'. Yet our passage is more difficult as the air is not a visible obstacle. Possibly the *finis* itself is regarded as a barrier to be got past, though this seems rather a modern attitude.

Alternatively, it might be relevant that the ancient javelin was fired from an *amentum* or thong, which as it unwound gave the missile greater accuracy, like rifling. See Sil. 13. 159 f. 'indignatus opem amenti socioque iuvare / expulsum nodo iaculum', Jüthner, op. cit. pp. 39 ff., E. N. Gardiner, *JHS* 27, 1907, 249 ff., *Athletics of the Ancient World*, 1930, pp. 169 ff., and especially H. A. Harris, *G & R*, second series 10, 1963, 26 ff. Perhaps *expedito* refers to the disentangling of the javelin from the thong; in this case it would properly be applicable merely to *iaculo*, and could be taken with *disco* only by way of zeugma. It is a further objection to this theory that *expedito* would refer to the release of the missile in flight, *trans finem* to the far end of the ground.

13. latet . . .: Horace ends his poem elegantly with an allusion to myth. At the beginning of the Trojan War Achilles lay hid at Scyros, disguised as a girl; there he fell in love with Deidamia, the daughter of King Lycomedes (Apollod. 3. 13. 8 with Frazer's notes). The legend may have been found in the *Cypria* or *Little Iliad*; it was the theme of Euripides's tragedy, *The Scyrians* (fr. 684 ff.; cf. also Soph. fr. 509 ff. N., Pearson 2. 191 ff.); it suited the Alexandrians and their imitators (Bion 2, Ov. *met.* 13. 162 ff., *trist.* 2. 411 f., Stat. *Ach.* 1. 283 ff.). It was the subject of paintings by Polygnotus and Athenion (Paus. 1. 22. 6, Plin. *nat.* 35. 134; cf. Philostr. Jun. *imag.* 1); there is a well-known Pompeian specimen from the Casa dei Dioscuri (A. Maiuri, *Roman Painting*, 1953, p. 73), as well as others elsewhere (W. Helbig, *Wandgemälde der vom Vesuv verschütteten Städte Campaniens*, Leipzig, 1868, nos. 1296–7, 1299–1302). The emperor Tiberius liked to puzzle *grammatici* with the conundrum 'quod Achilli nomen inter virgines fuisset' (Suet. *Tib.* 70. 3); cf. Sir Thomas Browne, *Urn Burial* 5, p. 119 Martin 'What song the *Syrens* sang, or what names *Achilles* assumed when he hid himself among women, though puzzling Questions are not beyond all conjecture'. For one answer cf. 1. 5. 4 n.

marinae: Thetis was a sea-nymph. The epithet adds heroic dignity, as does the periphrasis *filium Thetidis*; cf. 4. 6. 6 'filius . . . Thetidis marinae', Eur. *Andr.* 108 παῖς ἁλίας Θέτιδος.

15. funera: cf. Lucr. 5. 326 'bellum Thebanum et funera Troiae', Prop. 2. 6. 16 'his Troiana vides funera principiis'.

16. cultus: 'dress'; cf. Ov. *met.* 13. 163 (of Achilles at Scyros) 'dissimulat cultu natum', Stat. *Ach.* 1. 272, 1. 652, 2. 45. For the collocation with *virilis* cf. Tac. *dial.* 26. 2 (with Gudeman's parallels on 26. 3).

Lycias: the Lycians were allies of the Trojans, commanded by Glaucus and Sarpedon (Hom. *Il.* 2. 876). The poem is rounded off with an imitation of Pindar; cf. *N.* 3. 59 f. (also of Achilles) ὄφρα θαλασσίαις ἀνέμων ῥιπαῖσι πεμφθεὶς / ὑπὸ Τροίαν δορίκτυπον ἀλαλὰν Λυκίων τε προσμένοι καὶ Φρυγῶν.

9. VIDES VT ALTA

[Pasquali 75 ff.; V. Pöschl, *WS* 79, 1966, 365 ff.; N. Rudd, *AJPh* 81, 1960, 387 ff.; M. G. Shields, *Phoenix* 12, 1958, 166 ff.; D. West 1 ff.; Wilkinson 129 ff.]

1–8. *Mountain, woods, and rivers are covered in snow; so build up the fire, Thaliarchus, and produce more wine.* 9–12. *Trust the future to the gods, who can still the fiercest storms.* 13–24. *Enjoy every day as it comes, and do not reject love while you are young.*

The first two stanzas, perhaps the first three, are modelled on an ode by Alcaeus (338), partly preserved by Athenaeus:

> ὔει μὲν ὁ Ζεῦς, ἐκ δ' ὀράνω μέγας
> χείμων, πεπάγαισιν δ' ὑδάτων ῥόαι . . .
> κάββαλλε τὸν χείμων', ἐπὶ μὲν τίθεις
> πῦρ, ἐν δὲ κέρναις οἶνον ἀφειδέως
> μέλιχρον, αὐτὰρ ἀμφὶ κόρσᾳ
> μόλθακον ἀμφι⟨βάλων⟩ γνόφαλλον (a woollen fillet or cap).

Some features of the two poems are the same: the weather, the fire, the wine, perhaps part of the *paraenesis* or adjuration (9 n.). Horace even keeps something of the movement of his exemplar: 'dissolve frigus' follows the form, if not the meaning, of κάββαλλε τὸν χείμωνα, and *benignius* scans the same way as ἀφειδέως. Yet, taken as a whole, Alcaeus's poem must have been very different. Alcaeus was writing for a society where the symposium was an important institution, at which men could express their unsophisticated gladness in song. Horace, on the other hand, is complex, literary, and much more reflective.

It is too often supposed that in spite of the literary allusion Horace's opening scene is primarily drawn from life. Monte Soratte is sometimes visible from a few favoured parts of Rome (2 n.), and the modern tourist, as he surveys the horizon from the Gianicolo on a clear day, willingly imagines that he is re-creating the poet's experience. But we should not suppose that Horace saw the mountain twenty miles away on a winter evening through the narrow slit of an ancient window; he is simply giving local colour to a Greek theme (for the same technique cf. 1. 9. 7, 1. 11. 6, 1. 18. 2, 1. 37. 2, *epist.* 1. 10. 27, etc.). Others assume that the scene is set at a villa near Soracte (D. West 3 ff.); this suits the *silvae*, and no doubt the diligent searcher might find plural rivulets in the neighbourhood. Yet there is nothing in the rest of the poem which encourages us to look for this kind of verisimilitude; the *flumina* are surely nothing but the ῥόαι of Alcaeus. Horace is not describing a particular scene; rather he has composed a picturesque Christmas-card, based on Alcaeus, and containing among more conventional elements a single feature of familiar topography.

The second stanza is likewise based on literature rather than observation. Horace's friend Thaliarchus does not belong to the Roman world of Horace's political friends; instead he bears a Greek name, with associations of the symposium (8 n.). He is asked to put wood on the fire, though in real life the menial office would have been performed by a slave. Again the Sabine wine provides a single local allusion, although it is appropriately contained in a Greek type of jar.

The third stanza also provides surprises for the over-literal reader. Horace implies, even if he does not state, that a storm is raging (9 n.); this is inconsistent with the clear, cold day at the beginning of the poem. In the first stanza the trees bend under their load of snow; in the third they are shaken in the high wind. The contradiction may be derived from Horace's sources; Alcaeus has both rain and ice, and in sympotic poetry the storm outside is elsewhere contrasted with the snugness within (*epod.* 13. 1 ff., perhaps Anacreon 17). The seething sea also seems to be a traditional motif (cf. 1. 11. 4, *epod.* 13. 2), and may also come from Alcaeus; though Rome is so close to the Mediterranean, the ancient Romans, unlike their modern counterparts, were hardly aware of it. Horace's advice to Thaliarchus also contains some confusion. First of all he seems to imply 'The storm will soon blow over, and with it our troubles' (9 n.). However, in the last three stanzas he advises: 'Enjoy yourself while you can; you will not always be able to'. He has included two themes of Greek poetic moralizing which on close inspection seem inconsistent.

, The last three stanzas are in fact quite different from the first three. Lines 13–15 owe more to Epicurus than to Alcaeus. The vignette that follows has nothing to do with early Greek poetry. Alexandrian realism is mellowed with Italian humanity. The attitude to love, or at least the literary expression of it, is not found before Middle Comedy: Alcaeus would not have written about romantic assignations in public places with flirtatious girls who are neither secluded maidens nor coarse prostitutes. The scene is urban, and specifically Roman. And the weather has changed marvellously since the beginning of the poem. When Thaliarchus is encouraged to play his game of hide-and-seek we must no longer visualize snow-laden trees and frozen rivers. Now it is spring, and evening.

The Soracte Ode has been censured by scholars for its inconsistency: 'Hübsche Verse' says Wilamowitz 'aber noch kein Gedicht' (*Sappho und Simonides*, 1913, p. 311). This view is mistaken. Horace is not professing to describe something that really happened, or represent his emotions on any particular occasion. Rather he is weaving together varied strands from reading and experience; and though he does not describe life directly, he gives hints of sensitive and convincing attitudes. If he had regarded 'continuity' as all-important he was a skilful enough organizer to achieve it. But by blurring his outlines he writes more evocatively than if he had tried a more 'photographic' and 'representational' poem. It is no accident that there are so many confusions in the most imaginative poetry of his age, the eclogues of Virgil and the elegies of Propertius (not to mention Tibullus). Artistic harmony does not depend on the unities of time and place, and changes of direction can easily be paralleled in Horace. The wintry back-cloth at the beginning of the ode is poetically right for the middle-aged Horace (though one should beware of saying, with some scholars, that Soracte 'symbolizes' old age). After the *paraenesis* in the centre the spring scene at the close provides an appropriate contrast. This is a great poem.

Metre: Alcaic.

1. vides: Bentley preferred to take the opening sentence as a statement rather than a question, and he has been followed by almost all modern editors. In fact a question seems much more likely; cf. the common locutions *nonne vides ut . . .?* and *viden ut?* (see Norden on Virg. *Aen.* 6. 779). So in Greek Hom. *Il.* 7. 448 οὐχ ὁράᾳς; (*Od.* 17. 545, Call. *h.* 2. 4), Alcman 1. 50 ἦ οὐχ ὁρῆς;, *carm. pop. PMG* 7. 5 τὸ φῶς διὰ τᾶς θυρίδος οὐκ εἰσορῆς;

alta: *nix alta* normally means 'deep snow'; cf. *epod.* 6. 7 'per altas . . . nives', Virg. *georg.* 1. 310 'cum nix alta iacet'. However, Dryden renders in his fine translation 'Behold yon' Mountains hoary height Made higher with new Mounts of Snow'. There is probably something in this interpretation: the sharp dichotomy between 'deep' and 'high' is not present in the Latin. For a similar point cf. Sil. 4. 743 f. 'condiderat nix alta trabes, et vertice celso / canus apex structa surgebat ad astra pruina'.

stet: the word suggests fixity and strength; cf. 3. 3. 42 'stet Capitolium', Virg. *Aen.* 6. 471, Ov. *fast.* 5. 169 'nondum stabat Atlas'. Here the word suits the isolated ridge of Soracte, which is separated from the Sabine mountains by the Tiber; cf. Byron, *Childe Harold* 4. 665 ff. 'the lone Soracte's height, display'd Not *now* in snow, which asks the lyric Roman's aid For our remembrance, and from out the plain Heaves like a long-swept wave about to break And on the curl hangs pausing'.

stet nive candidum makes a single and characteristically Horatian

complex. For *stet candidum* cf. Sen. *Thy.* 117 f. 'Cithaeronis iuga /
stant parte nulla cana, deposita nive'. For *nive candidum* cf. 3. 25.
10 f. 'nive candidam / Thracen'. The ancient commentators took
nive closely with *stet*, which is explained by Porphyrio as *plenum sit*,
by ps.-Acro as *cooperiatur*; for instances of this usage cf. Enn. *ann.*
608 'stant pulvere campi', Virg. *Aen.* 12. 407 f., Sisenna, *hist.* 130
'caelum caligine stat', Prop. 4. 11. 4, Plin. *paneg.* 52. 1. Yet in our
passage the presence of *candidum* makes all the difference.

2. Soracte: Monte Soratte, 2,400 feet high, about 20 miles north of
Rome, 6 miles from Città Castellana (the site of the ancient Falerii).
At different times it has been called Monte S. Silvestro (after Pope
Sylvester I who hid there during the reign of Constantine), or Treste,
or Sant' Oreste. It is visible from the Gianicolo and the Pincio, some
tall buildings in Rome, much of the Campagna, and Tivoli (though
not, of course, from Horace's Sabine farm). It was associated with
Apollo, with the fire-walking Hirpini, with Soranus and Feronia and
the cult of the dead (Virg. *Aen.* 11. 785 with Servius, Str. 5. 2. 9).
Some scholars suppose that it has been introduced here because of its
funereal associations (Commager 272), but so melancholy a note
would be inappropriate at this place in the poem. There is no evidence that the mountain was so sinister that every mention of it
suggested thoughts of mortality.

3. laborantes: straining and bending under their load of snow, which
is a particular hazard to the evergreen trees of the south. For the
picture cf. Longus 3. 3 λάβροι μὲν οἱ χείμαρροι κατέρρεον, ἐπεπήγει δὲ
κρύσταλλος· τὰ δένδρα ἐῴκει κατακλωμένοις (this passage conceivably
contains a reminiscence of the lost third and fourth lines of Alcaeus's
poem; it might even be relevant that the scene is set in Lesbos). For
the verb cf. 2. 9. 7, Housman, *Shropshire Lad* 31 'On Wenlock Edge
the wood's in trouble; His forest fleece the Wrekin heaves'.

geluque . . . acuto: *gelu* in conjunction with *constiterint* probably
means 'ice' rather than simply 'cold'; cf. Ov. *trist.* 2. 196 'et maris
adstricto quae coit unda gelu', Luc. 5. 438 'immensumque gelu tegi-
tur mare'. *acuto* may refer to the biting or nipping coldness of the
ice; cf. Manil. 5. 70 'qua gelidus Boreas aquilonibus instat acutis',
Pind. *P.* 1. 20[b] χιόνος ὀξείας τιθήνα (schol. ad loc. ὅτι οἱ ἐφαπτόμενοι
ὅμοιόν τι πάσχουσι τοῖς κεντουμένοις). But Porphyrio offers an alternative interpretation that is quite attractive: 'utrum ad sensum
frigoris pertinet quod velut pungat, an quod fractum velut vitrum
acutum sit?' These explanations are not necessarily exclusive;
Horace may be combining the ideas of nipping cold and sharp ice. So
Wilamowitz on Pindar loc. cit. 'der Schnee sticht, wenn man auf ihn
tritt; er ist hart und kalt' (*Pindaros*, 1922, p. 299 n. 1).

M

4. flumina: frozen rivers are a conventional part of the poet's wintry scene (Virg. *georg.* 1. 310, 4. 135). Those who set the scene in Rome should note that even in antiquity the Tiber hardly ever froze, and when it did, the occurrence is mentioned with surprise: see Liv. 5. 13. 1 (of 399 B.C.), Aug. *civ.* 3. 17 (of 270 B.C.) 'hiems illa memorabilis tam incredibili immanitate saeviens ut . . . Tiberis quoque glacie duraretur, si nostris temporibus accidisset, quae isti et quanta dixissent'. Juvenal says with deliberate hyperbole 'hibernum fracta glacie descendet in amnem, / ter matutino Tiberi mergetur' (6. 522 f.).

  constiterint: πεπάγαισιν in Alcaeus. Cf. Enn. *var.* 12 'constitere amnes perennes', Ov. *trist.* 5. 10. 1, Gell. 17. 8. 16 'mare Bosporicum . . . gelu stringi et consistere', *Thes.l.L.* 4. 471. 60 ff.

  ligna: πῦρ in Alcaeus. Cf. 3. 17. 14, *epod.* 2. 43, Xenoph. 18. 1 πὰρ πυρὶ χρὴ τοιαῦτα λέγειν χειμῶνος ἐν ὥρῃ, Eur. *Cycl.* 331 καὶ πῦρ ἀναίθων χίονος οὐδέν μοι μέλει, Tennyson, *In Mem.* 107 'Bring in great logs and let them lie, And make a solid core of heat'. G. Bagnani, *Phoenix* 8, 1954, 23 ff. points out that the Roman *focus* had no chimney to create a draught and remove smoke; he suggests that it must have burned charcoal rather than logs. He overstates his case: *ligna* could mean bits of wood smaller than logs, and an abundance of firewood was one of the privileges of country life (D. West 4 ff.).

6. reponens: ἐπιτίθεις in Alcaeus. *re-* does not imply a repeated action; it may suggest that the wood is being put where it belongs, or perhaps that it is replacing burnt logs (thus E. S. Thompson, *CR* 16, 1902, 282).

  benignius: 'more lavishly'; cf. Varro, *Men.* 461 'ipsum avide vino invitari poclis large atque benigne'. *benignus* sometimes implies not so much kindness and amiability as objective openhandedness of a material sort; contrast *malignus*, 'mean' (cf. 1. 28. 23 ff.).

7. quadrimum: Alcaeus mentioned οἶνον μέλιχρον, but Horace, in the manner of later poetry, is more specific. His Sabine wine was of medium quality (1. 20. 1 n.), and suits his portrait of himself as a moderate man. The precise age may have been suggested by literary associations; cf. Theoc. 7. 147 τετράενες δὲ πίθων ἀπελύσατο κρατὸς ἄλειφαρ, 14. 15 f. ἀνῷξα δὲ Βίβλινον αὐτοῖς / εὐώδη τετόρων ἐτέων.

8. o: the interjection sounds a Greek note; cf. 1. 16. 1. Horace normally uses the vocative alone; this is the standard Latin practice. Exceptions occur obviously in prayers (1. 30. 1, 1. 35. 1), pseudo-prayers (1. 32. 13, 3. 13. 1, 3. 21. 1), and other artificial addresses (1. 14. 1); sometimes also where the friend is characterized feelingly (1. 1. 2, 1. 4. 14, 2. 7. 1, 4. 10. 1).

Thaliarche: though not common, this is a real Greek name (Pape–Benseler 479, *SEG* 20. 238, 20. 486). θαλία in Greek poetry means 'a festivity', with suggestions of joy and abundance; so Thaliarchus is sometimes said to be the συμποσίαρχος at a drinking-party. Yet nothing else in the ode suggests a large gathering, so the association may be indirect and derived from Greek poetry. Thaliarchus appears once as a καλός name on a fifth-century Athenian pyxis (D. M. Robinson and E. J. Fluck, *A History of Greek Love Names*, 1937, p. 183). But this by itself is not sufficient justification for suggesting a sentimental implication.

diota: a two-eared wine-jar; cf. Pl. *Hipp. mai.* 288 d οἶαι τῶν καλῶν χυτρῶν εἰσί τινες δίωτοι, Athen. 473 c καδίσκον καινὸν δίωτον, Theoc. 1. 28 ἀμφῶες (of a κισσύβιον). This is the only occurrence of the word in extant Latin (except for glosses, etc., evidently based on our passage).

9. permitte . . .: after giving particular instructions Horace turns to more general advice. Such a *paraenesis* is found often in Greek lyric poetry, obviously in Pindar, but see also Alcaeus 38. 4 ἀλλ᾽ ἄγι μὴ μεγάλων . . . Here, as at 1. 7. 17 ff., the *paraenesis* is set in the middle of the poem.

divis: cf. Hom. *Od.* 19. 502 ἐπίτρεψον δὲ θεοῖσιν, 21. 279, 22. 288, Theogn. 1047 f. νῦν μὲν πίνοντες τερπώμεθα καλὰ λέγοντες· / ἄσσα δ᾽ ἔπειτ᾽ ἔσται ταῦτα θεοῖσι μέλει, Aesch. *Pers.* 229, Pind. *O.* 13. 106, Bacch. 17. 46, Machon 111 Gow πιὼν καθεῦδε ταῦτ᾽ ἐπιτρέψας τῇ τύχῃ, Symm. *epist.* 2. 7. 3, Milton, *P.L.* 11. 555 'how long or short permit to Heaven'.

cetera: everything outside the symposium; cf. *epod.* 13. 7, Eur. *Alc.* 788 ff. εὔφραινε σαυτόν, πῖνε, τὸν καθ᾽ ἡμέραν / βίον λογίζου σόν, τὰ δ᾽ ἄλλα τῆς τύχης / . . . τὰ δ᾽ ἀλλ᾽ ἔασον ταῦτα, fr. 468 τὰ δ᾽ ἄλλα χαῖρε, κύλικος ἑρπούσης κύκλῳ, Amphis 21 K., Palladas, *anth. P.* 11. 62. 6.

qui simul . . .: the gods have power to still the storm; cf. 1. 12. 27 n. It may be asked why in our passage Horace should choose this relatively unimportant manifestation of divine omnipotence. The explanation surely lies in the ode's literary ancestry; it seems to have been a conventional feature in sympotic poems to say 'a storm is raging outside, but the gods will still it, and with it our present troubles'. See *epod.* 13. 1 ff. (which gives exactly the same sequence of thought as our poem): 'horrida tempestas caelum contraxit, et imbres / nivesque deducunt Iovem: nunc mare nunc siluae / Threicio Aquilone sonant . . . / tu vina Torquato move consule pressa meo. / cetera mitte loqui; deus haec fortasse benigna / reducet in sedem vice'. In our poem Horace keeps the traditional reference to storms, though strictly speaking it does not suit the weather of the first stanza.

10. stravere: cf. Theoc. 7. 57 f. χἀλκύονες στορεσεῦντι τὰ κύματα τάν τε
θάλασσαν / τόν τε νότον τόν τ᾽ εὖρον. Kiessling compares κάββαλλε τὸν
χείμωνα in Alcaeus's poem, but the context is different and the
resemblance may be fortuitous.

11. cupressi: Horace abruptly moves the scene from the sea to the
land; for other instances of such disconcerting variation cf. 1. 7.
10 n. The cypress is mentioned as a picturesque tree, which because
of its thin trunk and evergreen leaves makes a fine flurry in the
wind. Cf. Nonnus 3. 148 f. καὶ εὐπετάλου κυπαρίσσου / ὄρθριον ἐρρίπιζε
κόμην εὔοδμος ἀήτης, Tennyson, *The Princess*, 'Now sleeps the crim-
son petal, now the white; Nor waves the cypress in the palace walk'.

12. orni: a species of ash (strictly the 'manna-ash'), proverbially at
home on windy hillsides; cf. Virg. *ecl.* 6. 71 'deducere montibus ornos',
Avien. *orb. terr.* 676 'agitans aquilonibus ornos'. For *veteres* cf. Virg.
Aen. 10. 766 'annosam montibus ornum'.

13. quid sit futurum . . .: cf. Simon. 521 ἄνθρωπος ἐὼν μή ποτε φάσῃς
ὅ τι γίνεται, Philetaerus 7. 5 f. K. εἰς αὔριον δὲ μηδὲ φροντίζειν ὅ τι /
ἔσται, Theoc. 13. 4 τὸ δ᾽ αὔριον οὐκ ἐσορῶμες, Anacreontea 7. 9 f. τὸ
σήμερον μέλει μοι· / τὸ δ᾽ αὔριον τίς οἶδεν; / ὡς οὖν ἔτ᾽ εὐδία ᾽στιν, / καὶ
πῖνε καὶ κύβευε, anon. *anth. P.* 11. 56. 1 f. πῖνε καὶ εὐφραίνου· τί γὰρ
αὔριον ἢ τί τὸ μέλλον / οὐδεὶς γινώσκει, Palladas, ibid. 5. 72. 2 ff. ζωῆς
ἀνθρώποις ὀλίγος χρόνος. ἄρτι Λύαιος, / ἄρτι χοροὶ στεφανοί τε φιλαν-
θεές, ἄρτι γυναῖκες. / σήμερον ἐσθλὰ πάθω· τὸ γὰρ αὔριον οὐδενὶ δῆλον,
Monuments et Mémoires (Fondation Piot) 5, 1899, 59 (silver cup from
Boscoreale) ζῶν μετάλαβε· τὸ γὰρ αὔριον ἄδηλόν ἐστι. See further
1. 11. 8 n.

    fuge quaerere: *fuge* means 'forbear', and is probably a Grecism,
modelled on φεύγειν; cf. 2. 4. 22 'fuge suspicari', Lucr. 1. 1052 'illud in
his rebus longe fuge credere', *Thes.l.L.* 6. 1. 1491. 64. For similar
locutions cf. 2. 11. 3 'remittas quaerere', 1. 26. 3 n.

14. lucro adpone: 'credit to your account'; the tone is commercial.
Cf. *Sotadea* 6. 10 Powell ἡμέρας μιᾶς ἀλυπία μέγ᾽ ἐστὶ κέρδος, Plaut.
merc. 553 f. (to an old man) 'id iam lucrumst / quod vivis', Ter.
Phorm. 251, Cic. *epist.* 9. 17. 1 'de lucro prope iam quadriennium
vivimus', Ov. *trist.* 1. 3. 68, Sen. *ben.* 5. 17. 7.

16. puer: 'while you are young'; cf. *epist.* 1. 2. 67 f. 'nunc adbibe puro /
pectore verba puer'. For the commonplace cf. Pind. fr. 123. 1 χρῆν
μὲν κατὰ καιρὸν ἐρώτων δρέπεσθαι, θυμέ, σὺν ἁλικίᾳ, Antiphanes, *anth.*
P. 10. 100. 3 ff. ὅτ᾽ οὖν χρόνος ὥριος ἡμῖν, / πάντα χύδην ἔστω, ψαλμὸς
ἔρως προπόσεις. / χείμων τοὐντεῦθεν γήρως βαρύς, Eur. fr. 897. 9 f. τὸ δ᾽
ἐρᾶν προλέγω τοῖσι νέοισιν / μήποτε φεύγειν, Sen. *Phaedr.* 446 f.

tu: in Greek and Latin the pronoun is sometimes expressed only in the second of two parallel clauses; it has the effect of giving more body to the clause that lacks the verb. See K.–G. 1. 657, F. Leo, *Analecta Plautina* 1. 24 f. (= *Ausgewählte Schriften* 1. 96 f.).

choreas: one must not think of mixed couples revolving round a ball-room, but of young men dancing in a ring. We hear of Roman dances at a few religious ceremonies, and of less decorous solo performances at wild parties (Cic. *Mur.* 13 'nemo enim fere saltat sobrius', *Pis.* 19); female artistes also danced for the entertainment of men. But the dances here have less to do with Roman life than with the Greek poetic convention; cf. Nepos 15. 1. 2 'scimus etiam musicen nostris moribus abesse a principis persona, saltare vero etiam in vitiis poni; quae omnia apud Graecos et grata et laude digna ducuntur'. See further *RE* 4 A. 2247, G. Williams, *JRS* 52, 1962, 37 f.

17. donec: cf. 2. 3. 15, 4. 12. 26, *epod.* 13. 4, Theoc. 14. 68 ff. ἀπὸ κροτάφων πελόμεσθα / πάντες γηραλέοι, καὶ ἐπισχερὼ ἐς γένυν ἕρπει / λευκαίνων ὁ χρόνος· ποιεῖν τι δεῖ ἇς γόνυ χλωρόν, Prop. 2. 15. 23 with Enk's note, 4. 5. 59 'dum vernat sanguis, dum rugis integer annus', Philostr. *epist.* 17 (35) μηδὲν μέλλε, ὦ φθεγγόμενον ῥόδον, ἀλλ' ἕως ἔξεστι καὶ ζῆς, μετάδος ἡμῖν ὧν ἔχεις, Spenser, *F.Q.* 2. 12. 75 'Gather therefore the Rose, whilest yet is prime, For soone comes age, that will her pride deflowre: Gather the Rose of love, whilest yet is time, Whilest loving thou mayest loved be with equall crime', Herrick 'Gather ye rosebuds while ye may'.

virenti: less specifically a colour-word than English 'green', yet here obviously contrasted with *canities*. Cf. Theoc. 14. 70 (cited in previous note), André 349.

18. morosa: cf. Cic. *Cato* 65 'at sunt morosi . . . et difficiles senes'.

nunc: the word means of course not 'today' but 'while you are young'; cf. *epist.* 1. 2. 67 f. (cited 16 n.). Even so, there is some inconsistency with the weather of the opening stanza.

Campus: the Campus Martius, the park of Rome; by modern conventions editors should print with a capital letter. The word suggests the general social activities of the young (Pöschl, loc. cit., pp. 374 ff., D. West, loc. cit.). Editors generally assume that the associations are exclusively erotic, and that *composita hora* is to be taken with *Campus* and *areae* as well as with *susurri*. It is certainly true that young men seeking encounters with girls sauntered along the colonnades of the Campus; cf. Prop. 2. 23. 5 f. ' "quaenam nunc porticus illam / integit?" et "campo quo movet illa pedes?" ', 4. 8. 75 'tu neque Pompeia spatiabere cultus in umbra', Ov. *am.* 2. 2. 4, *ars* 1. 67, *trist.* 2. 286. Yet it may be doubted whether in our context *Campus* can be interpreted so narrowly; after all, *choreas* above

suggests the general gaiety of youth rather than anything specifically
to do with love.

areae: 'in urbe loca pura areae' (Varro, *ling.* 5. 38). The name could
be applied to open spaces round temples, and Ovid gives it to the
Forum Boarium (*fast.* 6. 478). One has to think of the part played by
a piazza in the social life of a modern Italian town.

19. sub noctem: 'approaching nightfall'. Cf. Pasquali 83 'di notte sì
per vero in solitarie piazze romane, dove cresce l'erba, s'incontrano
ancor oggi coppie di amanti, si ode ancor oggi il loro tenero sussurro,
ma di giorno non si fa l'amore in piazza nè a Roma nè altrove' (1920).

susurri: Orelli comments 'amator ad ianuam semiapertam amicae
hora constituta susurrat'. This is pure fiction: the scene is set in the
open air, and the *susurri* are the ψιθυρίσματα of both man and girl.
Cf. Hes. *th.* 205 παρθενίους τ' ὀάρους μειδήματά τ' ἐξαπάτας τε, Theoc.
27. 68 ἀλλήλοις ψιθύριζον, anon. *anth. Pl.* 202. 1 f. τὸν φιλοκώμων /
τερπόμενον νυχίοις ἠιθέων ὀάροις, Tib. 1. 1. 71 f. 'iam subrepet iners
aetas, nec amare decebit / dicere nec cano blanditias capite', 1. 8. 2,
Prop. 1. 11. 13, Claud. 14. 21 f.

20. composita . . . hora: cf. *serm.* 1. 5. 82 f., Juv. 3. 12 'ubi nocturnae
Numa constituebat amicae', Paul. Sil. *anth. P.* 5. 279. 5 ἆ πόσα τὴν
Κυθέρειαν ἐπώμοσεν ἕσπερος ἥξειν.

repetantur: the prefix means 'according to the compact' rather
than 'repeatedly'. The force of the verb carries on into the next
stanza, though there it is less appropriate.

21. nunc et latentis . . .: in spite of his sentimental subject Horace's
diction is austere and his word-order intricate; the tone is that of
a detached observer. Porphyrio drily comments: 'grate dictum. sic
enim puellae solent verecundiam sexus cum libidine miscentes abs-
condere se sequentibus amatoribus, et rursus ut inveniantur risu
se prodere'. For this motif cf. 2. 12. 26 f. 'aut facili saevitia negat /
quae poscente magis gaudeat eripi', Virg. *ecl.* 3. 64 f. 'malo me
Galatea petit, lasciva puella, / et fugit ad salices et se cupit ante
videri' (Servius ad loc. quotes our passage), Tib. 1. 9. 44 'et latuit
clausas post adoperta fores', Ov. *am.* 1. 5. 15 f. 'quae cum ita pugna-
ret tamquam quae vincere nollet / victa est non aegre proditione
sua', Maxim. *eleg.* 1. 67 ff. 'et modo subridens latebras fugitiva
petebat, / non tamen effugiis tota latere volens, / sed magis ex
aliqua cupiebat parte videri, / laetior hoc potius quod male tecta
fuit'.

proditor: used adjectivally; cf. Wackernagel, *Vorlesungen* 2. 54,
H.–Sz. 157 f. The word here is artistically juxtaposed with *latentis*.

22. angulo: some editors assume that the action has shifted indoors.

But in a Mediterranean country the scene should be set outside, open to the appraising eye of the passer-by.

23. pignus: a bracelet from the arm, a ring from the finger (see D.–S. 1. 293 ff., 1. 435 ff.). For engagement-rings cf. Juv. 6. 27 'digito pignus fortasse dedisti', J. Marquardt and A. Mau, *Das Privatleben der Römer*, 1886, p. 41 nn. 7 and 8. Here a more temporary commitment is implied; cf. Ov. *am.* 2. 15 (the present of a ring to a girl), Mart. 8. 5 'dum donas, Macer, anulos puellis, / desisti, Macer, anulos habere'.

24. aut: in the ancient manner Horace suggests alternative situations; it would seem more vivid to the modern point of view if he had concentrated either on the ring or the bracelet. In the same way the *Campus* and the *areae* are mentioned as alternatives. Even *lacertis* implies that the bracelet might have come off either arm (here a desire to avoid rhyme with *digito* may play a part). For a similar disjunction which seems undesirable to modern taste cf. Virg. *Aen.* 8. 23 'sole repercussum aut radiantis imagine lunae'.

male: negatives *pertinaci* but less bluntly than *non*; for such sophisticated understatements cf. the common use of *parum*. So *serm.* 1. 9. 65, 2. 5. 45, *epist.* 1. 19. 3, Petron. 87. 3 'male repugnanti gaudium extorsi'; cf. 'malcontent', 'maladroit'. Distinguish the use of *male* which intensifies words of bad sense: *serm.* 1. 3. 45, 1. 4. 66, *carm.* 4. 12. 7, Prud. *cath.* praef. 14 f. 'male pertinax / vincendi studium subiacuit casibus asperis', Sulpicius Lupercus, *anth. Lat.* 648. 5 ff. 'amnis insueta solet ire valle, / mutat et rectos via certa cursus, / rupta cum cedit male pertinaci / ripa fluento'. The last two passages are presumably modelled on our own, but *male* is used differently. For further details see Wackernagel, *Vorlesungen* 2. 255, J. B. Hofmann, *Lateinische Umgangssprache*, ed. 3, 1951, p. 145, E. Wölfflin, *Ausgewählte Schriften*, 1933, pp. 139 f., Bömer on Ov. *fast.* 1. 559.

10. MERCVRI FACVNDE NEPOS

[Fraenkel 161 ff.]

1–4. Mercury, originator of language and athletic contests, 5–8 I shall hymn you as the inventor of the lyre and the god of trickery. 9–12. You stole Apollo's cattle and quiver, 13–16 you escorted Priam through the Greek pickets, 17–20 you conduct the dead to the underworld.

Porphyrio calls our poem 'hymnus in Mercurium ab Alcaeo lyrico poeta'. Alcaeus's Hymn to Hermes occupied a prominent position in

the Alexandrian edition (second poem in the first book) and, like
Horace's, it was written in the Sapphic metre. The first stanza survives (308):

χαῖρε, Κυλλάνας ὀ μέδεις, σὲ γάρ μοι
θῦμος ὔμνην, τὸν κορύφαισιν †αὐγαῖς†
Μαῖα γέννατο Κρονίδᾳ μίγεισα
παμβασίληι.

Alcaeus described the stealing of Apollo's cattle; cf. Paus. 7. 20. 4
βουσὶ γὰρ χαίρειν μάλιστα Ἀπόλλωνα Ἀλκαῖος . . . ἐδήλωσεν ἐν ὕμνῳ
τῷ ἐς Ἑρμῆν, γράψας ὡς ὁ Ἑρμῆς βοῦς ὑφέλοιτο τοῦ Ἀπόλλωνος. He also
seems to have mentioned the theft of Apollo's quiver, which finds no
place in the Homeric hymn; see the evidence cited below on line 11.
For Alcaeus's hymn see further Page, Sappho and Alcaeus, pp. 252 ff.

It is most unlikely that Horace imitated Alcaeus in any detail. The
narrative in Alcaeus must have been short and perfunctory by
the standards of the Homeric hymn, but it probably found room for
the nursing of Hermes by the Horae (Page, op. cit., pp. 256 f.). Horace,
on the other hand, does not tell a story at all, but simply alludes;
'viduus pharetra risit Apollo' exhibits the point and compression of
a rhetorical age. The symmetry of Horace's poem and the delicacy
of his transitions are also very sophisticated: the stealthy thief gives
place to the stealthy escort of Priam, who is followed in turn by the
escort of the dead. The Homeric episode in the fourth stanza, which
cannot have belonged to traditional cult, sounds alien to Alcaeus
(Wilamowitz, Sappho und Simonides, 1913, p. 312). Moreover, the
picture of the ψυχοπομπός and the suggestion of rewards after death
belong to an age later than Alcaeus's.

For purposes of comparison other addresses to Hermes may be
more briefly mentioned. In the Fourth Homeric Hymn he is primarily
a cattle-thief, but also a musician (30 ff.), herald (331), politician
(367 ff.), and prophet (552 ff.). Pindaric and Alexandrian hymns to
Hermes are lacking, but the 'epyllion' of Eratosthenes seems to have
described an ascent to the stars and the music of the spheres.
Horace is imitated by Ovid in some elegant elegiacs, which, however,
show less insight and sympathy than their model (fast. 5. 663 ff.):

> clare nepos Atlantis ades, quem montibus olim
>   edidit Arcadiis Pleias una Iovi,
> pacis et armorum superis imisque deorum
>   arbiter, alato qui pede carpis iter,
> laete lyrae pulsu, nitida quoque laete palaestra,
>   quo didicit culte lingua docente loqui.

A simple inscription from Rome, discovered in the Villa Albani, also
mentions some of the Horatian attributes (carm. epig. 1528):

lucri repertor atque sermonis dator
infas palaestram protulit Cyllenius.
interpres divum caeli terraeque meator
sermonem docui mortales atque palaestram.
[caelorum incola toti]usque terrae,
sermonis dator atque somniorum,
Iovis nuntius et precum minister.

The 28th Orphic hymn is mainly a list of cult titles, easily paralleled in prose Hellenistic ἀρεταλογίαι; the 57th is addressed to Hermes Chthonios and, characteristically for its period, concentrates on the god's function of ψυχοπομπός; a third-century A.D. papyrus encomium refers to the traditional themes of the lyre and the gymnasium (Ox. pap. 1015 = GLP 130). Finally, a few lines may be cited from a magical papyrus to show an up-to-date view of Hermes which was alien to Horace's cool and rational mind: see pap. Brit. Mus. XLVI. 401 ff. = K. Preisendanz, Papyri Graecae magicae: die griechischen Zauberpapyri, 1928, i. 194:

> Ἑρμῆ κοσμοκράτωρ ἐνκάρδιε κύκλε σελήνης,
> στρογγύλε καὶ τετράγωνε, λόγων ἀρχηγέτα γλώσσης . . .
> πνεύματος ἡνίοχε, ἡλίου ὀφθαλμέ, μέγιστε,
> παμφώνου γλώττης ἀρχηγέτα, λαμπάσι τέρπων
> τοὺς ὑπὸ τάρταρα γαίης τε βροτοὺς βίον ἐκτελέσαντας.

Horace's hymn is simply a literary composition, but it retains some features conventional to the genre and expounded in Eduard Norden's famous book Agnostos Theos. After the opening vocative a characteristic of the god is stated in apposition (1 n.). This is followed by a relative clause; cf. 'our Father which art in heaven', Hom. Il. i. 37 (Chryses's prayer to Apollo) κλῦθί μευ, ἀργυρότοξ', ὃς Χρύσην ἀμφιβέβηκας, Norden, op. cit. 168 ff. canam (5) recalls the ἀείσομαι or ἄρχομ' ἀείδειν of the Homeric hymns, and the repeated te is equally stereotyped (9 n.). The subject-matter is as traditional as the form. After giving the god's ancestry (nepos Atlantis) Horace turns to his ἀρεταί and πράξεις; Mercury is λόγιος, ἐναγώνιος, κῆρυξ, the inventor of the lyre, δόλιος, διάκτορος, ψυχοπομπός (for these cult titles see Bruchmann 104 ff.). The third and fourth stanzas tell stories in however clipped a way; these are the vestiges of the so-called 'pars epica', which was a regular feature of the genre. A hymn often ended with a prayer, and though in our ode this is modified into a statement, one can still detect traces of its origin (17 n.).

Horace's ode must be regarded primarily as a literary imitation, yet it is noteworthy that on three other occasions he writes as if he had a close relationship with Mercury. He was a vir Mercurialis, born when Mercury was in the ascendant (2. 17. 29); Mercury stole him away from Philippi (2. 7. 13); Mercury is offered prayers for the fertility of his estate (*serm.* 2. 6. 5 ff.). Fraenkel objects that such matters are irrelevant to our poem, which must be regarded as an entity in itself; that is true, but one may distinguish the analysis of a finished work of art from speculations about its genesis. In an astrological age it is at least possible that Horace pretended an allegiance to the god of unassuming poetry, whimsical trickery, and gentle charm, who helped his lucky devotees to fall on their feet. The Hymn to Mercury could not be one of Horace's greatest poems: it is too outmoded in form and has not enough universal application. Yet the poet has recaptured very deftly the humour and the pathos of the old Greek stories.

Metre: Sapphic.

1. facunde: the word is somewhat prosaic, and is not found in Catullus, Lucretius, Virgil, Tibullus, Propertius, Lucan, Valerius Flaccus, Silius. It is used here to represent λόγιος, a standard epithet for Hermes; cf. Mart. 7. 74. 1 f. 'Cyllenes caelique decus, facunde minister, / aurea cui torto virga dracone viret'. For this aspect of Hermes see *act. apost.* 14. 12 ἐκάλουν τε τὸν Βαρνάβαν Δία, τὸν δὲ Παῦλον Ἑρμῆν, ἐπειδὴ αὐτὸς ἦν ὁ ἡγούμενος τοῦ λόγου, anon. *GLP* 136. 46 ff. ἔστιχεν Ἑρμῆς / οὐκ οἶος, σὺν τῷ γε Λόγος κίεν ἀγλαὸς υἱὸς / λαιψηραῖς πτερύγεσσι κεκασμένος, αἰὲν ἀληθής, / ἁγνὴν ἀτρεκέεσσιν ἔχων ἐπὶ χείλεσι πειθώ, / πατρῴου καθαροῖο νοήματος ἄγγελος ὠκύς. For statues of Hermes as an orator see Roscher 1. 2410, 2423.

nepos Atlantis: Hermes was the son of Maia, daughter of Atlas (*RE* 14. 527 ff., Pease on Cic. *nat. deor.* 3. 56); cf. especially Hes. *th.* 938, *h.Merc.* 1 Ἑρμῆν ὕμνει, Μοῦσα, Διὸς καὶ Μαιάδος υἱόν, *h.Hom.* 18. 3 f., Alcaeus 308 (above, p. 126). *nepos* has none of the prosaic note of English 'grandson'; cf. Ov. *fast.* 5. 663, Claud. *rapt. Pros.* 1. 89 'Atlantis Tegeaee nepos'.

It is a common usage in hymns and prayers to combine the vocative with an attribute in apposition (Norden, *Agnostos Theos*, p. 148). This phrase often describes the ancestry of the god; genealogy is an important part of mythology. Cf. especially Alcaeus 307 ὦναξ Ἄπολλον, παῖ μεγάλω Δίος, Sappho 1. 1 f. ποικιλόθρον' ἀθανάτΆφρόδιτα, / παῖ Δίος δολόπλοκε, Anacreon 348. 1 ff., Pind. *P.* 8. 1 f., *O.* 12. 1 f., anon. *PMG* 1018 (b). 1 f. (these passages show that *facunde* should be taken with *nepos* rather than with *Mercuri*). The 'appositional style' is reproduced in later odes; cf. Ronsard, *A Mercure* 'Facond neveu d'Atlas, Mercure', Gray, *Hymn to Adversity* 1 f. 'Daughter of Jove, relentless power, Thou tamer of the human breast', Wordsworth 'Stern daughter of the voice of God, Oh duty, if that name thou love', Shelley 'O wild west wind, thou breath of Autumn's being'. For another instance of genealogy cf. Milton, *L'Allegro* 1 f. 'Hence loathed Melancholy, Of Cerberus and blackest midnight born'.

2. feros cultus: there is no oxymoron; *cultus* is naturally used in anthropological or ethnographic contexts. Cf. Hirt. *Gall.* 8. 25. 2 '(Treverorum) civitas . . . cultu et feritate non multum a Germanis differebat', Virg. *Aen.* 5. 730. For the civilizing power of language cf. *serm.* 1. 3. 103 f., Cic. *de orat.* 1. 33 'quae vis alia potuit aut dispersos homines unum in locum congregare aut a fera agrestique vita ad hunc humanum cultum civilemque deducere?', *nat. deor.* 2. 148 with Pease's note. Serious thinkers in antiquity were under no illusions about the savagery of early man; cf. Lucr. 5. 925 ff. with Bailey's note, Diod. Sic. 1. 8. 1, W. K. C. Guthrie, *In the Beginning,* 1957, pp. 95 ff., Kern 292.

voce: cf. *carm. epig.* 1528 and Ov. *fast.* 5. 668 (see pp. 126 f.), Diod. Sic. 1. 16. 1 (the Egyptians on 'Hermes', i.e. Thoth) ὑπὸ γὰρ τούτου πρῶτον μὲν τήν τε κοινὴν διάλεκτον διαρθρωθῆναι καὶ πολλὰ τῶν ἀνωνύμων τυχεῖν προσηγορίας, τήν τε εὕρεσιν τῶν γραμμάτων γενέσθαι (cf. Pl. *Phil.* 18 b), 5. 75. 2, Diogenes of Oenoanda 10. 2 f. καὶ τῶν φθόγγων δὲ ἕνεκεν . . . μήτε τὸν Ἑρμῆν παραλαμβάνωμεν εἰς διδασκαλίαν, ὥς φασίν τινες, περιφανὴς γὰρ αὕτη γε ἀδολεσχία. See further Roscher 1. 2366, Gruppe 2. 1339 n. 2, Pease on Cic. *nat. deor.* 3. 56, A.-J. Festugière, *La Révélation d'Hermès trismégiste* 1, 1944, pp. 71 ff.

3. catus: to be taken absolutely and not with the ablatives, in spite of Ausonius's imitation 'Phegeus catus arte palaestrae' (93. 1). The word means 'sharp', both literally and metaphorically; cf. Varro, *ling.* 7. 46 'cata acuta. hoc enim verbo dicunt Sabini; quare catus Aelius Sextus [Enn. *ann.* 331] non ut aiunt sapiens sed acutus'. *catus* is unpoetical, but used elsewhere by Horace (3. 12. 10, *epist.* 2. 2. 39); its unpretentious tone suits Mercury.

decorae: cf. Virg. *Aen.* 4. 559 (on Mercury) 'et crinis flavos et membra decora iuventa' (Servius comments 'quia palaestrae deus est'), Diod. Sic. 1. 16. 1 (below, 4 n.). T. E. Page confuses the ethos of the *palaestra* and the playing-field: 'true physical beauty is impossible without proper physical exercise'.

4. more: 'rules' (νόμος). Cf. Pind. *O.* 6. 69 τεθμόν τε μέγιστον ἀέθλων, Prop. 3. 14. 1 'multa tuae, Sparte, miramur iura palaestrae', Luc. 4. 613 f. 'perfudit membra liquore / hospes Olympiacae servato more palaestrae'.

palaestrae: Hermes was the patron of athletic contests and his statue, sometimes in the form of a herm, was set up at gymnasia and wrestling-schools; hence he had the title ἐναγώνιος. Cf. Aesch. fr. 384

ἐναγώνιε Μαίας / καὶ Διὸς Ἑρμᾶ, Pind. *O.* 6. 79, *P.* 2. 10, Cic. *Verr.* 5.
185 'teque, Mercuri, quem Verres in domo et in privata aliqua
palaestra posuit', *Att.* 1. 10. 3, Diod. Sic. 1. 16. 1 (the Egyptians on
Hermes) καὶ παλαίστρας εὑρετὴν ὑπάρξαι καὶ τῆς εὐρυθμίας καὶ τῆς περὶ
τὸ σῶμα πρεπούσης πλάσεως ἐπιμεληθῆναι, anon. *GLP* 130. 9 γυμνασίων
δὲ πόληες ἐπίσκοπον ἀείδουσιν, *RE* 7. 2022. Philostratus describes a picture of Palaestra, daughter of Hermes (*imag.* 2. 32); cf. Serv. auct.
Aen. 8. 138 'amatam vero suam Palaestram remuneratus, omne
luctamen quod corpore conficitur palaestram vocari fecit'. See further
Gruppe 2. 1340 n. 2, *RE* 18. 2. 2495, Roscher 1. 2368 f., Farnell
5. 28 ff.

5. **magni Iovis**: cf. Alcaeus 307 παῖ μεγάλω Δίος, Bruchmann 133 f.
For the conjunction *Iovis et deorum* cf. orac. ap. Hdt. 1. 65. 3 Ζηνὶ
φίλος καὶ πᾶσιν Ὀλύμπια δώματ' ἔχουσι, Men. *dysc.* 151 νὴ τὸν Ἀπόλλω
καὶ θεούς, Plaut. *capt.* 922 'Iovi disque ago gratias', K.–S. 2. 25.

6. **nuntium**: Hermes appears from the Odyssey as the messenger or
'angel' of the gods; cf. 5. 29 Ἑρμεία, σὺ γὰρ αὖτε τά τ' ἄλλα περ
ἄγγελός ἐσσι, Hes. *th.* 939 κήρυκ' ἀθανάτων, *op.* 80, fr. 170, *h.Merc.* 3
ἄγγελον ἀθανάτων ἐριούνιον, Plaut. *Stich.* 274 'Mercurius, Iovi' qui
nuntius perhibetur', Virg. *Aen.* 4. 356 'interpres divum Iove missus
ab ipso', Gruppe 2. 1329 n. 4, Roscher 1. 2362 ff.

curvaeque lyrae: on the day of his birth Hermes made a lyre out of
a tortoise-shell; cf. *h.Merc.* 30 ff., Paus. 8. 17. 5, Roscher 1. 2372 f.,
1. 21. 12 n. Hence the lyre is *curvae* or 'concave'; cf. 3. 28. 11, *h.Merc.*
64 φόρμιγγα γλαφυρήν, Ov. *fast.* 5. 104 'inventor curvae, furibus apte,
fidis', Avien. *Arat.* 619.

parentem: cf. Cic. *fin.* 2. 1 'Socrates . . . parens philosophiae', *Tim.*
40 'quorum operum ego parens effectorque' (translating Plato's ὧν
ἐγὼ δημιουργὸς πατήρ τε ἔργων), Pind. *P.* 4. 176 f. ἀοιδᾶν πατὴρ . . .
Ὀρφεύς, Pl. *Phaedr.* 275 a πατὴρ . . . γραμμάτων, Galen 1. 246 K. οἱ
πατέρες αὐτῶν (τῶν ἀτόμων).

7. **iocoso . . . furto**: Mercury was famous already in Homer for
trickery, perjury, and theft (*Il.* 24. 24, *Od.* 19. 395 ff.). In the fourth
Homeric hymn he is called δολομήτης, ἠπεροπευτής, δολοφράδης, πολύ-
τροπος, αἱμυλομήτης, ποικιλομήτης, κακομήδης, κλεψίφρων, μηχανιώτης,
ληιστήρ; he was actually worshipped at Pellene under the title of
Δόλιος (Paus. 7. 27. 1). There was something engaging and humorous
about his conjuring tricks which appealed to the Greek mind; cf.
Philostr. *imag.* 1. 26 μάλα ἡδεῖαι αἱ κλοπαὶ τοῦ θεοῦ. φασὶ γὰρ τὸν
Ἑρμῆν ὅτε τῇ Μαίᾳ ἐγένετο, ἐρᾶν τοῦ κλέπτειν καὶ εἰδέναι τοῦτο, οὔτι πω
ταῦτα πενίᾳ δρῶν ὁ θεός, ἀλλ' εὐφροσύνῃ διδοὺς καὶ παίζων. The Christians were less impressed; cf. Lact. *inst.* 1. 10. 7 'fur ac nebulo

Mercurius quid ad famam sui reliquit nisi memoriam fraudum suarum, caelo scilicet dignus quia palaestram docuit et lyram primus invenit?'

9. te . . .: such an anaphora is a traditional feature of hymns: see the important discussion by Norden in *Agnostos Theos*, pp. 149 ff. Parallels are abundant in Hellenistic Greek and in Latin; one may note especially 1. 35. 5 ff., 2. 19. 17 ff., 3. 11. 1 ff. and 13 ff., 3. 13. 9 ff., 3. 21. 13 ff., Lucr. 1. 6 ff. 'te dea, te fugiunt venti, te nubila caeli / adventumque tuum, tibi suavis daedala tellus / summittit flores, tibi rident aequora ponti', Catull. 34. 13 ff., 61. 51 ff., Tib. 1. 7. 25 ff., 61 ff., Prop. 3. 17. 3 ff., Virg. *Aen.* 8. 293 ff. Early Greek instances are rare, and are not as a rule asyndetic (A. D. Nock, *CQ* 18, 1924, 185; to his examples one may add Archil. 94). Nock suggests an Oriental source, though he also sees the influence of rhetoric and popular acclamations. For Christian examples one may refer to the Te Deum and the Gloria ('tu solus sanctus, tu solus dominus, tu solus altissimus, Iesu Christe').

boves . . .: for the theft by Hermes of Apollo's cattle see *h.Merc.* 20 ff., Soph. *Ichneutae*, Eratosthenes fr. 1 Powell, Apollod. 3. 10. 2, Ov. *met.* 2. 680 ff., Antoninus Liberalis, *met.* 23. The episode was described by Alcaeus in his Hymn to Hermes (above, p. 126). See further T. W. Allen and W. R. Halliday, *The Homeric Hymns*, pp. 270 ff., N. O. Brown, *Hermes the Thief*, Wisconsin, 1947 (he reproduces a sixth-century Athenian vase picturing the episode), Gruppe 2. 1327 n. 2, Roscher 1. 2369 ff., J. D. Beazley, *Attic Red-Figure Vase Painters*, ed. 2, 1963, pp. 369 f., *Attic Black-Figure Vase Painters*, 1956, pp. 99, 602.

olim: 'once upon a time' (ποτε), appropriate in telling a story (Hand 4. 368 f., Fraenkel on Aesch. *Ag.* 1040). Cf. Don. *Andr.* 925 'etenim *olim* fabulae proprium est, ut Horatius, "olim / rusticus urbanum murem mus paupere fertur / accepisse cavo" ' (*serm.* 2. 6. 79 ff.).

reddidisses: represents the future-perfect *reddideris* of direct speech; cf. Cic. *Verr.* 2. 162 'nisi restituissent statuas vehementer minatur'.

10. per dolum: Hermes drove Apollo's cattle backwards, so that the tracks led in the wrong direction; cf. *h.Merc.* 76 δολίης δ' οὐ λήθετο τέχνης, 344 ff., Soph. *Ichn.* 112 ff., Antoninus Liberalis 23 (= Hes. fr. 256). The same story is told of Cacus (Liv. 1. 7. 5, Virg. *Aen.* 8. 209 ff., Prop. 4. 9. 12, Dion. Hal. *ant. Rom.* 1. 39. 2); see further Allen and Halliday on *h.Merc.* 77.

amotas: not simply a discreet euphemism, but a technical term of Roman lawyers. Cf. Gai. *inst.* 3. 195 'furtum . . . fit . . . cum quis intercipiendi causa rem alienam amovet', Ulp. *dig.* 29. 2. 71. 6

'amovisse eum accipimus qui quid celaverit aut interverterit aut consumpserit', 47. 9. 3. 5 'aliud autem esse rapi, aliud amoveri palam est, si quidem amoveri aliquid etiam sine vi possit' (*sine vi* implies *per dolum*).

puerum: the episode took place on the day that Hermes was born (*h.Merc.* 19 ff.). Latin has not distinct words for 'a baby' and 'a boy'.

11. terret: 'threaten' rather than 'terrify'; Mercury was anything but frightened.

viduus: χῆρος is similarly used in Greek (Headlam on Herodas 3. 35).

pharetra: in the Homeric hymn Hermes does not actually steal the quiver. Apollo simply says, after the quarrel about the cattle has been settled, δείδια . . . μή μοι ἀνακλέψῃς κίθαριν καὶ καμπύλα τόξα (514 f.). However, two accounts other than Horace's mention the theft of the quiver and Apollo's laughter; all three are presumably derived from Alcaeus's poem (cf. Porph. ad loc. 'fabula . . . ab Alcaeo ficta'). One of these is the scholium on Hom. *Il.* 15. 256: ἀπειλοῦντος δὲ τοῦ Ἀπόλλωνος ἔκλεψεν αὐτοῦ καὶ τὰ ἐπὶ τῶν ὤμων τόξα· μειδιάσας δὲ ὁ θεὸς ἔδωκεν αὐτῷ τὴν μαντικὴν ῥάβδον ἀφ' ἧς καὶ χρυσόρραπις ὁ Ἑρμῆς προσηγορεύθη. Philostratus purports to describe a picture of the story, though his account is obviously more circumstantial than anything possible for Alcaeus (*imag.* 1. 26): ἔτ' αὐτῶν ἀντιλεγόντων ἀλλήλοις ὁ Ἑρμῆς ἵσταται κάτοπιν τοῦ Ἀπόλλωνος καὶ κούφως ἐπιπηδήσας τοῖς μεταφρένοις ἀψοφητὶ λύει τὰ τόξα καὶ συλῶν μὲν διέλαθεν, οὐ μὴν ἠγνοήθη σεσυληκώς· ἐνταῦθα ἡ σοφία τοῦ ζωγράφου· διαχεῖ γὰρ τὸν Ἀπόλλω καὶ ποιεῖ χαίροντα· μεμέτρηται δὲ ὁ γέλως οἷος ἐφιζάνων τῷ προσώπῳ θυμὸν ἐκνικώσης ἡδονῆς. For other similar exploits of Hermes cf. Lucian, *dial. deor.* 7. 3 τῆς Ἀφροδίτης μὲν τὸν κεστὸν ἔκλεψε . . . τοῦ Διὸς δὲ γελῶντος ἔτι τὸ σκῆπτρον, εἰ δὲ μὴ βαρύτερος ὁ κεραυνὸς ἦν καὶ πολὺ τὸ πῦρ εἶχε, κἀκεῖνον ἂν ὑφείλετο.

13. quin et . . .: Horace sketches with great economy the moving scene in the *Iliad* where Hermes escorts the stricken Priam through the Greek lines to recover Hector's body from Achilles (*Il.* 24. 333 ff., *epod.* 17. 13 f.). The episode was repeatedly portrayed in works of art (*RE* 22. 1868 ff., Roscher 3. 2957 ff.).

14. dives: Priam had all the wealth of an eastern king; cf. *Il.* 18. 288 f. Πριάμοιο πόλιν . . . πολύχρυσον πολύχαλκον, 24. 544 ff. (Achilles to Priam) ὅσσον Λέσβος ἄνω, Μάκαρος ἔδος, ἐντὸς ἐέργει / καὶ Φρυγίη καθύπερθε καὶ Ἑλλήσποντος ἀπείρων, / τῶν σε, γέρον, πλούτῳ τε καὶ υἱάσι φασὶ κεκάσθαι, Eur. *Hec.* 492 f. In our context Priam's wealth suggests the large ransom which he is bringing; so Aeschylus in his

Phrygians described how Hector's body was weighed against gold
(schol. A *Il.* 22. 351, Roscher 3. 2659 f.).

15. **Thessalosque ignes**: the watch-fires of the pickets in front of the
Greek camp; this detail is not mentioned in the last book of the
Iliad. The Myrmidons, like Achilles, came from Phthia in Thessaly;
Horace suggests that Priam is on his way to Achilles.

16. **fefellit**: ἔλαθε. Cf. Hom. *Il.* 24. 336 ff. (Zeus to Hermes) βάσκ᾽
ἴθι, καὶ Πριάμου κοίλας ἐπὶ νῆας Ἀχαιῶν / ὡς ἄγαγ᾽ ὡς μήτ᾽ ἄρ τις ἴδῃ
μήτ᾽ ἄρ τε νοήσῃ / τῶν ἄλλων Δαναῶν πρὶν Πηλειωνάδ᾽ ἱκέσθαι, 24. 443 ff.

17. **tu . . .**: a hymn to Hermes might appropriately end with a prayer
for a peaceful death; cf. *Orph. h.* 28. 11 ff. κλῦθί μου εὐχομένου, βιότου
τέλος ἐσθλὸν ὀπάζων / ἐργασίαισι, λόγου χάρισιν καὶ μνημοσύνῃσιν. By
hinting at this conventional pattern Horace gives his poem a quiet
and serious ending. But as a rationalist and a sceptic he cannot himself make such a prayer to Mercury; instead he simply states what
Mercury is reputed to do.

Hermes was the ψυχοπομπός who escorted the dead to the underworld; cf. 1. 24. 15 ff., Hom. *Od.* 24. 9 f. ἦρχε δ᾽ ἄρα σφιν / Ἑρμείας
ἀκάκητα κατ᾽ εὐρώεντα κέλευθα (the book is late, and the belief non-
Homeric), Soph. *Ai.* 831 f., Lucian, *dial. deor.* 24. 1 τὸ δὲ πάντων
δεινότατον ὅτι μηδὲ νυκτὸς καθεύδω μόνος τῶν ἄλλων, ἀλλὰ δεῖ με καὶ
τότε τῷ Πλούτωνι ψυχαγωγεῖν καὶ νεκροπομπὸν εἶναι καὶ παρεστάναι τῷ
δικαστηρίῳ. οὐ γὰρ ἱκανά μοι τὰ τῆς ἡμέρας ἔργα, ἐν παλαίστραις εἶναι
κἂν ταῖς ἐκκλησίαις κηρύττειν καὶ ῥήτορας ἐκδιδάσκειν, ἀλλ᾽ ἔτι καὶ
νεκρικὰ συνδιαπράττειν μεμερισμένον. The evidence of literature is
reinforced by the tombstones: cf. Peek, *GV* 258. 3 f. = Kaibel, *EG*
411. 3 f. (Patara, 1st century B.C.) τὸν ὦ Μαίας κλυτὲ κοῦρε / Ἑρμείη
πέντοις χῶρον ἐπ᾽ εὐσεβέων, Peek, *GV* 1249. 9 f. (Crete, 100 B.C.)
Ἑρμῆ Μαιάδος υἱέ, ἄγ᾽ εὐσεβέων ἐπὶ χῶρον / ἄνδρα τὸν ἐν θηραῖς γ᾽ ὄντ᾽
ἀκ[ορε]στότατον, 1518. 7 f. (Eretria, 100 B.C.) ἀλλ᾽ Ἑρμῆ, Μαίης τέκος
ἄφθιτον, εὔφρονι θυμῷ / γαίης ἐγ κόλποις ἀμφαγάπαζε κόρον. Of representations in works of art one may refer in particular to the
Ephesus relief in the British Museum (Roscher 1. 2416). See further
Gruppe 2. 1321 n. 1, Roscher 1. 2373 ff.

laetis: cf. Virg. *Aen.* 6. 638 'devenere locos laetos'. The prefix of
reponis suggests 'to their appointed place'.

18. **virga**: cf. 1. 24. 15 n. Hermes is regularly equipped with a herald's
staff (κηρύκειον, *caduceus*), which had a characteristic loop on the end
(8). His magic wand (ῥάβδος, *virga*) was by origin identical with the
caduceus, but sometimes is regarded as distinct (Apul. *met.* 10. 30. 4
'caduceum et virgula', Roscher 3. 3231 = D.–S. fig. 4947). Cf. Hom.

Il. 24. 343 εἵλετο δὲ ῥάβδον τῇ τ' ἀνδρῶν ὄμματα θέλγει / ὧν ἐθέλει, τοὺς δ' αὖτε καὶ ὑπνώοντας ἐγείρει (so *Od.* 24. 2 ff., where Hermes drives the souls of the suitors), *h.Merc.* 529 f. (Apollo to Hermes) ὄλβου καὶ πλούτου δώσω περικαλλέα ῥάβδον, / χρυσείην τριπέτηλον ἀκήριον ἥ σε φυλάξει, *Orph. h.* 57. 6 ff., Virg. *Aen*: 4. 242 ff. 'tum virgam capit ; hac animas ille evocat Orco / pallentes, alias sub Tartara tristia mittit, / dat somnos adimitque et lumina morte resignat' (cf. Stat. *Theb.* 1. 306 ff.), Spenser, *F.Q.* 2. 12. 41. For further details cf. F. J. M. de Waele, *The Magic Staff or Rod in Graeco-Italian Antiquity*, 1927, pp. 29 ff., *RE* 11. 331 ff., 3 A. 1920, Roscher 1. 2365, Pease on Cic. *div.* 1. 30 and Virg. *Aen*. 4. 242.

levem: 'insubstantial'; cf. Ov. *met.* 10. 14 'perque leves populos simulacraque functa sepulcro', Sen. *Ag.* 757.

coerces: Mercury used his wand like a shepherd's staff; so more explicitly 1. 24. 16 ff. (see note).

19. aurea: Hermes is χρυσόρραπις in the *Odyssey*. He is still assigned a golden wand in a papyrus poem of the fourth century A.D. (*GLP* 136. 4 f.) δῶκε δέ οἱ ῥάβδον χρυσέην διακοσμήτειραν / πάσης εὐέργοιο νοήμονα μητέρα τέχνης, ibid. 18.

superis . . .: Mercury is an ambassador between Heaven and Hades; cf. *h.Merc.* 572 οἷον δ' εἰς Ἀίδην τετελεσμένον ἄγγελον εἶναι, Aesch. *cho.* 165 κῆρυξ μέγιστε τῶν ἄνω τε καὶ κάτω, Apollod. 3. 10. 2 Ζεὺς δὲ αὐτὸν κήρυκα ἑαυτοῦ καὶ θεῶν ὑποχθονίων τίθησι, Ov. *fast.* 5. 665 and *carm. epig.* 1528 (see pp. 126 f.), Cornutus, *nat. deor.* 16 διὰ δὲ τὸ κοινὸν αὐτὸν εἶναι καὶ τὸν αὐτὸν ἔν τε τοῖς ἀνθρώποις πᾶσι καὶ ἐν τοῖς θεοῖς . . ., Plut. *Is. et Osir.* 375 e, Apul. *apol.* 64, *met.* 11. 11. 1, Claud. *rapt. Pros.* 1. 89 f., Serv. auct. *Aen.* 8. 138 'alii Mercurium quasi Medicurrium a Latinis dictum volunt quod inter caelum et inferos semper intercurrat', Fulg. *myth.* 1. 18.

11. TV NE QVAESIERIS

[D. West 58 ff.]

1–3. *Do not investigate our horoscopes, Leuconoe; better to accept whatever happens.* 4–8. *Whether life is to be long or short, enjoy your wine today and distrust the morrow.*

The antecedents of this little poem are more complex than might appear at first sight. Some elements are obviously derived from convivial Greek lyric and epigram. Stormy weather is a traditional feature of drinking-songs (p. 117). The adjuration 'to cut short long hopes' suits the *paraenesis* of early lyric. It seems to have been a commonplace in sympotic verse to say 'do not ask or trouble about serious or worrying matters'; cf. 1. 9. 13 'quid sit futurum cras fuge quaerere', 2. 11. 3 f. 'remittas quaerere', *Anacreontea* 3. 10 f. τί Πλειάδων μέλει μοι; / τί γὰρ καλοῦ Βοώτου; In particular one may compare some elegant meiuric hexameters of the Roman period (anon. *GLP* 125. 8 ff.):

> μὴ κοπία ζητεῖν πόθεν ἥλιος ἢ πόθεν ὕδωρ
> ἀλλὰ πόθεν τὸ μύρον καὶ τοὺς στεφάνους ἀγοράσῃς.
> αὔλει μοι.

Similarly in our poem Horace expresses disregard for astrology; cf. Antip. Thess.· *anth. P.* 11. 23. 1 ff. ὠκύμορόν με λέγουσι δαήμονες ἀνέρες ἄστρων·/εἰμὶ μὲν ἀλλ' οὔ μοι τοῦτο, Σέλευκε, μέλει./ . . . πίνωμεν.

Yet the ode has one feature which is noteworthy in a drinking-poem: it is addressed to a woman. Perhaps Horace has chosen to do this because he is talking of horoscopes, and women were particularly interested in astrology. Yet there are also hints of a love-interest which, though not conspicuous, may have been more prominent in Horace's models. It is surely significant that Leuconoe consults astrologers not only in her own but on Horace's behalf (1 n.). Some of the parallels to *carpe diem* have a clear reference to love (8 n.), and this is the natural interpretation of the phrase in a poem addressed to a girl (D. West 64). Horace may be using a motif from a lost Greek prototype, something on the lines of Marvell's poem 'To his Coy Mistress', or Herrick's 'To the Virgins, to make much of Time'; for the general theme cf. Asclepiades, *anth. P.* 5. 85. 1 f. (above, 1. 4. 18 n.). A particularly illuminating parallel is provided by a little piece in the Virgilian appendix, *de rosis nascentibus*; this ends with the couplet (49 f.)

> collige, virgo, rosas dum flos novus et nova pubes,
> et memor esto aevum sic properare tuum.

Direct imitation of Horace is unlikely: the two poems are very different in subject and treatment, and 'collige virgo rosas' is much more explicit than 'carpe diem'. One should look rather for a common ancestry in Hellenistic erotic epigram. It may or may not be a coincidence that 'dum loquor' occurs in the elegiac poem (38) and 'dum loquimur' in Horace (7 n.).

The ode also contains several reminiscences of Epicurus. He seems to be the source of the maxim in line 3, 'put up with whatever happens' (see n.); he may also have commented on the advantages of not knowing the future (3 n.). *carpe diem* is perhaps Epicurean in expression as well as in spirit (8 n.). Epicurus's distrust of divination may therefore be relevant to the opening lines: cf. fr. 395. 16 ff. Ἐπικούρειόν ἐστι δόγμα ἀναιροῦν τὴν μαντικήν· εἱμαρμένης γάρ, φησι,

N

πάντα κρατούσης πρὸ καιροῦ λελύπηκας ⟨εἰπὼν τὴν συμφοράν⟩, ἢ χρηστόν
τι εἰπὼν τὴν ἡδονὴν ἐξέλυσας. λέγουσι δ' ὅτι καὶ ἃ δεῖ γενέσθαι ταῦτα καὶ
γενήσεται, fr. 27 μαντικὴ οὖσα ἀνυπαρκτός, εἰ καὶ ὑπαρκτή, οὐδὲν παρ'
ἡμᾶς ἡγητέα τὰ γινόμενα, Cic. div. 1. 5 with Pease's note. Yet it would
be wrong to interpret the poem as a whole as a rationalistic attack on
astrology. The undesirability of knowing the future is emphasized as
much as the impossibility. Distrust of prophecies merges into distrust of the future itself; and this too is an Epicurean doctrine (8 n.).

Horace's poem is outstandingly good. His theme may be traditional, but he relates it to the real life of his own times; as astrology
was a contemporary interest (see 2 n.), the reference comes in very
naturally. Even if the Tyrrhenian waves are derived from some
Greek commonplace, Horace's treatment is fresh and evocative. To
write in choriambs is something of a *tour de force*, but the metre is
handled without strain. The rapid movement of the poem suits the
suggestion that there is no time to lose; and 'carpe diem', however
hackneyed it later became, is a brilliant expression. In Greek epigram the topic encouraged sensuousness and sentimentality, but
here it is stated with unique brevity and authority. Horace nowhere
expresses his pessimism (admittedly conventional) with greater
energy and concentration.

Metre: Greater Asclepiad.

1. tu: the pronoun strikes a note of earnest admonition; the usage
is not particularly colloquial (as suggested by H.–Sz. 173).

quaesieris: the word well suits the consultation of astrologers; cf.
Prop. 2. 27. 1 f. 'at vos incertam, mortales, funeris horam / quaeritis,
et qua sit mors aditura via', Ov. *met.* 1. 148, Tac. *ann.* 3. 22. 2 'quaesi-
tumque per Chaldaeos in domum Caesaris'.

scire nefas: 'knowledge is forbidden'; cf. Porph. on *carm.* 3. 29. 31
'nefas est inquirere futura quae divi nescire nos voluerunt'. The
phrase is a conventional formula; cf. *carm.* 4. 4. 22, Ov. *fast.* 3. 325,
Luc. 1. 127, Stat. *Theb.* 3. 562 f. 'quid crastina volveret aetas / scire
nefas homini', Prud. *cath.* 3. 116. Cicero uses *nefas* to translate
ἀδύνατον (*Tim.* 6), but the word has moral overtones which ἀδύνατον
lacks: it suggests that something is a violation of a natural or divine
order.

quem mihi, quem tibi: consultations about a loved one must have
been common; for a satirical reference cf. Juv. 6. 565 ff. 'consulit . . .
an sit victurus adulter'.

2. Leuconoe: the lady is obviously fictitious, and it is not clear why
Horace calls her 'Leuconoe'. It may only be a pretty name that suits

a difficult metre. But more probably it conveys some particular nuance either by derivation or literary association. Yet no explanation that has been suggested seems completely convincing.

'Leuconoe' seems to be derived from νοῦς and νοεῖν. For similar names cf. *Alcinoe, Arsinoe, Autonoe, Chrysonoe, Philonoe, Thelxinoe* (F. Bechtel, *Die historischen Personennamen des Griechischen bis zur Kaiserzeit*, 1917, p. 337). Pape–Benseler connect 'Leuconoe' with νόα, an obscure word for a spring; this would suit the Attic deme Leuconoe, but is not a natural derivation for the woman's name.

The meaning of λευκο- is less clear, but it cannot in origin be derogatory; otherwise the name would not have been borne by several mythological heroines. This argument rules out any connection with λευκαῖς . . . φρασίν (Pind. *P.* 4. 109), an obscure phrase which has been variously interpreted as 'shallow', 'mad', and 'envious'. Perhaps the adjective refers to simplicity and innocence of character; it is used for instance of clear water (Hom. *Il.* 23. 282 λοέσσας ὕδατι λευκῷ). But even so it is difficult to see a really pointed application in this particular poem. Horace may be hinting that Leuconoe is a little too simple-minded; yet to consult astrologers was not the mark so much of guileless girls as sophisticated women. To trust the future may indeed be a sign of ingenuousness, but 'credula postero' only appears at the end of the poem. One might rather suggest, simply as a speculation, that a lost Greek epigram was addressed to a Leuconoe, who was of such purity and innocence of mind that she was reluctant to 'gather rose-buds'; and that Horace has overlaid this epigram with so many other features that the significance of the name has virtually disappeared.

If such a hypothesis is thought too fanciful, one might look for other forms of literary association. Leuconoe seems to have been a name for one of the Minyads who rejected the rites of Bacchus and were turned into bats (cf. ps.-Lact. Plac. *fab. Ov.* 4. 12, from where the name is restored by editors in Ov. *met.* 4. 168 for the corrupt *Leucothoe*). In a context urging the enjoyment of life an allusion to this legend might seem appropriate; yet there is a difference between Dionysiac ecstasy and the rational hedonism which Horace enjoins.

An attempt has been made to find a reference to star-gazing in the name. Meton, the great fifth-century astronomer, came from the deme Leuconoe; cf. Phrynichus 21 K. *A.* Τίς δ᾽ ἔστιν ὁ μετὰ ταῦτα φροντίζων; *B.* Μέτων | ὁ Λευκονοιεύς. *A.* οἶδ᾽, ὁ τὰς κρήνας ἄγων. Hence it has been suggested that the name is the equivalent of 'Miss Newton' (J. R. Smith, *CR* 33, 1919, 27 f.). This theory, if carefully phrased, is not absurd, but it depends on one unproved assumption: one has to posit that Meton was known familiarly in Hellenistic literature as ὁ Λευκονοιεύς, just as Epicurus was called

'Gargettius' (Cic. *epist.* 15. 16. 1, Stat. *silv.* 1. 3. 94, 2. 2. 113). Of course 'Leuconoe' is not the feminine of 'Leuconoeus', and even if it were the name would be, strictly speaking, irrational; it would have to acquire its effect simply by association. This is perhaps not altogether impossible; the athlete Hebrus is described as *Liparaeus* because the name suggests λιπαρός (3. 12. 6). Yet it must be recognized that the theory involves more than one step in the dark.

Babylonios: astrology originated in Babylonia and hence was often called Χαλδαική; the Chaldaei were, strictly speaking, the inhabitants of lower Mesopotamia, then the Babylonian priesthood, finally astrologers in general. The art spread over the Hellenistic world, notably to Egypt, in the wake of Alexander (cf. Leonidas, *anth. P.* 9. 80 for some unfriendly remarks). In the second century B.C. we find it practised at Rome: Cato (*agr.* 5. 4) and Ennius (*scaen.* 242 ff.) were hostile, as was the neo-Stoic Panaetius, and in 139 B.C. astrologers were expelled temporarily from the city (Val. Max. 1. 3. 3). In the next century opinion in the governing classes was much more favourable. Sulla believed in astrology; more significantly, so did Posidonius and Varro, as well as Nigidius Figulus; here as elsewhere the rationalism of Cicero is untypical (*div.* 2. 87–99). In 33 B.C. Octavian expelled the astrologers from Rome, but the effect did not last long. Maecenas seems to have been a believer (cf. 2. 17); Vitruvius (9. 6. 2), Propertius (4. 1), and Ovid (*Ib.* 209 ff.) all at least profess to take the art seriously; later in the reign Manilius began his remarkable poem. Augustus forbade the consultation of astrologers about death, but at the same time he published his own horoscope (Dio 56. 25. 5). Tiberius not only practised astrology himself, but allowed immense power to his astrologer Thrasyllus. The Julio-Claudian and Flavian emperors all consulted astrologers, and their experts (e.g. Balbillus) obtained great influence; the elder Pliny is an outstanding exception to the credulity of the age (*nat.* 2. 23). Astrology was regarded as the most scientific method of telling the future, one sanctioned by cool-headed statesmen and high-minded scholars. No doubt astrologers made mistakes, but so did doctors; the art itself was not to be impugned for that reason any more than medicine. See further A. Bouché-Leclercq, *L'Astrologie grecque*, 1899, pp. 543 ff., F. Cumont, *Astrology and Religion among the Greeks and Romans*, 1912, F. H. Cramer, *Astrology in Roman Law and Politics*, 1954.

3. numeros: astrological calculations; cf. Cic. *div.* 1. 36, 2. 17, Luc. 1. 641, Juv. 6. 576. Astrologers were often called *mathematici* (Mayor on Juv. 14. 248).

ut melius: *ut* is exclamatory; for its use with a comparative cf. Plaut. *truc.* 806 'ut facilius alia quam alia eundem puerum . . . parit'.

Withof proposed *utilius* (against the ancient commentators); but it is too calculating to confine the issue so explicitly to expediency.

It was a commonplace of ancient thought that it is better not to foresee the future (3. 29. 29 ff.). The point was no doubt made by Epicurus himself; it is found in a fragment of Diogenianus, the Epicurean of the second century A.D. (ap. Euseb. *pr. evang.* 138 b 1 ff.): τί γὰρ ὄφελος ἡμῖν ἦν προμανθάνειν τὰ πάντως ἐσόμενα δυσχερῆ ἃ οὐδὲ προφυλάξασθαι δυνατὸν ἂν εἴη; See also Aesch. *Pr.* 248, Cic. *div.* 2. 22 with Pease's note, 2. 105 'magnus Dicaearchi liber est nescire ea melius quam scire', *nat. deor.* 3. 14 with Pease's note, Plut. εἰ ἡ τῶν μελλόντων πρόγνωσις ὠφέλιμος (title of dialogue), ps.-Plut. *Apoll.* 107 a οἶμαι δὲ καὶ τὴν φύσιν ὁρῶσαν τό τ' ἄτακτον καὶ βραχυχρόνιον τοῦ βίου ἄδηλον ποιῆσαι τὴν τοῦ θανάτου προθεσμίαν. τοῦτο γὰρ ἦν ἄμεινον, Favorinus fr. 3 with Barigazzi's note, Origen, *in Gen.* 8 (12. 68 c Migne) πάντα γοῦν χρησίμως ὁ Θεὸς τὰ κατὰ τὸν κόσμον οἰκονομῶν, εὐλόγως ἡμᾶς καὶ πρὸς τὰ μέλλοντα ἐτύφλωσεν.

quicquid erit pati: cf. Virg. *Aen.* 5. 710 'quidquid erit, superanda omnis fortuna ferendo est', Ov. *epist.* 18. 51 'quidquid erit, patiar'.

Horace's sentiment may be Epicurean. This is suggested by a fine sentence in Cicero addressed to the Epicurean Paetus: 'tu tamen pro tua sapientia debebis optare optima, cogitare difficillima, ferre quaecumque erunt' (*epist.* 9. 17. 3). There is a similar aphorism in Plut. *tranq. an.* 474 c εὔχεται μὲν ὁ νοῦν ἔχων τὰ βελτίονα, προσδοκᾷ δὲ καὶ θάτερα, χρῆται δ' ἀμφοτέροις τὸ ἄγαν ἀφαιρῶν. It may be significant that Plutarch goes on to quote Epicurus fr. 490 in the next sentence.

4. seu . . .: this clause is best taken as the beginning of a new sentence which continues to 7 *reseces.* 'ut melius quidquid erit pati' is complete in itself and needs no development. This argument is particularly forcible if Horace is alluding to an Epicurean aphorism.

Many editors print a comma at *pati* and run on till 6 *Tyrrhenum* (cf. P. Veyne, *RPh* 41, 1967, 107). But the long sentence seems to straggle a little; and it ends with an adjective immediately preceded by its noun. Moreover, the pronounced break after 6 *Tyrrhenum* is very sudden and interrupts the flow of the long choriambic lines. A full stop after the third syllable in line 6 would be unparalleled in Horace's greater Asclepiads; the only full stops inside the line occur after the sixth syllable (1. 11. 3, 1. 11. 7, 1. 18. 11, 1. 18. 13); the pause after *aetas* (1. 11. 8) is distinctly slighter.

hiemes: Horace partly uses 'winters' as a conventional substitute for 'years' (cf. 1. 15. 35), but he also implies a great deal more. Mediterranean winters are associated with storm rather than snow (cf. χειμών). It seems likely that a Greek lyric poet (perhaps Alcaeus) mentioned the sea in a sympotic poem (cf. p. 117).

tribuit: if the tense is perfect it suits the astrological doctrine that one's span of life is allotted at birth; cf. Plin. *nat.* 2. 23 'semelque in omnes futuros umquam deo decretum, in reliquum vero otium datum'. An Epicurean should not talk in such terms, but Horace is not greatly concerned to deny Leuconoe's presuppositions.

5. debilitat: the sea is worn down by a barrier of rock. Some editors find the expression strange; they say that one would sooner expect the sea to wear down the land. Yet cf. Virg. *Aen.* 10. 304 'fluctusque fatigat'; in Greek κοπάζειν is used of stormy seas being calmed; in English one talks of the 'spent force' of the waves (cf. also A. H. Clough's 'tired waves vainly breaking').

pumicibus: the name is applied not only to pumice in the modern sense (which is particularly associated with the Lipari islands), but also in a more general sense to other volcanic rocks, such as are abundant on the west coast of Italy; cf. Plin. *nat.* 36. 154–5, *RE* 3. 473 f., D.–S. 4. 767 f. The essential characteristic of *pumex* is porosity (Ov. *met.* 8. 562 'pumice multicavo'); hence the word is used of the hiding-place of birds (Virg. *Aen.* 5. 214) and of bees (12. 587).

pumex would not be the right stone to mention if Horace were emphasizing the strength of the rocks. Rather he suggests the slow and steady process of erosion caused by the continuous interaction of rocks and sea; cf. Lucr. 1. 325 ff. 'nec porro quaecumque aevo macieque senescunt, / nec mare quae impendent vesco sale saxa peresa / quid quoque amittant in tempore cernere possis', Sidon. *carm.* 11. 28 'asper ab assiduo lympharum verbere pumex'. By this subtle touch the poet evokes a contrast (which he does not explicitly state) between the long-drawn-out conflicts of nature and the brevity of human life and happiness.

6. Tyrrhenum: Horace includes an Italian place-name, as often, to add local colour.

sapias: 'be sensible'; cf. 1. 7. 17, Mart. 4. 54. 3 'si sapis, utaris totis, Colline, diebus', J. B. Hofmann, *Lateinische Umgangssprache*, ed. 3, 1951, pp. 134, 200. Porphyrio (together with Prisc. *gramm.* 3. 247. 14 ff.) says that *sapias* here means 'if you were wise', and is subordinate to *liques* (so also P. Veyne, *RPh* 41, 1967, 107). But as the words are both subjunctive this is unlikely.

vina liques: 'strain your wine'. The ancients removed the sediment from wine by pouring it through either a strainer of metal or rush (*colum*) or a linen bag (*saccus*); see D.–S. 1. 1331 f., *RE* 4. 590 ff., G. Curtel, *La Vigne et le vin chez les Romains*, 1903, pp. 156 ff. This process often took place just before the actual drinking; cf. Pherecrates 41. 2 K. ἔγχει τ' ἐπιθεὶς τὸν ἠθμόν, Juv. 13. 44 f. 'et iam saccato nectare tergens / bracchia Volcanus Liparaea nigra taberna' (where *saccato* is Schurzfleisch's convincing emendation of *siccato*).

Commentators on our passage do not ask why Horace says 'vina liques' rather than 'vina bibas'. Probably they assume that the preparation implies the drinking. Yet a special point seems to be meant. Sediment could be removed not only by straining but by leaving the wine standing; cf. *serm*. 2. 4. 51 ff. 'Massica si caelo suppones vina sereno, / nocturna, si quid crassi est, tenuabitur aura / et decedet odor nervis inimicus: at illa / integrum perdunt lino vitiata saporem'. This method avoided the bad effects of straining. But Horace recommends immediate consumption: it is true that the wine may improve if you leave it standing, but you may not be there to drink it. Epicurean distrust of the morrow could not be expressed more vividly.

spatio brevi: 'within short limits'; the ablative is similar to the one sometimes found with *coercere* and *claudere*. It is correctly explained by A. O. Hulton, *CR* N.S. 8, 1958, 106 f.; he compares Liv. 2. 50. 7 'cogebantur breviore spatio et ipsi orbem colligere', Ov. *fast*. 6. 495 f. 'est spatio contracta brevi (terra)'. He rightly rejects the view of many commentators (following Porphyrio) that *spatio brevi* is ablative absolute (= 'the span of life being short').

7. reseces: the metaphor is from pruning vines.

dum loquimur: cf. Ov. *am*. 1. 11. 15 'dum loquor hora fugit', *Pont*. 4. 3. 58, Pers. 5. 153, Petron. 99. 3, Hier. *in Gal*. 3. 6 p. 528, *ros. nasc*. 37 f. 'ecce et defluxit rutili coma punica floris / dum loquor', Orient. *comm*. 2. 196. No instance of this *sententia* before Horace has been noticed by editors. Yet Horace is less pointed than some of his successors; 'dum loquimur' means not 'while I am speaking these words' but 'while we are holding this conversation'.

fugerit: 'will already have fled'; the future perfect emphasizes the speed of time's flight.

8. aetas: not 'life' (in which case *invida* would be inappropriate), but 'time'; cf. 2. 5. 13 f. 'currit enim ferox / aetas', Cic. *Tusc*. 1. 76 'volat enim aetas'. For similar aphorisms cf. Otto 112. Time is 'mean' because it will not let people enjoy themselves for long; cf. Erinna, *anth. P*. 7. 712. 3 βάσκανος ἔσσ', Ἀΐδα (for parallels see Gow–Page 2. 283), Strato, ibid. 12. 234. 4 ταῦτα δ' ὁμῇ φθονέων ἐξεμάρανε χρόνος.

carpe diem: Porphyrio correctly comments 'translatio . . . a pomis sumpta est quae . . . ideo carpimus ut fruamur'. The word suggests both that there is something desirable to be gained and that if time is wasted the pleasure will be lost. So Ov. *ars* 3. 79 f. 'nostra sine auxilio fugiunt bona: carpite florem / qui nisi carptus erit turpiter ipse cadet', Pers. 5. 151 'indulge genio, carpamus dulcia', Mart. 7.

47. 11. For similar expressions cf. Pind. fr. 123. 1 χρῆν μὲν κατὰ καιρὸν ἐρώτων δρέπεσθαι, θυμέ, σὺν ἁλικίᾳ, Aristaenetus 2. 1 δικαία δ᾽ ἂν εἴης ἀπ᾽ αὐτοῦ γε τοῦ ἔργου συνεῖναι ὅτι οὐ δεῖ τηρεῖν ὀπώραν. τοῖς σοῖς δίδου ὀπωρώναις τὴν ὥραν τρυγᾶν. μετ᾽ ὀλίγην ἔσῃ γεράνδρυον (a withered stump), *ros. nasc.* 49 f. (above, p. 135), Ronsard, *Sonnets pour Helene* 2. 43. 13 f. 'Vivez, si m'en croyez, n'attendez à demain : Cueillez dés aujourdhuy les roses de la vie'.

Yet though this is the meaning, Horace indulges in none of the lush elaborations of erotic epigram. *carpe* is connected with the Greek καρπίζειν, and might suggest to Horace's readers the words of a serious and austere philosopher. Cf. Epicurus, *epist.* 3. 126 ὥσπερ δὲ σιτίον οὐ τὸ πλεῖον πάντως ἀλλὰ τὸ ἥδιον αἱρεῖται (ὁ σοφός), οὕτω καὶ χρόνον οὐ τὸν μήκιστον ἀλλὰ τὸν ἥδιστον καρπίζεται.

postero: distrust of the morrow is a recurring theme in Horace; cf. especially 3. 29. 41 ff., *epist.* 1. 4. 13. The same thought is expressed by many writers, often in a light-hearted way; cf. *copa* 37 'pereat qui crastina curat', Petron. 99. 1 'ego sic semper et ubique vixi ut ultimam quamque lucem tamquam non redituram consumerem', above, 1. 9. 13 n. But in Horace one still finds something of the austere scepticism of Epicurus himself; cf. *epist.* 3. 127 μνημονευτέον δὲ ὡς τὸ μέλλον οὔτε ἡμέτερον οὔτε πάντως οὐχ ἡμέτερον, ἵνα μήτε πάντως προσμένωμεν ὡς ἐσόμενον μήτε ἀπελπίζωμεν ὡς πάντως οὐκ ἐσόμενον, fr. 204 γεγόναμεν ἅπαξ, δὶς δὲ οὐκ ἔστι γενέσθαι. δεῖ δὲ τὸν αἰῶνα μηκέτ᾽ εἶναι. σὺ δὲ τῆς αὔριον οὐκ ὢν κύριος ἀναβάλλῃ τὸν καιρόν. ὁ δὲ πάντων βίος μελλησμῷ παραπόλλυται καὶ διὰ τοῦτο ἕκαστος ἡμῶν ἀσχολούμενος ἀποθνῄσκει, fr. 490 ὁ τῆς αὔριον ἥκιστα δεόμενος ἥδιστα πρόσεισι πρὸς τὴν αὔριον, fr. 491. This is not hedonism but a serious and sensible attitude to life. Some readers associate Epicureanism with St. Paul's words in *1 Cor.* 15. 32 εἰ νεκροὶ οὐκ ἐγείρονται, φάγωμεν καὶ πίωμεν, αὔριον γὰρ ἀποθνῄσκομεν. A juster parallel would be *euang. Matth* 6. 34 μὴ οὖν μεριμνήσητε εἰς τὴν αὔριον, ἡ γὰρ αὔριον μεριμνήσει ἑαυτῆς· ἀρκετὸν τῇ ἡμέρᾳ ἡ κακία αὐτῆς.

12. QVEM VIRVM

[T. Birt, *Philologus* 79, 1924, 26 ff.; G. Daniels, *Die Strophengruppen in den Horazoden*, Diss. Königsberg, 1940, 2 ff.; Doblhofer, op. cit.; D. L. Drews, *CQ* 19, 1925, 159 ff.; G. E. Duckworth, *TAPhA* 87, 1956, 297 f.; Fraenkel 291 ff.; La Penna 95 ff.; A. Magariños, *Emerita* 10, 1942, 13 ff., ibid. 20, 1952, 78 ff.; T. Plüss, *Fleckeisens Jahrb.* 107, 1873, 111 ff.; O. Weinreich, *ZKG* 1942, 33 ff.]

1–12. *What man, hero, or god shall I sing?* 13–24. *I shall sing first of*

Jupiter, who has no equal or second, and also of Pallas, Liber, Diana, and Phoebus. 25–36. Among heroes I shall tell of Hercules and the Dioscuri; after them Romulus, or Numa's reign, or Tarquin's power, or Cato's death. 37–48. I shall tell of men of Rome who were sturdy in defeat and frugal in their lives, and in particular of Marcellus and Augustus. 49–60. May Augustus be Jupiter's vicegerent; Augustus will rule the world, while Jupiter shakes the heaven.

The ode opens with a reminiscence of the Second Olympian, where Pindar swiftly and splendidly asks and answers his own question (*O.* 2. 1 ff.):

> Ἀναξιφόρμιγγες ὕμνοι,
> τίνα θεόν, τίν᾽ ἥρωα, τίνα δ᾽ ἄνδρα κελαδήσομεν;
> ἤτοι Πίσα μὲν Διός, Ὀλυμπιάδα
> δ᾽ ἔστασεν Ἡρακλέης
> ἀκρόθινα πολέμου·
> Θήρωνα δὲ τετραορίας ἕνεκα νικαφόρου
> γεγωνητέον . . .

Other Pindaric allusions in the poem are few and unimportant (cf. the notes on 1 and 45). Some have thought it significant that the ode breaks up, with one possible exception (33–36), into five groups of three stanzas each; this pattern, coming after a Pindaric motto, might be meant to suggest the Pindaric scheme of strophe, antistrophe, and epode. Yet the differences between the two systems are very great; in Pindar the epode does not repeat the metrical arrangement of the strophe and antistrophe, and it need not end with a break in sense. Certainly from the point of view of subject-matter, the second Olympian has nothing to do with Horace's ode. The dark but consoling alternations of disaster and success in Pindar's myth, the concrete ecstasies of his eschatology, and the glittering self-confidence of his closing section have no parallel in our poem.

After his introduction, Horace celebrates the gods (13–24); as so often, a Hellenistic intermediary comes between the poet and his original. Horace was not the first to be impressed by the convenience of Pindar's question. Theocritus remembered it in opening two encomiastic poems, one to Hieron of Syracuse, one to Ptolemy Philadelphus:

> Αἰεὶ τοῦτο Διὸς κούραις μέλει, αἰὲν ἀοιδοῖς,
> ὑμνεῖν ἀθανάτους, ὑμνεῖν ἀγαθῶν κλέα ἀνδρῶν.
> Μοῖσαι μὲν θεαὶ ἐντί, θεοὺς θεοὶ ἀείδοντι·
> ἄμμες δὲ βροτοὶ οἵδε, βροτοὺς βροτοὶ ἀείδωμεν.
> (16. 1 ff.)

'Εκ Διὸς ἀρχώμεσθα καὶ ἐς Δία λήγετε, Μοῖσαι,
ἀθανάτων τὸν ἄριστον ἐπὴν †ἀείδωμεν ἀοιδαῖς·
ἀνδρῶν δ' αὖ Πτολεμαῖος ἐνὶ πρώτοισι λεγέσθω
καὶ πύματος καὶ μέσσος· ὃ γὰρ προφερέστατος ἀνδρῶν.
ἥρωες, τοὶ πρόσθεν ἀφ' ἡμιθέων ἐγένοντο,
ῥέξαντες καλὰ ἔργα σοφῶν ἐκύρησαν ἀοιδῶν·
αὐτὰρ ἐγὼ Πτολεμαῖον ἐπιστάμενος καλὰ εἰπεῖν
ὑμνήσαιμ'.   (17. 1 ff.)

The second of these two poems is particularly important to Horace's
structure and thought: it shares the tags 'Let us begin from Zeus'
(13 n.) and 'Zeus is the guardian of rulers' (50 n.), it deals with
divinized mortals (13 ff. Ptolemy Lagus, Alexander, Heracles), it
ends as it began, with Zeus.

Horace's celebration of the gods develops some stylistic features
appropriate to a hymn. One may note the relative clauses (14 ff.), the
archaic *unde*, and such formulas as *dicam* and *neque silebo* (which do
not refer to the future, but themselves constitute the very act of
praising). Again, the list of deities is a common feature of hymns (cf.
1. 2. 33 n.). The style is continued in the section dealing with heroes
(25–36), but here the poet seems to have met with special problems.
The status of hero was a peculiarly Greek one, and there were few
available candidates for a Roman poem. So Horace fills out his
three stanzas by mentioning several kings of Rome, including even
a Tarquin (34 n.); with more point and audacity he adds a legendary
figure from his own times, the younger Cato.

Horace thus glides naturally from 'heroes' to 'men', who form the
subject of the next three stanzas (37–48). Here he no longer depends
on classical Greek hymns or Hellenistic panegyrics, but on the
traditions of the Roman Republic, of which Augustus professed to be
the heir. Cicero both in his own speeches and in his philosophical
writings appeals repeatedly to the virtues and resolution of eminent
Romans (cf. *Sest.* 143, *off.* 1. 61, *Tusc.* 1. 110; see further *Brut.* 322 on
the necessity to the orator of *memoria rerum Romanarum*, Quint.
inst. 12. 4, below, 37 n.). Collections of *exempla* were used in the
rhetorical schools even before Valerius Maximus. Quintilian sums up
the Roman view (*inst.* 12. 2. 29 f.): 'quae sunt tradita antiquitus
dicta ac facta praeclare et nosse et animo semper agitare conveniet.
quae profecto nusquam plura maioraque quam in nostrae civitatis
monumentis reperientur. an fortitudinem iustitiam fidem continen-
tiam frugalitatem contemptum doloris ac mortis melius alii docebunt
quam Fabricii Curii Reguli Decii Mucii aliique innumerabiles? quantum enim Graeci praeceptis valent, tantum Romani, quod est maius,
exemplis.'

The list of men ends with a mention of the third-century Marcellus and an allusion to Augustus (47 n.). This leads naturally to the last group of three stanzas (49–60), which deal with Jupiter and Augustus, the two real subjects of the poem. These stanzas belong to a different sphere of ideas, the speculations of Hellenistic philosophers on the nature of kingship and its relation to the divinity. The description of Augustus as Jupiter's vicegerent jars with the republican tone of the previous section, where the Princeps is simply the greatest Roman. This is not so restrained a poem as is sometimes imagined; for a ruler to claim that he is God's vicegerent is not really a sign of modesty. The reminiscence of Alexander in the last stanza needs more emphasis than it sometimes receives. And though Horace's claims are formulated within a Hellenistic literary convention, they cannot be dissociated from the actual development of Hellenistic monarchy in the Roman world.

A clue to the date of the poem is given by the allusion to Marcellus in 46. Though Horace is primarily referring to the Roman hero of the Hannibalic war, he is no doubt also hinting at the Princeps's nephew and son-in-law (see note ad loc.). The young Marcellus probably died in September 23 B.C.; it is hardly possible that Horace could talk in the way he does after that date. Therefore the ode was written before Virgil's famous panegyric (*Aen.* 6. 860 ff.) as well as before Propertius's lament (3. 18). Virgil seems in fact to have known and used Horace's ode when writing the sixth book of the *Aeneid*; for a trivial similarity cf. 11 n. It is much more important that Virgil's procession of great Romans owes something to our poem. Both lists start with the kings of Rome, mentioning not only Romulus but Numa and Tarquin, both cite the conventional *exempla* of rhetoric (Regulus, Fabricius, Camillus) without much regard for chronological order, both give prominent positions to Marcellus and Augustus.

Horace's long and elaborate ode does not fulfil its considerable pretensions. It was an ambitious conception to use the Pindaric motto to link Augustus both with republican *exempla* and Hellenistic kingship theory. It cannot be denied that the poem has a certain movement, from the conventional mythology of classical Greek lyric to a modern and, in intention at least, serious political philosophy. Yet though Horace shows some ingenuity in linking diverse elements, he does not succeed in fusing them; they exist in unhappy juxtaposition, each occupying its own section of the poem. In particular, the catalogues of gods and men, though sanctioned by Greek hymns and republican oratory, lack colour and effective unity; Horace might have remembered Corinna's advice to Pindar, to sow with the hand and not with the sack (Plut. *bellone an pace* 348 a). Here Virgil, who had more room to manœuvre, a more flexible

metrical medium, and above all a strongly imagined setting for his
characters, makes a striking contrast. But perhaps one's main
quarrel with the poem is its essential implausibility. We cannot
apply the naïve assurance of this ode to our own world nor to the
complex and familiar facts of Augustan politics. We can accept the
encomia of Pindar, who was writing in a simpler age; but Horace's
exclamations evoke the derisive response of Ezra Pound:

> O bright Apollo,
> τίν' ἄνδρα, τίν' ἥρωα, τίνα θεόν,
> What god, man, or hero
> Shall I place a tin wreath upon!
>
> (*Hugh Selwyn Mauberley*)

Metre: Sapphic (not altogether appropriate for the matter in
hand).

1. **lyra vel . . . tibia:** for the conjunction cf. 1. 1. 32 ff., 3. 4. 1 ff.,
Pind. *O.* 3. 8, *I.* 5. 27 ff. Yet Pindar would never have offered his
Muse a choice of instruments; his odes really were intended to be
sung.

acri: λιγυρᾷ or λιγείᾳ, 'shrill', like *acutus*; cf. Theogn. 241 ff. καί σε
σὺν αὐλίσκοισι λιγυφθόγγοις νέοι ἄνδρες / . . . καλά τε καὶ λιγέα / ᾄσονται.
Quintilian cites our passage, praising the epithet as 'proprie dictum,
id est, quo nihil inveniri possit significantius' (*inst.* 8. 2. 9). Yet poets
of the Silver Age thought it equally appropriate to the sound of
a trumpet (*Thes.l.L.* 1. 360. 45 ff.).

2. **sumis celebrare:** cf. *epist.* 1. 3. 7 'quis sibi res gestas Augusti
scribere sumit?' *sumis* is livelier and more immediate than the
variant *sumes*. *sumis celebrare* gives a suggestion of futurity sufficient
to reproduce κελαδήσομεν and to balance *recinet*.

Clio: the Muse's name suggests the verb κλείειν, used of celebrating
heroic glory; cf. Hes. *th.* 66 f. πάντων τε νόμους καὶ ἤθεα κεδνὰ /
ἀθανάτων κλείουσιν, Pind. *N.* 3. 83 f. τίν γε μέν, εὐθρόνου Κλεοῦς
ἐθελοίσας, ἀεθλοφόρου λήματος ἕνεκεν / . . . δέδορκεν φάος, Plut. *quaest.*
conv. 743 d τῶν δ' ἄλλων ἥ τε Κλειὼ τὸ ἐγκωμιαστικὸν προσάγεται· κλέα
γὰρ ἐκάλουν τοὺς ἐπαίνους. She appears as the Muse of history in
paintings at Herculaneum and in Silver poets; cf. Val. Fl. 3. 15 f.,
Stat. *Theb.* 10. 630 f., *Thes.l.L.* Onom. 2. 494. 68 ff., Roscher 2. 3278.
Horace presumably means to suggest a connection between κλείειν
and *celebrare*; he may have pointed it by spelling the name *Cleo*, as
the meaningless variant *caelo* suggests.

3. **iocosa . . . imago:** cf. 1. 20. 6 n., 1. 20. 8 n.

5. aut . . . aut: the disjunctive belongs to the language of hymns and prayers; cf. Ar. *nub.* 270 ff. εἴτ᾽ ἐπ᾽ Ὀλύμπου κορυφαῖς ἱεραῖς χιονο-βλήτοισι κάθησθε, / εἴτ᾽ Ὠκεανοῦ πατρὸς ἐν κήποις ἱερὸν χορὸν ἵστατε Νύμφαις, / εἴτ᾽ ἄρα Νείλου προχοαῖς ὑδάτων χρυσέαις ἀρύτεσθε πρόχοισιν, / ἢ Μαιῶτιν λίμνην ἔχετ᾽ ἢ σκόπελον νιφόεντα Μίμαντος, / ὑπακούσατε, Theoc. 1. 123 ff., *Orph. h.* 42. 5 ff., 49. 5 f., Apul. *met.* 6. 4. 1 ff., Blake, *Poetical Sketches, To the Muses,* 'Whether on Ida's shady brow Or in the chambers of the East', 1. 30. 1 n. It is true that in our passage *recinet* breaks away from the stereotyped pattern of a κλητικὸς ὕμνος; yet the allusion to the sacral formula is still clear.

Heliconis: the Boeotian range between Lake Copais and the Gulf of Corinth, especially its eastern peak (Sagará 5,010 ft.). Here the Muses appeared to Hesiod (*th.* 22 ff.); here were the fountains of Aganippe and Hippocrene, and the stream of Permessus (Call. fr. 2 a. 16 ff.). Callimachus's Roman imitators exploited the poetical associations of the names (see Kambylis 102 ff., Boucher 183 f., Troxler-Keller 23 ff.). The local cult of the Muses was no doubt a tourist attraction, and the woods of the area are particularly mentioned (Paus. 9. 28. 1, Prop. 3. 3, Ov. *met.* 5. 265 ff.). See further Paus. 9. 28–31 (Frazer 5. 150 ff.), A. Conze, *Philologus* 19, 1863, Taf. IV (an excellent profile and map), E. Maass, *Hermes* 31, 1896, 382 ff. (allusions in the Latin poets).

6. **Pindo**: the passless range, rising to 8,000 ft., that divides Thessaly from Epirus and is the watershed of central Greece. Pindus had no traditional association with the Muses and poetry, though its wild and beautiful landscape is occasionally mentioned by the poets (cf. Pind. *P.* 9. 15, Call. *h.* 4. 138 f., 6. 82). Perhaps Horace has been influenced by Virgil, *ecl.* 10. 9 ff. 'quae nemora aut qui vos saltus tenuere, puellae / Naides, indigno cum Gallus amore peribat? / nam neque Parnasi vobis iuga, nam neque Pindi / ulla moram fecere, neque Aonie Aganippe'. This passage is adapted from Theoc. 1. 66 ff. πᾷ ποκ᾽ ἄρ᾽ ἦσθ᾽, ὅκα Δάφνις ἐτάκετο, πᾷ ποκα, Νύμφαι; / ἦ κατὰ Πηνειῶ καλὰ τέμπεα, ἦ κατὰ Πίνδω; / οὐ γὰρ δὴ ποταμοῖο μέγαν ῥόον εἴχετ᾽ Ἀνάπω. Virgil introduces the poetical names Parnassus and Aganippe because Gallus was a poet; as a result Pindus, which is simply retained from Theocritus, seems also to get poetical associations.

Haemo: here again Horace may be influenced by Virgil (*georg.* 2. 488 'gelidis convallibus Haemi'). Haemus (the Balkan range) was, like other parts of Thrace, associated with Orpheus. Heraclides Ponticus stated that Orpheus's writing tablets were preserved there in a shrine of Dionysus (schol. Eur. *Alc.* 968). See also Mela 2. 17 'montes . . . Haemon et Rhodopen et Orbelon, sacris Liberi patris et coetu Maenadum Orpheo primum initiante celebratos'. An inscription from Eski-Zaghra, a village on Haemus, celebrates Orpheus's power over nature (*BCH* 2, 1878, 401 Ἀπόλλωνος ἑταῖρον / 'Ορφέα δαιδαλέης θῆκεν ἄγαλμα τέχνης, / ὃς θῆρας καὶ δένδρα καὶ ἑρπετὰ καὶ πετεηνὰ / φωνῇ καὶ χειρῶν κοίμισεν ἁρμονίῃ).

7. unde . . .: cf. 3. 11. 13 f. (to the lyre) 'tu potes tigris comitesque silvas / ducere et rivos celeres morari'. The first extant reference to Orpheus's power over the natural world is Simonides 567. For further literary references see Aesch. *Ag.* 1630, Eur. *Ba.* 561 ff., Roscher 3. 1115 f., *RE* 18. 1. 1247 ff., Kern, *test.* 46 ff., I. M. Linforth, *The Arts of Orpheus*, 1941, pp. 32 ff. For pictures cf. Roscher 3. 1178, 1191, 1203, W. K. C. Guthrie, *Orpheus and Greek Religion*, 1935, pp. 20 ff., O. Kern, *MDAI(A)* 63/64, 1938/9, 107 ff.

We may contrast with this passage the moralizing Euhemerism of *ars* 391 ff. 'silvestris homines sacer interpresque deorum / caedibus et victu foedo deterruit Orpheus, / dictus ob hoc lenire tigres rabidosque leones'. There Horace speaks with the rationalism of the historians and philosophers (cf. Ar. *ran.* 1032, Diod. Sic. 4. 25. 2 f., 4. 48. 6 f., Quint. *inst.* 1. 10. 9, Paus. 9. 30. 4, Dio Chrys. 35. 9, 53. 8, Themistius, *or.* 30. 349 b, Palladius, *anth. Lat.* 628). Here he pretends to the enthusiastic credulity of high poetry.

vocalem: here a term of praise, 'sweet-voiced', apparently used on the model of φωνήεις (cf. Sappho 118 χέλυ δῖα . . . φωνάεσσα). Cf. Tib. 2. 5. 3 *chordae*, Ov. *met.* 5. 332 *ora*, 11. 317 *carmine, fast.* 2. 91 *Arion* (see Bömer's note), Sen. *Med.* 625 'ille vocali genitus Camena' (of Orpheus), Sidon. *epist.* 8. 9. 5 v. 5 'poeta vocalissimus', Milton, *Lycidas* 86 'vocall reeds'.

temere: 'pell-mell'; the word implies the haste and confusion of an unexpected journey. Horace is not taking the legend too seriously; cf. *auritas* below.

9. arte materna: Orpheus's mother is normally said to be the Muse Calliope (cf. Roscher 3. 1073 f., *RE* 18. 1. 1220, Kern, *test.* 24). One should probably attach no importance to a variant tradition in Eustath. *Il.* 10. 442 p. 817. 31 Καλλιόπης μὲν γὰρ ἢ Κλειοῦς ὁ 'Ορφεύς. Some writers make the Muse teach her son; cf. Asclepiades of Tragilus, *FGrH* 12 F 6b, Himerius, *or.* 13. 3, Iambl. *vit. Pyth.* 146 (Orpheus learnt the theory of numbers from her).

rapidos . . . cursus: earlier tradition usually confines itself to Orpheus's power of attracting beasts, trees, and rocks. For his halting rivers cf. 3. 11. 14 (7 n.), Ap. Rhod. 1. 26 f. πέτρας / θέλξαι ἀοιδάων ἐνοπῇ ποταμῶν τε ῥέεθρα, Prop. 3. 2. 3 f., *culex* 117 f., 278 f., Phaedr. 3 prol. 59, Sen. *Med.* 627 'restitit torrens, siluere venti',

Herc. f. 573, *Herc. O.* 1036 ff., Callist. *imag.* 7. 4. Virgil attributes the same effect to the songs of Damon and Alphesiboeus (*ecl.* 8. 4).

10. ventos: Orpheus's power over winds may have been mentioned by Simonides; cf. fr. 595 οὐδὲ γὰρ ἐννοσίφυλλος ἀήτα / τότ᾽ ὦρτ᾽ ἀνέμων, ἄτις κ᾽ ἀπεκώλυε / κιδναμένα μελιαδέα γᾶρυν / ἀραρεῖν ἀκοαῖσι βροτῶν. Add Antip. Sid. *anth.* P. 7. 8. 3 f. οὐκέτι κοιμάσεις ἀνέμων βρόμον, οὐχὶ χάλαζαν, / οὐ νιφετῶν συρμούς, οὐ παταγεῦσαν ἅλα with Gow–Page 2. 42, Sen. *Med.* 627 cited above.

11. blandum: cf. 1. 24. 13. θέλγειν is often used of the magic ἐπῳδαί of Orpheus (12 n.).

auritas: glossed by Serv. *georg.* 1. 308 'sensum audiendi habentes'; cf. 1. 24. 14 'auditam . . . arboribus fidem', Manil. 5. 327 'et sensus scopulis et silvis addidit aures'. But Horace surely means to suggest also the normal sense of *auritus*, 'long-eared'. The oaks 'prick up their ears', 'are all ears' to hear Orpheus; cf. also Plaut. *asin.* 4 'face nunciam tu, praeco, omnem auritum poplum', *mil.* 608 '(ne) nostro consilio venator adsit cum auritis plagis'. Horace is imitated by later poets; cf. Sidon. *carm.* 2. 72 'compulit auritas ad plectrum currere silvas', 23. 190 'aurita chelyn expetente silva', 16. 3 f. (of Amphion) 'chelyn quae saxa sequacia flectens / cantibus auritos erexit carmine muros' (cf. anon. *anth. Lat.* 114. 6), Milton, *P.L.* 7. 35 f. 'In Rhodope, where woods and rocks had ears To rapture'.

fidibus canoris: other writers use the same phrase of Orpheus; cf. Virg. *Aen.* 6. 120 'Threicia fretus cithara fidibusque canoris', Palladius, *anth. Lat.* 628. 1. Virgil may have borrowed from Horace (above, p. 145).

12. quercus: oaks, as the toughest of woodland trees, appear fairly constantly in accounts of Orpheus's attractive powers; cf. Nic. *ther.* 462, Damagetus, *anth.* P. 7. 9. 3, Antip. Sid. ibid. 7. 8. 1 f. οὐκέτι θελγομένας, ᾿Ορφεῦ, δρύας, οὐκέτι πέτρας / ἄξεις, anon. ibid. 7. 10. 7 f. πέτραι / καὶ δρύες, ἃς ἐρατῇ τὸ πρὶν ἔθελγε λύρῃ, Virg. *georg.* 4. 509 'agentem carmine quercus' (cf. also *ecl.* 6. 27 ff.), Prop. 2. 13. 5, Dio. Chrys. 35. 9, Clem. Alex. *protr.* 1. 1. 1 καὶ δὴ . . . τὰς φηγοὺς μετεφύτευε τῇ μουσικῇ, Sidon. *epist.* 8. 11. 3 v. 21 f., *Orph. Arg.* 434 ff., Dryden, *Song for Saint Cecilia's day*, 1687, 'And trees unrooted left their place Sequacious of the lyre'.

Some editors complain that Horace has already mentioned trees (8 *silvae*). Hence in 8 G. Wolff proposed *belvae*, or alternatively *cervae*; but *silvae* is supported by parallels (cf. de Jonge on Ov. *trist.* 4. 1. 17) and *temere insecutae* is more amusing if the word is kept. J. Jortin suggested replacing *quercus* by *cautes*; πέτραι are often mentioned in similar passages, though one might more pertinently compare Sen. *Herc. O.* 1048 f. 'abrupit scopulos Athos / Centauros obiter ferens', Sil. 11. 464 ff. But *quercus* certainly cannot be proved wrong.

13. quid prius . . .: the practice of beginning songs with Zeus was an old one; cf. Alcman 29 ἐγὼν δ' ἀείσομαι / ἐκ Διὸς ἀρχομένα, Pind. *N.* 2. 1 ff. ὅθεν περ καὶ 'Ομηρίδαι / . . . ἄρχονται, Διὸς ἐκ προοιμίου, 5. 25 f., Ion, *eleg.* 2. 6, Arat. *phaen.* 1 f. ἐκ Διὸς ἀρχώμεσθα, τὸν οὐδέποτ' ἄνδρες ἐῶμεν / ἄρρητον (with Erren's note), West on Hes. *th.* 34. Most significantly, the tag was used by Theocritus to introduce his praise of Ptolemy; cf. p. 144, Gow on Theoc. 17. 1. For Roman examples cf. Virg. *ecl.* 3. 60 'ab Iove principium', Val. Max. 1 praef. 'si prisci oratores ab Iove Optimo Maximo bene orsi sunt, si excellentissimi vates a numine aliquo principia traxerunt', Otto 178 f.

parentis: cf. Sen. *epist.* 107. 11 (translating Cleanthes's ὦ Ζεῦ) 'o parens celsique dominator poli'.

14. qui . . .: cf. 3. 4. 45 ff. 'qui terram inertem, qui mare temperat / ventosum . . .' (for the relative style see 1. 10, p. 127). Horace's description of the universal power of the supreme god draws on commonplaces of the Hellenistic age, and is itself echoed by Christian poets; cf. Arat. *phaen.* 2 ff., Cleanthes 1. 7 f. Powell σοὶ δὴ πᾶς ὅδε κόσμος ἑλισσόμενος περὶ γαῖαν / πείθεται ᾗ κεν ἄγῃς καὶ ἑκὼν ὑπὸ σεῖο κρατεῖται, 15 ff. οὐδέ τι γίγνεται ἔργον ἐπὶ χθονὶ σοῦ δίχα, δαῖμον, / οὔτε κατ' αἰθέριον θεῖον πόλον οὔτ' ἐνὶ πόντῳ, Cic. *leg.* 3. 3 'nam et hic (mundus) deo paret et huic oboedunt maria terraeque, et hominum vita iussis supremae legis obtemperat', Prud. *apoth.* 153, Victorin. *Macc.* 204 f.

res hominum ac deorum: cf. Hom. *Il.* 2. 669 ὅς τε θεοῖσι καὶ ἀνθρώποισιν ἀνάσσει, Virg. *Aen.* 1. 229 f. 'o qui res hominumque deumque / aeternis regis imperiis et fulmine terres', E. Kemmer, *Die polare Ausdrucksweise in der griechischen Literatur*, 1903, pp. 77 ff. For *res hominum* (= τὰ τῶν ἀνθρώπων, *res humanae*) cf. also *cons. Liv.* 62.

15. mare ac terras: for Jupiter as lord of land and sea, cf. A. Momigliano, *JRS* 32, 1942, p. 64 n. 45.

mundum: the sky, as often in Republican Latin; cf. F. Bücheler, *Kleine Schriften* 1, 1915, pp. 629 ff., Nettleship, *Latin Lexicography*, p. 529, Kroll, *Festschrift für P. Kretschmer*, 1926, pp. 120 ff. For the threefold division 'earth, sea, sky' cf. Norden on *Aen.* 6. 724, Pease on Cic. *nat. deor.* 1. 100, Bömer on Ov. *fast.* 5. 11. Here the word has some reference to climatic conditions; cf. the common use of *caelum.*

16. temperat: 'regulates', i.e. keeps in equilibrium by a judicious handling of the controls; cf. *epod.* 16. 56, *epist.* 1. 12. 16. *temperare* and its compounds represent the Greek κεραννύναι, κρᾶσις, etc.; they imply not simply mixture, but just the right mixture. Thus *temperamentum aeris* refers primarily to a properly balanced temperature (cf. Hippocr. *aer.* 12. 14 ἡ κρῆσις τῶν ὡρέων, Pl. *Phaed.* 111 b, Dion. Hal. *ant. Rom.* 1. 37. 5), *temperamentum* to a properly balanced disposition (Galen, *mixt.* 1. 509 ff. K.); cf. Shakespeare, *Julius Caesar* v. v. 73 f. 'The elements So mixt in him'.

The idea of a universe in equilibrium was particularly Stoic; cf. Cleanthes 1. 12 f. Powell ᾧ σὺ κατευθύνεις κοινὸν λόγον, ὃς διὰ πάντων / φοιτᾷ μιγνύμενος μεγάλῳ μικροῖς τε φάεσσιν, 20 ff. ὧδε γὰρ εἰς ἓν πάντα συνήρμοκας ἐσθλὰ κακοῖσιν / ὥσθ᾽ ἕνα γίγνεσθαι πάντων λόγον αἰὲν ἐόντα. See also Prop. 3. 5. 26, Ov. *am.* 3. 10. 21, *fast.* 4. 91, Manil. 2. 60 ff., Sen. *epist.* 71. 14, 73. 6 'anno temperantique annum deo privatim obligatus sum', Calp. 4. 92 ff. (influenced by Horace), Plin. *paneg.* 80. 4, Sidon. *carm.* 15. 53, Boeth. *cons.* 1 carm. 5. 18.

horis: 'seasons' (ὧραι); cf. 3. 13. 9 'hora Caniculae', *ars* 302 'sub verni temporis horam'. This use is not attested before Horace. For the idea cf. Hom. *Od.* 24. 344 Διὸς ὧραι, Paus. 1. 40. 4 (at Megara) ὑπὲρ δὲ τῆς κεφαλῆς τοῦ Διός εἰσιν ῟Ωραι καὶ Μοῖραι· δῆλα δὲ πᾶσι τὴν πεπρωμένην μόνῳ οἱ πείθεσθαι, καὶ τὰς ὥρας τὸν θεὸν τοῦτον νέμειν εἰς τὸ δέον, Cornutus, *nat. deor.* 9 (Zeus is the father) τῶν ῾Ωρῶν, τῶν κατὰ τὰς τοῦ περιέχοντος μεταβολὰς σωτηρίους, West on Hes. *th.* 901.

17. unde: 'from whom', archaic and grandiose, as is the verb *generatur*; cf. 1. 28. 28, 2. 12. 7, *serm.* 1. 6. 12 f. 'Valeri genus, unde Superbus / Tarquinius regno pulsus fugit', Fraenkel 102 n. 2, 293 n. 3, *Kl. Beitr.* 2. 479 ff., Löfstedt, *Syntactica* 2. 149 ff., H.–Sz. 208 ff.

nil maius: cf. Ov. *fast.* 5. 126, *met.* 2. 62, *trist.* 2. 38. Zeus was saved by Themis's good advice from begetting a son mightier than himself; cf. Pind. *I.* 8. 27 ff., Ov. *met.* 11. 224 ff.

18. nec viget . . .: cf. Mart. 12. 8. 1 f. 'terrarum dea gentiumque Roma, / cui par est nihil et nihil secundum', Milton, *P.L.* 8. 406 f. 'for none I know Second to me or like, equal much less'.

secundum. proximos: cf. Cic. *Brut.* 173 'duobus igitur summis, Crasso et Antonio, L. Philippus proximus accedebat, sed longo intervallo tamen proximus. itaque eum, etsi nemo intercedebat qui se illi anteferret, neque secundum tamen neque tertium dixerim', Virg. *Aen.* 5. 320 'proximus huic, longo sed proximus intervallo', Non. p. 524 M. 'proximum dicebant veteres non solum adhaerens et adiunctum, verum etiam longe remotum, si tamen inter duo discreta nihil medium exstitisset'. Quintilian follows this pattern with fair consistency in his judgements on authors; cf. *inst.* 10. 1. 53 'quamvis ei secundas fere grammaticorum consensus deferat, . . . arte deficitur

o

ut plane manifesto appareat quanto sit aliud proximum esse, aliud secundum', 73 f., 85 f.

19. proximos . . .: for the pre-eminence of Pallas cf. Hes. *th.* 896 ἴσον ἔχουσαν πατρὶ μένος καὶ ἐπίφρονα βουλήν, Pind. fr. 146 πῦρ πνέοντος ἅ τε κεραυνοῦ / ἄγχιστα δεξιὰν κατὰ χεῖρα πατρός, Aesch. *Eum.* 827 f., Call. *h.* 5. 132 f., Aristides 37. 2 (Athena) p. 304 Keil τοῦ πάντων δημιουργοῦ καὶ βασιλέως παῖς ἐστι μόνη δὴ μόνου . . . μόνη βεβαίως γνησία τοῦ πατρός, 37. 6 p. 305 Keil ἐστὶν αἰδέσιμος τῷ πατρὶ καὶ πάντων κεκοινώνηκε καὶ τὰ πρεσβεῖα μόνη κατείληφεν. In Greece she and her father often share a temple, and sometimes a cult-epithet as well (Farnell 1. 412, Gruppe 2. 1217). It is also relevant that Minerva and Juno were worshipped with Jupiter in Rome's most venerable temple on the Capitol.

21. proeliis audax: these words should be referred to Pallas; cf. Hes. *th.* 925 f. δεινὴν ἐγρεκύδοιμον ἀγέστρατον ἀτρυτώνην / πότνιαν, ᾗ κελαδοί τε ἄδον πόλεμοί τε μάχαι τε, *h.Ven.* 10 f., Lamprocles, *PMG* 735, Cic. *nat. deor.* 3. 53 with Pease's note, *Octavia* 546 'ferox armis dea', Firm. *err.* 16. 1 'numquam se intra feminei sexus verecundiam tenuit, sed arma semper strepitumque pugnarum et cruenta secuta est studia bellorum'. From Homer on, Athene was the warlike goddess *par excellence* (cf. Roscher 1. 678 ff., Gruppe 2. 1207 f.); she was worshipped as the defender of many Greek cities, and was almost always represented in art as armed (see Farnell 1. 308 ff., 406 ff., Plates 13 ff., Roscher 1. 689 ff.).

Some editors attribute the epithet to Liber, who otherwise has none (nor has Hercules in 25). For Bacchus's martial exploits cf. 2. 19. 21 ff., Eur. *Ba.* 302 Ἄρεώς τε μοῖραν μεταλαβὼν ἔχει τινα with Dodds's note, Farnell 5. 101, 292. In particular his conquests were often compared with those of Alexander and other conquerors, including Augustus (cf. E. Norden, *Kleine Schriften*, 1966, pp. 422 ff. = *RhM* 54, 1899, 466 ff.); in view of the tone of the latter part of our poem (58 n.) a similar reference has been thought appropriate in this passage (cf. Magariños, loc. cit., 17 ff.). However, if *proeliis audax* refers to Pallas, *neque* is in its usual position; if it refers to Bacchus, *neque* is abnormally postponed.

neque te silebo: for the formula of panegyric cf. 4. 9. 30 ff., *h.Ap.* 1 μνήσομαι οὐδὲ λάθωμαι Ἀπόλλωνος ἑκάτοιο, Xen. *Ag.* 8. 1 ἀλλὰ μὴν ἄξιόν γε αὐτοῦ καὶ τὸ εὔχαρι μὴ σιωπᾶσθαι, Virg. *Aen.* 10. 793 'non equidem nec te, iuvenis memorande, silebo', Auson. *Mos.* 115 'nec te, delicias mensarum, perca, silebo' with Hosius's parallels.

22. Liber: here apparently a protecting deity; elsewhere it suits Horace to represent him as a hero (25 n.).

saevis . . . beluis: θηροφόνος, θηροκτόνος; cf. Claud. *rapt. Pros.* 2.
20 f. (on Pallas and Diana) 'haec tristibus aspera bellis, / haec
metuenda feris'. Like the other deities mentioned here, Diana is
beneficent and protective to men; cf. 1. 21. 13 n.

23. certa: 'unerring'; cf. Catull. 68. 113, Virg. *Aen.* 11. 767, Ov. *am.*
1. 1. 25, Sen. *Phaedr.* 56. Cf. also Ov. *met.* 1. 458 of the *vulnera* Apollo
dealt the Pytho. The god's unerring bow is the weapon with which
he rids the world of monsters.

25. Alciden puerosque Ledae: Hercules and the Dioscuri are often
mentioned together as benefactors of mankind, who by their deeds
had won immortality; cf. 3. 3. 9 ff. (Pollux, Hercules, Bacchus, and
Quirinus), 4. 8. 29 ff. (Hercules, Dioscuri, and Liber), *epist.* 2. 1. 5 ff.
(Romulus, Liber, the Dioscuri), Pease on Cic. *nat. deor.* 2. 62. They
are also joined as θεοὶ ἀλεξίκακοι, cf. Ar. *eccl.* 1068 f., Lucian, *Alex.* 4.
Allusions in Latin authors are not simply literary; their popularity
at Rome is attested by the expletives *mehercule, ecastor,* and *edepol.*
The antiquity of the cult of the Dioscuri is confirmed by a late sixth-
century inscription from Lavinium CASTOREI PODLOVQVEIQVE QVROIS,
while their statue by the *lacus Iuturnae* at Rome dates from the
early fifth century (cf. S. Weinstock, *JRS* 50, 1960, 112 ff., A. Alföldi,
Early Rome and the Latins, 1965, pp. 268 ff., frontispiece and Plate 2).
pueros: cf. 1. 19. 2 n.

26. hunc . . .: variations on this theme are a commonplace from
Homer on; cf. *serm.* 2. 1. 26 f. 'Castor gaudet equis, ovo prognatus
eodem / pugnis', Hom. *Il.* 3. 237 (= *Od.* 11. 300) Κάστορά θ' ἱππόδαμον
καὶ πὺξ ἀγαθὸν Πολυδεύκεα, Ap. Rhod. 1. 146 f. κρατερὸν Πολυδεύκεα
. . . / Κάστορά τ' ὠκυπόδων . . . δεδαημένον ἵππων, Prop. 3. 14. 18 'hic
victor pugnis, ille futurus equis', Ov. *fast.* 5. 700 'Tyndaridae fratres,
hic eques, ille pugil', *met.* 8. 301 f. 'Tyndaridae gemini, spectandus
caestibus alter, / alter equo', Arnob. *nat.* 1. 36 'Tyndaridae Castores,
equos unus domitare consuetus, alter pugilator bonus et crudo
inexsuperabilis caestu'.
superare . . . nobilem: for the infinitive cf. Prop. 4. 10. 42.
pugnis: πυγμαχίᾳ: the word is instrumental from *pugnus*, not
pugna.

27. quorum: Castor and Pollux protected seamen; cf. 1. 3. 2 n., 3. 29.
64, *h.Hom.* 33. 6 f. σωτῆρας τέκε παῖδας . . . ὠκυπόρων . . . νεῶν, 33.
12 ff. οἱ δ' ἐξαπίνης ἐφάνησαν / ξουθῇσι πτερύγεσσι δι' αἰθέρος ἀΐξαντες. /
αὐτίκα δ' ἀργαλέων ἀνέμων κατέπαυσαν ἀέλλας, / κύματα δ' ἐστόρεσαν
λευκῆς ἁλὸς ἐν πελάγεσσι, / ναύταις †σήματα καλὰ πόνου σφισιν, *lyr. adesp.*
998, Theoc. 22. 6 ff., 17 f. καὶ ἐκ βυθοῦ ἕλκετε νῆας / αὐτοῖσιν ναύτῃσιν
ὀιομένοις θανέεσθαι, Catull. 4. 27, 68. 65, Prop. 1. 17. 18, *ILS* 4613b (an

early imperial dedication by the boatmen of Paris), Epictet. 2. 18. 29, *IG* iv². 511 πλωτήροιν Διοσκούροιν Σεκ. Πομ. Ἱλαρίανος Ἀλκάστου Λακεδαιμόνιος κατ' ὄναρ. See further Roscher 6. 948 ff., J. Rendel Harris, *The Cult of the Heavenly Twins*, 1906, H. Jaislé, *Die Dioskuren als Retter zur See*, Tübingen, 1907, Pease on Cic. *div.* 1. 75 and *nat. deor.* 2. 6, Bömer on Ov. *fast.* 5. 694.

alba . . . stella: in view of the parallels (1. 3. 2 n.), Horace is presumably talking about St. Elmo's fire rather than a constellation in the sky. However, the exact force of the adjective is uncertain. St. Elmo's fire is normally electric blue in colour, according to the experts; cf. also Val. Fl. 1. 569 ff. '(fax) puppe propinqua / in bifidum discessit iter fratresque petivit / Tyndareos, placida et mediis in frontibus haesit / protinus amborum lumenque innoxia fundit / purpureum, miseris olim implorabile nautis'. Yet in certain atmospheric conditions a whitish light cannot be excluded; in any case Horace probably knew about the phenomenon more from literature than autopsy. Moreover, *alba* may bring with it an idea of 'favourable' (André 27, 31).

29. defluit . . .: for the details of the calming of the storm cf. Virg. *Aen.* 5. 820 f. 'subsidunt undae tumidumque sub axe tonanti / sternitur aequor aquis, fugiunt vasto aethere nimbi', Sen. *Thy.* 588 f. 'si suae ventis cecidere vires, / mitius stagno pelagus recumbit', Stat. *Theb.* 9. 525 'ab infestis descendunt aequora saxis'.

30. concidunt: 'collapse'; the word is a violent one, more expressive than the simple *cado* and than Theocritus's ἀπολήγουσι (22. 18).

31. minax: 'overhanging' as well as 'threatening'.

quod: corrupted to the unmetrical *quia* in the bulk of the paradosis, as well as in Porphyrio. The corruption took place because *quia* encroached at the expense of *quod* in late Latin (H.–Sz. 586). Thus the scholiast on Juv. 6. 301, in citing Hor. *epod.* 8. 19, replaces relative *quod* by the meaningless *quia*. Other proposals are not plausible. *sicut* is not used elsewhere in the *Odes*, and its unnecessary length does not suit Horace's economical style. *sic di* is impossible; if *di* refers to the Dioscuri it is redundant, and a reference to other gods would be absurdly obscure.

voluere: gods find it easy to calm the winds and waves; cf. Hom. *Od.* 10. 21 f. (of Aeolus) κεῖνον γὰρ ταμίην ἀνέμων ποίησε Κρονίων, / ἠμὲν παυέμεναι ἠδ' ὀρνύμεν ὅν κ' ἐθέλῃσι, Hes. *th.* 252 ff. Κυμοδόκη θ', ἣ κύματ' ἐν ἠεροειδέι πόντῳ / πνοιάς τε ζαέων ἀνέμων σὺν Κυματολήγῃ / ῥεῖα πρηΰνει, Alcaeus 34. 7 ff. (above, 1. 3. 2 n.), Moschus 2. 115 ἡ δὲ τότ' ἐρχομένοιο γαληνιάασκε θάλασσα (see Bühler's note), *euang. Matth.* 8. 26 f. τότε ἐγερθεὶς ἐπετίμησεν τοῖς ἀνέμοις καὶ τῇ θαλάσσῃ, καὶ ἐγένετο γαλήνη μεγάλη. οἱ δὲ ἄνθρωποι ἐθαύμασαν λέγοντες· Ποταπός

ἐστιν οὗτος, ὅτι καὶ οἱ ἄνεμοι καὶ ἡ θάλασσα αὐτῷ ὑπακούουσιν;, BCH
51, 1927, 380 (Isis inscription from Cyme) ἐγὼ πραΰνω καὶ κυμαίνω
θάλασσαν, Apul. *met.* 4. 31. 5. Empedocles assured his pupil Pausanias
that he would have this divine power (cf. fr. 111. 3 ff., W. K. C.
Guthrie, *History of Greek Philosophy* 2, 1965, p. 134).

It is a commonplace that gods need only wish or think in order to
achieve their ends (often expressed in Greek by various sorts of
clauses containing ἐθέλειν); cf. Hom. *Il.* 20. 242 f. Ζεὺς δ' ἀρετὴν
ἄνδρεσσιν ὀφέλλει τε μινύθει τε, / ὅππως κεν ἐθέλῃσιν, Hes. *th.* 442 f.
ῥηιδίως ἄγρην κυδρὴ θεὸς ὤπασε πολλήν, / ῥεῖα δ' ἀφείλετο φαινομένην,
ἐθέλουσά γε θυμῷ, 446 f., *h.Merc.* 43 ff., Pind. *P.* 9. 67 ὠκεῖα δ' ἐπειγο-
μένων ἤδη θεῶν / πρᾶξις ὁδοί τε βραχεῖαι, Aesch. *supp.* 598 f., Call. *h.*
1. 87 f. (on Ptolemy Philadelphus) ἑσπέριος κεῖνός γε τελεῖ τά κεν ἦρι
νοήσῃ· / ἑσπέριος τὰ μέγιστα, τὰ μείονα δ', εὖτε νοήσῃ, Ov. *met.* 8. 619,
Liv. 1. 39. 4 with Ogilvie's note, Clem. Alex. *protr.* 4. 63. 3 ψιλῷ τῷ
βούλεσθαι δημιουργεῖ καὶ τῷ μόνον ἐθελῆσαι αὐτὸν ἕπεται τὸ γεγενῆσθαι,
West on Hes. *th.* 28 and 90, Pease on Cic. *nat. deor.* 2. 59, Otto 108.
A tantalizing fragment of Alcaeus may perhaps be an example of the
same formula (37. 7): θέοισι[. . . . .]ην ὡς κε θέλωσ[.

ponto: a local ablative, 'on the sea'; cf. Virg. *georg.* 1. 401 'campo
. . . recumbunt', *Aen.* 5. 481 'procumbit humi bos'.

33. Romulum . . .: the drift becomes obscure at this point. It is
clear that the ode has at least some tendency to fall into groups of
three stanzas (even if we do not speak of triads). And Romulus by
some accounts was deified; cf. 3. 3. 15 f., 1. 2. 46 n. There is therefore
good reason for assuming that here as elsewhere he is regarded as
a hero, and that this stanza goes with the two preceding ones. The
replacement of the doubting *an . . . an . . . an* by *et* and *-que* shows
that we have moved to a new start in 37.

Yet there are obvious difficulties in this view. The presence of
Cato is a notorious stumbling-block (35 n.). And by no stretch of the
imagination can Tarquinius Superbus be included among the *heroes*.
Perhaps the divisions of the poem are not quite so clear-cut as is
sometimes supposed. All we can say is that most of this stanza
refers to the remote past, and that Romulus serves as a link with the
stanzas concerned with undisputed *heroes*.

an . . . memorem: for such formulas of hesitation, often found in
hymns, cf. *h.Ap.* 19 ff. πῶς τ' ἄρ σ' ὑμνήσω πάντως εὔυμνον ἐόντα; κτλ.
(207 ff.), Pind. *I.* 7. 1–20, fr. 29, Aesch. *cho.* 855, Hyper. 6. 6 (a hymnal
trait in an *epitaphios logos*), Theoc. 22. 25. For a non-panegyric example cf. Theoc. 2. 65 and Gow's note.

34. Pompili: Numa Pompilius, the wise lawgiver of Roman tradition
(cf. Ogilvie on Liv. 1. 18–21).

superbos . . . fasces: 'Tarquin's haughty fasces' inevitably suggests the reign of the last Roman king (cf. Dion. Hal. *ant. Rom.* 4. 38. 2 on his private assumption of the *fasces* in initiating his usurpation). It is unreasonable to refer the phrase to the rule of Tarquinius Priscus; it is true that Priscus, as the first Etruscan king, was said to have introduced the *fasces*, but the reference in *superbos* cannot be resisted. In tradition at least, Rome under the last Tarquin rose to a dazzling and premature hegemony that it took her long to recover after the expulsion of the kings. The extent of his empire was something a Roman could take pride in.

35. Catonis: it is not clear what Cato is doing in this company. Whether or not we emphasize the 'triadic' structure of the poem it is manifest that his presence here totally disrupts the chronological sequence. If the text is good, Horace must be deliberately equating him with the heroic figures of legend.

It is at first sight surprising to find Cato referred to in such glowing terms in a poem in praise of Augustus; the tempered eulogy of Cato in a poem addressed to the ostentatiously intransigent Asinius Pollio (2. 1. 24) is not really a parallel. Octavian himself had written a *rescripta Bruto de Catone*, and was to recite it, with Tiberius's help, in his old age (Suet. *Aug.* 85. 1). Still, propaganda began to idealize Cato immediately after his death; cf. Plut. *Cato min.* 71. 1 (on hearing of his death the inhabitants of Utica hailed him as) τὸν εὐεργέτην καὶ σωτῆρα καὶ μόνον ἐλεύθερον καὶ μόνον ἀήττητον and, for a more grudging tribute from a hostile source, *bell. Afr.* 88. 5. Soon Cicero, Brutus, and M. Fadius produced their eulogies, and as the political issues of his day ceased to be relevant, this picture increasingly prevailed. Virgil makes him a judge in Elysium (*Aen.* 8. 670), implying already the attitude of later times (cf. Val. Max. 2. 10. 8 '(perfecta virtus) effecit ut quisquis sanctum et egregium civem significare velit, sub nomine Catonis definiat', Haterius ap. Sen. *suas.* 6. 2, Vell. 2. 35. 2 'homo Virtuti simillimus et per omnia ingenio dis quam hominibus propior'). Manilius, writing in Augustus's later years, includes Cato in a catalogue of Roman worthies (1. 797). In his more politic moments, the *princeps* himself could approve Cato's example; cf. his rebuke to a sycophantic detractor, 'quisquis praesentem statum civitatis commutari non volet et civis et vir bonus est' (Macr. *sat.* 2. 4. 18). See further R. Syme, *A Roman Post-Mortem, An Inquest on the Fall of the Roman Republic*, Sydney, 1950, p. 9, H. Fugier, *Recherches sur l'expression du sacré dans la langue latine*, 1963, p. 259, P. Pecchiura, *La figura di Catone Uticense nella letteratura latina*, Torino, 1965.

Conjectures have been attempted in order to resolve the puzzle. Hamacher proposed *catenis nobilitatum* (agreeing with *Regulum* in the next line). This disrupts the pattern of three-stanza groups and substitutes a clumsy and artificial phrase for what is crisp and incisive. Bentley's *anne Curti* is more plausible; this refers to M. Curtius, who flung himself armed and mounted into a chasm that opened in the Forum (cf. Val. Max. 5. 6. 2, *culex* 361 ff. 'hic Fabii Deciique, hic est et Horatia virtus, / hic et fama vetus nunquam moritura Camilli, / Curtius et . . .', Ogilvie on Liv. 1. 12). Yet *nobile letum* is so applicable to Cato's suicide that one is reluctant to reject the transmitted reading; cf. Cic. *epist.* 9. 18. 2 'ceteri quidem . . . foede perierunt. at Cato praeclare', Val. Max. 3. 2. 14 'clarissimi excessus . . . Vtica monumentum est', Dio 43. 11. 6 μεγάλην δόξαν καὶ ἀπ' αὐτοῦ τοῦ θανάτου ἔλαβεν, Daniels, loc. cit., p. 3 n. 2, H. Fugier, op. cit. above, p. 267.

37. Regulum . . .: historical *exempla* were freely used by the Greek orators (notably in panegyric) and recommended by rhetorical theorists (Volkmann 233 ff.). The Romans, with their idealization of their own past history, easily outdid the Greeks (cf. p. 144). The canon of great men was built up by historians, poets, and orators, notably Ennius, Cato, and Cicero (cf. Austin on Cic. *Cael.* 39). Collections of *exempla* also played a part (cf. C. Bosch, *Die Quellen des Valerius Maximus*, Stuttgart, 1929). See further H. Schoenberger, *Beispiele aus der Geschichte*, Augsburg, 1911, H. W. Litchfield, *HSPh* 25, 1914, 1 ff., Norden on Virg. *Aen.* 6. 752 ff., H. Kornhardt, *Exemplum*, Diss. Göttingen, 1936, Pease on Cic. *div.* 1. 29 and *nat. deor.* 2. 7.

M. Atilius Regulus was captured by the Carthaginians in Africa in 255, and about 250 was sent on parole to Rome to negotiate an exchange of prisoners (or perhaps peace); he advised against acceptance, and returned to Carthage where he died, tortured to death, according to the Roman story. For an extended treatment cf. 3. 5.

Scauros: for the Scauri as a type of morality cf. Val. Max. 4. 4. 11 'Fabricios Curios Scipiones Scauros', Juv. 2. 35, 11. 90 f. 'Fabios durumque Catonem / et Scauros et Fabricium'. The generalizing plural is common in lists of *exempla* (Gudeman on Tac. *dial.* 21. 12, K.–S. 1. 72), and one is at first sight tempted to take it in this way in our passage also. The alternation of singular and plural is not unusual; cf. Colum. 4. 11. 1 'Vergilius et Saserna Stolonesque et Catones', Juv. 8. 3 ff. 'Aemilianos / et Curios . . . umerosque minorem / Corvinum et Galbam', Pers. 3. 79. Yet here we have five singulars and only one plural; therefore it is also possible that Horace is thinking of more than one Scaurus.

Most editors assume that Horace is referring to the most famous bearer of the name, M. Aemilius Scaurus, *cos.* 115, *cens.* 109, and *princeps senatus*. His reputation for frugality and integrity went back to his own autobiography; cf. Val. Max. 4. 4. 11 'M. autem Scaurus quantulum a patre hereditatem acceperit in primo libro eorum quos de vita sua tres scripsit refert'. Cicero speaks warmly of his character (*Font.* 24, *Brut.* 111), and Valerius Maximus recounts how when his son showed cowardice against the Cimbri Scaurus drove him to suicide (5. 8. 4). No doubt when Valerius Maximus and Juvenal speak admiringly of *Scauri* they mean Aemilius (Mayor on Juv. 11. 91). See further M. Bloch, *Univ. de Paris, Bibliothèque de la Faculté des Lettres* 25, 1909, 1 ff., P. Fraccaro, *RAL*⁵ 20, 1911, 169 ff. = *Opuscula* 2, 1957, pp. 125 ff.

However, another Scaurus has claims to be considered (so Krebs, *RE* 2. 2525, Malcovati, *or. Rom.*, p. 214): this was M. Aurelius Scaurus, *cos.* 108. He showed a defiance and intransigence in defeat that make him a worthy companion of Regulus and Paullus. Cf. Liv. *per.* 67 'M. Aurelius Scaurus legatus consulis a Cimbris fuso exercitu captus est; et cum in consilium ab iis advocatus deterreret eos ne Alpes transirent Italiam petituri, eo quod diceret Romanos vinci non posse, a Boiorige, feroci iuvene, occisus est', Gran. Lic. p. 17 B. 'nihil indignum viro Romano qui tantis honoribus functus erat aut fecit aut dixit'.

It is not altogether easy to choose between these two Scauri; the former is the more characteristic hero of *exempla*, the latter is much better suited to our context. It is possible, of course, that Horace has confused the two; yet they were comparatively recent figures. It seems more likely that he is alluding vaguely to both at once: the choice between a real and a rhetorical plural may be rather an artificial one. Some commentators have seen an allusion to Aemilius's sons; as one was a coward and the other a voluptuary (Plin. *nat.* 36. 113) the reference would be very unhappy.

38. prodigum: the word, normally pejorative, is here used in a good sense. The paradox belongs to patriotic discourse; cf. Thuc. 2. 43. 1 προιέμενοι, 5 ἀφειδοῖεν ἂν τοῦ βίου, Hyper. 6. 26 τὸ ζῆν ἀνήλωσαν, Cic. *epist.* 1. 4. 3 'si vitam pro tua dignitate profundam', *Marc.* 31 'qui in causa animam profudit', *off.* 1. 84 'non modo pecuniam, sed etiam vitam profundere pro patria'. Horace's phrase was much imitated by later writers; cf. especially Sil. 15. 42 f. 'haec (Virtus) prodiga Paullum, / haec Decios Stygias Erebi detrusit ad undas'.

Paullum: L. Aemilius Paullus, *cos.* 219 and 216, shared responsibility for the defeat at Cannae. However, he fell on the battlefield, and Roman aristocratic tradition laid the blame on his more humble colleague C. Terentius Varro.

39. gratus: 'grateful' rather than 'pleasing'. Horace seems to mean that his song will be a χάρις to Rome's heroes.

insigni . . . **Camena**: *insigni* imitates naïve Pindaric self-glorifica-
tion; cf. *N.* 6. 28 f. εὔθυν᾽ ἐπὶ τοῦτον, ἄγε, Μοῖσα, / οὖρον ἐπέων /
εὐκλέα, *O.* 2. 89 f. τίνα βάλλομεν / ἐκ μαλθακᾶς αὖτε φρενὸς εὐκλέας
ὀιστοὺς ἱέντες; Heinze interprets 'quae insignes reddit', but this seems
less natural. *Camena* for 'poetry' is likewise modelled on the Pindaric
Μοῖσα (*N.* 3. 28); cf. *epist.* 1. 1. 1, K. F. Smith on Sulpicia ap. Tib.
4. 7. 3.

40. Fabriciumque: C. Fabricius Luscinus, *cos.* 282, 278, *cens.* 275,
defeated Pyrrhus at Beneventum. Traditionally he belongs to the
group in the next stanza, the exemplars of ancient Roman frugality;
cf. Cic. *Cael.* 39 'Camillos Fabricios Curios, omnisque eos qui haec ex
minimis tanta fecerunt', *off.* 3. 86, Val. Max. 4. 3. 6, Otto 129, Milton,
P.R. 2. 445 ff. 'Canst thou not remember Quintius, Fabricius, Curius,
Regulus? For I esteem those names of men so poor Who could do
mighty things, and could contemn Riches, though offered from the
hand of kings'.

41. incomptis: barbers came to Rome about 300 B.C. (Varro, *rust.* 2.
11. 10 'olim tonsores non fuisse adsignificant antiquorum statuae,
quod pleraeque habent capillum et barbam magnam'). Hence long or
uncombed hair was often associated with archaic virtue (Cic. *Cael.*
33, Virg. *Aen.* 6. 809 f., Bömer on Ov. *fast.* 2. 30, Mayor on Juv. 16.
31). See also Serv. *Aen.* 12. 100 'quae (calamistrata coma, cf. Cic.
Sest. 18 f.) etiam vituperationi est. unde e contra ad laudem est positum ab Horatio "hunc et incomptis Curium capillis" '.
    Curium: M' Curius Dentatus, *cos.* 290, 284, 275, 274, *cens.* 272,
a hero of the Samnite and Pyrrhic wars. He was repeatedly associated
with Fabricius and sometimes with Camillus (Otto 102).

42. utilem bello: the dry commendation suits military discourse. Cf.
Soph. *Ai.* 410 ἄνδρα χρήσιμον, Eur. *supp.* 887 πόλει παρασχεῖν σῶμα
χρήσιμον θέλων. So in Latin *epist.* 2. 1. 124 (of the poet) 'militiae quamquam piger et malus, utilis urbi', Prop. 3. 9. 19 'castrensibus utilis
armis', Ov. *am.* 2. 3. 7, *ars* 2. 710, *fast.* 3. 173, Oros. 4. 1. 1 'bello utiles
caesi', *Thes.l.L.* 2. 1842. 49 ff.
    tulit . . .: that poverty was the mother of effort and invention
was an old commonplace, converted by the Romans to the glory of
their frugal ancestors. Cf. Eur. fr. 641. 3 πενία δὲ σοφίαν ἔλαχε διὰ τὸ
συγγενές, Theoc. 21. 1 ff. ἁ πενία, Διόφαντε, μόνα τὰς τέχνας ἐγείρει· /
αὖτα τῶ μόχθοιο διδασκάλος, οὐδὲ γὰρ εὕδειν / ἀνδράσιν ἐργατίναισι
κακαὶ παρέχοντι μέριμναι (with Gow's note), Virg. *georg.* 1. 145 f.
'labor omnia vicit / improbus, et duris urgens in rebus egestas', Val.
Max. 4. 4. 11 '(modica fortuna) ut non abundantibus ita fidis uberibus
Publicolas, Aemilios, Fabricios, Curios, Scipiones, Scauros hisque

paria robora virtutis aluit', Sen. *contr.* 1. 6. 4 'quid tibi videntur illi ab
aratro, qui paupertate sua beatam fecere rem publicam?', 2. 1, Sen.
epist. 87. 41 'ut populus Romanus paupertatem, fundamentum et
causam imperii sui, requirat ac laudet', Luc. 1. 165 ff. 'fecunda virorum / paupertas fugitur totoque accersitur orbe / quo gens quaeque
perit; tum longos iungere fines / agrorum, et quondam duro sulcata
Camilli / vomere et antiquos Curiorum passa ligones / longa sub
ignotis extendere rura colonis', Apul. *apol.* 18, Lucian, *Timon* 31 ff.,
P. Vallette, *L'Apologie d'Apulée*, 1908, pp. 129 ff., Otto 268 f.

    Camillum: M. Furius Camillus, *cens.* 403, *cos. trib.* six times, *dict.*
five times, the conqueror of Veii and 'the second founder' of Rome
after its capture by the Gauls *c.* 390 (Otto 68).

43. saeva: 'stern', not 'savage'. *paupertas* is a harsh mother who
rears her children strictly. Bentley thought the epithet too strong
and proposed *sancta*. It is true that *paupertas* often suggests a modest
competence rather than total indigence (cf. Ar. *Plut.* 552 ff., Porph.
on *epist.* 2. 2. 199 'paupertas etiam honestae parsimoniae nomen est,
et usurpatur in fortuna mediocri'). But sometimes a harsh adjective
is appropriate; cf. 3. 16. 37 'importuna . . . pauperies', Hes. *op.* 717
οὐλομένην πενίην, Stob. 4. 32ᵃ. 17 Ἀρκεσίλαος τὴν πενίαν λυπρὰν μὲν
ἔλεγεν εἶναι, ὥσπερ καὶ τὴν Ἰθάκην, ἀγαθὴν δὲ κουροτρόφον, ἐθίζουσαν
συνεῖναι λιτότητι καὶ καρτερίᾳ καὶ καθόλου γυμνάσιον ἀρετῆς ἔμπρακτον.
Cf. also Sil. 15. 40 'Virtus . . . saeva' (the whole passage has several
reminiscences of our ode).

    avitus: the estate is a modest inherited one, not a *latus fundus*; cf.
epod. 2. 1 ff., Plin. *nat.* 18. 18 (in a context praising the good old days
and abusing *latifundia*) 'Manii quidem Curii post triumphos immensumque terrarum adiectum imperio nota dictio est perniciosum
intellegi civem cui septem iugera non essent satis; haec enim men-
sura plebei post exactos reges adsignata est', Pope, *Ode on Solitude*,
'Happy the man whose wish and care A few paternal acres bound'.

    apto: of a size to suit the ancestral estate; for this ideal cf. Cato,
agr. 3. 1 'ita aedifices, ne villa fundum quaerat ⟨neve fundus villam⟩',
Varro, *rust.* 1. 11. 1 'in modo fundi non animadverso lapsi multi,
quod alii villam minus magnam fecerunt quam modus ⟨fundi⟩
postulavit, alii maiorem, cum utrumque sit contra rem familarem ac
fructum. maiora enim tecta et aedificamus pluris et tuemur sumptu
maiore. minora cum sunt quam postulat fundus, fructus solent dis-
perire', Colum. 1. 4. 8 'eleganter igitur aedificet agricola nec sit
tamen aedificator, atque areae pedem tantum complectatur, quod
ait Cato, quantum ne villa fundum quaerat neve fundus villam',
Plin. *nat.* 18. 32 'modus hic probatur ut neque fundus villam quaerat
neque villa fundum, non, ut fecere iuxta diversis in eadem aetate

exemplis L. Lucullus et Q. Scaevola, cum villa Scaevolae fructus non
caperet, villam Luculli ager, quo in genere censoria castigatio erat
minus arare quam verrere', H. Kronasser, *WS* 79, 1966, 302.

Some editors think that the phrase does not sufficiently express
the modesty of the ancients; they therefore favour *arto*, 'strait',
'small' (first conjectured in the Milan edition of 1477). This can be
supported by an impressive list of parallels; cf. especially 3. 29. 14 f.
'mundaeque parvo sub lare pauperum / cenae', Varro, *ling.* 5. 92
'pauper a paulo (?) lare', Prop. 4. 10. 18 'parco . . . lare', Sen. *Phoen.*
594 'exiguo lare', Luc. 5. 527 f. 'o vitae tuta facultas / pauperis
angustique laris' (Cortius, *lares* codd.), Pers. 5. 109 'presso lare', Sil.
7. 173 'parvos . . . lares', Apul. *met.* 1. 21. 6 'exiguo lare', 1. 23. 6 'lare
parvulo', *apol.* 21 'gracili lare', Arnob. *nat.* 7. 12 'angusto lare'. For
the conjunction with *avitus* one might compare 2. 16. 13 f. 'cui
paternum / splendet in mensa tenui salinum'. In fact, however, in
our passage the idea of restriction is already conveyed by *avitus* (see
above), and does not need to be expressed again; the parallels from
the agricultural writers seem to defend *apto* quite conclusively.

44. cum lare fundus: cf. *serm.* 1. 2. 56 'patrium . . . fundumque
laremque', *epist.* 2. 2. 50 f. 'inopemque paterni / et laris et fundi'.

45. crescit . . . velut arbor: in this professedly Pindaric poem a Pindaric parallel is most relevant; cf. *N.* 8. 40 ff. αὔξεται δ' ἀρετά, χλω-
ραῖς ἐέρσαις / ὡς ὅτε δένδρεον †ἀίσσει†, / ⟨ἐν⟩ σοφοῖς ἀνδρῶν ἀερθεῖσ'
ἐν δικαίοις τε πρὸς ὑγρὸν / αἰθέρα. Virgil had recently used the old simile
in a different context; cf. *ecl.* 10. 73 f. 'Gallo, cuius amor tantum mihi
crescit in horas / quantum vere novo viridis se subicit alnus'.

occulto . . . aevo: 'by the imperceptible lapse of time'. One does
not see time passing or a tree growing, yet these things happen
slowly but surely (λεληθότως). See *epist.* 1. 1. 80 'occulto crescit res
faenore', Ar. *nub.* 1288 f. πλέον πλέον τἀργύριον ἀεὶ γίγνεται / ὑπορρέον-
τος τοῦ χρόνου, Lucr. 1. 314 'occulte decrescit vomer in arvis', Prop. 3.
25. 11 'at te celatis aetas gravis urgeat annis', Hier. *in Ephes.* 4. 16
p. 619 'parvulus crescat et occulto aevo in perfectam adolescat aetatem', anon. *anth. P.* 7. 564. 3 σῆμα δ' ἀμαλδύναντος ἀνωίστοιο χρόνοιο,
Shakespeare, *Henry V*, I. i. 63 ff. 'And so the prince obscured his
contemplation Under the veil of wildness; which no doubt Grew
like the summer grass, fastest by night, Unseen, yet crescive in his
faculty'.

46. Marcelli: M. Claudius Marcellus, *cos.* 222, 215, 214, 210, 208,
conqueror of the Insubres, the third person to win the *spolia opima*,
the captor of Syracuse, and the 'sword' of Rome against Hannibal.
After the Roman worthies of the previous stanzas no other Marcellus

could be understood here. Peerlkamp objects that the great Marcellus won such glory in his own life that it could not be said to increase with the lapse of time. Yet cf. Enn. *ann.* 372 (on Fabius Cunctator) 'ergo postque magisque viri nunc gloria claret', Sil. 6. 63 (on Regulus) 'longum semper fama gliscente per aevum'.

Some editors understand Horace to refer to M. Claudius Marcellus, the son of C. Marcellus (*cos.* 50 B.C.) and of Octavia, who married Augustus's daughter Julia in 25 B.C. and died late in 23 B.C. Homer had compared the rapid growth of a young man to that of a tree (*Il.* 18. 56 f. ὁ δ' ἀνέδραμεν ἔρνεϊ ἶσος· / τὸν μὲν ἐγὼ θρέψασα, φυτὸν ὣς γουνῷ ἀλωῆς); but in our passage the word *fama* makes a lot of difference. Jerome's use of *occulto aevo* (see above) might seem to support the view that a young man is meant; but perhaps he misunderstood Horace. It is a more important argument that a reference here to the young Marcellus would provide a natural transition to the *Iulium sidus* in the latter part of the stanza. But one should rather say that the mention of the elder Marcellus inevitably reminds the reader of the young Marcellus, and this supplies the connection of thought with *Iulium sidus*. For a similar association of ideas cf. 33 'Tarquini . . . Catonis'.

Peerlkamp tentatively proposed *Marcellis*, a conjecture commended by Housman in his lectures. This reading has the merit of providing a clear link both with the old Romans of the previous stanzas and with the *Iulium sidus* of the following line. Yet perhaps the singular *Marcelli* does the same thing rather more delicately. Moreover, the simile of the steadily growing tree is inappropriate to the Marcelli as a whole: after their glorious history in the third and early second centuries, they decayed for a hundred years, only to produce a late efflorescence of three successive consuls in the last years of the Republic.

47. Iulium sidus: Horace is thinking of Augustus himself. As elsewhere in this poem (cf. 35 f., Doblhofer 124) he foreshadows the content of the next stanza, which on any other interpretation would be too abrupt. A direct reference to Julius Caesar is unlikely; in the twenties Julius Caesar was long dead, and played down in official utterances (Syme, *The Roman Revolution*, pp. 317 f., op. cit. [above, 35], pp. 12 ff.). Even a reference to the Julian house as a whole is probably undesirable; it was Augustus himself who was pre-eminent, and everybody knew it.

The metaphor goes back to Homer, and was a regular feature of Pindaric and Alexandrian panegyric; cf. Hom. *Il.* 6. 401 Ἑκτορίδην ἀγαπητόν, ἀλίγκιον ἀστέρι καλῷ, 11. 62 ff., Alcman 3. 66 f. ὥ τις αἰγλάεντος ἀστὴρ / ὠρανῶ διαιπετής, Eur. *Hipp.* 1121 f. τὸν Ἑλλανίας /

φανερώτατον ἀστέρ᾽ Ἀθάνας, Call. fr. 67. 8 καλοὶ νησάων ἀστέρες ἀμφότεροι with Pfeiffer's note, Ap. Rhod. 1. 774 φαεινῷ ἀστέρι ἶσος, 2. 40 ff., Alcaeus, *anth. P.* 7. 1. 8 Μουσάων ἀστέρα καὶ Χαρίτων, Gow–Page 2. 17, 2. 48, Ov. *trist.* 2. 167 (of Drusus and Germanicus) 'sidus iuvenale', *Pont.* 3. 3. 2 'o sidus Fabiae Maxime gentis, ades'. The simile is applied to Augustus himself in an epigram inscribed in 7 B.C. at Philae by Catilius son of Nicanor (Kaibel, *EG* 978. 1 ff.): Καίσαρι ποντομέδοντι καὶ ἀπείρων κρατέοντι / Ζανί, τῷ ἐκ Ζανὸς πατρὸς Ἐλευθερίῳ, / δεσπότᾳ Εὐρώπας τε καὶ Ἀσίδος, ἄστρῳ ἁπάσας / Ἑλλάδος, ὃς σωτὴρ Ζεὺς ἀνέτειλε μέγας.

Horace may well be making a side-allusion to the comet that appeared in the summer of 44 B.C. and that was regarded as evidence for the apotheosis of the dead dictator (cf. Wagenvoort 1 ff.). Pliny (*nat.* 2. 93 f.) tells us that though Augustus in his writings paid lip-service to the popular idea that the comet signified Caesar's immortality, he secretly took it to be an omen for his own future: 'haec ille in publicum; interiore gaudio sibi illum natum seque in eo nasci interpretatus est; et, si verum fatemur, salutare id terris fuit.' Cf. also Serv. auct. *Aen.* 8. 681 'ipse vero Augustus in honorem patris stellam in galea coepit habere depictam', *ecl.* 9. 47 'quam (stellam) quidam ad inlustrandam gloriam Caesaris iuvenis pertinere existimabant', Magariños, loc. cit. 20, 1952, 85 f.

velut . . .: for a similar pre-eminence of Augustus over the Republican heroes cf. Prop. 3. 11. 65 ff. (*CQ* N.S. 18, 1968, 327 f.), Ov. *fast.* 1. 587 ff., especially 607 f. 'sed tamen humanis celebrantur honoribus omnes; / hic socium summo cum Iove nomen habet'.

48. luna: it was a commonplace in encomia, whether erotic, athletic, or political, that the person praised surpassed all rivals as the sun, moon, or Lucifer outshone other heavenly bodies. Cf. Sappho 34 ἄστερες μὲν ἀμφὶ κάλαν σελάνναν / ἂψ ἀποκρύπτοισι φάεννον εἶδος, / ὅπποτα πλήθοισα μάλιστα λάμπῃ / γᾶν . . . / ἀργυρία, 96. 6 ff. νῦν δὲ Λύδαισιν ἐμπρέπεται γυναί/κεσσιν ὥς ποτ᾽ ἀελίω / δύντος ἀ βροδοδά-κτυλος †μήνα / πάντα περρέχοισ᾽ ἄστρα, Pind. *I.* 4. 23 f. λάμπει / Ἀοσφόρος θαητὸς ὡς ἄστροις ἐν ἄλλοις, Bacch. 9. 27 ff. πενταέθλοισιν γὰρ ἐνέπρε-πεν ὡς / ἄστρων διακρίνει φάη / . . . εὐφεγγὴς σελάνα, Hermocles 11 f. Powell (on Demetrius Poliorcetes) ὅμοιον ὥσπερ οἱ φίλοι μὲν ἀστέρες, / ἥλιος δ᾽ ἐκεῖνος, Leonidas, *anth. P.* 9. 24, Pompon. *Atell.* 74 'simile est, quasi cum in caelo fulgit propter lunam lucifer', Meleager, *anth. P.* 12. 59 (see Gow–Page 2. 660), Lucr. 3. 1044, Ov. *epist.* 18. 71 ff., *met.* 2. 722 ff., Sen. *Med.* 93 ff., *Phaedr.* 743 ff., Sil. 7. 639 f., 16. 33 ff., Stat. *Theb.* 6. 577 ff., *silv.* 2. 6. 35 ff., Menander rhet. 378. 10 ff. Sp., 380. 29 ff. Sp. οὗτος δὲ ὅτι τῷ γένει πάντων κρείττων ἐστὶ καθάπερ καὶ ὁ ἥλιος τῶν ἀστέρων δέδεικται, 381. 6 ff. Sp., Philostr. *epist.* 9 (33), Q.

Smyrn. 1. 36 ff., Cypr. Gall. *genes.* 1116 f., Marc. Argent. *anth. P.* 5.
110. 5 f., Galfridus de Vino Salvo, *Poetria nova* 30 f. (to Innocent III)
'tu solus mundo quasi sol, illi quasi stellae, / Roma quasi caelum',
Sir Henry Wootton, *On his Mistress, the Queen of Bohemia*, 'You
meaner *Beauties* of the *Night*, That poorly satisfie our *Eyes* More by
your *number*, than your *light*, You *Common People* of the *Skies*;
What are you when the *Sun* shall rise?', S. G. P. Small, *YClS* 12,
1951, 115 f., Doblhofer 19 ff.

　　minores: cf. *epod.* 15. 1 f., Sen. *Phaedr.* 748 'nec tenent stellae
faciem minores', Petron. 89. 55 '(Phoebe) minora ducens astra', Sil.
7. 640 '(Lucifer) laudatur Veneri et certat maioribus astris' (vies with
the sun and moon), Stat. *silv.* 2. 6. 36 f., Boeth. *cons.* 1 *carm.* 5. 7.

49. pater atque custos: cf. Dio Chrys. 2. 75 κηδεμὼν καὶ πατὴρ κοινὸς
ἀνθρώπων καὶ θεῶν, A. Alföldi, *MH* 11, 1954, 143 f.

50. orte Saturno: Κρονίδη, Κρονότεκνε (*Orph. h.* 4. 8); for the solemn
patronymic cf. Enn. *ann.* 627 (= Bibac. *carm.* fr. 11) 'Saturno
sancte create', 456 'o genitor noster Saturnie, maxime divom', Cic.
poet. 29. 5 T. (*Tusc.* 2. 23), Virg. *Aen.* 4. 372, Carter 55.

　　The periphrastic expression belongs particularly to high epic
style; cf. *epod.* 13. 12, *serm.* 2. 6. 5, Enn. *ann.* 37 'Eurydica prognata',
Catull. 64. 324 'Opis carissime nato', Cic. *poet.* 29. 2 T (*Tusc.* 2. 23)
'generata Caelo', Virg. *Aen.* 1. 582 'nate dea', 6. 322. So Caelius in
mocking Caesar (Cic. *epist.* 8. 15. 2): 'vellem quidem Venere prognatus tantum animi habuisset in vestro Domitio quantum psacade
natus in hoc habuit.'

　　tibi: we find already in Homer the belief that kings are διοτρεφεῖς
and appointed by Zeus. The Alexandrian poets develop the idea
that the Ptolemies were under Zeus's special protection; in this they
were followed by the Romans of the imperial period. Philosophers
and sophists, particularly Stoics and neo-Pythagoreans, affirmed in
voluminous prose that the king or emperor was the vicegerent of
Zeus, responsible only to him, and with functions corresponding to
those of his overlord in the κόσμος. Cf. in Horace himself 3. 1. 5 f.
'regum timendorum in proprios greges, / reges in ipsos imperium est
Iovis'.

　　The material is so abundant that only a selection can be given
here. Cf. Hom. *Il.* 9. 98 f. λαῶν ἔσσι ἄναξ καί τοι Ζεὺς ἐγγυάλιξε /
σκῆπτρόν τ' ἠδὲ θεμίστας, ἵνα σφίσι βουλεύησθα, Hes. *th.* 96 ἐκ δὲ Διὸς
βασιλῆες, Call. *h.* 1. 73 f. σὺ δ' ἐξέλεο πτολιάρχους / αὐτούς, 79 f. " ἐκ δὲ
Διὸς βασιλῆες ", ἐπεὶ Διὸς οὐδὲν ἀνάκτων / θειότερον· τῷ καί σφε τεὴν
ἐκρίναο λάξιν, Theoc. 17. 73 f., Ov. *met.* 15. 858 ff. 'Iuppiter arces /
temperat aetherias et mundi regna triformis; / terra sub Augusto
est; pater est et rector uterque', *fast.* 2. 31 f., *sap. Sol.* 6. 3 ff., Philo,

leg. Gai. 49 f., *vit. Mos.* 1. 148 ff., 2. 2 ff., Paul, *Rom.* 13. 1 ff. οὐ γάρ
ἐστιν ἐξουσία εἰ μὴ ὑπὸ Θεοῦ, αἱ δὲ οὖσαι ὑπὸ Θεοῦ τεταγμέναι εἰσίν.
ὥστε ὁ ἀντιτασσόμενος τῇ ἐξουσίᾳ τῇ τοῦ Θεοῦ διαταγῇ ἀνθέστηκεν, Sen.
clem. 1. 1. 2, 1. 7. 1, Plin. *paneg.* 67. 5, 80. 4 f. 'quae ille mundi parens
temperat nutu, si quando . . . fata mortalium inter divina opera
numerare dignatus est; qua nunc parte liber solutusque tantum
caelo vacat, postquam te dedit qui erga omne hominum genus vice
sua fungereris', Dio Chrys. 1. 37 ff., 45, 84, 2. 71 f., Plut. *princ.*
inerud. 780 d, ps.-Ecphantus, *regn.* 2 pp. 79 ff. T., Diotogenes, *regn.* 1
pp. 71 ff. T., Sthenidas, pp. 187 f. T., *anth. Lat.* 256. 2 'commune
imperium cum Iove, Caesar, agis', 813 'Iuppiter in caelis, Caesar
regit omnia terris', 855, ps.-Aug. *quaest. test.* 91. 8 'rex . . . quasi
vicarius dei', Synes. *regn.* 8. 8b f., E. B. Goodenough, *YClS* 1, 1928,
55 ff., W. Theiler, *Schr. d. Königsb. gel. Ges.* 12, 1935, 268 f., W.
Schubart, *Archiv f. Papyrusforschung* 12, 1937, 1 ff., L. Delatte, *Les
Traités de la Royauté d'Ecphante, Diotogène et Sthénidas*, 1942, pp.
123 ff., A Alföldi, loc. cit. on 49 above, La Penna, loc. cit., O. Murray,
Journal of Theological Studies, N.S. 18, 1967, 337 ff.

The notion that God is the only ruler of princes became still more
important in the Middle Ages, and is familiar to us as the doctrine of
'the divine right of kings', though spiritual potentates naturally
raised similar claims; cf. Peter Damian on Hildebrand (cited in
W. Martens, *Gregor VII, sein Leben und Wirken*, 1894, 2. 205), Galfridus de Vino Salvo to Innocent III (*Poetria nova* 2068 ff.) 'non deus
es nec homo. quasi neuter es, inter utrumque, / quem deus elegit
socium. socialiter egit / tecum partitus tibi mundum. noluit unus /
omnia, sed voluit tibi terras et sibi caelum'. On the whole question
cf. F. Kern, *Gottesgnadentum und Widerstandsrecht*, 1954, especially
pp. 106 ff. Significantly enough, the first medieval monarch of the
West who claimed to rule *Dei gratia* was the usurper Pippin (cf. W.
Staerk, *Dei gratia*, Festschrift W. Judeich, Weimar, 1929, pp. 160 ff.).

Cicero's cool rationalism provides an apt comment on such theories
(*rep.* 1. 56): 'sive haec ad utilitatem vitae constituta sunt a principi-
bus rerum publicarum, . . . magna auctoritas est multique testes . . .
ita consensisse gentes decretis videlicet principum, nihil esse rege
melius, quoniam deos omnis censent unius regi numine; sive haec
in errore imperitorum posita esse et fabularum similia didicimus,
audiamus communis quasi doctores eruditorum hominum (i.e. the
philosophers), qui tanquam oculis illa viderunt quae nos vix audiendo
cognoscimus.'

cura: a political word; the *cura rei publicae* is the proper preoccupation of a statesman (cf. 3. 29. 26, *Thes.l.L.* 4. 1453. 20 ff., J.
Béranger, *Recherches sur l'aspect idéologique du principat*, 1953, pp.
196 ff.).

magni: this title is also applied to Augustus in the parodic oracle *serm.* 2. 5. 64. It had previously been given to Pompeius, first by the acclamation of his troops in Africa, but was otherwise not usual in Rome; in Greco-Egyptian texts it was a normal epithet of gods and their sons and it was also used as a cult-title by Antiochus III (cf. P. P. Spranger, *Saeculum* 9, 1958, 22 ff., H. J. Mette, *Hermes* 89, 1961, 332 ff., Doblhofer 50).

51. tu . . .: 'may Caesar be the vicegerent of your kingdom'; it is *secundo Caesare*, not *regnes*, that carries the weight of the sentence. The reiteration of the second person pronoun is characteristic of prayers; cf. 1. 10. 9 n.

secundo: cf. Leonidas, *anth. P.* 9. 25. 5 f. (on the poet Aratus) αἰνείσθω δὲ καμὼν ἔργον μέγα καὶ Διὸς εἶναι / δεύτερος, ὅστις ἔθηκ' ἄστρα φαεινότερα, Calp. *ecl.* 4. 93 f. 'Iuppiter ipse parens, cui tu iam proximus ipse, / Caesar, abes', Suet. *Aug.* 31. 5 'proximum a dis immortalibus honorem memoriae ducum praestitit, qui imperium populi Romani ex minimo maximum reddidissent'.

This passage is formally inconsistent with 18 'nec viget quicquam simile aut secundum'. But Horace is not here deliberately reformulating his position; he has simply used in different places two τόποι of such different provenance that the question of reconciling them does not present itself to him.

52. regnes: Jupiter is king as Zeus is ἄναξ and βασιλεύς (Bruchmann 124, 126).

53. Parthos Latio imminentis: the Parthians had given the Romans a fright when they invaded the province of Syria after Carrhae, and again in 41–40 B.C. when Pacorus and Labienus made substantial inroads on the Roman provinces in the East. Driven back a year later by Ventidius, they successfully defended their own territory against Antony. Nothing justifies the sensational picture of their threat to Latium, the Roman heartland; but autocratic governments commonly seek popular support by exaggerating the dangers of foreign enemies. Cf. D. C. Earl, *Political Thought of Sallust*, 1961, pp. 47 ff.

54. iusto . . . triumpho: the triumph is justified because of the enemies' aggression, a claim made by Augustus himself; cf. *res gest.* 26. 3 'Alpes . . . [pacari fec]i nulli genti bello per iniuriam inlato', Suet. *Aug.* 21. 2 'nec ulli genti sine iustis et necessariis causis bellum intulit'. This was the general Roman attitude; cf. Cic. *off.* 1. 35 ff., H. Drexler, *RhM* 102, 1959, 97 ff., P. A. Brunt, *JRS* 53, 1963, 170.

55. subiectos: 'immediately next to' (cf. ὑποκεῖσθαι). The prefix still conveys a hint of 'under'; cf. Manil. 1. 43 'feras gentes oriente sub ipso', Flor. *epit.* 2. 34. 62. *orae* seems to mean 'region', not 'edge' as in Prop. 2. 10. 17.

56. Seras et Indos: cf. 3. 29. 27, 4. 14. 42, Prop. 3. 4. 1 'arma deus Caesar ditis meditatur ad Indos', 4. 3. 8 'munito Sericus hostis equo', Luc. 1. 19 (if it were not for the civil war) 'sub iuga iam Seres, iam barbarus isset Araxes', Stat. *silv.* 4. 1. 41 f., Sil. 15. 79 f. (a passage with several reminiscences of our ode). The Indians sent ambassadors to Augustus (*carm. saec.* 55 f., *res gest.* 31. 1 'ad me ex In[dia regum legationes saepe missae sunt, non visae ante id t]em[pus] apud qu[em]q[uam] R[omanorum du]cem'); Florus (loc. cit. above) incredibly tells us that the Chinese did so too.

The Augustan references are the first mention of the Chinese, who early in the first century under the emperor Wu were organizing the silk route to Parthia. They were thought to live by the Eastern Ocean, north of India and the Himalayas and south-east of the Scyths. Their conquest and that of India did not seem a wild dream to people of Horace's age; the explorations that revealed the real east–west extent of central Asia belong to the next two centuries. Horace and his contemporaries studied their geography by the map of Eratosthenes (cf. J. Oliver Thomson, *History of Ancient Geography*, 1948, p. 135); according to this the Romans were already masters of most of the habitable parts of Africa and Europe and of a sizeable part of Asia. Agrippa had a map of the world set up in the portico of Octavia and asserted that it was only 480 miles from the Caspian to the Oceanus Sericus; cf. Plin. *nat.* 3. 17, 6. 37, *RE* 2 A. 1678 ff., M. Cary and E. H. Warmington, *The Ancient Explorers*, 1929, c. 12 § 14, P. Brunt, loc. cit. [above, 54], pp. 175 f.

57. te minor: cf. 3. 6. 5 (to the Romans generally) 'dis te minorem quod geris, imperas', Tert. *apol.* 30. 3 '(imperator) ideo magnus est quia caelo minor est'.

laetum: the εὔνοια felt by subjects for their rulers is a commonplace of Hellenistic and later panegyric; cf. the letter of Aristeas (265): τίς ἐστι βασιλεῖ κτῆσις ἀναγκαιοτάτη; τῶν ὑποτεταγμένων φιλανθρωπία καὶ ἀγάπησις. Rhetoricians gave rules for its expression (cf. Menander rhet. 377. 19 ff. Sp.), and inscriptions and papyri show that the lesson was well learnt (see the examples cited by W. Schubart, loc. cit. [above, 50 *tibi*], pp. 16 f.). For the use of the τόπος of Roman rulers cf. *epist.* 1. 16. 27 ff. 'tene magis salvum populus velit an populum tu, / servet in ambiguo qui consulit et tibi et urbi / Iuppiter', Virg. *georg.* 4. 560 f. 'victorque volentis / per populos dat iura', Stat. *silv.* 4. 3. 128 f. (on Domitian) 'en hic est deus, hunc iubet beatis / pro se Iuppiter imperare terris', *SIG³* 797. 5 ff. (Assos) Caligula's rule

P

is πᾶσιν ἀνθρώποις ἐλπισθεῖσα . . . οὐδὲν δὲ μέτρον χαρᾶς εὕρηκεν ὁ κόσμος. So in 9 B.C. the proconsul Paullus Fabius Maximus told the citizens of Asia that they found it hard to decide whether Augustus's birthday was more pleasant or more useful (*OGIS* 458. 4 f.); a few years later the citizens of Sardis expressed their delight at the majority of C. Caesar (*IGRR* 4. 1756. 8 f. ἥδονταί τε πάντες ἄνθρωποι συνδιεγειρομένας ὁρῶντες τῷ Σεβαστῷ τὰς ὑπὲρ τῶν παίδων εὐχάς). For further discussion and examples see Doblhofer 52 ff.

latum has comparable manuscript authority, and can also be supported by parallels; cf. 2. 2. 9 'latius regnes', Theoc. 17. 76 (the king whom Zeus loves) πολλᾶς δὲ κρατέει γαίας, πολλᾶς δὲ θαλάσσας, Virg. *Aen.* 1. 21 'populum late regem', 4. 199 'latis . . . regnis'. But it is hard to resist the special point of *laetum*, which is less likely to be the result of palaeographic accident.

aequus: the ruler must be just and impartial, like the highest god; cf. 3. 4. 48 (of Jupiter) 'imperio regit unus aequo', Virg. *Aen.* 10. 112 'rex Iuppiter omnibus idem', Stat. *Theb.* 1. 285 ff., 10. 884, Diotogenes, *regn.* 1 p. 72. 9 ff. Τ. καὶ μὰν τό τε δικασπολὲν καὶ διανέμεν τὸ δίκαιον, ξυνᾷ μὲν καθόλου, ἰδίᾳ δὲ καθ᾽ ἕκαστον, οἰκῆον βασιλέως, ὥσπερ θεῶ ἐν τῷ κόσμῳ.

58. tu . . .: Horace is surely recalling a famous anecdote about Alexander, recorded by Plutarch; cf. *fort. Alex.* 335 b Λυσίππου δὲ τὸν πρῶτον Ἀλέξανδρον πλάσαντος, ἄνω βλέποντα τῷ προσώπῳ πρὸς τὸν οὐρανόν (ὥσπερ αὐτὸς εἰώθει βλέπειν Ἀλέξανδρος ἡσυχῇ παρεγκλίνων τὸν τράχηλον) ἐπέγραψέ τις οὐκ ἀπιθάνως Αὐδασοῦντι δ᾽ ἔοικεν ὁ χάλκεος εἰς Δία λεύσσων, / Γᾶν ὑπ᾽ ἐμοὶ τίθεμαι· Ζεῦ, σὺ δ᾽ Ὄλυμπον ἔχε. The epigram is attributed by some to Asclepiades, by some to Archelaus (cf. *anth. Pl.* 120, Gow–Page 2. 146 f.). For other eulogies of Augustus that compare him with Alexander cf. E. Norden, loc. cit. [above, 21 *proeliis audax*], Magariños, loc. cit. 10, 1942, 17 ff., P. Brunt, loc. cit. [above, 54], p. 176, Doblhofer 129 ff.

59. parum castis . . . lucis: cf. Val. Fl. 5. 335 'castis Hecates excedere lucis', Tac. *Germ.* 40. 2 'est in insula Oceani castum nemus, dicatumque in eo vehiculum, veste contectum; attingere uni sacerdoti concessum'. Such sacred groves were subject to many taboos and easily polluted; cf. *ILS* 4912 'honce loucum ne quis violatod . . . seiquis scies violasit dolo malo Iovei bovid piaclum datod', Val. Fl. 5. 640 f., Stat. *silv.* 5. 5. 6 'numquid inaccesso posui vestigia luco?', Apollod. 3. 9. 2 καί ποτε λέγεται θηρεύοντας αὐτοὺς εἰσελθεῖν εἰς τὸ τέμενος Διός, κἀκεῖ συνουσιάζοντας εἰς λέοντας ἀλλαγῆναι, D.–S. 3. 1355. According to pseudo-Acro, who claims to be citing the records of the pontiffs and haruspices, it was only polluted groves that were struck by lightning; certainly such an event was regarded as a portent needing expiation (cf. *acta Arv.* a. 224. 15 f. 'immolav(erunt) quod ab ictu fulminis arbores luci sacri D(eae) D(iae) attactae arduerint').

Augustus himself had a particular devotion to Juppiter Tonans (Suet. *Aug.* 91. 2). In the Cantabrian war a thunderbolt had narrowly missed the *Princeps* and killed his linkboy (ibid. 29. 3). In return he vowed a temple, which was dedicated in 22 B.C.

13. CVM TV, LYDIA, TELEPHI

[Commager 152 ff.; D. West 65 ff.]

1–8. *When you praise Telephus, Lydia, I betray all the symptoms of jealous love.* 9–12. *I am inflamed when you show the marks of his violence and his passion.* 13–16. *Passion like his is barbarous and will not last.* 17–20. *True happiness belongs to those who never quarrel and whose love is broken only by death.*

The first two stanzas of this ode derive ultimately from an illustrious prototype. In one of her most famous poems Sappho described the symptoms of her own love (31, imitated in Catullus 51):

ἀλλ' ἄκαν μὲν γλῶσσα †ἔαγε†, λέπτον
δ' αὔτικα χρῷ πῦρ ὑπαδεδρόμηκεν,
ὀππάτεσσι δ' οὐδ' ἒν ὄρημμ', ἐπιρρόμ-
βεισι δ' ἄκουαι,
κὰδ δέ μ' ἴδρως ψῦχρος ἔχει, τρόμος δὲ
παῖσαν ἄγρει, χλωροτέρα δὲ ποίας
ἔμμι, τεθνάκην δ' ὀλίγω 'πιδεύης
φαίνομ' ἔμ' αὔτ[ᾳ.

In Alexandrian literature we find similar pathological catalogues, but there they serve a quite different purpose; instead of being autobiographical statements of the poet's own emotion they are used to justify arch inferences about other people (5 n.). Horace conflates these two approaches: he purports to be writing about himself (like Sappho), but he also uses words like *arguens*, which suggest rather an outside observer.

Another complication is caused by the juxtaposition of contrasting styles. For much of its length the poem moves in the epigrammatists' world of furtive tears and smouldering marrows, bruised shoulders and nectareous kisses. Telephus indeed belongs completely to this milieu, to which he owes his name (1 n.), his pink and white complexion (2 n.), and his violent habits (9 n., 11 n.). Yet Horace does not seek to describe this world with the elegant sensuousness of a Meleager. Rather he adopts a casual off-hand manner; one may note the number of colloquialisms (3 *vae*, 4 *bile tumet iecur*, 8 *macerer*, 13 *si me satis audias*). This conjunction of the 'poetical' and the colloquial has parallels elsewhere in Horace's love poetry; cf. particularly 1. 19. 9–12 ('in me tota ruens Venus . . .').

The last stanza strikes yet another note both in content and in style. Now Horace stops his game and talks about love in the terms of a different and more serious convention: his attitude here is shared by the elegists and goes back to Catullus (109. 5 f.):

> ut liceat nobis tota perducere vita
> aeternum hoc sanctae foedus amicitiae.

The bonds of love had been mentioned by the Greek epigrammatists in accounts of love-making; but Horace, like other Roman poets, uses the image to signify a lasting union (18 n.). One does not wish to exaggerate the moral elevation of the last stanza; but at least it trenchantly states an ideal that is remote from the world of Greek epigram.

The poem as a whole is better than it might appear at first sight. What might be thought disastrous incongruities turn out to be effective and deliberately pointed: the off-hand diction shows the poet scoffing at conventional prettiness, and the serious ending makes a telling contrast with the frivolities that have gone before. As for the earlier stanzas, there is no point in comparing Sappho's objectivity and intenseness with the maudlin sentimentality of our ode; the poems are doing different jobs, and it would be imprudent to suppose that Horace was unaware of his own absurdity. The post-romantic reader is confused because Horace sets his poem in an autobiographical framework: accustomed as we are to expect the sincere outpouring of heartfelt confessions, we find it hard to cope with irony at a literary convention when the theme is love and the irony expressed in the first person. It is particularly regrettable from our point of view that Horace seems to be challenging Sappho; yet in fact his wit is directed elsewhere. Our poem should be regarded as a skit on the absurdities of Hellenistic epigram, set off against a more serious and Roman attitude.

Metre: Fourth Asclepiad.

1. **tu**: the pronoun is emphatic; it is not praise of Telephus, but Lydia's praise of him that upsets the poet.

Lydia: cf. 1. 8. 1 n.

Telephi: also a lover at 3. 19. 26, 4. 11. 21, anon. *anth. P.* 12. 88. 4. At first sight it seems strange that the name is applied so often to a handsome youth; we more naturally associate it with the dishevelled hero of the Euripidean play. But the most significant thing about the Telephus of legend was not his rags (which were peculiar to Euripides), but the fact that he was cured by the spear that wounded him (cf. *corp. paroem. gr.* 2. 763 ff. ὁ τρώσας ἰάσεται). Perhaps it might be suggested that some Hellenistic poet gave the name Telephus to a love-lorn youth because he would be cured by 'a hair of the dog that bit him'. It is this feature of Telephus's story that the love poets seize on when they invoke his example; cf. Prop. 2. 1. 58 ff. 'solus amor morbi non habet artificem. / ... Mysus et Haemonia iuvenis qua cuspide vulnus / senserat, hac ipsa cuspide sensit opem', Ov. *am.* 2. 9. 7 f. 'quid? non Haemonius quem cuspide perculit heros / confossum medica postmodo iuvit ope?', *rem.* 43 ff. 'discite sanari per quem didicistis amare; / ... vulnus in Herculeo quae quondam fecerat hoste, / vulneris auxilium Pelias hasta tulit', Publil. 31 'amoris vulnus idem sanat qui facit', Lucian, *Nigrin.* 38 ΛΟΥΚ. Οὐκοῦν καὶ αὐτὸς ἡμῖν ἐρᾶν ὁμολογεῖς; ΕΤΑΙ. Πάνυ μὲν οὖν, καὶ προσέτι δέομαί γέ σου κοινήν τινα τὴν θεραπείαν ἐπινοεῖν. ΛΟΥΚ. Τὸ τοῦ ἄρα Τηλέφου ἀνάγκη ποιεῖν. ΕΤΑΙ. Ποῖον αὖ λέγεις; ΛΟΥΚ. Ἐπὶ τὸν τρώσαντα ἐλθόντας ἰᾶσθαι παρακαλεῖν, Chariton 6. 3. 7 φάρμακον γὰρ ἕτερον ἔρωτος οὐδέν ἐστι πλὴν αὐτὸς ὁ ἐρώμενος· τοῦτο δὲ ἄρα καὶ τὸ ᾀδόμενον λόγιον ἦν ὅτι ὁ τρώσας αὐτὸς καὶ ἰάσεται, Paul. Sil. *anth. P.* 5. 291. 5 f. Τήλεφον ὁ τρώσας καὶ ἀκέσσατο· μὴ σύ γε, κούρη, / εἰς ἐμὲ δυσμενέων γίνεο πικροτέρη, Macedonius, ibid. 5. 225. 5 f. Τήλεφός εἰμι, κόρη, σὺ δὲ γίνεο πιστὸς Ἀχιλλεύς· / κάλλει σῷ παῦσον τὸν πόθον, ὡς ἔβαλες.

In our passage the repetition of Telephus's name shows irritation at the way Lydia keeps going on about him; for such repetition in erotic contexts cf. Anacreon 359 Κλεοβούλου μὲν ἔγωγ' ἐρέω, / Κλεο-βούλῳ δ' ἐπιμαίνομαι, / Κλεόβουλον δὲ διοσκέω, Ov. *met.* 7. 707 f., Alciphron fr. 5. 2 Λαῒς ἐν τοῖς κουρείοις, Λαῒς ἐν τοῖς θεάτροις ... The parasite in Terence recommends Lydia's technique to his patron (*eun.* 440 ff. 'ubi nominabit Phaedriam, tu Pamphilam / continuo; si quando illa dicet "Phaedriam / intro mittamus comissatum", Pam-philam / cantatum provocemus; si laudabit haec / illius formam, tu huius contra').

2. cervicem: the singular is normal in the poets instead of the plural required by classical prose; cf. *Thes.l.L.* 3. 946. 13 ff., P. Maas, *ALL* 12, 1902, 500 ff.

roseam: cf. Virg. *Aen.* 1. 402 'rosea cervice'. Martial often uses the word of *pueri delicati*, but in less sentimental contexts it is more appropriate to a woman than a man; cf. André 112.

cerea: 'white as refined wax'; cf. Philodemus, *anth. P.* 9. 570. 1

Ξανθώ, κηρόπλαστε, μυρόχροε, μουσοπρόσωπε, Plin. *nat.* 37. 33 'candidum atque cerei coloris', Ennod. *opusc.* 3. 14 'frons cereae pulchritudinis et candoris illius quae [*sic*] solis passa radios colorem traxit ab aethere', André 157 f. Though firm and smooth texture may also be suggested, the word must primarily be a colour adjective to contrast with *roseam* (id. 324 f., 347). As a colour adjective *cereus* more often signified a yellowish pallor; this was admired in plums, but in human beings was rather a sign of disease (cf. Ov. *Pont.* 1. 10. 27 f. 'parvus in exiles sucus mihi pervenit artus / membraque sunt cera pallidiora nova').

Lilies, snow, or milk provided more standard and attractive contrasts to 'rosy' (cf. Rohde, *Roman³*, p. 163). Hence some editors have preferred the conventional *lactea*, attributed to our passage by the grammarian Caper (*gramm.* 7. 98); so Statius, in bemoaning the death of a *delicatus*, sighs sentimentally 'heu lactea colla / bracchiaque' (*silv.* 2. 1. 50 f.). Yet *cerea*, which is supported by the scholia and a testimonium as well as by the manuscripts, is a more interesting word and seems confirmed by the parallel in Philodemus.

3. vae: the word has a colloquial tone; it is found only here in Horace, once in Virgil (*ecl.* 9. 28), and never in Tibullus, Propertius, Lucan, Statius, Silius, or for that matter Cicero or Caesar. In archaic Latin *vae* is regularly followed by a dative; the absolute use is first seen in Catull. 64. 196 (see J. B. Hofmann, *Lateinische Umgangssprache*, 1951, p. 13).

4. difficili: 'hard to swallow', 'indigestible', cf. Juv. 13. 213 'difficili crescente cibo'. Most editors explain 'ill-tempered'; but that is not strong enough to describe Horace's emotional state.

bile: cf. *epod.* 11. 15 f. The word may have a prosaic flavour; it is freely used by Plautus and the satirists, but is not found in Virgil, Tibullus, Propertius, Ovid, Seneca's tragedies, or silver epic (in Statius only *silv.* 2. 1. 58).

tumet iecur: the ancients, at least from the time of Aeschylus, associated violent emotions with biliary disturbance. Hence the liver was connected with grief (Aesch. *Ag.* 432), anger (*serm.* 1. 9. 66 and elsewhere), and frustrated desire (1. 25. 15, 4. 1. 12, *epist.* 1. 18. 72, Theoc. 11. 15 f. ἔχθιστον ἔχων ὑποκάρδιον ἕλκος / Κύπριδος ἐκ μεγάλας, τό οἱ ἥπατι πᾶξε βέλεμνον, 13. 72, *Anacreontea* 31. 27 f., Hier. *epist.* 64. 1. 3 'voluptas et concupiscentia iuxta eos qui de physicis disputant consistit in iecore', *Thes.l.L.* 7. 1. 245. 71; so more generally σπλάγχνα in Theoc. 7. 99, Moschus 1. 17, Meleager, *anth. P.* 12. 80. 1 f., Gow on Theoc. loc. cit., Headlam on Herodas 1. 57). From Plato on, the psychologists elevated the θυμός to the area of the heart and lungs, but continued to regard the liver as the seat of the ἐπιθυμητικόν; see further R. B. Onians, *The Origins of European Thought*, ed. 2, 1954, pp. 84 ff., F. M. Cornford, *Plato's Cosmology*, 1937, pp. 286 ff.

For *tumet* cf. Herodas 1. 56 f. ἰδών σε καθόδῳ τῆς Μίσης ἐκύμηνε / τὰ σπλάγχν᾿, ἔρωτι καρδίαν ἀνοιστρηθείς and Headlam's note, Dion. Hal. *ant. Rom.* 11. 35. 4 οἰδῶν τε τὴν ψυχὴν καὶ ζέων τὰ σπλάγχνα διὰ τὸν ἔρωτα, Ov. *epist.* 16. 133 f. 'praecordiaque intima sensi / attonitus curis intumuisse novis'. *fervens* in our passage and *torrere* in 4. 1. 12 suggest that the cause was heat, as it was in the case of anger; cf. Ar. *Thesm.* 468 ἐπιζεῖν τὴν χολήν, Q. Smyrn. 5. 324, 1. 16. 22 n.

5. tum nec . . .: cf. 4. 1. 33 ff. 'sed cur heu, Ligurine, cur / manat rara meas lacrima per genas? / cur facunda parum decoro / inter verba cadit lingua silentio?'. Such lists of symptoms depend ultimately on Sappho's celebrated catalogue (above, p. 169). For their elaboration in Alexandrian and later authors cf. Call. *ep.* 43. 1 f. ἕλκος ἔχων ὁ ξεῖνος ἐλάνθανεν· ὡς ἀνιηρὸν / πνεῦμα διὰ στήθεων (εἶδες;) ἀνηγάγετο, Ap. Rhod. 3. 297 f. ἁπαλὰς δὲ μετετρωπᾶτο παρειὰς / ἐς χλόον, ἄλλοτ᾿ ἔρευθος, ἀκηδείῃσι νόοιο, Theoc. 2. 106 ff. πᾶσα μὲν ἐψύχθην χιόνος πλέον, ἐκ δὲ μετώπω / ἱδρώς μευ κοχύδεσκεν ἴσον νοτίαισιν ἐέρσαις, / οὐδέ τι φωνῆσαι δυνάμαν, Asclepiades, *anth. P.* 12. 135 οἶνος ἔρωτος ἔλεγχος· ἐρᾶν ἀρνεύμενον ἡμῖν / ἤτασαν αἱ πολλαὶ Νικαγόρην προπόσεις. / καὶ γὰρ ἐδάκρυσεν καὶ ἐνύστασε, καί τι κατηφὲς / ἔβλεπε, χὠ σφιγχθεὶς οὐκ ἔμενε στεφανός, Aedit. *epigr.* 1. 2 ff. 'verba labris abeunt, / per pectus manat subito ⟨subido⟩ mihi sudor: / sic tacitus, subidus, dum pudeo, pereo', Ov. *met.* 9. 535 ff. 'esse quidem laesi poterat tibi pectoris index / et color et macies et vultus et umida saepe / lumina' etc., Lucian, *Jup. trag.* 2 τὰ σημεῖα γὰρ ταῦτα, οἱ στεναγμοὶ καὶ τὰ δάκρυα καὶ τὸ ὠχρὸν εἶναι, οὐκ ἄλλου του ἢ ἐρῶντός ἐστιν, Plut. *Demetr.* 38. 4 (the physician Erasistratus discovered Antiochus's love for Stratonice by observing) τὰ τῆς Σαπφοῦς ἐκεῖνα . . . φωνῆς ἐπίσχεσις, ἐρύθημα πυρῶδες, ὄψεων ὑπολείψεις, ἱδρῶτες ὀξεῖς, ἀταξία καὶ θόρυβος ἐν τοῖς σφυγμοῖς, τέλος δὲ τῆς ψυχῆς κατὰ κράτος ἡττωμένοις ἀπορία καὶ θάμβος καὶ ὠχρίασις. See further A. Turyn, *Eos Suppl.* 6, 1929, 43 ff.

mens: cf. Ov. *met.* 3. 99 f. 'pariter cum mente colorem / perdiderat', Sen. *epist.* 22. 16 'non animus nobis, non color constat, lacrimae . . . cadunt'.

6. sede: cf. Cic. *parad.* 1. 15 'voluptas . . . mentem e sua sede et statu demovet'.

manet: the singular is found in the Bernensis, but otherwise has poor manuscript support. For the same metrical licence see p. xxxix. The plural after such a disjunction is not cited from the classical Latin poets, though it is attested occasionally in prose writers; cf.

Tac. *hist.* 3. 28 'neque Antonius neque Hormus . . . degeneravere'
(K.–S. 1. 48; cf. also K.–G. 1. 81).

7. furtim: cf. Meleager, *anth. P.* 5. 212. 2 ὄμμα δὲ σῖγα Πόθοις τὸ γλυκὺ
δάκρυ φέρει.

arguens: cf. *epod.* 11. 9 f. 'amantem languor et silentium / arguit',
Antiphanes, fr. 235 K. μηνύει, Asclepiades, *anth. P.* 12. 135 (cited on
5 above). So Callimachus does some detective work (*ep.* 43. 5 f.
ὤπτηται μέγα δή τι· μὰ δαίμονας οὐκ ἀπὸ ῥυσμοῦ / εἰκάζω, φωρὸς δ'
ἴχνια φὼρ ἔμαθον).

8. lentis: the word indicates the prolonged agony of Horace's love;
cf. 3. 19. 28, Tib. 1. 4. 81, 1. 10. 57 f. Ovid similarly uses the image of
a seasoned lover, as contrasted with a youth (*ars* 3. 573 ff.). One may
compare the Greek use of σμύχω (Theoc. 3. 17 with Gow's note) and
of τύφω (Meleager, *anth. P.* 12. 63. 6, Philodemus, ibid. 5. 124. 4 πῦρ
τύφεται ἐγκρύφιον, 5. 131. 4, 11. 41. 6; cf. Gow–Page 2. 339).

penitus: love was believed to attack the bones, and particularly
the marrow; cf. Archil. 104 δύστηνος ἔγκειμαι πόθῳ / ἄψυχος, χαλεπῆσι
θεῶν ὀδύνῃσιν ἕκητι / πεπαρμένος δι' ὀστέων, Eur. *Hipp.* 253 ff. χρῆν
γὰρ μετρίας εἰς ἀλλήλους / φιλίας θνητοὺς ἀνακίρνασθαι / καὶ μὴ πρὸς
ἄκρον μυελὸν ψυχῆς, Theoc. 3. 17 (of Eros) ὅς με κατασμύχων καὶ ἐς
ὀστίον ἄχρις ἰάπτει and Gow's note. To the passages there cited add
Catull. 35. 15, 61. 169 ff. 'illi non minus ac tibi / pectore uritur inti-
mo / flamma, sed penite magis', 64. 93, 66. 23 'quam penitus maestas
exedit cura medullas', Virg. *Aen.* 4. 66 with Pease's note, Prop. 1. 9.
29, 2. 34. 60, Ov. *epist.* 4. 15, 16. 276, Sen. *Phaedr.* 641 ff., Apul. *met.*
2. 7. 7 'ureris intime', Paul. Sil. *anth. P.* 5. 239. 3 f. ἤδη γὰρ μετὰ σάρκα
δι' ὀστέα καὶ φρένας ἕρπει / παμφάγον ἀσθμαίνων οὗτος ὁ πικρὸς Ἔρως.

macerer: this word originally meant 'steep' or 'soak'; in this sense
it was prosaic. It came to be used colloquially, particularly in
comedy, for 'enervate' or 'distress'; it is applied to love at *epod.* 14.
15 f. 'ureris ipse miser, me . . . Phryne macerat', Plaut. *cist.* 71 'ad
istam faciem est morbus qui me, mea Gymnasium, macerat'. The
original meaning may not always have been strongly felt, and there
seems to be no oxymoron with *ignibus*; cf. *Ciris* 244 'amor noto te
macerat igne'.

9. uror: Horace does not say what emotion inflames him, but love,
anger, and jealousy are obviously suggested by the context. In
erotic poetry *uri* normally refers to love, but there is no reason why
it should not here be used of a more complicated set of feelings; cf.
epist. 1. 2. 12 'hunc amor, ira quidem communiter urit utrumque'.

candidos: the word contrasts the normal whiteness of Lydia's
shoulders with the bruises Telephus inflicts. Neither the quarrel nor

the wounds are necessarily very serious; cf. Catull. 66. 13 'dulcia nocturnae portans vestigia rixae', Prop. 2. 15. 4, 3. 8. 21 f.

11. sive puer . . .: several similarities suggest that Horace is here remembering Lucr. 4. 1079 ff. 'quod petiere premunt arte faciuntque dolorem / corporis et dentis illidunt saepe labellis / osculaque adfligunt, quia non est pura voluptas / et stimuli subsunt qui instigant laedere id ipsum / quodcumque est, rabies unde illaec germina surgunt'.

Lovers' bites are a common theme in Latin love poetry; the motif is also found, though less commonly, in Greek erotic writing (Lucian, *dial. mer.* 5. 3 ἡ Δημώνασσα δὲ καὶ ἔδακνε μεταξὺ καταφιλοῦσα, Ach. Tat. 2. 37. 7 οὐ γὰρ μόνον ἐθέλει φιλεῖν τοῖς χείλεσιν, ἀλλὰ καὶ τοῖς ὀδοῦσι συμβάλλεται καὶ περὶ τὸ τοῦ φιλήματος στόμα βόσκεται καὶ δάκνει τὰ φιλήματα, Paul. Sil. *anth. P.* 5. 244. 1 f. μακρὰ φιλεῖ Γαλάτεια καὶ ἔμψοφα, μαλθακὰ Δημώ, / Δωρὶς ὀδακτάζει, C. Sittl, *Die Gebärden der Griechen und Römer*, 1890, p. 42 n. 5, *RE* Suppl. 5. 513). For eminent historical examples cf. Cic. *Verr.* 5. 32 'ne excitetur Verres, ne denudetur a pectore, ne cicatrices populus Romanus aspiciat, ex mulierum morsu vestigia libidinis atque nequitiae', Plut. *Pomp.* 2. 2 Φλώραν δὲ τὴν ἑταίραν . . . λέγουσαν, ὡς οὐκ ἦν ἐκείνῳ συναναπαυσαμένην ἀδήκτως ἀπελθεῖν.

12. memorem: for the sense 'reminding' cf. 3. 17. 4, *Thes.l.L.* 8. 661. 48.

13. si . . . audias: more urbane than *si sapis*, but still informal; cf. Cic. *epist.* 2. 18. 3 'sed si me audies, vitabis inimicitias', 7. 20. 1, *de orat.* 1. 68, *nat. deor.* 2. 168, Liv. 9. 9. 2.

14. perpetuum: cf. Plaut. *most.* 194 f. 'stulta es plane / quae illum tibi aeternum putes fore amicum et benevolentem', 247 'tibi fore illum amicum sempiternum', *Persa* 35 'emere amicum tibi me potis es sempiternum'.

15. laedentem oscula: *laedere* implies hurt as well as collision. Editors debate whether the *oscula* here are kisses or Lydia's lips; the former interpretation might perhaps be supported by Ach. Tat. 2. 37. 7 (cited on 11 above). Yet the nectar should belong to the girl rather than the man.

16. quinta parte: nectar was a very potent substance, and a little went a long way; even when diluted it was extremely sweet. Elsewhere honey is said to have a ninth of the sweetness of ambrosia, or to be a tenth part of immortality; cf. Ibycus 325 Ἴβυκος δέ φησι τὴν ἀμβροσίαν τοῦ μέλιτος κατ' ἐπίτασιν ἐννεαπλασίαν ἔχειν γλυκύτητα, τὸ μέλι λέγων ἔνατον εἶναι μέρος τῆς ἀμβροσίας κατὰ τὴν ἡδονήν, Schol.

Pind. *P.* 9. 112 ἔστι δὲ τοῦ μέλιτος εὑρετής, ὃ δὴ τῆς ἀθανασίας δέκατον μέρος ᾠήθησαν εἶναι. These striking parallels show that Lydia's kisses are a fifth as sweet as nectar. *imbuit* ('tinges') confirms this interpretation of *parte*; it does not suit nearly so well the other explanations that have been offered.

Many editors have seen a reference to the young Aristotle's πέμπτη οὐσία, a fifth, very pure element invoked to explain the autokinesis of the heavens and perhaps of the soul (cf. W. K. C. Guthrie, *History of Greek Philosophy* I, 1962, pp. 270 ff., H. J. Easterling, *MH* 21, 1964, 73 ff., *RE* 24. 1171 ff.). But *pars* is not a sensible translation of οὐσία; other writers use *corpus, genus, natura, elementum*. Nor can one legitimately speak at Horace's date of a 'quintessence'; the notion of the *quinta essentia* as an extractable element present in everything belongs to the alchemical writers and its poetic fortune began only in the Middle Ages (see M. Berthelot, *Les Origines de l'alchimie*, 1885, p. 262). In any case an analogy drawn from the obscurer tracts of natural philosophy is unexpected in Horace, who does not usually write like an ancient Donne.

Porphyrio comments 'eleganter quia in quinque partes amoris fructus esse partitus dicitur, visu alloquio tactu osculo concubitu'; cf. also Lucian, *am.* 53, Don. *eun.* 640 'CERTE EXTREMA LINEA et hoc recte, quia quinque lineae perfectae sunt ad amorem: prima visus, secunda alloquii, tertia tactus, quarta osculi, quinta coitus'. But these are the stages of love rather than the ingredients; nor could kissing be valued equally with seeing. In any case the scholastic division is more suited to a poet of the Middle Ages than to Horace; cf. *carmina Burana* 88. 8 'volo tantum ludere, / id est contemplari, / presens loqui, tangere, / tandem osculari; / quintum, quod est agere, / noli suspicari' (see further Curtius 512 ff.).

sui nectaris: Venus's nectar must in some sense symbolize love. Aphrodite was said to provide nectar as a drink or unguent for those she favoured; cf. Sappho 2. 13 ff. ἔνθα δὴ σὺ στέμ⟨ματ'⟩ ἔλοισα, Κύπρι, / χρυσίαισιν ἐν κυλίκεσσιν ἄβρως / ὀμ⟨με⟩μείχμενον θαλίαισι νέκταρ / οἰνοχόαισον, 96. 26 ff., Nossis, *anth.* P. 6. 275. 3 f. ἁδύ τι νέκταρος ὄσδει· / τούτῳ καὶ τήνα καλὸν Ἄδωνα χρίει.

For the association of the divine food and drink with kisses cf. Meleager, *anth.* P. 12. 68. 7 ff. γλυκὺ δ' ὄμμασι νεῦμα δίυγρον / δοίη, καί τι φίλημ' ἁρπάσαι ἀκροθιγές. / τἆλλα δὲ πάντ' ἐχέτω Ζεύς, ὡς θέμις· εἰ δ' ἐθελήσοι, / ἦ τάχα που κἠγὼ γεύσομαι ἀμβροσίας, 12. 133. 3 ff. Ζεῦ πάτερ, ἆρα φίλημα τὸ νεκτάρεον Γανυμήδευς / πίνεις, καὶ τόδε σοι χείλεσιν οἰνοχοεῖ; / καὶ γὰρ ἐγὼ τὸν καλὸν ἐν ἠιθέοισι φιλήσας / Ἀντίοχον, ψυχῆς ἡδὺ πέπωκα μέλι, Catull. 99. 2 'suaviolum dulci dulcius ambrosia', anon. *anth.* P. 5. 305. 2, Lucian, *dial. deor.* 5. 2, Apul. *met.* 2. 10. 4 'occursantis linguae inlisu nectareo', Alciphron 4. 11. 7 (1. 38. 7),

Philostr. *epist.* 60 (23) εἰ δὲ καὶ ἀποπίοις ποτέ, πᾶν τὸ καταλειπόμενον γίγνεται . . . ἥδιον . . . τοῦ νέκταρος. κάτεισι γοῦν ἐπὶ τὴν φάρυγγα ἀκωλύτοις ὁδοῖς, ὥσπερ οὐκ οἴνῳ κεκραμένον ἀλλὰ φιλήμασιν, Ach. Tat. 2. 38. 5 αὕτη δὲ παιδὸς φιλήματος εἰκών· εἰ νέκταρ ἐπήγνυτο καὶ χεῖλος ἐγίνετο, τοιαῦτα ἂν ἔσχες τὰ φιλήματα. In English the idea is most familiar from Ben Jonson's exquisite *Song to Celia*: 'Drinke to me, onely, with thine eyes, And I will pledge with mine; Or leave a kiss but in the cup, And I'll not look for wine. The thirst, that from the soule doth rise, Doth aske a drink divine: But might I of JOVE's *Nectar* sup, I would not change for thine.'

17. felices . . .: cf. Hom. *Od.* 5. 306 τρὶς μάκαρες Δαναοὶ καὶ τετράκις, Ar. *Plut.* 850 ff. οἴμοι κακοδαίμων, ὡς ἀπόλωλα δείλαιος, / καὶ τρισκακοδαίμων καὶ τετράκις καὶ πεντάκις / καὶ δωδεκάκις καὶ μυριάκις, Meleager, *anth. P.* 5. 195. 5, 12. 52. 3 f., Virg. *Aen.* 1. 94, Prop. 3. 12. 15, Tib. 3. 3. 26, Ov. *ars* 2. 447 f. 'o quater et quotiens numero comprendere non est / felicem', Prud. *perist.* 2. 529 f. 'o ter quaterque et septies / beatus', *Thes.l.L.* 6. 1. 444. 51 ff. The formula *felix qui* . . . is very common and was particularly used in the language of mystery cults; cf. Dodds on Eur. *Ba.* 72, Bömer on Ov. *fast.* 1. 297, Norden, *Agnostos Theos*, p. 100, G. L. Dirichlet, *De veterum macarismis*, Giessen, 1914, E. Lohmeyer on *euang. Matth.* 5. 3 (the beatitudes), B. Gladigow, *Hermes* 95, 1967, 404 ff.

18. irrupta: the word occurs only here, as an equivalent of ἄρρηκτος; cf. Hom. *Od.* 8. 274 f. κόπτε δὲ δεσμοὺς / ἀρρήκτους ἀλύτους (the chains used by Hephaestus to bind Ares and Aphrodite).

copula: Horace is no doubt imitating the phraseology of some Greek poem; cf. Lucr. 4. 1113 'usque adeo cupide in Veneris compagibus haerent', Paul. Sil. *anth. P.* 5. 255. 17 f. τρὶς μάκαρ, ὃς τοίοισι, φίλη, δεσμοῖσιν ἐλίχθη, / τρὶς μάκαρ, 5. 286. 5 f. εἴη μοι μελέεσσι τὰ Λήμνιος ἥρμοσεν ἄκμων / δεσμά, Irenaeus, ibid. 5. 249. 3 f. ἀγκὰς ἑλοῦσά μ' ἔχεις παρὰ σὸν λέχος· ἐν δ' ἄρα δεσμοῖς / κεῖμαι, ἐλευθερίης οὐκ ἐπιδευόμενος. These passages refer to love-making, and are meant to recall the licentious tale of Ares and Aphrodite (see the previous note). The Roman poets characteristically use the image to signify lifelong devotion; cf. Prop. 2. 15. 25 f. 'atque utinam haerentis sic nos vincire catena / velles, ut nunquam solveret ulla dies!', Tib. 2. 2. 19 f., 3. 11. 15 f. 'sed potius valida teneamur uterque catena / nulla queat posthac quam soluisse dies', Stat. *silv.* 5. 1. 43 f. 'vos collato pectore mixtos / iunxit inabrupta concordia longa catena'. The use of *copula*, in particular, to signify enduring bonds, especially those of matrimony, is common in Christian and legal writers; cf. *Thes.l.L.* 4. 917. 77 ff.

For the genesis and development of the Roman treatment of love as a *foedus amicitiae* cf. F. Leo, *RhM* 55, 1900, 604 f., R. Reitzenstein, *SHAW* 1912, 12. Abh., 9 ff., A. La Penna, *Maia* 4, 1951, 190 ff., G. Williams, *JRS* 48, 1958, 25, Boucher 85 ff., Lilja 172 ff.

nec malis . . .: 'and whom love, torn asunder by silly quarrels, will not separate sooner than the day of death (will separate them)'. From the prosaic standpoint *amor* is inappropriate as a subject of *solvet*, but the construction is made easier by the preceding *divolsus*. On the other hand it would be misleading to explain *divolsus amor* simply as the equivalent of *divolsio amoris*; in the normal *ab urbe condita* construction the noun and participle are not found in separate cola.

19. divolsus: for *divellere* with an abstract object cf. Cic. *Quinct.* 25 'affinitas . . . divelli nullo modo poterat', *har. resp.* 60, Tert. *anim.* 52. 3. *divellere* more often has a personal object, and Muretus proposed *divolsos*; cf. 1. 36. 18 f., 2. 17. 13 f. 'me nec Chimaerae spiritus igneae / divellet unquam'. But one may doubt Bentley's view that *divolsos* is more elegant; *irrupta copula* and *nec divolsus amor* seem to balance each other.

querimoniis: the absence of quarrels is an essential element in the popular ideal of conjugal love; cf. *CIL* 5. 124 'hanc sedem vivi sibi (posuerunt) uno animo laborantes / sine ulla querella', Lattimore 279 f. Cf. also Nepos, *Att.* 17. 2 'quod est signum aut nullam unquam inter eos querimoniam intercessisse, aut hunc ea fuisse in suos indulgentia ut quos amare deberet irasci eis nefas duceret'.

20. suprema citius . . . die: probably this means 'citius quam suprema dies solvet'; cf. the significant and important parallels Prop. 2. 15. 26, Tib. 3. 11. 16 (cited on 18 above). Alternatively one might interpret 'sooner than on the last day'; cf. 4. 14. 13 'plus vice simplici' ('with more than single requital'), Colum. *arb.* 3. 5 'nam ubi vinea fuit quod citius decimo anno severis aegrius comprehendet'. But unless a numerical expression is present, this brachylogy is rare in good authors.

suprema is the ordinary adjective for the day of death; *summa* would be grander. The words used in this clause are very simple and straightforward, their order complicated and exquisite.

14. O NAVIS REFERENT

[W. S. Anderson, *CPh* 61, 1966, 84 ff.; C. Carlsson, *Eranos* 42, 1944, 1 ff.; Commager 163 ff.; Fraenkel 154 ff.; Pasquali 19 ff.; L. P. Wilkinson, *Hermes* 84, 1956, 495 ff.]

1–3. Fresh waves will sweep you back to sea, o Ship, unless you make an effort to reach port betimes. 3–10. Your oars, mast, yard, keel, sails, and sacred images have all suffered in the storm. 11–16. Your proud past and gaudy paint will not save you; so unless you are looking for trouble, beware. 17–20. You who were once a weariness to me, but now my heart's desire, avoid the reef-strewn seas.

This poem is cited by Quintilian as an instance of allegory (*inst.* 8. 6. 44 'navem pro re publica, fluctus et tempestates pro bellis civilibus, portum pro pace atque concordia dicit'); he is echoed by the scholiasts. This interpretation is confirmed by line 17: Horace could not possibly say to a real ship 'nuper sollicitum quae mihi taedium'. A few other touches also suit the metaphor: *novi fluctus* (1 f.) and *iterum* (10) suggest a recrudescence of civil war, *fortiter* (2) the effort needed to achieve stability, *nobilis* (12) and *pictis* (14) the antiquity and outward splendour of the Roman state. But commentators, after the fashion of their kind, looked for hidden meanings on every side: ps.-Acro explained *funibus* as *administratoribus*, while to Cruquius in the sixteenth century the mast was Egypt and the haven Augustus. In fact the development of detail is of no more importance than in a Homeric simile.

Horace's ode is modelled on Alcaeus, and parts of two relevant poems survive. One of these (6) contains the words τόδ' αὖτε κῦμα τῶν προτέρων ὄνω / στείχει (τὼ προτέρω νέμω *vel sim. codd.*), and this may faintly have influenced Horace's *novi fluctus*. Another fragment of the same poem reads ἐς δ' ἔχυρον λίμενα δρόμωμεν, and this certainly lies behind *fortiter occupa portum*. The second of Alcaeus's poems is more complete (326):

> ἀσυννέτημμι τὼν ἀνέμων στάσιν·
> τὸ μὲν γὰρ ἔνθεν κῦμα κυλίνδεται,
> τὸ δ' ἔνθεν, ἄμμες δ' ὂν τὸ μέσσον
> νᾶϊ φορήμμεθα σὺν μελαίνᾳ
> χείμωνι μόχθεντες μεγάλῳ μάλα·
> πὲρ μὲν γὰρ ἄντλος ἰστοπέδαν ἔχει,
> λαῖφος δὲ πὰν ζάδηλον ἤδη,
> καὶ λάκιδες μεγάλαι κὰτ αὖτο,
> χόλαισι δ' ἄγκυραι . . .

Here the torn sail has obviously influenced Horace, though Alcaeus's treatment is much more vivid. For the obscure and non-Lesbian ἄγκυραι Unger plausibly conjectured ἄγκονναι (ropes of some sort, perhaps used to manœuvre the yard-arm; cf. Page, *Sappho and Alcaeus*, p. 187); if this is what Alcaeus wrote, it may have influenced Horace's *antemnae*.

These poems of Alcaeus were understood allegorically in antiquity, notably by Heraclitus, the author of the valuable but misguided *quaestiones Homericae* (ed. F. Buffière, 1962). His conclusion was correct; one of the fragments contains the word μοναρχίαν and an appeal to remember former toils and dead ancestors (Page, pp. 184 f.; other arguments are indecisive). Such allegorical interpretations were familiar to ancient poetry-readers, and anybody who had enjoyed a rhetorical education must have known about the figure (Volkmann 429 ff., F. Buffière, *Les Mythes d'Homère et la pensée grecque*, 1956, pp. 45 ff., L. Arbusow, *Colores rhetorici*, ed. 2, 1963, p. 86). In particular the explanation of Alcaeus's poem would be well known. This rules out strange theories that sometimes appear, according to which the existence of allegory is accepted, but not the conventional interpretation of the riddle; thus most recently W. S. Anderson, who sees a reference to the Ship of Love (loc. cit.).

The Ship of State was indeed a familiar topic in poetry: ἀεὶ οἱ ποιηταὶ τὰς πόλεις πλοίοις παραβάλλουσι (schol. Ar. *vesp.* 29). Theognis gives a plain man's version, which is less enigmatic than he imagines (671 ff.):

οὕνεκα νῦν φερόμεσθα καθ' ἱστία λευκὰ βαλόντες
Μηλίου ἐκ πόντου νύκτα διὰ δνοφερήν.
ἀντλεῖν δ' οὐκ ἐθέλουσιν· ὑπερβάλλει δὲ θάλασσα
ἀμφοτέρων τοίχων. ἦ μάλα τις χαλεπῶς
σῴζεται. οἳ δ' ἔρδουσι· κυβερνήτην μὲν ἔπαυσαν
ἐσθλόν, ὅτις φυλακὴν εἶχεν ἐπισταμένως . . .

The metaphor was used sporadically by the tragedians; see especially Aesch. *Th.* 2 f. and *passim*, Soph. *OT* 22 ff. It was familiar to philosophers, historians, and orators; see Pl. *rep.* 488, Plb. 6. 44. 3 ff., Cic. *Att.* 2. 7. 4, *epist.* 9. 15. 3 (from the familiar *gubernator rei publicae* comes the modern word 'governor'). The image was later taken over by the Church; cf. H. Rahner, *Griechische Mythen in christlicher Deutung*, ed. 3, 1966, pp. 294 ff. For bibliography see further Page, *Sappho and Alcaeus*, pp. 181 f., J. Svennung, *Catulls Bildersprache*, 1945, p. 94 n. 75, V. Pöschl, *Bibliographie zur antiken Bildersprache*, 1964, pp. 561 f., F. Fuhrmann, *Les Images de Plutarque*, 1964, pp. 234 ff.

Such, then, is the literary background to Horace's ode; the historical background is more difficult to determine. Porphyrio referred the poem to the campaign of Philippi (43–42), ps.-Acro to the period before the war against Sextus Pompeius (38–36); as none of Horace's other odes can be placed nearly as early, both dates are very unlikely. Others suggest a date following the defeat of Sextus Pompeius, and this seems much more possible. However, the seventh epode may belong to this period (note 3 *Neptuno super*, which seems to refer to the naval war of 36); and its mood of disgust, so strongly contrasted with the patriotism of our ode, might suggest some interval between the two poems. Yet if we move down to 33 and 32, when the war of Actium was impending, it is unlikely that Horace would have taken so despondent a view of the coming conflict.

Another date to be considered is 29 B.C. (compare the atmosphere of foreboding at the beginning of 1. 2 and in *Georgics* 1. 498 ff.). About that time Octavian implausibly pretended that he was contemplating abdication (Suet. *Aug.* 28. 1), and the news was greeted with alarm by his partisans. It is a singular circumstance that in the speech that Dio assigns to Maecenas on that occasion the image of the Ship of State is developed (52. 16. 3–4): καὶ διὰ ταῦθ᾽ ἡ πόλις ἡμῶν, ὥσπερ ὁλκὰς μεγάλη καὶ πλήρης ὄχλου παντοδαποῦ χωρὶς κυβερνήτου, πολλὰς ἤδη γενεὰς ἐν κλύδωνι πολλῷ φερομένη σαλεύει τε καὶ ᾄττει δεῦρο κἀκεῖσε, καθάπερ ἀνερμάτιστος οὖσα. μήτ᾽ οὖν χειμαζομένην ἔτ᾽ αὐτὴν περιίδῃς, ὁρᾷς γὰρ ὡς ὑπέραντλός ἐστι, μήτε περὶ ἕρμα περιρραγῆναι ἐάσῃς, σαθρὰ γάρ ἐστι καὶ οὐδένα ἔτι χρόνον ἀντίσχειν δυνήσεται. It would be very surprising if Dio had used Horace's poem either directly or indirectly; one may note that ὑπέραντλος is derived from Alcaeus himself. The possibility must be considered that Maecenas mentioned the Ship in some pamphlet which has influenced both Horace and Dio. Yet it must be admitted that the speech in Dio is a rhetorical composition which shows no other sign of historical foundation (cf. P. M. Meyer, *De Maecenatis oratione a Dione ficta*, 1891, F. G. B. Millar, *A Study of Cassius Dio*, 1964, pp. 102 ff.). The figure of the Ship of State must have been fairly trite in Hellenistic disquisitions on politics; its use by both Horace and Dio in the same context may be simply due to coincidence.

Horace's ode, though elegant as always, is less than a masterpiece. The poet's immediate impulse was not a worsening political situation (which is perhaps why the date is so uncertain), but a perverse determination to write allegory. Alcaeus knew what it was like to be swept along in a black boat: waves rolling down on both sides, the mast-hold awash with sea-water, huge rents in the sails. Horace can supply only a civil servant's inventory of the damage. His personification of the ship is stereotyped and unconvincing, more so than in 1. 3. Above all, Alcaeus gives a sense of immediacy and personal participation; Horace is so detached and disembodied that scholars debate whether he was on board or not. Yet in the last stanza he breaks away from the traditional form and shows serious and convincing attitudes, which could still move later generations. Horace was imitated by Longfellow in 'The Building of the Ship';

this poem was quoted in a private letter from Roosevelt to Churchill
in January 1941 (Churchill, *The Second World War* 3. 24), and subse-
quently repeated by Churchill in a broadcast speech:

> Sail on, O Ship of State!
> Sail on, O Union, strong and great!
> Humanity with all its fears,
> With all the hopes of future years,
> Is hanging breathless on thy fate!

But to those who have not lived through such situations this way of
talking may seem exaggerated.

Metre: Third Asclepiad.

2. fluctus: for the metaphor cf. 2. 7. 15 f. 'te rursus in bellum resorbens /
unda fretis tulit aestuosis', Quint. *inst.* 8. 6. 44 (cited above, p. 179),
Thes.l.L. 6. 1. 947. 54 ff. Palmer proposed *flatus*, but there is no more
difficulty in Horace's phrase than in Swift's imitation (on the state
of Ireland in 1726): 'Unhappy Ship, thou art return'd in Vain; New
Waves shall drive thee to the Deep again'.

o quid agis?: the question expresses anxiety at the rash behaviour
of a friend (cf. 'what are you up to?'). See Ter. *Andr.* 134 (when
Glycerium goes too near the burning pyre) ' "mea Glycerium"
inquit "quid agis? quor te is perditum?" ', Don. ad loc. *'quid agis*
quasi perturbatus', Cic. *Cat.* 1. 27 'si mecum patria, . . . si cuncta
Italia, si omnis res publica loquatur "M. Tulli, quid agis?" ', *Planc.*
33, Quint. *decl.* 338 p. 337 'quid agis, mulier? temere facis', *Thes.l.L.*
1. 1380. 6 ff.

occupa portum: 'make port before it is too late'; *occupa* implies
that the ship must anticipate the worsening waves. So *epist.* 1. 6. 32
'cave ne portus occupet alter': the other merchant must not reach
the market first.

3. nonne vides ut . . .: storms at sea were a set topic in ancient
poetry; cf. W.-H. Friedrich, *Festschrift Bruno Snell*, 1956, pp. 77 ff.,
M. P. O. Morford, *The Poet Lucan*, 1967, pp. 20 ff. Juvenal comments
scornfully 'omnia fiunt / talia tam graviter si quando poetica surgit /
tempestas' (12. 22 ff.).

4. nudum: probably understand *sit*; cf. *serm.* 2. 5. 42 f. 'nonne vides
. . . ut patiens, ut amicis aptus, ut acer?' Some understand *gemat*,
but groaning is associated primarily with mast and yards; moreover,
the loss of oars would diminish rather than increase creaking. The
sentence consists of three cola of increasing length (cf. 1. 21. 1 n.).

5. saucius: cf. Prop. 1. 16. 5 '(ianua) saucia rixis', Ov. *met.* 10. 372 f.,

Claud. 28. 138 'antemnis saucia fractis' (the whole passage is modelled on our own). τιτρώσκω is often used of ships (Hdt. 8. 18, Thuc. 4. 14. 1, etc.); cf. also Liv. 37. 24. 8 'multis ictibus vulnerata navis erat' (a Polybian passage).

6. antemnae: 'the yard' (κεραῖαι), i.e. the long cross-beams at the top of the mast to which the sail was attached. 'Each yard was formed of two spars lashed together, so as to avoid the waste of timber in tapering the thicker end of a single spar to balance with the thinner end' (C. Torr, *Ancient Ships*, 1894, p. 78). The *antemnae* are vividly portrayed on the tomb of Naevoleia Tyche at Pompeii (Torr, fig. 26 = D.–S. 4. 39 = Baumeister 3. 1619). Naturally they were vulnerable in a storm; cf. Plaut. *trin.* 837 'ruere antemnas, scindere vela'.

gemant: for the groaning of a ship's tackle under strain, cf. 3. 29. 57 f., Pacuv. *trag.* 336, Virg. *Aen.* 1. 87, Ov. *trist.* 1. 4. 9 f. 'pinea texta sonant, pulsi stridore rudentes, / ingemit et nostris ipsa carina malis', Sil. 17. 255 ff., Plin. *epist.* 9. 26. 4. The Romans wrongly connected *rudens* 'a rope' with *rudere* 'to bellow' (Isid. *orig.* 19. 4. 1).

There is nothing unusual about the verb of sound following *vides*; cf. Aug. *conf.* 10. 35. 54 'dicimus autem non solum "vide quid luceat" . . . sed etiam "vide quid sonet", "vide quid oleat", "vide quid sapiat", "vide quam durum sit"'. The turn of phrase is particularly easy as a visual scene has preceded; cf. Call. *h.* 2. 4 f. οὐχ ὁράᾳς· ἐπένευσεν ὁ Δήλιος ἡδύ τι φοῖνιξ / ἐξαπίνης, ὁ δὲ κύκνος ἐν ἠέρι καλὸν ἀείδει, Lucr. 1. 255 f., Virg. *Aen.* 4. 490 f. Elsewhere only the verb of hearing is expressed (*carm.* 3. 10. 5 ff.). See further Friedrich on Catull. 62. 9, Norden on Virg. *Aen.* 6. 256 ff.

funibus: the ship has lost its strengthening cables in the storm (and not merely sailed without them): *sine funibus* seems to describe a mishap, like *nudum remigio* and *saucius*. The ancients used ropes (sometimes called ὑποζώματα) to strengthen the fabric of their ships. These were attached beforehand in the case of warships (Torr, p. 42 nn. 102 and 103). But sometimes emergency measures were taken even while the ship was still at sea; cf. *act. apost.* 27. 16 βοηθείαις ἐχρῶντο ὑποζωννύντες τὸ πλοῖον, App. *civ.* 5. 91. 383.

The method of attachment is uncertain, and three main possibilities come under consideration. 1. Stem and stern may have been joined by cables down the middle of the ship. See especially Pl. *rep.* 616 c (the myth of Er) εἶναι γὰρ τοῦτο τὸ φῶς σύνδεσμον τοῦ οὐρανοῦ οἷον τὰ ὑποζώματα τῶν τριηρῶν, οὕτω πᾶσαν συνέχον τὴν περιφοράν; as this light is described above as 'straight, like a pillar' (φῶς εὐθύ, οἷον κίονα), one naturally thinks of a rope down the middle rather than round the circumference (though a combination of both methods is an obvious possibility; cf. Adam's note). This view is supported by

Athenaeus, *de machinis* (ed. Wescher, p. 24), who talks of 'under-girding' to describe the attachment of a rope lengthwise to a battering-ram: ὑποζώννυται δὲ ὅλος ὁ κριὸς ὅπλοις ὀκταδακτύλοις τρισί (cf. the parallel passage in Vitr. 10. 15. 6 'ita religati quemadmodum navis a puppi ad proram continetur'). For other evidence for this kind of cable cf. Ap. Rhod. 1. 367 ff. νῆα δ' ἐπικρατέως Ἄργου ὑπο-θημοσύνῃσιν | ἔζωσαν πάμπρωτον ἐυστρεφεῖ ἔνδοθεν ὅπλῳ | τεινάμενοι ἑκάτερθεν, Isid. *orig.* 19. 4. 4 'tormentum funis in navibus longis (Brewster, *longus* codd.) qui a prora ad puppim extenditur quo magis constringantur'. The device is not represented on Greek or Roman works of art, yet for an excellent Egyptian illustration cf. Torr, op. cit., fig. 4–5. It may be objected that the prefix of ὑπόζωμα does not suit this theory, yet however one explains the name, the evidence for such internal strengthening cables is incontrovertible.

2. Some authorities believe that the ὑποζώματα ran horizontally round the outside of the ships. The prefix is compatible with this view, as the rowing deck of an ancient warship projected outwards; ὑπαλοιφή is paint for the outside of the hull (Morrison, cited below). An important argument in favour of this theory is found in the measurements of a (fictitious) Egyptian ship, cited from Callixinus by Athenaeus (203 e–204 a); this was said to be 280 cubits long, 38 cubits broad, with twelve ὑποζώματα each of 600 cubits.

3. From the prefix of ὑπόζωμα one might naturally assume that the cable ran under the keel, holding the planks in like the hoop on a barrel. This process was known to English seamen as 'frapping'; Macleane quotes Captain Back, describing an Arctic voyage in 1837: 'A length of the stream chain-cable was passed under the bottom of the ship four feet before the mizen-mast, hove tight by the capstan, and finally immovably fixed to six ring-bolts on the quarter-deck. The effect was at once manifested by a great diminution in the working of the parts already mentioned, and in a less agreeable way by impeding her rate of sailing.' For this last reason it seems inconceivable that Athenian warships were permanently equipped with cables of this kind. Moreover, it would have been impossible to launch ships with the cables already in position.

For further details see Torr, op. cit., pp. 41 ff., F. Brewster, *HSPh* 34, 1923, 63 ff., *RE* Suppl. 4. 776 ff., Suppl. 5. 944 f., H. J. Cadbury in *The Beginnings of Christianity, Part I, The Acts of the Apostles*, edited by F. J. Foakes Jackson and K. Lake 5, 1933, pp. 345 ff., J. S. Morrison and R. T. Williams, *Greek Oared Ships, 900–322 B.C.*, 1968, pp. 294 ff.

7. **carinae**: if the first explanation given above of *funes* is correct, *carinae* may refer to the fore and aft sections of the keel, which would

be held together by a rope down the middle of the ship. A reference to several ships would make havoc of the metaphor. A 'plural for singular' (K.–S. 1. 84) would perhaps be inappropriate in this detailed inventory, where one expects plurals to mean what they say.

If the 'round-the-keel' explanation of *funes* is accepted the above interpretation of *carinae* might still be valid. On the other hand if the 'round-the-sides' explanation is preferred *carinae* presents difficulties. One could perhaps defend it by Sidon. *epist.* 8. 12. 5 'pandi carinarum ventres abiegnarum trabium textu pulpitabuntur'; there the word seems to mean 'sides'. But on this, and indeed any, hypothesis there is much to be said for the conjecture *cavernae* (considered, but not read, by Orelli). This word can refer to the ribs of a ship (and not just the empty space which they enclose). Cf. Lucr. 2. 553 f. 'disiectare solet magnum mare transtra cavernas / antemnas proram malos tonsasque natantis', Cic. *de orat.* 3. 180 'quid tam in navigio necessarium quam latera, quam cavernae (carinae *codd. dett.*), quam prora, quam puppis, quam antemnae, quam vela, quam mali?', Stat. *Theb.* 5. 389 'abiunctis regemunt tabulata cavernis', Serv. auct. *Aen.* 2. 19 'alii fustes curvos navium quibus extrinsecus tabulae adfiguntur cavernas appellarunt', *CGL* 5. 176. 19 'cavernas caverne proprie latera navis dicuntur', *Thes.l.L.* 3. 646. 10 ff.

8. imperiosius: 'too peremptory'. Some interpret 'if the sea turns more peremptory'; but the sentence is more vivid if Horace describes a present situation.

10. di: this should refer like *malus, lintea*, etc., to a part of the boat. Horace means the images of the gods on the stern, the so-called *tutela*; distinguish the figure-head on the prow, which often represented the ship's name. Cf. Eur. *IA* 239 ff. χρυσέαις δ᾽ εἰκόσιν κατ᾽ ἄκρα Νηρῆδες ἕστασαν θεαί, / πρύμναις σῆμ᾽ Ἀχιλλείου στρατοῦ, Virg. *Aen.* 10. 171, Ov. *trist.* 1. 4. 8 'pictos verberat unda deos', Val. Fl. 8. 202 f., Torr, op. cit., p. 67, *RE* Suppl. 5. 934. For an illustration of the Torlonia relief, with a winged figure on the stern, cf. R. Meiggs, *Roman Ostia*, 1960, plate XX (= D.–S. 4. 40). In a storm the projecting image might easily be broken off, to the derision of the cynical; cf. Ov. *am.* 2. 16. 28 'et subventuros auferet unda deos', Pers. 6. 29 f. 'iacet ipse in litore et una / ingentes de puppe dei', Sil. 14. 543 'tutelaeque deum fluitant'.

iterum: with *voces* as much as with *pressa*; if disaster comes a second time the gods will not listen so readily.

pressa: cf. Min. Fel. 28. 4 'si qui infirmior malo pressus et victus Christianum se negasset'. In our passage the word is particularly appropriate as it is sometimes applied to the sinking of ships. Heinsius proposed *prensa*; *prendere* and *deprendere* are often used of the sailor or traveller caught by surprise in a storm (cf. Bentley ad loc.). But *malo* is much less appropriate than *tempestate*.

11. Pontica: cf. 1. 35. 7 n.
   pinus: cf. Theophr. *hist. plant.* 5. 7. 1 ἐλάτη μὲν οὖν καὶ πεύκη καὶ κέδρος, ὡς ἁπλῶς εἰπεῖν, ναυπηγήσιμα. τὰς μὲν γὰρ τριήρεις καὶ τὰ μακρὰ πλοῖα ἐλάτινα ποιοῦσι διὰ κουφότητα, τὰ δὲ στρογγύλα πεύκινα διὰ τὸ ἀσαπές.

12. filia: for the grandiloquent personification cf. Catull. 64. 1 'Peliaco quondam prognatae vertice pinus', Mart. 14. 90. 1 (of a table) 'silvae filia Maurae', Symph. 52 (= *anth. Lat.* 286. 54) 'velox formosae filia silvae', Lycophron 24 αἱ Φαλακραῖαι κόραι (of Paris's ships). The lively Greek fancy often amused itself with the femininity of ships (Fraenkel 157 f.).
   nobilis: genitive.

13. iactes: cf. Ov. *epist.* 17. 51 'quod genus et proavos et regia nomina iactas'. The ship boasts of its distinguished ancestry, like the *phaselus* of Catullus 4. But Horace points out that lineage by itself is useless; for this topic of moralizing cf. Curtius 179 f., G. Highet, *Juvenal the Satirist*, 1954, p. 272.

14. nil . . .: the argument runs 'though you boast of inessential qualities the seaman does not trust them'. Of these inessential qualities lineage is mentioned in the concessive clause, paint in the main clause. At first sight this distribution seems incoherent, yet the technique is characteristic of Horace; cf. 1. 7. 10 n.
   pictis: the word suggests decoration. For other references to the painting of ships cf. Hom. *Il.* 2. 637 νῆες . . . μιλτοπάρῃοι, Virg. *Aen.* 8. 93 'pictasque innare carinas', Torr, op. cit., pp. 35 ff., Bömer on Ov. *fast.* 4. 275, G. Jacopi, *Monumenti Antichi* 39, 1943, 46 ff., especially 66 ff. (he provides a bibliography and illustrations). Sometimes the decoration took the form of an actual picture, especially on the stern (Torr, op. cit., p. 36).
   The paint on ships is sometimes regarded as a sign of empty show, and contrasted with more solid qualities. Cf. Prop. 4. 6. 49 f. 'quodque vehunt prorae Centaurica saxa minantis, / tigna cava et pictos experiere metus', Sen. *epist.* 76. 13: 'navis bona dicitur non quae pretiosis coloribus picta est . . . sed stabilis et firma et iuncturis aquam excludentibus spissa', Luc. 3. 510 ff. 'non robore picto / ornatas decuit fulgens tutela carinas, / sed rudis et qualis procumbit montibus arbor / conseritur, stabilis navalibus area bellis'. The topic is presumably Greek in origin; cf. Greg. Naz. *carm.* 1. 2. 9. 141 ff. (37. 678 f. Migne) μὴ ναῦν μιλτοπάρῃον εὔχροον ἢ παρασήμοις / κάλλεσιν

ἀστράπτουσαν ἄγειν ἐπὶ νῶτα θαλάσσης· / ἀλλ' ἐσθλὴν γόμφοισιν εὔπλοον
εὖ ἀραρυῖαν / χείρεσι ναυπηγοῖο, δι' οἴδματος ὦκα φέρουσαν.

15. tu . . .: 'unless the winds are due a laugh you had better look out'.
In spite of the compressed diction, the sarcastic form of the sentence
belongs to everyday speech. *tu* is peremptory and goes with *cave* (not,
as Heinze suggests, with *debes*). *debes* suggests more strongly than
'owe' the necessity of payment (cf. *ars* 63 'debemur morti nos nostraque') ; for the metaphor cf. γέλωτα ὀφλισκάνειν (Eur. *Med.* 404, Ar.
nub. 1035). For *ludibrium* cf. Luc. 8. 710 'ludibrium pelagi', Claud. 28.
139, Milton, *P.L.* 2. 181 f. 'the sport and prey Of racking whirlwinds'.
Yet here the word means not 'a laughing-stock' but 'mockery'.

16. cave: the sinister brevity suits an old-world oracle; cf. *serm.* 1. 4.
85 'hunc tu, Romane, caveto', Liv. 5. 16. 9 'Romane, aquam Al-
banam cave lacu contineri, cave in mare manare suo flumine sinas',
Hdt. 7. 148. 3 κεφαλὴν πεφύλαξο, Fraenkel 117 f. For absolute *cave* cf.
epod. 6. 11. For other warnings in nautical contexts cf. Archil. 57
A. 7 ἀλλὰ σὺ προμήθεσαι, perhaps Alcaeus 249. 6 f. ἐκ γᾶς χρῆ προΐδην
πλόον / αἴ τις δύναται καὶ παλάμαν ἔχῃ (for the latter cf. Page, *Sappho
and Alcaeus*, pp. 196 f., W. Barner, *Neuere Alkaios-Papyri aus Oxyrhynchos*, 1967, pp. 125 f.).

17. nuper: if the poem belongs to 29, *nuper* refers to the prolonged
anxieties of the period before Actium. If it belongs to 34 the word
refers to the war against Sextus Pompeius. Certainly it cannot
refer to Philippi; the issues of 42 were soon forgotten by the Augustan
poets, and *taedium* suits a frustrated spectator rather than a defeated
participant.

sollicitum . . . taedium: it is relevant that *taedium* is a lover's
word (Tib. 1. 4. 16, Ov. *epist.* 3. 139 'aut si versus amor tuus est in
taedia nostri'). The distinction between *sollicitudo* and *cura* may
seem thin; but the former emphasizes mental agitation, the latter
suggests positive 'caring'. The terse form of Horace's address is
not idiosyncratic or even specifically Roman; cf. Peek, *GV* 720. 2
Εὔτυχος ἡ γονέων ἐλπίς, ἔπειτα γόος.

18. desiderium: a lover's word for his heart's desire; Horace is an
ἐραστὴς τῆς πόλεως (cf. Thuc. 2. 43. 1 with Gomme's note, Wordsworth, *Poems dedicated to National Independence and Liberty* 17. 14
'Felt for thee as a lover or a child'). *desiderium* does not necessarily
imply that the loved one is absent or hard to win. *cura* is also a
lover's word, like μέλημα.

19. nitentes: gleaming treacherously in the bright sun; cf. Byron, *The
Isles of Greece* 'Eternal summer gilds them yet, But all, except their
sun, is set'. However, the adjective is a conventional one, and the

reader should visualize not white-washed villages but (imaginary) marble cliffs. Cf. 3. 28. 14 'fulgentis . . . Cycladas', Virg. *Aen.* 3. 126 'niveamque Parum', Ov. *epist.* 21. 82 'candida Delos', Antip. Thess. *anth. P.* 9. 421. 5 f. ἡ τότε λευκὴ / Δῆλος, Stat. *Theb.* 5. 182 f., Dionys. Perieg. 530, Sedul. *epist.* 2 p. 171 'Cycladas nitentes' (*ingentes* codd.).

20. Cycladas: the Cyclades were and are notorious for their winds. Cf. Liv. 36. 43. 1 'est ventosissima regio inter Cycladas fretis alias maioribus alias minoribus divisas', Antip. Thess. *anth. P.* 7. 639. 1 f. πᾶσα θάλασσα θάλασσα. τί Κυκλάδας ἢ στενὸν Ἕλλης / κῦμα καὶ Ὀξείας ἠλεὰ μεμφόμεθα;, Stat. *Ach.* 1. 389 f.

The specific mention of a particular set of islands is a little surprising. The Cyclades could not easily have been introduced into Alcaeus's ship-poem; in any case they were rather remote from his sphere of operations. A poet like Archilochus, who lived in the Cyclades, would hardly say 'avoid the Cyclades', though he could have mentioned some notorious reef. To use the Cyclades as a whole to typify dangerous rocks sounds the mark of a literary man who did not belong there, either an Alexandrian or Horace himself.

15. PASTOR CVM TRAHERET

[L. Alfonsi, *Aegyptus* 34, 1954, 215 ff.; Fraenkel 188 ff.; R. Helm, *Philologus* 90, 1935, 364 f.; T. Sinko, *Eos* 29, 1926, 135 ff.]

1–5. When Paris was carrying off Helen to Troy, Nereus prophesied: 5–8. 'Ill-omened is your marriage, and a Grecian host will punish it. 9–12. How much Trojan suffering you are responsible for. 13–20. Even now Pallas is arming against you, and Venus's help will do you no good; sometime you will be laid low. 21–32. The Greek heroes will press hard upon you, and you will run from Diomede like a panic-stricken stag. 33–36. Achilles's anger will adjourn Troy's fall for a time, but the date of her destruction is fixed.'

Porphyrio comments 'hac ode Bacchylidem imitatur. nam ut ille Cassandram facit vaticinari futura belli Troiani ita hic Proteum' (a slip for *Nereum*). Other prophecies to Paris are found as early as the *Cypria*; cf. Procl. *chrest.* 1 ἔπειτα δὲ Ἀφροδίτης ὑποθεμένης ναυπηγεῖται. καὶ Ἕλενος περὶ τῶν μελλόντων προθεσπίζει. καὶ Ἀφροδίτη Αἰνείαν συμπλεῖν αὐτῷ κελεύει. καὶ Κασσάνδρα περὶ τῶν μελλόντων προδηλοῖ. Cassandra's prophecy is also given by Pindar in his Eighth Paean (8a. 10 ff.) : σπεύδοντ᾽, ἔκλαγξέ θ᾽ ἱερ[ᾶς κόρας] / δαιμόνιον κέαρ ὀλοαῖσι στοναχαῖς ἄφαρ ... (the first word may imply that Paris was building his fleet). Euripides's *Alexander* seems to have included a prediction of Cassandra's at the time of Paris's recognition (cf. Nauck, p. 374). For other prophecies cf. Sinko, loc. cit. Horace's poem is unusual in two respects: the prophecy is assigned to Nereus and it takes place after the Rape.

Among the Alexandrian and Roman poets the prophecy was a familiar literary motif (Kroll 220–2, L. Hensel, *Weissagungen in der alexandrinischen Poesie*, Diss. Giessen, 1908); one thinks of Lycophron's *Alexandra*, and of the predictions of the Parcae in Catullus 64 and of Thetis in Stat. *Ach.* 1. 31 ff. Yet apart from a few idiomatic presents and a slight obscurity in the last stanza, Horace's ode shows none of the oracular manner cultivated by Hellenistic poets. It owes much more to a common type of early Greek lyric, the pastiche of epic narrative (Kroll 239 f.); see, for instance, the rambling dactyloid songs by Sappho on the wedding of Hector and Andromache (44), and by Ibycus on the Trojan war (282 a). In view of Porphyrio's note, it is particularly significant that Bacchylides wrote 'dithyrambs' on epic themes, which often contained speeches. One dithyramb that has been partly preserved in papyrus is called Ἀντηνορίδαι ἢ Ἑλένης ἀπαίτησις; it ends with a speech by Menelaus to the Trojans hinting at their doom (15. 50 ff.):

> ῏Ω Τρῶες ἀρηίφιλοι,
> Ζεὺς ὑψιμέδων ὃς ἅπαντα δέρκεται
> οὐκ αἴτιος θνατοῖς μεγάλων ἀχέων,
> ἀλλ' ἐν μέσῳ κεῖται κιχεῖν
> πᾶσιν ἀνθρώποις Δίκαν ἰθεῖαν, ἁγνᾶς
> Εὐνομίας ἀκόλουθον καὶ πινυτᾶς Θέμιτος.

The triviality of the genre can be seen from Alcaeus's sketchy narrative of the Trojan war (283. 3 ff.):

> κἈλένας ἐν στήθ[ε]σιν [ἐ]πτ[όαισε
> θῦμον Ἀργείας, Τροΐω δ' ὐ]π' ἀν[δρος
> ἐκμάνεισα ξ[εν]ναπάτα 'πὶ π[όντον
> ἕσπετο νᾶι.

(The poem trails on for several more stanzas.) For other instances of such naïve balladry cf. Alcaeus 42, Page, *Sappho and Alcaeus*, pp. 278 ff.

Many editors have found it difficult to believe that Horace wrote a poem that contains no reference, however oblique, to the contemporary world. Some have denied his authorship altogether; a more common move is to regard the poem as an allegory, like 1. 14. On this view, Paris and Helen stand for, or are at any rate intended to

make the reader think of, Antony and Cleopatra (for the comparison
of Antony with Paris cf. Plut. *comp. Dem. et Ant.* 3. 4 τέλος δέ, ὡς ὁ
Πάρις, ἐκ τῆς μάχης ἀποδρὰς εἰς τοὺς ἐκείνης κατεδύετο κόλπους· μᾶλλον
δὲ ὁ μὲν Πάρις ἡττηθεὶς ἔφυγεν εἰς τὸν θάλαμον, Ἀντώνιος δὲ Κλεοπάτραν
διώκων ἔφυγε καὶ προήκατο τὴν νίκην). Yet, if this is so, it is remarkable
that Horace has concentrated his attention so exclusively on Paris
and that he is so tender of Helen. Earlier authors, notably Alcaeus,
gave him plenty of precedents for assailing her as responsible for the
woes of Troy (cf. especially Alcaeus 42). If he had been concerned to
point a contemporary moral, he could easily have turned to abuse of
Helen ; his failure to do so is a strong indication that he had no such
thought.

Rather, the genesis of the poem is a literary one, the desire to
emulate the Greek lyrists in their rehandling of literary topics. One
cannot say how closely Horace imitated any particular ode of
Bacchylides, but he seems to have recaptured successfully the tepid
elegance of the Bacchylidean style. One may note the pervasive
attempt at epic colouring, and in particular the use of conventional
Homeric epithets (for Greek practice see A. E. Harvey, *CQ* N.S. 7,
1957, 206 ff.). The abruptness of the transitions and the dislocation of
the normal order are equally characteristic of the genre (the prophecy
of Paris's downfall precedes the account of the heroes who will
accomplish it). Yet the ode has some modern notes. It is more
allusive than Greek lyric, more rhetorical, and less picturesque. It
attempts one colloquialism (32 *tuae*) and three technicalities (15
carmina divides, 31 *sublimi anhelitu*, 33 *diem proferet*). On the other
hand, we find none of the Hellenistic intricacy of structure that
appears in Horace's two other narrative poems (3. 11 on Hypermestra, 3. 27 on Europa).

The ode is more persevering than successful ; Horace's ambition
was no doubt fired by the *Iliad* and archaic lyric, but here at least
his imagination seems to have been left untouched. The second
epistle of Book 1 shows what was real and deep in his appreciation ;
he could use a moralized Homer to deploy his own resources of
wisdom and urbanity. Our ode has, in contrast, hardly anything to
say. Moreover, the various scenes Horace chooses to depict are not
sharply realized ; it is characteristic that the most vivid stanza
presents the picture of an animal, not of an ancient hero (29 ff.).
Johnson made a significant comparison between our poem and
Gray's *The Bard*: 'There is in *The Bard* more force, more thought,
and more variety. But to copy is less than to invent, and the copy
has been unhappily produced at the wrong time. The fiction of
Horace was to the Romans credible ; but its revival disgusts us with
apparent and unconquerable falsehood' (*Lives of the Poets, Gray* 40).

In fact, Johnson's criticisms of Gray could equally be applied to Horace's own poem.

Metre: Second Asclepiad.

1. **pastor**: βουκόλος, 'herdsman', not 'shepherd'. The noun is sufficient to designate Paris, especially as Ida is mentioned in the context; cf. Bion 2. 10 f. ἅρπασε τὰν Ἑλέναν ποθ' ὁ βωκόλος, ἆγε δ' ἐς Ἴδαν, Cic. Att. 1. 18. 3, Prop. 2. 2. 13 f. 'divae quas pastor viderat olim / Idaeis tunicas ponere verticibus', Octavia 774, Stat. silv. 1. 2. 43 'Dardania pastor temerarius Ida', 1. 2. 214, Ach. 1. 20 f. Homer had told of the goddesses' coming to Paris's steading (Il. 24. 29 f.). Euripides gives a romantic picture of the solitary herdsman (Andr. 281 ff. βοτῆρά τ' ἀμφὶ μονότροπον νεανίαν / ἐρῆμόν θ' / ἑστιοῦχον αὐλάν, IA 180 f., 573 ff., 1291 f.). The theme was also a favourite with vase painters; cf. Roscher 3. 1582 ff. For a recent and admirably illustrated account of the development of the story cf. T. C. W. Stinton, Euripides and the Judgment of Paris, 1965.

traheret: ἥρπαζεν, cf. Hom. Il. 3. 443 f. οὐδ' ὅτε σε πρῶτον Λακεδαίμονος ἐξ ἐρατεινῆς / ἔπλεον ἁρπάξας ἐν ποντοπόροισι νέεσσι, Hdt. 2. 118. 2 Ἑλένης ἁρπαγήν. The word does not exclude Helen's consent.

navibus Idaeis: Paris made ready a fleet for the seizure of Helen (Hom. Il. 3. 444, 5. 62, 22. 115). In the Cypria it was built by Paris himself at Aphrodite's suggestion (Procl. chrest. 1); cf. Eur. Hec. 631 ff. Ἰδαίαν ὅτε πρῶτον ὕλαν / Ἀλέξανδρος εἰλατίναν / ἐτάμεθ', Ov. epist. 16. 105 ff., Sidon. carm. 9. 117 ff., RE 18. 4. 1502. According to Hellanicus, the building of the fleet was itself a defiance of an oracle (FGrH 4 F 142 Ἑλλάνικος δέ φησι χρησμὸν δοθῆναι τοῖς Τρωσὶν ἀπέχεσθαι μὲν ναυτιλίας, γεωργίᾳ δὲ προσέχειν, μὴ τῇ θαλάσσῃ χρώμενοι ἀπολέσωσιν ἑαυτούς τε καὶ τὴν πόλιν).

2. **Helenen**: Horace uses the Greek form of the accusative here, but the Latin Helenam at serm. 1. 3. 107 (cf. Neue–Wagener 1. 72). The difference of genre is significant.

perfidus hospitam: for the collocation, which heightens the emphasis of both epithets, cf. 3. 7. 13 'Proetum mulier perfida credulum'. The whole phrase renders Paris's Greek epithet ξεναπάτης (cf. Alcaeus 283. 5 above, Ibycus 282. 10, Eur. Tro. 866).

Paris's breach of hospitality was a serious aggravation of his offence; cf. 3. 3. 25 f. 'Lacaenae . . . adulterae / famosus hospes', Hom. Il. 13. 626 f. οἳ μευ κουριδίην ἄλοχον καὶ κτήματα πολλὰ / μὰψ οἴχεσθ' ἀνάγοντες, ἐπεὶ φιλέεσθε παρ' αὐτῇ, Aesch. Ag. 61 f., 401 f., 748, Hdt. 2. 115. 4, Prop. 2. 34. 7 'hospes (?) in hospitium Menelao venit adulter', Ov. epist. 8. 73, 13. 44, 17. 3 f., G. Glotz, La Solidarité de la famille dans le droit criminel en Grèce, 1904, p. 317 n. 3.

3. **ingrato**: the juxtaposition of the epithet with *celeres* suggests that it is the winds themselves that dislike their enforced idleness; cf. Virg. *Aen.* 1. 55 f. 'illi indignantes magno cum murmure montis / circum claustra fremunt'.

obruit . . . ventos: a respectful εὐφημία is expected when a prophet is uttering. The power to check the winds is given to Nereus in *Orph. h. 23*. 5 f. ὃς κλονέεις Δηοῦς ἱερὸν βάθρον, ἡνίκα πνοιὰς / ἐννυχίοις κευθμῶσιν ἐλαυνομένας ἀποκλείῃς. See further 1. 12. 29 n.

4. **fera . . . fata**: 'dire doom'. Yet *fata* keeps something of its original sense of 'utterance' (from *fari*); cf. Virg. *georg.* 4. 452 (of Proteus) 'sic fatis ora resolvit', *Aen.* 1. 261 f. 'fabor enim . . . et volvens fatorum arcana movebo'. For *fata canere* cf. *serm.* 1. 9. 29 f., Cic. *div.* 2. 98. The alliterative and slightly unusual form *fera fata* may be a borrowing from an old Roman poet; cf. also Tiberian. 4. 10 f. 'fera turbine certo / rerum fata rapi', Avien. *Arat.* 458 'natae fera fata retundunt'.

5. **Nereus**: Like other sea-gods (Proteus, Glaucus, Thetis, Triton), Nereus had the gift of prophecy. Hesiod speaks of his truthfulness as well as his mildness (*th.* 233 ff.): Νηρέα τ' ἀψευδέα καὶ ἀληθέα γείνατο Πόντος / πρεσβύτατον παίδων· αὐτὰρ καλέουσι γέροντα, / οὕνεκα νημερτής τε καὶ ἤπιος (cf. West ad loc.). After turning himself into many shapes he revealed to Hercules where to find the apples of the Hesperides; cf. Pherecydes, *FGrH* 3 F 16 (= schol. Ap. Rhod. 4. 1396), Apollod. 2. 5. 11. He gave instructions in prophecy to Theonoe (Eur. *Hel.* 13 ff.) and Glaucus was his προφήτης (Eur. *Or.* 363 f.).

Horace's lines are imitated by Spenser (*F.Q.* 4. 11. 18 f.). See also Goethe, *Faust* 8110 ff. (Nereus speaking):

> Wie hab' ich Paris väterlich gewarnt
> Eh sein Gelüst ein fremdes Weib umgarnt!
> Am griechischen Ufer stand er kühnlich da,
> Ihm kündet' ich, was ich im Geiste sah:
> Die Lüfte qualmend, überströmend Roth,
> Gebälke glühend, unten Mord und Tod:
> Troja's Gerichtstag, rhythmisch fest gebannt,
> Jahrtausenden so schrecklich als gekannt.

mala ducis avi domum: the poets use *avi, alite* (3. 3. 61), or *pennis* instead of the technical *auspiciis*; for the similar use of ὄρνις see Jebb on Soph. *OT* 520. *domum ducere* means 'to marry', whence the common *uxorem ducere* (*Thes.l.L.* 5. 1. 2142. 51 ff.). Horace is referring to the *auspicia nuptiarum*; cf. Catull. 61. 19 f. 'bona cum bona / nubet alite virgo', Pease on Cic. *div.* 1. 28. His phrase recalls *epod.* 10. 1 'mala soluta navis exit alite', where *mala* is similarly emphatic at the beginning, *epod.* 16. 13 f. 'secunda . . . alite'; for another phrase modelled on the tenth epode cf. 9 n. The conjunction of these two reminiscences suggests that our ode is early.

6. repetet: 'reclaim'; the word belongs to civil, criminal, and international law (cf. *res repetundae*). Here, as elsewhere in Latin, it is used sardonically with *milite*; cf. Ov. *epist.* 16. 341 (Paris to Helen) 'tot prius abductis ecqua est repetita per arma?', *carm. poet. min.* 5. 77. 65 'Graecia coniurat repetendam mille carinis'. In Greek ἀπαιτεῖν is repeatedly used in the Helen story of the peaceful negotiations for Helen's recovery; cf. Hdt. 1. 3. 2 ἀπαιτέειν τε Ἑλένην (5. 85. 1), Proclus, *chrest.* 1 (summary of the *Cypria*) τὴν Ἑλένην καὶ τὰ χρήματα ἀπαιτοῦντες. Sophocles wrote a play called Ἑλένης ἀπαίτησις, and this was also the Alexandrian sub-title of Bacchylides's *Antenoridae*. See further *RE* 18. 4. 1508 f.

7. coniurata: for the oath taken by Agamemnon's allies cf. Hom. *Il.* 2. 286 ff. οὐδέ τοι ἐκτελέουσιν ὑπόσχεσιν ἥνπερ ὑπέσταν / ἐνθάδ᾽ ἔτι στείχοντες ἀπ᾽ Ἄργεος ἱπποβότοιο, / Ἴλιον ἐκπέρσαντ᾽ εὐτείχεον ἀπονέεσθαι, Virg. *Aen.* 4. 425 f. 'non ego cum Danais Troianam exscindere gentem / Aulide iuravi', Ov. *am.* 2. 18. 1 f., Stat. *Ach.* 1. 35 f., Paus. 2. 22. 2. A Roman reader would no doubt think of the *sacramentum* administered to the Roman soldier at the beginning of a campaign. In particular he might remember the oath of loyalty to Octavian taken before the war of Actium; cf. *res gest.* 25. 2 'iuravit in mea verba tota Italia', Suet. *Aug.* 17. 2 'coniurandi cum tota Italia'.

rumpere: the verb goes more naturally with *nuptias* than with *regnum*; yet cf. Sen. *Herc. f.* 79 'Titanas ausos rumpere imperium Iovis'.

8. vetus: cf. Aesch. *Ag.* 710 Πριάμου πόλις γεραιά, Virg. *Aen.* 2. 363 'urbs antiqua ruit multos dominata per annos'.

9. heu . . . : cf. Virg. *Aen.* 8. 537 'heu quantae miseris clades Laurentibus instant', Ov. *epist.* 5. 120 (Cassandra of Paris's ship) 'heu quantum Phrygii sanguinis illa vehit', Drac. *rapt. Hel.* 628 ff.

quantus . . . sudor: cf. *epod.* 10. 15 'o quantus instat navitis sudor tuis', Hom. *Il.* 2. 388 ff. ἱδρώσει μέν τευ τελαμών . . . ἱδρώσει δέ τευ ἵππος (note the anaphora as in our passage), 4. 27 ἱδρῶ θ᾽ ὃν ἵδρωσα μόγῳ, καμέτην δέ μοι ἵπποι, Val. Fl. 5. 287 f. 'manet aegida sudor / et nostros iam sudor equos', Stat. *Theb.* 3. 210 f. 'quantus equis quantusque viris in pulvere crasso / sudor! io quanti crudele rubebitis, amnes!', 9. 150 f. 'subitusque recurrit / sudor equis sudorque viris'. Sweat is quite frequent in epic accounts of the battles of heroes; cf. Hom. *Il.* 16. 109 f., Enn. *ann.* 406, Virg. *Aen.* 9. 812. The collocation of horses and men is likewise Homeric; cf. *Il.* 2. 554 ἵππους τε καὶ ἀνέρας.

10. quanta: we might expect *quot*, but the poets sometimes use quantitative adjectives for numerical ones (a usage that becomes quite ordinary in later Latin); cf. Housman on Manil. 5. 170, Enk on Prop. 1. 5. 10, Shackleton Bailey, *Propertiana*, p. 270, Löfstedt, *Peregrinatio*, p. 147, J. Svennung, *Untersuchungen zu Palladius und zur lateinischen Fach- und Volkssprache*, 1935, pp. 322 ff. In our passage the presence of *quantus sudor* above makes the usage easier.

11. galeam . . . aegida . . . currus: cf. the description of Pallas in Hom. *Il.* 5. 738 ff. ἀμφὶ δ᾽ ἄρ᾽ ὤμοισιν βάλετ᾽ αἰγίδα . . . κρατὶ δ᾽ ἐπ᾽ ἀμφίφαλον κυνέην θέτο . . . ἐς δ᾽ ὄχεα φλογέα ποσὶ βήσετο. Pallas is constantly represented in art with a helmet.

aegida: cf. 3. 4. 57 'sonantem Palladis aegida'. The epithet there suggests that Horace took the aegis to be a shield. The oldest representations show it as a tasselled mantle, covering the breast, shoulders, and back; it could serve as a protection for the extended left arm, and as it had a border of lively looking snakes it could also inspire terror in close fighting (cf. the pictures in D.–S. 1. 102 f.). It was later reduced to the dimensions of a transverse scarf or breast-plate, usually adorned with a Gorgon's head.

12. currus: Athene was worshipped as Ἱππία and Χαλινῖτις, and was said to have invented the chariot; cf. Cic. *nat. deor.* 3. 59 with Pease's note, Farnell 1. 272 f., 408, N. Yalouris, *MH* 7, 1950, pp. 19 ff.

rabiem: the conception of fury as another weapon of war is non-Homeric; cf. Virg. *Aen.* 12. 108 'Aeneas acuit Martem', Ov. *met.* 13. 544 'seque armat et instruit iram'. Homer himself, however, is capable of attaching such an abstract to a list of concrete nouns; cf. *Il.* 4. 447 σὺν δ᾽ ἔβαλον ῥινούς, σὺν δ᾽ ἔγχεα καὶ μένε᾽ ἀνδρῶν. The zeugma gives an edge to the expression and is a mark of heightened style; cf. 1. 35. 33, Sen. *Ag.* 529 f. 'quicquid haut hasta minax, / haut aegide, haut furore Gorgoneo potest', H.–Sz. 833 f. So in English Milton has 'flown with insolence and wine' (*P.L.* 1. 502); later the figure became chiefly mock-heroic and finally facetious.

13. nequiquam . . .: sardonic Homeric humour; cf. *Il.* 3. 54 f. οὐκ ἄν τοι χραίσμῃ κίθαρις τά τε δῶρ᾽ Ἀφροδίτης / ἥ τε κόμη τό τε εἶδος, ὅτ᾽ ἐν κονίῃσι μιγείης, 5. 53 ff., Virg. *Aen.* 12. 52 f. 'longe illi dea mater erit, quae nube fugacem / feminea tegat'.

Veneris . . . ferox: the ἄναλκις θεά rescued Paris from Menelaus in *Il.* 3. 380 ff. τὸν δ᾽ ἐξήρπαξ᾽ Ἀφροδίτη / ῥεῖα μάλ᾽, ὥς τε θεός, ἐκάλυψε δ᾽ ἄρ᾽ ἠέρι πολλῇ, / κὰδ δ᾽ εἷσ᾽ ἐν θαλάμῳ εὐώδεϊ κηώεντι. Cf. Paris's boast in *Il.* 3. 439 f. νῦν μὲν γὰρ Μενέλαος ἐνίκησεν σὺν Ἀθήνῃ, / κεῖνον δ᾽ αὖτις ἐγώ· πάρα γὰρ θεοί εἰσι καὶ ἡμῖν, *Il. lat.* 332 ff. 'tristis Alexander "non me superavit Atrides, / o meus ardor" ait, "sed castae Palladis ira. / mox illum nostris succumbere turpiter armis / aspicies, aderitque meo Cytherea labori" '.

ferox means high-spirited, not fierce; so Paris in the *Iliad* is compared to a prancing stallion (6. 506 ff.).

14. pectes: cf. 4. 9. 13 f. (on 20 n.). The Romans thought careful combing of the hair effeminate (cf. Cic. *Cat.* 2. 22, Pers. 1. 15 ff., K. F. Smith on Tib. 1. 8. 9, above, 1. 12. 41 n.); so Juvenal is indignant that Otho carried a mirror in his knapsack (2. 99). Yet it was thought commendable for the Spartans to comb their hair at Thermopylae.

feminis: to be taken with *grata*. For the indiscriminate gallantries implied by the plural cf. Hom. *Il.* 3. 39 γυναιμανές, 11. 385 παρθενοπῖπα.

15. imbelli: cf. 1. 6. 10 n.

carmina divides: an elaborate expression, where the simple 'sing' would convey the sense. Horace may have in mind some technical term of Greek musical or metrical theory, but it is not clear what the precise idea is. (i) διαιρεῖν and similar verbs are used of division into rhythmical units of feet or *cola*; cf. Lucian, *imag.* 14 εὐκαίρῳ τῇ ἄρσει καὶ τῇ θέσει διαμεμετρῆσθαι τὸ ᾆσμα, Dion. Hal. *comp. verb.* 131 p. 85. 7 ff. (of lyric poems) τὰ δὲ κῶλα ἐξ ὧν συνέστηκε περίοδος ἐπὶ πολλῆς ἐξουσίας δέδοται [αὐτοῖς] ποικίλως διαιρεῖν, Plut. *Dem.* 20 (of the drunken Philip) ᾖδε τὴν ἀρχὴν τοῦ Δημοσθένους ψηφίσματος πρὸς πόδα διαιρῶν καὶ ὑποκρούων. The phrase would then mean 'to play rhythmically articulated tunes'. (ii) διαιρεῖν and διαίρεσις are also sometimes used of difference of pitch; cf. Aristoxenus, *elem. harm.* 29 ἀσύνθετον . . . διάστημα . . . ὃ ἡ φωνὴ μελῳδοῦσα μὴ δύναται διαιρεῖν εἰς διαστήματα . . . So *carmina divides* might mean 'give songs their various notes'. (iii) Perhaps Horace simply means that one part of the song is marked off from another by an intermezzo on the lyre. For a somewhat similar use cf. schol. Ar. *pax* 775 οὐ γὰρ διῄρηνται ἀλλ' ἐχόμεναι εἰσὶν ἀλλήλων (i.e. the strophe and antistrophe are not separated by an epirrhema).

Some editors do not acknowledge the technical flavour of the term, and explain that Paris divided his songs among a number of women; cf. 1. 36. 5 ff. 'caris multa sodalibus / nulli plura tamen dividit oscula / quam dulci Lamiae'.

It is an interesting coincidence that 'division' was used from the sixteenth century of the dividing of a succession of long notes into several short ones; cf. Shakespeare, *1 Henry IV*, III. i. 207 ff. 'ditties . . . Sung by a fair queen . . . With ravishing division to her lute', *OED* s.v. 'division' 7, 'divide' 11. But there is no evidence that this was an ancient sense of the term.

16. thalamo: after the duel with Menelaus, Aphrodite settles Paris in his bedroom (Hom. *Il.* 3. 382, quoted at 13 n.). Later writers were shocked; cf. Plut. *quaest. conv.* 655 a ὡς οὐκ ἀνδρὸς ἀλλὰ μοιχοῦ λυσσῶντος οὖσαν τὴν μεθημερινὴν ἀκρασίαν (so *audiend. poet.* 18 f.). For this moralizing attitude to Paris (which Homer does not express explicitly) see F. Buffière, *Les Mythes d'Homère et la pensée grecque*, 1956, pp. 330 ff. For the thought here cf. Solon 3. 28 f. (of δημόσιον κακόν) ὑψηλὸν δ᾽ ὑπὲρ ἕρκος ὑπέρθορεν, ηὗρε δὲ πάντως, / εἰ καί τις φεύγων ἐν μυχῷ ᾖ θαλάμου, Dem. 18. 97, Prop. 3. 18. 25 f.

gravis: the epithet renders the description of the spear in Homer as βριθὺ μέγα στιβαρόν (*Il.* 5. 746 and elsewhere).

17. calami: for Cretan archery in archaic times cf. Hom. *Il.* 10. 260, 23. 850 ff., A. M. Snodgrass, *Early Greek Armour and Weapons*, 1964, pp. 142 ff. For later evidence see Pind. *P.* 5. 41 Κρῆτες τοξοφόροι, Pl. *leg.* 625 d, Call. *ep.* 37. 1 ff., Virg. *ecl.* 10. 59 f. 'Partho torquere Cydonia cornu / spicula', *Aen.* 5. 306 f., Luc. 3. 185 f., Plin. *nat.* 16. 161, Paus. 1. 23. 4, Prud. *cath.* 5. 52, A. Magariños, *Emerita* 8, 1940, 87 f. Here, as elsewhere in Roman poetry, the epithet is merely conventional. *Cnosii* is the right spelling; after the short open vowel *Gnosii* is unlikely for Horace's odes (Housman, *CQ* 22, 1928, 7).

18. strepitum: ὅμαδον, κύδοιμον.

19. Aiacem: not the great Ajax but the son of Oileus; his epithet here recalls Homer's Ὀιλῆος ταχὺς Αἴας (cf. also *Il.* 14. 521 f.). The mention of the fastest runner on the Greek side heightens the picture of Paris's cowardice.

tamen . . . serus: 'though late, yet sometime'; cf. Virg. *ecl.* 1. 27 'libertas quae sera tamen respexit inertem', Tib. 1. 9. 4 'sera tamen tacitis Poena venit pedibus', Prop. 3. 15. 35 'sera tamen pietas: natis est cognitus error', Stat. *Theb.* 5. 181 'sera tamen mundo venerunt astra'. For the order here cf. Housman on Manil. 4. 413, Luc. 1. 333; as he remarks, 'talia passim fallunt interpretes, qui interdum admoniti repugnant, ut Meinekio Peerlkampius ad Hor. carm. I 15 19'. The idiom answers the Greek ὀψὲ μὲν ἀλλ᾽ ἔθανον (*anth. P.* 7. 349. 2); cf. also such expressions as Soph. *Tr.* 201 ἔδωκας ἡμῖν ἀλλὰ σὺν χρόνῳ χαράν. For the motif 'too late' cf. P. Courcelle, *REL* 38, 1960, 264 ff.

heu: the word expresses Nereus's grief at the tardiness of Paris's punishment. It is true that *heu* can be used to represent the sighs of the person addressed or spoken of, when the emotion of the speaker is quite different; cf. 4. 13. 17 f., *epod.* 15. 23 f. 'heu heu, translatos alio maerebis amores, / ast ego vicissim risero', Prop. 3. 25. 14 'a! speculo rugas increpitante tibi'. Sometimes such a *heu* is joined with *sero* (Prop. 2. 5. 8, Tib. 1. 8. 4); but it would be absurd for Paris to regret that he has died too late.

20. cultus: *cultus* and *crines* are both well-attested readings. Both occur in 4. 9. 13 ff. 'non sola comptos arsit adulteri / crines et aurum vestibus illitum / mirata regalesque cultus / et comites Helene Lacaena'. *adulteri crines* there might seem to support *adulteros crines* here, but in fact it could tell in favour of *cultus*; an easy explanation of the corruption would be an ancient scribe's memory, conscious or subconscious, of *adulteri crines*. The conjunction of either noun with *adulteros* produces a phrase that is recherché but quite legitimate.

In point of sense there is little to help one choose between the two readings. Paris's gorgeousness is a frequent theme; cf. Hom. *Il.* 6. 513 τεύχεσι παμφαίνων ὥς τ' ἠλέκτωρ ἐβεβήκει, Eur. *IA* 73 f. ἀνθηρὸς μὲν εἱμάτων στολῇ, / χρυσῷ τε λαμπρός, βαρβάρῳ χλιδήματι, Ov. *epist.* 16. 193 f. (Paris to Helen) 'cum videas cultus nostra de gente virorum', Apul. *met.* 10. 30. 2 'pulchre indusiatus adulescens', Drac. *Romul.* 8. 482 ff. 'vestibus indutus Tyriis et murice regni . . .'; he is magnificently dressed on the Karlsruhe vase (Roscher 3. 1619). For the conjunction of *cultus* with the rare word *collines* cf. Plaut. *Poen.* 306 'pulcrum ornatum turpes mores peius caeno conlinunt'. Heinze argues that Paris would not wear his gorgeous clothes in battle, but *cultus* can be used of 'get-up' in general, including hair and accoutrements (cf. Val. Fl. 5. 354, Stat. *Theb.* 2. 242, Sil. 15. 694 f. 'gemmiferi spolium cultus auroque rigentes / exuvias'). Even if *adulteros cultus* suggests a dress inappropriate for fighting, this point is not really relevant in a piece of emotive writing that could disregard the realities of Homeric warfare.

Editors generally prefer *crines*, and can cite very relevant passages in its support; cf. Hom. *Il.* 3. 54 f. (on 13 above), 16. 795 f. μιάνθησαν δὲ ἔθειραι / αἵματι καὶ κονίῃσι, 22. 401 f., Pind. *N.* 1. 68 βελέων ὑπὸ ῥιπαῖσι κείνου φαιδίμαν γαίᾳ πεφύρσεσθαι κόμαν, Virg. *Aen.* 12. 98 'foedare in pulvere crines', *Il. lat.* 3. 323 'Iliacoque tuos foedaret pulvere crines'. Cf. also Ar. *Ach.* 849 Κρατῖνος ἀεὶ κεκαρμένος μοιχὸν μιᾷ μαχαίρᾳ.

From the point of view of euphony, the assonance 'adu*lt*eros cu*lt*us pu*lv*ere' seems agreeable; cf. 3. 11. 35 'splendide mendax', Catull. 11. 4 'tunditur unda', Gell. 13. 21(20), Enk on Prop. 2. 8. 16, N. Herescu, *La Poésie latine*, 1960, pp. 82 ff. The rhyme *crines . . . collines* raises doubts (cf. O. Skutsch's paper cited on 1. 1. 6); yet they could be easily resolved by reading *crinis*.

21. exitium: applied to Odysseus because he survived other heroes, stole the Palladium, and was finally responsible for the introduction of the wooden horse into Troy (Hom. *Od.* 8. 494). Cicero drew a moral for Plancus's benefit (*epist.* 10. 13. 2): 'qui enim M. Antonium oppresserit, is bellum confecerit; itaque Homerus non Aiacem nec Achillem, sed Vlixem appellavit πτολιπόρθιον'.

22. genti: the dative is poetical; cf. 2. 1. 13, Hes. *th.* 326 Καδμείοισιν ὄλεθρον, Eur. *Tro.* 814 Λαομέδοντι φόνον, Enn. *scaen.* 46 (= *trag. inc.* 16) 'eum (Paridem) esse exitium Troiae, pestem Pergamo', Plaut. *Bacch.* 944, 947, 1054, Löfstedt, *Syntactica* 1². 195 f. *gentis* is quite as well attested and was preferred by Bentley; cf. Ov. *met.* 13. 500 'exitium Troiae nostrique orbator Achilles', Sen. *Herc. f.* 358 'nostri generis exitium ac lues', *Tro.* 892 f. (of Helen) 'pestis exitium lues / utriusque populi', *dial.* 6. 17. 5 'Dionysius . . . libertatis iustitiae legum exitium'. But the more recherché expression is surely right.

Nestora: Agamemnon says of him αἰ γὰρ Ζεῦ τε πάτερ καὶ Ἀθηναίη καὶ Ἄπολλον / τοιοῦτοι δέκα μοι συμφράδμονες εἶεν Ἀχαιῶν· / τῷ κε τάχ᾽ ἠμύσειε πόλις Πριάμοιο ἄνακτος (Hom. *Il.* 2. 371 ff.). Cicero recalled the passage in *Cato* 31 'dux ille Graeciae nusquam optat ut Aiacis similis habeat decem, sed ut Nestoris'. The ruins of an important thirteenth-century palace complete with Linear B Tablets have been excavated by Blegen north of Navarino, the Pylos of the battle of 425 B.C. (cf. A. J. E. Wace and F. H. Stubbings, *A Companion to Homer*, 1962, pp. 422 ff.).

24. te: this reading has rather better support than the variant *et* and seems more vigorous in sense (*te* is repeated in 27). It is true that after the plural *urgent* one might expect *et* rather than a second *te*; but the force of this argument is probably destroyed by the presence of *impavidi*. However, it remains possible, even if not likely, that Horace wrote *et*; for a glyconic beginning with a trochee cf. the last line of this poem. In that case *te* would be a metrical interpolation by an ancient editor (cf. 1. 13. 6 n.).

Sthenelus: the son of Capaneus; in the *Iliad* he is not shown fighting himself, but drives Diomede's chariot.

sciens . . .: cf. Hom. *Il.* 5. 549 μάχης εὖ εἰδότε πάσης. The whole phrase resembles Hom. *Od.* 9. 49 f. ἐπιστάμενοι μὲν ἀφ᾽ ἵππων / ἀνδράσι μάρνασθαι καὶ ὅθι χρὴ πεζὸν ἐόντα.

25. imperitare: epic in tone; cf. *serm.* 1. 6. 4 'olim qui magnis legionibus imperitarent' (see Lejay's note), Lucr. 3. 1028 (in a passage full of Ennian phrases) 'magnis qui gentibus imperitarunt'. Like the archaism *induperator*, the frequentative made available to dactylic poetry parts of an essential verb that would otherwise have been unmanageable (see Ernout–Robin on Lucr. 1. 355).

26. non auriga piger: Homeric litotes.

Merionen: like Sthenelus, Meriones is in some accounts a hench-man of Diomede; cf. 1. 6. 15 n.

27. nosces: sinister; cf. Hector on Achilles, Hom. *Il.* 18. 268 ff. εἰ δ' ἄμμε κιχήσεται ἐνθάδ' ἐόντας / αὔριον ὁρμηθεὶς σὺν τεύχεσιν, εὖ νύ τις αὐτὸν / γνώσεται.

furit . . . : the following lines contain a number of reminiscences of the single combat between Paris and Menelaus in *Iliad* 3. Heinze suggests that Horace substituted Diomede for Menelaus because the latter's glory was rather tarnished in the post-epic tradition, particularly in Euripides. Yet conceivably Diomede already appeared in Bacchylides.

The prophetic presents here and at *urgent* in 23 indicate greater excitement and a more vivid imagining than the futures that Nereus began with; cf. ps.-Acro 'Sthenelus sciens: bene vaticinantem ut praesentia videre facit futura', E. Wistrand, *Horace's Ninth Epode*, 1958, pp. 49 ff., H. D. Jocelyn, *The Tragedies of Ennius*, 1967, pp. 209, 215, 227, R. Führer, op. cit. (above, p. 105), p. 127.

reperire: cf. Hom. *Il.* 3. 449 f. Ἀτρείδης δ' ἀν' ὅμιλον ἐφοίτα θηρὶ ἐοικώς, / εἴ που ἐσαθρήσειεν Ἀλέξανδρον θεοειδέα. The infinitive with *furit* recalls that with μεμαώς in Homer; cf. also Manil. 5. 660 'pontum vinclis artare furentes', *Thes.l.L.* 6. 1. 1626. 20 ff. *reperire* is the Homeric κιγχάνειν; cf. above on *nosces*.

28. melior patre: Horace is giving a glancing reference to *Iliad* 4, where Agamemnon says in reproach to Diomede τοῖος ἐὼν Τυδεὺς Αἰτώλιος· ἀλλὰ τὸν υἱὸν / γείνατο εἶο χέρεια μάχῃ, ἀγορῇ δέ τ' ἀμείνω (399 f.; cf. Athene's criticisms at 5. 800). Though Diomede makes no reply, Sthenelus retorts ἡμεῖς τοι πατέρων μέγ' ἀμείνονες εὐχόμεθ' εἶναι (405). Horace pointedly gives the proud epithet to the modest Diomede rather than the boastful Sthenelus; the former's conduct is praised in Pl. *rep.* 389 e, Plut. *aud. poet.* 29 a–c, *schol. Il.* 4. 412 ἔστι δὲ ἐπίδειξις χρηστοῦ ἤθους. Cf. also Stat. *Ach.* 1. 468 f., Auson. 223. 1 'conditur hic genitore bono melior Diomedes'. For similar comparisons cf. Hom. *Il.* 1. 404, 6. 479, *Od.* 2. 276, Mayor on Juv. 14. 213.

29. cervus uti . . . : cf. Hom. *Il.* 3. 21 f. τὸν δ' ὡς οὖν ἐνόησεν ἀρηίφιλος Μενέλαος / . . . ὥς τε λέων ἐχάρη μεγάλῳ ἐπὶ σώματι κύρσας, / εὑρὼν ἢ ἔλαφον κεραὸν ἢ ἄγριον αἶγα / πεινάων, 13. 101 f. Horace characteristically thinks of the wolves of his native land rather than of lions or panthers; cf. 4. 4. 50 ff., 1. 22. 14 n.

30. visum: cf. Hom. *Il.* 3. 30 f. τὸν δ' ὡς οὖν ἐνόησεν Ἀλέξανδρος θεοειδὴς / ἐν προμάχοισι φανέντα, κατεπλήγη φίλον ἦτορ, / ἂψ δ' ἐτάρων ἐς ὅμιλον ἐχάζετο κῆρ ἀλεαίνων.

graminis immemor: cf. Theoc. 4. 14 οὐκέτι λῶντι νέμεσθαι, *epitaph.*

R

Bion. 23 f. αἱ βόες αἱ ποτὶ ταύροις / πλαζόμεναι γοάοντι καὶ οὐκ ἐθέλοντι νέμεσθαι, Virg. *ecl.* 8. 2 'immemor herbarum . . . iuvenca', *georg.* 3. 498 f. 'immemor herbae / victor equus'. The Latin phrase is an odd one, and one suspects a common source, perhaps the passage from the *Eclogues*, but conceivably the *Io* of Calvus.

31. sublimi . . . anhelitu: Horace is translating the Greek medical expression μετέωρον πνεῦμα, which is used of shallow, panting breath; cf. ps.-Hippocr. *epid.* 7. 41 πνεῦμα μετέωρον κατὰ ῥῖνα σπώμενον, Philodemus, *ira* p. 27 W. τὸ μετεωρότερον ἄσθμα τῶν [χίλ]ια δεδραμηκότων στάδια καὶ τὴν πήδ[ησι]ν τῆς καρδίας, Galen, *diff. spir.* 3. 10 (= 7. 946 K.) τοῖς κυναγχικοῖς οὐ πάνυ τὸ πνεῦμα μετέωρον (see the whole context, in which the word occurs several times in this sense). So in the poets Eur. *HF* 1092 f. καὶ πνοὰς θερμὰς πνέω / μετάρσι᾽ οὐ βέβαια πνευμόνων ἄπο, Men. fr. 23. 5 τὸ πνεῦμ᾽ ἔχοντ᾽ ἄνω, Sosicrates fr. 1. 3 K. γίνεται τὸ πνεῦμ᾽ ἄνω, Ap. Rhod. 2. 207 f. ἐξ ὑπάτοιο / στήθεος ἀμπνεύσας, Stat. *Theb.* 11. 239 'nuntius exanimi suspensus pectora cursu', *silv.* 3. 10. 19 f. Note that glosses give μετέωρος as a translation of *sublimis* (*CGL* 2. 190. 43, 2. 370. 8) and ἄσθμα as a translation of *anhelitus* (2. 247. 38 etc.).

Some commentators more prettily picture a stag holding its head high; but one cannot ignore the correspondence of *sublimis* with the technical μετέωρος, especially in view of the parallels in the Greek poets. Nor can we argue that Horace is using both images together; the two interpretations are too different in tone to be thought of simultaneously.

32. non hoc . . . : cf. Helen's reproach ἦ μὲν δὴ πρίν γ᾽ εὔχε᾽ ἀρηιφίλου Μενελάου / σῇ τε βίῃ καὶ χερσὶ καὶ ἔγχει φέρτερος εἶναι (Hom. *Il.* 3. 430 f.), also Ov. *epist.* 16. 351 ff.

tuae: 'your darling'. The semi-colloquialism is a mark of ταπείνωσις; it is more suited to elegy than to high poetry (cf. Ov. *rem.* 573 'ut posses odisse tuam, Pari', below, 1. 25. 7 n.).

33. iracunda . . . : the end of Nereus's speech, like the beginning, refers not to Paris but to Troy. The words are cryptic, as befits a prophecy. Though the first clause is concessive, it is paratactically expressed (there would be a μέν in Greek); and Paris cannot know how Achilles's wrath could postpone Troy's fall.

iracunda . . . classis: 'the anger of the fleet'; cf. 1. 37. 12 n.

diem proferet: 'will grant an adjournment'. The phrase is technical in business and juridical contexts; cf. *Thes.l.L.* 5. 1. 1051. 22 ff. For the legal allusion cf. *Gerichtstag* in Goethe's imitation (5 n.).

34. matronis: the Τρωάδες ἑλκεσίπεπλοι are seen in Roman terms. So

Ennius translates Κορίνθιαι γυναῖκες (Eur. *Med.* 214) 'quae Corinthum arcem altam habetis matronae opulentae optimates' (*scaen.* 259).

classis: probably this refers to the beached ships round which the Achaean camp was built; Horace may have remembered Call. *h.* 3. 232 νῆες . . . ἀμφ' Ἑλένῃ Ῥαμνουσίδι θυμωθεῖσαι (though Nereus was foretelling a different wrath). Alternatively one might interpret *classis* in its old sense of 'army'.

Achillēī: Horace seems to have invented or adopted this genitive (and *Vlixēī*) as convenient for ending iambic lines in the epodes (cf. also 3. 16. 41 *Alyattēī*). Outside his works *Achillei* is found in two inscriptional poems, *Vlixei* once in Ausonius; cf. Neue–Wagener 1. 507 f., M. Leumann, *MH* 2, 1945, 246, 252.

35. certas: Orelli argues against Markland's *denas* that a prophecy is more menacing if it does not date its own fulfilment (cf. Aesch. *Ag.* 126 χρόνῳ μὲν ἀγρεῖ Πριάμου πόλιν ἅδε κέλευθος). For the fixed date of Troy's fall cf. Hom. *Il.* 4. 164 (= 6. 448) ἔσσεται ἦμαρ ὅτ' ἄν ποτ' ὀλώλῃ Ἴλιος ἱρή.

uret . . .: cf. Hom. *Il.* 21. 375 f. ὁπότ' ἄν Τροίη μαλερῷ πυρὶ πᾶσα δάηται / δαιομένη, δαίωσι δ' ἀρήιοι υἷες Ἀχαιῶν, Fraenkel on Aesch. *Ag.* 818.

36. Iliacas: the glyconic with a short second syllable, though common in Greek, is against Horace's normal practice; for other possible instances cf. above, 24 n., 1. 23. 1 n. Some explain the oddity as a sign of early composition; others emend to *Pergameas, Dardanias*, or *barbaricas*. But J. P. Postgate pointed out that in Homer Ἴλιος is repeatedly treated as if it began with a consonant, in fact a digamma (*CQ* 16, 1922, 33); cf., for instance, *Il.* 21. 558 φεύγων πρὸς πεδίον Ἰλήιον, 22. 17 γαῖαν ὀδὰξ εἷλον πρὶν Ἴλιον εἰσαφικέσθαι, and especially 4. 164 (above, 35 n.). This is a useful observation in view of the many Homeric touches elsewhere in the poem. Editors also complain of the repetition *Ilio . . . Iliacas*, yet such infelicities sometimes occur in Horace (1. 29. 16 n.).

16. O MATRE PVLCHRA

[Commager 136 ff.; Fraenkel 207 ff.; E. A. Hahn, *TAPhA* 70, 1939, 213 ff.; P. Rabbow, *Antike Schriften über Seelenheilung und Seelenleitung, I. Die Therapie des Zorns*, 1914.] McKay, AJP 83(1962) 298 ff

1–4. O fairer daughter of a fair mother, you may censor my libellous iambics—whether by fire or water. 5–16. Anger is a maddening passion

*that drives us headlong into danger, the result of the leonine element in
our natures.* 17–22. *It has before now ruined heroes and cities; so
restrain your temper.* 22–28. *I too when young was driven by anger to
write lampoons; now I want peace, provided that when I recant you
give me your affection in return.*

According to the ancient commentators, this graceful poem has
some connection with a palinode to Helen by Stesichorus. The story
went that Stesichorus lost his sight because he criticized Helen in a
poem, and recovered it when he wrote a recantation; cf. *epod.* 17.
42 ff. 'infamis Helenae Castor offensus vice / fraterque magni Castoris, victi prece, / adempta vati reddidere lumina'. Classical scholars
have long been familiar with three lines of such a poem (192):

$$Οὐκ ἔστ' ἔτυμος λόγος οὗτος·$$
$$οὐδ' ἔβας ἐν νηυσὶν εὐσέλμοις$$
$$οὐδ' ἵκεο πέργαμα Τροίας.$$

It is now known that in fact Stesichorus wrote two palinodes to
Helen, one beginning

$$Δεῦτ' αὖτε, θεὰ φιλόμολπε$$

and the other

$$Χρυσόπτερε παρθένε$$

(193, C. M. Bowra, *CR* N.S. 13, 1963, 245 ff.). Obviously, neither is
very closely related to our poem. Horace probably borrows a motto
from Stesichorus for his opening line (1 n.), and at the end he coins
the word *recantare* as an equivalent of παλινῳδεῖν (27 n.). That, it
seems, is the whole extent of the borrowing.

This formal debt has led commentators to believe that Horace's
ode is itself primarily a palinode. The centre of the ode (5–21) is
occupied by a hyperbolical and mock-heroic development on the
power and danger of anger. Commentators assume that in it Horace
is making excuses for his own lampoons. He is thought to be saying,
'Please forgive me, for I was angry when I wrote'. This interpretation is entirely wrong. In fact Horace is addressing a *dissuasio* to the
lady; he is arguing, 'Anger is a terrible thing, so do not be angry
with me'.

A brief consideration of the movement of the poem will show that
this must be so. In the first stanza the lady must already be angry;
she is to be allowed to take the most drastic measures against the
offending lampoons. Then comes the *locus de ira*, which if read without prejudice is seen to be directed at the lady, the only person of
whose anger we are aware. Such a sermon, with its wealth of moral
maxims and mythological instances, should here as elsewhere be
designed to alter the behaviour of the person addressed. It is not

irrelevant that we find a very close parallel to the thought of 5–12 in one of the homilies of St. Basil (10 = 31. 356 c Migne): οὔτε γὰρ ξίφους ἀκμὴ οὔτε πῦρ οὔτε ἄλλο τι τῶν φοβερῶν ἱκανὸν τὴν ὑπὸ τῆς ὀργῆς ἐκμανεῖσαν ψυχὴν ἐπισχεῖν· οὐ μᾶλλόν γε ἢ τοὺς ὑπὸ δαιμόνων κατασχεθέντας, ὧν οὐδὲν οὔτε κατὰ τὸ σχῆμα οὔτε κατὰ τὴν ψυχῆς διάθεσιν οἱ ὀργιζόμενοι διαφέρουσιν.

But the most decisive point comes at 22 'compesce mentem'. On the conventional interpretation Horace is saying, 'I am sorry I was angry, but anger is uncontrollable. Restrain your anger'; here the abruptness of *compesce mentem*, which *ex hypothesi* is the first mention of the lady's anger, is surely intolerable, though Heinze seems alone in expressing surprise. Matters are made worse when Horace adds by way of afterthought, 'I too was angry', though, again *ex hypothesi*, he has been talking of little else for most of the poem. But if the *locus de ira* is directed at the lady, *compesce mentem* follows perfectly naturally; so does *me quoque*, and so does the final proviso.

The poem then is not a palinode, but for the most part a little discourse *de ira*. In a civilized modern society, perhaps deficient in τὸ θυμοειδές, anger attracts few ministrations from psychiatrist or priest. It was very different in antiquity, and from the time of the *Iliad* anger was a subject of perennial interest. When Cicero exerted himself to moderate the passion of his brother, he referred to a large literature on the topic (*ad Q. fr.* 1. 1. 37 'qua re illud non suscipiam, ut quae de iracundia dici solent a doctissimis hominibus ea nunc tibi exponam, cum et nimis longus esse nolim et ex multorum scriptis ea facile possis cognoscere'). Extant treatises were written by Philodemus, Seneca (*de ira = dial.* 3–5), Plutarch, and Libanius. All of them describe the violence of anger; they never consider that violence as an excuse for bad temper, but use it as an argument for restraint. Seneca may speak for them all (*dial.* 5. 3. 1): ' "non est" inquis "dubium quin magna ista et pestifera sit vis: ideo quemadmodum sanari debeat monstra".' This relation must also hold good in Horace.

The question of who the girl is has been fantastically debated. Porphyrio and ps.-Acro identify her with the Tyndaris of the next poem (Stesichorus, they argue, wrote about Helen and Helen was a Tyndaris, i.e. a daughter of Tyndareus). The commentator Cruquianus provides a further identification with the unattractive Canidia of *serm.* 1. 8 and *epod.* 5 and 17; he is no doubt influenced by the allusion to Stesichorus in *epod.* 17 (above, p. 202). Modern commentators sometimes elaborate these biographical extravaganzas yet further (cf. E. A. Hahn, loc. cit.). We need not pursue them in multiplying fantasies on things the ode itself shows to be irrelevant.

Throughout the poem Horace does not put a foot wrong. The formal opening stanza seems to combine allusions to Stesichorus (1 n.) and a Hellenistic commonplace about burning objectionable poems (3 n.). The disquisition on anger is developed with an elegant pomposity that amusingly parodies a whole genre of writing. The surprise turn at the end (22 n.) is graceful and wholly characteristic of its author. As so often in Horace, the interest turns out to be literary rather than autobiographical. The ode is one of the most agreeable poems in the collection.

Metre: Alcaic.

1. o matre . . . pulchrior: these words seem to be a typical Horatian 'motto' modelled on Stesichorus (Ritter). The words are perfectly suited to Helen, daughter of Leda; cf. Ov. *epist.* 16. 85 f. 'pulchrae filia Ledae / ibit in amplexus, pulchrior illa, tuos'. They therefore hang together with the delicate suggestion of παλινῳδία in the last stanza.

For similar eulogies cf. Pl. *symp.* 214 b ὦ 'Ερυξίμαχε βέλτιστε βελτίστου πατρὸς καὶ σωφρονεστάτου χαῖρε, Theoc. 17. 56 f. σὲ δ', αἰχμητὰ Πτολεμαῖε, / αἰχμητᾷ Πτολεμαίῳ ἀρίζηλος Βερενίκη (ἔτεκεν), Catull. 34. 5 f. 'o Latonia, maximi / magna progenies Iovis', Milton, *To Mr. Lawrence*, 'Lawrence, of virtuous father virtuous son'. For other similar locutions cf. Plaut. *asin.* 614 'oh melle dulci dulcior tu es', *truc.* 371, Catull. 22. 14, 27. 4, 39. 16, 99. 2, H. D. Jocelyn, *The Tragedies of Ennius*, 1967, p. 211.

2. voles: sc. *ponere*, which should be supplied also with *libet* in 4.

modum: the word often comes close to meaning *finis*; cf. 2. 6. 7 f. 'sit modus lasso maris et viarum / militiaeque', 3. 15. 2 'tandem nequitiae fige modum tuae', Cic. *Verr.* 2. 118 'modum aliquem et finem orationi nostrae criminibusque faciamus', *Thes.l.L.* 8. 1259. 58 ff. Yet in all these places the word suggests a limitation rather than an irrevocable conclusion. In our passage Horace with urbane humour uses the more moderate word, only to reveal in the following clause the drastic kind of limitation that he has in mind.

3. pones: the future is a polite imperative.

iambis: for their ferocious character cf. *ars* 79 'Archilochum proprio rabies armavit iambo', Meleager (?), *anth. P.* 7. 352. 7 ὑβρι-στῆρας ἰάμβους, Catull. 36. 5 (cited below), fr. 3, Hadrian, *anth. P.* 7. 674. 1 λυσσῶντας ἰάμβους, Julianus, ibid. 7. 69. 3 f. θυμὸν ἰάμβων / δριμύν, πικροχόλου τικτόμενον στόματος, 7. 70. 3 f. ἰάμβων / ἄγριον . . . φλέγμα.

sive flamma . . .: Horace seems to be recalling Lesbia's vow to burn Catullus's poems if he were reconciled to her (36. 4 ff. 'vovit, si sibi restitutus essem / desissemque truces vibrare iambos, / electissima pessimi poetae / scripta tardipedi deo daturam / infelicibus ustulanda lignis'). In both passages destruction is a penalty for libel, not for badness, as in most instances of the motif.

This piece of academic humour may go back to an anecdote about Plato; cf. Diog. Laert. 3. 5 κατέφλεξε τὰ ποιήματα εἰπών· "Ἡφαιστε, πρόμολ' ὧδε· Πλάτων νύ τι σεῖο χατίζει (cf. 6. 95). Here we have already the mock pomposity of language that characterizes most occurrences of this theme. Cf. also Isoc. panath. 232 πολλάκις ὁρμήσας ἐξαλείφειν αὐτὸν ἢ κατακάειν μετεγίγνωσκον, Tib. 1. 9. 49 f. 'illa velim rapida Volcanus carmina flamma / torreat et liquida deleat amnis aqua', Ov. trist. 4. 10. 61 f. 'quae vitiosa putavi / emendaturis ignibus ipse dedi', 5. 12. 61, Lucil. anth. P. 11. 214 γράψας Δευκαλίωνα, Μενέστρατε, καὶ Φαέθοντα / ζητεῖς τίς τούτων ἄξιός ἐστι τίνος. / τοῖς ἰδίοις αὐτοὺς τιμήσομεν· ἄξιος ὄντως / ἐστὶ πυρὸς Φαέθων, Δευκαλίων δ' ὕδατος, Mart. 5. 53. 3 f. 'materia est, mihi crede, tuis aptissima chartis / Deucalion vel si non placet hic Phaethon', 9. 58. 7 f., 14. 196, Juv. 7. 24 f. 'quae / componis dona Veneris, Telesine, marito', Galen 7. 507 K. εἰ δ' ἄχρηστον, . . . καλείτωσαν ἐπὶ τὰς βίβλους τὸν "Ἡφαιστον, M. Aurelius ap. Fronto 68 N. (= 62 van den Hout) 'paululum misere scripsi quod aut lymphis aut Volcano dicarem', Auson. 335 (p. 127. 10 Sch.), Ronsard, Odes 2. 22. 1 ff. (the whole poem is full of borrowings from our ode), Herrick, To Vulcan, 'Thy sooty godhead I desire Still to be ready with thy fire: That sho'd my Booke despisèd be Acceptance it might find of thee'.

4. Hadriano: the Adriatic was notoriously stormy and the epithet perhaps suggests the lady's own temper; cf. 1. 33. 15, 3. 9. 22 f. 'improbo / iracundior Hadria', 1. 3. 15 n. The feature is not Hellenistic, but Italian.

5. non . . .: anger and madness are very frequently associated in ancient moralizing; cf. epist. 1. 2. 62 'ira furor brevis est', Philemon fr. 184 K. μαινόμεθα πάντες ὁπόταν ὀργιζώμεθα, Philodemus, ira 16. 26 ff., Cic. Tusc. 4. 52, 4. 77, Sen. dial. 3. 1. 2 'quidam itaque ex sapientibus viris iram dixerunt brevem insaniam', 4. 36. 5, 5. 1. 5, epist. 18. 14 (citing Epicurus) 'immodica ira gignit insaniam', Apoll. Ty. epist. 86, Galen, anim. pass. 5. 22 K. (= p. 16. 23 ff. Marquardt), Themistius, or. 1 p. 7 b H., Basil, hom. 10 (= 31. 356 b Migne), Stob. 3. 20. 68 (= Cato, dicta 56 J.), Otto 177.

With rhetorical hyperbole Horace describes anger as even more violent than frenzy. The fiction is conventional to the commonplace; cf. Euenus fr. 5 πολλάκις ἀνθρώπων ὀργὴ νόον ἐξεκάλυψεν / κρυπτόμενον, μανίας πουλὺ χερειότερον.

Dindymene: Cybele, the goddess of Mount Dindymus in Phrygia, her central cult place; cf. Hdt. 1. 80. 1 μητρὸς Δινδυμήνης, Catull. 63. 13 'Dindymenae dominae'. For the madness induced in her followers cf. Lucr. 2. 621, Catull. 63 passim, anon. anth. P. 6. 51. 3 f. (a dedication to Rhea of Dindymos) σοὶ τάδε θῆλυς Ἄλεξις ἑῆς οἰστρήματα λύσσης / ἄνθετο, χαλκοτύπου παυσάμενος μανίας, Erycius, ibid. 6. 234. 6 ἐκ λύσσας ἄρτια παυσάμενος. She and the other deities mentioned in this stanza are no doubt among the demons that St. Basil speaks of (above, p. 203).

adytis: unsupported by an adjective the word seems bare, and incola Pythius is a rather odd phrase; it may however be justified by IG 5 (1) 497 Καρνείου Βοικέτα (from Sparta). If emendation is needed, Palmer's adyti . . . Pythii would be acceptable, but less change is involved in his adytis . . . Pythiis. In support of Pythius some editors cite Taulantius incola (Luc. 6. 16, Sil. 15. 294); but these passages are irrelevant.

quatit: ταράσσει, cf. Lact. inst. 2. 14. 14 'spiritus . . . tenues . . . mentes furoribus quatiunt', Hor. serm. 2. 3. 295 'mentem concussa', Cic. div. 1. 38 'vis illa terrae quae mentem Pythiae divino adflatu concitabat', 1. 66. Prophetic madness was a feature of many cults of Apollo; see Dodds 69 ff.

6. incola: of his shrine at Delphi; cf. Catull. 64. 228 'incola Itoni', Gratt. 437 f. 'loci . . . incola sancte', Min. Fel. 7. 5 '(templa) augusta numinibus incolis praesentibus inquilinis'. So in Greek Simon. 531. 6 ἀνδρῶν ἀγαθῶν ὅδε σηκὸς οἰκέταν εὐδοξίαν Ἑλλάδος εἵλετο, IG 5(1) 497 (cited above).

7. Liber: the reference is to the Bacchants' orgiastic rites; cf. the verb bacchari, 'to rave'.

non . . .: the Corybantes were youths associated with various gods of orgiastic cult, most often with Cybele, but sometimes with Dionysus (cf. Eur. Ba. 125 with Dodds's note on 120–34). They are sometimes confused with other similar groups, especially with the Curetes, the attendants of Rhea, the mother goddess of Crete (cf. Lucr. 2. 629 ff. and Bailey's note on pp. 899 f.). See further Str. 10. 3. 7–23, I. M. Linforth, Corybantic Rites in Plato, Univ. Calif. Publ. Phil. 13, 1944–50, 121 ff., Dodds, The Greeks and the Irrational, pp. 77 ff.

The Corybantes are not, as some editors believe, themselves maddened (κορυβαντιῶντες); like the other figures in this stanza, they are producers of madness. Cf. Eur. Hipp. 141 ff. ἢ γὰρ ἔνθεος, ὦ κούρα, / εἴτ' ἐκ Πανὸς εἴθ' Ἑκάτας / ἢ σεμνῶν Κορυβάντων φοι/τᾷς ἢ ματρὸς ὀρείας;, Philostr. epist. 69 (15) οἱ τελούμενοι τῇ Ῥέᾳ μαίνονται πληγέντες τὰ ὦτα κτύποις ὀργάνων. Occasionally, but untypically, κορύβας is used of a victim of madness (Philodemus, *rhet.* 1. 60. 30 Sudhaus, Lucian, *hist. conscr.* 45). But it is perverse to attribute this rare sense to Horace here.

acuta: conventional of cymbals; cf. Ov. *met.* 6. 589, Philippus, *anth. P.* 6. 94. 2 ὀξύδουπα, anon. ibid. 6. 51. 5 ὀξύφθογγα.

8. sic: this word implies that bursts of passion clash cymbals, and Bentley protested at so extraordinary a notion. Yet the abrupt metaphor can be paralleled in the rationalizations of popular philosophy; cf. Lucr. **3.** 992 f. 'sed Tityos nobis hic est in amore iacentem / quem volucres lacerant', Cic. *Pis.* 46 'sua quemque fraus, suum facinus, suum scelus, sua audacia de sanitate ac mente deturbat; hae sunt impiorum furiae, hae flammae, hae faces'. For a more regular form of comparison cf. Plut. *amat.* 763 a τί τοσοῦτον ἢ Πυθία πέπονθεν ἁψαμένη τοῦ τρίποδος; τίνα τῶν ἐνθεαζομένων οὕτως ὁ αὐλὸς καὶ τὰ μητρῷα καὶ τὸ τύμπανον ἐξίστησιν;

Bentley himself proposed *si* (which is also found in at least one manuscript). It is true that *si* sometimes comes close to meaning 'when'. Yet it retains a note of caution that is inappropriate in describing the standing activity of Corybantes (when do they ever do anything but clash cymbals?).

geminant: 'redouble'; cf. Virg. *Aen. 5.* 227 'ingeminat clamor', 1. 1. 8 n. Here the object states the source of the sound; cf. Stat. *silv.* 4. 5. 60 'barbiton ingemina sub antro', 'make your lyre sound again' (wrongly interpreted in *Thes.l.L.* 7. 1. 1518. 8). The word is in our passage often interpreted 'join' (thus *Thes.l.L.* 6. 2. 1739. 1 ff.); cf. Stat. *Theb.* 8. 221 'gemina aera sonant'. A clear instance of such a use is hard to find. Editors compare *ars* 13 'serpentes avibus geminentur'; but that suggests monstrous Siamese twins, and is irrelevant to the banging of cymbals.

aera: cf. Eur. *Cyc.* 205 οὐ κρόταλα χαλκοῦ τυμπάνων τ' ἀράγματα, *Hel.* 1346 f. χαλκοῦ δ' αὐδὰν χθονίαν / τύπανά τ', D.–S. 1. 1697 f.

9. tristes: 'glowering', 'scowling'; cf. Sen. *dial.* 3. 1. 3 '(furentium) tristis frons'. The plural refers to fits of anger; cf. 17 below, 3. 27. 70.

quas . . .: it is a commonplace in these discussions that the angry man is heedless of possible damage to himself; cf. Heraclitus fr. 85 (cited in Plut. *Coriol.* 22. 2) θυμῷ μάχεσθαι χαλεπόν· ὅτι γὰρ ἂν θέλῃ, ψυχῆς ὠνεῖται, Theophr. fr. 154 τὸ γὰρ τιμωρεῖσθαί τινα κακῶς ἑαυτὸν ποιοῦντα, δίκην διδόναι οὐχ ἧττον ἢ λαμβάνειν ἐστίν, Philodemus, *ira* 13. 11 ff. τ[ί γ]ὰρ [δ]εῖ λέγειν τὸ μηδ' ἀπ[ω]σμένους ἀλλ' ἐπιφερομένους ἐνίοτε διὰ τὴν ἀνεπιστασίαν εἰς ξύλα καὶ τοίχους καὶ τάφρους ἤ τι τοιοῦτον ἐνπίπτειν;, 33. 1 ff. βιαζομένης καὶ πολλ[ά]κις ἀνόπλους καὶ πρὸς τ[ὴν] φυλακὴν ἀποτυ[φλ]ούσης [καὶ τὸ σ]ῶμα συντριβούσης [καὶ μὴ]ν μᾶλλον α[ὐ]τοὺς [τῶν ἐναν]τίων κα[κ]ῶς δι[ατιθείσης], Sen. *dial.* 3. 1. 1 'in ipsa

inruens tela et ultionis secum ultorem tracturae avidus (adfectus)',
3. 5. 2, 3. 11. 8, Plut. *cohib. ira* 463 a ἀγωνίζεται γάρ, οὐχὶ μὴ παθεῖν
αὐτός, ἀλλὰ παθεῖν κακῶς ἐπιτρίψας ἕτερον, Basil, *hom.* 10 (= 31. 356 b
Migne) εἰς πρόϋπτον κακὸν ἑαυτοὺς πολλάκις ἐμβάλλουσι, 356 c (above,
p. 203), H. Ringeltaube, *Quaestiones ad veterum philosophorum de
affectibus doctrinam pertinentes*, Diss. Göttingen, 1913, pp. 87 f.

We find in other contexts similar lists of ineffective deterrents,
presumably also derived from Hellenistic moralizing, at *serm.* 1. 1.
38 f., 2. 3. 54 f., *epist.* 1. 1. 46, Sen. *Phaedr.* 700 ff.

Noricus: Noricum was the Alpine territory occupied by the modern
Tyrol, Styria, and Carinthia; its iron was the basis of the 'Hallstatt'
civilization of about 800 B.C. The area was not conquered by Rome
till 15 B.C., but was already subject to commercial penetration. For
the excellence of its most famous product cf. Plin. *nat.* 34. 145,
Petron. 70. 3 'quia bonam mentem habet, attuli illi Roma munus
cultros Norico ferro'. See further *RE* 17. 1042 f., O. Davies, *Roman
Mines in Europe*, 1935, pp. 173 f., R. J. Forbes, *Studies in Ancient
Technology* 9, 1964, pp. 268 ff.

Horace is the first extant author to refer to the iron of Noricum
(*epod.* 17. 71 'ense pectus Norico recludere'). The epithet is still
novel and adventurous, a Roman substitute for the Greek 'Scythian'
or 'Chalybian'. Later it became more hackneyed; cf. Ov. *met.* 14.
712, Mart. 4. 55. 11 f., Rut. Nam. 1. 351 f.

10. ensis: the poetical word; both Cicero and Seneca use predominantly *ensis* in verse, but only *gladius* in prose. Cf. the tables in
Thes.l.L. 5. 2. 608. 40 ff.

naufragum: used in its active sense of 'wrecking ships'; cf. Tib.
2. 4. 10, Sil. 17. 634, *navifragus* Virg. *Aen.* 3. 553, Ov. *met.* 14. 6,
Auson. 157. 8, 396. 40, *carm. Bob.* 25. 4; so in Greek anon. *anth. P.* 9.
105. 2 ναυηγῶν ἀνέμων. For rather similar doublets see further A.
Debrunner, *Griechische Wortbildungslehre*, 1917, § 117.

11. nec . . .: cf. Liban. 8. 322. 10 f. οὐκ ἀξιοῦσι δεδοικέναι τοῦ Διὸς τὸ
πῦρ. The attitude Horace describes was exemplified in the next
century by Caligula, who challenged Jupiter to mortal combat for
thundering during a theatrical performance (Sen. *dial.* 3. 20. 8).

12. ruens: Jupiter is καταιβάτης (cf. Aesch. *Pr.* 359), the god who
descends in the form of a thunderbolt; cf. Cook, *Zeus* 2. 13 ff. *ruere* is
used of the sky or the aether in Lucr. 1. 1097, Virg. *georg.* 1. 324 'ruit
arduus aether', Val. Fl. 1. 828 f. The word vividly describes the sudden violence of a Mediterranean thunderstorm. The effect is here
enhanced by the weak caesura after *ipse*; cf. Virg. *Aen.* 2. 465 f. 'ea
lapsa repente ruinam / cum sonitu trahit'.

13. fertur . . .: Horace's use of a mythological parallel to dignify advice to a contemporary reflects the practice of archaic lyric (cf. I. 7. 21 n.); but in content his myth here owes much more to philosophy. Plato had twisted the crude legends of archaic Greece to recommend a more modern morality, and the technique must have proved congenial to the popular teachers of the Hellenistic age. Horace's point here is that anger is something θηριῶδες (*insani leonis* bears the weight of the sentence); by an unfortunate contingency something bestial has found its way into beings very different from the beasts.

Prometheus: Horace's fable has several parallels. See Pl. *Prot.* 320 d–321: Epimetheus uses up on the animals such qualities as speed and strength, so that there is nothing left for man; Prometheus gives man 'wisdom' in compensation. Philemon describes how Prometheus gave each kind of animal a special quality, whereas he made men all different from each other (fr. 89 K.). Closest of all to our passage is one of Aesop's fables (228 Hausrath = 383 Halm): there Prometheus at first created too many animals and did not have enough stuff left over for men; he therefore had to transform some beasts into men, and the resulting creatures have human forms but bestial souls.

The ancients seem to have found amusement in attributing such disastrous fits of absent-mindedness to the foreseeing god; cf. Prop. 3. 5. 7 ff. 'o prima infelix fingenti terra Prometheo! / ille parum cauti pectoris egit opus: / corpora disponens mentem non vidit in arte. / recta animi primum debuit esse via', Phaedrus 4. 16 (he causes homosexuality through an oversight), Strato, *anth. P.* 12. 220 (he is responsible for hairiness), Ach. Tat. 2. 21. 1 f. (he allows the lion to be afraid of a cock). For more general allusions to Prometheus as the creator of man cf. Heraclid. Pont. fr. 66 Wehrli, Erinna, *anth. P.* 6. 352. 1 f., Men. fr. 718. 5 f. Körte, Mayor on Juv. 14. 35, *RE* 23. 696 ff., Themist. 359d.–360a. See also below, 14 n.

principi: 'original'; the word is occasionally used of things. Lewis and Short I A cite five examples, to which one can add Val. Fl. 1. 532 *cursu*, Stat. *Theb.* 12. 664 *lancea*.

14. limo: for mud or clay as the original matter of man, cf. Hes. *op.* 61 f. γαῖαν ὕδει φύρειν, ἐν δ' ἀνθρώπου θέμεν αὐδὴν / καὶ σθένος, Aesch. fr. 369 ἐκ πηλοπλάστου σπέρματος θνητὴ γυνή, Soph. fr. 441 N. (= 482 P.) καὶ πρῶτον ἄρχου πηλὸν ὀργάζειν χεροῖν (all three passages deal with the creation of Pandora), Ar. *av.* 686 πλάσματα πηλοῦ, Call. fr. 483 εἴ σε Προμηθεὺς / ἔπλασε, καὶ πηλοῦ μὴ 'ξ ἑτέρου γέγονας, 192. 3 ὁ πηλὸς ὁ Προμήθειος (i.e. 'men'), Ov. *met.* 1. 82 f., Apollod. 1. 7. 1 with Frazer's notes, Juv. 14. 35 'meliore luto finxit praecordia Titan' with

Mayor's note, Otto 202, Headlam on Herodas 2. 28, S. Thompson, *A Motif Index of Folk Literature* 1, 1955, A 1241. Horace's word is taken up in Prud. *cath.* 11. 50 ff. 'te creator arduus / spiravit et limo indidit / sermone carnem glutinans'. Pausanias actually saw some stones at Panopeus which were the remnants of Prometheus's clay (10. 4. 4).

coactus: Bentley, following Scaliger, objects that Prometheus manufactured man on his own initiative, 'non alterius iussu et imperio'. This is not necessarily true; in some versions he acted under divine instruction (Pl. loc. cit., Aesop, loc. cit. κατὰ πρόσταξιν Διός, Steph. Byz. s.v. Ἰκόνιον). But whether true or not, it misses the point of *coactus*, which here as often elsewhere refers to the constraint imposed by the limiting possibilities of a situation; cf. Cic. *Mur.* 6, *dom.* 93, *Flacc.* 14, *Rab. Post.* 5, *off.* 1. 83 'gravioribus . . . morbis periculosas curationes et ancipites adhibere coguntur', Hdt. 5. 101. 2 ἠναγκάζοντο ἀμύνεσθαι. Prometheus was, it seems, driven to desperate expedients by the scarcity of raw materials.

particulam: μόριον; cf. Pl. *Tim.* 42 e–43 a (of the subordinate deities) πυρὸς καὶ γῆς, ὕδατός τε καὶ ἀέρος ἀπὸ τοῦ κόσμου δανειζόμενοι μόρια, Cic. *Tim.* 47 'particulas ignis et terrae et aquae et animae a mundo . . . mutuabantur'. The word may be an innovation of Cicero's, and it usually has a flavour of technical rhetoric or philosophy (so even *Pis.* 85 'cognoscis ex particula parva scelerum et crudelitatis tuae genus universum'). Hence in our passage the diminutive has no particular note of contempt or humour.

undique: 'from anywhere and everywhere'; cf. Thuc. 2. 53. 3 πανταχόθεν ἐς αὐτὸ κερδαλέον. Prometheus was not in a position to pick and choose.

15. desectam: ἀποτμηθεῖσαν. One thinks of the plastic surgery in Plato's most exuberant creation myth (*symp.* 190–1).

et: = *etiam*. Alternatively one might interpret 'fertur coactus esse et adposuisse' (for the omission of *esse* cf. Catull. 67. 19 'virgo quod fertur tradita nobis'). Yet as the whole relevance of the sentence lies in the *adposuisse* clause, it is desirable to take the first part as subordinated. It is impossible to regard the skeleton of the sentence as 'fertur addere et adposuisse'; even if the variation in tense were swallowed (cf. 3. 20. 11 ff.), *coactus* would be left very bare and far too emphatic.

insani leonis: cf. (of the constellation) 3. 29. 19 'stella vesani leonis'. For lions as the animal type of anger cf. Tyrtaeus 10 (cited by Chrysippus 2. 255. 22 von A.) αἴθωνος δὲ λέοντος ἔχων ἐν στήθεσι θυμόν, Pl. *rep.* 588 d, 589 b, 590 a, 620 b εἰκοστὴν δὲ λαχοῦσαν ψυχὴν ἑλέσθαι λέοντος βίον· εἶναι δὲ τὴν Αἴαντος τοῦ Τελαμωνίου, Philodemus, *ira* 27. 19 f. βριμώσεως θηριώδους οὐδὲ παυομένης ὡς τῆς τῶν λεόντων, Lucr. 3. 296 ff., 741 f. 'acris violentia triste leonum / seminium sequitur', Sen. *dial.* 4. 16. 1, Stat. *silv.* 2. 5. 1, Clem. Alex. *protr.* 1. 4. 1, Aug. *in evang. Io.* 10. 1 v. 11. Ael. *nat. anim.* 7. 23 deals with the vengefulness of lions.

16. vim: = *violentiam*.

stomacho: here the seat of anger; in 1. 6. 6 it means anger itself, cf. *stomachor*. Cf. 1. 13. 4 n. and see the discussion in R. B. Onians, *The Origins of European Thought*, ed. 2, 1954, pp. 84 ff.

17. irae Thyesten . . .: for sermonizing anaphora in an *exemplum* cf. Liban. 8. 323. 11 ff. ὀργὴ τὴν Μήδειαν ὥπλισε κατὰ τῶν τέκνων, ὀργὴ τὴν Πρόκνην κατὰ τοῦ μηδὲν ἠδικηκότος "Ἴτυος . . . The anger of Thyestes is specifically 'thirst for revenge' as in the philosophic definitions; cf. Arist. *rhet.* 1378ᵃ30 with Cope's note, Rabbow, op. cit., pp. 2 ff., 171 ff. Reflection on such *exempla* is recommended by the moralists (Sen. *dial.* 5. 14 ff., Rabbow, op. cit., pp. 74 ff.).

Thyesten: Thyestes seduced the wife of his brother Atreus. Atreus banished Thyestes from Mycenae. Thyestes tried to murder Atreus through the agency of Atreus's son Pleisthenes, but the young man was killed by his father without being recognized. Atreus called Thyestes to Mycenae and served him a meal of his own children. Thyestes cursed Atreus's race, and his son Aegisthus later murdered Atreus's son, Agamemnon. The subject was popular with the Romans: Ennius wrote a *Thyestes*, and Accius an *Atreus*; in 29 B.C. Varius produced another *Thyestes* (p. 81).

There is some difficulty about Horace's version of the story. The anger referred to must be that of Thyestes; there would be no point in saying that Atreus's anger destroyed Thyestes. Yet it is Atreus who usually illustrates the evils of vengeful anger; cf. Cic. *Tusc.* 4. 77 (citing Acc. *trag.* 59) 'ut facile appareat Atrei filios esse, eius qui meditatur poenam in fratrem novam: "maior mihi moles, maius miscendumst malum . . ."', Sen. *Thy.* 712 ff., 737. We hear, it is true, of Thyestean curses (*epod.* 5. 86), but they were made after and not before the ruin of Thyestes's family.

It is not clear how the difficulty should be resolved. Horace might have made a mistake either about identity (like ps.-Acro ad loc.) or about chronology; but this may not seem likely for a well-educated man who had seen these stories performed on the stage. Or perhaps Varius introduced a new form of the legend in which Thyestes's anger played a more significant part (suggested by Vollmer on Stat. *silv.* 5. 1. 57). Alternatively one might look here for the construction by which one member of a pair may be put for both, or even for the other member; it may be relevant that both brothers are mentioned by Philodemus (*ira* 14. 10 ff.). Cf. Virg. *georg*. 3. 89 'domitus Pollucis habenis'; Servius comments 'atqui Castor equorum domitor fuit. sed fratrem pro fratre posuit poetica licentia, ut *quas illi Philomela dapes* pro *Progne*, item *revocato a sanguine Teucri* pro *Dardani*; aut certe ideo Pollucem pro Castore posuit, quia ambo licenter et Polluces et Castores vocantur; nam et ludi et templum et stellae Castorum nominantur'. So *Remus* is sometimes used for *Romulus*. See further Bell 9 ff., Housman on Luc. 7. 871.

18. altis urbibus: for the idea cf. 4. 15. 19 f. 'non ira, quae procudit enses / et miseras inimicat urbes', Sen. *dial*. 3. 2. 2 'aspice nobilissimarum civitatum fundamenta vix notabilia: has ira deiecit'.

The transition from individual to city or vice versa is common; cf. Theogn. 1103 f. ὕβρις καὶ Μάγνητας ἀπώλεσε καὶ Κολοφῶνα / καὶ Σμύρνην· πάντως, Κύρνε, καὶ ὔμμ᾽ ἀπολεῖ, Soph. *Ant*. 296 f. τοῦτο (gold) καὶ πόλεις / πορθεῖ, τόδ᾽ ἄνδρας ἐξανίστησιν δόμων, 673 f. αὕτη (anarchy) πόλεις τ᾽ ὄλλυσιν, ἥδ᾽ ἀναστάτους / οἴκους τίθησιν, Catull. 51. 13 ff. 'otium, Catulle, tibi molestum est . . . / otium et reges prius et beatas / perdidit urbes', Prop. 2. 6. 15 f., Liban. 8. 324. 2 ff. ὀργὴ Τυδέα διεκώλυσεν ἀθανασίας τυχεῖν. ὀργῇ Καμβύσης τὰ πολλὰ ἐκεῖνα ἐξήμαρτε. δι᾽ ὀργὴν ἡ πόλις ἡ τῶν Ἀθηναίων δέκα στρατηγῶν ἀγαθῶν ἑαυτὴν ἀπεστέρησε.

altis is probably 'great and proud' rather than merely a translation of Homer's αἰπὺ πτολίεθρον; cf. Sall. *Jug*. 42. 4 'quae res plerumque magnas civitatis pessum dedit, dum alteri alteros vincere quovis modo et victos acerbius ulcisci volunt'.

ultimae: 'primary', i.e. those that one arrives at last in going backwards from the event to its original cause; we use 'ultimate' in the same way. The phrase means 'last (i.e. immediately preceding) cause' in Liv. 7. 9. 2 'ea ultima fuit causa . . . cur . . . bellum indiceretur'.

19. stetere: anger is the appointed or determined cause of the downfall of cities; the use of *stare* is like that in Virg. *Aen*. 10. 467 'stat sua cuique dies'.

causae: Horace is assuming the judicious gravity of a historian; cf. 2. 1. 2 (to Pollio) 'bellique causas'. Thucydides and his Hellenistic admirers had attempted to trace αἰτίαι in human affairs; the pseudo-scientific approach brought some insight and some over-simplification. The gain in sophistication leaves its trace on Roman poetry: Homer is content with a naïve τίς δ᾽ ἄρ σφῶε θεῶν ἔριδι ξυνέηκε μάχεσθαι;, but Virgil must ask 'Musa, mihi causas memora'. See further M. Pohlenz, *Causa civilium armorum, ΕΠΙΤΥΜΒΙΟΝ Heinrich Swoboda dargebracht*, 1927, pp. 201 ff., E. Fraenkel, *JRS* 35, 1945, 3.

20. imprimeret . . .: the site of a destroyed city was ploughed over; cf. Mod. *dig.* 7. 4. 21 'si . . . aratrum in ea (civitate) inducatur, civitas esse desinit, ut passa est Carthago', Prop. 3. 9. 41 f. 'moenia cum Graio Neptunia pressit aratro / victor Palladiae ligneus artis equus', Manil. 4. 557 f., Sen. *clem.* 1. 26. 4 'inicere tectis ignem, aratrum vetustis urbibus inducere potentiam putat', Isid. *orig.* 15. 2. 4, Jeremiah 26. 18 'Zion shall be plowed like a field'. A slightly different metaphor is used in Aesch. *Ag.* 525 f. Τροίαν κατασκάψαντα τοῦ δικηφόρου / Διὸς μακέλλῃ, τῇ κατείργασται πέδον.

21. hostile . . .: this line has no regular caesura (cf. p. xli). In order to provide one, the *ex-* of *exercitus* has to be felt as partly detached; this is very bold in a secondary compound where the rest of the word has no meaning *per se.*

22. compesce: a strong word, cf. *epist.* 1. 2. 62 f. 'animum rege, qui nisi paret, / imperat; hunc frenis, hunc tu compesce catena', Sen. *dial.* 4. 18. 1 'aliter iram debemus repellere, aliter compescere', 4. 33. 6; the same idea is differently expressed in Sen. *dial.* 5. 1. 1 'iram . . . refrenare et impetus eius inhibere'. Editors have compared Hom. *Il.* 9. 255 f. σὺ δὲ μεγαλήτορα θυμὸν / ἴσχειν ἐν στήθεσσι, Soph. *OC* 874, Neophron fr. 2. 4. The metaphor is in fact more vivid and more like Hom. *Il.* 9. 496 δάμασον θυμὸν μέγαν, Plut. *cohib. ira* 453 c εὐήνιον . . . ἐποιήσω τὸν θυμόν, 459 b δαμάζοντος καὶ καταθλοῦντος ἀσκήσει τὸ ἄλογον καὶ δυσπειθές, Greg. Naz. *contra iram* 65 ff. (= 37. 818 Migne) (anger is like a bolting horse). The popularity of the image among the moralists presumably owes much to Plato's picture of the chariot of the soul in the *Phaedrus* (246 f.).

mentem: 'mood', here furious; cf. *epist.* 1. 2. 60, Catull. 15. 14 'mala mens furorque vecors', inc. Tib. 3. 9. 7 f.

me quoque: it is a disarming rhetorical trick to appeal to one's own experience to illustrate a point. Cf. 1. 33. 13 f., Cic. *Mur.* 63 'fatebor enim, Cato, me quoque in adulescentia diffisum ingenio meo quaesisse adiumenta doctrinae', Liban. 8. 315. 17 ff. Here Horace elegantly binds his poem together by giving as his illustration the very offence that had provoked the lady in the first place. The urbane effrontery is worthy of Cicero.

pectoris . . . fervor: ancient physiological theory explained anger as a boiling up of blood round the heart; cf. Arist. *anim.* 403^{b}1 ζέσιν τοῦ περὶ καρδίαν αἵματος ἢ θερμοῦ, Basil, *hom.* 10 (= 31. 356 c Migne) περιζεῖ μὲν τῇ καρδίᾳ τὸ αἷμα, ὥσπερ βίᾳ πυρὸς κυκώμενον καὶ παφλάζον, Chaucer, *Parson's Tale* 535 f. 'Ire, after the philosophre, is the fervent blood of man yquyked in his herte . . . For certes, the herte of man, by eschawfynge and moevynge of his blood, wexeth so trouble that he is out of alle juggement of resoun'. The 'choleric', those with a surplus of hot and dry in the *temperamentum* of the body, were particularly liable to boil over.

23. temptavit: 'afflicted'; the word is often used of disease.

dulci iuventa: cf. Maecen. ap. Serv. *Aen.* 8. 310 '(vinum) dulcis iuventae reducit bona', Prud. *cath.* 9. 43 'exitu dulcis iuventae'. The sentimental and conventional phrase (cf. πολυήρατος ἥβη) is here given an edge; what Horace enjoyed about youth was its turbulent ferocity. Aristotle notes that the young are most subject to anger (*rhet.* 1389ª9 ff.), and also comments on the pleasure of anger, quoting with approval Hom. *Il.* 18. 109 f. (χόλος) πολὺ γλυκίων μέλιτος καταλειβομένοιο / ἀνδρῶν ἐν στήθεσσιν ἀέξεται (*rhet.* 1378ᵇ1 ff.); cf. also Sen. *dial.* 4. 32. 1, Greg. Naz. op. cit. [above, 22] 515 (= 37. 848 Migne), Rabbow, op. cit., pp. 13 f.

iuventa: cf. 3. 14. 27 'calidus iuventa', *ars* 115 f. 'adhuc florente iuventa / fervidus'. In his youth, the impeccable Cato was moved to similar excesses; cf. Plut. *Cato min.* 7. 2 ὀργῇ καὶ νεότητι τρέψας ἑαυτὸν εἰς ἰάμβους πολλὰ τὸν Σκηπίωνα καθύβρισε, τῷ πικρῷ προσχρησάμενος τοῦ Ἀρχιλόχου, τὸ δὲ ἀκόλαστον ἀφεὶς καὶ παιδαριῶδες.

24. celeres: partly because they were an over-hasty expression of anger (so Wickham). There is also a play on the swift movement of the iambic line; cf. *ars* 251 f., Ter. Maur. 2182 f. 'adesto, iambe praeceps, et tui tenax / vigoris adde concitum celer pedem', Auson. 413. 1 f. 'iambe Parthis et Cydonum spiculis, / iambe pinnis alitum velocior', Sidon. *epist.* 8. 4. 2, 8. 11. 7.

25. furentem: the word corresponds to the previous *fervor*; cf. Comm. *apol.* 4 'dum furor aetatis primae me portabat in auras'.

26. mutare: here 'to give in exchange' as in 1. 29. 14 f.

tristia: beside *mitibus* the word suggests a harsh, sour taste; cf. Virg. *georg.* 1. 75 'tristisque lupini', 2. 126 'tristis sucos'.

27. recantatis: a new coinage of Horace's on the model of παλινῳδεῖν (cf. Pl. *Alc.* 2. 142 d ἐνίοτε παλινῳδοῦσιν ἀνευχόμενοι ἅττ' ἂν τὸ πρῶτον εὔξωνται). The noun παλινῳδία is used by Cicero in his letters (*Att.* 4. 5. 1). Horace's innovation provided English with a new word in the sixteenth century (Fraenkel 209).

28. animumque reddas: sc. *tuum. animum* here means 'affection', as at 4. 1. 30 'spes animi credula mutui', Plaut. *asin.* 141 'amans ego animum meum isti dedi'. For another sense cf. 1. 19. 4.

17. VELOX AMOENVM

[Fraenkel 204 ff.; G. L. Hendrickson, *CPh* 26, 1931, 7 ff.; F. Klingner, *Römische Geisteswelt*, ed. 3, 1965, pp. 412 ff. (= *Philologus* 90, 1935, 289 ff.); Troxler-Keller 108 ff.]

1–12. *Faunus often leaves Arcadia and visits my Sabine farm, playing on his pipe and bringing protection to the goats.* 13–28. *The gods care for me as man and as poet. Come, Tyndaris, share this heaven-sent bounty and peace, and sing of mythological themes to Anacreon's lyre. Here at least you will be free of the jealous violence of your metropolitan lover.*

This subtle and most original poem falls roughly into two sections. First in the descriptive part Horace tells how Faunus's epiphanies bring protection to his farm; secondly, combining themes from pastoral and from erotic epigram, he promises the same peace to Tyndaris. Certain specific features occur in both sections: freedom from fear (8, 24), the heat of the summer's day (2, 18), the music of pipe or lyre (10, 18). Out of his varied themes Horace has created a rich and complex structure; he moves with extraordinary ease from the realistic country scene at the beginning up to the emphatic affirmation of the central sentence (13 f.), and down to the contrasting vignette at the close.

The poem illustrates a feeling for country life that began in the urban conglomerations of the Hellenistic age and that finds expression in bucolic poetry and often in the Anthology (cf. Vischer 130 ff.). In particular, some of the details in Horace have parallels in an epigram of the third century B.C. by Nicaenetus of Samos (Gow–Page 1. 146):

οὐκ ἐθέλω, Φιλόθηρε, κατὰ πτόλιν, ἀλλὰ παρ᾽ ῞Ηρῃ
δαίνυσθαι, ζεφύρου πνεύμασι τερπόμενος.
ἀρκεῖ μοι λιτὴ μὲν ὑπὸ πλευροῖσι χάμευνα·
ἐγγὺς γὰρ προμάλου δέμνιον ἐνδαπίης,
καὶ λύγος, ἀρχαῖον Καρῶν στέφος. ἀλλὰ φερέσθω
οἶνος καὶ Μουσέων ἡ χαρίεσσα λύρη,
θυμῆρες πίνοντες ὅπως Διὸς εὐκλέα νύμφην
μέλπωμεν νήσου δέσποτιν ἡμετέρης.

The same tone recurs in the *Anacreontea*, which Horace no doubt attributed to Anacreon (18 n.). See, for instance, 17, 18, 30, and 39; 30 was freely rendered by Cowley, whose version begins 'Underneath this myrtle shade, On flow'ry beds supinely laid, With

S

od'rous oils my head o'erflowing And around it roses growing, What
should I do but drink away The heat and troubles of the day?'
Such poems are distinguished by an agreeable ἀφέλεια, but Horace
seeks more complicated harmonies.

A romantic note is introduced by Tyndaris, who puzzles commentators. We must not think of her as an actual person, or assimi-
late the ode to the class of 'invitation poems'. Rather she is a dream
figure, belonging to the world of Alexandrian pastoral (10 n.). Her
prototype is Theocritus's Galatea; Horace's theme is 'Come live
with me and be my love', ἀλλ' ἀφίκευσο ποθ' ἁμέ, καὶ ἕξεις οὐδὲν
ἔλασσον (Theoc. 11. 42). Compare also Virgil's imitations:

> hic ver purpureum, varios hic flumina circum
> fundit humus flores, hic candida populus antro
> imminet et lentae texunt umbracula vites.
> huc ades; insani feriant sine litora fluctus.
>
>   (ecl. 9. 40 ff.)
>
> hic gelidi fontes, hic mollia prata, Lycori,
> hic nemus; hic ipso tecum consumerer aevo.
>
>   (10. 42 f.)

hic is there repeated as in our poem (cf. ἐντὶ . . . ἐντὶ in Theoc. 11.
45 ff.).

Finally, in the last two stanzas Horace gives the poem another
twist; it transpires that Tyndaris is not an Arcadian shepherdess
but an urban *hetaera*, like the Phyllis to whom Horace gives a rustic
party in 4. 11. The mixture of the two worlds is not wholly unparalleled, and has some Alexandrian antecedents (see Gow on Theoc.
3, p. 64). Later Alciphron in one of his letters of courtesans (4. 13)
described a picnic in the grotto of the nymphs; but in spite of the
conventionally idyllic setting the detail is realistic and even vulgar.
The Roman elegiac poets come nearer to Horace. Gallus claimed to
have carved Lycoris's name on trees (cf. Serv. *ecl.* 10. 46). Tibullus
sets Delia in an orchard, and implausibly imagines her picking
apples for Messala (1. 5. 31 f.). Propertius continues the convention
(2. 30. 25 f.): 'libeat tibi, Cynthia, mecum / rorida muscosis antra
tenere iugis'. Ovid too invites his lady to Sulmo (*am.* 2. 16); but,
however conventionalized, she is a less romantic and more everyday
figure than Horace's Tyndaris. See also Aristaenetus 1. 3 for another
idealized picture of love in the country.

Yet in spite of these literary complications Horace's poem reveals
a warm Italian feeling for nature, less ecstatic perhaps than Virgil's
(*georg.* 2. 143 ff., 516 ff.), but not less authentic. The idyllic Arcadian
Lycaeus is linked with the prosaic Sabine place-names, Lucretilis
and Ustica. The goats straggle and smell, and though they are safe

from wolves they are not so unrealistic as to lie down with them. In expressing his exuberant gratitude for the opulence of nature Horace uses not the conventional bucolic conceits, but the naturalized Italian image of the cornucopia. Above all he conveys a very personal joy and pride in his beloved estate: 'It is *his* field, *his* garden, *his* vineyard, and *his* orchard that bear everything in plenty' (Fraenkel 206). By comparison Tyndaris leaves the poet unmoved; similarly in Ovid's elegy mentioned above, the accents of genuine love are reserved for Sulmo. Horace's more perfect poem might be compared to a landscape by Claude or Poussin; there too the human figures may be beautiful, but they only appear because a landscape without figures seemed inconceivable.

Metre: Alcaic.

1. **velox:** like a mountain goat; cf. Ov. *fast.* 2. 285 f. 'ipse deus velox discurrere gaudet in altis / montibus, et subitas concipit ipse fugas', Swinburne, *Atalanta* 'And Pan by noon and Bacchus by night Fleeter of foot than the fleet-foot kid'.

amoenum: cf. *epist.* 1. 14. 19 f. 'nam quae deserta et inhospita tesqua / credis, amoena vocat mecum qui sentit', 1. 16. 15 'hae latebrae dulces, etiam, si credis, amoenae'. The modern pilgrim will agree with Horace; yet the attitude might seem an unconventional one in the poet's own time.

Lucretilem: cf. Paul. Fest. 106 L. (= 119 M.) 'Lucretilis mons in Sabinis' (thus also Porphyrio). We may be sure that the mountain had no poetical associations until Horace linked it with the legendary Lycaeus (cf. 1. 21. 6 n.).

It is much less certain precisely what Horace means by the name. The *Liber pontificalis* 34. 27 (Silvester) records a donation to a church of a 'possessio in territorio Sabinense quod appellatur Duas casas sub monte Lucreti'. The name 'duas casas' may well survive in the chapel of the Madonna della Casa near Rocca Giovane. This is situated to the west of the valley of the Licenza less than a mile to the south-west of the villa attributed to the poet (an attribution that is plausible without being certain). The evidence of the *Liber pontificalis* makes it very likely that Lucretilis is to be looked for on the western side of the Licenza valley (see Capmartin de Chaupy, *Découverte de la Maison de Campagne d'Horace*, Rome, 3, 1769, pp. 157 ff., H. Nissen, *Landeskunde* 2, 1902, pp. 616 f., *RE* 1 A. 1590 ff., and for maps ibid. 2553 f., Wickham, vol. 2, pp. 296 ff.).

We cannot with certainty proceed much further. Lucretilis must be a conspicuous feature; people who live in hill country do not give a name to every knoll and spur. One possible candidate is the

Colle Rotondo, a detached and conspicuous hill (3,335 ft.), which lies
within a mile to the west of Horace's supposed villa and is even
closer to the Madonna della Casa. But Horace is more probably
referring to the range to the west of the Colle Rotondo, which
culminates in the present Monte Gennaro (4,164 ft.), four miles to the
west of the villa. It is the range rather than a single hill whose name
one would expect to be familiar to Horace's readers. Present-day
travellers to Greece are sometimes surprised to find that Olympus
and Parnassus are not single peaks but mountainous complexes.

2. mutat: 'takes in exchange' (by the common Latin idiom); so in
Greek ἀμείβειν and ἀλλάσσειν, used with a plain accusative, can
mean 'to go to' (1. 37. 24 n.). The gods went on progress from one
favourite shrine to another (1. 30. 2 n.). For such visits by Faunus
(Pan) cf. 3. 18 (where he is summoned to the Sabinum), Theoc. 1.
123 ff., 7. 111 ff., Nicias, *anth. Pl.* 189. 1 f. μίμνω / ἐνθάδε, Μαιναλίαν
κλιτὺν ἀποπρολιπών, Virg. *georg.* 1. 16 ff. 'ipse, nemus linquens patrium
saltusque Lycaei, / . . . adsis, o Tegeaee, favens', Sil. 13. 345 f., Stat.
silv. 1. 3. 78 'silvis accersere Pana Lycaeis' (to Vopiscus's house at
Tibur), Rut. Nam. 1. 233.

    Lycaeo: there is an assonance with Lucretilis; y was pronounced
ü. Lycaeus is a mountain in the west of Arcadia, near Bassae; the
present road from Karytaina to Andritsaina scrambles dangerously
along its flank. It was said to be Pan's birthplace and he had a
temple on the summit (Paus. 8. 38. 5, Pind. fr. 100 b, schol. Stat.
Theb. 2. 206). Hence it was one of the god's favourite haunts; cf.
Theoc. 1. 123. Pan was associated with mountains in general (*h.Pan*
6 f.); hence he is called ὀρειβάτης and other similar names.

    Faunus: Faunus and the Fauni were ancient woodland spirits of
Italy. They were associated with divination, with the aboriginal
inhabitants of Latium, with the mysterious god of the Lupercalia. At
an early stage Faunus was identified with the Greek Pan. For details
and bibliography see Pease on Cic. *nat. deor.* 2. 6, *div.* 1. 101, Bömer
on Ov. *fast.* 2. 271, Farnell 5. 431 ff., 464 ff., R. Herbig, *Pan*, 1949.

    Faunus seems to have been one of Horace's favourite gods; per-
haps, like some of the ancients, he connected his name with *favere*.
Faunus is to receive a sacrifice at the coming of spring (1. 4. 11 f.); he
saves Horace from the falling tree (2. 17. 27); he is addressed with an
elegant hymn at his December festival (3. 18). The plastic Greek
imagination contributes most of the detail to Horace's picture; and
it may be significant that Pindar had a personal cult of Pan (*P.* 3.
77 ff.). However, it would be quite wrong to regard Horace's Faunus
as an alien poetical fancy; he remains a truly Italian deity, sanctified
by deeply rooted local cults.

3. **defendit**: 'wards off', ἀμύνει; cf. *serm.* 1. 3. 14, Cic. *Cato* 53 'nimios solis defendit ardores', Prop. 1. 20. 11, Stat. *silv.* 3. 1. 70 'patulas defendimus arbore soles'. For the dative *capellis* cf. Virg. *ecl.* 7. 47 'solstitium pecori defendite', *georg.* 3. 155, Sil. 5. 490 f.

capellis: Pan was the protector of sheep and goats, and was worshipped as νόμιος (*h.Pan* 5, Paus. 8. 38. 11). At Aule in Arcadia ὅσα ἂν ἐνταυθοῖ τῶν ζώων καταφύγῃ ὥσπερ οὖν ἱκέτας ὁ θεὸς δι᾽ αἰδοῦς ἄγων εἶτα μέντοι σώζει τὴν μεγίστην σωτηρίαν αὐτά (Ael. *nat. anim.* 11. 6). See further Virg. *ecl.* 2. 33, *georg.* 1. 17, Theaetetus, *anth. Pl.* 233. 2 εὐκεράου μαλοφύλαξ ἀγέλας, below, 10 n.

4. **usque**: the word is in some relation with *saepe*: Faunus often visits Lucretilis and stays a good long time. *usque* does not mean 'always', as the god's protection depends on his *praesentia*; this is brought out by *utcumque* in 10.

pluviosque ventos: contrasted with *aestatem*. In a Mediterranean climate rain is a typical phenomenon of winter.

5. **impune**: for an even more startling consequence of Faunus's protection cf. 3. 18. 13 'inter audaces lupus errat agnos'. Horace is using language appropriate to the Golden Age; cf. *epod.* 16. 51 f. 'nec vespertinus circumgemit ursus ovile, / nec intumescit alta viperis humus', Theoc. (?) 24. 86 f. ἔσται δὴ τοῦτ᾽ ἆμαρ ὁπηνίκα νεβρὸν ἐν εὐνᾷ / καρχαρόδων σίνεσθαι ἰδὼν λύκος οὐκ ἐθελήσει with Gow's note (cf. also E. Norden, *Die Geburt des Kindes*, ed. 2, 1931, p. 52 n. 1), Virg. *ecl.* 4. 22 'nec magnos metuent armenta leones', 24 f. 'occidet et serpens, et fallax herba veneni / occidet', 5. 60 f., *Sib. or.* 3. 788 f. ἠδὲ λύκοι τε καὶ ἄρνες ἐν οὔρεσιν ἄμμιγ᾽ ἔδονται / χόρτον, παρδάλιές τ᾽ ἐρίφοις ἅμα βοσκήσονται, Sen. *Herc. O.* 1056 ff., Calp. *ecl.* 1. 37 ff. (an oracle of Faunus foretells a golden age), Babrius 102, Lact. *inst.* 7. 24. 7 ff. (citing Virgil and the Sibylline oracles), Mart. Cap. 9. 907, Gatz 171 ff. Christian readers are most familiar with Isaiah 11. 6 ff. 'The wolf also shall dwell with the lamb, and the leopard shall lie down with the kid; and the calf and the young lion and the fatling together. . . . And the suckling child shall play on the hole of the asp, and the weaned child shall put his hand on the cockatrice' den. They shall not hurt nor destroy in all my holy mountain.'

tutum: Bentley objected to the tautology after *impune*, and read *totum* with a manuscript of Lambinus. He compared especially Pers. 5. 32 f. 'totaque impune Subura / permisit sparsisse oculos iam candidus umbo'. *totum* would be reinforced by *deviae*; the goats wander all over the place, even off the beaten track. The theory is not absurd, but in this poem the pleonasm has point (cf. 14 ff.). *tutus* means not just 'safe' but 'protected', from *tueor*; cf. 4. 5. 17 'tutus bos etenim rura perambulat'.

arbutos: much liked by goats; cf. Virg. *ecl.* 3. 82 'dulce ... depulsis arbutus haedis', *georg.* 3. 300 f. 'iubeo frondentia capris / arbuta sufficere', Colum. 7. 6. 1.

7. olentis uxores mariti: mock-pompous poetic diction. The billy-goat is often described as the husband of the flock, sometimes even in technical contexts; cf. Theoc. 8. 49 ὦ τράγε, τᾶν λευκᾶν αἰγῶν ἄνερ, Leonidas, *anth. P.* 9. 99. 1 ἴξαλος εὐπώγων αἰγὸς πόσις, anon. *anth. Pl.* 17. 5, Virg. *ecl.* 7. 7 'vir gregis ipse caper', *georg.* 3. 125 'quem ... pecori dixere maritum', Ov. *fast.* 1. 334 'lanigerae coniuge ... ovis', Colum. 7. 6. 4 'maritos gregum', Petr. 133 v. 14 'hircus, pecoris pater', Mart. 7. 95. 13, 14. 140. 1, Juv. 8. 109 'pater armenti', *pervig. Ven.* 83 'cum maritis ecce balantum greges', Sidon. *carm.* 9. 238 'olidae marem capellae'. The formula is given an even more grotesque varia-tion in Stat. *silv.* 4. 5. 18 'nec vacca dulci mugit adultero'. See also Chaucer, *Nun's Priest's Tale*, 2865 ff. 'This gentil cok hadde in his governaunce Sevene hennes for to doon al his plesaunce, Whiche were his sustres and his paramours', Milton, *L'Allegro* 52 '(The cock) Stoutly struts his dames before', 1. 25. 14 n.

8. viridis: a conventional epithet of snakes; cf. Pind. *O.* 8. 37 γλαυκοὶ δὲ δράκοντες (though that presumably refers to the colour of their eyes; cf. schol. ad loc. γλαυκοὶ δὲ δράκοντες: φοβεροί), Stat. Theb. 1. 711, 2. 279, 5. 549 f., Claud. 3. 290 'virens ... hydra', André 340. In fact vipers, which Horace is probably thinking of, are not charac-teristically green. But descriptions of snakes in the ancient poets owe more to tradition than autopsy (cf. Kroll 286 ff.).

9. Martialis: because sacred to Mars; cf. Virg. *Aen.* 9. 566 'Martius ... lupus', 8. 630 f. (the she-wolf suckles Romulus and Remus 'Mavortis in antro'), Liv. 10. 27. 9 'hinc victor Martius lupus ... gentis nos Martiae et conditoris nostri admonuit', Ov. *fast.* 3. 37 f., Roscher 2. 2430.

haediliae: 'kids'; cf. *CGL* 3. 432. 38 'αιριφιον haedilia' (*Thes.l.L.* 6. 3. 2487. 76 ff.); the word is not found elsewhere, but is correctly formed, cf. *porciliae*. It is true that the feminine *haeda* never occurs, whereas *porca* does; but *haedilla* is found in inscriptions and in the pre-Vulgate translation of the Bible, the Itala. A few manuscripts, puzzled by the unfamiliar word, have the unmetrical *haedilia*, 'pens for goats'.

Some editors have believed in an (otherwise unknown) mountain Haedilia from which the wolves make forays. But in a context re-ferring to goats and wolves it would be a fantastic coincidence if *haediliae* were a place-name.

10. dulci: cf. Pind. *O.* 10. 93 γλυκύς τ' αὐλός.

Tyndari: the very name may strike a pastoral note; the Arcadian Evander was son of Timandra, daughter of Tyndareus. Its position between *dulci* and *fistula* suggests that Faunus's pipe had a particular appeal for Tyndaris.

fistula: for Pan's pipe cf. *h.Pan* 15 f. δονάκων ὕπο μοῦσαν ἀθύρων / νήδυμον, Eur. *El.* 702 ff. εὐαρμόστοις ἐν καλάμοις / Πᾶνα μοῦσαν ἡδύθροον / πνέοντ᾽, ἀγρῶν ταμίαν, Virg. *ecl.* 2. 32 f., Mart. 9. 61. 11 f., Paus. 8. 36. 8 οἱ περὶ αὐτοῦ (τοῦ Μαινάλου) καὶ ἐπακροᾶσθαι συρίζοντος τοῦ Πανὸς λέγουσι, 8. 38. 11. Lucretius (4. 580 ff.) offers a rationalistic explanation for the rustic belief in the piping of Pan. In particular Pan protected animals by his music; cf. Anyte, *anth. Pl.* 231 a. Τίπτε κατ᾽ οἰόβατον, Πὰν ἀγρότα, δάσκιον ὕλαν / ἥμενος, ἀδυβόᾳ τῷδε κρέκεις δόνακι; β. Ὄφρα μοι ἐρσήεντα κατ᾽ οὔρεα ταῦτα νέμοιντο / πόρτιες ἠυκόμων δρεπτόμενοι σταχύων, anon. *anth. Pl.* 17.

11. Vsticae cubantis: Ustica 'reclines', i.e. slopes; cf. Porph. ad loc. 'Vstica mons in Sabinis est, quem cubantem suaviter dixit ad resupinam regionem eius attendens'. There is no certain parallel for this use of *cubare* (Lucr. 4. 517 is obscure and probably irrelevant). For the sense one may compare 3. 4. 23 'Tibur supinum', Virg. *georg.* 2. 276 'tumulis acclive solum collesque supinos' (3. 555). Ps.-Acro suggests (among other possibilities) that Ustica was a valley; in that case *cubantis* would have to mean 'low-lying' (cf. Virg. *Aen.* 3. 689 'Thapsumque iacentem'). Yet this does not provide the expected contrast with *valles*; resounding rocks suit a hill much better than a low-lying area; and one should draw a distinction between *cubare* ('recline, as at table') and *iacere* ('to lie flat').

Ustica cannot be identified precisely; one looks for a fairly prominent feature not too far from Horace's villa. The resonance of the whole area is remarkable (pointed out already by Capmartin de Chaupy, op. cit. [above, 1], 3. 336 f.); conceivably we should look for something on the eastern side of the valley. Yet Ustica might well be the rocky hill to the north, on which stands the modern village of Licenza (there is no suggestion of a village in Horace's time). Today, when workmen near 'Horace's villa' want their lunch, they simply shout to their womenfolk in Licenza, half a mile to the north (information supplied from personal observation by Mr. Robert Wells).

12. levia . . . saxa: cf. Hom. *Od.* 3. 293 λισσὴ . . . πέτρη, Aesch. *supp.* 794 ff. λισσὰς . . . πέτρα.

13. di me tuentur: Horace often makes this assertion. The gods protected him as a child (3. 4. 17 ff.), saved him from the tree (2. 13, 2. 17. 27 ff.), from Philippi (2. 7. 13 f.), from shipwreck (3. 4. 28).

Conventionally the gods protect the good man (cf. 1. 22. 1) and the poet (Kroll 30 f., K. F. Smith on Tib. 2. 5. 113–14). For a reference to our passage cf. [Gallican.] *Avid.* 11. 8 (professedly a letter from M. Aurelius to his wife) 'esto igitur secura; "di me tuentur, dis pietas mea cordi est" '.

14. cordi est: the phrase seems to have been used in old Latin in speaking of the gods; cf. Cato, *orig.* 12 'Iuppiter, si tibi magis cordi est nos ea tibi dare potius quam Mezentio, uti nos victores facias', Liv. 9. 8. 8.

hic . . .: 'here you will see plenty flowing to the full, rich with a horn that lavishes the glories of the fields'. The opulence of the pleonasm suits the scene of abundance that Horace is describing.

In this line *hinc* has overwhelming manuscript support, and is backed by Porphyrio and ps.-Acro; they comment 'scilicet de Sabino fundo'. Yet *hinc . . . hic . . . hic* gives an unexpected asymmetry; the series should start with *hic,* as in the parallel passages in the *Eclogues* (above, p. 216). Moreover, in this context *hinc* would naturally be interpreted *ob pietatem meam* (Bentley); cf. *Querol.* p. 3. 8 'parvas mihi litterulas non parvus indulsit amor. hinc honos atque merces, hinc manabit praemium'. But in our passage such an interpretation is quite impossible, as it destroys the connection with *hic* in lines 17 and 21. It looks as if an ancient editor has consciously or unconsciously substituted *hinc* in an attempt to provide a more explicit connection.

copia: *copia* is abstract with *manabit,* but with *benigno . . . cornu* suggests the personified goddess Copia; cf. *carm. saec.* 59 f. 'beata pleno / Copia cornu', *epist.* 1. 12. 28 f. 'aurea fruges / Italiae pleno defundit Copia cornu', Ov. *met.* 9. 89, Sidon. *carm.* 11. 114 'patulo Fortunae copia cornu'. For such a blend of abstraction and personification cf. 1. 18. 16 n.

15. ad plenum: cf. Virg. *georg.* 2. 243 f. 'huc ager ille malus dulcesque a fontibus undae / ad plenum calcentur' ('till the strainer is full', Conington). The use of *ad,* 'up to', is like that in the old adverbs *adfatim* and *admodum* (cf. W. M. Lindsay, *Syntax of Plautus,* 1907, p. 84) and the later *ad infinitum.* In our passage the phrase simply means 'abundantly'; there is nothing to be literally filled, as the harvest fruits are spilling out of the horn, not going into it.

16. ruris honorum: it is uncertain whether the phrase is to be taken with *benigno* or *opulenta.* For the former cf. *serm.* 2. 3. 3 'vini somnique benignus'; on this view *cornu* must be taken with *opulenta* (cf. Virg. *Aen.* 1. 447 ('templum) donis opulentum'). For the latter cf. Stat. *Theb.* 6. 91 'largae . . . opulentior umbrae', Virg. *georg.* 2. 468 'dives opum'; this necessitates taking *benigno cornu* as 'from generous horn', as in *epist*. 1. 12. 29 (cited on *copia* above). With *manabit* the separative ablative is rather less natural (in spite of 3. 11. 19 f. 'saniesque manet / ore trilingui', where a preceding *exeatque*, if that is the correct emendation, would ease the construction). Moreover, the word-order raises doubts.

honorum: 'splendours'; for the concrete use cf. *serm*. 2. 5. 12 f. 'dulcia poma / et quoscumque feret cultus tibi fundus honores', *epod*. 11. 6, Virg. *georg*. 2. 404 'silvis aquilo decussit honorem', Stat. *silv*. 4. 5. 1 'parvi beatus ruris honoribus', *Theb*. 10. 788 'veris honore', Sil. 3. 487 'nullique aestatis honores', *Thes. l.L.* 6. 2923. 49 ff., Pope, *Od*. 11. 235 'The leafy honours scattering on the ground', *OED* s.v. *honour* 6 b. Cf. in Greek Aristaenetus 1. 10 (Acontius to the trees) καὶ τοὺς κλάδους ἁπλῶς ὁ πόθος κόμης ὑμᾶς καὶ ἀγλαίας ἐψίλου.

cornu: the horn of plenty is particularly associated with Amalthea's goat, which suckled Zeus. Cf. Anacreon 361. 1 f. ἐγὼ δ' οὔτ' ἂν Ἀμαλθίης / βουλοίμην κέρας, Phocylides 7. 2 ἀγρὸν γάρ τε λέγουσιν Ἀμαλθείης κέρας εἶναι, schol. Call. *h*. 1. 49. According to other accounts, the horn belonged to the river-god Achelous and was broken off by Hercules; cf. Ov. *fast*. 5. 121 with Bömer's note, Porph. ad loc., Ov. *met*. 9. 88 f. It is first mentioned in Latin by Plaut. *Pseud*. 671 'haec allata cornu Copiaest, ubi inest quicquid volo'; for other examples cf. Bömer, loc. cit., Otto 94.

The cornucopia was an attribute of Earth and of Fortuna; cf. Roscher 1. 927 ff., 5. 342 ff. For its antiquity as an emblem of fertility cf. Cook, *Zeus* 1. 501 f. It was important in Augustan symbolism, and appears on the so-called Ara Pacis.

17. reducta valle: 'convalle longe in montes recedente ac propterea secreta' (Orelli). The phrase is conventional and occurs again in *epod*. 2. 11, Virg. *Aen*. 6. 703, 8. 609. Yet it exactly describes the Digentia valley.

Caniculae: the name is used both for Sirius and for the whole constellation Canis Major, of which Sirius is the brightest star. The diminutive form is characteristic of Roman star-names, cf. *iugulae*, *suculae*, *vergiliae*. The constellation's heliacal rising towards the end of July coincided with the hottest days, the so-called 'dog days'; cf. 3. 13. 9 f., Virg. *georg*. 2. 353, Tib. 1. 1. 27 with K. F. Smith's note, *RE* 3 A. 342.

18. vitabis: cf. Tib. 1. 1. 27 'Canis aestivos ortus vitare sub umbra', Ov. *am*. 3. 5. 7, Symm. *epist*. 7. 35, Sidon. *epist*. 2. 2. 2 'fallis clementissimo recessu inclementiam canicularem'. In particular, the picture belongs to idyllic pastoral. We are reminded of Thyrsis singing to the goatherd under the elm at midday and of Tityrus piping under

his beech-tree; cf. also Anyte (cited on 10 above), anon. *anth. Pl.*
227. 5 ff. χὼ ποιμὴν ἐν ὄρεσσι μεσαμβρινὸν ἀγχόθι παγᾶς / συρίσδων,
λασίας θάμνῳ ὕπο πλατάνου· / καῦμα δ᾽ ὀπωρινοῖο φυγὼν κυνὸς αἶπος
ἀμείψεις / ὥριον.
    fide Teia: the lyre of Anacreon of Teos; cf. *epod.* 14. 10 f. He was
famous above all for light love-poetry (cf. 4. 9. 9). Like Horace here,
he was regarded as a harmless character; cf. Critias 8. 1 f. γυναικείων
μελέων πλέξαντά ποτ᾽ ᾠδάς / ... φιλοβάρβιτον, ἡδύν, ἄλυπον. The
pastoral note of the *Anacreontea* is even more relevant to our poem.

    19. dices: for such mythological songs cf. 3. 28. 11 ff. But one may
doubt the validity of L. Müller's generalization 'die Hetären liebten
Lieder mythologischen Inhalts'. For the use of *dico* in the sense of
'sing' cf. 1. 21. 1 n.
    laborantis: for the use of *labor* and *laboro* referring to the torments
of love cf. Enk on Prop. 1. 6. 23. So in Greek cf. Ar. *eccl.* 975 διά τοι
σὲ πόνους ἔχω, *Anacreontea* 33. 13 ff. εἰ τὸ κέντρον / πονεῖ τὸ τᾶς
μελίττας, / πόσον δοκεῖς πονοῦσιν, / ῎Ερως, ὅσους σὺ βάλλεις;
    in uno: cf. *epod.* 11. 4 'mollibus in pueris aut in puellis urere'. *in*
and the ablative with verbs of emotion is idiomatic (cf. K.–S. 1. 563,
Butler and Barber on Prop. 2. 8. 36).

    20. vitream: the epithet perplexed the ancient commentators; cf.
Porph. 'vitream Circen parum decore mihi videtur dixisse pro candida', ps.-Acro 'aut pulchram aut procurato lucentem nitore aut mari
vicinam'. The meaning 'glittering' is no doubt present; cf. Call.
fr. 238. 16 ὑάλοιο φαάντερος οὐρανός, Ov. *met.* 13. 791 'splendidior vitro',
Rufinus, *anth. P.* 5. 48. 1 ὄμματα μὲν χρύσεια καὶ ὑαλόεσσα παρειή.
    But ancient glass was more exotic and sinister than the modern
product. The characteristic glass known to Horace was the mould-
pressed *millefiori* ware of various colours and complicated decoration; glass-blowing was not invented till some years after his death
and colourless glass two centuries later (cf. D. B. Harden, *G & R* 3,
1934, 140 ff.). Though *millefiori* glass was translucent, it was complex,
distorting, and enigmatic. *vitream* suits the *femme fatale* in the dark
wood; Statius at least seems to have found something sinister in
Horace's epithet (cf. *silv.* 1. 3. 85 'vitreae iuga perfida Circes').
Circe was δολοφρονέουσα, the very opposite of Penelope. Some editors
compare Publil. 189 'Fortuna vitrea est', but that passage indicates
rather a dangerous brittleness.
    Others associate the epithet with the sea; cf. 3. 28. 10 'viridis
Nereidum comas', Stat. *silv.* 1. 5. 15 f. 'ite deae virides, liquidosque
advertite vultus / et vitreum Veneris crinem redimita corymbis',
Claud. *rapt. Pros.* 2. 53 f. 'soror vitrei libamina potat / uberis' (of
Tethys), André 188. Circe was the daughter of the Oceanid Perse

(Hom. *Od.* 10. 139, *RE* 19. 938). She also had a love-affair with the
marine deity Glaucus, which was perhaps described by the third-
century poetess Hedyle (cf. Ov. *met.* 14. 1 ff., Athen. 297 b, Gruppe
1. 708 n. 2). However, there is no justification, at least in extant
literature, for regarding Circe herself as a lady of the sea. Yet it is
quite possible that Horace has conflated the attributes of Circe and
the sea nymph Calypso (cf. Prop. 3. 12. 31 'thalamum Aeaeae flentis
fugisse puellae', 1. 16. 17 n.) ; strictly speaking it was the latter who
shared Penelope's love for Odysseus. So Plutarch makes Odysseus
refuse immortality from Circe, not Calypso (*brut. anim.* 985 f, 988 f) ;
cf. E. Kaiser, *MH* 21, 1964, 199.

21. innocentis: not just a poeticism ; cf. Hermippus fr. 82. 5 K. Χῖον
ἄλυπον, Plin. *nat.* 23. 34 'innocentius iam est quodcumque et ignobilius
(vinum)', 46 'innocentius pice sola conditum'. Lesbian wine did not go
to the head ; Philodemus, *anth. P.* 11. 34. 7 mentions it in a list of
things contrasted with τὰ πρὸς μανίαν. Cf. also Athen. 45 e προλαμ-
βανέτω . . . τὸν καλούμενον πρότροπον, τὸν γλυκὺν Λέσβιον, ὄντα εὐστό-
μαχον. καὶ ὁ γλυκάζων δ' οἶνος οὐ βαρύνει τὴν κεφάλην, ὡς Ἱπποκράτης
ἐν τῷ Περὶ διαίτης (2. 332) φησί, Plin. *nat.* 14. 73 'in summa gloria . . .
fuere Thasium Chiumque . . . his addidit Lesbium Erasistrati maximi
medici auctoritas'. The virtues of Lesbian are also implied in the
story of Aristotle's designation of his successor ; cf. Gell. 13. 5. 5
'vinum ait quod tunc biberet non esse id ex valetudine sua, sed
insalubre esse atque asperum ac propterea quaeri debere exoticum
vel Rhodium aliquod vel Lesbium'. Whereupon with the words ἡδίων
ὁ Λέσβιος he rejected Eudemus of Rhodes and gave the job to
Theophrastus of Eresus.

In spite of having a natural taste of sea-water (Plin. loc. cit.),
Lesbian ranked as one of the most agreeable of Greek wines, and
Athenaeus (28 e–30 b) provides an anthology of commendations, e.g.
Clearchus fr. 6 K., Eubulus fr. 124 K. Λέσβιον γέροντα, νεκταροσταγῆ,
Archestratus fr. 59. 10 f., 19 ἀλλ' οὐδὲν τἄλλ' ἐστὶν ἁπλῶς πρὸς Λέσβιον
οἶνον ; cf. also Longus 4. 10 ἀνθοσμίας οἶνος Λέσβιος, ποθῆναι κάλλιστος
οἶνος. Horace more normally offers a choice Italian vintage, Caecuban
to Lyde in 3. 28, Alban to Phyllis in 4. 11 ; but perhaps the Greek
wine suits the pastoral note.

Lesbii: both Horace and Virgil maintain the republican genitive in
-*i* of nouns in -*ius* and -*ium*. The -*ii* here is due to the fact that
Lesbium is really an adjective.

22. duces: the word implies a leisurely process ; cf. 4. 12. 14, 3. 3. 34 f.,
4. 1. 21 f. 'illic plurima naribus / duces tura', *serm.* 2. 6. 62 'ducere
sollicitae iucunda oblivia vitae', Prop. 2. 9. 21 'multo duxistis pocula
risu'.

Semeleius ... Thyoneus: both names are metronymics; cf. *h. Hom.* 1. 21 σὺν μητρὶ Σεμέλῃ ἥνπερ καλέουσι Θυώνην, Apollod. 3. 5. 3 ὁ δὲ (Διόνυσος) ἀναγαγὼν ἐξ Ἅιδου τὴν μητέρα, καὶ προσαγορεύσας Θυώνην, μετ᾽ αὐτῆς εἰς οὐρανὸν ἀνῆλθεν. They recur together in *anth. Lat.* 751 'Semeleie Bacche ... laete Thyoneu'. Horace is not wholly serious in accumulating these pretentious ἐπωνυμίαι.

Thyoneus is not attested in Greek, though Dionysus was Θυωνίδας at Rhodes (Hesychius), and Oppian used Θυωναῖος (*cyn.* 1. 27). In Latin it is not rare; cf. Ov. *met.* 4. 13, Val. Fl. 1. 726, Stat. *Theb.* 5. 265 f.

23. cum Marte: 'along with Mars'. Bacchus and Mars would not of course be fighting each other, but co-operating to turn the party into a riot.

24. nec metues ...: the violent quarrels of jealous lovers are a motif of New Comedy, flowing from there to the Anthology and Roman elegy. The tearing of clothes is normal to the topic. Cf. Prop. 2. 5. 21 'nec tibi periuro scindam de corpore vestes', Tib. 1. 10. 61 f. 'sit satis e membris tenuem rescindere vestem, / sit satis ornatus dissoluisse comae', Ov. *am.* 1. 7. 47 'aut tunicam a summa diducere turpiter ora', *ars* 3. 569, Lucian, *dial. mer.* 8. 1 ὅστις δὲ ... μήτε ζηλοτυπεῖ μήτε ὀργίζεται μήτε ἐρράπισέ ποτε ἢ περιέκειρεν ἢ τὰ ἱμάτια περιέσχισεν, ἔτι ἐραστὴς ἐκεῖνός ἐστιν;, Headlam on Herodas 2. 69.

25. suspecta: used of jealousy; cf. 2. 4. 22 ff. 'fuge suspicari / cuius octavum trepidavit aetas / claudere lustrum', Juv. 11. 188.

Cyrum: the name seems to belong to Hellenistic erotic verse; cf. 1. 33. 6, Numenius, *anth. P.* 12. 28, Fronto, ibid. 12. 174, and Κῦρις in Strato, ibid. 12. 206 and 215.

male: intensifies *dispari*; cf. 1. 9. 24 n.

26. incontinentis ... manus: cf. Tib. 1. 10. 56 'flet sibi dementes tam valuisse manus', Ov. *am.* 1. 7. 1 ff. 'adde manus in vincla meas (meruere catenas), / ... nam furor in dominam temeraria bracchia movit; / flet mea vesana laesa puella manu', Philostr. *epist.* 61 (64) φεῦ ἀναιδοῦς παλάμης, Paul. Sil. *anth. P.* 5. 248. 1 ὦ παλάμη πάντολμε, Agathias, ibid. 5. 218. 4 παντόλμοις χερσίν. Propertius characteristically uses similar phrases of Cynthia's hands, not his own; cf. 1. 6. 16 'insanis ora notet manibus', 3. 8. 3 f., 3. 16. 10 'in me mansuetas non habet illa manus', 4. 8. 64.

27. haerentem ... crinibus: cf. *serm.* 1. 10. 49 'haerentem capiti multa cum laude coronam'.

28. immeritam: the phrase involves a natural personification that is found in various styles; cf. Cic. *epist.* 7. 18. 4 'epistulam tuam ...

concidi innocentem', *serm*. 2. 3. 7 f. 'culpantur frustra calami, im-
meritusque laborat / iratis natus paries dis atque poetis', Prop. 2. 4. 3
'immeritos corrumpas dentibus ungues', *moretum* 108 'immeritoque
furens dicit convicia fumo', *Thes.l.L.* 7. 1. 456. 54 ff.

18. NVLLAM VARE SACRA

[S. Eitrem, *Annuaire de l'institut de philologie et d'histoire orientales et slaves* 5,
1937, 343 ff.; Pasquali 1 ff.]

1–2. '*Plant no tree rather than the vine' on your estate at Tibur, Varus.*
3–6. *Wine relieves anxiety and hardship.* 7–11. *One should not misuse
the gifts of Bacchus, but be warned by the Centaurs and Sithonians.*
11–16. *I shall do you no injury, Bacchus, so restrain your orgiastic
music; in your revel-rout are vices like self-love, pride, and indiscretion.*

The Varus of this ode is described as 'Varus Quintilius' by the
superscriptions of one family of manuscripts; this information is not
found in the text of either ps.-Acro or Porphyrio (though it appears
as a heading to the Acro scholia in cod. A). For Horace's literary
friend Quintilius see below on 1. 24; as is there observed, we have no
evidence earlier than the fourth century that he bore the cognomen
Varus. Yet editors generally accept the identification of the Varus of
our poem and the Quintilius of 1. 24: Horace's Varus lived at
Tibur (2), and one can point at Tivoli to a so-called Villa of Quintilio
Varo, a church of Santa Maria di Quintiliolo, and already in the
tenth century a *fundus Quintiliolus* (cf. T. Ashby, *PBSR* 3, 1906,
155 ff., *RE* 24. 901). But these names are likely to be derived from
a greater magnate than Horace's friend, for instance the Quintilius
Varus who lost Germany. As for Horace's poem, more attention
ought to be given to yet another Varus, who was surely the first to
spring to mind when this name was mentioned in early Augustan
society.

This was P. Alfenus Varus, who was born in Cremona (Porph. *serm.*
1. 3. 130) not later than 82 B.C. (he became consul suffect in 39). In
view of his rare name, age, literary interests, and Transpadane origin
he may well be the Alfenus of Catullus 30 ('Alfene immemor atque
unanimis false sodalibus'), possibly also the Varus of Catullus 10 and
22. He studied law under Ser. Sulpicius Rufus, and became one of
the most eminent jurists of his day; some of his rulings are cited in
the Digest. In 41 B.C. he distributed land or exacted money in Gallia
Transpadana (Broughton, *MRR* 2. 377); he was criticized by one

Cornelius for his severity (Serv. auct. *ecl.* 9. 10), but was honoured by
Virgil with unconvincing eulogies (*ecl.* 6. 6–12, 9. 26–9). Porphyrio
identifies him with the Alfenus of *serm.* 1. 3. 130 ff. 'ut Alfenus vafer,
omni / abiecto instrumento artis clausaque taberna, / sutor erat';
but though *vafer* suits a lawyer, the impertinence to a living consular
would be unparalleled in Horace, and the imperfect *erat* tells against
the identification. Of course it cannot be proved that the jurist is the
Varus of our poem; one can only emphasize that he was a patron of
letters (Virgil, loc. cit.), grand enough to have a house at Tibur,
and to receive an ode in the distinguished company of Horace's
First Book; 'arcanique Fides prodiga' (16) would be agreeably
humorous if addressed to a tight-lipped lawyer. A more substantial
argument may be added: Horace's poem to Varus and Catullus's to
Alfenus are both written in Greater Asclepiads, a rare and difficult
metre. Horace may be delicately recalling that the formidable old
jurist was once teased with classic virtuosity by a young Transpadane contemporary, now a generation dead.

Our ode begins with a reminiscence of Alcaeus 342 (also in Greater
Asclepiads) μηδ' ἐν ἄλλο φυτεύσῃς πρότερον δένδριον ἀμπέλω. If Horace
is indeed echoing Catullus (as suggested above), his subject-matter
is largely determined by his metre; but by referring to Tibur he
characteristically gives his Greek allusions an Italian flavour. We
only have the first line of Alcaeus's poem, so we do not know
whether Horace's imitation extended any further. Certainly a close
resemblance is impossible.

In lines 3–6 Horace gives some conventional praises of wine. Such
lists may have originated in the ἀρεταλογίαι of the dithyramb (cf.
Norden, *Agnostos Theos*, p. 160); in our poem the address to Bacchus
in lines 6 and 11 ff. suggests a hymn (cf. note on 4 *aliter*). The praise
of wine is also found in other contexts in Greek choral lyric; see
especially Pind. fr. 124 a.b, Bacch. fr. 20 B (below, 4 n., 5 n.). Horace
later developed the theme in his charming epistle to Torquatus,
another lawyer (1. 5. 16 ff.):

> quid non ebrietas dissignat? operta recludit,
> spes iubet esse ratas, ad proelia trudit inertem,
> sollicitis animis onus eximit, addocet artis.
> fecundi calices quem non fecere disertum?
> contracta quem non in paupertate solutum?

See also Maecenas ap. Serv. auct. *Aen.* 8. 310 'idem umor ministrat
faciles oculos, pulchriora reddit omnia, et dulcis iuuentae reducit
bona', Ov. *ars* 1. 237 ff., Plut. *quaest. conv.* 715–16.

At line 7 Horace changes his tune and warns against the misuse
of wine. The style alters with the subject-matter: now it is elaborate,

compressed, and allusive; the transitions are abrupt; the long
sentences and the enjambement (contrast 1–6) give an impression of
rapidity. The Hellenistic poets (following Euripides) and the Romans
after them showed a morbid interest in the orgiastic cult of Bacchus,
and the similar rites of Cybele; the thyrsus and the cista, the drone
of the pipe and the boom of the tambourine, all stimulated their
taste for the grotesquely picturesque (see below, 13 n., Pease on
Virg. *Aen.* 4. 301). Horace hints at some obscure irregularity of the
Sithonians with all the knowing learning of an Alexandrian poet. He
adjures Bacchus alike with the brusqueness and the preciosity of a
Callimachus. Even the revel-rout that escorts the god is not a thiasos
of ululating Maenads but a motley troop of sophisticated abstractions.

It may be asked what the ode is about. Certainly Horace is not
offering an opinion on horticultural priorities; he dedicates the
poem to Varus by way of compliment, and then ignores him. He is
not criticizing Antony (Eitrem), or contemporary Bacchic cult
(Pasquali). He is not rejecting an emotional or 'Dionysiac' response
to life; in other poems he is capable of saying just the opposite (2. 19,
3. 25). Rather he is elaborating variations on an old commonplace
which praised the moderate, but not excessive, use of wine (7 n.).
Drunkenness, and not ecstasy, was the sin of the Centaurs (8), and
tempts its victims to breaches of security (16).

A poem of this sort makes little appeal to moderns. It depends for
its effect on an intricate network of allusions, some of which are now
obscure. Its subject veers disconcertingly, though not untypically of
its author. It contains no sentiments to which every bosom returns
an echo: dithyrambic exhortations to sobriety sound very odd unless
one realizes that Horace is playing a complicated literary game. In
many other poems, of course, he is equally artificial; but where
the commonplaces are less esoteric it is easier to persuade oneself
that he is speaking from the heart. But though the ode lacks that
reference to life which must be demanded from the greatest poetry,
one should not underestimate its ingenuity. Horace's tapestry tells
no story, points no moral, and is not particularly beautiful; but one
may admire all the same the ποικιλία of the needlework.

Metre: Greater Asclepiad.

1. **sacra**: the adjective is lacking in Alcaeus, who is writing a matter-
of-fact drinking song. Horace strikes a more solemn note; cf. Enn.
scaen. 124 'Lyaeus vitis inventor sacrae'. Similarly in Greek, Hom.
Od. 13. 372 ἱερῆς παρὰ πυθμέν' ἐλαίης, Eur. fr. 765 οἰνάνθα τρέφει τὸν
ἱερὸν βότρυν.

severis: 'plant'; the word could be used both for σπείρειν and φυτεύειν. Ps.-Acro glosses by *posueris*, and quotes Virg. *georg.* 2. 319 f. 'optima vinetis satio, cum vere rubenti / candida venit avis'; so ibid. 2. 275 'densa sere', Acc. *trag.* 240 f. 'Dionyse . . . vitisator'.

arborem: δένδριον in Alcaeus. The vine was regarded as a tree by the early Romans: cf. Plin. *nat.* 14. 9 'vites iure apud priscos magnitudine quoque inter arbores numerabantur'. Gaius remarks that a man lost a case about the cutting down of vines because he used the word *vites* instead of *arbores*; he gives as a reason 'quod lex XII tabularum ex qua de vitibus succisis actio conpeteret generaliter de arboribus succisis loqueretur' (*inst.* 4. 11). On the other hand cf. Cic. *nat. deor.* 2. 85 'quae procreatio vitis aut arboris'.

2. circa: 'in and around'; cf. 4. 2. 30 f. 'circa nemus uvidique / Tiburis ripas', Plin. *nat.* 19. 46 'quod circa Syriam nascitur' (which does not imply that Syria is excluded), A. Goldbacher, *WS* 20, 1898, 281 f. In our passage the preposition is largely determined by *moenia*, with which it bears its normal sense.

mite: Tivoli is climatically mild compared with the plain and the mountains; for fruit-growing there cf. 1. 7. 13 n. For *mite solum* cf. Stat. *silv.* 1. 3. 15 'ingenium quam mite solo' (also of Tibur), 3. 5. 79, *Thes.l.L.* 8. 1158. 30 ff.

Catili: the legendary founder of Tibur; cf. 1. 7. 13 n. There was a *mons Catilli* at Tibur (Serv. auct. *Aen.* 7. 672), presumably the modern Monte Catillo. Horace's scansion is unparalleled: in Virgil (*Aen.* 7. 672) and Silius the name is *Cātillus*, in Statius (*silv.* 1. 3. 100) *Cătillus*.

3. siccis . . .: 'for the abstemious heaven has ordained nothing but hardship'. Horace is criticized by John of Salisbury, *Policraticus* 739 d 'est autem via omnibus praeclusa disciplinis, si comes sapientiae sobrietas amovetur, quam utique tenere non possunt qui clamitant apud insulsos omnia siccis dura esse proposita'.

nam: for postponed *nam* cf. *epod.* 14. 6, 17. 45, *carm.* 4. 14. 9. This word-order is first attested in Catullus (23. 7, 37. 11, 64. 301); cf. the Hellenistic practice of postponing καί and ἀλλά. See further Norden, *Aen.* 6, pp. 402 ff., M. Platnauer, *Latin Elegiac Verse*, 1951, p. 94, Boerma on *catalepton* 4. 10, H.–Sz. 506.

deus: not 'Bacchus' but 'God' in a general sense; cf. 1. 3. 21, 1. 34. 13 n., 3. 29. 30, *Thes.l.L.* 5. 1. 889. 18.

4. mordaces: cf. 2. 11. 17 f. 'dissipat Euhius / curas edaces', Virg. *Aen.* 1. 261 'haec te cura remordet', Ov. *am.* 2. 19. 43, Maxim. *eleg.* 5. 63, Boeth. *cons.* 3 *carm.* 3. 5. So Alcaeus 70. 10 χαλάσσομεν δὲ τὰς θυμοβόρω λύας, ps.-Theogn. 1324, West on Hes. *th.* 567.

aliter: 'except by drinking'; Horace's language is elliptical, but one should not suspect corruption. For the thought cf. Eur. *Ba.* 283 οὐδ' ἐστ' ἄλλο φάρμακον πόνων. In a hymn to Bacchus the same idea might be expressed by 'sine te'; cf. 1. 26. 9 n.

sollicitudines: μέριμναι. Cf. *Cypria* fr. 13 οἰνόν τοι, Μενέλαε, θεοὶ ποίησαν ἄριστον / θνητοῖς ἀνθρώποισιν ἀποσκεδάσαι μελεδῶνας, Alcaeus 346. 3 f. οἶνον γὰρ Σεμέλας καὶ Διὸς υἷος λαθικάδεον / ἀνθρώποισιν ἔδωκ', Theogn. 883, Pind. fr. 124. 5 ἀνίχ' ἀνθρώπων καματώδεες οἴχονται μέριμναι, Eur. *Ba.* 381, anon. *anth. P.* 9. 524. 12 (of Bacchus) λαθικηδέα λυσιμέριμνον, Palladas, ibid., 11. 55. 1, above, 1. 7. 22 n.

5. post vina: after the drinking of wine. For this abbreviated construction cf. 3. 7. 6, 3. 21. 19, Sen. *Herc. O.* 79 'post feras, post bella, post Stygium canem', Sil. 10. 590, Mart. 1. 1. 6, 3. 68. 5, Tac. *hist.* 3. 49. 1 'post Cremonam', Archipoeta 10. 72 'Nasonem post calicem carmine preibo'. So in Greek Hom. *Il.* 18. 96 αὐτίκα γάρ τοι ἔπειτα μεθ' Ἕκτορα πότμος ἑτοῖμος, Babrius 12. 8 πρῶτον βλέπω σε σήμερον μετὰ Θρᾴκην. See further Peerlkamp's note on our passage, Housman on Luc. 5. 473, Mayor on Juv. 1. 169 'ante tubas', H.–Sz. 243, 827, Schwyzer 2. 486.

Horace repeatedly uses the plural *vina* in the nominative and accusative, and in these cases Virgil uses only the plural. Metrical convenience plays an important part, but the construction would hardly have been so common but for the tendency of such neuter plurals in -a to be used collectively. See P. Maas, *ALL* 12, 1902, 521, Löfstedt, *Syntactica* 1². 48.

gravem militiam: the adjective is not a standing epithet of *militia*; rather the harshness of military service and restricted means is part of the complaint.

pauperiem: the word has no relevance to the prosperous Varus but belongs to a *communis locus* on wine. Cf. 3. 21. 18 'viresque et addis cornua pauperi', *epist.* 1. 5. 19 f. (quoted above, p. 228), Theogn. 1129 ἐμπίομαι πενίης θυμοφθόρου οὐ μελεδαίνων, Pind. fr. 124 b. 8 ὃς μὲν ἀχρήμων, ἀφνεὸς τότε, Bacch. fr. 20 B. 13 χρυσῷ δ' ἐλέφαντί τε μαρμαίρουσιν οἶκοι (what a man thinks when he is drinking), *carm. pop.* PMG 879 Σεμέλη' Ἴακχε πλουτοδότα, Ar. *eq.* 92 f. ὅταν πίνωσιν ἄνθρωποι τότε / πλουτοῦσι, Macedonius, *anth. P.* 11. 63. 2 ἐλπίσιν ἡμερίδων ῥίψατε τὴν πενίην.

crepat: 'prates of' (παταγεῖ, κροτεῖ); cf. *epist.* 1. 7. 84 'sulcos et vineta crepat mera'. The variant *increpat* would mean 'criticizes'; it is a strong argument against this reading that ps.-Acro glosses *crepat* by *increpat*. In the next line one must understand *dicit* out of *crepat*; if one reads *increpat* (which is definitely a word of blame) the next line becomes much more difficult.

T

6. pater: Servius comments on *georg.* 2. 4 '*pater* licet generale sit omnium deorum, tamen proprie Libero semper cohaeret: nam Liber pater vocatur'. See further Lucil. 19 ff., Wissowa 26 f.

Venus: for the association of Venus and Bacchus cf. 1. 19. 2 n.

7. ac: Latin sometimes uses a continuative particle where a modern language might prefer an adversative one (Hand 1. 486). The variant *at* is weakly supported, and is perhaps too blunt; Horace is not preaching a sermon but simply developing his account of Bacchus. In support of *ac* Bentley quotes *epist.* 1. 1. 13 'ac ne forte roges', 1. 19. 26, 2. 1. 208.

ne . . .: 'in case a man is inclined to transgress'.

modici: cf. 1. 27. 3 f. 'verecundumque Bacchum / sanguineis prohibete rixis', Ov. *Pont.* 1. 10. 29 'non haec immodico contraxi damna Lyaeo'. *transiliat* implies transgression. For the theme cf. Hom. *Od.* 21. 293 f. οἶνός σε τρώει μελιηδής, ὅς τε καὶ ἄλλους / βλάπτει, ὃς ἄν μιν χανδὸν ἕλῃ μηδ' αἴσιμα πίνῃ, Theogn. 211 f. οἶνόν τοι πίνειν πουλὺν κακόν· ἢν δέ τις αὐτὸν / πίνῃ ἐπισταμένως, οὐ κακὸς ἀλλ' ἀγαθός, 479 f. ὃς δ' ἂν ὑπερβάλλῃ πόσιος μέτρον, οὐκέτι κεῖνος / τῆς αὑτοῦ γλώσσης καρτερὸς οὐδὲ νόου, Panyassis fr. 14. 4 f. K. πάσας δ' ἐκ κραδίης ἀνίας ἀνδρῶν ἀλαπάζει / πινόμενος κατὰ μέτρον, ὑπὲρ μέτρον δὲ χερείων, Mnesitheus ap. Athen. 36 a τὸν οἶνον τοὺς θεοὺς / θνητοῖς καταδεῖξαι τοῖς μὲν ὀρθῶς χρωμένοις / ἀγαθὸν μέγιστον, τοῖς δ' ἀτάκτως τοὔμπαλιν, Vitalis, *anth. Lat.* 633. 15 f. (clearly modelled on our passage) 'vina sitim sedent . . .: hos fines transiluisse nocet'.

munera: 'rites'; cf. Virg. *Aen.* 6. 637 'perfecto munere divae'. The use with *transiliat* is made possible by the presence of *modici*; *modum transilire* is a natural expression. The word is generally interpreted as 'gifts', which is certainly the most obvious meaning when combined with *Liberi*; cf. 4. 15. 26 'inter iocosi munera Liberi', Virg. *georg.* 2. 4 f. 'tuis hic omnis plena / muneribus', Lygd. 6. 17 f., Ov. *ars* 1. 565, Mart. 8. 68. 4, Hes. *op.* 614 δῶρα Διωνύσου, Bacch. fr. 20 B. 9 Διονυσίοισι δώροις. But this sense seems impossible with *transiluisse*; one needs a word which refers to what the drinker does and not what Bacchus does. Müller, the first editor to feel the difficulty, proposed *munia* (*officia*, ἔργα); this avoids the strange ambiguity of *munera*, and *munia Liberi* would be exposed to corruption. One might also consider *moenia*, which would suit *transiliat*; yet no parallel presents itself for the metaphor.

Liberi: an Italian god of fruitfulness, early identified with Dionysus, though he had nothing to do with wine. Cf. Latte 70, Bömer on Ov. *fast.* 3. 512, A. Brühl, *Liber Pater*, 1953. The Romans connected Liber with *libertas*; hence the use of the name is significant here.

8. Centaurea . . .: at the wedding of Hippodamia to Pirithous (ruler of the Lapiths) the Centaurs got drunk and started a brawl in which they were defeated. See Hom. *Od.* 21. 295 f. οἶνος καὶ Κένταυρον, ἀγακλυτὸν Εὐρυτίωνα, / ἄασ᾽ ἐνὶ μεγάρῳ μεγαθύμου Πειριθόοιο (the first three words of this sentence became proverbial; cf. Call. *ep.* 61. 3, Alcaeus of Messene, *anth. P.* 11. 12. 1, Nicarchus, ibid. 11. 1. 3, Gow–Page 2. 10). The battle was portrayed in the Parthenon metopes, now in the British Museum, and on the temple of Zeus at Olympia (B. Ashmole and N. Yalouris, *Olympia: the Sculptures of the Temple of Zeus*, 1967, pl. 62 ff.).

rixa . . . debellata: though the fight began as a *rixa* (a word appropriate to a tavern brawl) it ended as a serious battle in which some of the participants were killed. Bacchus was traditionally ζηλοδοτήρ (anon. *anth. P.* 9. 524. 7).

super mero: 'in their cups'. Oudendorp proposed *super merum*, which would be normal; cf. Curt. 8. 4. 30 'super vinum', Stat. *Theb.* 2. 161 'super hesternas . . . mensas' (Mulder cites parallels), Plin. *epist.* 4. 22. 6 'super cenam' (so Juv. 15. 14, Suet. *Cal.* 22. 1), Flor. *epit.* 4. 2. 69. But *super* is used by poets with the ablative in a local sense (1. 9. 5, H.–Sz. 281); perhaps Horace has sought here to vary the normal prose usage.

mero is unmixed wine (ἄκρητος). Heinze points out that Horace uses the word (*a*) of wine before it is served (1. 9. 8, 3. 29. 2), (*b*) of wine in sacrifice (1. 19. 15 n.), (*c*) where the context suggests heavy drinking (1. 13. 10, 1. 36. 13, 2. 12. 5).

9. Sithoniis: Sithonia was the middle of the three promontories of Chalcidice; the name could be loosely applied to Thrace in general. Horace must be alluding to some specific story about the Sithonians to balance the one about the Centaurs; cf. Ov. *fast.* 3. 719 f. (on Bacchus) 'Sithonas et Scythicos longum est narrare triumphos / et domitas gentes, turifer Inde, tuas'. For allusions to Sithonian scandals cf. Porph. ad loc. 'Sithonii Thraces sunt qui per vinolentiam incitati etiam inlicitos concubitus audent' (probably based simply on our passage), Nonnus 48. 93 ff. (Sithon falls in love with his daughter Pallene, and is killed by Dionysus). At first sight Horace might seem to be alluding simply to the Lycurgus legend (cf. Hyg. *fab.* 132. 1 'Lycurgus Dryantis filius Liberum de regno fugavit; quem cum negaret deum esse, vinumque bibisset, et ebrius matrem suam violare voluisset, tunc vites excidere est conatus'). Yet as Nonnus explicitly associates incest with Sithon, it looks as if Horace is thinking of a similar story.

non levis: cf. Eur. *Hec.* 722 δαίμων . . . ὅστις ἐστί σοι βαρύς, Theoc. 3. 15 νῦν ἔγνων τὸν Ἔρωτα· βαρὺς θεός.

Euhius: as the poem grows more tempestuous Horace no longer uses the kindly names of *Bacche pater* and *Liber*, but the orgiastic cult-titles *Euhius* and *Bassareus*.

10. cum fas . . . : 'when in their eagerness for lust they separate right and wrong by a narrow line'. Horace says with urbane understatement that the Sithonians made no distinction between right and wrong. *libidinum* depends on *avidi*, and refers to the act rather than the desire; so Plin. *nat.* 22. 87 'mulieres libidinis avidissimas'. Others take *avidi* absolutely; then *exiguo fine libidinum* is supposed to mean 'by the slenderness of the line imposed by their lusts'. But *avidi* is oddly unspecific.

For *exiguo fine* cf. Cic. *rep.* 4. 4 'Lacedaemonii ipsi, cum omnia concedunt in amore iuvenum praeter stuprum, tenui sane muro dissaepiunt id quod excipiunt', Ov. *rem.* 325 f. 'qua potes in peius dotes deflecte puellae / iudiciumque brevi limite falle tuum', Lucian, *hist. conscr.* 7 ἀγνοοῦντες ὡς οὐ στένῳ τῷ ἰσθμῷ διώρισται καὶ διατετείχισται ἡ ἱστορία πρὸς τὸ ἐγκώμιον, ἀλλά τι μέγα τεῖχος ἐν μέσῳ ἐστίν αὐτῶν. See further Liv. 1. 33. 8 'discrimine recte an perperam facti confuso', Lucian, *Nigrinus* 31 μηδὲ χρῆσθαι ἴσασι ταῖς ἐπιθυμίαις, ἀλλὰ κἂν ταύταις παρανομοῦσι καὶ τοὺς ὅρους συγχέουσι. For the thought in general cf. Liv. 39. 8. 6 (the Bacchanalia scandal) 'cum vinum [animos] et nox et mixti feminis mares, aetatis tenerae maioribus discrimen omne pudoris exstinxissent . . .'.

11. non ego te . . . : it does not seem to be understood that this is a deprecation, expressed paratactically; Horace says 'I shall not offend you, so do not hurt me'. For a somewhat similar apology cf. 1. 23. 9 ff. 'atqui non ego te . . . frangere persequor: / tandem desine matrem / tempestiva sequi viro', Pease on Virg. *Aen.* 4. 425. Müller, alone among editors, sees some of the drift; at least he comments on *saeva tene* (13) 'hartes Asyndeton; zu ergänzen durch *itaque*'. But he is wrong in supposing that the *non ego* clause refers allegorically to drunkenness; there is no point in saying 'I'll not get drunk, so don't make me drunk'. Horace purports to be thinking of a real profanation of the Bacchic rites.

candide: the word refers to good looks: cf. Ov. *fast.* 3. 772 'candide Bacche', Lygd. 6. 1, Sen. *Oed.* 509, anon. *anth. P.* 9. 524. 2 ἀγλαόμορφον, Dryden, *Alexander's Feast* 48 'Bacchus ever Fair, and ever Young'. Horace is no longer thinking of 'Bacchus pater', the bearded god, but of Dionysus in his other traditional aspect as a handsome youth; for this dichotomy see Cornutus, *nat. deor.* 30, Macr. *sat.* 1. 18. 9 (who says in contradiction to Horace that Bassareus was a bearded Bacchus), Roscher 1. 1089 ff.

Bassareu: a title of Dionysus. A Bassaris was a Thracian Maenad;

βάσσαρα is said to have been a Thracian name for the fox, whose skin the Maenads wore (Roscher 1. 751). A Roman Bacchic inscription of the second century A.D. mentions ἀρχιβάσσαροι and ἀρχιβάσσαραι (*AJA* 37, 1933, 215 ff.).

12. invitum quatiam: the exact meaning is uncertain. Horace may be alluding to the shaking of the thyrsus by Bacchus's worshippers; cf. Eur. *Ba*. 80 ff. ἀνὰ θύρσον τε τινάσσων . . . Διόνυσον θεραπεύει, 553 f. μόλε χρυσῶπα τινάσσων, / ἄνα, θύρσον κατ' 'Ολύμπου, Catull. 64. 256 'tecta quatiebant cuspide thyrsos', Val. Fl. 2. 269 'pampineamque quatit ventosis ictibus hastam'. The thyrsus was the ritual staff of Dionysus, with ivy-leaves fastened to the tip (Dodds on Eur. *Ba*. 113, D.–S. 5. 295). Dionysus was said in some sense to be present in the thyrsus (Dodds, loc. cit. 'to carry it was to carry deity'); hence Horace could speak of 'shaking the god'.

Alternatively one might suppose that Horace refers to the shaking of the god in the λίκνον or *vannus*. This was a winnowing-basket which could be used as a cradle for infants; cf. *RE* 13. 536 ff., J. Harrison, *JHS* 23, 1903, 294 ff., Frazer on Apollodorus 3. 10. 2, M. P. Nilsson, *The Dionysiac Mysteries of the Hellenistic and Roman Age*, 1957, pp. 21 ff., B. C. Dietrich, *CQ* N.S. 8, 1958, 244 ff. Plutarch talks of waking the god of the winnowing-fan; cf. *Is. et Osir.* 365 a ὅταν αἱ Θυιάδες ἐγείρωσι τὸν Λικνίτην (with Hopfner's note). But there is nothing in ἐγείρειν to suggest a violent movement, such as is implied by *quatiam*.

variis obsita frondibus: the sacred emblems (*orgia*) of Bacchus were kept not only in the λίκνον but also in the κίστη; cf. Theoc. 26. 7 ἱερὰ δ' ἐκ κίστας πεπονημένα χερσὶν ἑλοῖσαι, Catull. 64. 259 'pars obscura cavis celebrabant orgia cistis', Tib. 1. 7. 48, Val. Fl. 2. 267, O. Jahn, *Hermes* 3, 1869, 317 ff., *RE* 3. 2591 ff., Nilsson, op. cit., p. 96. The neuter plural *obsita* is deliberately secretive; cf. Apul. *met.* 11. 11. 2 'ferebatur ab alio cista secretorum capax penitus celans operta magnificae religionis'. For the emblems cf. Clem. Alex. *protr.* 2. 22. 4 (pomegranates and poppies), Aug. *civ.* 7. 21 (a phallus), Apul. *apol.* 55 'Liberi patris mystae qui adestis scitis quid domi conditum celetis'.

13. sub divum rapiam: cf. *epist.* 1. 6. 24 'in apricum proferet aetas'. It was *nefas* to betray the rites of Bacchus to the uninitiated; cf. Eur. *Ba*. 472 ἄρρητ' ἀβακχεύτοισιν εἰδέναι βροτῶν, Theoc. 26. 14 τά τ' οὐχ ὁρέοντι βέβαλοι, Catull. 64. 260 'orgia quae frustra cupiunt audire profani'.

Berecyntio: the Berecyntes were a Phrygian tribe, and *Berecyntius* was used as a poetical equivalent for *Phrygius*. The adjective properly belongs to Cybele, but was transferred from her to Bacchus; for the association of the two gods cf. Pind. fr. 70b. 6 ff., Eur. *Ba*.

78 f. (with Dodds's note), Prop. 3. 17. 33 ff., Str. 10. 3. 13 ff. For the
Berecyntian pipe cf. 3. 19. 18 f., 4. 1. 22 f., Ov. *met.* 11. 16, *fast.*
4. 181 (with Bömer's note), Str. 10. 3. 17. Persius mocks the affectation: 'cludere sic versum didicit: "Berecyntius Attis"' (1. 93).

Roman poets were fond of describing the wild music of Cybele and
Bacchus. See especially Varro, *Men.* 131 ff. 'Phrygius per ossa cornus
liquida canit anima / . . . tibi typana non inani sonitu matri' deum /
tonimus ⟨chorus⟩ tibi nos', Lucr. 2. 618 ff. 'tympana tenta tonant
palmis et cymbala circum / concava, raucisonoque minantur cornua
cantu, / et Phrygio stimulat numero cava tibia mentis', Catull.
63. 21 f. 'ubi cymbalum sonat vox, ubi tympana reboant, / tibicen ubi
canit Phryx curvo grave calamo', 64. 261 ff. (the only one of these
parallels to concern Bacchus) 'plangebant aliae proceris tympana
palmis / . . . multis raucisonos efflabant cornua bombos / barbaraque
horribili stridebat tibia cantu'.

14. cornu: a Phrygian *tibia*. The *tibia* was nothing like the modern
flute (K. Schlesinger, *The Greek Aulos*, 1939): it was held outwards
like a clarinet or oboe, and not cross-ways; it was sounded by a reed
(again like a clarinet or oboe); it was played in pairs (hence *tibiae*
in the plural is the normal prose form). Norman Douglas says that
it was still used in Sicily in his time, but was hard to find in the Sila
(*Old Calabria*, p. 192).

In the *cornu* one of the two pipes was curved at the far end, and
sounded a deep note (*RE* 2. 2420); for illustrations cf. D.–S. 5. 312,
Baumeister 1. 557. It is very confusing that the name *cornu* is also
applied to the curved trumpet used in the Roman army.

tympana: the *tympanum* was a wooden hoop, covered on one side
with hide (Eur. *Ba.* 124 βυρσότονον κύκλωμα). It was associated with
the cults of Cybele and Dionysus; see Dodds on Eur. *Ba.* 59 and 120.

subsequitur: Bacchus was normally followed by a different set of
attendants; cf. Anacreon 357. 1 ff. ὦναξ ᾧ δαμάλης ῎Ερως / καὶ
Νύμφαι κυανώπιδες / πορφυρῆ τ᾽ Ἀφροδίτη / συμπαίζουσιν. But here the
thiasos consists of abstract vices; cf. Sil. 15. 96 f. (on the train of
Voluptas) 'Ebrietas tibi foeda comes, tibi Luxus et atris / circa te
semper volitans Infamia pennis'. Some abstractions are of course
found in archaic poetry (West on Hes. *th.* pp. 33 f., Pease on Cic. *nat.
deor.* 2. 61), but the list here is Hellenistic in spirit.

caecus: lovers are often said to be blind (*serm.* 1. 3. 38 f., *Thes.l.L.*
3. 44. 36 ff., Otto 30), but in antiquity the epithet was seldom given
to the god (Gow on Theoc. 10. 20). Here Horace applies the commonplace to self-love, using *caecus* in its sense of 'morally blind'; cf.
Pl. *leg.* 731 e (also on self-love) τυφλοῦται γὰρ περὶ τὸ φιλούμενον ὁ
φιλῶν, Sen. *epist.* 109. 16 'quos amor sui excaecat'. For later references

to the blindness of love cf. M. B. Ogle, *AJPh* 41, 1920, 240 ff., E.
Panofsky, *Studies in Iconology*, 1939, pp. 95 ff., E. Wind, *Pagan Mysteries in the Renaissance*, 1958, 57 ff., W. Deonna, *Le Symbolisme de l'œil*, 1965, pp. 243 f.

15. vacuum: cf. Juv. 14. 57 f. 'vacuumque cerebro / . . . caput'. But the adjective is less commonplace with *vertex*; Horace has combined two ideas with epigrammatic alliteration.

plus nimio: 'much too much'; the ablative indicates 'measure of difference', not comparison (K.–S. 1. 402). The idiom is popular, though in prose the word-order would naturally be *nimio plus*. See also 1. 33. 1, *epist.* 1. 10. 30, Owen on Ov. *trist.* 2. 210, Ogilvie on Liv. 2. 37. 4.

Gloria: κενοδοξία, 'vainglory'; cf. *glorior, gloriosus.*

verticem: for the high head as a sign of pride cf. 1. 1. 36, 3. 16. 19 'late conspicuum tollere verticem', Rhianus 1. 9 ff. Powell ὃς δέ κεν εὐοχθῇσι, θεὸς δ' ἐπὶ ὄλβον ὀπάζῃ / καὶ πολυκοιρανίην, ἐπιλήθεται οὔνεκα γαῖαν / ποσσὶν ἐπιστείβει θνητοὶ δέ οἱ εἰσὶ τοκῆες, / ἀλλ' ὑπεροπλίῃ καὶ ἁμαρτωλῇσι νόοιο / ἶσα Διὶ βρομέει, κεφαλὴν δ' ὑπέραυχον ἀνίσχει.

16. arcanique: cf. 3. 21. 15 f. 'arcanum iocoso / consilium retegis Lyaeo', *epod.* 11. 13 f., Hom. *Od.* 14. 466 καί τι ἔπος προέηκεν ὅ πέρ τ' ἄρρητον ἄμεινον, Alcaeus 366 οἶνος ὦ φίλε παῖ καὶ ἀλάθεα, Bury on Pl. *symp.* 217 e, Gow on Theoc. 29. 1, Eratosth. fr. 36. 3 f. Powell τὰ δὲ καὶ κεκρυμμένα φαίνει / βυσσόθεν, K. F. Smith on Tib. 1. 9. 25–6, Plin. *nat.* 14. 141, Sen. *epist.* 83. 10 'huic autem neminem commissurum arcana quae per vinum eloqui possit', Vitalis, *anth. lat.* 633. 6. The Romans valued the ability to keep a secret; cf. *serm.* 1. 4. 84 f., *carm.* 3. 2. 25, *epist.* 1. 18. 38. For the other point of view cf. Plut. *quaest. conv.* 715 f ἔστι δὲ παρρησίας καὶ δι' αὐτὴν ἀληθείας γονιμώτατος, ἧς μὴ παρούσης, οὐδὲν ἐμπείριας οὐδ' ἀγχινοίας ὄφελος. ἀλλὰ πολλοὶ τῷ ἐπιόντι χρώμενοι μᾶλλον κατορθοῦσιν ἢ εἰ κρύπτουσιν ἐπιβούλως καὶ πανούργως τὸ παριστάμενον.

Fides: often applied to 'fidele silentium' (*Thes.l.L.* 6. 1. 681. 78 ff.); according to Silius (2. 481), Fides is 'arcanis dea laeta'. As the word can mean 'trustworthiness' in a neutral sense, it can also be qualified by derogatory adjectives; cf. 3. 24. 59 'periura patris fides', Sall. *Jug.* 108. 3 'Punica fide'. However, the usage is stranger when the word is personified; cf. 1. 17. 14 n., 1. 35. 21 'rara Fides'.

perlucidior: cf. 3. 13. 1 'splendidior vitro' (so Ov. *met.* 13. 791), Call. fr. 238. 16 τόφρα δ' ἔην ὕαλοιο φαάντερος οὐρανὸς ἠνοψ, Ov. *epist.* 15. 157 'nitidus vitroque magis perlucidus omni', below 1. 19. 6 n. It was an old commonplace that wine makes a man's mind transparent: cf. Alcaeus 333 οἶνος γὰρ ἀνθρώπω δίοπτρον, Aesch. fr. 393 κάτοπτρον εἴδους χαλκός ἐστ', οἶνος δὲ νοῦ. Μέθη was portrayed by the

painter Pausias ἐξ ὑαλίνης φιάλης πίνουσα· ἴδοις δὲ κἂν ἐν τῇ γραφῇ
φιάλην τε ὑάλου καὶ δι' αὐτῆς γυναικὸς πρόσωπον (Paus. 2. 27. 3).

19. MATER SAEVA CVPIDINVM

1–4. *Venus and her train again assail me, though I had given up love.*
5–8. *It is Glycera who inflames me.* 9–12. *Venus's onslaught is so
violent that I cannot sing of martial themes.* 13–16. *Prepare a sacrifice,
my slaves; an offering will make her coming more gentle.*

The poem opens with the lyric theme of the renewed assault of
love; cf. Alcman 59a Ἔρως με δηῦτε Κύπριδος ϝέκατι / γλυκὺς κατείβων
καρδίαν ἰαίνει, Sappho 130 Ἔρος δηῦτέ μ' ὁ λυσιμέλης δόνει / γλυκύπικρον
ἀμάχανον ὄρπετον, Anacreon 358 σφαίρῃ δηῦτέ με πορφυρέῃ / βάλλων
χρυσοκόμης Ἔρως /... συμπαίζειν προκαλεῖται, 413 μεγάλῳ δηῦτέ μ'
Ἔρως ἔκοψεν ὥς τε χαλκεὺς / πελέκει. Here Horace suggests that he is
too old for such amusements (4 *finitis ... amoribus*), but he succumbs
all the same; for this motif cf. 3. 26, 4. 1, Philodemus, *anth. P.* 11. 34,
11. 41. Horace seems particularly close to our poem in 4. 1, where
he actually repeats the line *mater saeva Cupidinum*; however, in that
ode 'love' partly stands for 'love-poetry', whereas here there is no
such complication.

In the rest of the poem Horace shows his usual skill in harmonizing
diverse themes. The comparison of Glycera with Parian marble
recalls some descriptions in the Anthology (6 n.). In the third stanza
the ode veers from an old Greek motif (*Cyprum deseruit*) to the
mundane problems of contemporary foreign policy; and though the
recusatio is a Callimachean topic, Horace's light-hearted treatment
is his own. The pretty vignette at the end of the poem is again very
Roman (*verbenas, bimi ... meri, hostia*). Yet the contrast between
the savage and gentle aspects of love is a literary topic going back to
Greek tragedy; cf. Soph. fr. 855. 5 f. N. (= 941. 5 f. P.) ἐν κείνῃ τὸ
πᾶν / σπουδαῖον, ἡσυχαῖον, ἐς βίαν ἄγον, Eur. *Hipp.* 443 ff. Κύπρις γὰρ
οὐ φορητὸς ἦν πολλὴ ῥυῇ, / ἢ τὸν μὲν εἴκονθ' ἡσυχῇ μετέρχεται· / ὃν δ'
ἂν περισσὸν καὶ φρονοῦνθ' εὕρῃ μέγα / ... καθύβρισεν.

Needless to say the ode has no bearing on real life; we need weave
no fantasies about Horace's romance with Glycera. The poem is in
fact much too detached to be a love poem; it is not about a girl,
but about literature and Horace. The pomposity of the opening
stanza and the high tragic tone of the ninth line dissolve, as so
often, in a display of charm and humour. When the goddess of

Cyprus descends on Horace he dreads her onslaught; yet being less obstinate than Hippolytus, he decides on a policy of appeasement.

Metre: Fourth Asclepiad.

1. mater . . . Cupidinum: the locution is found in both classical and Hellenistic Greek poetry; cf. Pind. fr. 122. 4 μᾶτέρ' ἐρώτων, Bacch. 9. 73, Philodemus, *anth. P.* 10. 21. 2 Κύπρι Πόθων μῆτερ ἀελλοπόδων, *Orph. h.* 55. 8, Babrius 32. 2. Similar expressions recur in the Latin poets, especially Ovid; cf. Carter 102.

saeva: 'merciless'. Such epithets are not so often used of Venus as of her son; yet cf. 1. 33. 10 ff., Eur. *Med.* 640 δεινὰ Κύπρις, *Hipp.* 563, Theoc. 1. 100 f. Κύπρι βαρεῖα, / Κύπρι νεμεσσατά, Ap. Rhod. 1. 802 f., Asclepiades, *anth. P.* 12. 50. 2 χαλεπὴ Κύπρις, Tib. 1. 2. 98 'quid messes uris acerba tuas?', 1. 6. 84 'infidis quam sit acerba monet', Opp. *hal.* 4. 2 ὀλοῆς τ' Ἀφροδίτης, Agathias, *anth. P.* 5. 280. 7 Κύπρις . . . παλίγκοτος.

Cupidinum: the Hellenistic age gave Aphrodite an escort of *amorini*, such as frequently appear in art (cf. Roscher 1. 1365 ff., 6. 191). For the plural cf. Headlam on Herodas 7. 94, Ellis on Catull. 3. 1, Pease on Cic. *nat. deor.* 3. 60, *Thes.l.L.* Onom. 2. 749. 50 ff., 76 ff., T. G. Rosenmeyer, *Phoenix* 5, 1951, 11 ff.

2. Thebanae . . .: Dionysus and Aphrodite are often associated in literature as the gods of wine and love; cf. Otto 366, Pease on Cic. *nat. deor.* 2. 60. The connection is less conspicuous in art and cult; yet Aphrodite is found on vase paintings among the Maenads, and the two gods occasionally share a temple (cf. Dodds on Eur. *Ba.* 402).

puer: an archaism for *filius*; cf. 1. 12. 25, 4. 6. 37 'Latonae puerum', 4. 8. 22 f., *ars* 83, *carm.* 3. 11. 23 'Danai puellas', Liv. Andr. *carm.* fr. 3 'mea puera, quid verbi ex tuo ore supera fugit?', 14 'sancte puer, Saturni filia, regina', Naev. *carm.* fr. 29 'prima incedit Cereris Proserpina puer'. For the description of Bacchus as the son of Semele cf. 1. 17. 22 n., Ar. *Thesm.* 991, Eur. *Ba.* 581, anon. *PMG* 879 Σεμελήϊ' Ἴακχε πλουτοδότα, Acc. *trag.* 241 'Semela genitus', Dracont. 10. 587 'puer Semeleie Bacche', Bruchmann 90 f.

3. Licentia: 'wantonness', specified by the addition of *lasciva*, which in Horace usually has an erotic sense. Cicero uses the personification humorously when he calls Clodius's Statue of Liberty a *simulacrum . . . Licentiae* (*dom.* 131). For a closer parallel to our passage cf. Claud. 10. 78, where Licentia lives in Venus's garden.

4. animum reddere: 'to surrender my heart once more' (contrast 1. 16. 28 n.).

5. urit: for the flames of love cf. Brandt on Ov. *am.* 1. 1. 26, Gow on Theoc. 7. 55, Pease on Virg. *Aen.* 4. 2. *nitor* refers to a cold brilliance, and is not something that would normally burn.

Glycerae: Horace uses the name again in 1. 30, 1. 33, and 3. 19. Like its diminutive Glycerium, it was frequently affected by *hetaerae*, presumably by way of advertisement; cf. Machon 411 with Gow's note, Str. 9. 2. 25, Lucian, *dial. mer.* 1, Aristaenetus 1. 22, Auson. 18. 1 'Laidas et Glyceras, lascivae nomina famae', Pape–Benseler 1. 253. A Glycera was one of the inmates in the brothel of Africanus and Victor at Pompeii (J. P. V. D. Balsdon, *Roman Women*, 1963, p. 225).

6. Pario marmore: the statuary marble *par excellence*, because of its dazzling whiteness (Diod. Sic. 2. 52. 9, Str. 10. 5. 7, D.–S. 3. 1602 f., *RE* 18. 4. 1791, 3 A. 2261 ff.). The most prized kind was called λύγδος (connected with λευκός) or λυχνίτης. Pliny prosaically points out that whiter marbles had lately been discovered, particularly that of Carrara (*nat.* 36. 14). This did not diminish the poets' attachment to Parian marble as the type of brilliance; cf. Pind. *N.* 4. 81 στάλαν . . . Παρίου λίθου λευκοτέραν, Theoc. 6. 37 f. τῶν δέ τ᾽ ὀδόντων / λευκοτέραν αὐγὰν Παρίας ὑπέφαινε λίθοιο, Poseidippus or Asclepiades, *anth. P.* 5. 194. 3 f., Philodemus, ibid. 5. 13. 3, *Anacreontea* 15. 27, Sen. *Phaedr.* 797 'lucebit Pario marmore clarius', Petron. 126. 17 'iam mentum, iam cervix, iam manus, iam pedum candor . . . Parium marmor extinxerat', *anth. Lat.* 130. 4 'et vibret Parium nitens colorem'. For other instances of the comparison of women with statues cf. Rohde, *Roman*[3], pp. 165 f., André 41, Nonnus 42. 424 f. τεοῦ χροὸς εἶδος ἐλέγχει / μάρμαρα τιμήεντα.

purius: such exaggerated comparisons belong to the language of love, at least in literature; cf. Theoc. 11. 20 λευκοτέρα πακτᾶς ποτιδεῖν, Catull. 17. 15 f. 'et puella tenellulo delicatior haedo, / adservanda nigerrimis diligentius uvis', Virg. *ecl.* 7. 37 'Nerine Galatea, thymo mihi dulcior Hyblae', Ov. *met.* 13. 789 ff. 'candidior foliis nivei Galatea ligustri . . .', Mart. 1. 115. 2 f. 'loto candidior puella cycno, / argento, nive, lilio, ligustro', Longus 1. 18 χείλη μὲν ῥόδων ἀπαλώτερα καὶ στόμα κηρίων γλυκύτερον, τὸ δὲ φίλημα κέντρου μελίττης πικρότερον, Gregor. in Hermog. (Walz, *Rhet.* 7. 1236) αἰσχρῶς μὲν κολακεύει τὴν ἀκοὴν ἐκεῖνα, ὅσα εἰσὶν ἐρωτικά, οἷον τὰ Ἀνακρέοντος, τὰ Σαπφοῦς, οἷον γάλακτος λευκοτέρα, ὕδατος ἀπαλωτέρα, πηκτίδων ἐμμελεστέρα, ἵππου γαυροτέρα, ῥόδων ἁβροτέρα, ἱματίου ἑανοῦ μαλακωτέρα, χρυσοῦ τιμιωτέρα, Löfstedt, *Syntactica* 1². 318 ff., Bowra 232.

7. grata protervitas: a slight oxymoron. The quality was less agreeable to moralists; cf. Prud. *praef.* 10 ff. 'tum lasciva protervitas / et luxus petulans (heu pudet ac piget!) / foedavit iuvenem nequitiae sordibus ac luto'. Neither the noun nor the adjective *protervus* belongs to high poetry.

8. lubricus aspici: 'slippery to the sight'. *lubricus* brilliantly reinforces the image of *marmor*; Glycera's face is as dazzling as a marble floor, and as treacherous. Congreve in his imitation makes the point less tersely: 'Each Look darts forth a thousand Rays, Whose Lustre an unwary Sight betrays, My Eye-balls swim, and I grow giddy while I gaze'.
There may be some relevance in a comic fragment (*adesp.* 222 K.) quoted by Plut. *amat.* 769 b; the manuscripts there read a nonsensical οἰκειότητος ἐμβλέπων ὠλίσθανον, for which Headlam, referring to our passage, conjectured εἰς λειότητα δ' ἐμβλέπων ὠλίσθανον (on Herodas 6. 44).

9. in me . . .: the phrase is a strong one; cf. Eur. *Hipp.* 443 (cited above, p. 238), ps.-Phocyl. 193 μηδ' ἐς ἔρωτα γυναικὸς ἅπας ῥεύσῃς ἀκάθεκτος, Ach. Tat. 1. 9. 1 ὅλος γάρ μοι προσέπεσεν ὁ ῎Ερως. There is a similar use of ἁθρόος; cf. Theoc. 25. 252 ἀθρόος ἆλτο, 13. 50 with Gow's note. Racine exploited Horace's line in *Phèdre* 1. 3. 154 'C'est Vénus tout entière à sa proie attachée'. Note that *ruens* represents Euripides's ῥύῃ because of its similar sound, though its meaning is quite different; cf. 1. 24. 3 n.

10. Cyprum deseruit: such locutions originate in the κλητικὸς ὕμνος ('leave Cyprus and come here'); cf. 1. 17. 2 n., 1. 30. 2 n.
Scythas: cf. intr. p. xxxiv.

11. versis animosum equis: after Carrhae the Parthians' ungentlemanly tactics became a stock theme. For the oxymoron cf. 2. 13. 16 ff. 'timet . . . celerem fugam / Parthi', Virg. *georg.* 3. 31 'fidentemque fuga Parthum versisque sagittis', Sen. *Oed.* 118 f. 'versas equitis sagittas, / terga fallacis metuenda Parthi'.

12. Parthum: the collective singular is an old construction in Latin; Varro mentions that 'Romanus sedendo vincit' was a 'vetus proverbium' (*rust.* 1. 2. 2). It seems to have been both archaic and colloquial, and is consequently affected by the historians (except Sallust) and avoided by Cicero (except in his letters); cf. K.–S. 1. 67 f., K.–G. 1. 14, H.–Sz. 13 f., Norden on Virg. *Aen.* 6. 851, and especially Löfstedt, *Syntactica* 1². 12 ff. It is particularly common in military contexts, where it is convenient to think of a mass rather than a collection of individuals. A refusal to individualize is especially useful when thinking of enemies, and *hostis* and the names of hostile peoples are consequently very often employed in the singular. Cf. also Rose Macaulay, *Staying with Relations*, p. 19 'Squealings and tramplings came from the forest on the left. Isie said, "Plenty of pig in there." And Catherine surmised, from her use of the singular number, that she would fain pursue these animals and take their lives.'

quae nihil attinent: 'things of no importance'; cf. *Anacreontea* 50. 3 f. τί δέ μοι λόγων τοσούτων / τῶν μηδὲν ὠφελούντων; *attinere* is an unpoetical word, used at *epod.* 4. 17, *serm.* 2. 2. 27, twice in Lucretius, and once in Ovid (cf. Axelson 101). Here the colloquial and off-hand phrase makes a piquant contrast with the portentous 'in me tota ruens Venus'; such fluctuations of style are common in Horace and Maas was wrong to doubt the text.

13. vivum . . . caespitem: fresh turfs. A Roman sacrifice normally needed an altar (unless it were a simple domestic offering of meal or incense); cf. Latte 386, *RE* 2. 338 f. In early Rome such altars were naturally made of turf; cf. Tert. *apol.* 25. 13 'temeraria de caespite altaria', Serv. *Aen.* 12. 119 'Romani enim moris fuerat caespitem arae superimponere et ita sacrificare'. The custom was maintained if no permanent altar was available (and private citizens would not normally possess one).

See 3. 8. 2 ff., Ov. *trist.* 5. 5. 9 'araque gramineo viridis de caespite fiat', Juv. 12. 2 f. with Mayor's note, [Capitol.] *Max. Balb.* 11. 5, Auson. 152. 11 ff. 'nec tus cremandum postulo / nec liba crusti mellei, / foculumque vivi caespitis / vanis relinquo altaribus', Prud. *perist.* 5. 50 ff., Gow on Theoc. 26. 5, *Thes.l.L.* 3. 111. 25 ff., D.-S. 1. 347. Christians naturally disapproved; cf. Lact. *inst.* 6. 24. 28 'neque verbenis opus est neque februis neque cespitibus quae sunt utique vanissima', *cod. Theod.* 16. 10. 12. 1 f. (8 Nov. A.D. 392) 'nullus omnino . . . sensu carentibus simulacris vel insontem victimam caedat vel secretiore piaculo larem igne, mero genium, penates odore veneratus accendat lumina, imponat tura, serta suspendat. . . . si quis . . . erecta effossis ara cespitibus vanas imagines humiliore licet muneris praemio . . . honorare tentaverit, is . . . ea domo seu possessione mulctabitur'.

14. verbenas: plants used to garland the altar; cf. 4. 11. 6 f., Virg. *ecl.* 8. 65, Ov. *met.* 7. 242, Don. *Andr.* 726 'verbenae sunt omnes herbae frondesque festae ad aras coronandas', Nettleship, *Latin Lexicography*, p. 606. Celsus mentions some of the plants (2. 33. 3): 'verbenarum (folia) . . . cuius generis sunt olea, cupressus, myrtus, lentiscus, tamarix, ligustrum, rosa, rubus, laurus, hedera, punicum malum'. Here one should perhaps think especially of myrtle, which was sacred to Venus (Plin. *nat.* 15. 119). Plin. *nat.* 25. 105 adds vervain (*verbenaca, verbena officinalis*); but *verbenae* should not be thought of as restricted to vervain.

15. bimi: strictly wine that is two years old (*bis-hiems*). The date is perhaps calculated from the vintage rather than from the transfusion from *dolium* to *amphora*; cf. *CIL* 4. 5520 'C. Pomponio C. Anicio cos. ex fund. Badiano diff. id. Aug. bimum'.

meri: wine for sacrifice had to be unmixed with water; cf. Fest. 474. 31 ff. L. (= 348. 19 ff. M.) 'spurcum vinum est quod sacris adhiberi non licet, ut ait Labeo Antistius lib. X commentari iuris pontificii, cui aqua admixta est defrutumve, aut igne tactum est, mustumve antequam defervescat', Plin. *nat.* 14. 119.

16. mactata . . . hostia: this must refer to a blood sacrifice and not simply to incense and wine. The argument in prose would have run: 'I shall offer Venus wine, incense, and a victim; then she will visit me more gently'. For the poetical σχῆμα cf. 1. 7. 10 n.

For blood-sacrifices to Venus cf. Plaut. *Poen.* 449 ff. 'di illum infelicent omnes qui post hunc diem / leno ullam Veneri unquam immolarit hostiam . . . / nam ego hodie infelix dis meis iratissumis / sex immolavi agnos nec potui tamen / propitiam Venerem facere uti esset mihi', Prop. 4. 5. 65 f., Mart. 9. 90. 16 ff., Tac. *hist.* 2. 3. 5, Farnell 2. 756 f.

lenior: cf. 3. 18. 3 'lenis incedas', Tib. 2. 1. 79 f. 'at ille / felix cui placidus leniter adflat Amor'. For similar prayers for the peaceful advent of a deity cf. Anacreon 357. 6 f. σὺ δ' εὐμενὴς / ἔλθ' ἡμίν, Pl. *leg.* 712 b ἵλεως εὐμενής τε ἡμῖν ἔλθοι, Sen. *Phaedr.* 437 'beatis mitior rebus veni', Stat. *silv.* 3. 1. 39 'placatus mitisque veni'. Here Horace is particularly thinking of Euripides's *Hippolytus* (above, p. 238).

20. VILE POTABIS

[E. Ensor, *CR* 16, 1902, 209 ff.; Fraenkel 214 ff.; A. O. Prickard, *CR* 25, 1911, 269 f.; R. Reitzenstein, *Aufsätze*, pp. 16 f.; K. P. Schulze, *BPhW* 36, 1916, 285 ff., 317 ff.]

1–8. *You shall have cheap wine which I laid down at the time of your ovation, Maecenas.* 9–12. *It is all very well for you to drink vintage wines, but they are too grand for me.*

The circumstances of this poem were examined by Ernest Ensor in an ingenious though inevitably speculative article (see above). The *vile Sabinum* was laid down at the time when Maecenas was applauded in the theatre after a dangerous illness. Horace elsewhere recounts the episode in conjunction with his own escape from a falling tree; he comments 'utrumque nostrum incredibili modo / consentit astrum,

(2. 17. 21 f.). We are not told why these events are connected
in so incredible a fashion; after all, most men have narrow escapes
from death at one time or another. In an astrological context
it is natural to suppose (though nothing is explicitly stated) that
the association is one of time: the two events seem to have taken
place on the same day, or at any rate near enough for a poet's purposes. Ensor himself suggests that the year might have been different
though the day was the same; but such a view finds no support in
astrological theory.

The date of the escape from the tree was 1 March (3. 8. 1 'Martiis
caelebs quid agam Kalendis'); admittedly there is no evidence in the
Fasti for theatrical performances on that date, but the point cannot
be regarded as decisive. A clue to the year may be given in 3. 8. 9:
'hic dies anno redeunte festus / corticem adstrictum pice dimovebit /
amphorae fumum bibere institutae / consule Tullo'. Ensor argues not
without plausibility that Tullus is the familiar consul of 33 B.C.
rather than the remote figure of 66; it would be a characteristic
Horatian touch if the wine dated the escape. If the escapes of Horace
and Maecenas were simultaneous, the wines could even be regarded
as the same; it might be significant that in both cases Horace
describes his careful measures to ensure preservation (1. 20. 2 f.
'Graeca . . . testa / conditum levi', 3. 8. 10 'adstrictum pice'). The
date of 3. 8 is probably about 25 B.C. (intr. p. xxxiii), perhaps eight
years after the event it described (anno redeunte in no way implies
a first anniversary). A Sabine wine, though vile by Maecenas's high
standards, could have kept for that period (1 n.).

Yet already we are in danger of exaggerating the element of literal
truth in Horace's poem. It is not an invitation in the strict sense,
asking Maecenas on a definite occasion to a particular party (1 n.).
Moreover, it is absurd for the poet to say that in entertaining his
fastidious patron he cannot provide Falernian; elsewhere he offers
a nine-year-old Albanum even to a young woman called Phyllis
(4. 11. 2). The whole business of the commemorative 'bottling'
may be no less of a literary convention; in that case it is absurd to
debate whether the wine of two invitation poems is or is not the
same.

The invitation-poem was in fact a minor category of Hellenistic
epigram, and we are lucky to have one of the prototypes, which
Horace must have known well. This is a poem by Philodemus, the
most important Epicurean of the Ciceronian age, the author of some
admirable epigrams preserved in the Greek Anthology, as well as
of much tedious philosophy recovered from Herculaneum. In this
epigram Philodemus invites to dinner his patron, L. Calpurnius Piso,
the consul of 58 B.C. (anth. P. 11. 44):

Αὔριον εἰς λιτήν σε καλιάδα, φίλτατε Πείσων,
ἐξ ἐνάτης ἕλκει μουσοφιλὴς ἕταρος,
εἰκάδα δειπνίζων ἐνιαύσιον· εἰ δ' ἀπολείψεις
οὔθατα καὶ Βρομίου Χιογενῆ πρόποσιν,
ἀλλ' ἑτάρους ὄψει παναληθέας, ἀλλ' ἐπακούσῃ
Φαιήκων γαίης πουλὺ μελιχρότερα·
ἢν δέ ποτε στρέψῃς καὶ ἐς ἡμέας ὄμματα, Πείσων,
ἄξομεν ἐκ λιτῆς εἰκάδα ποτέρην.

Here the situation is much the same as in our ode. The poet writes with affection to a more important friend. He emphasizes the humbleness of his house and his supper, but offers good talk in compensation. Finally he suggests, just like Horace, that his patron enjoys a higher standard of living.

The claim to simplicity was taken over by the Latin poets in their invitations; Horatian modesty should be regarded in part at least as a literary topic. Thus it was part of the convention to ask one's guest for a valuable present which one cannot afford oneself (4. 12. 16); Catullus carries this motif to an absurd conclusion, and says that he himself will be responsible for the perfume if Fabullus brings the dinner (13). Even in the fifth century Sidonius still keeps up the theme of simplicity (*carm.* 17. 15 ff.): 'vina mihi non sunt Gazetica Chia Falerna / quaeque Sarepteno palmite missa bibas / . . . tu tamen ut venias petimus; dabit omnia Christus, / hic mihi qui patriam fecit amore tuo'. But the most illuminating parallel to our ode is Horace's own epistle to Torquatus (1. 5. 1 ff.):

> si potes Archiacis conviva recumbere lectis
> nec modica cenare times holus omne patella,
> supremo te sole domi, Torquate, manebo.
> vina bibes iterum Tauro diffusa palustris
> inter Minturnas Sinuessanumque Petrinum . . .

In both poems Horace addresses a man of much higher social position than himself: Torquatus was the last survivor of the great patrician gens of the Manlii Torquati. In both he emphasizes the simplicity of his arrangements, and suggests that his grand friend was used to better things. Most significant of all, in the epistle, as in our ode, the modest wine has particular associations for the guest. T. Manlius Torquatus, the first and greatest of the Torquati, fought his most important battle in 340 B.C. between Sinuessa and Minturnae (Liv. 8. 11. 11, cf. *CQ* N.S. 9, 1959, 73 f.); obviously, both Horace and Torquatus must have known all about this battle, and the wine is specified with carefully contrived tact. The resemblance to our ode suggests that it was a conventional feature of the invitation-poem to offer graceful compliments to one's guest, and in particular to give him wine with sentimental value.

Our poem has no exceptional literary merit. Horace tries hard to give his traditional topic a realistic and Roman flavour; the names of the wines, the applause in the theatre, and Maecenas's ancestral river (5 n.) all add something that would not be found in a conventional Greek epigram. Yet the poem suffers by comparison with the epistle; the more spacious form allows Horace to develop a real picture of upper-class Roman society which would be impossible in the narrower framework of this short ode. In the epistle, too, the tact is more subtle, and is relieved with friendly banter; the ode spends too much time on blatant flattery of Maecenas's ovation. One also prefers Philodemus's references to good fellowship, though Horace greatly improved on Philodemus's ending. The last sentence of the ode is in fact most elegantly balanced, and this gives the poem such charm as it possesses.

Metre: Sapphic.

1. **vile . . .:** the first five words are all edged to suggest a lack of sophistication.

potabis: the word implies deep drinking and is more humorous than *bibes*; though the wine is unpretentious there will be no shortage of supplies. The tense is polite and urbane. Some commentators call it a 'future of invitation' (cf. *epist.* 1. 7. 71 'post nonam venies', Plaut. *Curc.* 728 'tu, miles, apud me cenabis', Prop. 3. 23. 15 'venies hodie; cessabimus una'). But no time and place are specified, and *potabis* by itself can hardly mean 'come and have a drink'.

The full formula would rather run 'You will dine with me tomorrow and you will drink Sabine'; cf. *epist.* 1. 5. 3 f. (above, p. 245), Mart. 11. 52. 1 ff. 'cenabis belle, Iuli Cerealis, apud me; / condicio est melior si tibi nulla, veni. / . . . prima tibi dabitur ventri lactuca movendo / utilis et porris fila resecta suis'. In our passage *potabis* corresponds not so much to Martial's *cenabis* (where *belle* makes a difference), but rather to his *dabitur*.

modicis: reinforces the point of *vile* and refers to the quality of the tankards (cf. μέτριος). So in *epist.* 1. 5. 2 (p. 245), *modica* corresponds to *Archiacis* and refers to quality.

Sabinum: a light wine of medium quality at the best. Martial calls a Sabine wine *plumbea*, but that was newly bottled (10. 49. 3 ff.); a Sabine wine is four years old in 1. 9. 7, and it could keep from seven to fifteen years (Galen ap. Athen. 27 b). The word suggests honesty, simplicity, and, above all, Horace's gratitude to his patron for his Sabine farm. But the grapes were not home-grown; Horace says that his estate would produce pepper and frankincense sooner than the vine (*epist.* 1. 14. 23).

2. cantharis: the *cantharus* was a large two-handled drinking-cup; cf. G. M. A. Richter and M. J. Milne, *Shapes and Names of Athenian Vases*, 1935, pp. 25 f., fig. 167, R. M. Cook, *Greek Painted Pottery*, 1960, pp. 238 f. It was made sometimes of earthenware, sometimes of metal (cf. *epist.* 1. 5. 23 f.). It was particularly associated with Bacchus; cf. Plin. *nat.* 33. 150 'C. Marius post victoriam Cimbricam cantharis potasse Liberi patris exemplo traditur' (so Val. Max. 3. 6. 6). The word suggests unsophisticated jollity; the sybaritic Maecenas will down his drink from large tankards in true rustic style.

Graeca . . . testa: commentators miss the point: a Greek jar was impregnated with salt which would act as a preservative. Greek wines were frequently mixed with salt water, and any wine so mixed might be characterized as Greek: cf. Cato, *agr.* 24 'vinum Graecum hoc modo fieri oportet. uvas Apicias percoctas bene legito. ubi delegeris, in eius musti culleum aquae marinae veteris Q. II indito vel salis puri modium . . .', 105 (how to make a Greek-type wine if one lives far from the sea), 112. 1 'vinum Coum si voles facere, aquam ex alto marinam sumito mari tranquillo, cum ventus non erit, dies LXX ante vindemiam, quo aqua dulcis non perveniet', Plaut. *rud.* 588 'quasi vinis Graecis Neptunus nobis suffudit mare'. See further Plin. *nat.* 14. 73, Galen 10. 833 K., Athen. 32 e, H. Warner Allen, *A History of Wine*, 1961, pp. 70 f. So in our passage *Graeca*, like *levi*, emphasizes the care taken to preserve a wine of great sentimental value but relatively little staying-power.

There is evidence elsewhere for pouring new wine into old vessels. Columella says that if you want to preserve wine you should mix with it lees from a good wine, or pour the new wine into vessels recently emptied (12. 28. 4); however, neither of these recommendations is directly relevant to our passage. Commentators quote the ethical commonplace (perhaps Stoic) that young minds are like new jars, which retain the flavour of their first contents; cf. *epist.* 1. 2. 69 f. 'quo semel est imbuta recens servabit odorem / testa diu', Lucr. 6. 17 ff., Philo, *quod omnis probus liber sit* 15 ὥσπερ γάρ, φασί, τὰ καινὰ τῶν ἀγγείων ἀναφέρει τὰς τῶν πρώτων εἰς αὐτὰ ἐγχυθέντων ὀσμάς, Quint. *inst.* 1. 1. 5 'natura tenacissimi sumus eorum quae rudibus animis percepimus, ut sapor quo nova imbuas ⟨vasa⟩ durat', Epictetus fr. 10. It is generally supposed, on the strength of these passages, that Horace chooses a Greek jar for flavouring purposes (Porph. 'ut inde adduceret aliquid suavitatis'). But it may be doubted whether an earthenware pot, even when unglazed, could allow very precise discrimination; the ethical writers may be referring

U

to perfume and fish-sauce, not to different types of wine. In any case
if Horace were thinking simply of taste his reason for specifying
a Greek jar would not be clear; Greek wines, like Italian, might be
good, bad, or indifferent.

Other interpretations may be briefly dismissed. Some scholars,
who rightly find difficulty in the 'flavouring' theory, suggest that
Horace means some very ordinary type of jar (cf. A. Goldbacher,
WS 20, 1898, 282 ff., K. P. Schulze, loc. cit., pp. 285 f.). But *Graeca*
is too comprehensive to convey such a notion; and in view of the
word's proximity to *ego ipse*, one more naturally assumes that it is
a term of commendation. Commager hints at a symbolic significance
in Horace's behaviour (p. 326): he is a poet pouring new Italian
themes into old Greek forms. This kind of interpretation ought to
be rejected without hesitation. If the wine in the first stanza has
to suggest so subtle an overtone, so must the wines of the last (if
the poem is not to dissolve in anticlimax); but nobody, it is to be
hoped, will argue that 'Falernian' stands for the Campanian school
of poetry.

ego ipse: cf. Rufinus, *anth. P.* 5. 74. 1 f. πέμπω σοι, 'Ροδόκλεια, τόδε
στέφος, ἄνθεσι καλοῖς / αὐτὸς ὑφ' ἡμετέραις πλεξάμενος παλάμαις.

3. conditum levi: 'bottled and sealed'. After the new wine had fer-
mented in the big *dolium* it was transferred ('diffusum') to small
lagoenae or *amphorae*; *testa* must refer to one of these (so 3. 14. 20,
3. 21. 4). The cork was smeared with pitch to keep out the air; cf.
3. 8. 9 ff. (above, p. 244), Petron. 34. 6 'statim allatae sunt amphorae
vitreae diligenter gypsatae', D.–S. 5. 920. The date was then added:
cf. *ILS* 8580 'Ti. Claudio P. Quinctilio cos. [13 B.C.] a.d. xiii k. Iun.
vinum diffusum quod natum est duobus Lentulis cos. [18 B.C.]
autocr.' Horace, however, indicates the year not by the consuls but
by the polite allusion which follows.

datus . . . plausus: Horace recalls how when Maecenas had recovered from a serious illness the crowd applauded his arrival in the
Theatre of Pompey; cf. 2. 17. 25 f. 'cum populus frequens / laetum
theatris ter crepuit sonum'. Maecenas's undeniable gifts were not
such as to attract the man in the street, but he cannot have been
indifferent to popular acclaim; this demonstration must have been
one of the red-letter days in his neurotic life. Politicians attached
considerable importance to ovations in the theatre (ἐπισημασίαι);
cf. Cic. *Sest.* 115–27, *Att.* 1. 16. 11, 2. 19. 3, F. F. Abbott, *TAPhA* 38,
1907, 49 ff., *RLAC* 2. 95 f.

5. clare Maecenas eques: *clare* has negligible manuscript support, but
was defended by Bentley among others; the only reading with
authority is *care*. The first thing to make clear is that the adjective

does not go with *Maecenas*, as this would leave *eques* strangely isolated; it must be taken primarily with *eques*. For this poetical mannerism cf. 3. 24. 42 'magnum pauperies opprobrium', 4. 8. 31, Virg. *ecl.* 3. 3, *georg.* 2. 146 f., 4. 168.

It might be urged that *care* is a livelier and warmer word, supported not only by 2. 20. 7 'dilecte Maecenas', but also by φίλτατε Πείσων in Philodemus's invitation-poem (above, p. 245). Though *care eques* is undoubtedly a strange expression it could be argued that the presence of *Maecenas* mitigates the oddity. In any case might there not be an element almost of oxymoron in *care eques*? Maecenas is both a knight and a friend; so at 1. 1. 2 'dulce decus meum' he is both dear to Horace and a source of glory.

This defence seems unavailing. It would only work if being an *eques* were a mark of high distinction; then Horace might say 'though you are so important you are still very dear to me'. That would be a possible thing to say to some *equites*, but not to Maecenas; he was one of the greatest men in Rome and his retention of equestrian status could only be reckoned as a mark of self-abnegation. When Horace contrasts his own poor wine with Maecenas's grand way of living, nothing should be said to minimize Maecenas's importance. It makes much more point to suggest that Maecenas was a very special sort of *eques*; cf. 3. 16. 20 'Maecenas equitum decus', Prop. 3. 9. 1 'Maecenas, eques Etrusco de sanguine regum'. When Maecenas appeared in the theatre in the *quattuordecim ordines*, behind the senate, he was all the more conspicuous because of his relatively unimportant company. That effect is marked by *clare*, which was a word normally reserved for senators; *equites* were conventionally called *splendidi*.

paterni fluminis: commentators from Porphyrio point out that the Tiber, like Maecenas, came from Etruria; cf. 3. 7. 28 'Tusco denatat alveo', *serm.* 2. 2. 32 f. 'amnis . . . Tusci', Virg. *georg.* 1. 499 'Tuscum Tiberim', Augustus, *epist.* fr. 32 M. (to Maecenas) 'Tiberinum margaritum'. They do not mention the even more relevant fact that the river rose in the *territorium* of Arezzo, Maecenas's home town; cf. Plin. *nat.* 3. 53 'finibus Arretinorum profluit'.

6. ripae: some commentators say that this refers to stone quays, which would re-echo the sound; but one does not suppose that there was an extended embankment at this date, certainly not on the right bank. There is a parallel, which might reasonably be regarded as a reminiscence, in Shakespeare, *Julius Caesar* 1. i. 44 ff. 'And when you saw his chariot but appear, Have you not made an universal shout, That Tiber trembled underneath her banks, To hear the replication of your sounds Made in her concave shores?'

iocosa: cf. 1. 12. 3 f., Soph. *Phil.* 188 f. ἁ δ᾽ ἀθυρόστομος / ἀχώ, Lucian or Archias, *anth. Pl.* 154. 3 f. παντοίων στομάτων λάλον εἰκόνα, ποιμέσιν ἡδὺ / παίγνιον, Lucr. 4. 582 'noctivago strepitu ludoque iocanti'; for other epithets cf. *RE* 5. 1928 f. For instances of pointed repartees by Echo cf. Call. *ep.* 28. 5 f., Ov. *met.* 3. 379 ff., Gauradas, *anth. Pl.* 152, F. L. Lucas on Webster, *Duchess of Malfi* v. iii. 21 (a full collection of material), S. Körner, *Eos* 34, 1932–3, 111 f., W. A. Ringler, *The Poems of Philip Sidney*, 1962, p. 402.

7. **Vaticani montis:** Maecenas was presumably given his ovation in the Theatre of Pompey on the Campus Martius, the only permanent theatre of which we know at that date; its shape still determines the building line of some little streets south of S. Andrea della Valle. The echo would naturally come from the long line of the Gianicolo, which is directly opposite on the other side of the Tiber, and not from the modern Vatican, which is too far north. The name *ager Vaticanus* was applied to the whole area on the right bank of the Tiber south of the Ponte Milvio; there is no evidence in antiquity for its restriction to the modern Vatican. See A. Elter, *RhM* 46, 1891, 112 ff.; he quotes from Fea on the echo of the Gianicolo 'hodieque notant qui in eo colle et declivitate versantur, ad vocum strepitum, horologiorum et molarum sonum. ipse expertus sum'.

The second syllable of *Vaticani* is here short; it is long in Mart. 1. 18. 2, 6. 92. 3, 10. 45. 5, 12. 48. 14, Juv. 6. 344.

8. **imago:** cf. Serv. auct. *georg.* 4. 50 'quae Graece ἠχώ, Latine imago dicitur'. Horace characteristically uses the austere Latin word; so Cic. *Tusc.* 3. 3 'ea virtuti resonat tamquam imago', Varro, *rust.* 3. 16. 12 'ubi non resonent imagines'. The genitive *montis* is unscientific, but legitimate for a poet; cf. Aesch. *Pers.* 390 f. ἀντηλάλαξε νησιώτιδος πέτρας / ἠχώ, Auson. 418. 10 'redit et nemorum vocalis imago'.

For a similar echo cf. *consol. ad Liv.* 220 (on the funeral of Drusus) 'at vox adversis collibus icta redit'. Juvenal sneers at the noise from the circus reverberating across the city (11. 197 f.). But when civilization was collapsing Rutilius Namatianus took a fonder view: 'pulsato notae redduntur ab aethere voces, / vel quia perveniunt vel quia fingit amor' (1. 203 f.).

9. **Caecubum:** Caecuban and Formian wine came from Latium, on the Roman side of the Liris, Calenian and Falernian from Campania; therefore their arrangement forms a chiasmus (the alliteration increases the artistry). All four are famous wines, much better than Sabinum. But Horace makes no further discrimination. He causes confusion among some commentators because of his mannered distribution: he really means 'You can drink Caecuban, Calenian,

Falernian, and Formian, but I have none of them' (Prickard, loc.
cit.). This type of structure can easily be paralleled (1. 7. 10 n.); so
far from causing difficulty, it should be regarded as conspicuously
Horatian.

Other interpretations are less attractive. J. Gow argued that Caecuban is the best sort of Formian, Calenian the best sort of Falernian;
'so a modern might say: "You drink Chambertin and Chateau Lafitte,
but I have neither Bordeaux nor Burgundy" ' (CR 26, 1912, 50 f.).
But there is no evidence that Formian and Falernian were more
comprehensive terms than Caecuban and Calenian; Pliny and
Athenaeus clearly imply that they all belonged to the same level.

Those who read *tum* (see below) favour the view that Falernian
and Formian were even better than Caecuban and Calenian; this
is contradicted by the evidence. Caecuban belonged to the very
highest class, particularly before Pliny's day (*nat*. 14. 61); Horace
drinks it to celebrate victory (1. 37. 5, *epod*. 9. 1, 9. 36), and in the
Postumus ode it is described as 'better than a pontiffs' feast' (2. 14.
25 ff.). For praises of Calenian wine (from Cales = Calvi) cf. 1. 31. 9 f.,
4. 12. 14; Pliny says that it was once rated very high (*nat*. 14. 65).
Falernian is mentioned by Horace more often than any other wine,
but that does not imply that it was the best of all; Athenaeus
thought that Calenian was more healthy (27 a), and Pliny values
Caecuban more highly (*nat*. 14. 62). Formian wine is less often mentioned (cf. 3. 16. 34 f. 'nec Laestrygonia Bacchus in amphora /
languescit mihi'); Athenaeus says that it matured quickly and was
oily (26 e). One might try to argue that Caecuban and Calenian were
even better than Falernian and Formian; one certainly cannot
maintain that the last two were superior.

The four wines are all alluded to in a different way: Caecuban
(wine), Calenian wine-press, Falernian vines, Formian hills. For the
same sort of *variatio* cf. *epist*. 1. 2. 51 ff. 'iuvat illum sic domus et
res / ut *lippum* pictae tabulae, fomenta *podagram*, / *auriculas*
citharae collecta sorde dolentis'.

prelo domitam Caleno: cf. Prop. 4. 6. 73 'prelis elisa Falernis',
Sil. 7. 165 'nullum dant prelis nomen praeferre Falernis'. The *prelum*
or press-beam (derived from *premo*) might be a huge piece of
machinery as much as 25 feet long. See Cato, *agr*. 18, Plin. *nat*.
18. 317, A. G. Drachmann, *Ancient Oil Mills and Presses*, 1932,
pp. 50 ff., R. J. Forbes, *Studies in Ancient Technology* 3, 1955,
pp. 133 ff., *RE* 6 A. 1727 ff. (for illustration see 1743). A press has
been reconstructed in the House of the Mysteries at Pompeii.

10. tu bibes: 'you can drink' (i.e. in your own house). The future is
concessive, of a type used elsewhere where a strong contrast is being

drawn (1. 7. 1 n.). This explanation may seem difficult in view of
1 *potabis*, which is a future of a very different category; but as *bibes*
is overshadowed by an emphatic *tu*, the awkwardness may not have
been obvious to ancient ears. Several conjectures have been put
forward, of which *bibas* (Keller) would be acceptable; for the concessive subjunctive cf. 1. 31. 9 f. (in a similar context) 'premant
Calena falce quibus dedit / Fortuna vitem'.

Instead of *tu* some scholars have wrongly preferred *tum*. It is
sometimes suggested that this was the reading implied by Porphyrio
in his note on *serm.* 2. 2. 48, but this view rests on a misunderstanding; and even as a conjecture *tum* must certainly be ruled out.
To drink Caecuban after Sabine would be an unorthodox procedure
(*evang. Ioh.* 2. 10 πᾶς ἄνθρωπος πρῶτον τὸν καλὸν οἶνον τίθησιν, καὶ ὅταν
μεθυσθῶσιν τὸν ἐλάσσω); but this point at least might be met by
arguing that the Sabine has a special and sentimental value (Ensor,
loc. cit., p. 210). The other objections to *tum* are insurmountable.
It implies that Falernian and Formian were clearly superior to
Caecuban and Calenian; and this was certainly not the case (9 n.).
The emphatic *tu* is necessary to balance *mea*, and cannot be the
fortuitous result of textual corruption. The whole point of the poem
is the strong contrast between Horace's simplicity and Maecenas's
luxury; cf. 1. 31. 9 ff., 2. 16. 33 ff. (*te ... mihi*), Philodemus, above,
p. 245.

11. temperant: with *pocula* one expects this to mean 'qualify', 'make
mild', and the agent that produces the effect should be water, not
wine; cf. Lygd. 6. 58 'temperet annosum Marcia lympha merum',
Fraenkel 344. The paradox emphasizes the bland character of these
first-class wines; for a more commonplace expression cf. Sil. 7. 169
'pocula nec norant sucis mulcere Lyaei'.

12. colles: the word evokes a vivid picture of the sunny vine-clad
hills that rise suddenly from the coast behind Formiae.

21. DIANAM TENERAE

[Fraenkel 209 f.; Wilamowitz, *Hellenistische Dichtung* 2. 290 f.]

1–4. *Girls, sing of Diana, and you, boys, of Apollo and Latona.*
5–12. *Girls, praise Diana as goddess of the woods; boys, praise Tempe
and Delos and Apollo's bow and lyre.* 13–16. *Your prayer will move
him to avert all peril from Rome and Caesar.*

This poem has obvious affinities with cult-songs. These played a central part in Greek religious life, and naturally continued in the Hellenistic and Roman periods (cf. Wilamowitz's note in Norden, *Agnostos Theos*, p. 392). Alcman, Anacreon, Telesilla, and Timotheus wrote hymns to Artemis. We find a later mention in an inscription from Magnesia (after 129 B.C.), recording a school holiday on the occasion of such a performance (*SIG*³ 695. 28 ff.): συντελείτω δὲ ὁ νεωκόρος καὶ χοροὺς παρθένων ἀδουσῶν ὕμνους εἰς Ἄρτεμιν Λευκοφρυήνην, ἀνιέσθωσαν δὲ οἱ παῖδες ἐκ τῶν μαθημάτων. A paean in honour of T. Flamininus shows the pattern of such compositions; cf. p. 173 Powell:

Πίστιν δὲ Ῥωμαίων σέβομεν
τὰν μεγαλειοτάταν ὅρκοις φυλάσσειν.
μέλπετε κοῦραι
Ζῆνα μέγαν Ῥώμαν τε
Τίτον θ' ἅμα Ῥωμαίων τε
πίστιν· ἰὴ ἰὲ Παιάν·
ὦ Τίτε σῶτερ.

Religious songs are also attested in Rome, though little is known about them. In 217 B.C., during certain expiatory rites, 'acta... obsecratio est pueris ingenuis itemque libertinis, sed et virginibus patrimis matrimisque pronuntiantibus carmen' (Macr. *sat.* 1. 6. 14). In 207 B.C. Livius Andronicus composed a hymn for a girls' choir (Liv. 27. 37. 13); cf. 31. 12. 9 for another hymn in 200 B.C. Horace himself speaks of such *carmina* as necessary for the state; cf. *epist.* 2. 1. 132 ff. 'castis cum pueris ignara puella mariti / disceret unde preces, vatem ni Musa dedisset? / poscit opem chorus et praesentia numina sentit, / caelestis implorat aquas, docta prece blandus, / avertit morbos, metuenda pericula pellit, / impetrat et pacem et locupletem frugibus annum'. He was thinking especially of his own *carmen saeculare*; that was, however, too Hellenized to be representative, and was not an integral part of the ceremonies for which it was composed (cf. Fraenkel 380).

For the double chorus of girls and boys see especially Soph. *Tr.* 207 ff. ἐν δὲ κοινὸς ἀρσένων / ἴτω κλαγγὰ τὸν εὐφαρέτραν / Ἀπόλλωνα προστάταν, / ὁμοῦ δὲ παιᾶνα παι/ᾶν' ἀνάγετ', ὦ παρθένοι, / βοᾶτε τὰν ὁμόσπορον / Ἄρτεμιν Ὀρτυγίαν, ἐλαφαβόλον, / ἀμφίπυρον, / γείτονάς τε Νύμφας, *AA* 1894, 81 (twin choirs of nine boys and nine girls in the cult of Zeus Sosipolis at Magnesia on the Maeander). In Latin the double choir is found in Catullus's hymn to Diana (34), in his hexameter *epithalamium* (62), and in Horace's own *carmen saeculare* (cf. 4. 6. 31 f.). See also the prediction of the oracle in Phlegon on the worship of Apollo in Rome (*FGrH* 257 F 37, p. 1190. 18 ff.): καὶ ἀειδόμενοί τε Λατῖνοι / παιᾶνες κούροισι κόρῃσί τε νηὸν ἔχοιεν / ἀθανάτων.

χωρὶς δὲ κόραι χορὸν αὐταὶ ἔχοιεν / καὶ χωρὶς παίδων ἄρσην στάχυς, ἀλλὰ γονήων / πάντες ζωόντων, οἷς ἀμφιθαλὴς ἔτι φύτλη (*patrimi et matrimi*). Even in the *carmen Arvale* there seems to have been alternate singing, though not by boys and girls: 'semunis alternei advocapit cunctos' (cf. E. Norden, *Aus altrömischen Priesterbüchern*, 1939, pp. 184 ff.).

But though Horace's poem draws on the techniques of hymns, it could not conceivably have been sung. This is shown not simply by the artificial style and metre, but by the mode of addressing the boys and girls. Horace's *dicite* is of course intended to recall the way in which genuine cult-songs open (1 n.), but it can only be spoken by the poet, not by the chorus; it is absurd to suppose that the boys tell the girls to hymn Diana and the girls tell the boys to hymn Apollo. The poem is no more a real hymn than those of Callimachus, in which we find similar addresses (2. 8 οἱ δὲ νέοι μολπήν τε καὶ ἐς χορὸν ἐντύνασθε, 5. 137 ff., 6. 1 f., 118 f., Wilamowitz, op. cit. 2. 15). One may further note that though Horace appears to ask for a song of praise, the song of praise is nothing other than the ode itself (for the same technique cf. 1. 26, p. 302, 1. 32, p. 359).

Horace's ode was influenced by Catullus 34, and invidious comparisons are provoked. Both poems begin with a mention of mixed choirs, though in Catullus only Diana is praised. Catullus, like Horace, goes on in the manner of hymns to describe the goddess's sphere of operation: 'montium domina ut fores / silvarumque virentium / saltuumque reconditorum / amniumque sonantum'. The note is fresh and joyful, fit for the voices of an innocent young choir; the Cisalpine poet knew from the woods and rivers of his own country what Diana was about. Horace on the other hand is formal and involved; his praise of the deities evokes no definite feelings; his place-names (except for Algidus) are derived from poetry and add no particularity. There is another significant gulf between the last stanza and Catullus's final prayer 'Romulique / antique ut solita es bona / sospites ope gentem'. There is, it is true, something touching in Horace's suggestion that the prayers of a sinless new generation will be needed to move Apollo (*vestra* in 16 is in a position of emphasis). Still, the coupling of a single autocrat with the ancient Roman people is frankly shocking, though Horace is no doubt reflecting contemporary cult.

Metre: Third Asclepiad.

1. **Dianam . . .**: Diana, Apollo, and Leto often form a trinity in cult; cf. *h.Ap.* 158 f. (on the song of the Delian girls) αἵ τ' ἐπεὶ ἄρ πρῶτον μὲν Ἀπόλλων' ὑμνήσωσιν, / αὖτις δ' αὖ Λητώ τε καὶ Ἄρτεμιν ἰοχέαιραν, *CIL* 6. 32, R. Herzog, *Philologus* 77, 1912, 1 ff., *RE* 2. 1366, Ogilvie on

Liv. 5. 13. 6. Diana and Latona stood one on each side of Apollo in his temple on the Palatine (1. 31. 1 n.), and another group of the three deities together with the Muses was set up near the portico of Octavia (Plin. *nat.* 36. 34); see further Roscher 2. 1975 f., L. R. Taylor, *The Divinity of the Roman Emperor*, 1931, pp. 131 f.

In this stanza Diana is merely named, Apollo has an epithet, Latona is fully praised in two lines. For this structure cf. 1. 2. 38 ff. 'clamor galeaeque leves / acer et Marsi peditis cruentum / vultus in hostem', E. Lindholm, *Stilistische Studien*, 1931, pp. 157 ff., especially pp. 181 ff., Fraenkel on Aesch. *Ag.* 1243. The pattern is repeated on a larger scale in the whole poem. Latona gets her two lines of praise and is then dismissed, Diana has a whole stanza, developing 1, and Apollo two stanzas, developing 2.

The first stanza is very artfully composed. The four names are placed at the beginnings and ends of lines. *tenerae* is applied to the maidens but hints also at Diana, *intonsum* is applied to Apollo but hints also at the boys.

Dianam: the first syllable is here long, the more archaic and hymnal form (cf. 2. 12. 20, 4. 7. 25, *carm. saec.* 70); it is short in 3. 4. 71, *epod.* 5. 51, 17. 3, *ars* 16, 454; cf. *Thes.l.L.* Onom. 3. 127. 27 ff.

dicite: the word has no prosaic feeling and is often applied to singing; cf. in Greek Hom. *Od.* 1. 10 τῶν ἁμόθεν γε, θεά, θυγάτερ Διός, εἰπὲ καὶ ἡμῖν, Call. *h.* 4. 257 εἶπαν Ἐλειθυίης ἱερὸν μέλος, Antip. Sid. *anth. P.* 7. 2. 6 (of Homer) τὰν Αἴαντος ναύμαχον εἶπε βίαν, Nonnus 43. 392 γάμιον μέλος εἶπεν.

Cult-songs often open with an apparently similar command; cf. Isyllus 37 p. 133 Powell (the first line of the paean) ἰὲ Παιᾶνα θεὸν ἀείσατε λαοί, anon. *PMG* 934. 1 f. Παιᾶνα κλυτόμητιν ἀείσατε, / κοῦροι, Macedonius (?) 1 ff. p. 138 Powell, anon. 1 f. p. 140 Powell ὑμνεῖτε ἐπὶ σπονδαῖς Ἀπόλλωνος κυανοπλοκάμου / παῖδα Σέλευκον. In these passages the members of the chorus seem to be encouraging each other (see also Bacch. 13. 190 νίκαν τ᾽ ἐρικυδέα μέλπετ᾽, ὦ νέοι, E. Norden, op. cit. [above, p. 254], pp. 193 ff.); in our poem this is impossible.

2. intonsum: ἀκερσεκόμην (Hom. *Il.* 20. 39, Pind. *I.* 1. 7). The epithet is appropriate because Phoebus is perpetually youthful: cf. *h.Ap.* 449 f. ἀνέρι εἰδόμενος αἰζηῷ τε κρατερῷ τε / πρωθήβῃ, χαίτῃς εἰλυμένος εὐρέας ὤμους, Ap. Rhod. 2. 708 f. αἰεί τοι, ἄναξ, ἄτμητοι ἔθειραι, / αἰὲν ἀδήλητοι, Tib. 1. 4. 37 f. Long hair is a constant attribute of Apollo; cf. *epod.* 15. 9 '(dum) intonsos ... agitaret Apollinis aura capillos' (i.e. 'for ever'), Tib. 2. 3. 12, 2. 5. 121, Ov. *met.* 1. 564 f.

All early Greek statues of κοῦροι have long hair, and were formerly taken to represent Apollo (cf. G. Richter, *Kouroi*, 1960, pp. 1 f.).

In the fifth and early fourth centuries Apollo, like other youths, normally wore his hair short; yet there are exceptions (cf. especially the recently discovered Apollo from the Piraeus, Richter, op. cit., 159 bis, pp. 136 f.). In Hellenistic and later sculpture the hair clusters long on his neck or is gathered up in a knot on the top of the head; cf. Roscher 1. 450, 456, 458.

Cynthium: Cynthus is the one and only hill of Delos (only 350 ft.); here Apollo and Diana (Cynthia) are said to have been born (cf. *h.Ap.* 17, 25 ff.). *Cynthius* as an ἐπίκλησις of Apollo is common in Hellenistic and Roman poetry; cf. *Thes.l.L.* Onom. 2. 792. 68 ff.

3. supremo: cf. 1. 32. 13, Pind. *N.* 1. 60 Διὸς ὑψίστου, Paus. 1. 26. 5 Διὸς βωμὸς Ὑπάτου. In Latin the archaic superlative *supremus* is particularly used of Jupiter (11 out of 13 cases in Plautus).

4. dilectam penitus: Apollo and Diana, unlike most of Zeus's children, were not the result of a casual amour. In Hes. *th.* 918 Leto appears in the list of the wives Zeus had before Hera, and in *h.Ap.* 5 ff. she is clearly an honoured member of the court at Olympus; cf. also Call. *h.* 4. 55 ff.

penitus: cf. *h.Ap.* 138 φίλησε δὲ κηρόθι μᾶλλον, Pind. *P.* 2. 74 οὐδ' ἀπάταισι θυμὸν τέρπεται ἔνδοθεν, Eur. *Or.* 1122 ἔνδοθεν κεχαρμένην.

5. vos . . .: for Diana as goddess of rivers cf. Pind. *P.* 2. 7 ποταμίας ἕδος Ἀρτέμιδος, Catull. 34. 9 ff. (above, p. 254), Virg. *Aen.* 1. 498 f. 'qualis in Eurotae ripis aut per iuga Cynthi / exercet Diana choros', Menander rhet. 3. 334. 29 f. Sp. (of Alcman) τὴν μὲν γὰρ Ἄρτεμιν ἐκ μυρίων ὀρέων, μυρίων δὲ πολέων, ἔτι δὲ ποταμῶν ἀνακαλεῖ, Max. Tyr. 2. 1 ἱερὰ δὲ Ἀρτέμιδος πηγαὶ ναμάτων καὶ κοῖλαι νάπαι καὶ εὔθηροι λειμῶνες. Shrines to Artemis were frequent on the banks of the Alpheus, at Letrinoi (Paus. 6. 22. 9), at Olympia, and at the river mouth (Str. 8. 3. 12). The Ephesian Artemis is sometimes represented with the rivers Cenchreus and Cayster reclining at her feet, and sometimes with the rivers Claseas and Marnas (Head 577). Cf. also Roscher 1. 560 f.

For the woods cf. 3. 22. 1, *carm. saec.* 1, *h.Ven.* 18 ff. τῇ ἅδε . . . ἄλσεα . . . σκιόεντα, Virg. *Aen.* 9. 405, 11. 557, Sen. *Phaedr.* 409, Serv. *georg.* 3. 332 'omnis lucus Dianae (est consecratus)'. The goddess was called *Nemorensis* in her cult at Aricia, and δρυμονία in *Orph. h.* 36. 12.

For the mountains cf. Alcaeus 304. 6 οἰοπό]λων ὀρέων κορύφαισ' ἔπι and the passages cited by Page, *Sappho and Alcaeus*, pp. 263 f.; add Eur. *Phoen.* 151 f., Catull. 64. 300 'cultricem montibus Idri', *Orph. h.* 36. 10 ἢ κατέχεις ὀρέων δρυμούς, Christodorus, *anth. P.* 2. 306 f. Φοίβου δ' οὐρεσίφοιτος ὁμόγνιος ἵστατο κούρη / Ἄρτεμις. The Ephesian Artemis is sometimes represented with a recumbent figure of Mt. Peion, 'holding a cultus statue of Artemis beneath a mountain on which runs a boar pierced by a spear' (Head, loc. cit.).

5. coma: *comam* has stronger manuscript support and was defended by Bentley. But Diana's praises would be too meagre if she were merely described as *laetam fluviis* and the rest of the stanza celebrated the foliage of the woods.

6. gelido: punning when linked with *Algido*, which itself means 'chill'; cf. 3. 23. 9 'nivali . . . Algido', Fronto, p. 31 N. (= p. 31 van den Hout) 'iam conticinum atque matutinum atque diluculum usque ad solis ortum, gelidum, ad Algidum maxime', Prud. *c. Symm.* 2. 534 'gelido . . . Algidus axe'. For similar puns cf. Virg. *Aen.* 1. 366 'novae Karthaginis arcem' (Serv. ad loc. 'Karthago enim est lingua Poenorum nova civitas'), 7. 740 'maliferae . . . Abellae' (the name of the town comes from the same root as 'apple', cf. A. Meillet and J. Vendryes, *Traité de grammaire comparée des langues classiques*, ed. 3, 1960, p. 19). See further J. S. T. Hanssen, *SO* 26, 1948, 113 ff.

prominet: 'stands out conspicuously' on the mountain top; Artemis was particularly worshipped on the summit of mountains (cf. Page, loc. cit.).

Algido: probably the curving wall of heights that limits the Alban hills on the east and south-east, from Tusculum to Velitrae. In its northern section Monte Porzio, Compatri, and Rocca Priora are now favourite places of *villeggiatura* in the Roman summer; the highest point here is Monte Salomone near Rocca Priora. Further south, the ridge rises higher, at Castel Lariano and Monte Peschio (*c.* 3,070 ft.). At Castel Lariano ruins of several old walls of large square blocks have been thought to be the remains of the sanctuary of Diana; cf. *RE* 1. 1476. For the cult cf. *carm. saec.* 69; for the woods of oak and ilex cf. 3. 23. 9 f., 4. 4. 57 f., Liv. 3. 25. 7.

Horace characteristically links the Italian name with those of the poetical mountains of Greek legend. An eighteenth-century ear was more aware of his audacity here than we are; cf. Addison, *A Discourse on Antient and Modern Learning*, 1734, p. 33, 'How oddly, therefore, must the Name of a paultry Village sound to those who were well acquainted with the Meanness of the Place; and yet how many such Names are to be met with in the Catalogues of *Homer* and *Virgil*? Many of their Words must therefore very much shock the Ear of a *Roman* or *Greek*, especially whilst the Poem was new; and appear as meanly to their own Countrymen, as the Duke of *Buckingham's Putney Pikes* and *Chelsea Curiaseers* do to an *Englishman*'.

7. nigris . . . viridis: probably both adjectives are felt in both clauses; both mountains are green and their woods are dark (cf.

1. 17. 5 f. 'arbutos / quaerunt latentis et thyma deviae (capellae)',
3. 4. 18 f. 'sacra / lauroque collataque myrto', *carm. saec.* 31 f. 'aquae
salubres / et Iovis aurae'). Some editors think *nigris* applies only to
Erymanthus's woods and that the contrasting *viridis* takes its
place in the next clause; the fact that *nigris* precedes *aut* makes this
less likely.

nigris refers to the dark appearance of massed and distant trees;
cf. 4. 12. 11 f. 'nigri / colles Arcadiae', Pind. *P.* 1. 27 Αἴτνας ἐν μελαμ-
φύλλοις . . . κορυφαῖς.

Erymanthi: the wildest and most impassable mountain of Arcadia
(7,290 ft.). It was a traditional haunt of Artemis (Hom. *Od.* 6. 102 f.,
RE 6. 569 f.). Cf. also Rufinus, *anth. P.* 5. 19. 5 ὁ δενδροκόμης Ἐρύμανθος.

8. Gragi: a mountainous area in Lycia, west of the mouth of the
Xanthus, rising at its highest point to 6,500 ft.; seven impressive
headlands run from it into the sea. Though Apollo had an important
cult at Patara in Lycia, we do not often hear of Artemis there; yet
cf. Soph. *OT* 207 f. Ἀρτέμιδος αἴγλας, ξὺν αἷς / Λύκι' ὄρεα διᾴσσει. The
mountain sounds a suitable haunt for a huntress; cf. Eur. fr. 669.
1 f. πέλας δὲ ταύτης δεινὸς ἵδρυται Κράγος / ἔνθηρος, Steph. Byz. s.v.
Κράγος· . . . ἐνταῦθα δ' εἶναι καὶ τὰ ἐπονομαζόμενα θεῶν ἀγρίων ἄντρα
(cf. Artemis's cult-title Ἀγροτέρα), Str. 14. 3. 5. Most editors spell
the name *Cragi*; the manuscripts here have *Gragi*, the form generally
favoured by the manuscript tradition where the name occurs in
Latin (cf. *Agrigentum* for Ἀκράγας).

9. Tempe: cf. 1. 7. 3 n.

10. Delon: a cult-centre from early times; cf. *h.Ap.* 146 f. ἀλλὰ
σὺ Δήλῳ, Φοῖβε, μάλιστ' ἐπιτέρπεαι ἦτορ, / ἔνθα τοι ἑλκεχίτωνες Ἰάονες
ἠγερέθονται κτλ. Apart from the Homeric hymn to Apollo, Delos was
celebrated in poetry by Pindar, who wrote four Paeans for performance there (4, 5, 7b, 12), and by Bacchylides (17, a dithyramb
for the Ceans at the Delian festival, cf. also fr. 65); tradition also
attributed poems, supposed ancient, to the Sibyl, Olen, Eumelus,
and Melanopus. Extant praises of Delos are found in Callimachus's
fourth *Hymn* and in Aristides 44 K.; see also Str. 10. 5. 2 τετίμηται δὲ
ἐκ παλαιοῦ διὰ τοὺς θεοὺς ἀπὸ τῶν ἡρωικῶν χρόνων ἀρξαμένη, Wilamowitz, op. cit. 2. 63.

In the second century Delos had a period of great prosperity as
a slave market and free port. But it suffered terribly in the first
Mithridatic War, when 20,000 of its inhabitants are said to have
been massacred, and from a pirate raid in 69 B.C. By Horace's time
any hope of recovery had been finally destroyed by the refoundation

of Corinth, and the island was largely deserted and once more abandoned to Apollo; cf. Antip. Thess. *anth. P.* 9. 408. 3 ff. οἳ ἐμὲ δειλήν, / ὅσσαις Ἑλλήνων νηυσὶ παραπλέομαι, / Δῆλος ἐρημαίη, τὸ πάλαι σέβας, Gow–Page, *Philip* 2. 95.

mares: ἄρσενες, cf. p. 253.

11. **insignem:** editors generally assume that the epithet refers to Apollo, with *umerum* as an accusative of respect. If this is what Horace meant the expression is strangely ambiguous and Peerlkamp's *umeros* would seem the minimum needed for clarity (for the plural cf. 3. 4. 60, Virg. *Aen.* 4. 149). But why should *insignem* not simply qualify *umerum*? Apollo's shoulder is as fit a subject of song as the Nereids' green hair (3. 28. 10).

pharetra fraternaque . . . lyra: for the conjunction of these two attributes of Apollo, cf. 2. 10. 17 ff., *h.Ap.* 131 εἴη μοι κίθαρίς τε φίλη καὶ καμπύλα τόξα, Call. *h.* 2. 18 f. ὅτε κλείουσιν ἀοιδοὶ / ἢ κίθαριν ἢ τόξα, Λυκώρεος ἔντεα Φοίβου, Ov. *rem.* 705. The statue of Apollo at Delos held a bow in the left hand and in the right carried the three Graces holding musical instruments, one a syrinx, one a lyre, and one a flute (cf. R. Pfeiffer, *Ausgewählte Schriften*, 1960, pp. 55 ff.).

We are not of course to think of Apollo as hung about simultaneously with the bow and the lyre, each of them suspended from a shoulder. In art he appears as the archer or as the *citharoedus*, but not as both at once.

12. **fraterna:** invented by his half-brother Mercury, son of Jupiter and Maia. Hermes gave Apollo the lyre to win his forgiveness for stealing his cattle (*h.Merc.* 475 ff.). Hermes's lyre was in fact a different instrument from the cithara of Apollo (cf. D.–S. 3. 1437 ff., W. D. Anderson, *Ethos and Education in Greek Music*, 1966, pp. 3 ff.); but Horace does not distinguish them. In this he resembles the artists of Campanian wall-paintings, whose representations are so vague that it is impossible to tell which instrument they intend to portray.

13. **hic . . . hic:** the reiterated demonstrative is characteristic of the sacral style; cf. Democr. fr. 30 πάνθ᾽ οὗτος οἶδε καὶ διδοῖ καὶ ἀφαιρεῖται καὶ βασιλεὺς οὗτος τῶν πάντων, Lygd. 6. 13 ff. 'ille facit mites animos deus, ille ferocem / contudit . . .; / Armenias tigres et fulvas ille leaenas / vicit', Aristides 43. 29 f. K. οὗτος ἁπάντων εὐεργέτης . . ., οὗτος πρύτανις . . . ἁπάντων . . ., οὗτος δοτὴρ ἁπάντων, οὗτος ποιητής, Norden, *Agnostos Theos*, pp. 163 ff. (a notable account of the ' "Er"-Stil der Prädikation').

bellum . . . : both Apollo and Diana are *dei averrunci*, averters of evil; cf. Macr. *sat.* 1. 17. 14 f. 'nam ὡς ἀπελαύνοντα τὰς νόσους Ἀπόλλωνα tanquam Ἀπέλλωνα cognominatum putant, . . . ut Apollinem apellentem mala intellegas, quem Athenienses Ἀλεξίκακον appellant'. *aversio* often involves the idea that the evil must go somewhere else ; enemies, especially public ones, were suitable recipients.

Examples are numerous in many languages; cf. i. 28. 27, 3. 27. 21 f. 'hostium uxores puerique caecos / sentiant motus orientis Austri', *epod.* 5. 51 ff., Aesch. *Ag.* 1571 ff. ἰόντ' / ἐκ τῶνδε δόμων ἄλλην γενεὰν / τρίβειν θανάτοις αὐθένταισιν, Soph. *OT* 159 ff. where Athene, Artemis, and Phoebus are invoked as ἀλεξίμοροι, Philippus, *anth. P.* 6. 240. 2 ff. Ἄρτεμις, ἣ θαλάμους τοὺς ὀρέων ἔλαχες, / νοῦσον τὴν στυγερὴν αὐθήμερον ἐκ βασιλῆος / ἐσθλοτάτου πέμψαις ἄχρις Ὑπερβορέων, Orph. *h.* 3. 14, 11. 23, 36. 16, Catull. 63. 92 f. 'procul a mea tuus sit furor omnis, era, domo : / alios age incitatos, alios age rabidos', Virg. *georg.* 3. 513, Liv. 5. 18. 12 'precibusque ab dis petitum ut exitium ab urbis tectis templisque ac moenibus Romanis arcerent Veiosque eum averterent terrorem', Tib. i. 1. 33 f. with K. F. Smith's note, Prop. 3. 8. 20, Ov. *epist.* 16. 217, *am.* 2. 10. 16 f., 3. 11. 16, *ars* 3. 247 f., *fast.* 3. 494, *paneg. lat.* 11(3). 16. 2, Ronsard, *Prière à Dieu pour la famine* 51 ff. 'Ou bien sur les Tartares, Turcs, Scythes et Barbares, Qui n'ont la connoissance Du bruit de ta puissance, O Seigneur, hardiment Espan ce chastiment', anon. (prayer to the saint who deals with arson) 'O heiliger Sankt Florian, / verschon dies Haus, zünd andre an!', anon. (1659) 'Raine, raine, goe to Spain: Faire weather come againe', I. and P. Opie, *The Lore and Language of Schoolchildren*, 1959, pp. 218 f., Fraenkel 410 f., O. Weinreich, *Gebet und Wunder*, *Tübinger Beiträge zur Altertumswissenschaft*, Heft 5, 1929, 174 ff., ZKG 61, 1942, 44 ff.

As both Apollo and Diana are often invoked to avert trouble, some editors, Bentley among them, wish to give Diana something to do in this stanza ; hence they conjecture *haec bellum.* But such a division of function shows disregard for poetic structure (1 n.) and for the hymnal style (above, *hic* n.). Moreover, it is surely far more appropriate, in view of Apollo's importance in Augustan Rome, that he should have the last part of the poem to himself.

bellum lacrimosum: cf. Hom. *Il.* 5. 737 πόλεμον . . . δακρυόεντα, 19. 318 πολύδακρυν Ἄρηα, Anacreon 382 δακρυόεσσάν τ' ἐφίλησαν αἰχμήν. But in Roman poets of this age the epithet is not merely decorative.

miseram: cf. Hom. *Od.* 12. 342 λιμῷ δ' οἴκτιστον θανέειν καὶ πότμον ἐπισπεῖν, Thuc. 3. 59. 3, Dion. Hal. *ant.* 6. 86. 3, Cic. *Att.* 5. 21. 8 'fames, qua nihil miserius est', Sall. *epist. Pomp.* 1, Liv. 21. 41. 11, 27. 44. 8.

famem pestemque: cf. Hes. *op.* 243 λιμὸν ὁμοῦ καὶ λοιμόν, *carm. Arval.* 4 'neve lue rue, Marmar, sins incurrere in pleores', Fest. 230. 29 f. L. (= 210. 22 f. M.) 'avertas morbum mortem labem nebulam impetiginem', Cato, *agr.* 141. 2 'uti tu morbos visos invisosque,

viduertatem vastitudinemque, calamitates intemperiasque pro-
hibessis defendas averruncesque', Liv. 5. 31. 5, Luther's litany, 'a
peste et fame . . ., a bello et cede . . . libera nos, Domine' (the words
'a peste, fame et bello' were added to the Roman litany in 1847, cf. L.
Eisenhofer, *Handbuch der katholischen Liturgik* 1, 1932, p. 200). For
similar collocations cf. Jeremiah 14. 12, Ezekiel 5. 17, 14. 21, R. H.
Charles, *Commentary on the Revelation of St. John*, 1920, 1. 156 ff.

14. pestem: a poetical equivalent for the prose *pestilentiam*. Power
to heal and send disease is constantly attributed to Apollo and to
Artemis (13 n.). Apollo's hymn, the paean, is defined in the *Etymo-
logicum Magnum* as ὕμνος ἐπὶ ἀφέσει λοιμοῦ ᾀδόμενος, and he was the
first god mentioned in the Hippocratic oath.

populo: alliteration is very common in prayers; cf. Cato, loc. cit.
above, Appel 160 ff.

principe: the *princeps* replaces the *patres*, who are frequently
linked with the *populus*; cf. Lucil. 1229 'populusque patresque',
Virg. *Aen.* 4. 682, 9. 192, Val. Fl. 8. 281, Stat. *silv.* 1. 4. 115, Mart.
7. 5. 1, 8. 49(50). 7, 9. 48. 7, 12. 2(3). 15, Auson. *Mos.* 409; the phrase
is a poetical equivalent for the official *senatus populusque Romanus.*
The more regular formula under the Empire is perhaps reflected
in Apul. *met.* 11. 17. 3 'fausta vota praefatus principi magno sena-
tuique et equiti totoque Romano populo' (cf. Dio 51. 19. 7). Horace
no doubt aims at brevity, but his disregard for the senate seems a
constitutional enormity. Even a century later the omission could
give offence; cf. Suet. *Nero* 37. 3 'et in auspicando opere Isthmi
magna frequentia clare ut sibi ac populo Romano bene res verteret
optavit, dissimulata senatus mentione'.

22. INTEGER VITAE

[Commager 130 ff.; Fraenkel 184 ff.; G. L. Hendrickson, *CJ* 5, 1910, 250 ff.;
C. Josserand, *AC* 4, 1935, 357 ff.; Pasquali 470 ff.; R. Reitzenstein, *Hermes* 57,
1922, 358 ff.; P. Shorey, *CJ* 5, 1910, 317 ff.]

*1–8. The man who is pure of heart needs no weapons even when travelling
through the most dangerous territory. 9–16. For instance, when I was
singing of Lalage in the Sabine woodland a monstrous wolf fled from
me although I was unarmed. 17–24. Set me in the most distant and uninhabitable lands and I shall go on loving Lalage.*

This ode is addressed to Fuscus, whom Porphyrio rightly identifies
as Aristius Fuscus. He was a close friend of Horace's (*serm.* 1. 9. 61

'mihi carus', *epist.* 1. 10. 3 'paene gemelli'). He wrote comedies (Porph. on *epist.* 1. 10) and seems to have had a sense of humour: it was he who refused to rescue Horace from the 'importunate man' in the Sacra Via (*serm.* 1. 9. 60 ff.). Horace says elsewhere that he was a town-lover, who disliked the countryside (*epist.* 1. 10); here he amuses him with an account of the perils of his Sabine estate. Fuscus was a schoolmaster by profession (Porph. on *serm.* 1. 9. 60 'prae-stantissimus grammaticus illo tempore'); in *epist.* 1. 10. 45 Horace teases him for his stern discipline ('nec me dimittes incastigatum...'; cf. *CQ* N.S. 9, 1959, 74 f.). Fuscus is mentioned with Asinius Pollio and others as a critic who approved of Horace's poetry (*serm.* 1. 10. 83 ff.). He may also have written on grammar; cf. *gramm.* 7. 35. 2 'Abnesti Fusti (*Aristi Fusci* Haupt, *Aufusti* Usener) grammatici liber est ad Asinium Pollionem'.

Horace's ode starts with the proposition that the pure in heart need no weapons even when travelling through the most dangerous country. Bias is supposed to have thought that a good conscience is without fear (Stob. 3. 24. 11), and even Epicurus affirmed that a good man would disregard danger (fr. 99). But Horace's maxim seems more characteristically Stoic: *non eget* gives a hint of Stoic self-sufficiency (2 n.), and the reference to the Syrtes suggests the Stoic hero, Cato (5 n.). For similar sentiments cf. Sen. *Thy.* 380 ff. 'mens regnum bona possidet. / nil ullis opus est equis, / nil armis et inertibus / telis quae procul ingerit / Parthus cum simulat fugas', Claud. 17. 193 ff. (on Justice) 'nitidis quisquis te sensibus hausit, / inruet intrepidus flammis, hiberna secabit / aequora, confertos hostes superabit inermis. / ille vel Aethiopum pluviis solabitur aestus; / illum trans Scythiam vernus comitabitur aer'. In the past many people have taken this absurdity to be the true meaning of Horace's poem; cf. Lact. *inst.* 5. 17. 18 'recte igitur Flaccus tantam esse dixit in-nocentiae vim ut ad tutelam sui non egeat nec armis nec viribus quacumque iter fecerit'. The ode was even supplied with mournful music by F. F. Flemming (cf. the *Scottish Students' Song-book*), and sung at German and Scandinavian funerals.

As an illustration of his general maxim Horace says that when he was singing about Lalage a wolf met him and ran away (9–16). An epigram in the Greek Anthology describes how the chaste priest of Cybele (ἁγνὸς Ἄτυς) frightened off a lion with his tambourine (Dios-corides 6. 220; cf. 217–19, 237, Varro, *Men.* 364; see H. W. Prescott, *CPh* 20, 1925, 276 f.). To Horace it is not the eunuch *gallus* but the lover who is pure of heart; his weapon is not the tambourine but a simple love-song (cf. Josserand, loc. cit.). He is applying to himself, not without amusement, the elegists' commonplace that the lover is a sacred person under divine protection; cf. especially Prop. 3. 16. 11 ff. :

nec tamen est quisquam sacros qui laedat amantes:
  Scironis media sic licet ire via.
quisquis amator erit, Scythicis licet ambulet oris:
  nemo adeo ut feriat barbarus esse volet.
luna ministrat iter, demonstrant astra salebras;
  ipse Amor accensas percutit ante faces.
saeva canum rabies morsus avertit hiantis;
  huic generi quovis tempore tuta via est.

For other variations on this theme cf. Poseidippus, *anth. P.* 5. 213. 3 f.
εἰπὲ δὲ σημεῖον μεθύων ὅτι καὶ διὰ κλωπῶν / ἦλθον, Ἔρωτι θρασεῖ
χρώμενος ἡγεμόνι, anon. 12. 115. 4 τὸν ἔρωθ' ὅπλον ἄτρωτον ἔχων, Tib.
1. 2. 27 f. 'quisquis amore tenetur eat tutusque sacerque / qualibet;
insidias non timuisse decet', Ov. *am.* 1. 6. 13 f. 'nec mora, venit amor;
non umbras nocte volantis, / non timeo strictas in mea fata manus',
Longus 3. 5 ἔρωτι δὲ ἄρα πάντα βασιμά, καὶ πῦρ καὶ ὕδωρ καὶ Σκυθικὴ
χιών.
    At the end of the poem Horace returns to the theme of sojourning
in remote areas (17–22); the grandiloquent lines balance 5–8 and
form a frame round the story of the Sabine wolf. In the last two
lines 23–4 he points the moral. To achieve symmetry with the opening
stanza we expect Horace to say that he will keep his heart pure; this
is what is required by the principles of 'Ring-Composition' (for
which see Fraenkel on Aesch. *Ag.* 205, V. Buchheit, *Studien zum
Corpus Priapeorum*, 1962, p. 39, Newman 59). Instead he makes the
less pretentious statement: 'I shall go on loving Lalage'. The *integer
vitae* is thus revealed as the lover; the poem which began so pom-
pously is shown to be not so earnest after all.
    Some commentators, while rightly dismissing the most solemn
interpretations, still believe that the ode contains some serious note.
They point to other places where Horace claims to be under special
protection: 1. 17. 13 f. 'di me tuentur, dis pietas mea / et Musa cordi
est', 2. 17. 28 (Faunus saves the poet from a falling tree), 3. 4. 9 ff.
(doves protect the infant Horace); see further K. F. Smith on Tib.
2. 5. 113–14. Though Horace would not literally regard the poet as
sacred, he might (it is argued) use the old idea to represent the
happiness and security that poetry gave him. Yet one feels that this
approach should not be pressed. The type of poetry alluded to is love-
poetry, not the most serious sort; and in the last two lines the emphasis
is on the love rather than the poetry.
    The ode is one of Horace's most charming and most perfect. It
does not describe a real event literally: few poems do. There was
no such person as Lalage: the name, and indeed the whole circumstance, is chosen because it suits the artistic needs of the poem (cf.
23 n.). Horace may have glimpsed a wolf shambling off in the middle

                                                            x

distance, but the incident was a trivial one at best. Yet the ode is not just a conventional exercise devoid of personality. Only a poet could have expressed so agreeable a blend of self-mockery and self-satisfaction.

Metre: Sapphic. The first stanza is quoted in Lily's Latin Grammar to illustrate this metre; cf. Shakespeare, *Tit. Andr.* IV. ii. 20 f. (after quoting the first two lines) 'O 'tis a verse in Horace; I know it well. I read it in the grammar long ago'.

1. **integer vitae**: the genitive is slightly mannered, and *vita* would have been more normal; cf. *carm. epig.* 667. 1 f. (on a priest from Arles) 'integer adque pius vita et corpore purus / aeterno hic positus vivit Concordius aevo'. *integer mentis* and *integer animi* seem to have belonged to spoken Latin (*serm.* 2. 3. 65, 2. 3. 220); the poets extended the construction to *aevi* (Enn. *scaen.* 414, Virg. *Aen.* 2. 638, Ov. *met.* 9. 441). See further H.–Sz. 74 f., Löfstedt, *Syntactica* I². 172 ff.

scelerisque purus: this phrase is likewise poetical; cf. Stat. *Theb.* 11. 450 f. 'puraeque nefandi / sanguinis . . . hastae', Sil. 12. 370, Paul. Nol. *carm.* 10. 213. Such genitives are found in Greek with ἁγνός (Eur. *Hipp.* 316), ἀκήρατος (ibid. 949), and καθαρός (Pl. *rep.* 496 d), and in Latin with *solutus* (3. 17. 16), *vacuus* (*serm.* 2. 2. 119), *liber* (*ars* 212), *orbus, cassus, privus, nudus* (K.–S. 1. 441 f.).

The labelling of these genitives is not very important. The ancient reader, who did not think in grammatical categories, would be less aware than we are of the distinction between the two types. He would rather appreciate the elegance of the chiasmus: *integer* and *purus* are similar in meaning and combined elsewhere (Cic. *Tusc.* 1. 41, *nat. deor.* 2. 31, 2. 71). The syntax is interesting because of its stylistic significance: the important thing to realize about the first line is that it is grandiloquent.

2. **non eget**: ancient moral philosophers were fond of enumerating the things which the good man can do without. Cynics and Stoics in particular emphasized the importance of self-sufficiency (αὐτάρκεια).

Mauris: to be taken with *arcu* as well as *iaculis*. The *iaculum* (ἀκόντιον) was a typically Moroccan weapon; cf. Str. 17. 3. 7 (of the Moors) μάχονται δ' ἱππόται τὸ πλέον ἀπὸ ἄκοντος, *bell. Afr.* 7. 5, Sil. 3. 339 'iaculove . . . Mauro', Herodian, *hist.* 1. 15. 2 συνῆσαν δὲ παιδεύοντες αὐτὸν Παρθυαίων οἱ τοξικὴν ἀκριβοῦντες καὶ Μαυρουσίων οἱ ἀκοντίζειν ἄριστοι.

3. **venenatis**: poisoned arrows were barbarous; cf. Pease on Cic. *div.* 2. 135, *nat. deor.* 2. 126, *RE* 19. 1427 f. In the present context, after *Mauris*, one naturally thinks of North Africa; for the use of poison

in this area cf. Sil. 1. 219 (of Numidia) 'nec fidens nudo sine fraudibus ensi', 15. 681.

gravida . . .: 'with its brood of arrows'. The word properly means 'heavy with child'; here it gives a more sinister note than the objective *gravi*. Cf. [Liv. Andr.] *trag.* p. 4 'pressaque iam gravida crepitant tibi terga pharetra', Sil. 7. 445.

5. sive . . .: Horace no doubt remembers Catull. 11. 2 ff. 'sive in extremos penetrabit Indos / . . . sive in Hyrcanos Arabasve molles, / seu Sagas sagittiferosque Parthos, / sive quae septemgeminus colorat / aequora Nilus, / sive trans altas gradietur Alpes . . .'. For similar lists of diverse journeys in remote areas cf. *epod.* 1. 11 ff. 'te vel per Alpium iuga / inhospitalem et Caucasum / vel occidentis usque ad ultimum sinum / forti sequemur pectore', *carm.* 2. 6. 1 ff. 'Septimi, Gadis aditure mecum et / Cantabrum indoctum iuga ferre nostra et / barbaras Syrtes ubi Maura semper / aestuat unda', 3. 4. 29 ff., Prop. 1. 6. 1 ff., 3. 22. 7 ff. One may note that the Syrtes, the Caucasus, and India are mentioned in other places besides our ode.

Hendrickson, loc. cit., calls attention to the fact that some such passages refer specifically to lovers; cf. Virg. *ecl.* 10. 64 ff., Ov. *am.* 2. 16. 21 ff. 'cum domina Libycas ausim perrumpere Syrtes . . .', Sen. *Phaedr.* 613 ff. But at this stage of the poem Horace is emphasizing heroic achievement; the *integer vitae* is seen as the Stoic good man, and has not yet emerged as the lover. On the other hand the topic of the 'lover in distant lands' is very relevant to the balancing lines 17–22.

Syrtis: the *magna Syrtis* is the gulf of Sirte or Sidra where Cyrenaica and Tripolitania meet; the *parva Syrtis* is the gulf of Gabes, where Tunisia and Tripolitania meet. The name was often applied, as here, to the land as well as to the sea (cf. Butler on Apul. *apol.* 72). Libya was infested by wild animals (Hdt. 2. 32. 4 θηριώδης, Plin. *nat.* 5. 26, Luc. 9. 607 ff., Dio Chrys. 5. 5 ff., Apul. *apol.* 72), and must have been dangerous to the traveller.

Commentators do not mention that in 47 B.C. a very famous march was made round the Great Syrtis. Cato set out from Berenice (Benghazi) with 10,000 men, and reached Leptis in Tripolitania in 30 days (Str. 17. 3. 20, Plut. *Cato min.* 56. 3 f., *RE* 22. 200). His sufferings and endurance were described by Livy (*epit.* 112 'laboriosum M. Catonis in Africa per deserta . . . iter'), and in the ninth book of Lucan; cf. also Sen. *epist.* 104. 33 'vides posse homines laborem pati: per medias Africae solitudines pedes duxit exercitum. vides posse tolerari sitim: in collibus arentibus sine ullis inpedimentis victi exercitus reliquias trahens inopiam umoris loricatus tulit, et quotiens aquae fuerat occasio novissimus bibit', Sidon. *epist.* 8. 12. 3 'et cum

nec duodecim milium obiectu sic retarderis, quid putamus cum exercitu M. Catonis in Leptitana Syrte fecisses?' These accounts must
go back to the panegyrics written soon after Cato's death by Cicero,
Brutus, and others (cf. E. Meyer, *Caesars Monarchie*, 1919, pp. 434 ff.,
M. Gelzer, *Caesar*, 1960, pp. 279 ff., P. Pecchiura, *La figura di Catone
Uticense nella letteratura latina*, 1965, pp. 25 ff.). When Horace was
at Athens in 44 Cato's recent march was surely idealized in Stoic
and Republican circles. It is difficult to see how he could talk of an
integer vitae marching through the Syrtes without remembering this
familiar event; this point remains valid even when it is conceded that
the Syrtes belonged to the conventional topic of 'journeys in remote
areas' (see above).

   aestuosas: probably this refers to the heat rather than the boiling
tides of the Syrtes; cf. Apul. *apol.* 72 'hiemem alteram propter Syrtis
aestus et bestias opperiendum'. This coheres with the usual meaning
of the word; cf. 1. 31. 5 'aestuosae . . . Calabriae', Catull. 7. 5 'oraclum
Iovis inter aestuosi', 46. 5 'Nicaeaeque ager uber aestuosae', Cic.
Att. 5. 14. 1 'aestuosa et pulverulenta via'. Horace is thinking of the
horrors of a land journey, though admittedly the tides of the Syrtes
were reputed to swirl over the land. One may also see a contrast with
the frosty Caucasus, and a parallel with the heat of 21 f.

   It could be argued on the other side that the seething tides of the
Syrtes were notorious. Cf. 2. 6. 3 f. 'barbaras Syrtes ubi Maura semper / aestuat unda', Ap. Rhod. 4. 1235 ff., Sall. *Jug.* 78. 3, Str. 17. 3. 20,
Luc. 5. 484 f. 'non rupta vadosi / Syrtibus incerto Libye nos dividit
aestu', H. Weld-Blundell, *ABSA* 2, 1895–6, 115 ff. For the use of
aestuosus in such contexts cf. 2. 7. 16 'unda fretis tulit aestuosis',
Val. Max. 9. 8 ext. 1 'angusti atque aestuosi maris'.

   6. inhospitalem: ἄξενον. The Black Sea (Euxine) was originally called
ἄξενος (Str. 7. 3. 6), and the adjective was applied to the Crimea by
Euripides (*IT* 94), to the Phasis by Theocritus (13. 75), to the Sym-
plegades by Apollonius (fr. 5. 4 Powell). Prometheus is chained τῷδ᾽
ἀπανθρώπῳ πάγῳ (Aesch. *Prom.* 20); so Varro in his *Prometheus liber*
(*Men.* 426) talks of 'late incolens / Scytharum inhospitalis campis
vastitas'. See also *epod.* 1. 12 'inhospitalem et Caucasum', Sen. *Med.*
43, *Thy.* 1048, Serv. *Aen.* 4. 367.

   7. Caucasum: the range, like the whole Caspian area, was notorious
for its wild beasts, particularly tigers; cf. Sen. *Herc. f.* 1208 f., Sil.
4. 331 'ubi Caucaseis tigris se protulit antris', 5. 148, 15. 81, Lact.
inst. 5. 11. 4 'quis Caucasus, quae India, quae Hyrcania tam im-
manes, tam sanguinarias umquam bestias aluit?'

   Of the three places mentioned by Horace, the Syrtes are associated
with Cato, the Hydaspes with Alexander; for the sake of symmetry

the Caucasus should perhaps also be connected with some great man, though in view of the commonplace (5 n.) the point cannot be pressed. The first general to reach the Caucasus was Pompey (Plut. *Pomp.* 34); yet though he may have received eulogies from Theophanes and others, he is hardly a typical enough hero to put beside Alexander and Cato. Perhaps one should rather see a reference here also to Alexander; it may be significant that the second and third clauses are separated by *vel* rather than *sive*. Alexander had nothing to do with the real Caucasus, but the Hindu-Kush was identified with the Caucasus by his panegyrists; cf. Str. 11. 5. 5 καὶ ἦν μὲν ἐνδοξότερον τὸ τὸν Ἀλέξανδρον μεχρὶ τῶν Ἰνδικῶν ὁρῶν καταστρέψασθαι τὴν Ἀσίαν ἢ μεχρὶ τοῦ μυχοῦ τοῦ Εὐξείνου καὶ τοῦ Καυκάσου, ἀλλὰ ... χαριεῖσθαί τι τῷ βασιλεῖ ὑπέλαβον τοὔνομα τοῦ ὄρους μετενέγκαντες εἰς τὴν Ἰνδικήν.

fabulosus: 'about which stories are told' (cf. 3. 4. 9 ff. 'fabulosae ... palumbes'); these are the first appearances of the word in Latin, and it might even be a coinage of Horace's own (on the lines of μυθώδης). Ancient writers on India were famous for their τερατολογία (notably about animals). Of historians before Alexander one may mention Scylax and Ctesias, of later authors Onesicritus, Megasthenes, Cleitarchus, Curtius (8. 9), and the authors of the Alexander-Romance; the genre is parodied in Lucian's *Vera Historia*. Cf. Str. 2. 1. 9 ἅπαντες μὲν τοίνυν οἱ περὶ τῆς Ἰνδικῆς γράψαντες ὡς ἐπὶ τὸ πολὺ ψευδολόγοι γεγόνασι, Rohde, *Roman*[3], pp. 178 ff., M. Braun, *History and Romance in Graeco-Oriental Literature*, 1938, R. Wittkower, *JWI* 5, 1942, 159 ff., R. Merkelbach, *Die Quellen des griechischen Alexanderromans*, 1954, pp. 40 ff., L. Pearson, *The Lost Histories of Alexander the Great*, 1960.

8. lambit: this verb is used elsewhere of licking flames (*serm.* 1. 5. 74, Lucr. 5. 396, Virg. *Aen.* 2. 684, 3. 574), but is not found before Horace of a river. For later parallels cf. Stat. *Theb.* 4. 51 f. 'quos pigra vado Langia tacenti / lambit', Amm. Marc. 27. 4. 6, Avien. *orb. terr.* 495, 1077. The usage does not seem to be Greek.

Hydaspes: a river of the Punjab ('land of the five rivers'), now the Jhelum, once also called Bitasta (Sanskrit *Vitasta*, whence *Hydaspes*). It flows into the Chenab (Acesines), which flows into the Indus; it was not the biggest river of the system, but the richest in associations. Here in 326 B.C. Alexander the Great, in one of his greatest battles, defeated the elephants of Porus; here he founded the city of Bucephala in memory of his horse Bucephalas; finally he sailed down the river in splendour with Onesicritus at the helm (Arr. *Ind.* 18. 9). Hence *Hydaspes* is used by the poets as a romantic place-name; cf. Virg. *georg.* 4. 211 'Medus Hydaspes'.

9. **namque:** like καὶ γάρ introduces a particular instance (*exemplum*, παράδειγμα) which illustrates a preceding general maxim. Fraenkel quotes Hom. *Il.* 24. 601 f. νῦν δὲ μνησώμεθα δόρπου. / καὶ γὰρ τ᾽ ἠύκομος Νιόβη ἐμνήσατο σίτου, Alcaeus 38 ἀλλ᾽ ἄγι μὴ μεγάλων . . . / καὶ γὰρ Σίσυφος Αἰολίδαις βασίλευς . . ., anon. *PMG* 869. 1 f. ἄλει μύλα ἄλει· / καὶ γὰρ Πιττακὸς ἄλει, Prop. 4. 7. 1 ff.

me: grandiloquently emphatic (= ἐμέ, not με).

silva . . . in Sabina: Horace humorously suggests that the familiar Sabine woodland is comparable with savage places like the Caucasus. He himself owned 'silva iugerum / paucorum' (3. 16. 29 f., cf. *serm.* 2. 6. 3 'paulum silvae'); he addresses his bailiff as 'vilice silvarum' (*epist.* 1. 14. 1), and mentions his cornel- and plum-trees, oaks and holm-oaks (*epist.* 1. 16. 9 f.). But here he is clearly referring to wilder forest outside his own estate. The area must have been far more wooded than it is now; the face of Italy has been changed by the depredations of men and goats.

lupus: wolves were common in ancient Italy (J. Aymard, *Essai sur les chasses romaines*, 1951, pp. 9 ff.), and played a big part in folklore (Bömer on Ov. *fast.* 4. 766, G. Binder, *Die Aussetzung des Königskindes Kyros und Romulus*, Meisenheim, 1964, pp. 78 ff.). For Sabine wolves cf. 1. 17. 9. Fraenkel quotes two modern pieces of evidence: in October 1950 a soldier was killed by a wolf in the Abruzzi, and in February 1956 a postman was devoured by wolves near Mandela, only a few miles from Horace's estate.

10. **meam canto Lalagen:** Lalage encourages the romantic tendencies of commentators. Dacier explains 'Fuscus Aristius étoit amoureux de Lalage'. Ritter takes a less frivolous view: 'Lalagen non esse meretricem sed honestam puellam de qua in matrimonium ducenda Flaccus aliquamdiu cogitavit'. Others suggest that she is the Livia Lalage found by chance in an inscription from Rome (*CIL* 6. 3940). In fact we need look for no autobiographical information. When Horace says that he 'sang of Lalage' he means that he was composing a love-poem, but not even this is likely to have been literally accurate.

Lalage is in fact a rarely attested name; cf. 2. 5. 16, Prop. 4. 7. 45, *priap.* 4. 3, Herodian, *Gramm. Graec.*, ed. A. Lentz, 3. 310. It is connected with λαλαγεῖν 'to chatter', a by-form of λαλεῖν.

11. **terminum:** the word is more evocative than the English 'boundary'; it suggests that Horace is an intrepid pioneer venturing outside the safe precincts of his estate (cf. 1. 17. 5 ff.). The *terminus* (cf. Greek τέρμα) was a concrete object, a stone or a tree. It was of great importance in law and religion; the man who removed landmarks was accursed (cf. 2. 18. 24).

curis . . . expeditis: there is something to be said for the weakly supported *expeditus*, which was approved by Bentley. Strictly speaking *expedire* means 'to disentangle'; the object should be not the shackles but the thing that is disentangled. For the use with *cura* cf. Ter. *Phorm.* 823 'cura sese expedivit', Cic. *Att.* 16. 15. 6 'consenti in hac cura ubi sum ut me expediam', Aug. *epist.* 31. 4 'vos autem audio curis eius modi expeditiores liberioresque vivere', Pelag. *in Eph.* 6. 14, p. 383. 17 'ab omnibus curis saeculi expediti'. In favour of *expeditis* editors quote Catull. 31. 7 'o quid solutis est beatius curis?; this is not a useful parallel as *curas solvere* means to 'dissipate cares'. Better evidence is provided by Ter. *Hec.* 291 'rem cognosces, iram expedies, rursum in gratiam restitues'.

Bentley failed to make clear that *expeditus* has no serious manuscript authority. It is also worth noting that the rhyme *curis...* *expeditis* is very typical of Horace's Sapphics, yet this fact might in itself have contributed to a corruption. Bentley ingeniously attributed *expeditis* to an *eruditulus* who remembered 1. 8. 12 'saepe trans finem iaculo nobilis expedito'; such a person might not have realized that *ultra terminum* goes with *vagor*.

13. portentum: τέρας, πέλωρον, something that goes against the normal laws of nature; the word here has a mock-heroic tone.

militaris: at this date the Roman army was still primarily recruited from the stalwart rustics of Italy; cf. 2. 1. 34 f. 'Dauniae . . . caedes', 3. 5. 9 'sub rege Medo Marsus et Apulus'. The Apulians had a particular reputation for hardiness, at least in an Apulian poet; cf. 3. 16. 26 'impiger Apulus', *epod.* 2. 42 'pernicis uxor Apuli'.

14. Daunias: 'the land of Daunus' (nom. fem.); the Greek accidence strikes a mock-heroic note and reinforces the legendary associations of the name. Horace is speaking of the northern part of Apulia, which included his native Venusia; this is called Δαυνία by Strabo (6. 3. 2, 6. 3. 9), and *Apulia Dauniorum* by Pliny (*nat.* 3. 103). The Daunii were a mysterious tribe who were said to have been brought across the Adriatic by Diomedes; the legend assigned him a father-in-law called Daunus. See Str. 6. 3. 9, Aug. *civ.* 18. 16, Bömer on Ov. *fast.* 4. 76, G. Giannelli, *Culti e miti della magna Grecia*, ed. 2, 1963, pp. 53 ff.

It may well be relevant that Pythagoras is said to have tamed a monster called the 'Daunian bear' (Iambl. *vit. Pyth.* 60 τὴν μὲν γὰρ Δαυνίαν ἄρκτον . . . κατασχών, Porph. *Pyth.* 23). Of course wolves were common in Apulia (1. 33. 7 f. 'Apulis . . . lupis'), and a wolf is perhaps found on third-century B.C. coins of Venusia (Head 50). Yet Horace's other parallel for the Sabine wolf is not a wolf but a lion; and the sentence is more symmetrical if an animal other than a wolf is referred to here also. If the story of the 'Daunian bear' was familiar to Horace's readers they might first think of bears.

alit: τρέφει. A wild beast is a θρέμμα; so in Latin Stat. *silv.* 1. 3. 6 'Nemeae frondentis alumnus', Claud. 24. 280 'horribiles Libyae . . . alumnos'. See below, 16 n.

aesculetis: cf. 1. 28. 26 f. 'Venusinae . . . silvae'; for the lost forests of Italy cf. A. J. Toynbee, *Hannibal's Legacy*, 1965, 2. 593 ff. See also Norman Douglas, *Old Calabria*, pp. 106 f. (quoting an 'old writer') 'in this province there is excellent hunting of divers creatures, as wild Hoggs, Staggs, Hares, Foxes, Porcupines, Marmosets. There are also ravenous beasts, as Wolves, Bears, Luzards . . .'.

15. Iubae: the son of the Juba who was King of Numidia and committed suicide in 46 B.C. after Thapsus. Juba II fought for Octavian at Actium and was thereafter restored to his father's kingdom (Dio 51. 15. 6, doubted by S. Gsell, *Histoire ancienne de l'Afrique du Nord* 8, 1928, 207 ff.). He married Cleopatra Selene, the daughter of Antony and Cleopatra; for a coin bearing portraits of both see Head 888. In 25 B.C. he was translated to Gaetulia and Mauretania (Dio 53. 26. 2, cf. Str. 17. 3. 7); in modern terms he moved from eastern Algeria to western Algeria and Morocco. Lions, which are mentioned below, are conventionally Gaetulian (1. 23. 10, 3. 20. 2, Virg. *Aen.* 5. 351); they are found on the coins both of Juba I in Numidia and Juba II in Mauretania (Head 885, 888).

Juba did more than rule over lions; he also wrote about them. Aelian tells what is clearly one of his tales (*nat. anim.* 7. 23): a lion wounded by an ἀκόντιον (= *iaculum*) singled out its assailant a year later and killed him. Solinus tells another (27. 15 f., cf. Plin. *nat.* 8. 48): a Gaetulian woman begged some attacking lions for mercy, and was spared. It seems likely that many of the tall stories about wild animals in Pliny and Aelian are derived from the same source (M. Wellmann, *Hermes* 27, 1892, 389 ff., F. Münzer, *Beiträge zur Quellenkritik der Naturgeschichte des Plinius*, 1897, pp. 411 ff., *FGrH* 275 F 47–61). So Horace is perhaps not just using a poetical periphrasis for Morocco; he may be hinting that his wolf was a more terrible *portentum* than anything in the zoological sections of Juba's Λιβυκά. But this point cannot be put strongly as the date of the work is unknown.

Juba was, in fact, unusually research-minded for a king (Plut. *Sert.* 9. 5 τοῦ πάντων ἱστορικωτάτου βασιλέων). Besides his book on Africa (Λιβυκά) he wrote on Assyria and Arabia, on Roman history and antiquities, on grammar and agriculture, on painting in nine books and on the theatre in seventeen. He discovered the properties of the plant euphorbia, which was long used in medicine (*RE* 6. 1171);

he named it after his doctor Euphorbus (brother of Augustus's doctor Antonius Musa), and naturally composed a monograph on the subject. He was an art-collector and patron of literature; the epigrammatist Crinagoras wrote for him (*anth. P.* 7. 633, 9. 235). Horace and Fuscus must have been familiar with his works, and may even have met him in Rome, where he lived before his restoration. See further F. Jacoby, *RE* 9. 2388 f. (= *Griech. Historiker*, 1956, pp. 168 ff.).

16. **arida nutrix**: an oxymoron; a *nutrix* was primarily a wet-nurse (*assa nutrix* was used of a nursemaid). Richer women in antiquity were reluctant to feed their own babies; hence the importance of the faithful nurse (reflected, for instance, in tragedy). See Favorinus ap. Gell. 12. 1, *RE* 17. 1491 ff., W. Braams, *Jenaer medizin-historische Beiträge*, 1913, Heft 5, *RLAC* 1. 381 ff.

For *nutrix* and similar words applied to regions cf. Hom. *Il.* 8. 47 μητέρα θηρῶν (of Ida), Pind. *P.* 2. 1 f. Συράκοσαι . . . ἀνδρῶν ἵππων τε σιδαροχαρμᾶν δαιμόνιαι τροφοί, Ap. Rhod. 4. 1561 Λιβύη θηροτρόφῳ, Vitr. 8. 3. 24 'cum esset enim Africa parens et nutrix ferarum bestiarum', Juv. 7. 148 f. 'nutricula causidicorum / Africa', *orac. Sib.* 3. 469. It is a curious circumstance that the passage of Vitruvius cited above occurs in a context which explicitly mentions Juba's father and his capital of Zama. It is even possible that both Horace and Vitruvius are imitating some expression of Juba's own (cf. E. Wistrand, *Eranos* 29, 1931, 81 ff.).

17. **pone me . . .**: the imperative is equivalent to a conditional clause, though more rhetorical, and the repetition of *pone* increases the pomposity of the passage. Cf. Sen. *dial.* 7. 25. 1–2 'pone in opulentissima me domo, pone aurum argentumque ubi in promiscuo usu sit: non suspiciam me ob ista quae etiam si apud me extra me tamen sunt . . . pone in stramentis splendentibus et delicato apparatu: nihilo me feliciorem credam quod mihi molle erit amiculum'. For an imitation of Horace's lines cf. Petrarch, *Canzoniere* 145, J. B. Leishman, *Translating Horace*, 1956, pp. 94 ff.

pigris: the dead and barren steppes of the North; cf. Lucr. 5. 746 'bruma nives affert pigrumque rigorem', Hor. *carm.* 2. 9. 5 'stat glacies iners', 4. 7. 12 'bruma recurrit iners', Ov. *am.* 3. 6. 94 'pigra . . . hiems'. Yet here Horace seems to be influenced by γῆ ἀργός (= ἀεργός), the opposite of γῆ εἰργασμένη; this view is supported by the fact that other geographers' expressions are alluded to below (*latus, nimium propinqui, domibus negata*).

nulla . . . aura: it is a geographer's point to comment on treelessness; cf. Hdt. 4. 21 πᾶσαν ἐοῦσαν ψιλὴν καὶ ἀγρίων καὶ ἡμέρων δενδρέων, Plin. *nat.* 16. 2. The breeze is the giver of life, particularly from the Mediterranean standpoint; cf. Pl. *leg.* 845 d οὔτε γὰρ γῆν οὔτε ἥλιον οὔτε πνεύματα τοῖς ὕδασι ξύντροφα τῶν ἐκ γῆς ἀναβλαστανόντων ῥᾴδιον φθείρειν, Call. fr. 110. 53 θῆλυς ἀήτης, Lucr. 1. 11 'genitabilis aura favoni', Sen. *nat.* 5. 18. 13, Plin. *nat.* 16. 93, Longus 3. 12 τὰ δὲ (ἄνθη) ἄρτι ὁ Ζέφυρος τρέφων καὶ ὁ ἥλιος θερμαίνων ἐξῆγεν. The Roman poets often make pretty allusions to the subject; cf. *carm. saec.* 31 f. 'nutriant fetus et aquae salubres / et Iovis aurae', Catull. 62. 41, 64. 282 'aura parit flores tepidi fecunda Favoni', Prop. 4. 7. 60, Ov. *met.* 1. 108, *fast.* 5. 209 f., Sen. *Phaedr.* 11 f., *pervig. Ven.* 14 f. Kroll suggests that the theme is derived from Hellenistic poetry; perhaps Sappho is just as likely (cf. 2. 10 f.), with Catullus the intermediary.

19. latus: in a geographical sense, like πλευρά; cf. 3. 24. 38 'Boreae finitimum latus', Pers. 6. 76 'omne latus mundi', Juv. 8. 117.

nebulae: cf. 3. 3. 54 ff. 'visere gestiens / qua parte debacchentur ignes, / qua nebulae pluviique rores'.

malusque Iuppiter: Jupiter was the Indo-European sky-god, the gatherer of the clouds and the wielder of the lightning, who had his dwelling in the mountain tops (for abundant material see Cook's *Zeus*). When the poets discuss the weather they are much more ready than prose authors to introduce a personal Jupiter.

21. nimium propinqui: cf. Arist. *meteor.* 363ª14 ἐκεῖνος δ᾽ ὁ τόπος διὰ τὴν τοῦ ἡλίου γειτνίασιν οὐκ ἔχει ὕδατα καὶ νομάς, Prop. 2. 18. 11, Tib. 2. 3. 56, Sen. *Oed.* 122 f., *Thy.* 602, Plin. *nat.* 2. 189 'namque et Aethiopas vicini sideris vapore torreri', Ach. Tat. 4. 5. 1 'Ἰνδῶν γὰρ ἡ γῆ γείτων ἡλίου, Serv. *Aen.* 4. 481 'et dicta Aethiopia a colore populorum quos solis vicinitas torret', Macr. *somn.* 2. 10. 11 'Aethiopes . . . quos vicinia solis usque ad speciem nigri coloris exurit', Shakespeare, *Merchant of Venice* II. i. 1 ff. 'Mislike me not for my complexion, The shadow'd livery of the burnisht sun, To whom I am a neighbour and near bred'. On the other side cf. Str. 15. 1. 24 (= Onesicritus, *FGrH* 134 F 22) φησὶ γὰρ μήτε ἐγγυτέρω τοῖς Αἰθίοψιν εἶναι τὸν ἥλιον ἢ τοῖς ἄλλοις, ἀλλὰ μᾶλλον κατὰ κάθετον εἶναι καὶ διὰ τοῦτο ἐπικαίεσθαι πλέον . . . μήτε τὸ θάλπος εἶναι τοῦ τοιούτου πάθους (colouring) αἴτιον· μηδὲ γὰρ τοῖς ἐν γαστρί, ὧν οὐχ ἅπτεται ἥλιος.

22. terra domibus negata: i.e. 'uninhabitable'; cf. Cypr. *heptat. deuteron.* 37 'informes heremi terras domibusque negatas'. Horace seems to be translating ἀοίκητος, a word much used by Greek geographers; he connects the word too specifically with οἶκος (rather than with οἰκεῖν). *inhabitabilis* appears from Cicero as a more correct translation (cf. also 4. 14. 5 f. 'qua sol habitabiles / illustrat oras').

The idea of uninhabitable areas was an old one; cf. Hdt. 5. 10 (on the lands to the north of Thrace) τὰ ὑπο τὴν ἄρκτον ἀοίκητα δοκέει εἶναι διὰ τὰ ψύχεα, Anaxagoras A 67 ἃ μὲν ἀοίκητα γένηται ἃ δὲ οἰκητὰ μέρη τοῦ κόσμου κατὰ ψύξιν καὶ ἐκπύρωσιν καὶ εὐκρασίαν. The belief is particularly associated with the doctrine of the zones, which was current long before Eratosthenes (J. O. Thomson, *History of Ancient Geography*, 1948, see index). Cf. especially Arist. *meteor.* 362ᵇ5 ff. ταῦτα δ' οἰκεῖσθαι μόνα δυνατόν, καὶ οὔτ' ἐπέκεινα τῶν τροπῶν· σκιὰ γὰρ οὐκ ἂν ἦν πρὸς ἄρκτον, νῦν δ' ἀοίκητοι πρότερον γίγνονται οἱ τόποι πρὶν ἢ ὑπολείπειν ἢ μεταβάλλειν τὴν σκιὰν πρὸς μεσημβρίαν· τά θ' ὑπὸ τὴν ἄρκτον ὑπὸ ψύχους ἀοίκητα, Lucr. 5. 204 f., Cic. *nat. deor.* 1. 24 with Pease's note, Virg. *georg.* 1. 233 ff., Str. 2. 3. 1 τὰ μὲν πρὸς τῷ ἰσημερινῷ καὶ τῇ διακεκαυμένῃ ζώνῃ διὰ καῦμα ἀοίκητά ἐστι, τὰ δὲ πρὸς τῷ πόλῳ διὰ ψῦχος, Plin. *nat.* 2. 172. As exploration advanced the falsity of these statements became apparent, and seems to have been recognized by Eratosthenes (?), Polybius, and Posidonius (Str. 2. 3. 2, Cleomedes 1. 6. 31 ff., W. W. Tarn, *CQ* 33, 1939, 193). Yet they went on being made.

23. dulce ridentem: the phrase comes from Catullus's Sapphics 51. 4 f. 'spectat et audit / dulce ridentem'. *dulce loquentem* comes not from Catullus but from Catullus's source: πλάσιον ἆδυ φωνείσας ὑπακούει / καὶ γελαίσας ἱμέροεν (Sappho 31. 3 ff.). In our poem *loquentem* is an effective climax because it reminds us of Lalage's name (10 n.). For a similar declaration of fidelity cf. Aristaenetus 2. 21 ἔστω τοίνυν ἔργον ἐν μόνον ἐπιδέξιον ἐμοὶ φιλεῖν Δελφίδα καὶ ὑπὸ ταύτης φιλεῖσθαι καὶ λαλεῖν τῇ καλῇ καὶ ἀκούειν λαλούσης (cf. F. Wilhelm, *RhM* 57, 1902, 606). The use of the verb λαλεῖν suggests that Aristaenetus and Horace may have been influenced by a common source, presumably a lost Hellenistic poem.

23. VITAS INVLEO

[Fraenkel 183 f.; H. J. Rose, *HSPh* 47, 1936, 2 f.]

1–8. *You shrink from me, Chloe, like a timid fawn that starts at every sound.* 9–12. *Yet I am no savage beast, and you are old enough for love.*

This ode is modelled on a theme in Anacreon. In discussing whether does have horns, Aelian quotes a tantalizing fragment (408):

ἀγανῶς οἷά τε νεβρὸν νεοθηλέα
γαλαθηνὸν ὅς τ' ἐν ὕλῃ κεροέσσης
ἀπολειφθεὶς ἀπὸ μητρὸς ἐπτοήθη.

Elsewhere Anacreon addressed a girl as a high-spirited filly (417):

πῶλε Θρῃκίη, τί δή με
λοξὸν ὄμμασι βλέπουσα
νηλέως φεύγεις, δοκεῖς δέ
μ' οὐδὲν εἰδέναι σοφόν;

This poem was also imitated by Horace, with a signal diminution of its tact and charm, in 2. 5.

In 1954 there was published a relevant new fragment of Anacreon (*Ox. pap.* 2321, Anacreon 346, Bowra 286 ff.):

φοβερὰς δ' ἔχεις πρὸς ἄλλῳ
φρένας, ὦ καλλιπρό[σ]ωπε παίδ[ων·
καί σε δοκεῖ μὲν ἐ[ν δό]μοισι[ν
πυκινῶς ἔχουσα [μήτηρ
ἀτιτάλλειν· σ[– – –
τὰς ὑακιν[θίνας ἀρ]ούρας
ἴ]να Κύπρις ἐκ λεπάδνων
– – – α[ς κ]ατέδησεν ἵππους.

Here too, as in Horace, we have a shy adolescent, a nervous mother, and an association with fine young animals.

Horace's ode is not drawn directly from life; one need pay no attention to the heading in the manuscripts, 'Ad Chloen meretricem fugientem se', 'Ad Chloen quam ad matrimonium hortatur'. Yet some of the poem's images suggest a fresh eye: the lizards parting the undergrowth, the fawn trotting at her mother's heels. And Horace has transferred to Latin poetry not just a conventional lyric theme, but something of the spirit of old Ionia. The poem is tender, humorous, and discreetly sensuous; these are the qualities of Anacreon.

Metre: Third Asclepiad.

1. **vitas**: the paradosis is *vitat*, which is also cited by Diom. *gramm.* I. 522 and interpreted by Porphyrio and ps.-Acro. It is not quite impossible that Horace should begin a line with a trochee (cf. I. 15. 36 n.). Nor can we say that he would not under any circumstances first speak of Chloe in the third person, and only address her in the third stanza (although 8 *tremit* of the fawn makes this much more difficult). But the conjunction of the two oddities discredits the manuscript reading; the corruption is presumably due to assimilation to *tremit*.

inuleo: 'a fawn' (Hesychius, ἰνούλεους· νεβρός). See also *h.Cer.* 174 ff. αἱ δ' ὥς τ' ἢ ἔλαφοι ἢ πόρτιες ἤαρος ὥρῃ / ἄλλοντ' ἂν λειμῶνα

κορεσσάμεναι φρένα φορβῆ, / ὡς αἱ . . . ἤιξαν κοίλην κατ᾽ ἀμαξιτόν,
Sappho 58. 16 ἴσα νεβρίοισιν, Bacch. 13. 84 ff. καί τις ὑψαυχὴς κό⟨ρα⟩ /
. . . πόδεσσι ταρφέως / ἠΰτε νεβρὸς ἀπεν[θὴς] / ἀνθεμόεντας ἐπ[᾽ ὄχθους] /
κοῦφα σὺν ἀγχιδόμ[οις] / θρῴσκουσ᾽ ἀγακλειτα[ῖς ἑταίρα]ις, Dionys.
perieg. 843 f. σὺν καὶ παρθενικαὶ νεοθηλέες οἷά τε νεβροὶ / σκαίρουσιν,
Agathias, anth. P. 5. 292. 12, Vulg. prov. 5. 18 f. 'et laetare cum
muliere adulescentiae tuae; cerva carissima et gratissimus inulus,
ubera eius inebrient te in omni tempore', cant. 2. 9 'similis est dilectus
meus capreae hinuloque cervorum', 2. 17, 8. 14.

inuleus is derived from ἔνελος, which one would expect to become
*ĕnulus or, with a different suffix, *ĕnuleus. The long i- is attested
only here; Scaliger introduced it by conjecture, probably wrongly,
in Prop. 3. 13. 35, where the manuscripts suggest atque hinuli. It is
taken to be a metrical licence (Heraeus in Walde–Hofmann 1. 647);
but the quantity, as well as the initial aspirate often found with this
word, may arise from confusion with hinnuleus, 'hinny' (Greek
ἴννος), the offspring of a stallion and an ass. H. J. Rose, loc. cit.,
suggested that Horace meant 'hinny' here, and was thinking primarily of the πῶλος Θρηκίη of Anacreon 417. But the mountain scene
and the parallel of Anacreon 408 make 'fawn' much more likely.

Chloe: the name suggests greenness and immaturity (χλόη).
Horace uses it again in 3. 7. 10, 3. 9. 6, 3. 26. 12; it belongs to a
fictional shepherdess in Longus (cf. 1. 6 ποιμενικὸν ὄνομα), and was
borrowed from him in the twelfth-century verse novel of Nicetas
Eugenianus (6. 439). For a less frivolous Chloe cf. 1 Cor. 1. 11.

2. pavidam: not merely a standing epithet; the mother is alarmed
about her young.

aviis: ἀβάτοις.

3. non sine: the litotes is urbane as well as metrically convenient; cf.
Wackernagel, Vorlesungen 2. 297 ff.

vano: the fawn is so childish that it is startled without cause; cf.
Cic. Cael. 36 'qui propter nescioquam, credo, timiditatem et nocturnos
quosdam inanis metus tecum semper pusio cum maiore sorore cubi-
tabat', Virg. georg. 3. 79 (of a thoroughbred foal) 'nec vanos horret
strepitus', Sen. Oed. 700 f. 'qui pavet vanos metus, / veros meretur'.
For the hiatus at the end of the line cf. p. xl.

4. aurarum . . .: cf. Ap. Rhod. 3. 954 f. ἢ θάμα δὴ †στήθεων ἐάγη†
κέαρ, ὁππότε δοῦπον / ἢ ποδὸς ἢ ἀνέμοιο παραθρέξαντα δοάσσαι, Virg.
Aen. 2. 726 ff. 'et me . . . nunc omnes terrent aurae, sonus excitat omnis',
Sil. 6. 58 f. 'sonus omnis et aura / exterrent pennaque levi commota
volucris', Claud. 20. 452 f., Sidon. epist. 4. 15. 3 'extremus autumnus
. . . viatorum sollicitas aures foliis toto nemore labentibus crepulo

fragore circumstrepit', Tasso, *Ger. Lib.* 7. 24 'E se pur la notturna aura percote Tenera fronde mai d' olmo o di faggio, O se fèra od augello un ramo scote, Tosto a quel picciol suon drizza il viaggio', Spenser, *F.Q.* 3. 7. 1 'Like as a Hind forth singled from the heard, That hath escaped from a ravenous beast, Yet flyes away of her owne feet affeard, And every leafe, that shaketh with the least Murmure of winde, her terrour hath encreast'. For further parallels see Nisbet on Cic. *Pis.* 99.

siluae: for the diaeresis cf. *epod.* 13. 2 'nunc mare nunc siluae', M. Platnauer, *Latin Elegiac Verse*, 1951, pp. 70 f. The form is an artificial poeticism, not a genuine variant (Sommer 131); it has been taken to point to an early date for this ode (cf. p. xxix).

5. mobilibus . . . foliis: cf. Ov. *am.* 3. 5. 35, Plin. *nat.* 17. 91, Auson. 417. 93 f.

veris inhorruit adventus foliis: if the reading of the manuscripts is correct it presumably means 'spring's arrival has come with a shiver on the fluttering leaves'. For another case of *inhorruit* with the cause of the shivering as subject cf. Petron. 123. 233 f. 'et velut ex alto cum magnus inhorruit auster / et pulsas evertit aquas'. The ablative *foliis* is probably local ('on the leaves'); for other ablatives with *inhorruit*, all rather different, cf. Virg. *georg.* 1. 314 'spicea iam campis cum messis inhorruit' (also local, but with another kind of subject), Ov. *Ib.* 201 'tristis hiems Aquilonis inhorruit alis' ('because of the wings of the wind'), Virg. *Aen.* 3. 195 'inhorruit unda tenebris' (instrumental).

veris adventus is in itself a natural expression; cf. Colum. 10. 80 'veris et adventum nidis cantabit hirundo'. So in Greek Alcaeus 367. 1 ἦρος ἀνθεμόεντος †ἐπάιον ἐρχομένοιο, Stesich. 212. 3 ἦρος ἐπερχομένου, Ar. *nub.* 311 ἦρί τ᾽ ἐπερχομένῳ. In the spring, when the leaves are out, a wood is a noisier place than in the winter. Cf. Swinburne, *Atalanta*, 'When the hounds of spring are on winter's traces, The mother of months in meadow or plain Fills the shadows and windy places With lisp of leaves and ripple of rain'.

The most important difficulty in the manuscript reading is that the first *seu* clause does not seem on all fours with the second one. If the text is sound Horace is not referring to the noise of the leaves sprouting (which would be absurd), but to their rustling in the wind; he must be using a variation for 'veris adventu (i.e. post veris adventum) folia inhorruerunt'. The trouble about this is that while the darting of the lizards is the immediate cause of the fawn's alarm, the coming of spring is a remoter cause. Yet while this difficulty is a real one, it should not be exaggerated. It may be relevant that Horace talks of lizards in the plural, and not (as a modern poet might) of a single lizard; this also, though in a different way, may have the effect of generalizing the situation, and not confining it to a particular momentary occurrence.

Other ways round the difficulty seem less satisfactory. Some scholars suggest that *veris adventus* equals *Favoni adventus* (so Lambinus, Bell 190); but though the spring and the zephyr come together, 'the coming of spring' can hardly without more ado mean 'the coming of the zephyr'. Fraenkel looks for an immediate cause of a different kind and thinks that *adventus* may suggest the sudden epiphany of a god which makes the leaves quiver (Call. *h.* 2. 1 ff., Ov. *fast.* 3. 329); yet in that case the lizards in the second clause would come as an anticlimax.

Some eminent scholars have felt the difficulty so great that they have resorted to conjecture. *vitis . . . ad ventum* was proposed by Muretus, but a vine does not suit the mountain scene. *vepris* ('a thorn-bush') was conjectured for *veris* independently by Gogau, Salmasius, and Bentley; together with *ad ventum* this gives a reading that deserves serious consideration. For the combination of *vepris* with *rubus* cf. Plin. *nat.* 12. 89 'densissimis in vepribus rubisque', Colum. 7. 6. 1 'nec rubos aversatur nec vepribus offenditur', Sen. *Phaedr.* 1103 'acutis asperi vepres rubis'. Yet *vepres* is normally listed among the *semper pluralia*, though admittedly *veper* was used by an Aemilius (anon. *gramm.* 5. 592. 20). Moreover, the diminutive *veprecula* suggests that the nominative singular should rather be *vepres*, and *vepris* is condemned by Prob. *gramm.* 4.198.16; cf.,however, Prop. 4. 10. 44 for *torquis* (also condemned by some grammarians). In addition to these oddities of accidence (never desirable in a conjecture), a more general point may be made. We find references to the rustling of pines (Pl. *anth. Pl.* 13. 1 f., Theoc. 1. 1 f., anon. *anth. Pl.* 12. 1 f.), cornfields (Virg. *georg.* 3. 198 ff.), reeds (Ov. *met.* 1. 707 f.), and the golden bough (Virg. *Aen.* 6. 209). But though a thorn-bush does rustle in certain circumstances, it is not typically associated with rustling in the conventionally minded ancient poets (though it must be admitted that other rustling plants equally lack parallels).

Schrevel and Desprez made a proposal that deserves mention: nam seu mobilibus veris inhorruit / ad ventum foliis seu virides rubum / dimovere lacertae' (so Arthur Palmer). The nominative to *inhorruit* is here *rubus*, supplied from the second clause; the construction is a little clumsy, but is theoretically not impossible. Yet *veris* seems unhappily placed, as its position leaves it obscure whether it is to be taken with *ventum* or *foliis*. Alternatively, on the same lines Desprez tried 'nam seu mobilibus veris inhorruit / adventu foliis' (again supplying *rubus* from the second clause). Yet the double ablative causes doubt; and the thorn-bush still rustles, even if less obtrusively than with Gogau's conjecture.

7. lacertae: cf. Virg. *ecl.* 2. 9 'nunc viridis etiam occultant spineta lacertos', *copa* 28 'nunc varia (?) in gelida sede lacerta latet'.

8. corde: cf. Hom. *Il.* 13. 282 ἐν δέ τέ οἱ κραδίη μεγάλα στέρνοισι πατάσσει, Tib. 1. 10. 12 'corde micante'. For *genibus* cf. Hom. *Il.* 3. 34 ὑπό τε τρόμος ἔλλαβε γυῖα.

9. atqui . . .: the style is deprecatory; so *non ego te* (cf. 1. 18. 11). The theme may belong to everyday colloquial speech ('I'll not eat you'). But Horace humorously dresses it up in pompous language; hence the conventional epithets of the tiger and lion, the pretentious infinitive with *persequor*, the artificial hyperbaton of the last lines.

non ego . . .: cf. Theoc. 11. 24 φεύγεις δ' ὥσπερ ὄις πολιὸν λύκον ἀθρήσασα, Ov. *met.* 1. 504 ff. (Apollo to Daphne) 'non insequor hostis; / nympha, mane! sic agna lupum, sic cerva leonem, / sic aquilam penna fugiunt trepidante columbae'. So Ausonius in professorial vein to a pupil who keeps out of his way (404. 15 ff.): 'non ut tigris te, non leonis impetu, / amore sed caro expeto. / . . . cur me supino pectoris fastu tumens / spernis poetam consulem?'

aspera: cf. Stat. *Theb.* 4. 315 f. 'raptis velut aspera natis . . . tigris', Hor. *carm.* 3. 2. 10 f. 'asperum / tactu leonem'. For the tiger as a type of savagery cf. Pease on Virg. *Aen.* 4. 366.

10. Gaetulus: from Juba's kingdom; cf. 1. 22. 15 n.

frangere: the word suggests the crunch of bones; cf. Hom. *Il.* 11. 113 f. ὡς δὲ λέων ἐλάφοιο ταχείης νήπια τέκνα / ῥηιδίως συνέαξε λαβὼν κρατεροῖσιν ὀδοῦσιν, Val. Fl. 2. 459 f. '(taurus) frangentem morsu super alta leonem / terga ferens', Stat. *Theb.* 11. 28 'armenti reges magno leo fregit hiatu', Claud. 22. 21 (of lions) 'alacres ardent qui frangere tauros'.

11. matrem: cf. Hes. *op.* 520 f. ἥ τε δόμων ἔντοσθε φίλη παρὰ μητέρι μίμνει / οὔπω ἔργα ἰδυῖα πολυχρύσου Ἀφροδίτης, Anacreon 346. 4, 408. 3 (above, p. 273), Catull. 62. 21 f. 'qui natam possis complexu avellere matris, / complexu matris retinentem avellere natam'.

12. tempestiva . . . viro: ὡρία or ὡραία; cf. 3. 19. 27, Hdt. 1. 107. 2 Μανδάνην . . . ἐοῦσαν ἀνδρὸς ὡραίην, Virg. *Aen.* 7. 53 'iam matura viro, iam plenis nubilis annis', Honestus, *anth. P.* 5. 20. 4. In 3. 11. 11 f. Lyde is likened to a filly 'nuptiarum expers et adhuc protervo / cruda marito'. The emphatic *viro* balances *me* (1) as *matrem* (11) balances *matrem* (3).

sequi: cf. Semonides 5 ἄθηλος ἵππῳ πῶλος ὡς ἅμα τρέχει.

24. QVIS DESIDERIO

[R. Kassel, *Untersuchungen zur griechischen und römischen Konsolationslitera-tur*, 1958; Pasquali 237 ff.; R. Reitzenstein, *Aufsätze*, pp. 2 f.; M. Siebourg, *Neue Jahrb.* 25, 1910, 271 ff.]

1–4. *Who can restrain grief at such a loss? Dictate me a lament, Melpomene.* 5–8. *Quintilius is dead, he whose virtues will never be matched.* 9–12. *None mourns him more than you, Virgil, but the gods reject your prayers.* 13–20. *If you were Orpheus himself, you could not recall the dead to life. Only fortitude can give relief in inevitable ills.*

The friend whose death Horace laments here is called simply Quintilius by Horace, Philodemus, Jerome, and Probus (*vit. Verg.* 1); Porphyrio (on *ars* 438), Serv. *ecl.* 5. 20, and some of the Virgil lives give him the *cognomen* Varus. Porphyrio and Jerome state that he came from Cremona; this would explain his friendship for Virgil, who was educated there. We may suspect some confusion with Alfenus Varus, the jurist (p. 227), who is also said to have come from Cremona (Porph. on *serm.* 1. 3. 130). Perhaps the birth-place of Quintilius has been misrepresented (through confusion with Alfenus), or else the *cognomen* (through confusion with Alfenus and with the general who lost Germany).

Porphyrio says that he was a Roman *eques* (*ars* 438). Some of the Acro scholia on the same passage say that he was a poet, but this is probably due to confusion with Varius (p. 81). He seems to be mentioned together with Varius in the περὶ κολακείας and περὶ φιλαργυρίας of Philodemus (cf. A. Körte, *RhM* 45, 1890, 172 ff.). Servius remarks (*ecl.* 6. 13) 'sectam Epicuream quam didicerant tam Vergilius quam Varus docente Sirone'; the passage of Virgil un-doubtedly refers to Alfenus Varus, but the note may be information about Quintilius, or indeed about Varius. For a supposed connection of Quintilius with Tivoli see p. 227. Jerome says that Quintilius died in 23/2 B.C., but this may be no more than an inference from the dating of the *Odes*. It is more significant that Horace praised his dead friend many years later as that rarest of paragons, a sensitive and honest critic (*ars* 438 ff.):

> Quintilio siquid recitares, 'corrige sodes
> hoc' aiebat 'et hoc'. melius te posse negares
> bis terque expertum frustra, delere iubebat
> et male tornatos incudi reddere versus.
> si defendere delictum quam vertere malles,
> nullum ultra verbum aut operam insumebat inanem,
> quin sine rivali teque et tua solus amares.

Y

Life in the ancient world was even more precarious than today,
and the literature of grief took many shapes. The sepulchral epitaph
in prose or verse, unmetrical or highly wrought, proclaimed in conventional truisms the virtues of the deceased and the desolation of
the bereaved. Pindar and Simonides wrote more elaborate θρῆνοι,
which they embellished with sombre maxims on the mortality of
human kind. The ἐπιτάφιος λόγος of the Athenian democracy was
a collective celebration of the nation's war dead, but the indivi-
dualistic Romans honoured the more private virtues (as in the
Laudatio Turiae, ILS 8393). From the fourth century on the ἐπική-
δειον became a minor literary form : Erinna wrote a famous lament
for her friend Baucis, Aratus commemorated his brother and a
friend, and Euphorion the astronomer Protagoras. The poem of
Parthenius on his dead wife Arete was imitated by Calvus in his
elegy on Quintilia (see R. Pfeiffer, Ausgewählte Schriften, 1960,
pp. 145 ff.). Other Latin poets attempted the genre : Catullus wrote on
his brother (101), Virgil on Marcellus (Aen. 6. 860 ff.), Propertius
on Paetus (3. 7), Marcellus (3. 18), and Cornelia (4. 11), Ovid on
Tibullus (am. 3. 9), an anonymous author on Maecenas, Statius with
impartial fluency on his father, his son, and a friend's parrot (silv.
5. 3, 5. 5, 2. 4).
    Meanwhile the philosophers had elaborated and organized the
clichés of consolation. The περὶ πένθους of the Academic Crantor was
particularly famous and much plundered by his successors ; in Latin
the Consolatio of Cicero must also have been influential. Formal
specimens of the genre survive in Cicero's letters (epist. 5. 16), in
Seneca's treatises to Marcia and to Polybius, as well as in two of his
epistles (63 and 99), in pseudo-Plutarch's λόγος παραμυθητικὸς πρὸς
Ἀπολλώνιον, a dreary congeries of all possible topics, and in the
much more affecting consolation addressed to his wife by the real
Plutarch. Verse specimens are provided by Ovid in a tactful letter
(Pont. 4. 11), in the anonymous consolatio ad Liviam, which develops
the standard themes at tiresome and tasteless length, and by Statius,
who was always ready to oblige a friend on the loss of a father or
slave-boy (silv. 3. 3, 2. 1, 2. 6). Nor were the rhetoricians idle :
Menander (3. 413 f., 419 ff. Sp.) supplied a convenient catalogue of
suitable arguments. But the noblest of all ancient consolations is a
real prose letter, sent to Cicero on the death of his daughter by the
great lawyer Servius Sulpicius Rufus (Cic. epist. 4. 5). For a detailed
bibliography see further R. Kassel, op. cit.
    Horace's poem may be regarded as an epicedion; but as such it
naturally includes some of the themes of consolatio. It is true that
the first stanzas do not mention Virgil; yet it was a rule of consolatio
that the comforter should begin by showing he shared the grief

(Theon 2. 117. 16 ff. Sp. οἱ γὰρ ἀνιώμενοι . . . πεφύκασιν . . . παρὰ . . .
τῶν συνολοφυρομένων εὐμενέστερόν πως προσιέναι, ὡς παρ' οἰκείων, τὰς
παρηγορίας, διόπερ μετὰ τοὺς θρήνους ἐποιστέον τῶν λόγων τοὺς νουθετι-
κούς, ps.-Dion. Hal. *rhet.* 6. 4 p. 281. 8 ff., Siebourg, loc. cit., Kassel,
op. cit., p. 51, p. 98 n. 1). The rest of the ode develops three standard
consolatory arguments, that mourning is pointless, death irrevocable,
and fortitude the best relief. The poet includes a σχετλιασμός against
the gods, as enjoined by Menander rhetor in his treatment of μονῳδία
(3. 435. 9 ff. Sp.). The refined ἀδύνατον of the fourth stanza gives
rhetorical point to a standard *exemplum*, and is particularly suitable
to a poet who had written about Orpheus (13 n.); but the ghastly
picture of Mercury herding the dead belongs to mystical hymn
rather than consolation. On the other hand the firm adjuration at
the end of the poem admirably reproduces the humanity and
rationalism of the best Hellenistic moral philosophy.

The ode is perhaps too austere and formal for most modern taste.
Landor puts in the mouth of Boccaccio the same sort of criticism
that Johnson applied to *Lycidas*: 'Did he want anyone to help him
to cry? What man immersed in grief cares a quattrino about Melpomene, or her father's fairing of an artificial cuckoo and a gilt
guitar? What man, on such an occasion is at leisure to amuse himself
with the little plaster images of Pudor and Fides, of Justitia and
Veritas, or disposed to make a comparison of Virgil and Orpheus?'
(*Pentameron* 4). But an ancient would have no feeling that rhetoric
or abstraction or mythology were not to the point. Nor does Landor
do justice to the tact of the poem, far removed from the philosophic
rigours of the 'solacium . . . quasi castigatorium et nimis forte'
deplored by Pliny (*epist.* 5. 16. 10). Shelley by his imitation in
Adonais showed a juster appreciation of the ode, though it failed
to teach him brevity or restraint:

> I weep for Adonais—he is dead!
> O, weep for Adonais! though our tears
> Thaw not the frost which binds so dear a head!
> And thou, sad Hour, selected from all years
> To mourn our loss, rouse thy obscure compeers,
> And teach them thine own sorrow, say: 'With me
> Died Adonais; till the Future dares
> Forget the Past, his fate and fame shall be
> An echo and a light unto eternity!'

Metre: Second Asclepiad.

1. quis desiderio . . .: Horace is defending the right to weep without
restraint; cf. Euphorion 21 Powell (from the *epicedion* on Protagoras)

τῷ καὶ μέτρια μέν τις ἐπὶ φθιμένῳ ἀκάχοιτο, | μέτρια καὶ κλαύσειεν· ἐπεὶ
καὶ πάμπαν ἄδακρυν | Μοῖραι ἐσικχήναντο, cons. Liv. 7 f. 'et quisquam
leges audet tibi dicere flendi | et quisquam lacrimas temperat ore
tuas?', Ov. rem. 127 f., Stat. silv. 2. 6. 1 f. 'saeve nimis, lacrimis
quisquis discrimina ponis / lugendique modos', 5. 5. 59 ff., 2. 1. 14 ff.
with Vollmer's note. Philosophers took a tougher line; even those
who, like Crantor, rejected the brutalities of Stoic ἀπάθεια, nevertheless urged the necessity of modus. Cf. Pl. rep. 387 e, Sen. dial. 12. 1. 4
'spero ut desiderio tuo velis a me modum statui', 6. 7. 1, ps.-Plut.
Apoll. 102 d τὸ δὲ πέρα τοῦ μέτρου παρεκφέρεσθαι καὶ συναύξειν τὰ
πένθη παρὰ φύσιν εἶναί φημι καὶ ὑπὸ τῆς ἐν ἡμῖν φαύλης γίγνεσθαι δόξης,
carm. epig. 1212. 15 'sum defleta satis, finem decet esse dolori', Hier.
epist. 39. 5. 2 'ignoscimus matris lacrimis, sed modum quaerimus in
dolore'. Similarly, Horace's poem proceeds at the end to a firmer
attitude.

   pudor aut modus: for this conjunction cf. Sen. Thy. 26 f., Mart.
8. 64. 15. pudor is not so much shame (αἰσχύνη) as αἰδώς, the fear of
going too far; cf. Luc. 9. 706 f. 'sed (quis erit nobis lucri pudor?)
inde petuntur / huc Libycae mortes et fecimus aspida mercem'.

   2. tam cari capitis: the phrase is strongly emotional; cf. Catull.
68. 119 f. 'nam nec tam carum confecto aetate parenti / una caput
seri nata nepotis alit', Virg. Aen. 4. 354 'capitisque iniuria cari',
Prop. 2. 1. 36, 3. 4. 20, 4. 11. 55, Val. Fl. 2. 404 (Hypsipyle to Jason)
'carius o mihi patre caput', 4. 24 (of Hylas), 8. 346 f. 'illud carum
caput ire cruenta / sub freta', Thes.l.L. 3. 404. 4 ff. For similar
phrases in Greek cf. Hom. Il. 8. 281 φίλη κεφαλή, Od. 1. 343 τοίην γὰρ
κεφαλὴν ποθέω, Soph. Ant. 1 ὦ κοινὸν αὐτάδελφον Ἰσμήνης κάρα; see
further Th. Wendel, Die Gesprächsanrede, Tübinger Beiträge zur
Altertumswissenschaft, Heft 6, 1929, p. 33, R. B. Onians, The Origins
of European Thought, ed. 2, 1954, pp. 97 ff.

   praecipe: in early Greece the Muse taught the poet what to sing; cf.
Hom. Od. 8. 481 (ἀοιδοὺς) οἵμας Μοῦσ' ἐδίδαξε, 488 ἢ σέ γε Μοῦσ' ἐδίδαξε,
Διὸς πάις, ἢ σέ γ' Ἀπόλλων, Solon 1. 51 Ὀλυμπιάδων Μουσέων πάρα
δῶρα διδαχθείς, Dodds 100 n. 116. praecipe in particular suggests
the ancient method of teaching: first the master spoke a sentence
(dictare) and then it was reproduced by the class (recitare).

   3. Melpomene: like other poets Horace sometimes speaks vaguely
of 'the Muse' (cf. 3. 3. 70) and sometimes of a particular Muse, such
as Clio (1. 12. 2), Polyhymnia and Euterpe (1. 1. 33), Calliope (3. 4. 2),
Thalia (4. 6. 25); Melpomene is mentioned again in 3. 30. 16 and 4. 3. 1.
For this indifference, which reflects the early Greek practice, cf.
schol. Ap. Rhod. 3. 1c 'Ριανὸς δὲ ἐν α' Ἡλιακῶν φησι μηδὲν διαφέρειν
εἰ μίαν ἐπικαλεῖται τῶν Μουσῶν τις· πάσας γὰρ σημαίνει διὰ μιᾶς· λέγει

δὲ οὕτως· Πᾶσαι δ᾽ εἰσαίουσι, μιῆς ὅτε τοὔνομα λέξεις. See further Wilamowitz, *Die Ilias und Homer*, 1916, p. 474 n. 1.

Poets could of course already play with the idea that different Muses had different provinces; cf. Prop. 3. 3. 33 'diversaeque novem sortitae iura puellae' and the Herculaneum paintings in Roscher 2. 3273 ff. (see also *RE* 16. 727 ff., G. M. A. Grube, *The Greek and Roman Critics*, 1965, p. 5 n. 3, citing Pl. *Phaedr.* 259 b–d). But the assignment of provinces was still vague; certainly in our passage we can draw no inference from the fact that Melpomene later became the Muse of tragedy. If Horace thought about the question at all, he may well have taken Melpomene to be the Muse of μολπή and therefore relevant to lyric; cf. schol. Ap. Rhod. 3. 1b λέγεται . . . εὑρηκέναι . . . Μελπομένην ᾠδήν, Honestus (Gow–Page, *Philip* 1. 274. 2448 f.) σύνφθογγόν με λύρης χορδῇ κεράσασαν ἀοιδὴν / λεύσσεις ἐν δισσοῖς Μελπομένην μέλεσιν, anon. *anth. P.* 9. 504. 4 Μελπομένη θνητοῖσι μελίφρονα βάρβιτον εὗρε. See further Fraenkel 306 n. 2.

cui . . .: the goddess is told, as often, that she has the power to fulfil the prayer; cf. 1. 28. 28 n.

liquidam: properly 'clear' (cf. *liquere*). But Roman poets seem to have used the word as an equivalent of λιγύς or λιγυρός because of the resemblance in sound; cf. Host. *carm.* fr. 3 'vocesque liquatae', Varro, *Men.* 131 'Phrygius per ossa cornus liquida canit anima', Lucr. 2. 146, 4. 981, 5. 1379, Virg. *georg.* 1. 410, Ov. *am.* 1. 13. 8, Prud. *c. Symm.* 1. 637. The sense of λιγύς is better rendered by *acutus* (3. 4. 3) or *argutus* (Prop. 1. 18. 30). Here the use of the word reminds one of the Linus song (*carm. pop.* PMG 880 ὦ Λίνε πᾶσι θεοῖσι / τετιμένε, σοὶ γὰρ ἔδωκαν / πρώτῳ μέλος ἀνθρώποισι / φωναῖς λιγυραῖς ἀεῖσαι).

pater: Zeus and Mnemosyne were the parents of the Muses.

5. ergo: 'and so'. The word expresses rueful realization that something has turned out the way it has; there is also a suggestion that nothing can now be done about it. Cf. *serm.* 2. 5. 101 f. 'ergo nunc Dama sodalis / nusquam est. unde mihi tam fortem tamque fidelem?', Prop. 3. 23. 1 f. 'ergo tam doctae nobis periere tabellae, / scripta quibus pariter tot periere bona', Virg. *Aen.* 6. 456 f. So in Greek we find ἄρα 'expressing the surprise attendant on disillusionment' (Denniston 35). Cf. also Malherbe, *Consolation à M. du Périer* 1 'Ta douleur, du Périer, sera donc éternelle?'

Roman poets sometimes begin poems with this exclamatory *ergo*. Cf. Prop. 3. 7, Ov. *am.* 2. 7, *trist.* 3. 2; so Nicias, *anth. P.* 6. 127 with ἄρα. Campbell therefore suggested transposing the first two stanzas. But in that case the first stanza would strangely disrupt the eulogies of lines 8 and 9.

perpetuus sopor: cf. 3. 11. 38 'longus . . . somnus'. Sleep was a euphemism for death from early times; Homer and Hesiod already make them brothers, and the motif is common both in high poetry and in inscriptions. See B. Lier, *Philologus* 62, 1903, 595 n. 46, M. B. Ogle, *The Sleep of Death*, *MAAR* 11, 1933, 81 ff., Pease on Cic. *div.* 1. 63, Lattimore 78, 164. The comparison is often found in consolations; cf. ps.-Plut. *Apoll.* 107 d ἀλλὰ μήν γ' ὅτι ἥδιστός ἐστιν ὁ βαθύτατος (ὕπνος), τί δεῖ καὶ λέγειν, Kassel, op. cit., pp. 77 f. But here the consoling optimism of *sopor* is qualified by *perpetuus*; cf. Hom. *Il.* 11. 241 κοιμήσατο χάλκεον ὕπνον, h.*Merc.* 289 μὴ πύματόν τε καὶ ὕστατον ὕπνον ἰαύσῃς, *epitaph.* Bion. 104 εὕδομες εὖ μάλα μακρὸν ἀτέρμονα νήγρετον ὕπνον, *OGIS* 383. 43 f. (the Antiochus inscription) εἰς τὸν ἄπειρον αἰῶνα κοιμήσεται, Diotimus, *anth. P.* 7. 173. 3 f., Philodemus, ibid. 9. 570. 5, Catull. 5. 6, Virg. *Aen.* 10. 745 f., 'olli dura quies oculos et ferreus urget / somnus', Cumont 349 ff., 367 ff.

6. urget: cf. 4. 9. 27, Virg. *Aen.* 10. 745 f. (cited above), Petron. *anth. Lat.* 651. 3 f. 'prostrata sopore / urget membra quies', Prud. *cath.* 10. 59 f. 'fore protinus omnia viva, / quae nunc gelidus sopor urget', Auson. 151. 10.

cui . . .: the recital of the virtues of the dead is natural alike in lament, funeral speech, and consolation; cf. Kassel, op. cit., p. 52 n. 2. In our passage the virtues appear as a train of deities; cf. *carm. saec.* 57 ff., 1. 18. 14 n. Here Horace owes more to Greek poetry than to Roman religion; even the old Roman goddess Fides seems no better than the company she keeps. Horace's conception may or may not have had antecedents in Hellenistic epigram; certainly it had an influence on English poetry. Cf. Collins, *How Sleep the Brave*, 'There Honour comes, a pilgrim gray, To bless the turf that wraps their clay; And Freedom shall a while repair To dwell a weeping hermit there'.

Pudor: Αἰδώς; for the personification cf. Hes. *op.* 200, Soph. *OC* 1268, Eur. *Hipp.* 78, fr. 436, ps.-Dem. 25. 35 καὶ Δίκης γε καὶ Εὐνομίας καὶ Αἰδοῦς εἰσι πᾶσιν ἀνθρώποις βωμοί. Αἰδώς was worshipped at Sparta and Athens (see Farnell 5. 474). *Pudor* has no Latin cult, and seems to be first personified by the Augustan poets; cf. Ov. *am.* 1. 2. 31 f. 'Mens Bona ducetur manibus post terga retortis / et Pudor et castris quicquid Amoris obest', *fast.* 5. 29 (Pudor and Metus attend on Maiestas), Mart. 10. 78. 3.

Iustitiae soror: cf. Petron. 124. 252 f. 'huic comes it submissa Fides et crine soluto / Iustitia', Sil. 2. 486 '(Fides) Iustitiae consors', Cic. *off.* 1. 23 'fundamentum autem est iustitiae fides'. *Iustitia* is again the Greek Δίκη, rather than a Roman goddess (see Farnell 5. 475, *RE* 10. 1339, Roscher 3. 2131 f.). Yet a statue was dedicated to Iustitia

Augusta on 8 Jan. A.D. 13 (*Fasti Praenestini, inscr. Ital.* 13. 2 p. 113 'signum Iustitiae Augus[tae . . . Ti. Caesar dedicavit Planco] et Silio cos.') ; for other traces in Roman cult cf. *carm. epig.* 867 'Iustitiae Nemesi Fatis quam voverat aram / numina sancta colens Cammarius posuit' (translating a Greek dedication δεσποίνῃ Νεμέσει καὶ συννάοισι θεοῖσιν), *ILS* 2924 'I]ovis et Iustitiae', 3790a and 5525a (statues of Iustitia Augusta).

Waddel conjectured *Iustitia et soror*; he argued that *Iustitia* as the prime virtue ought to have her own place on the list and not simply appear in the genitive case. But if a fourth nominative is introduced the sentence seems to straggle a little (more so than in *carm. saec.* 57 ff.). Perhaps *Iustitiae soror* includes the notion of *Iustitia*, just as at 3. 29. 64 *geminusque Pollux* includes the notion of Castor.

From Homer on (5 n.) we find related things or qualities placed on a family tree (cf. West on Hes. *th.*, pp. 33 ff.) ; thus panic is the son of Ares (*Il.* 13. 299), dust the brother of mud (Aesch. *Ag.* 494 f.), utility the mother of justice (Hor. *serm.* 1. 3. 98). See especially Pind. *O.* 13. 6 f. Εὐνομία . . . κασιγνήτα τε, βάθρον πολίων ἀσφαλές, / Δίκα καὶ ὁμότροφος Εἰρήνα, Claud. 22. 30 '(Clementiae) germana Fides'. Such metaphors had a particular appeal to the medieval mind; cf. Curtius 131 ff.

7. incorrupta: cf. Stat. *silv.* 2. 3. 68 'incorrupte fidem'. The epithet suits the quality better than the personification; cf. 1. 18. 16 n.

Fides: a Roman deity of great antiquity; cf. *RE* 6. 2281 ff. Πίστις is rarely personified (but cf. Theogn. 1137 Πίστις μεγάλη θεός).

nuda: cf. Apul. *met.* 10. 12. 4 'procedit in medium nuda veritas', Aug. *epist.* 242. 5; for the 'naked truth' see *OED* s.v. *naked* 6b. Similarly Ovid lists his own virtues as 'nulli cessura fides, sine crimine mores, / nudaque simplicitas purpureusque pudor' (*am.* 1. 3. 13 f.). Truth is represented as naked in Botticelli's *Calunnia* in the Uffizi, his reconstruction of the celebrated painting of Apelles described in Lucian, *calumn.* 5.

Veritas: cf. the boast of a dead man in *carm. epig.* 512. 4 'fydes in me mira fuit semper et veritas omnis'; to judge from the *ars poetica* (above, p. 279), Quintilius seems to have deserved the praise.

Ἀλήθεια and Veritas both belong to the poets and philosophers, not to ordinary cult; cf. Pind. *O.* 10. 3 f., Cebes 18. 2 (Education is the mother of Truth and Persuasion), Varro, *Men.* 141 'cana Veritas, Attices philosophiae alumna', Phaedrus, *app.* 4 (a fable on the genesis of Veritas and Mendacium), Gell. 12. 11. 7 'alius quidam veterum poetarum . . . Veritatem Temporis filiam esse dixit' (cf. Otto 343), Mart. 10. 72. 11 'siccis rustica Veritas capillis'. See further Farnell 5. 446, *RE* 8 A. 1551 f.

8. parem: cf. Milton, *Lycidas* 8 f. 'For Lycidas is dead, dead ere his prime, Young Lycidas, and hath not left his peer'.

9. bonis flebilis occidit: cf. Aesch. *Pers.* 674 ὦ πολύκλαυτε φίλοισι θανών, Val. Fl. 3. 202 f. 'flebilis urbi / conciderit', *inscr. Christ.* Rossi 2 p. 69 n. 37. 10 'conspicuus vixit, flebilis occubuit'. *flebilis* is often found on sepulchral inscriptions (*Thes.l.L.* 6. 1. 891. 24 ff.).

10. nulli . . .: cf. Eur. *Alc.* 264 οἰκτρὰν φίλοισιν, ἐκ δὲ τῶν μάλιστ' ἐμοί. For the phrasing cf. 1. 36. 6 n.

11. frustra . . .: to be taken in the first instance with *pius*, though the effect of the word colours the whole sentence; cf. Ov. *met.* 5. 152 'hac pro parte socer frustra pius et nova coniunx / cum genetrice favent ululatuque atria complent', E. Wölfflin, *ALL* 2, 1885, 11, *Thes.l.L.* 6. 1. 1435. 75 ff. For the uselessness of piety cf. Virg. *Aen.* 11. 843 f. 'nec tibi desertae in dumis coluisse Dianam / profuit', *cons. Liv.* 131 ff., *carm. epig.* 1225. 7 f. 'quos non ille prius (pius *Burmann*), qua non ego voce rogavi / infelix superos? nec valuere preces'.

non ita creditum: 'not entrusted to their care on these terms'. Virgil by his vows has entrusted Quintilius to the gods' care and now reclaims him in vain; cf. 1. 3. 5 ff. Some editors have assumed on the basis of this similarity that Quintilius perished on a journey; but we cannot be so specific.

13. quid? si . . .: the uselessness of lamenting inevitable loss is a commonplace from Homer on (cf. *Il.* 24. 550 οὐ γάρ τι πρήξεις ἀκαχήμενος υἷος ἑῆος, / οὐδέ μιν ἀνστήσεις). Cicero calls it 'consolatio pervulgata quidem illa maxime' (*epist.* 5. 16. 2), and philosophers constantly inveighed against 'tristitia supervacua stultaque' (Sen. *dial.* 12. 16. 7). See Kassel, op. cit., pp. 70 f., and, for the occurrence of the theme in epitaphs, B. Lier, *Philologus* 62, 1903, 571 f.

The lively *quid? si . . .* adds urgency to the following rhetorical question; cf. *serm.* 2. 3. 159 f., *epist.* 1. 19. 12 ff., Virg. *Aen.* 4. 311 ff. 'quid? si non arva aliena domosque / ignotas peteres, et Troia antiqua maneret, / Troia per undosum peteretur classibus aequor?'

Threicio . . .: Politian imitated this phrase at the beginning of his ode to Horace: 'vates Threicio blandior Orpheo / seu malis fidibus sistere lubricos / amnes, seu tremulo ducere pollice / ipsis cum latebris feras'.

Orpheo: 'if only I were as persuasive as Orpheus' is a common wish; cf. Eur. *Alc.* 357 ff. εἰ δ' Ὀρφέως μοι γλῶσσα καὶ μέλος παρῆν, / ὥστ' ἢ κόρην Δήμητρος ἢ κείνης πόσιν / ὕμνοισι κηλήσαντά σ' ἐξ Ἅιδου λαβεῖν, / κατῆλθον ἄν, *IA* 1211 ff., *epitaph. Bion.* 115 ff. εἰ δυνάμαν δέ,/ὡς Ὀρφεὺς καταβὰς ποτὶ Τάρταρον . . . κἠγὼ τάχ' ἂν ἐς δόμον ἦλθον / Πλουτέος ὥς κέ σ' ἴδοιμι, Ronsard, *Odes* 2. 3. 49 ff. The theme is also found in epitaphs; cf. *carm. epig.* 492. 7 f. Statius uses it to express the ineffectiveness of consolation; cf. *silv.* 2. 1. 10 ff., 5. 1. 23 ff.

Horace gives the commonplace a particular point and delicacy of application by using the second person. He seems to be hinting at, and implicitly contradicting, the story of the recovery of Eurydice, which Virgil had told in the *Georgics*. His view of the power of poetry is more commonsensical than his friend's.

14. arboribus: cf. 1. 12. 7 n.

fidem: the singular is poetic, first found in Varius, *trag.* 4 'nervis septem est intenta fides'; see *Thes.l.L.* 6. 1. 692. 59 ff.

15. vanae . . . imagini: the phrase answers both Homer's νεκύων ἀμένηνα κάρηνα (*Od.* 10. 521) and his βροτῶν εἴδωλα καμόντων (*Od.* 11. 476); cf. Lucr. 1. 123 'quaedam simulacra modis pallentia miris', Virg. *Aen.* 6. 292 f. 'tenues sine corpore vitas / . . . volitare cava sub imagine formae', Ov. *fast.* 5. 463, Dante, *purg.* 2. 79 'O ombre vane, fuor che ne l'aspetto', *inf.* 6. 34 ff. 'Noi passavam su per l'ombre che adona / la greve pioggia, e ponevam le piante / sopra lor vanità che par persona'. Milton exploited the image in his description of the insubstantial inhabitants of Limbo (*P.L.* 3. 444 ff.).

sanguis: cf. Virg. *Aen.* 6. 401 'exsanguis...umbras'. Horace may be recalling that the shades in the *Nekyia* must drink blood before they can speak (Hom. *Od.* 11. 152 ff.).

16. virga: cf. 1. 10. 18 n. The scene here is a much grimmer one; Horace chooses his details with an eye to pathos and horror. In our poem Mercury's wand, instead of glittering, inspires terror; and the *niger grex* is more sinister and humiliated than the *levis turba* of 1. 10. We may note too that the central figure in Horace's picture here is not so much Mercury as the single shade trying to escape and being herded back.

Mercury is here the shepherd of the dead; cf. Lucian, *cat.* 3 (as Hermes arrives breathless from efforts to restrain a runaway soul) ὥσπερ τι αἰπόλιον ἀθρόους αὐτοὺς τῇ ῥάβδῳ σοβῶν, Milton, *Epitaphium Damonis* 23 ff. 'at non ille, animas virga qui dividit aurea, / ista velit, dignumque tui te ducat in agmen, / ignavumque procul pecus arceat omne silentum'. Hades himself uses his wand for a like purpose in Pind. *O.* 9. 33 ff. οὐδ' Ἀΐδας ἀκινήταν ἔχε ῥάβδον, / βροτέα σώμαθ' ᾇ κατάγει κοιλὰν πρὸς ἄγυιαν / θνᾳσκόντων.

semel: 'once for all'; cf. 4. 7. 21 ff., Prop. 4. 11. 3 f. 'cum semel infernas intrarunt funera leges, / non exorato stant adamante viae', Fraenkel on Aesch. *Ag.* 1018, 1. 28. 16 n.

17. non lenis: the gods of the underworld are conventionally

inexorable; cf. 2. 3. 24, Hom. *Il.* 9. 158 Ἀΐδης τοι ἀμείλιχος ἠδ' ἀδά-
μαστος, *Orph. h.* 87. 9 (to Thanatos) οὔτε γὰρ εὐχαῖσιν πείθῃ μόνος οὔτε
λιταῖσιν, Peek, *GV* 971. 3 f. = Kaibel, *EG* 345. 3 f. μῆτερ ἐμή, θρήν[ων
ἀ]ποπαύεο, λ[ῆ]ξον ὀδυρμῶν / κ[αὶ] κοπετῶν· Ἀΐδης οἰκ[τ]ον ἀπο-
στ[ρέφεται, *carm. epig.* 1212. 5 f., West on Hes. *th.* 769.

  fata recludere: 'to open the gates of death'. *recludere* implies the
common image of the gates of Hades; cf. *pap. gr. mag.* 82. 340 f.
Ἑρμῇ καταχθονίῳ Θωούθ καὶ Ἀνούβιδι κραταιῷ τῷ τὰς κλεῖδας ἔχοντι
τῶν καθ' Ἄιδου, H. Usener, *Kleine Schriften* 4, 1913, pp. 226 ff.,
O. Weinreich, *Tübinger Beiträge zur Altertumswissenschaft*, Heft 5,
1929, 436 ff. The gates are often said to stand wide open for the reception of newcomers (cf. especially Virg. *Aen.* 6. 127 'noctes atque
dies patet atri ianua Ditis', Val. Fl. 4. 231 'reclusaque ianua leti').
But gates can imprison as well; cf. Prop. 4. 11. 2 'panditur ad nullas
ianua nigra preces'.

  fata is a strangely bold object for *recludere*; one would naturally
expect the phrase to mean 'to disclose what is fated', which is nonsense. *recludere* must keep up the image of the herdsman, relent-
lessly penning up the flock entrusted to him. But instead of saying
saepta or *clathra*, Horace uses the more poetical *fata*, to suggest
the immutable laws that prevent escape from death.

  18. nigro . . . gregi: blackness is commonly an attribute of everything associated with death; Horace uses *niger* and *ater* indifferently
to express this idea. For the general practice of Latin poets see
André 51, 54 f., 60, 362 ff. For the grandiose dative of the end of
motion see 1. 28. 10 n.

  compulerit: the word suits *gregi*; cf. Virg. *ecl.* 2. 30 'haedorumque
gregem viridi compellere hibisco', 7. 2 (cf. Serv. ad loc. 'compellere
proprie est in unum locum vel diversa vel diversorum animalia
cogere').

  19. durum: sed levius . . .: for this movement of thought with
similar γνῶμαι, cf. Soph. fr. 237 N. (= 258 P.) ἔχει μὲν ἀλγείν', οἶδα.
πειρᾶσθαι δ' ⟨ὅμως⟩ / ἐκ τῶν τοιούτων χρή τιν' ἴασιν λαβεῖν, fr. 526 N.
(= 585 P.) ἀλγεινά, Πρόκνη, δῆλον· ἀλλ' ὅμως χρέων / τὰ θεῖα θνητοὺς
ὄντας εὐπετῶς φέρειν, Eur. *Hel.* 252 f. ἔχεις μὲν ἀλγείν', οἶδα· σύμφορον
δέ τοι / ὡς ῥᾶστα τἀναγκαῖα τοῦ βίου φέρειν.

  That we must bear what is incurable was a common topic of
consolation (see Pasquali 257 n. 1). Sometimes there was added the
nuance that we find here, that our power of endurance is itself a cure
for grief; cf. Archil. fr. 7. 5 ff. ἀλλὰ θεοὶ γὰρ ἀνηκέστοισι κακοῖσιν, / ὦ
φίλ', ἐπὶ κρατερὴν τλημοσύνην ἔθεσαν / φάρμακον, Pind. *P.* 2. 93 f.
φέρειν δ' ἐλαφρῶς ἐπαυχένιον λαβόντα ζύγον / ἀρήγει, Publil. 206 'feras,
non culpes, quod mutari non potest', Sen. *epist.* 107. 9 'optimum

est pati quod emendare non possis', Kassel, op. cit., pp. 54 ff., Otto 134. A fifteenth-century manuscript of Donatus tells us, among other fictions, that the γνώμη was a favourite of Virgil's own, and cites *Aen.* 5. 709 f. (E. Diehl, *Die Vitae Vergilianae und ihre antiken Quellen*, 1911, p. 36).

25. PARCIVS IVNCTAS

[F. O. Copley, *Exclusus Amator*, 1956; Pasquali 440 ff.; T. Plüss, *Fleckeisens Jahrb.* 127, 1883, 493 ff.]

1–8. *Now few young men seek admittance to your room, Lydia; your front-door stays shut, and you seldom hear the lover's lament.* 9–20. *You will be punished for your haughtiness when you unsuccessfully seek clients on a gusty night; then you will whimper that young men reject withered garlands.*

This ode is an elaboration of a traditional motif: the rejected lover tells his beloved that her beauty will fade, and then she will be sorry. The theme in itself is psychologically plausible, but became stereotyped as a literary convention. See, for instance, the epigram by Julianus, *anth. P.* 5. 298; the late date (sixth century A.D.) is irrelevant as the subject-matter is obviously derived from a Hellenistic model:

ἱμερτὴ Μαρίη μεγαλίζεται· ἀλλὰ μετέλθοις
κείνης, πότνα Δίκη, κόμπον ἀγηνορίης·
μὴ θανάτῳ, βασίλεια· τὸ δ' ἔμπαλιν, ἐς τρίχας ἥξοι
γῆραος, ἐς ῥυτίδας σκληρὸν ἵκοιτο ῥέθος·
τίσειαν πολιαὶ τάδε δάκρυα· κάλλος ὑπόσχοι
ψυχῆς ἀμπλακίην, αἴτιον ἀμπλακίης.

Pasquali compared Propertius 3. 25. 11 ff.:

at te celatis aetas gravis urgeat annis
et veniat formae ruga sinistra tuae.
vellere tum cupias albos a stirpe capillos,
a! speculo rugas increpitante tibi,
exclusa inque vicem fastus patiare superbos,
et quae fecisti facta quereris anus.

Catullus's fine eighth poem, for all its directness of language, is set in the traditional mould: 'at tu dolebis cum rogaberis nulla. / scelesta vae te, quae tibi manet vita? / quis nunc te adibit? cui videberis bella? / quem nunc amabis? cuius esse diceris?' (8. 14 ff.).

See also *carm.* 4. 10 (Ligurinus), Ov. *med. fac.* 47 f., Rufinus, *anth. P.* 5. 92. 5 f. ὦ ῥυτίδες καὶ γῆρας ἀνηλεές, ἔλθετε θᾶσσον, | σπεύσατε· κἂν ὑμεῖς πείσατε τὴν Ῥοδόπην, Aristaenetus 2. 1 μετ᾽ ὀλίγον ἔσῃ γεράνδρυον.

In other poems the poet less plausibly exults that the lady has already turned old. This is the theme of 4. 13. 1 ff.: 'audivere, Lyce, di mea vota, di / audivere, Lyce: fis anus, et tamen / vis formosa videri.' See also 3. 15. 4 f. 'maturo propior desine funeri / inter ludere virgines', Tib. 1. 6. 81 f. 'hanc animo gaudente vident iuvenumque catervae / commemorant merito tot mala ferre senem', Rufinus, *anth. P.* 5. 21. 3 ff. νῦν ῥυτίδες καὶ θρὶξ πολιὴ καὶ σῶμα ῥακῶδες, | καὶ στόμα τὰς προτέρας οὐκέτ᾽ ἔχον χάριτας. | μή τις σοί, μετέωρε, προσέρχεται, ἢ κολακεύων | λίσσεται; ὡς δὲ τάφον νῦν σε παρερχόμεθα, 5. 27, Macedonius, 5. 271, Agathias, 5. 273.

Our ode also has affinities with the type of poem conveniently known as *paraclausithyron* (for which see *RE* 18. 3. 1202, Copley, op. cit., C. M. Bowra, *AJPh* 79, 1958, 376 ff.). This was a lament supposed to be sung by the excluded lover; though it had its origins in folk-song, it became as conventional an exercise as serenade in opera. The essential theme already appears in Alcaeus (374 δέξαι με κωμάσδοντα δέξαι, λίσσομαί σε λίσσομαι), and was greatly developed by Comedy (cf. Ar. *eccl.* 952 ff., Plaut. *Curc.* 147 ff.), but for extant Greek examples one must turn especially to the Anthology; see, for instance, Asclepiades, 5. 167. 1 f. ὑετὸς ἦν καὶ νὺξ καὶ τὸ τρίτον ἄλγος ἔρωτι, | οἶνος· καὶ βορέης ψυχρός, ἐγὼ δὲ μόνος, 5. 189. 1 f. νὺξ μακρὴ καὶ χεῖμα, μέσην δ᾽ ἐπὶ Πλειάδα δύνει· | κἀγὼ πὰρ προθύροις νίσσομαι ὑόμενος. The Roman poets showed their ingenuity by handling this well-worn topic in an individual idiom. Lucretius is austere and descriptive: 'at lacrimans exclusus amator limina saepe / floribus et sertis operit postisque superbos / unguit amaracino et foribus miser oscula figit' (4. 1177 ff.). In Propertius a door repeats a lover's romantic lament: 'me mediae noctes, me sidera prona iacentem, / frigidaque Eoo me dolet aura gelu' (1. 16. 23 f.). Ovid engages the concierge with witty rhetoric (*am.* 1. 6), or trips through the commonplaces in the fluent narrative of the *Metamorphoses* (14. 698 ff.). Horace himself supplies an elegant parody of the genre: 'non hoc semper erit liminis aut aquae / caelestis patiens latus' (3. 10. 19 f.). Persius is moral and derisive: 'an rem patriam rumore sinistro / limen ad obscenum frangam, dum Chrysidis udas / ebrius ante fores exstincta cum face canto?' (5. 164 ff.). Milton is equally disapproving: 'Or Serenate, which the starv'd Lover sings To his proud fair, best quitted with disdain' (*P.L.* 4. 769 f.).

Sometimes the *paraclausithyron* contains elements from the first-mentioned type of poem, i.e. predictions that the beauty of the lady will fade, and prayers that she will then suffer in turn. See, for

instance, an epigram attributed to Callimachus, though its authorship is doubtful (*ep.* 63):

οὕτως ὑπνώσαις, Κωνώπιον, ὡς ἐμὲ ποιεῖς
κοιμᾶσθαι ψυχροῖς τοῖσδε παρὰ προθύροις·
οὕτως ὑπνώσαις, ἀδικωτάτη, ὡς τὸν ἐραστὴν
κοιμίζεις· ἐλέου δ' οὐδ' ὄναρ ἠντίασας.
γείτονες οἰκτείρουσι· σὺ δ' οὐδ' ὄναρ. ἡ πολιὴ δὲ
αὐτίκ' ἀναμνήσει ταῦτά σε πάντα κόμη.

Rufinus, like Horace in our poem, says that the lady is already growing old, and will soon be older (*anth. P.* 5. 103):

μέχρι (ἄχρι Bothe) τίνος, Προδίκη, παρακλαύσομαι; ἄχρι τίνος δὲ
γουνάσομαι, στερεή, μηδὲν ἀκουόμενος;
ἤδη καὶ λευκαί σοι ἐπισκιρτῶσιν ἔθειραι,
καὶ τάχα μοι †δώσεις† ὡς Ἑκάβη Πριάμῳ.

See also Ov. *ars* 3. 69 ff. 'tempus erit quo tu quae nunc excludis
amantes, / frigida deserta nocte iacebis anus, / nec tua frangetur
nocturna ianua rixa, / sparsa nec invenies limina mane rosa'.

Horace combines these various themes in his usual manner,
though without achieving complete consistency. In lines 1–8 he
exults that Lydia is now less attractive; here the tone is dry and
sardonic. But the rest of the ode is more ferocious, and belongs
mainly to the category where the rejected lover prays for revenge.
Here Horace owes much to Catullus, who in his invective against
Lesbia had raised Italian *diffamatio* to the level of literature. Other
elements, and particularly lines 7–8, recall the traditional lament of
the excluded lover; but the poem as a whole is not a *paraclausithyron*.
One is not meant to suppose that Horace is lying at the door as he
utters the poem; Lydia would now be glad to admit lovers, and the
savagery of the last three stanzas implies that the relationship has
been broken off. Of course the unreality of the situation is obvious,
as in most ancient poems of the same type: one must not assume
that Asclepiades or Propertius really lay about on doorsteps. Horace
does not even persuade us, as do Catullus and Propertius, that his
conventional formulas reflect real feelings. He is simply exhibiting
his usual virtuosity in weaving together diverse poetical strands.

Yet the literary merit of the ode is considerable. It contains a forceful realism of Alexandrian origin, which appears but seldom in our
author. It is true that we are given no account of the details of
ugliness, such as is found in the poem to Lyce (4. 13. 10 ff.), in *epodes* 8
and 12, and in some of the Greek parallels. On the other hand the
impressionistic sketch of the *angiportus* is much more effective than
any delineation of ῥυτίδες and πολίη. And the opening stanza wins

the attention because it is set for once not in an idyllic grotto but
in a real city street. The rowdy young men throwing stones at a
shuttered window, the prostitute whining in a passage-way on a
gusty night, these are convincing vignettes of metropolitan life, such
as one rarely finds in the Augustans. In spite of its conventionalism
and inhumanity this is a good poem.

Metre: Sapphic.

1. parcius: 'more sparingly'; cf. Virg. *ecl.* 3. 7 'parcius ista viris
tamen obicienda memento', Prop. 2. 24. 10. The word has a dry,
ironic note which *rarius* would lack: the young men now show more
restraint. In the first two lines note the alliteration of the hard *c*s (and
qu), perhaps representing the thud of stone on wood; in lines 3 and 4
the *m*s and *n*s are rightly smoother.

iunctas . . . fenestras: one should picture a window without glass,
but with joining shutters, perhaps latticed; as the scene is set at
night the shutters have been closed by a bar. Moonlight or daylight
could come in by the *rimae* of the lattice; cf. Philodemus, *anth. P.*
5. 123. 1 f. νυκτερινὴ δίκερως φιλοπάννυχε φαῖνε Σελήνη, / φαῖνε δι'
εὐτρήτων βαλλομένη θυρίδων, Prop. 1. 3. 31 'diversas praecurrens luna
fenestras' (*diversas* is the opposite of *iunctas* in our poem), Ov. *Pont.*
3. 3. 5 'nox erat et bifores intrabat luna fenestras', Pers. 3. 1 f. 'iam
clarum mane fenestras / intrat et angustas extendit lumine rimas'.
When Ovid goes to bed in the middle of the day 'pars adaperta fuit,
pars altera clausa fenestrae / quale fere silvae lumen habere solent'
(*am.* 1. 5. 3 f.). See further Blümner 102 f.

2. iactibus: the young men throw pebbles at the shutters to attract
Lydia's attention; ancient streets must have supplied plenty of
ammunition for such purposes. *iactibus* is supported by the overwhelming preponderance of the manuscripts, as well as by the
ancient commentators; note especially ps.-Acro 'iactibus: id est
ictibus lapidum'. *ictibus* has negligible authority here; the word
would be more appropriate if the door were being battered and not
the window.

Bentley half-heartedly proposed *vectibus*; cf. Virg. *Aen.* 2. 492
'ariete crebro'. For the use of crowbars and similar implements by
iuvenes protervi cf. 3. 26. 7, Copley, op. cit., p. 148 n. 26. But the
crowbar was naturally used against the door rather than the window,
and it is absurd to suggest that it was the normal means of entry
to Lydia's bedroom. Heinsius proposed *tactibus*; cf. Claud. 18. 92 f.
(on the ageing Lais) 'iam turba procax noctisque recedit / ambitus,
et raro pulsatur ianua tactu'. But Claudian is talking of a door, not
a window.

If *iactibus* is right Lydia must be sleeping upstairs, which is what one would expect in any case. Cf. the serenade in 3. 7. 29 f. 'prima nocte domum claude neque in vias / sub cantu querulae despice tibiae'; add Ar. *eccl.* 697 ff. παρ' ἐμοὶ δ' ἑτέρα / φήσει τις ἄνωθ' ἐξ ὑπερῴου καὶ καλλίστη καὶ λευκοτάτη, Asclepiades, *anth. P.* 5. 153. 1 f. Νικαρέτης τὸ Πόθοις μεμελημένον ἡδὺ πρόσωπον / πυκνὰ δι' ὑψορόφων φαινόμενον θυρίδων, Fraenkel in *Greek Poetry and Life* (Essays presented to G. Murray), 1936, pp. 262 ff. The man might climb up by a ladder (S. Trenkner, *The Greek Novella in the Classical Period*, 1958, p. 129), or the girl descend by a rope (Prop. 4. 7. 18 'alterna veniens in tua colla manu'). One must not think of a prosperous mansion of the Pompeii type looking inwards on a courtyard, but rather of the ordinary man's house with upper windows facing a street (J. Marquardt and A. Mau, *Das Privatleben der Römer*, 1886, p. 247 n. 6, D. S. Robertson, *Handbook of Greek and Roman Architecture*, ed. 2, 1943, pp. 307 ff., R. Meiggs, *Roman Ostia*, 1960, pp. 235 ff.).

iuvenes protervi: Horace is no doubt thinking of the κῶμος or *comissatio* when noisy roisterers roamed the streets on the way to see their girl-friends; cf. Headlam on Herodas 2. 34, Bömer on Ov. *fast.* 5. 339, *RE* 4. 618 f., 11. 1286 ff., Yeats, *Byzantium* 'Night resonance recedes, night-walkers' song After great cathedral gong'. Of course the *comissatio* was not simply a Grecizing poetical convention, but took place in real Roman life; cf. Gell. 4. 14. 5 'apud eos dixit comissatorem Mancinum ad aedes suas venisse; eum sibi recipere non fuisse e re sua, sed cum vi irrumperet lapidibus depulsum', Apul. *apol.* 75 'diebus ac noctibus ludibrio iuventutis ianua calcibus propulsata'.

3. somnos adimunt: not simply 'wake you up' but 'deprive you of your night's rest'. Cf. Prop. 2. 19. 5 f. 'nulla neque ante tuas orietur rixa fenestras / nec tibi clamatae somnus amarus erit', 3. 10. 25 f. 'dulciaque ingratos adimant convivia somnos', *Thes.l.L.* 1. 683. 66.

amatque: 'keeps to'; cf. Prop. 2. 6. 24 'et quaecumque viri femina limen amat', Virg. *Aen.* 3. 134, 5. 163. Horace uses an expression appropriate to a chaste woman; for a somewhat similar point cf. Catull. 67. 38 (of the *ianua*) 'cui numquam domini limine abesse licet'.

4. ianua: the closed door was a motif in the *paraclausithyron*; see Plaut. *Curc.* 147 'pessuli, heus pessuli, vos saluto libens ...', Prop. 1. 16. 25 f. 'tu sola humanos numquam miserata dolores / respondes tacitis mutua cardinibus', Ov. *am.* 1. 6 with its refrain 'tempora noctis eunt, excute poste seram', Strato, *anth. P.* 12. 252. 4 φωλήσω γε θύραις νυκτὸς ἀνοιγομέναις. Horace reverses the conventional situation:

the door is shut and the hinges are silent because nobody wants to enter.

limen: the ancient threshold was not simply an imaginary line but a block of wood, designed to fit the door precisely in a day of uneven floors. It was big enough to hurt one's toes on: cf. Novius, *Atell.* 50 'inferum autem (limen) digitos omnis ubi ego diffregi meos'. It played an important part, originally religious, in Roman life (K. Meister, *Die Hausschwelle, SHAW* 15, 1924–5, 3. Abh.). It is often mentioned in Roman amatory poetry (3. 10. 19 f., *epod.* 11. 22, Ov. *met.* 14. 709 f.); the οὐδός does not seem to appear in similar contexts in Greek (Meister, p. 22).

5. multum: to be taken with *faciles* ('pretty compliant'). The idiom is colloquial (cf. Italian 'molto bene' etc.); here the forthright and sardonic tone suits the mood of the poem. The usage is normally confined by Horace to participles and words like *similis* and *dissimilis*; yet see *serm.* 2. 3. 147 f. 'hunc medicus multum celer atque fidelis / excitat hoc pacto' (where Heinze implausibly takes *multum* with *excitat*). See further E. Wölfflin, *Ausgewählte Schriften*, 1933, pp. 133 f.

Porphyrio takes *multum* with *movebat* ('often moved'), and he has been followed by some modern editors. It could be argued that on this interpretation the contrast with *parcius* is expressed more clearly. On the other hand it is infelicitous to have two adverbs, *prius* and *multum*, both modifying *movebat*.

facilis: accusative plural, agreeing with *cardines* (thus Porphyrio, rightly); cf. Juv. 4. 63 'facili patuerunt cardine valvae', Ser. Samm. 484. The word also suggests the compliance of a *meretrix*; cf. 3. 7. 32 'difficilis mane', Mart. 3. 69. 5 'nequam iuvenes facilesque puellae'. Some editors see an inconsistency with Lydia's hard-heartedness in the next sentence, but Horace has simply described two conventional attributes of the courtesan.

Many editors think that *facilis* is nominative, and is applied to the door; cf. Ov. *am.* 1. 6. 2 'difficilem . . . forem', Sen. *Tro.* 404 'custos non facili Cerberus ostio', *dial.* 5. 37 'difficilem ianuam'. But the sentence is better bound together if *cardines*, which comes at the end and after the verb, is qualified by an adjective that precedes the verb.

The ancient *cardines* were vertical poles to which the door-panels (*fores*) were attached; they were made of hard wood (Plin. *nat.* 16. 210), and often turned in sockets set in the threshold and lintel (D.–S. 1. 920 f.). Squeaking was hard to avoid (Blümner 19 n. 7), and is often mentioned in erotic contexts. See Ar. *Thesm.* 487 f. ἐγὼ δὲ καταχέασα τοῦ στροφέως ὕδωρ / ἐξῆλθον ὡς τὸν μοιχόν, Lys. 1. 14

ἐρομένου δέ μου τί αἱ θύραι νύκτωρ ψοφοῖεν, Dioscorides, *anth. P.*
12. 14. 3 f. οὐκέτι νύκτωρ | ἥσυχα τῇ κείνου μητρὶ μένει πρόθυρα, Plaut.
Curc. 94 'num muttit cardo', 158, Tib. 1. 2. 10, 1. 6. 12, 1. 8. 60,
Ov. *am.* 1. 6. 49, G. E. Duckworth, *The Nature of Roman Comedy*,
1952, p. 117. Lydia had less reason for secrecy than a married woman,
but even a *meretrix* might have a *custos* or a *vir*, and in the poetical
convention *furtivus amor* was more romantic (Copley, op. cit.,
pp. 36 ff.).

6. minus et minus: for similar locutions cf. E. Wölfflin, *Ausgewählte
Schriften*, 1933, pp. 311 ff.

7. me tuo . . .: note the restraint of Horace's seven words compared
with the lengthy *querimoniae* of Propertius or Ovid; such is the
difference between the lyric and elegiac manner. *me tuo* means 'I that
am yours'; *me* is indignantly emphatic. Horace reproduces the lively
idiom of Roman lovers; cf. Plaut. *Amph.* 542 'ut quom apsim me ames,
me tuam te apsenti tamen', Ter. *eun.* 664 'tam infandum facinus, mea
tu, ne audivi quidem', *ad.* 289, Catull. 66. 91 'unguinis expertem non
siris esse tuam me', Ov. *Pont.* 1. 10. 1, *Lydia* 41 'luna, tuus tecum est:
cur non est et mea mecum?' No Greek parallel presents itself.

longas . . . noctes: the night seems long to the rejected lover. Cf.
Asclepiades, *anth. P.* 5. 189. 1 νὺξ μακρὴ καὶ χεῖμα, Hor. *epist.* 1. 1. 20
'ut nox longa quibus mentitur amica', Prop. 1. 12. 13 f. 'nunc primum
longas solus cognoscere noctes / cogor', Ov. *am.* 2. 19. 22, *epist.*
16. 317, *Priap.* 47. 5. For a similar complaint from the woman's point
of view cf. anon. *PMG* 976 δέδυκε μὲν ἁ σελάνα . . .

Bentley proposed and printed *longam . . . noctem*: in the *paraclausithyron* the lover should be thinking only of the present. Editors
have paid little attention, but his difficulty seems a real one. One
should perhaps regard *noctes* as an exaggerated expression designed
to convey the length of the night. Alternatively one might suggest
that *noctes* here, like Greek νύκτες sometimes, is singular in sense.
Thus μέσαι νύκτες is the normal expression for 'midnight'; cf. also
Prop. 1. 16. 23 'mediae noctes'. So ἐκ νυκτῶν means 'by night';
cf. Hom. *Od.* 12. 686 ἐκ νυκτῶν δ' ἄνεμοι χαλεποί, Aesch. *cho.* 288,
Theogn. 460, Eur. *Rhes.* 13, Theaetetus, *anth. P.* 7. 444. 2. In Ar. *nub.* 2
τὸ χρῆμα τῶν νυκτῶν ὅσον naturally means 'how long the night is' and
not 'how long the nights are'. Cf. also Pind. *P.* 4. 256 ἆμαρ ἢ νύκτες,
N. 6. 6 μετὰ νύκτας, Pl. *symp.* 217 d διελεγόμην ἀεὶ πόρρω τῶν νυκτῶν,
223 d καὶ καταδαρθεῖν πάνυ πολὺ ἅτε μακρῶν τῶν νυκτῶν οὐσῶν, Blaydes
on Ar. loc. cit., Löfstedt, *Syntactica*, 1². 33. Yet it must be admitted
that there is no adequate parallel to this usage in Latin; *mediae
noctes* is a special case.

pereunte: of love and cold.

9. invicem: the contrast is with lines 7–8, not (as one might expect) with the opening of the poem. For the same motif cf. Asclepiades, *anth. P.* 5. 164. 3 f. ταὐτὰ παθοῦσα / σοὶ μέμψαιτ' ἐπ' ἐμοῖς στᾶσα παρὰ προθύροις, Theoc. 23. 33 ἥξει καιρὸς ἐκεῖνος (cf. Ov. *ars* 3. 69 'tempus erit'), Catull. 8. 14 'at tu dolebis', Hor. *epod.* 15. 24 'ast ego vicissim risero', Prop. 3. 25. 15 'inque vicem', Agathias, *anth. P.* 5. 280. 5 εὑρήσεις τὰ ὅμοια.

moechos . . .: 'you will weep the insolence of wenchers'. 'moechos . . . arrogantes' means 'moechorum arrogantiam', just as 'ab urbe condita' means 'from the foundation of the city'; cf. 1. 37. 13 n. *moechi* are properly men who commit adultery with married women, but here the word is used imprecisely; cf. Catull. 37. 16 'semitarii moechi'. *moechus* is a loan-word from Greek, often found in Latin comedy, but not attested in the higher styles of prose and poetry; however, it is used in Catull. 11. 17, 68. 103.

anus: a common object of ridicule in the lower categories of ancient literature; cf. Grassmann (see index under 'vetula-Skoptik'). For the theme here cf. especially Epicrates, fr. 2. 3. 21 ff. K. (on the elderly Lais) ἐξέρχεταί τε πανταχόσ' ἤδη πετομένη, / δέχεται δὲ καὶ στατῆρα καὶ τριώβολον, / προσίεται δὲ καὶ γέροντα καὶ νέον, Nicarchus, *anth. P.* 11. 73. 1 f. γραῖα καλὴ (τί γάρ;) οἶσθας ὅτ' ἦν νέα· ἀλλὰ τότ' ᾔτει· / νῦν δ' ἐθέλει δοῦναι μισθὸν ἐλαυνομένη.

arrogantes: contrasts with the conventional haughtiness of the courtesan; cf. 3. 26. 12 'tange Chloen semel arrogantem'.

10. solo: 'deserted'; cf. Ter. *eun.* 845 'in angiportum quoddam desertum'. Loneliness is one of the torments of the excluded lover (Asclepiades, *anth. P.* 5. 167. 2 ἐγὼ δὲ μόνος); here Horace hopes that Lydia will be repaid in kind.

levis: 'worthless'; Porphyrio explains 'nullius ponderis'. Cf. Catull. 72. 5 f. 'etsi impensius uror / multo mi tamen es vilior et levior'.

angiportu: a narrow lane (στενωπός); in spite of ps.-Acro, it was not necessarily a cul-de-sac (*RE* 1. 2190 f., P. W. Harsh, *CPh* 32, 1937, 44 ff.). Rome must have been a warren of such alleys. Horace is saying that Lydia will be a prostitute of the most despised sort, totally distinct from the fashionable demi-mondaine she has been. He no doubt remembers Catullus's *diffamatio* of Lesbia: 'nunc in quadriviis et angiportis / glubit magnanimi Remi nepotes' (58. 3 f.).

11. Thracio . . .: 'while the Thracian wind revels more wildly as the moonless nights draw near'. The poet specifies the climatic conditions of a time that is still in the future; so *epod.* 10. 9 f. Bentley asked with eighteenth-century common sense why Lydia would go out in such windy weather, but Horace is creating atmosphere, not describing facts. The excluded lover is sometimes assailed by the cold

north wind (3. 10. 4, Asclepiades, *anth. P.* 5. 167. 2); Horace says that Lydia will suffer in turn.
To the Greeks all the winds had their home in Thrace (Hom. *Il.* 9. 5), but Boreas in particular; cf. Hes. *op.* 553 Θρηικίου Βορέω, Aesch. *Ag.* 654 Θρήικιαι πνοαί, Call. *h.* 3. 114. Winds from the N. or NNW. were known as Θρακίας or Στρυμωνίας; cf. *RE* 8 A. 2335 ff. The Romans took over the epithet (Sen. *nat.* 5. 16. 6), though to them it was less appropriate; Thrace was always the Siberia of the ancients. So *epod.* 13. 3 'Threicio Aquilone', Sil. 1. 587 'Thracius . . . Boreas' (of the Provençal mistral).

bacchante: the Thracian wind is pictured as a Thracian bacchanal; somewhat similarly Antipater of Sidon described it as a cruel barbarian (*anth. P.* 7. 303. 1 ff. Κλεόδημον . . . / ὁ Θρῄξ ἐτύμως Βορέης βάλεν εἰς ἁλὸς οἶδμα). For the use of *bacchari* of winds cf. 3. 3. 55, *ciris* 480, Ov. *trist.* 1. 2. 29. So Anacreon 347. 17 πόντον . . . θυίοντα.

sub interlunia: 'approaching the period when there is no moon'; the plural is poetic. The *interlunium* (μεσοσέληνον) was the period between the waning of the old moon and the appearance of the new; the expressions σύνοδος, *coitus*, and *silentium lunae* are also used. Cf. Milton, *Samson Agonistes* 86 ff. 'The Sun to me is dark And silent as the Moon When she deserts the night, Hid in her vacant interlunar cave'. This period was supposed to be stormy; cf. Arist. *gen. an.* 738ᵃ20 ff. αἱ δὲ τῶν μηνῶν σύνοδοι ψυχραὶ διὰ τὴν τῆς σελήνης ἀπόλειψιν, διόπερ καὶ χειμερίους συμβαίνει τὰς συνόδους εἶναι τῶν μηνῶν μᾶλλον ἢ τὰς μεσότητας, Theophrast. *vent.* 17, Arat. *phaen.* 1151 f. ὅτε σφαλερώτερος αἰθὴρ / ὀκτὼ νύξι πέλει χήτει χαροποῖο σελήνης (cf. schol.), Veg. *mil.* 4. 40 'interluniorum autem dies tempestatibus plenos et navigantibus quam maxime metuendos non solum peritiae ratio sed etiam volgi usus intellegit'. In Horace's poem the darkness of the moonless night also adds to the gloom of the scene.

13. tibi: emphatic; Horace says 'you will suffer then as others have done in the past'.

14. matres . . . equorum: poetic diction for 'mares'; cf. 1. 17. 7 n. The mannered circumlocution is Hellenistic; cf. Arat. *phaen.* 947 πατέρες βοόωσι γυρίνων ('the fathers of the tadpoles'), Agathias, *anth. P.* 5. 292. 4 ὄρνιθες δροσερῶν μητέρες ὀρταλίχων. For the subject-matter cf. Arist. *hist. an.* 572ᵃ8 ff. τῶν δὲ θηλειῶν ὁρμητικῶς ἔχουσι πρὸς τὸν συνδυασμὸν μάλιστα μὲν ἵππος ἔπειτα βοῦς. αἱ μὲν οὖν ἵπποι αἱ θήλειαι ἱππομανοῦσιν· ὅθεν καὶ ἐπὶ τὴν βλασφημίαν τὸ ὄνομα αὐτῶν ἐπιφέρουσιν ἀπὸ μόνου τῶν ζῴων τὴν ἐπὶ τῶν ἀκολάστων περὶ τὸ ἀφροδισιάζεσθαι (cf. *gen. an.* 773ᵇ25, Ael. *hist. anim.* 4. 11), Virg. *georg.* 3. 266 'scilicet ante omnes furor est insignis equarum . . .'.

furiare: ἐκμαίνειν. This is the first extant occurrence of this rare verb; the scholiasts comment 'verbum fictum' and 'novo verbo'. Cf. Virg. *Aen.* 2. 407 'furiata mente Coroebus'; there Serv. auct. comments 'quidam sane participium volunt *furiata* a verbo figurato apud Horatium *furiare*'.

15. circa: περί. The word is thus used in medical contexts: cf. Cels. 2. 6. 6 'dolores etiam circa coxas et inferiores partes orti', *Thes.l.L.* 3. 1085. 62. For *iecur* cf. 1. 13. 4 n.

ulcerosum: the first occurrence of this word in extant Latin. Porphyrio glosses 'ulceratum ex contemptu'; rather 'ex insatiata libidine'. For the ulcers of love cf. Lucr. 4. 1068 'ulcus enim vivescit et inveterascit alendo'.

17. laeta: the word does not simply reinforce *gaudeat* below, but means something like 'exuberant'. So Virg. *georg.* 3. 63 f. 'superat gregibus dum laeta iuventas, / solve mares'.

pubes: ἥβη. The word is capable of a sexual implication that *iuventus* lacks.

hedera: 'rejoices in green ivy rather than dark myrtle, but consecrates withered leaves to winter's comrade, the East wind'. Horace describes women of three ages in terms appropriate to garlands. *virenti* means 'fresh and young' (like evergreen leaves in the spring), *pulla* 'dark', almost 'dingy' (like the same leaves in late summer), while *aridas* obviously refers to the 'sere and yellow leaf' of autumn. For the same threefold division cf. Strato, *anth. P.* 12. 215 νῦν ἔαρ εἶ, μετέπειτα θέρος· κἄπειτα τί μέλλεις, / Κῦρις; βούλευσαι, καὶ καλάμη γὰρ ἔσῃ, anon. ibid. 5. 304 ὄμφαξ οὐκ ἐπένευσας· ὅτ' ἦς σταφυλή, παρεπέμψω. / μὴ φθονέσῃς δοῦναι κἂν βραχὺ τῆς σταφίδος. Similarly Donne makes a contrast between 'Yong Beauties', 'Autumnall face', and 'Winter-faces' (*Elegy* 9).

Most editors interpret 'rejoices rather in green ivy *and* dark myrtle' (thus Porphyrio). It is alleged in favour of this explanation that *atque* cannot here mean *quam*. Yet the construction is legitimate for Horace even after a positive; cf. *epod.* 12. 14, E. Wölfflin, *Ausgewählte Schriften*, 1933, p. 166, *Thes.l.L.* 2. 1084. 38 ff. It can be argued, moreover, that the sentence is much less compressed and forceful if the ivy and myrtle are put on the same level. On such an interpretation *pulla* and *virenti* would simply make a picturesque colour contrast, appropriate to garlands but not to women. This blurs the much more significant opposition between *virenti* and *aridas*.

19. aridas frondes: the young ivy and mature myrtle still serve to garland lovers (cf. on 1. 38. 5), but not withered leaves. For the metaphor cf. 4. 13. 9 f. (referring to Cupid) 'importunus enim transvolat aridas / quercus', Archil. 113 οὐκέθ' ὅμως θάλλεις ἀπαλὸν χρόα· κάρφεται γὰρ ἤδη, Aesch. *Ag.* 79 f. φυλλάδος ἤδη / κατακαρφομένης. The whole theme may be paralleled from the Greek Anthology; see especially anon. 12. 107. 3 f. εἰ δ' ἕτερον στέρξειε παρεὶς ἐμέ, μύρτον ἕωλον / ἐρρίφθω ξηροῖς φυρόμενον σκυβάλοις ('let him be cast aside like stale myrtle mixed with dry rubbish'). Add Marcus Argentarius, ibid. 5. 118. 2 ff. στέφανον / ὃν νῦν μὲν θάλλοντα, μαραινόμενον δὲ πρὸς ἠῶ / ὄψεαι, ὑμετέρης σύμβολον ἡλικίης, Macedonius, ibid. 11. 374. 7 f. ὡς δὲ ῥόδον θαλέθεσκες ἐν εἴαρι· νῦν δ' ἐμαράνθης, / γήραος αὐχμηρῷ καρφομένη θέρει, Strato, ibid. 12. 234. 1 f. εἰ κάλλει καυχᾷ, γίνωσχ' ὅτι καὶ ῥόδον ἀνθεῖ· / ἀλλὰ μαρανθὲν ἄφνω σὺν κοπρίοις ἐρίφη.

sodali: livelier than *amico* or *comiti*; the wind and the winter are boon-companions. See 3. 18. 6 f. 'Veneris sodali ... craterae'; for the similar use of ἑταῖρος cf. Hom. *Od.* 17. 271 (φόρμιγξ) ἦν ἄρα δαιτὶ θεοὶ ποίησαν ἑταίρην, Allen and Halliday's note on *h.Merc.* 31.

20. **Euro**: this admirable conjecture was made at the beginning of the 16th century. *Hebro* is the only reading with authority, and is supported not only by the manuscripts but by the scholia (Porph. 'vel quod frigidus sit Hebrus hiemis sodalis dicitur vel quod septem-trionalis sit, ubi frigus maximum est'). The corruption is to be ex-plained by the common phonetic confusion of *b* and *v*; the Hebrus is in fact known to Byzantine writers as Εὗρος. There is evidence in Latin inscriptions for this kind of change already in the first cen-tury A.D.

The Hebrus (Maritza) is the largest river in Thrace, and is men-tioned in poetry as early as Alcaeus 45. 1. It is traditionally asso-ciated with cold (*RE* 7. 2588 f.); one may note especially *epist.* 1. 3. 3 'Hebrusque nivali compede vinctus', *epist.* 1. 16. 13, Theoc. 7. 112. The conventional nature of these remarks is shown by the parallels to the first of these passages, which editors fail to cite; cf. Flaccus, *anth. P.* 7. 542. 1 Ἕβρου χειμερίοις ... κρυμοῖσι δεθέντος, Philippus, ibid. 9. 56. 1, Germanicus, *carm. poet. min.* 4. 111. 1 f.

A mention of the Hebrus could only be justified here on one of the following assumptions: (1) Horace might be describing a scene on the banks of the Hebrus. This is absurd; though no place is named, and Rome need not be specifically intended, there is nothing in the metropolitan atmosphere to transport us to Thrace. The fact that the Thracian north wind is mentioned does not put the poem near the Thracian river. (2) A Greek prototype might have been set on the banks of the Hebrus. This is still difficult; Aenos and Cypsela were not very important cities, and neither is associated with a poet. (3) The Hebrus might stand for any cold wintry river. But it would be hard to produce a convincing parallel for such a use of metonymy.

There is one striking parallel for 'hiemis sodali' as applied to a river: Claudian says of the Rhine and Danube 'ambo Boreae Martique sodales' (26. 339). But it is an important consideration on the other side that Horace himself describes a wind as the companion of a season: 'iam veris comites ... / impellunt animae lintea Thraciae' (4. 12. 1 f.). The east wind is naturally associated with cold, and here comes in very naturally after the gusty scene in the third stanza. It would be futile to object that *Euro* is inconsistent with *Thracio vento*; indeed such variety is characteristic of Horace's lyric style.

dedicet might seem at first sight to suit *Hebro*. There is some evidence for the dedication of garlands to rivers and fountains; cf. Str. 6. 2. 9 (on the Eurotas and Alpheius) τῶν ἐπιφημισθέντων στεφάνων ἑκατέρῳ καὶ ἐρριφέντων εἰς τὸ κοινὸν ῥεῦμα ἀναφαίνεται κατὰ τὸν ἐπιφημισμὸν ἑκάτερος ἐν τῷ οἰκείῳ ποταμῷ, Varro, *ling.* 6. 22 'in fontes coronas iaciunt'. Yet as Horace's leaves are withered and his intention derisive, a reference to real religious rites is unnecessary. One should rather see a satire on the convention by which a lover 'dedicated' his garland on his lady's door. Cf. Athen. 670 d στεφανοῦσι δὲ τὰς τῶν ἐρωμένων θύρας ἤτοι τιμῆς χάριν ... ἢ οὐ τοῖς ἐρωμένοις ἀλλὰ τῷ Ἔρωτι ποιούμενοι τὴν τῶν στεφάνων ἀνάθεσιν, Meleager, *anth. P.* 5. 191. 5 ff. ἐπὶ προθύροισι μαράνας / δάκρυσιν ἐκδήσω τοὺς ἱκέτας στεφάνους, / ἐν τόδ' ἐπιγράψας· Κύπρι, σοὶ Μελέαγρος ὁ μύστης / σῶν κώμων στοργῆς σκῦλα τάδ' ἐκρέμασεν, Paul. Silent. ibid. 6. 71. 1 σοὶ τὰ λιποστεφάνων διατίλματα μύρια φύλλων.

It might be urged in favour of *Hebro* that it is picturesque to imagine the garlands floating downstream. Against this Heinze argues with some force that if the Hebrus were covered with ice (as *hiemis sodali* would suggest), the effect would be lost. On the other hand a withered garland might naturally be the sport of the wind; cf. Eur. *Ba.* 350 καὶ στέμματ' ἀνέμοις καὶ θυέλλαισιν μέθες (apparently of woollen fillets), Ov. *epist.* 5. 109 f. 'tu levior foliis tum cum sine pondere suci / mobilibus ventis arida facta volant'. See also Soph. *El.* 435 f. (of κτερίσματα) ἀλλ' ἢ πνοαῖσιν ἢ βαθυσκαφεῖ κόνει / κρύψον νιν (where Jebb comments that the passage is wretchedly enfeebled by the conjecture ῥοαῖσιν). One may further compare the Anthology passage which associates a discarded lover with dry rubbish (above, 19 n.).

Some editors attach importance to Virg. *Aen.* 1. 316 f. 'vel qualis equos Threissa fatigat / Harpalyce volucremque fuga praevertitur Hebrum'; as the Hebrus is a slow river (cf. Servius ad loc.), Rutgers seemed to have some solid reason for proposing *Eurum* (cf. 7. 807 'cursuque pedum praevertere ventos', 8. 223 'ocior Euro', *Thes.l.L.* 5. 2. 1079. 46 ff.). Yet the transmitted text finds striking support

in Sil. 2. 73 ff. 'quales Threiciae . . . cursuque fatigant / Hebrum';
Virgil and Silius, in the manner of Roman poets, could easily have
been indifferent to the finer points of geography. But though the
parallel from Virgil fails, this has no real bearing on the issue here.

26. MVSIS AMICVS

[G. Carlsson, *Eranos* 42, 1944, 7 ff.; M. Treu, *Würzburger Jahrbücher* 4, 1949/50,
219 ff.; Wilkinson 11 ff.]

1–6. *The Muses enable me to live without troubling about remote
foreign affairs. 6–12. Dear Muse, you who love poetry and make my
praises worth something, sing a modern song for my friend Lamia.*

The ode is written for a member of the Aelii Lamiae, a distinguished
family from Formiae, towards the southern border of Latium. Their
rise to fame begins with L. Aelius Lamia, who was relegated for
rallying the *equites* in Cicero's favour at the time of his exile; later he
held the aedileship in 45 B.C. and the praetorship in 42. His son
Lucius was legate of Hispania Citerior in 24 B.C. and defeated the
Astures and Cantabri (Cassiod. ·*chron. min.* 2. 135, cf. Dio 53. 29. 1,
PIR² 1. A 199). A third-generation Lucius was son of the legate;
he became consul in A.D. 3, governor of Africa in A.D. 15–16, and died
an old man in 32 as *praefectus urbi* (Tac. *ann.* 6. 27. 2). The Lamiae
rose high in the first century of the Empire, and Juvenal speaks of
them as the summit of nobility; they paid the penalty of eminence
in the reign of Domitian (Juv. 4. 154, 6. 385).

Horace mentions Lamiae in two other odes (1. 36 and 3. 17) and in
epist. 1. 14. The Lamia of the epistle is described as grieving in-
consolably for his brother; this behaviour suggests a young man, who
might well be the future consul of A.D. 3. The Lamia of 1. 36 is certainly a young man, the contemporary of the gay Numida; he too
could be the consul of A.D. 3, though he might be the brother who
died. Editors commonly assume that our ode is also addressed to one
of these brothers, but Horace's odes in general are written for
principes viri rather than their sons (who figure more prominently
in the epistles). This handsome tribute was probably written for
Lucius the legate, who was more a contemporary of Horace's; the
same is true of 3. 17.

An Alcaic model has been claimed for our ode (M. Treu, loc. cit.).
In Alcaeus 48, line 6 ends with θάλασσαν, 7 with φέρεσθαι (cf. 1 f.
of our poem), 10 f. refer to Babylon and Ascalon (cf. 3 f.), while 17
mentions garlands, presumably real ones (unlike Horace's). Such

scattered words are far too indefinite to prove imitation; certainly the whole movement of the poem is quite alien to Alcaeus. The opening lines about scattering care to the winds could be Alcaic, but they may be simply derived from the *Anacreontea* (2 n.). In any case, Horace's adaptation, with its reference to political cares, is Roman and original.

Commentators make heavy weather about the subject of the poem. When Horace talks of banishing cares, this is not (as some suppose) because Lamia is a melancholic person; rather the man of affairs is being teased for his unrealistic political anxieties, which are contrasted with the carefree happiness of the poet. And in fact poetry is the unifying theme of the ode; it is because he is under the protection of the Muses that Horace is carefree himself, and it is for the same reason that he can honour his friend in verse (thus rightly Wilkinson, loc. cit). Some scholars further suggest that the poem was an early one, when Horace was excited at his invention of the Latin Alcaic; but this may attach too much significance to the metrical abnormalities (pp. xli f.). The anxieties caused by Tiridates seem to be those of 26–25 rather than those of 31–30, when the world had other things to think about. Yet it remains true that Horace is not celebrating his friend so much as his own power to celebrate his friend; contrast the genial and jocular 3. 17, with its cheerful allusions to Lamia's Laestrygonian ancestry. As a result the ode lacks content, in spite of all its elegance. Poetry is not the best subject for poetry, and Horace's greatest odes are not written simply about themselves.

Metre: Alcaic.

1. **Musis amicus:** Horace was beloved by the Muses, and hence confident of their help; cf. Hom. *Od.* 8. 63 τὸν περὶ Μοῦσ' ἐφίλησε, Hes. *th.* 96 f. ὁ δ' ὄλβιος ὅν τινα Μοῦσαι / φίλωνται, Corinna 674 Θέσπια καλλιγένεθλε φιλόξενε μωσοφίλειτε, Ar. *ran.* 229, Call. fr. 1. 37 f. Μοῦσαι γὰρ ὅσους ἴδον ὄθματι παῖδας / μὴ λοξῷ, πολιοὺς οὐκ ἀπέθεντο φίλους, Theoc. 1. 141 τὸν Μοίσαις φίλον ἄνδρα, 11. 6 πεφιλημένον ἔξοχα Μοίσαις, *ep.* 21. 4, Philodemus, *anth. P.* 11. 44. 2 μουσοφιλὴς ἐτάρος, Virg. *Aen.* 9. 774 'amicum Crethea Musis', *Thes.l.L.* 1. 1903. 70 ff. In other passages the poet is described as the squire or attendant of the Muses; cf. Hes. *th.* 100 Μουσάων θεράπων with West's note, Lucr. 3. 1037 'Heliconiadum comites'. *amicus* will also have something of this implication, as if Horace were a favoured client.

In our passage some interpret 'lover of the Muses' (φιλόμουσος); but this is not the natural meaning of *Musis amicus* (cf. *serm.* 2. 3. 123 'dis inimice senex'). Nor does it cohere so well with the prayer formula *sine te.* Elsewhere Horace says 'vestris amicum fontibus et choris' (3. 4. 25); that probably means 'a welcome visitor to your springs' (cf. *epitaph. Bion.* 76 ἀμφότεροι παγαῖς πεφιλημένοι).

tristitiam: Horace thought of poets as serene and happy people; he did not take the view that they learn in suffering what they teach in song. For a more realistic interpretation of the phenomena see Juv. 7. 56 f. '(vatem egregium) anxietate carens animus facit'. Juvenal meant financial worries, but the point could be extended; cf. Archil. 20 (when grieving for his brother-in-law's death) καί μ' οὔτ' ἰάμβων οὔτε τερπωλέων μέλει, Catull. 65. 3 f. 'nec potis est dulcis Musarum expromere fetus / mens animi, tantis fluctuat ipsa malis', 68. 7 f., Ov. *epist.* 15. 14, Sidon. *epist.* 8. 9. 2 'nosti enim probe laetitiam poetarum, quorum sic ingenia maeroribus ut pisciculi retibus amiciuntur; et si quid asperum aut triste, non statim sese poetica teneritudo a vinculo incursi angoris elaqueat'.

2. tradam . . .: cf. *Anacreontea* 36. 13 f. τὸ δ' ἄχος πέφευγε μιχθὲν / ἀνεμοτρόφῳ θυέλλῃ, 48. 4 ff. ὅτ' ἐγὼ πίω τὸν οἶνον, / ἀπορίπτονται μέριμναι / πολυφρόντιδές τε βουλαὶ / ἐς ἁλικτύπους ἀήτας, 57. 9 ff. ἐμῶν φρενῶν μὲν αὔραις / φέρειν ἔδωκα λύπας, / λύραν δ' ἑλὼν ἀείδω / ἐρωτικὰς ἀοιδάς. Of course it is a commonplace to talk of speaking words to the winds; cf. Hom. *Od.* 8. 408 f. ἔπος δ' εἴπερ τι βέβακται / δεινόν, ἄφαρ τὸ φέροιεν ἀναρπάξασαι ἄελλαι, Gow on Theoc. 22. 167, Brandt on Ov. *am.* 1. 4. 11 f., *ars* 1. 388, A. Zingerle, *Ovidius und sein Verhältnis zu den Vorgängern und gleichzeitigen römischen Dichtern*, 1869, pp. 39 ff., Fordyce on Catull. 30. 10, Otto 364 f., *OED* s.v. 'wind' 20e, 25b. For modern instances of flinging care to the winds cf. Ronsard, *A un sien ami, fasché de suivre la court* 6 ff. 'Il vaut mieux que tu jettes Les soigneuses sagettes Qui ton cœur vont grevant, Aux Scythes et aux Gétes, A l'abandon du vent', Milton, *P.L.* 9. 989 'And fear of death deliver to the winds', E. Stemplinger, *Horaz im Urteil der Jahrhunderte*, 1921, p. 15. For various things that are cast to the winds cf. Jebb on Soph. *El.* 435 f.

protervis: the word suggests capricious violence. For similar expressions cf. *epod.* 16. 22 'Notus . . . aut protervus Africus', 17. 34 'iniuriosis . . . ventis', Lucr. 6. 111 'petulantibus Euris' (*auris* codd.), Virg. *Aen.* 1. 536 'procacibus Austris', Ov. *epist.* 11. 14 'Eure proterve'. For Greek parallels cf. Eupolis 320 K. ὥσπερ ἀνέμου 'ξαίφνης ἀσελγοῦς γενομένου, Pollux 1. 111 Εὔπολις δὲ καὶ ἄνεμον ἀσελγῆ εἶπε τὸν βίαιον· εἴη δ' ἂν ὅμοιον καὶ τὸ ὑβριστὴς ἄνεμος (he may be thinking of Hes. *th.* 307, on Typhoeus, δεινόν θ' ὑβριστὴν ἄνεμόν θ', where ὑβριστήν τ' ἄνομόν θ' is the correct reading), Theodoridas, *anth. P.* 7. 738. 2 ὑβριστής τ' ὤλεσε Λὶψ ἄνεμος.

Creticum: the Cretan sea counted as stormy (cf. Soph. *Tr.* 118 f. πολύπονον ὥσπερ πέλαγος / Κρήσιον, and the scholion); thus it is an appropriate home for *protervi venti*. It is also a long way from Rome and Horace; cf. Tib. 1. 5. 35 f. 'quae nunc Eurusque Notusque / iactat odoratos vota per Armenios', Ov. *am.* 2. 8. 19 f. 'animi periuria puri / Carpathium tepidos per mare ferre Notos'.

3. portare: for the infinitive cf. Theoc. 29. 35 αἰ δὲ ταῦτα φέρην ἀνέμοισιν ἐπιτρέπῃς, K.–G. 2. 6, K.–S. 1. 681. *portare* is on the whole avoided by the best prose writers, and might seem to have a colloquial character; yet the poets show no inhibitions about its use (Axelson 30 f.).

quis . . .: cf. 2. 11. 1 f. 'quid bellicosus Cantaber et Scythes / . . . cogitet . . . remittas / quaerere', Theogn. 763 f. πίνωμεν χαρίεντα μετ' ἀλλήλοισι λέγοντες / μηδὲν τὸν Μήδων δειδιότες πόλεμον, Ronsard, *Odes* 5. 17. 56 ff., 'Celuy n'a soucy quel Roy Tyrannise sous sa loy Ou la Perse, ou la Syrie . . .', Milton, *To Cyriack Skinner*, 'Let Euclid rest and Archimedes pause, And what the Swede intend, and what the French', E. Stemplinger, *Horaz im Urteil der Jahrhunderte*, 1921, p. 137. Later Greek poets expressed their quietism by an indifference to scientific speculation; cf. p. 135. A Roman, writing to a man of affairs, professed instead a disregard for the more abstruse aspects of foreign politics.

sub Arcto: 'under the Bear', i.e. in the Far North. Cf. Val. Fl. 5. 317 'Aeeten media regnare sub Arcto', *Thes.l.L.* 2. 471. 45 f.

4. gelidae . . . orae: probably genitive; cf. Luc. 5. 55 'gelidae dominum Rhascypolin orae'. One could in theory see a dative of the agent; yet a genitive helps to bind the sentence together, and the vagueness of *gelidae orae* suits the unknown king (*quis . . . rex*) better than the country threatened. Cotiso of Dacia gave trouble at a date when Parthia was rent by civil war, and the Scythians are said to have helped restore Phraates (above, pp. xxxii f.). In our ignorance of the period we cannot say whom Horace is pointing at, or indeed whether he is thinking of any particular individual.

metuatur: i.e. by Rome and her client states. In such contexts a reference to foreign danger is appropriate; cf. 2. 11. 1 (quoted above, 3 n.), 3. 29. 26 ff. 'urbi sollicitus times / quid Seres et regnata Cyro / Bactra parent Tanaisque discors', 4. 5. 25. It would be wrong to think here of a king frightening his own subjects (cf. 3. 1. 5 f.).

5. quid . . .: Horace is playfully overstating the anxieties of a Roman politician; the ancients did not have news of the latest threat to Cambodia served up on their breakfast tables.

Tiridaten: cf. p. xxxii.

unice . . .: 'supremely indifferent'. The adverb is intensive and does not imply that only Horace is *securus*. It has here a rather casual and colloquial flavour; cf. Cic. *epist.* 6. 1. 6 'quem semper unice dilexisti', 13. 15. 1 'Precilium tibi commendo unice'. *unus* similarly has the sense 'especially'; cf. Shackleton Bailey, *Propertiana*, pp. 171 f.

6. securus: the construction with a dependent question is characteristically Horatian; cf. *serm.* 2. 4. 50 'quali perfundat piscis securus olivo', *epist.* 2. 1. 176 'securus cadat an recto stet fabula talo'. It is imitated by Persius, significantly in an Horatian passage (6. 12 f. 'hic ego securus volgi et quid praeparet Auster / infelix pecori'); cf. also Auson. 363. 4 f. 'quid proceres vanique levis quid opinio vulgi / * * * securus'.

fontibus: water is associated with prophecy, and the Muses' streams appear as early as Hesiod; cf. *th.* 5 f. καί τε λοεσσάμεναι τέρενα χρόα Περμησσοῖο / ἢ Ἵππου κρήνης ἢ Ὀλμειοῦ ζαθέοιο with West's notes. The motif is particularly emphasized by the Alexandrians and their Roman imitators, who introduce various kinds of symbolism (the inspiring draught, the untouched spring, the small fountain contrasted with the sea or the big river). See further M. Ninck, *Die Bedeutung des Wassers im Kult und Leben der Alten, Philologus* Suppl. 14, 1921, pp. 90 ff., Kroll 28 ff., W. Wimmel, *Kallimachos in Rom,* 1960, pp. 222 ff., Kambylis 23 ff., Boucher 185 f., 215 ff., Commager 11 ff.

integris: 'pure', καθαροῖς; cf. Alcaeus, *anth. P.* 7. 55. 5 f. (on Hesiod) τοίην γὰρ καὶ γῆρυν ἀπέπνεεν ἐννέα Μουσέων / ὁ πρέσβυς καθαρῶν γευσάμενος λιβάδων. Yet in our passage Horace is hinting that the Muses like the unhackneyed; the point is made more explicitly in Lucr. 1. 927 ff. (Horace's immediate model) 'iuvat integros accedere fontis / atque haurire, iuvatque novos decerpere flores / insignemque meo capiti petere inde coronam / unde prius nulli velarint tempora Musae', Manil. 2. 53 f. 'integra quaeramus rorantis prata per herbas / undamque occultis meditantem murmur in antris'. The uncontaminated spring is a Callimachean motif; cf. *ep.* 28. 3 f. οὐδ' ἀπὸ κρήνης / πίνω, *h.* 2. 110 ff. Δηοῖ δ' οὐκ ἀπὸ παντὸς ὕδωρ φορέουσι μέλισσαι, / ἀλλ' ἥτις καθαρή τε καὶ ἀχράαντος ἀνέρπει / πίδακος ἐξ ἱερῆς ὀλίγη λιβὰς ἄκρον ἄωτον. For other instances of the theme cf. *serm.* 2. 4. 94 f. 'fontis ut adire remotos / atque haurire queam vitae praecepta beatae', *epist.* 1. 3. 10 f. 'Pindarici fontis qui non expalluit haustus, / fastidire lacus et rivos ausus apertos', Virg. *georg.* 2. 175 'sanctos ausus recludere fontis', Prop. 3. 1. 3 'primus ego ingredior puro de fonte sacerdos', Stat. *Ach.* 1. 9 f. 'da fontis mihi, Phoebe, novos ac fronde secunda / necte comas'.

7. apricos: sometimes applied to people or things that delight in the sun; cf. Ov. *met.* 4. 331 'aprica pendentibus arbore pomis', Serv. *Aen.* 5. 128, *Thes.l.L.* 2. 318. 47 ff.

flores: suggested by Lucretius's flowers (above, 6 n.). Claudian, like Lucretius, made the flowers for his poetic garland grow by the fountain (*carm. min.* 30. 5 ff. 'floribus illis / quos neque frigoribus Boreas nec Sirius urit / aestibus, aeterno sed veris honore rubentes / fons Aganippea Permessius educat unda'); so also Milton, *P.L.* 3. 29 f. 'but chief Thee, Sion, and the flowery brooks beneath', Gray, *Progress of Poesy* 3 ff. 'From Helicon's harmonious springs A thousand rills their mazy progress take; The laughing flowers that round them blow Drink life and fragrance as they flow'. Horace uses the traditional association of the Muses' spring with flowers, but without any picturesque scene-painting or even an explicit connection. For a humorous, though ineffectual, protest at the trite association of flowers and fountains cf. Antiphanes fr. 209. 7 ff. K. οἱ νῦν δὲ κισσόπλεκτα καὶ κρηναῖα καὶ / ἀνθεσιπότατα μέλεα μελέοις ὀνόμασιν / ποιοῦσιν ἐμπλέκοντες ἀλλότρια μέλη.

The garland as a symbol of the encomium is Greek; cf. Sappho 55. 2 f. οὐ γὰρ πεδέχῃς βρόδων / τὼν ἐκ Πιερίας (a passage commonly misinterpreted), Pind. *O.* 6. 86 f. ἀνδράσιν αἰχματαῖσι πλέκων / ποικίλον ὕμνον, 9. 48 f., *N.* 7. 77 ff. εἴρειν στεφάνους ἐλαφρόν· ἀναβάλεο· Μοῖσά τοι / κολλᾷ χρυσὸν ἔν τε λευκὸν ἐλέφανθ' ἁμᾷ / καὶ λείριον ἄνθεμον ποντίας ὑφελοῖσ' ἐέρσας, fr. 179 ὑφαίνω δ' Ἀμυθαονίδαισιν ποικίλον / ἄνδημα, Antip. Sid. *anth. P.* 7. 14. 3 f. Πειθὼ / ἔπλεκ' ἀείζωον Πειρίδων στέφανον, Synes. *hymn.* 1. 8 f. βασιλῆι θεῶν / πλέκομεν στέφανον, C. M. Bowra, *Pindar*, 1964, p. 16.

9. Piplea: 'lady of Pipla'. Πίμπλεια (or Πίμπλα) was a place in Pieria near Mt. Olympus. Pieria was associated with the Muses as early as Hesiod (cf. *op.* 1, *th.* 53 with West's note), and at least from Hellenistic times the name Πίμπλεια was attached to a local fountain ('drink deep or taste not the Pierian spring'). See further *RE* 20. 1387 ff., Roscher 3. 2508 f.

The form of the name in our passage has caused doubt. The omission of the *m* is attested in Greek and regular in Latin; the termination in -*ea* is normal both for the adjectival form and the place-name (cf. Catull. 105. 1 'Pipleum ... montem', Stat. *silv.* 2. 2. 37 'superet Piplea sitim'). But the name for the Muse is usually Πιμπληίς (cf. *RE* 20. 1389, Varro, *ling.* 7. 20 'ita enim ab terrestribus locis aliis cognominatae Libethrides, Pipleides, Thespiades, Heliconides', Mart. 11. 3. 1 'mea ... Pimpleide'; cf. also *carm.* 4. 3. 17 'Pieri'). Hence many editors have followed Heinsius and Bentley in reading *Piplei* here. They claim support from Porphyrio, but his note permits no certain inference ('Piplea dulcis: Pipleides Musae dicuntur a Pipleo fonte Macedoniae'). On the other hand in favour of *Piplea* cf. Hesych. Πιπλίαι· αἱ Μοῦσαι ἐν τῷ Μακεδονικῷ Ὀλύμπῳ ἀπὸ κρήνης

Πιπλείας. Other pieces of evidence have no importance, as they could well be derived from the vulgate text of Horace; cf. ps.-Acro ad loc. 'Pipleae Musae dictae . . . a Pipleo fonte Macedoniae', *CGL* 5. 617. 44 'camena vel piplia est musa'.

dulcis: cf. *epist.* 1. 19. 5 'vina fere dulces oluerunt mane Camenae', Virg. *georg.* 2. 475 'dulces ante omnia Musae', *catal.* 5. 12 'dulces Camenae'.

sine te: cf. especially Pind. *pae.* 7b. 18 ff. τ]υφλα[ὶ γὰ]ρ ἀνδρῶν φρένες, / [ὅ]στις ἄνευθ᾽ Ἑλικωνιάδων / βαθεῖαν ε . . [. .] . ων ἐρευνᾷ σοφίας ὁδόν, Call. fr. 228. 1 ἀγέτω θεός—οὐ γὰρ ἐγὼ δίχα τῶνδ᾽ ἀείδειν. The locution is common in hymns and other religious contexts (see Norden, *Agnostos Theos*, pp. 157 n. 3, 159, 175, 349 f.); cf. 1. 30. 7, Mimnermus 1. 1 τίς δὲ βίος τί δὲ τερπνὸν ἄτερ χρυσῆς Ἀφροδίτης;, Aesch. *supp.* 823 f. τί δ᾽ ἄνευ σέθεν / θνατοῖσι τέλειόν ἐστιν;, *Ag.* 1487 τί γὰρ βροτοῖς ἄνευ Διὸς τελεῖται;, Pind. *N.* 7. 2 f., Ariphron, *PMG* 813. 10, Cleanthes 1. 15 Powell οὐδέ τι γίγνεται ἔργον ἐπὶ χθονὶ σοῦ δίχα, δαῖμον, *Orph. h.* 16. 5, 68. 8, Catull. 61. 61 ff. 'nil potest sine te Venus / . . . commodi capere', Lucr. 1. 22 f. 'nec sine te quicquam dias in luminis oras / exoritur', Stat. *silv.* 1. 4. 19 f. 'quamquam mihi surda sine illo (Phoebo)/plectra', *euang. Ioh.* 1.3 καὶ χωρὶς αὐτοῦ ἐγένετο οὐδὲ ἕν, Prud. *cath.* 3. 11, Ven. Fort. *carm.* 3. 9. 72, Book of Common Prayer, Collect for the nineteenth Sunday after Trinity, 'O God, for as much as without thee we are not able to please thee'.

Virgil addresses similar flattery not to the Muse but to Maecenas (*georg.* 3. 42 'te sine nil altum mens incohat'). So Stat. *silv.* 4. 7. 21 (to Vibius Maximus) 'torpor est nostris sine te Camenis'.

mei . . . honores: 'praises bestowed by me'. Cf. Pind. *N.* 9. 10 ἐπασκήσω κλυταῖς ἥρωα τιμαῖς, *I.* 1. 34 γαρύσομαι τοῦδ᾽ ἀνδρὸς ἐν τιμαῖσιν ἀγακλέα τὰν Ἀσωποδώρου πατρὸς αἶσαν, 2. 34 εἴ τις εὐδόξων ἐς ἀνδρῶν ἄγοι τιμὰς Ἑλικωνιάδων, *paneg. Mess.* 192 'nec solum tibi Pierii tribuentur honores', 1. 1. 8 n.

10. prosunt: the variant *possunt* (mentioned with approval by Lambinus and read by Bentley) deserves the most serious consideration. It has little authority, being found in the lemma of the scholion in A and in a few inferior manuscripts; the attached note is inconclusive —'hoc ait quia sine Musa non multum honoris vult intellegi Lamiae carmina sua posse conferre'. Yet *possunt* suits precisely the religious formula *sine te*; cf. Catull. 61. 61 ff. (cited on 9 above), Prop. 2. 30. 40 'nam sine te nostrum non valet ingenium' (Propertius is treating Cynthia as a Tenth Muse). If *possunt* had respectable manuscript support, one would prefer it without hesitation.

novis: the boast of novelty is found also in the Greek poets; cf. Hom. *Od.* 1. 351 f. τὴν γὰρ ἀοιδὴν μᾶλλον ἐπικλείουσ᾽ ἄνθρωποι, / ἥ τις

ἀκουόντεσσι νεωτάτη ἀμφιπέληται, Alcman 4. 1. 5 f. γαρύματα μαλσακὰ
[– – –] | νεόχμ' ἔδειξαν, 14 (a). 2 f. μέλος | νεοχμὸν ἄρχε παρσένοις
ἀείδην, Pind. O. 9. 48 f. αἴνει δὲ παλαιὸν μὲν οἶνον, ἄνθεα δ' ὕμνων |
νεωτέρων, Timotheus 791. 202 f. ἀλλ' ὦ χρυσεοκίθαριν ἀέ/ξων μοῦσαν
νεοτευχῆ, 791. 211 ff., 796. 1 f. οὐκ ἀείδω τὰ παλαιά. | καινὰ γὰρ ἀμὰ
κρείσσω, anon. PMG 851(b) σοί, Βάκχε, τάνδε Μοῦσαν ἀγλαΐζομεν, | . . .
καινὰν ἀπαρθένευτον, οὔ τι ταῖς πάρος | κεχρημέναν ᾠδαῖσιν, ἀλλ' ἀκήρα-
τον | κατάρχομεν τὸν ὕμνον, 1027(a) νεόχυτα μέλεα. The motif was
a favourite with the Alexandrians, and is strongly suggested by
Callimachus in the prologue to the *Aetia* and elsewhere; cf. also
Nossis, *anth. P.* 7. 414. 3 f. ἀλλὰ Φλυάκων | ἐκ τραγικῶν ἴδιον κισσὸν
ἐδρεψάμεθα, Opp. *cyn.* 1. 20 f. τρηχεῖαν ἐπιστείβωμεν ἀταρπὸν | τὴν
μερόπων οὔπω τις ἐῇς ἐπάτησεν ἀοιδαῖς.

The Roman poets repeatedly make the same claim; cf. the passages
from Lucretius, Virgil, and Propertius quoted above on *integris*.
Add Lucr. 1. 117 f. 'Ennius . . . primus amoeno / detulit ex Helicone
perenni fronde coronam', 4. 1 ff., 5. 336 f. 'hanc (rerum naturam)
primus cum primis ipse repertus / nunc ego sum in patrias qui possim
vertere voces', Virg. *ecl.* 3. 86 'Pollio et ipse facit nova carmina',
6. 1 f. 'prima Syracosio dignata est ludere versu / nostra . . . Thalia',
georg. 3. 10 f. 'primus ego in patriam mecum, modo vita supersit, /
Aonio rediens deducam vertice Musas', 3. 292 f. 'iuvat ire iugis, qua
nulla priorum / Castaliam molli devertitur orbita clivo', Hor. *carm.*
3. 1. 2 f., 3. 25. 8, 3. 30. 13 f. 'princeps Aeolium carmen ad Italos / de-
duxisse modos', *epist.* 1. 19. 21 ff. 'libera per vacuum posui vestigia
princeps. / . . . Parios ego primus iambos / ostendi Latio', Manil. 1. 6
'nulli memorata priorum', 3. 1 ff., *Aetna* 7 f.

These claims mean different things; the didactic poets boast of
novelty in subject-matter, the others of introducing new genres or
metres to Latin literature. In the latter case the boast of originality
is often conjoined, to our sense oddly, with an epithet or phrase
referring to a Greek original; so here Horace claims both novelty
and the plectrum of Alcaeus. See further Kroll 12 ff., Wimmel
op. cit. [above, 6 *fontibus*], pp. 94 ff., 109 ff., Kambylis 155 ff., Newman 341 ff. For later developments of the theme cf. Ariosto, *Orlando
Furioso* 1. 2 'Cosa non detta in prosa mai ne in rima', Milton, *P.L.*
1. 16 'Things unattempted yet in prose or rhyme', Curtius 86.

11. sacrare: 'hallow'; cf. Ov. *Pont.* 4. 8. 63 f. 'et modo, Caesar, avum,
quem virtus addidit astris, / sacrarunt aliqua carmina parte tuum',
Stat. *silv.* 4. 7. 7 f. 'si tuas cantu Latio sacravi, / Pindare, Thebas'.
The term is vague and grandiose, and may include the notion of
conferring immortality by song; cf. *Thes.l.L.* 4. 384. 43 ff. (especially
70 ff.) for a similar use of *consecrare*.

12. **decet:** perhaps Horace's friend was himself a poet; cf. ps.-Acro on *ars* 288 'praetextas et togatas scripserunt Aelius Lamia, Antonius Rufus, Cn. Melissus, Afranius, Pomponius'.

27. NATIS IN VSVM

[Fraenkel 179 ff.; Pasquali 504 ff.]

1–8. *Cups are for drinking from, not fighting with; check your barbarous brawling and lie down quietly.* 9–12. *Do you want me to join in the drinking? Then let Megylla's brother tell us who he is in love with.* 13–18. *Don't you want to? I shan't drink otherwise. Your love is sure to be respectable. Tell me your secret; I shan't divulge it.* 18–24. *Heavens! what a monster! Unhappy boy, no magic will free you from her bondage.*

Porphyrio comments 'protreptice ode est haec ad hilaritatem (an odd remark), cuius sensus sumptus est ab Anacreonte ex libro tertio'. There is no need to assume that the resemblance was close or sustained. Porphyrio seems to be alluding to the surviving fragment 356(*b*), together with its immediate context:

> ἄγε δηῦτε μηκέθ' οὕτω
> πατάγῳ τε κἀλαλητῷ
> Σκυθικὴν πόσιν παρ' οἴνῳ
> μελετῶμεν, ἀλλὰ καλοῖς
> ὑποπίνοντες ἐν ὕμνοις.

Anacreon is apparently, like Horace, describing a developing situation; in the first place he called for drink (ἄγε δὴ φέρ' ἡμίν, ὦ παῖ, / κελέβην), but in the fragment cited the carousal has gone further than he intended. It may also be significant that Anacreon somewhere used the word ἀκινάκης for a dagger (5 n.).

After the second stanza Horace's ode veers characteristically from Persian daggers to Megylla's brother. Now we have left Anacreon far behind, and find ourselves in the intimate, playful world of comedy, epigram, and elegy, where ingenuous youths are inextricably ensnared by dangerous courtesans. For the atmosphere one may compare the idyll of Theocritus where the drinkers are invited to toast their loves (14. 18 ff.):

> ἤδη δὲ προιόντος ἔδοξ' ἐπιχεῖσθαι ἄκρατον
> ὧτινος ἤθελ' ἕκαστος· ἔδει μόνον ὧτινος εἰπεῖν.
> ἁμὲς μὲν φωνεῦντες ἐπίνομες, ὡς ἐδέδοκτο·
> ἁ δ' οὐδὲν παρεόντος ἐμεῦ. τίν' ἔχειν με δοκεῖς νῶν;

And Callimachus indulges in embarrassing speculations about the
emotional life of a party-goer (*ep.* 43):

> ἕλκος ἔχων ὁ ξεῖνος ἐλάνθανεν· ὡς ἀνιηρὸν
> πνεῦμα διὰ στηθέων (εἶδες;) ἀνηγάγετο,
> τὸ τρίτον ἡνίκ' ἔπινε, τὰ δὲ ῥόδα φυλλοβολεῦντα
> τὠνδρὸς ἀπὸ στεφάνων πάντ' ἐγένοντο χαμαί·
> ὤπτηται μέγα δή τι· μὰ δαίμονας οὐκ ἀπὸ ῥυσμοῦ
> εἰκάζω, φωρὸς δ' ἴχνια φὼρ ἔμαθον.

For a similar inquisitiveness in a Latin poet cf. Catull. 6 [17 n.].

The two parts of the poem are ingeniously linked and filled out:
Horace seems to take a hint from Anacreon in describing a changing
situation and his own reaction to it. For a simpler form of the same
technique in early Greek poetry cf. A. L. Wheeler, *AJPh* 51, 1930,
217 ff. (on the *epithalamium*), P. von der Mühll, *Hermes* 75, 1940,
422 ff. (who is wrong to exclude Anacreon; cf. Fraenkel 179 n. 2).
The Hellenistic poets took over the 'running commentary' on a
sacral scene; see, for instance, the opening of the second hymn of
Callimachus, where Apollo's gradual approach is described. But they
also sometimes use a similar technique in representing a scene from
everyday life. Sometimes too a rapid series of stage directions has
to be inferred, including even the words of the person addressed;
we seem to be looking at a one-man act or overhearing a telephone
conversation. See Theoc. 15. 29 ff.:

> κινεῦ δή· φέρε θᾶσσον ὕδωρ. ὕδατος πρότερον δεῖ,
> ἃ δὲ σμᾶμα φέρει. δὸς ὅμως· μὴ δὴ πολύ, λᾳστρί.
> ἔγχει ὕδωρ. δύστανε, τί μευ τὸ χιτώνιον ἄρδεις;

For another instance of this device cf. Asclepiades, *anth. P.* 5. 181. 1 ff.
(a master sends his slave to do some shopping and inspects the bill):

> τῶν †καρίων† ἡμῖν λαβὲ †κώλακας† · ἀλλά ποθ' ἥξει;
> καὶ πέντε στεφάνους τῶν ῥοδίνων. τί τὸ πάξ;
> οὐ φῂς κέρματ' ἔχειν; διολώλαμεν. οὐ τροχιεῖ τις
> τὸν Λαπίθην; λῃστήν, οὐ θεράποντ', ἔχομεν.
> οὐκ ἀδικεῖς οὐδέν; φέρε τὸν λόγον. ἐλθὲ λαβοῦσα,
> Φρύνη, τὰς ψήφους. ὦ μεγάλου κινάδους.

See further Meleager, *anth. P.* 5. 182, 184, Gow–Page 2. 132, P.
Pöstgens, *Tibulls Ambarvalgedicht, Kieler Arb. zu klass. Philol.*,
1940, 80 ff., Boucher 361 ff., F. R. B. Godolphin, *AJPh* 55, 1934, 62 ff.

The technique was taken over by the Latin poets, though nowhere
so strikingly as in our ode. Sometimes we are given a commentary
on a public ceremony (Catull. 61 on the marriage of Torquatus,
Tib. 2. 1 on the Ambarvalia), once on the aftermath of a battle

(Hor. *epod.* 9) ; sometimes we hear a developing series of instructions (Catull. 42 to the *hendecasyllabi*, Hor. *carm.* 3. 19 and 3. 28 giving directions for a party) ; sometimes we have to infer an intervention by the person addressed (as at Prop. 1. 15. 25). One may compare especially Horace's own seventh epode, where the poet tries to restrain a gathering of citizens intent on war (13 ff.) :

> furorne caecus an rapit vis acrior
> an culpa? responsum date.
> tacent et albus ora pallor inficit
> mentesque perculsae stupent.

Perhaps the best English parallels are to be found in Browning's monologues; cf. *Mr. Sludge, the Medium*:

> 'Get up?'
> You still inflict on me that terrible face?
> You show no mercy? . . .
> You'll tell? Go tell then! who the devil cares
> What such a rowdy chooses to . . . Aie-aie-aie!
> Please, sir! your thumbs are through my windpipe, sir!

Our ode is one of the cleverest that Horace ever wrote. The two parts of the monologue, despite their different provenance, are harmonized without strain. The movement of the poem is conversational, but this is belied by the amusingly high-flown diction; such phrases as *cessat voluntas*, as well as the opening γνώμη, are far removed from the limpid simplicities of Anacreon. In his lively transitions and heightened colloquialisms Horace is rather imitating Callimachus, who had more influence on his style than is always realized. The cross-examination of the unfortunate youth offends insular standards of manners, but this view would not be shared in all modern countries, and certainly not in the ancient world. It is true that the poet deploys his mastery of technique on a theme that means nothing much either to him or to us. But within its chosen limits, this amusing and original poem is completely successful.

Metre : Alcaic.

1. **natis**: 'made for', 'meant for'. This pompous expression is most naturally used of people; cf. Pl. *epist.* 9. 358 a ἕκαστος ἡμῶν οὐχ αὑτῷ μόνον γέγονεν, Cic. *fin.* 2. 45 'non sibi se soli natum meminerit sed patriae, sed suis' (see Reid ad loc., Gudeman on Tac. *dial.* 5. 5). So of animals Chrysipp. 2. 332. 30 f. von A. οὐ δι' ἄλλο τι πλὴν θύεσθαι ἐγεγόνει (the hog), Sen. *epist.* 84. 4, Juv. 1. 141 'animal propter convivia natum' (see Mayor's note). But the usage is sometimes extended to things; cf. Cic. *Brut.* 283 '(foro) nata eloquentia est', Prop. 2. 22. 4

'exitio nata theatra meo'. The word is naturally used by Cicero to suggest a teleological view of the universe (*nat. deor.* 2. 159 'cervices ... (boum) natae ad iugum'); Pease compares Pangloss in Voltaire, *Candide,* c. 1 'les nez ont été faits pour porter des lunettes'.

in usum laetitiae: the phrase helps the grandiloquent tone of the γνώμη, as *laetitia* seems half personified, like Εὐφροσύνη; cups are for her use, not that of the war-god.

scyphis: ablative of instrument. *scyphi* were large two-handled cups without a stem (cf. *epod.* 9. 33, Athen. 498 a–500 c, D.–S. 4. 1159 ff.); they varied considerably in size, and not all were as big as Trimalchio's, which held three gallons (Petron. 52. 1). The *scyphus* belonged particularly to Hercules, and was said to have been the death of Alexander (cf. Sen. *epist.* 83. 23 'Alexandrum ... intemperantia bibendi et ille Herculaneus ac fatalis scyphus condidit').

For cups used as weapons in drunken brawls cf. Prop. 3. 8. 4, Plin. *nat.* 14. 147 'Tergilla Ciceronem M. f. binos congios simul haurire solitum ipsi obicit, Marcoque Agrippae a temulento scyphum impactum', Lucian, *Hermotimus* 12, Athen. 482 c, Macedonius, *anth. P.* 11. 59. 2 ἔργα κυπελλομάχου στήσομεν εἰλαπίνης. Such behaviour was particularly associated with the battle of the Lapiths and Centaurs; cf. Virg. *georg.* 2. 457, Ov. *met.* 12. 242 f., Mart. 8. 6. 7, Lucian, *symp.* 44 f.; a Lapith is shown on a Parthenon metope wielding a cup.

2. Thracum: the Thracians, like other Northern barbarians, were associated with heavy drinking (Pl. *leg.* 637 d, Athen. 442 f πάντες οἱ Θρᾷκες πολυπόται, 1. 36. 14 n.). Xenophon gives an amusing account of a Thracian symposium at which toasts were drunk from large horns; even the author ὑποπεπωκὼς ἐτύγχανεν (*anab.* 7. 3. 21–33). Ammianus comments on the turbulent drinking bouts of the Thracian Odrysae 'ipsi inter epulas post cibi satietatem et potus suis velut alienis corporibus imprimerent ferrum' (27. 4. 9). For bibliography see *RE* 6 A. 402.

3. verecundum: for this picture of the wine-god cf. 1. 18. 7 f., Alexis fr. 284 K. ὁ γὰρ διμάτωρ Βρόμιος οὐ χαίρει συνὼν / ἀνδράσι πονηροῖς οὐδ' ἀπαιδεύτῳ βίῳ. A different situation earns Bacchus the opposite epithet in *epod.* 11. 13.

4. prohibete: 'defend from'; cf. *epist.* 1. 1. 31 'corpus prohibere cheragra'.

5. vino . . .: it is a commonplace that the symposium should be peaceful; cf. 3. 8. 15 f., Theogn. 493 f. ὑμεῖς δ' εὖ μυθεῖσθε παρὰ κρητῆρι μένοντες, / ἀλλήλων ἔριδας δὴν ἀπερυκόμενοι, Phocylides 14 χρὴ δ' ἐν συμποσίῳ κυλίκων περινισσομενάων / ἡδέα κωτίλλοντα καθήμενον οἰνοποτάζειν, Bacch. 14. 12 ff. οὔτ' ἐν βαρυπενθέσιν ἁρμό/ζει μάχαις φόρμιγγος

ὀμφὰ / καὶ λιγυκλαγγεῖς χοροί, / οὔτ᾽ ἐν θαλίαις καναχὰ / χαλκόκτυπος,
Dionysius Chalcus (fifth century) 2. 3 κυλίκων ἔριδας διαλύσατε,
Cratin. jun. fr. 4 K. πίνειν μένοντα τὸν καλῶς εὐδαίμονα / πρέπει· μάχαι
δ᾽ ἄλλοισι καὶ πόνοι μέλοι, Anacreontea 40. 13 στυγέω μάχας παροίνους.
Xenophanes went so far as to ban songs about the battles of the
Titans, Giants, and Centaurs (1. 21 ff.).

lucernis: lamplight can stand for the symposium because respectable Romans did not drink *de die* or work after dark; cf. Cic. *Cael.* 67
'lux denique longe alia est solis, alia lychnorum' (Austin translates
'candlelight'), Blümner 135 ff.

Medus acinaces: the *acinaces* was a long straight dagger used by
the Persians and Scyths (for illustrations see D.–S. 1. 31 f.). Norden
suggests that it was mentioned by Anacreon (*Agnostos Theos*,
p. 163 n. 1); this is supported by a one-word fragment that he does
not cite, τὠκινάκη (Anacreon 465). Saglio assumes that Romans wore
this outlandish weapon to parties, Heinze that the *acinaces* was
a trophy hung on the dining-room wall. Such seriousness about
Realien mistakes Horace's purpose. In fact his exotic and recherché
expression reinforces *Thracum* and *barbarum*; he is not describing
a scene from real life.

For the use of daggers at an Eastern party cf. *1 Esdras* 3. 21 καὶ
οὐ μέμνηται (ὁ οἶνος) ὅταν πίνωσιν φιλιάζειν φίλοις καὶ ἀδελφοῖς, καὶ
μετ᾽ οὐ πολὺ σπῶνται μαχαίρας.

6. immane quantum: ὑπερφυὲς ὅσον. For his comic hyperbole Horace
uses a grecism of the historians, not elsewhere found in poetry; cf.
Sall. *hist.* 2. 44 'immane quantum animi exarsere', *Thes.l.L.* 7. 1.
441. 54 ff., K.–S. 1. 13 f., H.–Sz. 537.

7. sodales: intimate friends (ἑταῖροι), especially sympotic ones. The
word suggests membership of a club, here a drinking club.

8. cubito . . .: at formal dinner-parties the men of antiquity re-
clined, resting on their left elbows; cf. *serm.* 2. 4. 39, Petron. 27. 4
'hic est, inquit, apud quem cubitum ponitis', Ach. Tat. 1. 5. 3,
Lucian, *Lexiph.* 6, Alciphron 3. 29 (65) where Πηξάγκωνος is the name
of a parasite. So Lucius while still a donkey is taught table manners:
'et primum me quidem mensam (?) accumbere suffixo cubito . . .
perdocuit' (Apul. *met.* 10. 17. 3).

9. severi: genitive. For dry Falernian cf. Plin. *nat.* 14. 63 'tria eius
genera, austerum, dulce, tenue', Athen. 26 c εἴδη δ᾽ αὐτοῦ δύο, ὁ
αὐστηρὸς καὶ ὁ γλυκάζων, Galen 10. 832 K., 14. 19 f., 267 f. Here
Horace, with a poet's originality, represents the Greek αὐστηρός not
by the conventional *austerus*, but by the calque *severus*; this properly translates αὐστηρός in its metaphorical senses, but not in its

primary sense of 'dry' (so at 3. 21. 8 *languidiora* represents μαλακώ-
τερα; cf. 1. 7. 19 n.). Horace is being deliberately paradoxical as the
word is often used of water-drinkers; cf. *epist.* 1. 19. 9, Catull. 27.
5 ff. 'at vos quo lubet hinc abite, lymphae, / vini pernicies, et ad
severos / migrate'. Perhaps 'austere' gives the right note in English;
the mannered diction would be understood only by the learned.

10. **dicat**: speculations about the loves of guests were a regular feature
of the symposium (cf. pp. 309 f.). Here Horace, like Alcibiades in the
Symposium, usurps the function of the συμποσίαρχος, who can make
people reveal such secrets, if necessary under the penalty of a for-
feit; cf. 1. 4. 18 n.

Opuntiae: for the geographical epithet cf. 2. 5. 20 'Cnidiusve Gyges',
3. 9. 9 'Thressa Chloe', 14 'Thurini Calais filius Ornyti', 3. 12. 6
'Liparaei nitor Hebri', Alciphron 3. 12(48). 3 τὸ ἐκ Κεραμεικοῦ πορνί-
διον, ἡ μέτοικος ἡ Φενεᾶτις, 3. 26(62). 2 μοιχὸς πολιορκεῖ τὴν οἰκίαν, ὁ
Ἠλεῖος νεανίσκος. But though natural in Hellenistic literature, the
specification here removes the characters from the real world of
Roman society. Moreover, in the context of the symposium Megylla
must be an *hetaera*, and an elegant young Roman would not care
to know her brother.

11. **Megyllae**: some *deteriores* have the spelling *Megillae*; both ter-
minations are found in nicknames (cf. Schwyzer 1. 485, A. Fick and
F. Bechtel, *Die griechischen Personennamen*, 1894, p. 198). Μέγιλλα
occurs in Lucian, *dial. mer.* 5. 1, Μέγυλλος quite often (cf. Pape–
Benseler 879), while Μέγυλλος is attested as a Megarian name (*IG* 7.
12, 13, 27, 29).

beatus . . . pereat: both words are felt with both clauses. For the
sentimental oxymoron cf. Tib. 2. 5. 109 f. 'iaceo cum saucius annum, /
et faveo morbo, cum iuvat ipse dolor', Apul. *met.* 4. 31. 1 'per tuae
sagittae dulcia vulnera'; Plut. *quaest. conv.* 681 b τὸ διὰ τῶν ὀμμάτων
ἐκπῖπτον . . . τοὺς ἐρῶντας ἐκτήκει καὶ ἀπόλλυσι μεθ᾽ ἡδονῆς ἀλγηδόνι
μεμιγμένης.

13. **cessat voluntas?**: the question is addressed to the young man,
not, as Heinze would have it, to the company at large. The phrase is
pretentious and stylized; such words did not pass human lips at a
real symposium (cf. Val. Max. 5. 2. 2 'ne patriae grata voluntas
cessasse videretur', Stat. *Theb.* 4. 690 'cesset ni vestra voluntas').

14. **Venus**: perhaps 'lady-love' (1. 33. 13 n.); for *domare* applied to
the girl cf. Prop. 1. 9. 6 'dicere quos iuvenes quaeque puella domet'.
domare is more normally used of love or Aphrodite; cf. Hom. *Il.*
14. 198 f., Sappho 102. 2 πόθῳ δάμεισα παῖδος βραδίναν δι᾽ Ἀφροδίταν,
Archil. 118 δάμναται πόθος. But here a reference to the girl seems more

direct and natural, as well as agreeing better with *quaecumque*; it is her name that is uncertain and that Horace wants to know.

15. non erubescendis . . .: cf. Ov. *epist.* 4. 33 f. 'at bene successit, digno quod adurimur igni. / peius adulterio turpis adulter obest'.

16. ingenuo: 'honourable'; there were degrees of respectability among *hetaerae*. Horace is not necessarily suggesting that the girl is 'free-born', that is, better than a *libertina. ingenuo* must be more general in sense, to balance *non erubescendis*.

semper: this may mark a climax, 'this love of yours is respectable, as indeed all your loves are'. Yet a reference to other loves seems slightly irrelevant. This leads one to suspect that *semper* here means not 'always', but 'at all events'. Lejay supposed a similar use of *usque* at *serm.* 2. 1. 75 ff. 'tamen me / cum magnis vixisse invita fatebitur usque / invidia'. 'Toujours' is similarly used, and so sometimes 'always' ('if there is no bus, you can always walk').

17. peccas: literally 'stumble'; the word suggests naughtiness rather than sin. Cf. 1. 33. 9, *serm.* 1. 2. 62 f., Chariton 1. 2. 6 ὁ Χαιρέας νεωτερικῶν ἁμαρτημάτων οὐκ ἄπειρος, Enk on Prop. 2. 6. 40, R. Pichon, *De sermone amatorio apud Latinos elegiarum scriptores*, 1902, p. 228.

quicquid habes: εἴ τι ἔχεις; cf. in a similar context Catull. 6. 15 f. 'quare quicquid habes boni malique / dic nobis'.

18. depone: 'entrust'; cf. *serm.* 2. 6. 46 'et quae rimosa bene deponuntur in aure', 1. 3. 5 n.

tutis: cf. Enn. *ann.* 240 f. '(cui) cuncta malaque et bona dictu / evomeret si qui vellet tutoque locaret'.

a miser!: *a* is very rare in Horace and shows an affectation of strong emotion. Here he is thinking of the Greek ἆ δειλέ, found in Homer and Hellenistic poets (cf. Gow on Theoc. *ep.* 6. 1).

19. laborabas: 'you have been involved all the time'. The imperfect is here used to express realization of the nature of the case, like the Greek imperfect with ἄρα (cf. Denniston 35 f., K.–G. 1. 146, Fraenkel 324 n. 3).

Charybdi: Charybdis was commonly used by the orators and poets as a symbol of rapacity. In particular the image was applied to *hetaerae*. See especially a striking passage by Anaxilas (fr. 22. 8 ff. K.), which also includes the Chimaera : ἔστι δὲ σκοπεῖν ἀπ' ἀρχῆς πρῶτα μὲν τὴν Πλαγγόνα, / ἥτις ὥσπερ ἡ Χίμαιρα πυρπολεῖ τοὺς βαρβάρους. / . . . πάντα τὰ σκεύη γὰρ ἕλκων ᾤχετ' ἐκ τῆς οἰκίας. / . . . ἡ δὲ Φρύνη τὴν Χάρυβδιν οὐχὶ πόρρω που ποιεῖ, / τόν τε ναύκληρον λαβοῦσα καταπέπωκ' αὐτῷ σκάφει; So also Alciphron 1. 6. 2 ἄλλος ἄλλο δῶρον ἀποφέρει· ἡ δὲ εἰσδέχεται καὶ ἀναλοῖ Χαρύβδεως δίκην, Sidon. *epist.* 9. 6. 2

'sumptuositas domesticae Charybdis'; cf. Otto 82, *Thes.l.L.* Onom.
2. 384. 14 ff., Pape–Benseler 1675, F. Leo, *Plautinische Forschungen*,
ed. 2, 1912, p. 150. For other such names cf. E. K. Borthwick, *CR*
N.S. 17, 1967, 250 ff.
    Erotic writers also use Charybdis to typify an overwhelming power
of attraction; cf. Plaut. *Bacch.* 470 f. 'meretricem indigne deperit . . .
acerrume aestuosam: absorbet ubi quemque attigit', Philost. *epist.*
50(49) ἕλκεις με ἀπὸ τῶν ὀμμάτων καὶ σύρεις μὴ θέλοντα, ὥσπερ τοὺς
πλέοντας ἡ Χάρυβδις ἀνερρόφει . . .

20. flamma: cf. Prop. 2. 34. 86 'Varro Leucadiae maxima flamma
suae', *carm. poet. min.* 3. 18. 320 'venisti, mea flamma, Paris', Prior
'But Chloe is my real flame'. Our passage is presumably the source
of the English usage, serious in the eighteenth century, jocular in
Victorian times.

21. quae saga . . .: love-magic was a popular theme in ancient
poetry; one may recall particularly the second idyll of Theocritus
and Virgil's eighth eclogue, Dido's rites in *Aeneid* 4, and the
poems of the elegists (Prop. 4. 5, Ov. *am.* 1. 8). A fragment of a mime
of Sophron (*GLP* 73) shows that magic was already a theme for
literature in the fifth century, but its main expansion came later,
in poetry as in life; cf. Dodds 194 f., 204 ff.
    For spells to loose from love cf. *epod.* 5. 71 f., Tib. 1. 2. 59 f., Plin.
nat. 28. 262. The poets in general reject the idea that love can be
cured by magic (cf. Gow on Theoc. 11. 1). Ovid especially is sceptical
of the claims both of aphrodisiac and anaphrodisiac magic; cf. *ars*
2. 99 ff. 'fallitur Haemonias siquis decurrit ad artes. / . . . ut ameris,
amabilis esto', *rem.* 248 ff., 289 f.
    Thessalis: Thessaly was the land of potent herbs (*venenis*; cf.
Bömer on Ov. *fast.* 5. 401) and of witches' magic; cf. Ar. *nub.* 749 f.,
Pl. *Gorg.* 513 a with Dodds's note, Plaut. *Amph.* 1043 'ego pol illum
ulciscar hodie Thessalum veneficum', Plin. *nat.* 30. 6 'quando trans-
isset (ars magica) ad Thessalas matres, quarum cognomen diu opti-
nuit in nostro orbe', Kroll 164, Gow–Page 2. 577. This is the scene
of Lucan's sixth book, where Sextus Pompeius consults the witches,
and of most of Apuleius's *Metamorphoses* (cf. 2. 1. 2 'reputansque me
media Thessaliae loca tenere, qua artis magicae nativa cantamina
totius orbis consono ore celebrentur'). Strictly speaking *Thessalis* is
inconsistent with *magus*, which suggests a Persian wizard; for a
similar conflation cf. *epod.* 5. 42 ff. 'Ariminensem Foliam / . . . quae
sidera excantata voce Thessala / lunamque caelo deripit', Prud.
perist. 10. 868 ff. 'quousque tandem summus hic nobis magus /
inludet, inquit, Thessalorum carmine / poenam peritus vertere in
ludibrium?'

deus: for the hyperbolical climax cf. Lucian, *asin.* 6 θεραπεῦσαι δέ σε οὐδεὶς ἀλλ᾽ οὐδὲ θεὸς ἰατρός, Chariton 4. 4. 4 τίς σε θεῶν δυνήσεται σῶσαι;

23. illigatum: the serpentine tail of the Chimaera constricted its victim; cf. Lucian, *Menipp.* 43 μικροῦ δεῖν τῇ Χιμαίρᾳ προσδεθέντα παρέλυσε τῆς καταδίκης. For a close parallel to our passage cf. anon. *anth. P.* 11. 52 παιδείῳ, Θρασύβουλε, σαγηνευθεὶς ὑπ᾽ ἔρωτι | ἀσθμαίνεις, δελφὶς ὥς τις ἐπ᾽ αἰγιαλοῦ | κύματος ἱμείρων· δρέπανον δέ σοι οὐδὲ τὸ Περσέως | ἀρκεῖ ἀποτμῆξαι δίκτυον ᾧ δέδεσαι. Add Ter. *hec.* 297.

24. Chimaera: the Chimaera was part lion, part snake, and part goat; cf. Hom. *Il.* 6. 181, Lucr. 5. 905. It was killed by Bellerophon, mounted on the winged horse Pegasus.

The myth is particularly pointed here as the name was applied to *hetaerae*. Cf. Anaxilas (19 n.), *schol. Town.* on *Il.* 6. 181 οἱ δὲ πανδοκεῖς εἶναι λέγουσι ⟨Λέοντα⟩ καὶ Δράκοντα καλουμένους, μέσην δὲ αὐτῶν πανδοκευτρίαν Χίμαιραν, ἢ τοὺς παριόντας ᾗψε μεληδὸν καὶ τοῖς ἄλλοις παρεῖχε παρατιθέναι, Athen. 583 e. A Christian author who had read his Horace used the allegory in warning a young man not to marry; cf. Valer. *ad Rufin.* 2 (= 30. 255 Migne) 'chimaeram nescis esse miser quod petis, et scire debes quod triforme monstrum illud insignis venustetur facie leonis, olentis maculetur ventre capri, anguis insidietur cauda virulentae'.

28. TE MARIS ET TERRAE

[P. H. Callahan and H. Musurillo, *CPh* 59, 1964, 262 ff.; Lattimore, op. cit.; W. J. Oates, *The influence of Simonides of Ceos upon Horace*, Diss. Princeton, 1932; T. Sinko, *Eos* 31, 1928, 41 ff.; B. G. Weiske, *Jahns Jahrb.* 12. 1, 1830, 349 ff.; Wilamowitz, *Kleine Schriften* 2, 1941, pp. 249 ff. (= *De tribus carminibus Latinis*, Göttingen, 1893, pp. 3 ff.); Wilkinson 109 ff.]

1–6. *Though your mind ranged the universe, Archytas, you are confined in a narrow tomb on the Matine shore.* 7–16. *Even men privileged by the gods died in the end, such as your teacher Pythagoras.* 17–20. *Some die in war, some in shipwreck, but none escapes.* 21–36. *I am no exception; I was drowned at sea. Throw sand on my corpse, passer-by. If you do, may you grow rich; if not, perhaps you will suffer the same fate yourself.*

This poem is a monologue (Weiske, loc. cit.), spoken by the corpse of a drowned man. First the dead man apostrophizes the great Pythagorean, Archytas of Tarentum (1 n.), as he lies buried in his grave. Then at 23 he turns to a passing *nauta* and asks for burial himself. The structure of the poem causes perplexity because we do not know till 21 that the speaker is not Horace but a corpse.

Some scholars have wrongly supposed that the ode is a dialogue. On this theory 1–20 (or less plausibly 1–16) are spoken by a passing *nauta* to the corpse of Archytas; in 21–36 Archytas asks the *nauta* for burial. This view has some attractions: the characters are reduced from three to two, and it is a piquant idea that Archytas, who counted the sand (1), should ask for sand-burial (23). However, the first sentence of the ode rules out this interpretation; when the speaker says 'a little dust confines you', he must mean that Archytas has been buried (2 n.). For other implausible theories see Orelli–Hirschfelder 164 ff., Oates, op. cit., pp. 57 ff. (who gives a history of the problem in some detail).

The poem includes many traditional elements from Greek sepulchral epigram; such epitaphs were often written for purely literary purposes, as can be seen from the seventh book of the *Anthology*. For an unusually interesting elaboration of this kind of poem cf. Prop. 1. 21, which shares with our ode a certain abruptness and obscurity. The first part of Horace's ode is reminiscent of the kind of epigram where the dead man is addressed in his grave. One may note the opening accusative *mensorem* (= τόν ποτε μετρήσαντα), and the summary of Archytas's past achievements (cf. Lattimore 285 ff.). A string of commonplaces follows: 'you who ranged so far have come to so little' (3 n.); 'your accomplishments avail you nothing' (4 n.); 'even the most privileged die in the end' (7 n.); 'all must die alike' (15 n., 16 n.); 'death is irrevocable' (16 n.); 'it comes by one means or another' (17 n.); 'some die old, some young' (19 n.).

Other elements in this part of the poem owe more to diatribe than to epigram. The Pythagoreans were the butts of Greek rationalism from the time of Xenophanes (6); plain men scoffed at their mysticism about number, their abstention from meat and beans, and their doctrine of transmigration (10 n.). Old and Middle Comedy provide some unfriendly *testimonia* (Diog. Laert. 8. 37–8, Diels–Kranz 1. 478 ff.); see also Gow on Theoc. 14. 5, Pfeiffer on Call. fr. 553. The mockery was intensified by the Cynics and sillographers of the Hellenistic period; their σπουδαιογέλοιον has left its influence on Lucian, especially in his *Somnium* (J. Bompaire, *Lucien Écrivain*, 1958, pp. 178 ff.). Eminent Romans, such as Ennius (significantly a south Italian), Varro, Nigidius Figulus, and in the Augustan age Q. Sextius, were interested in Pythagoreanism; even Ovid gives a surprisingly sympathetic account (*met.* 15. 60 ff.); for the importance of the school in Italy see Carcopino, *La Basilique pythagoricienne de la Porte Majeure*, 1927, pp. 161 ff. But the satirizing Horace has

no use for the pretensions of the creed; cf. *epod.* 15. 21 'nec te Pythagorae fallant arcana renati', *serm.* 2. 6. 63 'faba Pythagorae cognata',
epist. 2. 1. 52 'quo promissa cadant et somnia Pythagorea'.

At 21 the ode veers; it transpires that the speaker who has supplied
these reflections on mortality is himself a drowned man. Horace
now weaves in themes from the other type of Greek epitaph, where
the dead man does the speaking himself. Addresses by drowned
voyagers were particularly common; see especially *anth. P.* 7. 263–92,
Lattimore 199 ff. Hence we find the appeal to the passing *nauta*
(23); the sudden appearance of this man mystifies some, but he is
simply the ξεῖνος (*hospes*) or ὁδίτης (*viator*) of epitaph, treated in a
lively and semi-dramatic way. Similarly expressions like 'sic' (25 n.),
'quamquam festinas' (35 n.), 'non est mora longa' (35 n.), have
associations with sepulchral epigram, even if they are not used
here with their usual intention.

The two parts of the poem do not perfectly cohere, and Wilamowitz made an interesting attempt to find a unity (249 ff., Oates,
op. cit., pp. 56 ff.). The story went that Simonides buried a dead
man (not apparently a voyager), who in gratitude saved him from
travelling on a doomed ship; cf. *anth. P.* 7. 77 οὗτος ὁ τοῦ Κείοιο
Σιμωνίδεω ἐστὶ σαωτήρ, / ὃς καὶ τεθνηὼς ζῶντ' ἀπέδωκε χάριν, Cic. *div.*
1. 56 'illa duo somnia quae creberrime commemorantur a Stoicis' (cf.
Pease ad loc., Chrysipp. 2. 344 von A.), Val. Max. 1. 7 ext. 3, Liban.
8. 42 F. (who locates the incident at Tarentum). According to Wilamowitz Tarentum is in fact the unifying factor in Horace's poem:
first the scene is set at the grave of Tarentum's most famous son,
then we are given the Simonidean motif of the corpse at Tarentum.
Unfortunately the allusion to Simonides is far from obvious (F.
Jacoby, *Gnomon* 10, 1934, 481 ff., *Kleine philologische Schriften*, 1961,
2. 279 ff.); and it is quite uncertain whether Simonides himself ever
described the episode (it looks suspiciously like the story of his rescue
by the Dioscuri from the house of the Scopadae). In any case Libanius
is the only source who mentions Tarentum, and he may have been
influenced by the miraculous rescue of Arion.

The Ode to Archytas is often dismissed as a chaotic youthful
experiment, but such a view is unconvincing. The poem is undeniably bizarre in conception, but it is original and imaginative
as few other Latin writings. The long rambling sentences catch the
variety and impetuosity of the living voice better than the congested
involutions of Horace's maturity. Admiration for Archytas gives
place to derision; the style is now grandiloquent (7 ff.), now satiric
(11 ff.), now 'poetical' in an Alexandrian manner (21 f.). The tempestuous dactyls evoke the wind beating on the woods of Horace's
childhood, or blowing the sand about a drowned man on the

Calabrian shore—the sand which Archytas once had counted (1 n.), and which now stifles him. Anybody who likes this poem has discovered something about poetry.

Metre: First Archilochian.

1. te: Archytas, who lived in the first half of the 4th century B.C., was the most impressive of all Pythagoreans, and for some years the uncrowned philosopher-king of Tarentum. He was an eminent mathematician, who tackled the problem of doubling the cube (T. Heath, *History of Greek Mathematics*, 1921, 1. 246 ff.); he also distinguished harmonic progressions from arithmetic and geometric ones. He must have been an important influence on his friend Plato, whom on one occasion he saved from Dionysius II of Syracuse. He was an innovator in practical as well as theoretical mechanics, and constructed a flying wooden pigeon (Gell. 10. 12. 9 f.). This great and good man also invented the rattle; cf. Arist. *pol.* 1340ᵇ26 ff. δεῖ . . . καὶ τὴν Ἀρχύτου πλαταγὴν οἴεσθαι γενέσθαι καλῶς, ἣν διδόασι τοῖς παιδίοις ὅπως χρώμενοι ταύτῃ μηδὲν καταγνύωσι τῶν κατὰ τὴν οἰκίαν· οὐ γὰρ δύναται τὸ νέον ἡσυχάζειν. See further Diog. Laert. 8. 79–83, *RE* 2. 600ff., W. K. C. Guthrie, *History of Greek Philosophy* 1, 1962, pp. 333 ff.; E. Frank, *Platon und die sogennanter Pythagoreer*, 1923, P. Wuilleumier, *Tarente*, 1939, pp. 67 ff., 574 ff., A. Olivieri, *Civiltà greca nell'Italia meridionale*, 1931, pp. 61 ff.; *testimonia* and fragments in Diels–Kranz 1. 421 ff.

maris: the sea was proverbially boundless; cf. the Delphic oracle ap. Hdt. 1. 47. 3 οἶδα δ' ἐγὼ ψάμμου τ' ἀριθμὸν καὶ μέτρα θαλάσσης, Otto 138, E. Salzmann, *Sprichwörter und sprichwörtliche Redensarten bei Libanius*, Diss. Tübingen, 1910, p. 89; cf. also the proverb κύματα μετρεῖ (Gow on Theoc. 16. 60, *CR* 45, 1931, 10 ff.). 'Sea and land' make a conventional pair (E. Kemmer, *Die polare Ausdrucksweise in der griechischen Literatur*, 1903, p. 160).

terrae: a *terrae mensor* is quite literally a γεωμέτρης; for Archytas's geometrical work see, for instance, Diels–Kranz 1. 425 ff. (A. 14). But here Horace rather means that Archytas measured the whole world; cf. Pl. *Theaet.* 173 e ἡ δὲ διάνοια . . . πανταχῇ πέτεται κατὰ Πίνδαρον "τά τε γᾶς ὑπένερθε" καὶ τὰ ἐπίπεδα γεωμετροῦσα, "οὐρανοῦ θ' ὕπερ" ἀστρονομοῦσα. Perhaps more relevant to Archytas is the skit on his master Pythagoras by Hermias, *irris. gentil. philos.* 17 (H. Diels, *Doxographi Graeci*, 1879, pp. 655 f.) τὸν μὲν δὴ κόσμον ὁ Πυθαγόρας μετρεῖ . . . εἰς δὲ τὸν αἰθέρα αὐτὸν αὐτὸς ἀνέρχομαι καὶ τὸν πῆχυν παρὰ Πυθαγόρου λαβὼν μετρεῖν ἄρχομαι τὸ πῦρ . . . ἐπὶ τὸ ὕδωρ στέλλομαι καὶ . . . μετρῶ τὴν ὑγρὰν οὐσίαν . . . τὴν δὲ γῆν ἅπασαν ἡμέρᾳ μιᾷ περιέρχομαι συλλέγων αὐτῆς τὸν ἀριθμόν. No doubt similar remarks were made about many philosophers; cf. Cicero's fine sentence (*off.* 1. 154) 'quis enim est tam cupidus in perspicienda cognoscendaque rerum natura, ut si ei tractanti contemplantique res cognitione dignissimas subito sit allatum periculum discrimenque patriae cui subvenire opitularique possit, non illa omnia relinquat atque abiciat, etiamsi dinumerare se stellas aut metiri mundi magnitudinem posse arbitretur?' Palladas gives the commonplace a cynical twist (*anth. P.* 11. 349. 1 f.): εἰπὲ πόθεν σὺ μετρεῖς κόσμον καὶ πείρατα γαίης / ἐξ ὀλίγης γαίης σῶμα φέρων ὀλίγον.

numeroque carentis: ἀναρίθμου.

harenae: counting the sand was proverbially impossible: cf. Hom. *Il.* 9. 385 οὐδ᾿ εἴ μοι τόσα δοίη ὅσα ψάμαθός τε κόνις τε, Hdt. 1. 47. 3 (quoted above), Pind. *O.* 2. 98 ἐπεὶ ψάμμος ἀριθμὸν περιπέφευγεν, *P.* 9. 46 ff., Archimedes, *psamm.* οἴονταί τινες, βασιλεῦ Γέλων, τοῦ ψάμμου τὸν ἀριθμὸν ἄπειρον εἶμεν τῷ πλήθει, anon. *anth. P.* 12. 145. 4, anon. *PMG* 1007, Catull. 7. 3, Virg. *georg.* 2. 106, *ep. Hebr.* 11. 12 καὶ ὡς ἡ ἄμμος ἡ παρὰ τὸ χεῖλος τῆς θαλάσσης ἡ ἀναρίθμητος (quoting *genesis* 22. 17, 32. 12), Otto 159, J. Svennung, *Catulls Bildersprache*, 1945, p. 84.

In his Ψαμμίτης or 'Sand-Reckoner' Archimedes achieved the impossible; he showed that the sand could be counted even if the whole universe were filled with it. He solved his problem partly by a system of proportion: there are 10,000 grains of sand to a poppy seed, 40 poppy seeds to a finger's breadth, etc., etc. But his main difficulty was how to express very large numbers in a language that stops at 10,000; this he did by multiplying a myriad myriads by itself, and so on again and again (thus foreshadowing index numbers). This noble achievement of the human mind is still extant, but forms no part of a classical education. See Wilamowitz, *Griechisches Lesebuch* 1. 2. 242 ff., T. L. Heath, *Archimedes*, pp. 221 ff.

There is no evidence that Archytas had previously counted the sand; Archimedes does not mention him, and his own treatise is said to show characteristic originality. But it would be rash to assume that Horace has simply confused Archytas and Archimedes. Obviously he had heard of the Ψαμμίτης; Silius can say of Archimedes 'non illum mundi numerasse capacis harenas / vana fides' (14. 350 f.). So Horace ascribed the counting of the sand to Archytas, as the sort of thing that mathematicians did. A poet would have no respect for facts in a matter of this kind.

2. cohibent: 'confine' (stronger than the common κατέχει); cf. Kaibel, *EG* 594. 8 = Peek, *GV* 1283. 8 τύμβῳ εἰναλέῳ πεπεδημένος, *carm. epig.* 1312. 3 f. 'quam genuit tellus Maurusia quamque coercens / detinet ignoto tristis harena solo'. The grave seems particularly narrow for the man of great gifts, and above all for the far-ranging physicist. Cf. anon. *anth. P.* 7. 94 ἐνθάδε πλεῖστον ἀληθείας ἐπὶ τέρμα περήσας / οὐρανίου κόσμου κεῖται Ἀναξαγόρας, 7. 84 ἢ ὀλίγον τόδε σᾶμα, τὸ δὲ κλέος οὐρανόμηκες / τοῦ πολυφροντίστου τοῦτο Θάλητος ὄρη, Antip. Sid. ibid. 7. 2. 9 f. (on Homer), Antip. Thess. ibid. 7. 18. 1 f. (on Alcman), 7. 629. 1 (to Socrates) ἢ χθαμαλὴν ὑπέδυς ὁ τόσος κόνιν;, Stat. *silv.* 2. 7. 95, Shakespeare, *I Henry IV* v. iv. 89 ff. 'When that this body did contain a spirit A kingdom for it was too small a bound; But now two paces of the vilest earth Is room enough', Lattimore 172 f., 228 f.

Some interpret 'the lack of the dust of burial confines you in this world'; this suits the theory that the poem is a dialogue between a passer-by and the unburied Archytas (above, p. 318). One would have to explain the construction as an instance of *res pro defectu rei*; cf. Ar. *Plut.* 147 f. ἔγωγέ τοι διὰ μικρὸν ἀργυρίδιον / δοῦλος γεγένημαι, Rennie on Ar. *Ach.* 615. But the present case is considerably more difficult. In the context *cohibent* naturally points a contrast between the soaring mind and the cramping grave.

3. pulveris: the covering dust of the grave (κόνις); the word is appropriate here because it is derogatory, and also because it balances *harenae*. Cf. Luc. 8. 867 f. (on Pompey) 'pulveris exigui sparget non longa vetustas / congeriem bustumque cadet', Claud. 5. 452. In funereal contexts *pulvis* more normally refers to the ashes of the dead.

exigui: the adjective is conventional; cf. *anth. P.* 7. 21. 5 γῆς ὀλίγον μέρος, 7. 136. 1 βαιὸς τάφος, 7. 137. 5 ὀλίγην . . . κόνιν, 7. 276. 4 ὀλίγη . . . ψαμάθῳ, 7. 655. 1 γαίης μικρὴ κόνις, 7. 656. 1 τὴν ὀλίγην βῶλον, 8. 136. 3 τυτθὴ κόνις. Distinguish references to the 'little dust' of the cremated body (Gow–Page 2. 424).

litus: the variant *latum* is too imprecise, and it is desirable that we should be prepared a little for the washed-up corpse (22). Greek sepulchral epigrams are often set near the sea, sometimes in the case of drowned men (*anth. P.* 7. 267, 7. 278, 7. 287, Kaibel, *EG* 186 = Peek, *GV* 1334), but not necessarily so; cf. *anth. P.* 7. 4 (Homer), 7. 71 (Archilochus), 7. 78 (Eratosthenes), 7. 142 (Achilles), 7. 146 (Ajax), 7. 345 (Philaenis). See also [Hdt.] *vit. Hom.* 36 ἐπ' ἀκτῆς ἐτάφη, Cic. *Sest.* 140 (on Opimius) 'cuius . . . sepulcrum desertissimum in litore Dyrrachino relictum est'.

Matinum: the ancient scholia give imprecise accounts of this place-name: it is a mountain or promontory or perhaps a plain in Apulia (Porph. and ps.-Acro ad loc., ps.-Acro 3. 4. 15), or it is a mountain or plain or *saltus* in Calabria (Porph. 4. 2. 27, *epod.* 16. 28, ps.-Acro ad loc., 1. 31. 5, 4. 2. 27). These accounts are not so contradictory as they may appear; by some definitions Apulia extended to the Gulf of Taranto (*RE* 2. 289).

On balance it seems most likely that the Matine shore was not too far from Tarentum (C. Bulle, *Philologus* 57, 1898, 340 ff., Sinko, loc. cit., pp. 41 ff.). Horace refers elsewhere to the Matine bee (4. 2. 27), and Tarentum was famous for its honey (2. 6. 15, 3. 16. 33, Virg. *georg.* 4. 125 ff.). Archytas is most likely to have been buried near his native city; if his tomb was near the exclusive resort of Tarentum it might be a known landmark to the poet and his readers. There is an inland town called Matino, which can be traced back to the tenth century, in the Salentine peninsula (the 'heel' of Italy); but this is further from Tarentum than one would wish, and the name may have no significance.

Editors generally associate the *litus Matinum* with the modern village of Mattinata, up the Adriatic on the Gargano promontory. This probably is a mistake. Pliny gives a list of communities in the neighbourhood: 'Metinates ex Gargano, Mateolani, Neretini, Natini' (*nat.* 3. 105). The Metinates may well have come from Mattinata (cf. *RE* 15. 1406); but for the last name *Netini* (cf. Str. 6. 3. 7 Νήτιον, *RE* 16. 1805) seems preferable to the variant *Matini* (the list is in rough alphabetical order). A passage from Lucan is also relevant: 'sic ubi depastis summittere gramina campis / et renovare parans hibernas Apulus herbas / igne fovet terras, simul et Garganus et arva / Volturis et calidi lucent buceta Matini' (9. 182 ff.). If the *litus Matinum* was in Gargano the sequence of names is very strange, but Lucan is probably proceeding from north to south.

It must be conceded that there are real difficulties, though perhaps not insuperable ones, in assigning the *litus Matinum* to the south coast. Horace refers in our poem to Illyrian waves (22); but this could include the Gulf of Taranto as well as the Adriatic. The mention of Venusia (26) is more awkward; but if the *nauta* is thought of as sailing to Dyrrachium he would have reason to fear east winds blowing towards Venusia. The greatest difficulty of all lies in *epod.* 16. 27 f. 'quando / Padus Matina laverit cacumina'; this seems to imply something much higher than the low ridges near the south coast. Yet it is possible that Horace's main contrast is between the river of the north and the hills (however low) of the extreme south.

4. munera: often used of the tribute paid to the dead; cf. Catull. 101. 3, Virg. *Aen.* 4. 624, 11. 26, *carm. epig.* 1192. 6.

nec . . . prodest: a commonplace of laments. Cf. Hom. *Il.* 5. 53 f. ἀλλ' οὔ οἱ τότε γε χραῖσμ' Ἄρτεμις ἰοχέαιρα / οὐδὲ ἐκηβολίαι, Prop. 3. 18. 11 f. 'quid genus aut virtus aut optima profuit illi / mater et amplexum Caesaris esse focos', 4. 11. 11 f. 'quid mihi coniugium Paulli, quid currus avorum / profuit?' (with Fedeli's note), Ov. *am*. 3. 9. 21 'quid pater Ismario quid mater profuit Orpheo?', *consol. ad Liv*. 41 f., *carm. epig*. 543, Julianus, *anth. P*. 7. 562. 1 f. ὦ φθέγμα Κρατεροῖο, τί σοι πλέον εἴ γε καὶ αὐδῆς / ἔπλεο καὶ σιγῆς αἴτιον ἀντιπάλοις;, Milton, *Lycidas* 64 'Alas what boots it ...?', Landor, *Rose Aylmer*, 'Ah what avails the sceptred race, Ah what the form divine?', 1. 24. 11 n.

5. **aerias**: for astronomical activity attributed to Archytas cf. Prop. 4. 1. 77 'me creat Archytae suboles, Babylonius Orops', Sinko, loc. cit., pp. 44 ff. *aerius* (as well as *aetherius*) is sometimes used of heavenly bodies; cf. Catull. 66. 5 f. 'ut Triviam furtim . . . / dulcis amor gyro devocet aerio', Cinna fr. 11. 2 'carmina quis ignis novimus aerios', *Thes.l.L*. 1. 1062. 82 ff., 1. 1063. 33 ff., Call. *h*. 4. 176 τείρεσιν, ἡνίκα πλεῖστα κατ᾽ ἠέρα βουκολέονται.

In the present passage, where *domos* suggests 'heaven', there are at first sight some attractions in Meineke's emendation *aetherias*; cf. 1. 3. 29 f. 'post ignem aetheria domo / subductum', *Thes.l.L*. 5. 1. 1978. 58 ff. In particular, *aetherius* is appropriate where the mortal body is contrasted with the immortal soul; cf. Ov. *Pont*. 4. 13. 25 f. 'nam patris Augusti docui mortale fuisse / corpus, in aetherias numen abisse domos', *carm. epig*. 1340. 4 'spiritus ae]thereas ardet adire domos', Lattimore 31 ff. *aetherias* has a certain irony that *aerias* lacks; yet in view of the interchange of these words elsewhere one is not justified in emending here.

temptasse: the word suggests audacity; Archytas was like a Titan or giant assailing the ramparts of heaven. Cf. Ov. *fast*. 1. 297 f., Ptolemy (the astronomer), *anth. P*. 9. 577 οἶδ᾽ ὅτι θνατὸς ἐγὼ καὶ ἐφάμερος· ἀλλ᾽ ὅταν ἄστρων / μαστεύω πυκινὰς ἀμφιδρόμους ἕλικας, / οὐκέτ᾽ ἐπιψαύω γαίης ποσίν, ἀλλὰ παρ᾽ αὐτῷ / Ζανὶ θεοτρεφέος πίμπλαμαι ἀμβροσίης.

animoque . . . percurrisse: cf. Lucr. 1. 74 'atque omne immensum peragravit mente animoque', Cic. *fin*. 2. 102 (also on Epicurus) 'qui innumerabiles mundos infinitasque regiones, quarum nulla esset ora, nulla extremitas, mente peragravisset', *nat. deor*. 1. 54 and 2. 153 (with Pease's notes), Ov. *met*. 15. 63 (on Pythagoras) 'mente deos adiit', Manil. 1. 13 f., 1. 97 'caelum ascendit ratio', Sen. *dial*. 8. 5. 6, Nemesius 40. 532 c Migne (above, p. 44), Prud. *apoth*. 806, Paul. Nol. *carm*. 15. 190. For further instances of this common figure see R. M. Jones, *CPh* 21, 1926, 97 ff., A.-J. Festugière, *La Révélation d'Hermès Trismégiste* 2, 1949, pp. 441 ff., Russell on Longinus 35. 2–36. *percurrisse* suggests an explorer traversing unknown territories; cf. Wordsworth, *Prelude* 3. 62 ff. (on Newton's statue) 'The marble index of a mind for ever Voyaging through strange seas of thought alone'.

J. S. Morrison suggests that Horace refers to a less intellectual and more mystic progress; he argues that Er's journey εἰς τόπον τινὰ δαιμόνιον (Pl. *rep.* 614 c) may be derived from a similar journey in Archytas (*CQ* N.S. 8, 1958, 215 f.). In favour of his theory one might cite Cic. *Lael.* 88 (a saying attributed to Archytas himself): 'si quis in caelum ascendisset naturamque mundi et pulchritudinem siderum perspexisset, insuavem illam admirationem ei fore, quae iucundissima fuisset si aliquem cui narraret habuisset'. For supernatural flights of the soul attributed to Pythagoras and others see Jones, loc. cit., Festugière, loc. cit., P. Boyancé, *RA* 25, 1927, 377, J. D. P. Bolton, *Aristeas of Proconnesus*, 1962, pp. 146 ff. It is not always easy to distinguish the 'soaring of the mind' from the 'flight of the soul', but the parallels suggest that in the present passage Horace means the former. He is thinking of Archytas at this stage as a mathematician and astronomer; it is only below that he considers him as a Pythagorean and mystic.

rotundum: for the same idea cf. Virg. *Aen.* 4. 451 'caeli convexa', Enn. *scaen.* 381 'caeli ingentes fornices', H. D. Jocelyn, *The Tragedies of Ennius*, 1967, p. 254. Yet *rotundus* is a prosaic word, not used by Virgil, but naturally found in scientific or philosophical contexts (see Pease on Cic. *nat. deor.* 1. 18). Perhaps one might see a hint at the doctrine of the spheres, which was a theory held among others by the Pythagoreans (Arist. *cael.* 290ᵇ12 ff., Aetius 2. 7. 7 = G. S. Kirk and J. E. Raven, *The Presocratic Philosophers* frr. 330 and 332; cf. Wuilleumier [above, 1 n.], pp. 581 f.). In the procession of souls in the *Phaedrus*, which Morrison, loc. cit., connects with Archytas, Plato says ἄκραν ἐπὶ τὴν ὑπουράνιον ἁψῖδα πορεύονται (247 a).

6. morituro: probably ablative, agreeing with *animo*. Almost all editors take the word with *tibi*; but in that case *profuit* would have been desirable (pointed out by Ritter). *animo* is much closer than *tibi*; and the five words *animo . . . morituro* give a chiastic pattern.

7. occidit: it was a commonplace in consolatory literature to remark that even the greatest men have died; cf. Porph. ad loc. 'haec autem ad solacium mortis dicuntur', Menander rhet. 3. 414. 4 ff. Sp. ὅτι πέρας ἔστιν ἅπασιν ἀνθρώποις τοῦ βίου ὁ θάνατος καὶ ὅτι ἥρωες καὶ θεῶν παῖδες οὐ διέφυγον. See Hom. *Il.* 18. 117 οὐδὲ γὰρ οὐδὲ βίη Ἡρακλῆος φύγε κῆρα, / ὅσπερ φίλτατος ἔσκε Διὶ Κρονίωνι ἄνακτι, 21. 107 κάτθανε καὶ Πάτροκλος ὅ περ σέο πολλὸν ἀμείνων, Alcaeus 38. 5 ff. καὶ γὰρ Σίσυφος Αἰολίδαις βασιλεύς . . . , *trag. adesp.* 372 ποῦ γὰρ τὰ σεμνὰ κεῖνα, ποῦ δὲ Λυδίας / μέγας δυνάστης Κροῖσος ἢ Ξέρξης . . .;, Lucr. 3. 1025 'lumina sis oculis etiam bonus Ancu' reliquit', 3. 1042 'ipse Epicurus obit decurso lumine (limite?) vitae', Virg. *Aen.* 10. 470 f., Prop. 3. 18. 27, Hor. *carm.* 4. 7. 25 f., Marc. Aur. 6. 47 ἐκεῖ δὴ μεταβαλεῖν ἡμᾶς δεῖ, ὅπου τοσοῦτοι μὲν δεινοὶ ῥήτορες, τοσοῦτοι δὲ σεμνοὶ φιλόσοφοι, Ἡράκλειτος, Πυθαγόρας, Σωκράτης . . . , Marc. Argent. *anth. P.* 11. 28. 5 f. εἰ δέ σοι ἀθανάτου σοφίης νόος, ἴσθι Κλεάνθης / καὶ Ζήνων Ἀίδην τὸν βαθὺν ὡς ἔμολον, anon. ibid. 7. 157. 4, Peek, *GV* 1804. 10 οὐδ' Ἀχιλεὺς δ' ἔφυγεν Μοῖρ[α]⟨ν ὁ π⟩αῖ⟨ς⟩ Θέτιδος, *IG* 14. 1806 εὐψύχι Μίδων· οὐδεὶς ἀθάνατος· καὶ ὁ Ἡρακλῆς ἀπέθανε (so 12. 2. 384. 7 f.), Dunbar, *Lament for the Makers* 'He has done petuously devour The noble Chaucer, of makaris flour . . .', Villon, *Le Testament* 357 ff. ('Mais ou est le preux Charlemaigne?'). See further below on Tithonus (8) and Minos (9), B. Lier, *Philologus* 16, 1903, 575 ff., Lattimore 250 ff., Cumont 480 n. 3.

Pelopis genitor: Tantalus; cf. 2. 18. 37. *genitor* is an epic word, already used by Ennius, but not found in comedy or normally in classical prose.

conviva deorum: Tantalus was on dining-out terms with Zeus and ate his ambrosia, which ought to have ensured immortality. Cf. Pind. *O*. 1. 54 f. εἰ δὲ δή τιν' ἄνδρα θνατὸν Ὀλύμπου σκοποὶ / ἐτίμασαν, ἦν Τάνταλος οὗτος, 1. 60 ff., Eur. *Or*. 8 f. θεοῖς, ἄνθρωπος ὤν, / κοινῆς τραπέζης ἀξίωμ' ἔχων ἴσον, Gallus, *anth. Pl*. 89. 1 οὗτος ὁ πρὶν μακάρεσσι συνέστιος, Ov. *met*. 6. 172 f., Hyg. *fab*. 82. 2 (for such dinners in general see Gudeman on Tac. *dial*. 12. 6, Rhianus 1. 16 Powell). It is curious to find Tantalus in this list of privileged persons who died; as one of the great sinners he usually plays a more monitory role, and the positive horrors of his punishment are stressed.

'conviva deorum' would normally be heroic rather than satiric; cf. Stat. *Theb*. 6. 282 'sed pius et magni vehitur conviva Tonantis', Mart. 9. 91. 5, *anth. Lat*. 931. 9 f. 'Tantalus infelix, dicunt, conviva deorum, / nunc quoque apud Manes victima sacra Iovi es'. Prudentius somewhat surprisingly transfers the epithet *conviva dei* to Judas Iscariot (*psych*. 531).

8. Tithonus: in this context even stranger than Tantalus; according to the legend he was given immortality, though not eternal youth (see the discussion in *CR* 59–61). Cf. 2. 16. 30 'longa Tithonum minuit senectus', *h.Ven*. 218 ff., Mimnermus 4, Roscher 5. 1024 f., Tennyson, *Tithonus*, 'Me only cruel immortality Consumes. I wither slowly in thine arms'. Even the story that Tithonus was turned into a cicada does not help us here; *occidit et* must mean 'also died' (κάτθανε καὶ).

The crucial piece of evidence does not seem to have been deployed; see ps.-Dion. Hal. *rhet*. 6. 5, p. 282. 6 ff. (hints for funeral speeches) εἰ μὲν νέος ὢν τοῦτο πάθοι ὅτι θεοφιλής· τοὺς γὰρ τοιούτους φιλοῦσιν οἱ θεοί. καὶ ὅτι καὶ τῶν παλαιῶν πολλοὺς ἀνήρπασαν, οἷον τὸν Γανυμήδην, τὸν Τιθωνόν, τὸν Ἀχιλλέα. (Cf. also *schol. Od.* 5. 1, on the Tithonus legend, ἡ δὲ θεραπεία τοῦ μύθου ὅτι τοὺς ἔτι νέους ὄντας καὶ αἰφνιδίως ἀποθνήσκοντας ἔλεγον ἁρπάζεσθαι παρὰ τῆς 'Ηοῦς.) This rationalization of the story protects Horace's text but not his logic. *remotus in auras* refers to a special privilege of Tithonus (cf. *conviva deorum* and *Iovis arcanis . . . admissus*); the phrase implies a belief in Tithonus's immortality. Horace seems to have conflated an archaic legend ('Tithonus was immortal') with a topic of Hellenistic consolations ('Tithonus died young').

remotus in auras: a curious expression. One is familiar with passages where a dead person is said to be wafted away by the winds (1. 2. 48 n.). This treatment was accorded to Memnon, the son of Aurora (Q. Smyrn. 2. 553 οἳ καὶ ἀνηρείψαντο θοῶς 'Ηώιον υἷα), and Tithonus himself was carried through the air in a chariot (Eur. *Tr.* 885 f., Stat. *silv.* 1. 2. 44 f.). Yet *remotus in auras* does not mean the same as *raptus ab auris*. One might sooner be tempted to compare such passages as Kaibel, *EG* 723 τίς βροτὸς οὐκ ἐδάκρυσε ὅτι τὸ σὸν κάλλος ἀπῆλθεν ἐς ἀέρα / ἣν ἥρπασαν ἀπὸ γονέων Μοῖραι κατ' ἐρείπαν;, yet here ἀέρα seems to mean 'the upper air', almost 'heaven' (5 n.), and there is no parallel for *in auras* in this sense. However, it may be relevant that Aurora lived in the east ἐπὶ πείρασι γαίης (*h.Ven.* 227), where the ὠκεανίδες αὖραι breathed round the Islands of the Blest (D. S. Robertson, *CR* 61, 1947, 50). It is less likely to be important that the ancients sometimes associated *aura* and *aurora* (Robertson, ibid., citing *Prisc. gramm.* 3. 509. 27 f.).

9. Iovis arcanis . . .: Horace is alluding to the story of Minos in the dry terminology of a Roman *consilium*. Cf. Hom. *Od.* 19. 178 f. τῇσι δ' ἐνὶ Κνωσὸς μεγάλη πόλις, ἔνθα τε Μίνως / ἐννέωρος βασίλευε Διὸς μεγάλου ὀαριστής, [Pl.] *Min.* 319 c τὸν Μίνων συγγίγνεσθαι ἐνάτῳ ἔτει τῷ Διὶ ἐν λόγοις καὶ φοιτᾶν παιδευθησόμενον ὡς ὑπὸ σοφιστοῦ ὄντος τοῦ Διός, *RE* 15. 1902 ff. See further Cic. *nat. deor.* 1. 18 'tamquam modo ex deorum concilio . . . descendisset' (with Pease's note), Petron. 76. 10 'consiliator deorum', Otto 109.

Editors do not observe that Minos belongs to the *communis locus*; cf. Peek, *GV* 709. 7 f. ἀλλ' οὐκ εὐσεβίη τις ἀλεύεται ἄσστροφα Μοιρῶν / δόγματα· καὶ Μείνως ἦλθεν εἰς Ἀίδην, 1249. 19 (from Itanos in Crete) θνήσκει μὲν γὰρ ἄναξ Μίνως [ὃς ἐδέσποσ]ε Κρήτης.

habentque: so often ἔχει, especially in sepulchral inscriptions. Cf. Theogn. 1036 ὅταν αὐτὸν ἔχῃ Τάρταρος ἠερόεις, Virg. *Aen.* 5. 733 f. 'non me impia namque / Tartara habent', Henry on *Aen.* 4. 633. The Pythagoreans no doubt talked excessively of Tartarus.

10. Panthoiden: the grandiloquent epic patronymic of the Trojan Euphorbus, who was killed by Menelaus (Hom. *Il.* 17. 81 Πανθοίδην Εὔφορβον). For the satiric nickname for Pythagoras cf. Call. fr. 191.

58 ff. ξύοντα τὴν γῆν καὶ γράφοντα τὸ σχῆμα / τοὐξεῦρ' ὁ Φρὺξ Εὔφορβος
ὅστις ἀνθρώπων / τρίγωνα καὶ σκαληνὰ πρῶτος ἔγραψε, Pers. 6. 10 f.
'cor iubet hoc Enni, postquam destertuit esse / Maeonides Quintus
pavone ex Pythagoreo', Lucian, dial. mort. 20. 3 χαῖρε ὦ Εὔφορβε ἢ
Ἄπολλον ἢ ὅ τι ἂν θέλῃς, gall. 4, Tert. anim. 31. 3 'cum Pythagoran
Euphorbum mihi opponis'. Horace is alluding to the story that when
Pythagoras saw various shields dedicated in the Heraeum at Argos
he recognized one of them as Euphorbus's. He verified his assertion
by looking at the name on the back; conclusive proof was thus
obtained that he had lived a previous life as Euphorbus. Cf. schol.
Town. on Il. 17. 28, Max. Tyr. 10. 2, Ov. met. 15. 160 ff., Gell. 4. 11. 14,
E. Rohde, Psyche, ed. 9, 1925, Appendix X; Pausanias was shown the
shield (2. 17. 3).

    iterum: cf. Alcaeus 38. 7 f. (on Sisyphus) ἀλλὰ καὶ πολύιδρις ἐὼν
ὑπὰ κᾶρι [δὶς] / δυννάεντ' Ἀχέροντ' ἐπέραισε.

    Orco demissum: the phrase is epic; cf. Hom. Il. 1. 3 ψυχὰς Ἄιδι
προΐαψεν. The use of the dative of end of motion in such locutions is
archaic and grandiose; cf. serm. 2. 5. 49, Fest. 304. 2 L. (= 254. 34 M.)
'ollus Quiris leto datus', Plaut. capt. 692 with Lindsay's note, Virg.
Aen. 2. 85, 2. 398, 9. 527, K.–S. 1. 320, H.–Sz. 100 f., Löfstedt, Syntactica 1². 187 ff.

11. clipeo . . .: 'by unhooking the shield and appealing to the
evidence of the Trojan age'. Editors interpret 'having borne witness
to the Trojan age'; but the historicity of the Trojan war was not in
dispute. Horace's words could not mean 'having borne witness that
he was alive at the Trojan age'.

13. nervos atque cutem: this suggests Pythagoras's own point of
view. Cf. Max. Tyr. 7. 5 τὸ δέρμα τοῦτο καὶ τὰ ὀστᾶ καὶ τὰς σάρκας.

14. iudice te: Horace's language is prosaic, more reminiscent of the
Satires than the Odes.

    non sordidus auctor: 'no mean authority'; for the litotes cf. Virg.
Aen. 11. 339 (on Drances) 'consiliis habitus non futtilis auctor',
Liv. 30. 45. 5. Pythagoreans showed a veneration for their founder
that seemed excessive even by ancient standards; their most decisive
argument was αὐτὸς ἔφα.

15. naturae: i.e. 'an authority on nature'; Pythagoras was alleged
to have written a Φυσικόν (Diog. Laert. 8. 1. 6). For the genitive
cf. Cic. Balb. 20 'auctorem antiquitatis', Apul. apol. 40 'omnis vetu-
statis certissimus auctor Homerus', Nettleship, Latin Lexicography,
p. 363.

    verique: cf. Petron. 132. 15 'ipse pater veri doctos Epicurus amare /
iussit'.

sed: the contrast is with *concesserat. sed* sometimes cuts short a rambling digression (δ' οὖν, 'however that may be').

una: when combined with *omnes* this must mean 'one for all alike'. It is wrong to interpret with some editors 'one continuous' (as in Catull. 5. 6 'nox est perpetua una dormienda'). Cf. rather Simon. 522. 1 πάντα γὰρ μίαν ἱκνεῖται δασπλῆτα Χάρυβδιν, *anth. P.* 7. 270. 2 ἐν πέλαγος, μία νύξ, ἐν σκάφος ἐκτέρισεν, Sil. 13. 525 'domus omnibus una', *carm. epig.* 995. 22 'hic omnis exitus unus habet', 1097. 2 'haec domus, haec requies omnibus una manet', B. Lier, *Philologus* 62, 1903, 563 f., 567 ff., Otto 228, Lattimore 250 ff. Horace seems to be imitated by Gray, *Elegy* 33 ff. 'The boast of heraldry, the pomp of pow'r, And all that beauty, all that wealth e'er gave Awaits alike the inevitable hour. The paths of glory lead but to the grave' (note that 'hour' is the subject).

16. et calcanda . . . : is this a second subject of *manet,* or does one understand *calcanda est?* On the former assumption Horace is combining two themes, death's universality (*omnes via leti manet*) and its irrevocability (*calcanda semel,* to be taken adjectivally). On the latter assumption he is dealing now only with irrevocability; and this strangely disrupts the thought of the whole passage. Admittedly *via manet* is less natural than *nox manet,* but it can be explained as a kind of zeugma.

For the thought that the road to death is universal cf. Teles, p. 29 ἢ οὐ πανταχόθεν, φησὶν ὁ Ἀρίστιππος, ἴση καὶ ὁμοία ἡ εἰς Ἅιδου ὁδός; (for parallels see Hense's note), Prop. 3. 18. 22 'est mala, sed cunctis ista terenda via est', Antip. Thess. *anth. P.* 11. 23. 3 εἰς Ἅιδην μία πᾶσι καταίβασις, Tymnes, ibid. 7. 477. 3 f. ἔστι γὰρ ἴση | πάντοθεν εἰς Ἅιδην ἐρχομένοισιν ὁδός, Sen. *dial.* 11. 9. 9, Maxim. *eleg.* 6. 5, *carm. epig.* 998. 2, *gnom. Vat.* 115 (cf. Sternbach's note), B. Lier, loc. cit. [above, 15 *una*], 564 ff., 574.

semel calcanda adds a fresh point : one cannot even come back from Hades, much less go there again. For this commonplace cf. Aesch. fr. 239 ἁπλῆ γὰρ οἶμος εἰς Ἅιδου φέρει (though that passage is ambiguous), Catull. 3. 12 'unde negant redire quemquam', West on Hes. *th.* 769–73, Gow on Theoc. 12. 19. Yet *semel* surprisingly contradicts 10 f. 'Panthoiden iterum Orco / demissum'. Horace there accepted that Pythagoras received special privileges; he did not bluntly deny the possibility of visiting Orcus twice, but rather said that even in this extreme case death catches up in the end.

One might consider emending *semel* to *simul,* in the sense of 'for all alike'; cf. Pind. *I.* 7. 42 θνάσκομεν γὰρ ὁμῶς ἅπαντες, anon. *anth. P.* 7. 342. 2 πάντας ὁμῶς θνητοὺς εἰς Ἅιδης δέχεται. Then one would understand not *manet* but *est,* which on grounds of latinity might be preferable. Yet it must be admitted that *simul* would most naturally be taken as 'simultaneously', which is absurd.

17. dant alios . . .: for this topic cf. Semon. 1. 12 ff. τοὺς δὲ δύστηνοι νόσοι | φθείρουσι †θνητῶν· τοὺς δ' Ἄρει δεδμημένους | πέμπει μελαίνης Ἀΐδης ὑπὸ χθονός, | οἱ δ' ἐν θαλάσσῃ λαιλάπι κλονεύμενοι | . . . θνήσκουσιν, Pl. *anth. P.* 7. 265. 2 ὡς ἁλὶ καὶ γαίῃ ξυνὸς ὕπεστ' Ἀΐδης, Sen. *contr.* 7. 1. 9, Petron. 115. 16 'sed non sola mortalibus maria hanc fidem praestant. illum bellantem arma decipiunt, illum diis vota reddentem penatium suorum ruina sepelit. ille vehiculo lapsus properantem spiritum excussit, cibus avidum strangulavit, abstinentem frugalitas', Stat. *silv.* 2. 1. 213 ff. 'hos bella, hos aequora poscunt, / his amor exitio, furor his et saeva cupido, / ut sileam morbos . . .', Firm. *mathes.* 1. 9. 1.

Here the theme is treated very economically, and *alios* (= 'some') is picked up by *nautis*, not by another *alii*. There is no reason to suspect corruption or interpolation. Campbell transposed 17–18 with 19–20 (besides making other changes); the mention of the sea would then naturally lead to 21. But 'nullum . . . fugit' comes more effectively as the climax to this group of four lines.

Furiae: goddesses here of strife, not vengeance; cf. Hom. *Il.* 18. 535 ἐν δ' Ἔρις ἐν δὲ Κυδοιμὸς ὁμίλεον, ἐν δ' ὀλοὴ Κήρ. Such a portrayal of a Fury appears in Virgil's Allecto 'cui tristia bella / iraeque insidiae-que et crimina noxia cordi' (*Aen.* 7. 325 f.).

spectacula: in a bitter figure the Romans sometimes likened great military exploits, particularly those of the civil war, to the contests of the arena, where the vilest slaves were butchered for the pleasure of a sadistic proletariat. The point was made by the unenchanted Caelius, Cic. *epist.* 8. 14. 4 (50 B.C.): 'uterque et animo et copiis est paratus. si sine tuo periculo fieri posset, magnum et iucundum tibi Fortuna spectaculum parabat.' The gods were assigned the role of the bloodthirsty spectators; cf. 1. 2. 37, Sen. *dial.* 1. 2. 7 'ego vero non miror si aliquando (dei) impetum capiunt spectandi magnos viros conluctantis cum aliqua calamitate', Luc. 6. 3 'parque suum videre dei', Paul, *1 Cor.* 4. 9 ὁ Θεὸς ἡμᾶς τοὺς ἀποστόλους ἐσχάτους ἀπέδειξεν, ὡς ἐπιθανατίους, ὅτι θέατρον ἐγενήθημεν τῷ κόσμῳ καὶ ἀγγέλοις καὶ ἀνθρώποις, Nonnus 17. 157 τεύχων κῶμον Ἄρηι.

19. senum ac iuvenum . . .: cf. Hom. *Od.* 11. 38 νύμφαι τ' ἠίθεοί τε πολύτλητοί τε γέροντες, Virg. *georg.* 4. 474 f. 'matres atque viri . . . pueri innuptaeque puellae' (so *Aen.* 6. 306 f.), Maxim. *eleg.* 6. 7, Coripp. *bell. Afr.* 5. 1016, Ven. Fort. *carm.* 9. 2. 51 f.

20. caput: Proserpine cut off a lock of hair (as an ἀπαρχή) from people about to die. Cf. Eur. *Alc.* 74 στείχω δ' ἐπ' αὐτὴν ὡς κατάρξωμαι ξίφει (with Dale's note), Virg. *Aen.* 4. 698 f. 'nondum illi flavum Proserpina vertice crinem / abstulerat, Stygioque caput damnaverat Orco' (with Pease's note), Stat. *silv.* 2. 1. 147.

Proserpina: Persephone was presumably an important deity in Pythagorean cult. She had a special place at Tarentum, as in general in the Dorian colonies of South Italy; cf. Val. Max. 2. 4. 5, Headlam on Herodas 1. 32, Wuilleumier, op. cit. [above, 1 n.], pp. 502 ff., G. Giannelli, *Culti e miti della magna Grecia*, ed. 2, 1963, pp. 31 ff.

fugit: 'stops at'; the perfect is gnomic. *fugere* seems an odd verb to apply to Proserpine. Elsewhere, when similar expressions are used, there is some particular reason for Death's reluctance; cf. Ap. Rhod. 1. 689 f. εἰ καί με τὰ νῦν ἔτι πεφρίκασιν / Κῆρες (Hypsipyle), Sen. *Herc. f.* 1173 ff., *Herc. O.* 766 ff. 'mors refugit illum victa quae in regno suo / semel est nec audent fata tam vastum nefas / admittere', Luc. 2. 75 f. 'mors ipsa refugit / saepe virum', Apul. *met.* 4. 7. 1 f. 'anum quandam curvatam gravi senio, . . . Orci fastidium'. Ps.-Acro comments 'figura ypallage *fugit Proserpina* pro *fugerunt Proserpinam*', but not even Virgil wrote like this.

21. me quoque: the corpse adduces his own drowning as another instance of human mortality. *quoque* in no way implies that Archytas was drowned.

devexi . . . Orionis: the constellation of Orion sets in November; the period is associated with storm (see Gow on Theoc. 7. 53 f., Pease on Virg. *Aen.* 4. 52). The hexameter-ending Ὠρίωνος is found in the manuscripts of Homer and Hesiod, representing an original Ὠαρίωνος, and was taken over by the Hellenistic and Roman poets. For variations in the quantity of the first syllable cf. Bömer on Ov. *fast.* 5. 493.

rabidus: this reading has negligible manuscript support compared with *rapidus*, and is tacitly rejected by almost all editors (Müller and Campbell are exceptions). Yet cf. 1. 3. 14 'rabiem Noti', Virg. *Aen.* 5. 802 'rabiem tantam caelique marisque', Ov. *met.* 5. 7 'ventorum rabies', Sen. *Ag.* 484 'quid rabidus ora Corus oceano exerens'. For *rapidus* cf. Virg. *Aen.* 6. 75 'rapidis ludibria ventis', Prop. 2. 16. 45 'haec videam rapidas in vanum ferre procellas', Rut. Nam. 1. 463 (with Helm's note). *rapidus* of the wind seems to imply 'tearing' or 'snatching', and is very appropriate in the passages cited; yet it does not suit *obruit* particularly well. Moreover, the word does not naturally qualify nouns denoting persons, and the wind here is personified as a *comes* (cf. 1. 25. 19 n.). *rapidus* and *rabidus* are constantly confused in medieval manuscripts (Lachmann on Lucr. 4. 712, Housman on Manil. 1. 396, 2. 211, 5. 208, Shackleton Bailey, *Propertiana*, pp. 203, 317). See especially *ars* 393 'dictus ob hoc lenire tigres rabidosque leones'; here the variant *rapidosque* has substantial manuscript support, and if it had appeared in the tradition as a whole would no doubt give widespread satisfaction.

23. at tu . . .: Horace suggests that the corpse suddenly sees a passing merchant, and asks him for burial. There is no strong break at this point; that has already come at 21 *me quoque*. ἀλλά is similarly used when the speaker turns to somebody to express a wish; cf. Denniston 16, Bühler on Moschus, *Europa* 27.

The ancient world had deep-rooted anxieties about the unburied corpse; cf. the cases of Hector, Polynices, Palinurus, Aeneas, Pompey. This was why drowning caused such horror; cf. the curses of Archilochus (79*a*), Thyestes (Enn. *scaen.* 362 ff., probably Euripidean), and Horace on the imaginary Mevius (*epod.* 10). To go down with one's ship was not a glamorous death (cf. Arginusae); Cicero illustrates the injustice of fate by the case of M. Marcellus, who 'periit in mari' (*Pis.* 44). There was a duty to bury even the body of a stranger; cf. Simonides (above, p. 319), Greg. Naz. *anth. P.* 8. 210. 1 f. πολλάκι ναυηγοῖο δέμας κατέχωσεν ὁδίτης | κύμασι πλαζόμενον, πολλάκι θηρολέτου, schol. ad Soph. *Ant.* 255 οἱ νεκρὸν ὁρῶντες ἄταφον καὶ μὴ ἐπαμησάμενοι κόνιν ἐναγεῖς εἶναι ἐδόκουν . . . λόγος δὲ ὅτι Βουζύγης Ἀθήνησι κατηράσατο τοῖς περιορῶσιν ἄταφον σῶμα.

nauta: not an able-bodied seaman but a merchant-adventurer; cf. Ulp. *dig.* 4. 9. 1. 2 'nautam accipere debemus eum qui navem exercet. quamvis nautae appellantur omnes qui navis navigandae causa in nave sint; sed de exercitore solummodo praetor sentit'.

vagae . . . harenae: the corpse does not insist on earth but will be content with sand, even though it may blow away again. Cf. Prop. 1. 17. 8 'haecine parva meum funus harena teget?', 3. 7. 26 'Paetum sponte tua, vilis harena, tegas' (see Shackleton Bailey's note), Petron. 114. 11 'aut praeteriens aliquis tralaticia humanitate lapidabit, aut quod ultimum est iratis etiam fluctibus, imprudens harena componet'.

ne parce: 'do not grudge'. *parcere*, like φείδεσθαι, sometimes means simply 'refrain'; the use is in the main ante-classical (Cato, *agr.* 1. 1) and poetical (3. 8. 26), but cf. also Liv. 34. 32. 20. Here the idea of meanness is more evident; this is reinforced by *malignus, vagae harenae*, and the diminutive *particulam*.

24. capiti: cf. Zonas, *anth. P.* 7. 404. 1 f. ψυχράν σευ κεφαλᾶς ἐπαμήσομαι αἰγιαλῖτιν | θῖνα κατὰ κρυεροῦ χευάμενος νέκυος.

inhumato: the hiatus after *capiti* is strange, and the fact that both vowels are the same perhaps aggravates the difficulty. For other striking instances of hiatus in Horace's epodic poems see *epod.* 5. 100 'et Esquilinae alites' (but here the last syllable of *Esquilinae* is presumably shortened in the Greek manner), *epod.* 13. 3 'Threicio Aquilone sonant ' (also Greek in feeling). Other cases occur after exclamations like *o* and *heu*, and in the middle of elegiambi (*epod.* 11). Peerlkamp proposed *intumulato*. This word is only attested at Ov. *epist.* 2. 136 'occurramque oculis intumulata tuis'; yet Orelli begs the question when he comments 'vereor ne verbum sit ab Ovidio primo formatum'. It is relevant that the verb *tumulo* already occurs at Catull. 64. 153 'neque iniecta tumulabor mortua terra'. Yet *intumulata* lacks precision: it suggests the absence of a burial-mound, whereas the corpse in Horace's poem is content with three handfuls of dust. Moreover, Horace uses elision sparingly in these short dactylic lines; there is no other instance except *iterum Orco* and *exitiost*.

particulam: cf. Zonas, *anth. P.* 7. 404. 7 ὥστ᾽ ἔχε μὲν ψαμάθου μόριον βραχύ, πουλὺ δὲ δάκρυ, / ξεῖν᾽, ἐπεὶ εἰς ὀλοὴν ἔδραμες ἐμπορίην. Symbolical burial was enough; cf. Soph. *Ant.* 256 λεπτὴ δ᾽ ἄγος φεύγοντος ὡς ἐπῆν κόνις.

25. sic: 'if you do as I ask'; cf. 1. 3. 1 n. The idiom suits the style of sepulchral inscriptions; cf. *carm. epig.* 1181. 5 ff. 'te pie possessor sive colone precor / ne patiare meis tumulis increscere silvas. / sic tibi dona Ceres larga det et Bromius', 1943. 7 ff. 'tu quoque praeteriens tumulum qui perlegis istum, / parce meos cineres pedibus calcare protervis: / sic tibi ab aethereas lux multa superfluat auras', Lattimore 120 f. For another supplication to a merchant cf. Plaut. *rud.* 629 ff. 'teque oro et quaeso, si speras tibi / hoc anno multum futurum sirpe et laserpicium / eamque eventuram exagogam Capuam salvam et sospitem . . .'.

minabitur: cf. 4. 14. 28 '(Aufidus) diluviem meditatur agris', Virg. *georg.* 1. 462 'quid cogitet umidus Auster'.

26. Hesperiis: the western waves make an artistic contrast with the east wind. 'Hesperia' was a Greek name for Italy (Dion. Hal. *ant. Rom.* 1. 35. 3), derived by the Hellenistic poets perhaps from Stesichorus (Bömer on Ov. *fast.* 1. 498). It was taken over by Ennius (*ann.* 23 'est locus Hesperiam quam mortales perhibebant'), and by many Roman poets (*RE* 8. 1243); later it was applied to Spain (cf. 1. 36. 4 n.).

27. plectantur: 'let them suffer'. *plecti* means 'to be beaten' (cf. πλήσσω); hence in slaves' language 'to be punished' or especially to take the rap' (cf. *epist.* 1. 2. 14 'quidquid delirant reges, plectuntur Achivi', Palmer on Ov. *epist.* 11. 110). In our passage both meanings are present. The word is found only in the passive in classical Latin; it is used by Cicero even in serious contexts and by Ovid, but not by Virgil, Propertius, Lucan, or Statius.

te sospite: for the form of prayer which suggests an alternative victim for the deity's wrath cf. 1. 21. 13 n. Here the woods are mentioned as wild country that can be damaged without loss; cf. *Orph. h.* 36. 16 πέμποις δ' εἰς ὀρέων κεφαλὰς νούσους τε καὶ ἄλγη.

merces: cf. Heliodorus 6. 7. 1 σοὶ μὲν ἐπ' αἰσίοις ὁ ἔκπλους στέλλοιτο, καὶ Ἑρμῆς μὲν Κερδῷος Ποσειδῶν δὲ Ἀσφάλειος συνέμποροι καὶ πομποὶ γίγνοιντο, πᾶν μὲν ἐπὶ πέλαγος εὔρουν καὶ εὐήνεμον παραπέμποντες, πάντα δὲ ὅρμον εὐλίμενον καὶ πᾶσαν πόλιν εὐπρόσοδον καὶ φιλέμπορον ἀποφαίνοντες. For good wishes to the passer-by in epitaphs cf. Leonidas, *anth. P.* 7. 163. 8 καί σοί, ξεῖνε, πόροι πάντα Τύχη τὰ καλά, Antip. Sid. ibid. 7. 164. 9 f. καὶ σόν, ὁδῖτα, / οὔριον ἰθύνοι πάντα Τύχη βίοτον, *carm. epig.* 11. 3 'bene rem geras et valeas, dormias sine qura', Lattimore 235 ff.

28. unde potest: the sacral *unde* means 'from whom', and refers to the gods of the next line; cf. 1. 12. 17, 2. 12. 7 f. For the allusion to divine power cf. *epod.* 17. 45 'et tu—potes nam—solve me dementia', *serm.* 2. 3. 283 f., Hom. *Il.* 16. 515 δύνασαι δὲ σὺ πάντοσ' ἀκούειν, Hes. *th.* 420 (on Hecate) καί τέ οἱ ὄλβον ὀπάζει, ἐπεὶ δύναμίς γε πάρεστιν (with West's note), Theogn. 14, Eur. *Suppl.* 65 f., Plaut. *Amph.* 139, Virg. *Aen.* 6. 117 'potes namque omnia' (with Norden's note), Call. *h.* 4. 226, Agathias, *anth. P.* 6. 76. 5 ἀλλὰ θεά, δύνασαι γάρ . . . See further Norden, *Agnostos Theos*, pp. 154, 221, Appel 153, above, 1. 12. 31 n.

defluat: cf. Bion 1. 55 τὸ δὲ πᾶν καλὸν ἐς σὲ καταρρεῖ. If the god is the subject the verb can be *defundere* (*epist.* 1. 12. 29) or καταχεῖν (Hom. *Il.* 2. 670).

aequo: 'favourable' (Housman on Manil. 4. 174).

29. sacri: not just because Tarentum was founded by a god (as some editors explain). See Eustath. *Il.* 1. 366 ἱερὰ δὲ οὐ μόνον ἡ ῥηθεῖσα Θήβη ἀλλὰ καὶ πᾶσα πόλις, ὡς φυλακτικὴ τῶν ἐντὸς ὅπερ θεῖον τῷ ὄντι ἐστίν.

custode: often applied to gods (*Thes.l.L.* 4. 1576. 72 ff.). Poseidon was the father of Taras, the legendary founder of Tarentum; he had a cult there (Wuilleumier, op. cit. [above, 1 n.], p. 479, Giannelli, op. cit. [20 n.], pp. 15 ff.). The Roman colony of 122 B.C. was called Neptunia.

30. neglegis . . .: 'do you think nothing of the fact that you are doing a wrong that will one day hurt your innocent descendants?' The sentence in substance, though not in form, is the protasis of a condition: the argument is 'even if you don't mind hurting your descendants, perhaps you will be paid out yourself'. Some commentators translate *neglegis* 'are you unaware . . .?' (cf. Tib. 2. 3. 46 '(ut) neglegat hibernas piscis adesse minas'); but this interpretation does not tie up the sentence with what follows. Others, while rightly interpreting *neglegis* as *leve putas*, wrongly take *te* as ablative with *natis* (cf. 'nate dea'). But *neglegis committere* would naturally mean 'neglect to commit' (cf. Cic. *Phil.* 3. 20 'diem edicti obire neglexit'), and that is nonsense here. Moreover, the adjective *immeritis* suggests that *natis* is a noun rather than a participle; and if *te* were anything but enclitic, this would blur the contrast between *natis* and *te ipsum* in the next sentence.

immeritis . . . natis: cf. Hom. *Il.* 4. 162 σὺν σφῆσιν κεφαλῆσι γυναιξὶ τε καὶ τεκέεσσιν, Solon 1. 31 f. ἀναίτιοι ἔργα τίνουσιν / ἢ παῖδες τούτων ἢ γένος ἐξοπίσω, Theogn. 205 f., Fraenkel on Aesch. *Ag.* 535 f., Pease on Cic. *nat. deor.* 3. 90. Such curses are often found in Greek public inscriptions; cf. E. Ziebarth, *Hermes* 30, 1895, 57 ff. They are also used in epitaphs to threaten those who may violate the grave; cf. Peek, *GV* 2035. 28 ἀλλ' ἐγ γένους ὄλοιτο πάνρειζον γένος, Lattimore 108 ff. See further Plut. *sera num. vind.* 561.

31. postmodo: ἐξοπίσω, 'one day', to be taken with *nocituram*. For the use of the word in threats cf. Catull. 30. 12 'quae te ut paeniteat postmodo facti faciet tui', Ov. *Ib.* 53 f. 'postmodo si perges, in te mihi liber iambus / tincta Lycambeo sanguine tela dabit'.

fraudem: the word refers to any wrongful act, not necessarily involving deceit. Müller suggests that the wrong is done only to the descendants as the *nauta* has no legal obligation to the corpse. But he has a moral obligation; *nocituram* would lose its point if all it says were implicit in *fraudem*.

fors et: the expression is cautious but sinister. The use of *fors* for 'perhaps' is attested a number of times in Latin verse, and may be an archaism (Austin on Virg. *Aen.* 2. 139). Sometimes *fors* is followed by *et*, as here (Hand 2. 711 f., *Thes.l.L.* 6. 1. 1136. 51 ff.); in such places *et* may simply mean *etiam*. Yet this may lay too much stress on the word; cf. Serv. *Aen.* 2. 139 'alii iungunt *forset*, ut sit *forsan*', 11. 50 'potest et unum esse *forset*, id est *forsitan*'. Note especially Prop. 2. 9. 1 f. 'iste quod est ego saepe fui, sed fors et in hora / hoc ipso eiecto carior alter erit'; here the rhythm suggests that *et* is to be taken with *fors* rather than *in hora*. So in our passage though *et* might mean *etiam*, this interpretation is not helped by the word's position at the end of the line.

32. debita iura: 'rights unpaid' (Gow); *debeo* (**dehabeo*) means 'to withhold'. This seems the best interpretation of a difficult phrase; the expression is not on all fours with *vicesque superbae*, but an element of imbalance is possible. Others suggest that *iura* is a calque for δίκαι, 'retribution', though the Latin word properly does not bear this sense. Others again interpret 'due deserts'; yet *iura* are not *merita*.

vicesque: ἀμοιβαί, requital'. Cf. 4. 14. 13, Ov. *met.* 14. 35 f., Serv. *Aen.* 2. 433 'legimus etiam poenas *vices* dici' (he quotes our passage). For a similar prayer cf. Simon. *anth. P.* 7. 516 οἱ μὲν ἐμὲ κτείναντες ὁμοίων ἀντιτύχοιεν, / Ζεῦ Ξένι᾿· οἱ δ᾿ ὑπὸ γᾶν θέντες ὄναιντο βίου. See also some anonymous epigrams where the dead man prays that his murderer, who has buried him for the wrong reasons, may meet with similar treatment: *anth. P.* 7. 310. 2 τοίης ἀντιτύχοι χάριτος, 7. 356. 2 τοίου καὐτὸς ὄναιο τάφου, 7. 359. 4 τῶν αὐτῶν μετέχοις ὧνπερ ἐμοὶ παρέχεις, 7. 360. 2 ταὐτὸ δὲ καὶ σὺ πάθοις.

superbae: i.e. because of his own high-handed behaviour the *nauta* may meet with the same treatment. Note that English 'proud' refers primarily to an internal feeling, while *superbus* (etymologically connected with *super*) describes rather an external relationship. The best commentary is Liv. 1. 49. 1 'inde L. Tarquinius regnare occepit, cui Superbo cognomen facta indiderunt quia socerum gener sepultura prohibuit, Romulum quoque insepultum perisse dictitans'. For the combination of *vices* with a qualitative adjective cf. 1. 4. 1 n.

33. precibus non linquar inultis: 'if you abandon me my curses will not be unfulfilled'. For *linquar* cf. Hom. *Od.* 11. 72 (Elpenor speaking) μή μ᾿ ἄκλαυτον ἄθαπτον ἰὼν ὄπιθεν καταλείπειν, Cic. *Mil.* 33 'tu P. Clodi cruentum cadaver ... nocturnis canibus dilaniandum reliquisti', Virg. *Aen.* 10. 599 'alitibus linquere feris', Maecen. ap. Sen. *epist.* 92. 35 'nec tumulum curo; sepelit natura relictos'. *precibus inultis* is strange because *inultus* normally means 'unavenged' (of injuries), or 'unpunished' (of persons), rather than 'unfulfilled' (of curses etc.).

Others interpret *precibus* not as 'curses' but as 'prayers'; but by this stage the corpse has assumed a threatening tone, and in combination with *non ... inultis* the more sinister interpretation seems preferable. Heinze, on the other hand, takes *precibus inultis* as dative and compares phrases like 'leaving somebody to his tears'; but these are not Latin phrases.

34. piacula nulla: cf. Hom. *Od.* 11. 73 (the unburied Elpenor again) μή τοί τι θεῶν μήνιμα γένωμαι, *epod.* 5. 89 f. Such expiations were not just a poetical convention; cf. Cic. *leg.* 2. 57 'itaque in eo qui in nave necatus, deinde in mare proiectus esset, decrevit P. Mucius familiam puram, quod os supra terram non extaret; porcam heredi esse contractam, et habendas triduum ferias et porco femina piaculum faciundum. si in mari mortuus esset, eadem praeter piaculum et ferias', S. P. C. Tromp, *De Romanorum piaculis*, 1921, H. Fugier, *Recherches sur l'expression du sacré dans la langue latine*, 1963, pp. 331 ff.

35. quamquam festinas ...: cf. [Quint.] *decl. maior.* 5. 6 'hinc et ille

venit affectus quod ignotis cadaveribus humum congerimus; et insepultum quodlibet corpus nulla festinatio tam rapida transcurrit
ut non quantulocumque veneretur aggestu'. Similar expressions are
used in epitaphs that ask the attention of the passer-by; cf. Asclepiades, *anth. P.* 13. 23. 1 ἰὼ παρέρπων, μικρόν, εἴ τι κἀγκονεῖς, / ἄκουσον,
Pacuv. p. 32 Morel 'adulescens tam etsi properas hoc te saxulum /
rogat ut se aspicias', Prop. 4. 7. 83 f. 'hic carmen media dignum me
scribe columna, / sed breve, quod currens vector ab urbe legat',
Peek, *GV* 1324. 1 (= Kaibel, *EG* 288. 1) κἤν σπεύδῃς, ὦ ξεῖνε, 1325. 1
κἄν τροχάδην βαίνῃς, φίλε ὦ παροδεῖτα, βαιὸν ἐπίσχε.

non est mora longa: 'it does not take long (to do as I ask)'. Such
phrases are found in epitaphs which the passer-by is asked to read;
cf. *carm. epig.* 513. 2 'cur tantum properas? non est mora dum legis:
audi'.

36. ter: three handfuls of dust were enough. Cf. Soph. *Ant.* 431
χοαῖσι τρισπόνδοισι τὸν νέκυν στέφει.

curras: the merchant may sail with the corpse's blessing. For
currere of a sea-voyage cf. *epist.* 1. 11. 27, *Thes.l.L.* 4. 1515. 25 ff.; the
verb is particularly appropriate of a busy merchant (cf. *serm.*
1. 1. 29 f. 'per omne / audaces mare qui currunt', Cic. *epist.* 16. 9. 4
'solent nautae festinare quaestus sui causa'). For a similar reference
to a sea-voyage in sepulchral epigram cf. Julianus, *anth. P.* 7. 584
πλώεις ναυηγόν με λαβὼν καὶ σήματι χώσας; / πλῶε, Μαλειάων ἄκρα
φυλασσόμενος· / αἰεὶ δ' εὐπλοίην μεθέποις φίλος· ἦν δέ τι ῥέξῃ / ἄλλο
Τύχη, τούτων ἀντιάσαις χαρίτων.

29. ICCI BEATIS

1–5. *Iccius, it seems you are eyeing the treasures of Araby the Blest,
and planning a campaign against the sheikhs of Sheba.* 5–10. *Some
captive virgin will be your handmaid, some emir's page your cup-
bearer.* 10–16. *Water can flow uphill now that you are exchanging your
moral-philosophy books for uniform.*

This poem is addressed to one Iccius; the indexes of *CIL* record
the name six times in Gallia Narbonensis (cf. *L'Année épigr.*, 1961,
no. 162). Horace's friend appears again in *epist.* 1. 12 (written in
20 B.C.), where he is described as agent for Agrippa's Sicilian property. In the epistle as in the ode Horace mocks the philosophical
studies of his ambitious young acquaintance. He suggests that Iccius
is dissatisfied with his income, and maliciously consoles him with

edifying maxims. Even in so acquisitive a milieu, Iccius must have kept up his interest in higher things (*epist.* 1. 12. 14 ff.):

> cum tu inter scabiem tantam et contagia lucri
> nil parvum sapias et adhuc sublimia cures . . .
> quid velit et possit rerum concordia discors,
> Empedocles an Stertinium deliret acumen.

Our poem was written some years earlier than the epistle, at the time of the Arabian expedition of 26–25 B.C. This was led by Aelius Gallus, the prefect of Egypt and father by adoption of Sejanus (*RE* 1. 493). The aim of the campaign was partly to break the Arabian stranglehold on the eastern trade-route, partly aggrandisement and loot. Strabo, who was a friend of Aelius Gallus (2. 5. 12, 17. 1. 46), gives the show away: ἦν δέ τι καὶ τὸ πολυχρημάτους ἀκούειν ἐκ παντὸς χρόνου, πρὸς ἄργυρον καὶ χρυσὸν τὰ ἀρώματα διατιθεμένους καὶ τὴν πολυτελεστάτην λιθείαν, ἀναλίσκοντας τῶν λαμβανομένων τοῖς ἔξω μηδέν (16. 4. 22). Extravagant reports of victory were concocted: Strabo records a remarkable battle where 10,000 Arabians were killed for the loss of two Romans. Augustus in his *Res Gestae* claimed that the army reached Mariba in the Yemen (26. 5 'in Arabiam usque in fines Sabaeorum processit exercitus ad oppidum Mariba'); this was probably Ma'rib, the capital of the Sabaei (A. Dihle, *Umstrittene Daten*, 1964, 80 ff. against *RE* 1 A. 1354 ff., *CAH* 10. 877). But something went wrong with the campaign: Dio says that most of the army perished (53. 29. 4), and even Strabo admits heavy losses in the long march (16. 4. 24). The expedition yielded little but an antidote against snake-bite, which the commander-in-chief courteously sent to Augustus (Galen 14. 203). For further details see Plin. *nat.* 6. 160 ff., E. Glaser, *Skizze der Geschichte und Geographie Arabiens* 2, 1890, pp. 43 ff., *RE* 1 A. 1343 ff., J. G. C. Anderson, *CAH* 10. 248 ff., F. Altheim and R. Stiehl, *Die Araber in der alten Welt* 2, 1965, pp. 49 ff., S. Jameson, *JRS* 58, 1968, 71 ff.

Horace's attitude to the Arabian war suits his period and new-found status. Amiable frivolity would have been intolerable when citizen militias bled under their own walls; even Alcaeus's ode to his mercenary brother Antimenidas is more grandiloquent than ironic (350). If Aristotle ever wrote to his nephew Callisthenes he presumably did not make urbane jokes but asked for hard facts. Hellenistic states were defended by professional armies, and the Alexandrian poets reveal no contact with bookish young amateur officers. But in the first century B.C. a distant campaign was an interesting introduction to a public career (cf. Cic. *Mur.* 11–12); it was sometimes lucrative, one had an opportunity of impressing the right people, and the risk though real was not inordinate. Love and war were romantically linked, perhaps by Gallus, certainly by Virgil (*ecl.* 10), and Propertius (3. 12). Horace himself in an apparently serious poem describes a king's daughter sighing on the ramparts at the sight of a lion-hearted Roman chevalier challenging her betrothed (3. 2. 6 ff.).

In our ode Horace plays with the prevailing clichés. He evokes the romance of the East in a few deft strokes, but he seems rather amused at Iccius's journey to Samarkand. He teases his earnest young friend with a cultivated humour worthy of his epistles, or of Cicero's. Perhaps in fact the most illuminating analogy is Cicero's correspondence with the brilliant young jurist Trebatius, who served with Caesar in 54–53 B.C.: 'in Britannia nihil esse audio neque auri neque argenti. id si ita est, essedum aliquod capias suadeo et ad nos quam primum recurras' (*epist.* 7. 7. 1); 'est quod gaudeas te in ista loca venisse ubi aliquid sapere viderere. quod si in Britanniam quoque profectus esses, profecto nemo in illa tanta insula peritior te fuisset' (7. 10. 1); 'Balbus mihi confirmavit te divitem futurum. id utrum Romano more locutus sit, bene nummatum te futurum, an quo modo Stoici dicunt, omnis esse divites qui caelo et terra frui possint, postea videbo' (7. 16. 3). Horace has transferred to poetry the ironic banter of a civilized and serene governing class. Though unpretentious, the ode is perfect of its kind.

Metre: Alcaic.

1. beatis: Horace is alluding to Arabia Felix (ἡ εὐδαίμων Ἀραβία); this name was applied to the Arabian peninsula, as opposed to Arabia Deserta farther north (*RE* 6. 885 f.). The adjective is found as early as Eur. *Ba.* 16, though there without any precise geographical significance. Southern Arabia was famous for its incense, and its perfumed breezes enraptured the passing voyager; cf. Hdt. 3. 107 ff., 3. 113 ἀποζεῖ δὲ τῆς χώρας τῆς Ἀραβίας θεσπέσιον ὡς ἡδύ, Agatharchides ap. Diod. Sic. 3. 46, Plin. *nat.* 12. 51 ff. Moreover, it lay on the trade-route to the East (M. Cary and E. H. Warmington, *The Ancient Explorers*, 1929, chapter 4, section 8); the ancients assumed too readily that the country's exotic re-exports were locally produced. See further *RE* 2. 355 ff., Otto 33 f., Milton, *P.L.* 4. 162 f. 'Sabaean odours from the spicy shore Of Araby the Blest'.

nunc: whereas formerly the young Stoic regarded riches as anything but *beatae*.

invides: Horace maliciously suggests that Iccius is impelled by the least philosophic motives. For similar gibes at friends cf. 4. 12. 25 'pone moras et studium lucri', *epist.* 1. 5. 8 'mitte levis spes et certamina divitiarum'. For greed as a cause of war cf. Shackleton Bailey, *Propertiana*, p. 222, Boucher 20; in the case of the Arabian expedition the economic interpretation seems for once to have been correct.

2. gazis: the Persian word keeps up the oriental colouring (cf. Austin on Virg. *Aen.* 2. 763).

acrem militiam: grandiose; cf. 3. 2. 2 'robustus acri militia puer'. Horace suspects that the Arabs will have little to fear from Iccius.

3. non ante devictis: cf. 3. 24. 1 f. 'intactis . . . thesauris Arabum', Prop. 2. 10. 16 'et domus intactae te tremit Arabiae'. The Southern Arabians were left unconquered even by Alexander and the Diadochi, and the peninsula formed no part of Trajan's province of Arabia (A.D. 106). See Gibbon, *Decline and Fall*, chapter 50, p. 340 Bury: 'the arms of Sesostris and Cyrus, of Pompey and Trajan, could never achieve the conquest of Arabia; the present sovereign of the Turks may exercise a shadow of jurisdiction, but his pride is reduced to solicit the friendship of a people whom it is dangerous to provoke and fruitless to attack'.

Sabaeae: the south-west corner of Arabia, the Sheba of the Bible, roughly the modern Yemen.

4. regibus: more prosaic sources speak of a single king called Sabos (Str. 16. 4. 3, 16. 4. 24, Dio 53. 29. 3). Though the Sabaean kingdom had been displaced in 115 B.C. by the Himyarites, the royal title remained 'King of Saba'. See further *RE* 1 A. 1387, A. Grohmann, *Kulturgeschichte des alten Orients* 3. 4: *Arabien*, 1963, pp. 28, 121 ff., P. K. Hitti, *History of the Arabs*, 1964, pp. 54 ff.

horribilique Medo: Aelius Gallus was nowhere near either the Medes or the Parthians.

5. nectis catenas: interrogative, like all the other sentences in this poem. Before guards were armed with rifles, prisoners-of-war had to be shackled; for a few details cf. Mommsen, *Strafrecht*, p. 300, D.–S. 1. 969, 5. 897. The confident aggressor prepared his chains beforehand; cf. Hdt. 1. 66. 3, Plb. 3. 82. 8, Flor. *epit.* 1. 42. 2 (M. Antonius in the Bellum Creticum), Tac. *ann.* 2. 18. 1 (the Germans), Grotius, *Annales et Historiae de rebus Belgicis*, 1657, p. 118 (the Spanish Armada) 'laquei certe, et plura necis instrumenta, aut servitutis, inter spolia visitata sunt, quae in victos, ut non dubio eventu, paraverant' (imitating Tacitus, loc. cit.), S. Runciman, *History of the Crusades* 1, 1951, p. 179 'To their delight they found among the Turkish dead the ropes brought to bind the prisoners that the Sultan had hoped to take'.

quae tibi virginum . . . : the genitive is grandiose; its conjunction with the nominative *barbara* makes the style still more mannered.

sponso necato is not pathetic, as some scholars suggest. Rather Horace sees the studious young Iccius in heroic guise, slaying an enemy warrior and winning his bride as a submissive slave. Cf. Hom. *Il.* 19. 291 f. (Briseis speaking) ἄνδρα μὲν ᾧ ἔδοσάν με πατὴρ καὶ πότνια μήτηρ / εἶδον πρὸ πτόλιος δεδαιγμένον ὀξέι χαλκῷ.

7. ex aula: the boy has been a royal page. Cf. *Dan.* 1. 3 f. καὶ εἶπεν ὁ βασιλεὺς Ἀβιεσδρὶ τῷ ἑαυτοῦ ἀρχιευνούχῳ ἀγαγεῖν αὐτῷ . . . νεανίσκους ἀμώμους καὶ εὐειδεῖς . . . καὶ ἰσχύοντας ὥστε εἶναι ἐν τῷ οἴκῳ τοῦ βασι-λέως, Liv. 45. 6. 7 'pueri regii apud Macedonas vocabantur principum liberi ad ministerium electi regis', Curt. 8. 6. 2, Headlam on Herodas 1. 29.

8. ad cyathum: the cyathus was a ladle used to transfer wine from the mixing-bowl to the drinking-cup (D.–S. 1. 1675 ff.). Hence *stare ad cyathum* was to serve the wine; cf. Prop. 4. 8. 37 'Lygdamus ad cyathos', Juv. 13. 43 f. 'nec puer Iliacus formosa nec Herculis uxor / ad cyathos', Auson. 345. 19 'stat Iovis ad cyathum'. This office was entrusted by rich Romans to handsome slave-boys; cf. Cic. *fin.* 2. 23 'adsint etiam formosi pueri qui ministrent', Juv. 5. 56 'flos Asiae ante ipsum' (with Mayor's note), *CIL* 6. 8817 'Liarus Antoniae Drusi glaber ab cyato'. The tone of our passage is not only romantic but erotic; cf. Suet. *Jul.* 49. 2 'C. Memmius etiam ad cyathum . . . Nicomedi stetisse obicit' (the associations of Ganymede are significant).

unctis: for the long hair of *pueri delicati* cf. Vollmer on Stat. *silv.* 3. 4, Mart. 9. 16. 6 'Ganymedeas . . . comas', Philo, *vit. cont.* 51, Greg. Naz. *or.* 14(= 16). 17 παῖδας δὲ παρεστάναι, τοὺς μὲν ἐν κόσμῳ καὶ ἐφεξῆς, ἀνέτους τὰς κόμας καὶ θηλυδρίας καὶ τῇ κατὰ πρόσωπον κουρᾷ περιειργασμένους, πλεῖον ἢ ὅσον συμφέρει λίχνοις ὀφθαλμοῖς κεκοσμη-μένους, Blümner 271, 396 n. 10.

9. Sericas: for the extravagance of the geography cf. 1. 12. 56 n. For Chinese bows cf. Chariton 6. 4. 2 φαρέτρα καὶ τόξον αὐτῷ παρήρτητο, Σηρῶν ἔργον πολυτελέστατον.

10. arcu paterno: for the Persian education in archery cf. Hdt. 1. 136. 2, Str. 15. 3. 18.

quis neget . . .: after Iccius's personality-change Horace decides that water may flow uphill. Similarly Archilochus was induced by an eclipse to list impossibilities that might now happen (74). For Horace's illustration cf. Eur. *Med.* 410 ἄνω ποταμῶν ἱερῶν χωροῦσι παγαί; this famous line was often imitated (Otto 139, Pease on Cic. *div.* 1. 78, Virg. *Aen.* 4. 489). For ἀδύνατα in general cf. K. F. Smith on Tib. 1. 4. 65–6, Shackleton Bailey, *Propertiana*, p. 277, Gow on Theoc. 1. 132, H. V. Canter, *AJPh* 51, 1930, 32 ff., E. Dutoit, *Le Thème de* *l'adynaton dans la poésie antique*, 1936, Curtius 94 ff., G. O. Rowe *AJPh* 86, 1965, 387 ff.

arduis . . . montibus: probably ablative ('on the mountains'). Many editors think that the case is dative ('to the mountains'), but then *arduis* would be less pointed; Horace pictures streams flowing up a steep slope. *pronos* means that they formerly hurried downhill; cf. Claud. 3. 159 f. 'versaque non prono curvavi flumina lapsu / in fontes reditura suos'.

12. Tiberim: Horace characteristically develops the trite Greek ἀδύνατον with a fantastic Italian scene; cf. 1. 33. 7 n., *epod.* 16. 27 ff. 'quando / Padus Matina laverit cacumina / in mare seu celsus procurrerit Appenninus', Sil. 5. 253 f. 'Thrasymennus in altos / ascendet citius colles'.

13. coemptos undique: in the ancient world a library even of standard texts was built up laboriously and piece-meal, like an art-collection.

nobilis: genitive; *libros* is already qualified by *coemptos*. Cf. Cic. *Phil.* 5. 13 'Phaedri philosophi nobilis'.

14. Panaeti: Panaetius was born at Rhodes about 185 B.C.; about 144 he came to Rome and joined the circle of Scipio Aemilianus; from 129 to 109 he was head of the Stoa. His most famous work was the three books περὶ τοῦ καθήκοντος (Gell. 13. 28. 1 'tribus illis inclitis libris'), which lie behind Cicero's *de officiis*; so Horace may here be suggesting that Iccius has abandoned the *honestum*. For details see P. M. van Straaten, *Panaetii Rhodii Fragmenta*, ed. 3, 1962, M. Pohlenz, *Die Stoa* 1, 1948, pp. 191 ff., 2, 1949, pp. 97 ff., A. E. Astin, *Scipio Aemilianus*, 1967, pp. 294 ff.

domum: i.e. *scholam*; cf. Sen. *epist.* 29. 11 'idem hoc omnes tibi ex omni domo conclamabunt, Peripatetici Academici Stoici Cynici', *Thes.l.L.* 5. 1. 1981. 1 ff. See also Hor. *epist.* 1. 1. 13 'quo me duce, quo lare tuter', Cic. *div.* 2. 3 'totaque Peripateticorum familia' (with Pease's parallels).

15. mutare: Iccius is not selling his books to buy breastplates, as some surprisingly suppose, but temporarily abandoning them; cf. Marvell, *Horatian Ode* 5 f. 'Tis time to leave the books in dust And oil the unused armour's rust'.

Hiberis: for details see O. Davies, op. cit. [above, p. 208], pp. 106 f.

16. pollicitus meliora: *pollicitus* refers not to a verbal undertaking, but to the raising of expectations by general demeanour. No parallel presents itself; yet cf. 'promise', 'versprechen'. *meliora* strikes a philosophical note (τὰ κρείττω); cf. *serm.* 2. 2. 6 'adclinis falsis animus meliora recusat', Ov. *met.* 7. 20 'video meliora proboque'.

tendis: the word is a little strange after 9 *tendere*, and it can hardly be given its common sense of 'strive to'; one might sooner have expected *pergis*, 'proceed to' (cf. 2. 18. 16 'novaeque pergunt interire lunae'). Yet for *tendis* cf. *epist.* 2. 2. 56 f. '(anni) eripuere iocos Venerem convivia ludum: / tendunt extorquere poemata'. For non-rhetorical repetition in the *Odes* see W. C. Helmbold, *CPh* 55, 1960, 173 f. His material disproves Housman's assertion that 'Horace was as sensitive to iteration as any modern' (Lucan, p. xxxiii).

30. O VENVS REGINA

[Fraenkel 197 ff.; R. Reitzenstein, *Aufsätze*, pp. 10 f.]

1–4. O Venus, leave Cyprus and visit Glycera. 5–8. Come with Cupid, the Graces and Nymphs, Iuventas, and Mercury.

In form this poem is a κλητικὸς ὕμνος to Venus, but it has a more complicated ancestry than might appear at first sight. The prototype seems to be Alcman 55 Κύπρον ἱμερτὰν λιποῖσα καὶ Πάφον περιρρύταν. In this poem, as in Horace's, there was a mention of Cyprus and Paphos; cf. also Menander rhet. 3. 334. 27 ff. Sp. (an obscure and apparently corrupt passage) ἅμα μὲν γὰρ ἐκ πολλῶν τόπων τοὺς θεοὺς ἐπικαλεῖν ἔξεστιν ὡς παρὰ τῇ Σαπφοῖ καὶ τῷ Ἀλκμᾶνι πολλαχοῦ εὑρίσκομεν ... τὴν δὲ Ἀφροδίτην Κύπρου Κνίδου Συρίας πολλαχόθεν [ἀλλαχόθεν] ἀνακαλεῖ. We do not know the setting of Alcman's poem, but presumably it was a genuine cult-hymn, or something very near it.

Horace's ode may also have been influenced by a poem of Sappho's (2), deciphered by Medea Norsa on a potsherd and first published in 1937. The text in places is very uncertain; for a discussion see Page, *Sappho and Alcaeus*, pp. 34 ff.

> δεῦρύ μ᾽ ἐκ Κρήτας ἐπ[ὶ τόνδε] ναῦον
> ἄγνον, ὅππ[αι τοι] χάριεν μὲν ἄλσος
> μαλί[αν], βῶμοι δὲ τεθυμιάμε-
> νοι [λι]βανώτῳ.

In both Sappho and Horace the goddess is asked to leave her traditional haunts. In both she seems to be summoned to a holy place (ναῦον, aedem), which is described as lovely (χάριεν, decoram), and where incense is being burned. It is also possible that Sappho's poem, like Horace's, mentions the attendants of the goddess; Athenaeus, who quotes part of it, uses the paraphrase τούτοισι τοῖς ἑταίροις ἐμοῖς γε καὶ σοῖς. It should be observed that Sappho has already

C c

broken away from the old-world piety of the cult-hymn; she is more interested in her own feelings and experiences than in the deity to whom the poem is formally addressed (Page, op. cit. p. 42).

The κλητικὸς ὕμνος was further secularized by the Alexandrian Posidippus, to whom Horace is primarily indebted (Reitzenstein, loc. cit.):

> ἃ Κύπρον ἅ τε Κύθηρα καὶ ἃ Μίλητον ἐποιχνεῖς
> καὶ τὸ καλὸν Συρίης ἱπποκρότου δάπεδον,
> ἔλθοις ἵλαος Καλλιστίῳ ἣ τὸν ἐραστὴν
> οὐδέποτ' οἰκείων ὦσεν ἀπὸ προθύρων (anth. P. 12. 131).

Here the intention is not religious at all. The poem is nothing more than an elegant epigram, and its subject is not Aphrodite but the *hetaera* Callistion.

Where does Horace's poem fit in this series? Fraenkel regards it as serious and moving: 'Horace the poet understood and enjoyed the beauty of a scene in which the Olympians grant to a mortal the blessings of their presence, their παρουσία' (p. 198). That can hardly be right: Horace is imitating Posidippus's epigram, and one is therefore inclined to look for a sophisticated adaptation of the original hymnal form. Ps.-Acro took a much more cynical view: he supposed that Mercury was summoned by the courtesan as the god of gain. This interpretation deserves more consideration than it has usually received. It is true that in Greek cult Aphrodite and Hermes are sometimes found together (8 n.), but this association does not particularly suit the world of Glycera. The name occupies a prominent place in a single line at the end; if we do not give it a special point the ode becomes simply an ineffective imitation of a familiar Greek epigram. It is perhaps better to assume that so far from returning to Alcman Horace has gone one better than Posidippus.

Metre: Sapphic.

1. **regina . . .**: cf. Pind. fr. 122. 17 ὦ Κύπρου δέσποινα, Ar. *Lys.* 833 f. ὦ πότνια Κύπρου καὶ Κυθήρων καὶ Πάφου / μεδέουσ'. For the appositional style in prayers cf. 1. 10. 1 n. Archaic deities were not regarded as omnipresent (Norden, *Agnostos Theos*, p. 168); it was common for worshippers to mention alternative cult-centres where they might be found (Menander rhet., cited above). The formula was taken over by later poets; cf. 3. 26. 9 ff., 3. 28. 13 ff., Theoc. 15. 100 f. δέσποιν' ἃ Γολγώς τε καὶ Ἰδάλιον ἐφίλησας / αἰπεινάν τ' Ἔρυκα, χρυσῷ παίζοισ' Ἀφροδίτα, Catull. 64. 96 'quaeque regis Golgos quaeque Idalium frondosum'. Elsewhere Catullus ends the list of addresses with humorous bathos: 'quae sanctum Idalium Uriosque apertos /

quaeque Ancona Cnidumque harundinosam / colis quaeque Ama-
thunta quaeque Golgos / quaeque Durrachium Hadriae tabernam'
(36. 12 ff.).

Cnidi: in Caria, opposite Rhodes. Aphrodite had three shrines
there (Paus. 1. 1. 3), and was represented on the coinage from the
seventh century to the Roman Empire (Head 615 ff.). Tourists of
the imperial period could still admire the best statue in the world, the
naked Aphrodite of Praxiteles (Plin. *nat.* 36. 20, Lucian, *am.* 11,
imag. 4, Gow–Page 2. 68). It was celebrated in an epigram by Plato
which had many imitators (*anth. Pl.* 159 ff.). For an illustration
of the Vatican copy cf. G. M. A. Richter, *Handbook of Greek Art*,
1959, p. 130; for a reproduction on Cnidian coinage cf. Roscher
1. 416.

Paphique: the town in south-west Cyprus where Aphrodite landed
from the foam. There she had an ancient cult (derived from the
Phoenician Astarte); cf. Hom. *Od.* 8. 362 f. ἡ δ' ἄρα Κύπρον ἵκανε
φιλομμειδὴς Ἀφροδίτη / ἐς Πάφον, ἔνθα τέ οἱ τέμενος βωμός τε θυήεις,
Hes. *th.* 193, *h.Ven.* 58 f., Eur. *Ba.* 402 ff. The goddess's bloodless
rites and archaic cone excited wonder even in Tacitus's day (*hist.*
2. 3). See further *RE* 18. 3. 951 ff.

2. sperne: the word need not imply contempt; cf. 3. 2. 24 'spernit
humum'. For similar expressions applied to gods, sometimes in
κλητικοὶ ὕμνοι, cf. Alcaeus 34 a 1 νᾶσον Πέλοπος λίποντες, Theogn. 1277
τῆμος "Ερως προλιπὼν Κύπρον, περικαλλέα νῆσον, Aesch. *Eum.* 9,
Theoc. 1. 125, 7. 115 f., Catull. 61. 27 f. 'perge linquere Thespiae / rupis
Aonios specus', Virg. *georg.* 1. 16 ff., *Aen.* 4. 143 f., Stat. *Theb.* 5. 61
'illa Paphon veterem centumque altaria linquens'.

Cypron: Peerlkamp sees some awkwardness; Paphos was in
Cyprus but Cnidus was not. The imbalance is somewhat different in
Alcman 55 (above, p. 343), Sappho 35 ἤ σε Κύπρος καὶ Πάφος ἤ
Πάνορμος, Aesch. (?) fr. 463 Κύπρου Πάφου τ' ἔχουσα πάντα κλῆρον.
These passages were censured or explained away by ancient com-
mentators (cf. Eustath. *Il.* 2. 625 ἐμπεριέχεται γὰρ ἡ Πάφος τῇ
Κύπρῳ); perhaps Horace is replacing one sort of incongruity by
another. Yet in view of his models one might almost have expected
him to write *Cypri* and *Cnidon*.

3. ture: For the use of incense in the worship of Venus cf. 1. 19. 14,
4. 1. 22, Sappho 2 (above, p. 343), Pind. fr. 122. 3 ff. αἵ τε τᾶς χλωρᾶς
λιβάνου ξανθὰ δάκρη / θυμιᾶτε, πολλάκι ματέρ' ἐρώτων οὐρανίαν πτά-
μεναι / νοήματι πρὸς Ἀφροδίταν, Empedocles fr. 128, Virg. *Aen.* 1. 415
'ipsa Paphum sublimis abit, sedesque revisit / laeta suas, ubi templum illi, centumque Sabaeo / ture calent arae sertisque recentibus
halant'. Here Glycera can rival even the exotic rites of Paphos.

decoram: cf. Lucr. 2. 352 'deum . . . delubra decora'. But the word is particularly suited to a shrine of Venus.

4. aedem: in the singular in classical Latin this word means not 'house', but 'shrine'. Probably Horace suggests that the courtesan's room is itself a shrine, fit for occupation either by Glycera or Venus. Others think of a literal *aedicula*, where Glycera sacrificed to Venus; *aedes* need imply nothing more than a little domestic altar (*Thes.l.L.* 1. 913. 50 ff.). Yet this is perhaps a less pointed interpretation; a domestic altar would not be particularly beautiful whereas the room as a whole might derive loveliness from its occupant.

5. fervidus . . .: often in prayers a god is asked to bring his retinue; cf. Ar. *eq.* 586 ff. δεῦρ' ἀφικοῦ λαβοῦσα . . . Νίκην, *Thesm.* 1146 f. ἔχουσα δέ μοι μόλοις Εἰρήνην φιλέορτον. Aphrodite is represented with a κῶμος both in literature and art; Eros appears in her train as early as Hes. *th.* 201 τῇ δ' "Ερος ὡμάρτησε καὶ "Ιμερος ἕσπετο καλός (cf. West's note). For Dionysus, Eros, the nymphs, and Aphrodite cf. Anacreon 357; for Venus, the nymphs, and Graces cf. 1. 4. 6 n.

solutis . . . zonis: *discinctae*. This seems to have been a traditional dress of the Graces, and Seneca mentions an unconvincing explanation without conviction (*ben.* 1. 3. 5): 'in quibus nihil esse adligati decet, nec adstricti: solutis itaque tunicis utuntur; perlucidis autem, quia beneficia conspici volunt'. Such literary allusions seem to have influenced Botticelli's Primavera; cf. E. Wind, *Pagan Mysteries in the Renaissance*, 1958, p. 104. Peerlkamp comments censoriously on our passage 'parum honeste, praesente Mercurio et Iuventa'. In fact in Roman times the Graces were normally portrayed naked (Paus. 9. 35. 6 f., Roscher 1. 883 f.).

6. properentque: for the word order cf. 2. 19. 31 f. 'et recedentis trilingui / ore pedes tetigitque crura', Orelli on our passage, Leo, *Analecta Plautina* 1, 1896, 31 ff. (= *Ausgewählte kleine Schriften*, 1960, 1. 104 ff.).

7. comis: Porphyrio comments 'scire autem debemus Venerem non tantum concubituum verum etiam dominam esse omnium elegantiarum'. *comis* is a prosaic word, used by Horace in his satires, Ovid in his elegies, and Martial, but otherwise avoided by the major Latin poets (Axelson 101).

sine te: for this hymnal formula cf. 1. 26. 9 n.

Iuventas: originally a respectable Roman deity, the protector of young men, and the recipient of an ancient chapel on the Capitoline; Augustus took the cult seriously and assigned its festival to 18 October, the day on which he assumed the *toga virilis*. Yet Iuventas is often given the gayer qualities of Hebe; cf. Cic. *nat. deor.* 1. 112

'(the poets speak of) Iuventatem aut Ganymedem pocula mini-
strantem' (with Pease's note), Serv. auct. *Aen.* 5. 134 'Hebe Graece
est Iuventas', *RE* 10. 1361, Roscher 2. 764 ff. For Hebe's association
with Aphrodite cf. *h.Ap.* 195 Ἁρμονίη θ' "Ήβη τε Διὸς θυγάτηρ τ'
Ἀφροδίτη.

8. Mercuriusque: Peitho was a traditional member of Aphrodite's
train; cf. Aesch. *supp.* 1040, Paus. 1. 43. 6, Hor. *epist.* 1. 6. 38 'Suadela
Venusque'. Hermes could naturally be given the same function;
cf. Cornutus, *nat. deor.* 24 (Ἀφροδίτη) παρέδρους δὲ καὶ συμβώμους τὰς
Χάριτας ἔχει καὶ τὴν Πειθὼ καὶ τὸν Ἑρμῆν διὰ τὸ πειθοῖ προσάγεσθαι καὶ
λόγῳ καὶ χάρισι τοὺς ἐρωμένους, Plut. *conj. praec.* 138 c οἱ παλαιοὶ
τῇ Ἀφροδίτῃ τὸν Ἑρμῆν συγκαθίδρυσαν, Apul. *met.* 6. 7. 3 'scis nempe
sororem tuam Venerem sine Mercuri praesentia nihil umquam fecisse'.
The association was not merely literary; there were joint cults of
the two gods, some apparently of considerable antiquity, at Argos
(Paus. 2. 19. 6), Megalopolis (id. 8. 31. 6), Cnidos, and Lesbos (cf.
Farnell 2. 653). A late and eccentric tradition makes Hermes the
son of Aphrodite and Dionysus (*Orph. h.* 57. 3 f.). Yet here a special
point may be intended (above, p. 344).

31. QVID DEDICATVM

[P. Veyne, *Latomus* 24, 1965, 932 ff.]

1–3. *What is my prayer as I make libation at Apollo's new temple?*
3–15. *I do not ask for wealth.* 15–20. *I am content with little, and pray
for enjoyment of what comes to hand, for health of body and mind and
for an old age that leaves opportunities for poetry.*

Horace gives his poem a very Roman setting, in the glittering new
temple of Apollo on the Palatine, dedicated on 9 October 28 B.C.
(1 n.). The temple was also celebrated by Propertius in two poems,
one a graceful trifle (2. 31), the other a more pretentious composition
in which the poet figures as a priest and sings the glories of Actium
(4. 6). In our ode Horace's solemn appearance as a *vates* might lead
one to expect something similarly patriotic and conventional. Instead he chooses as the purported occasion of the poem not the
temple's dedication day, but the festival of the Meditrinalia two days
later (2 n.), and he takes the opportunity to utter not a public hymn,
but a private prayer.

First of all Horace explicitly rejects the prayers of the average

man. This theme belongs to a conventional type of priamel (cf.
1. 1, pp. 2 f.). One may compare *epod.* 1. 25 ff., 2. 49 ff., Anacreon 361
ἐγὼ δ᾽ οὔτ᾽ ἂν Ἀμαλθίης / βουλοίμην κέρας οὔτ᾽ ἔτεα / πεντήκοντά τε
κάκατόν / Ταρτησσοῦ βασιλεῦσαι, Pind. *N.* 8. 37 ff. (cited above, p. 3),
Alpheius, *anth. P.* 9. 110 οὐ στέργω βαθυληΐους ἀρούρας, / οὐκ ὄλβον
πολύχρυσον, οἷα Γύγης. / αὐτάρκους ἔραμαι βίου, Μακρῖνε· / τὸ Μηθὲν
γὰρ ἄγαν ἄγαν με τέρπει. However, the poem also draws on philosophic discussions on propriety in prayer, such as are found in the
Laws (687 c–688 b, 801 a–b) and in the pseudo-Platonic *Second
Alcibiades*. The commonplaces were later exploited by Persius
(*sat.* 2) and Juvenal (*sat.* 10). Horace himself touched on the theme
again in the eloquent conclusion to *epist.* 1. 18 (104 ff.):

> me quotiens reficit gelidus Digentia rivus . . .,
> quid sentire putas, quid credis, amice, precari ?

In the last stanza Horace gives his own prayer: one may note
alike his brevity and the wide range of his thought. He asks in
Epicurean spirit that he may have enjoyment of what lies ready to
hand (τὰ εὐπόριστα). He makes the conventional prayer for a 'healthy
mind in a healthy body', one that was particularly appropriate in
addressing the god of healing (Wissowa 294) on the occasion of the
Meditrinalia. Finally, he begs that his old age may not lack the lyre.
The theme was conventional in archaic and Hellenistic poetry (20 n.),
but here it seems completely authentic. In front of the statue of
Apollo Citharoedus (1 n.) even a sceptical poet might offer a personal
prayer that his capacity for poetry should not fail.

The ode might easily be underrated. In spite of the disconcertingly
pompous opening, it is very different from artificial laureate work.
The topic about rejected prayers is developed with varied pictures
of Italian life, the cornfields of Sardinia, the pastures of Calabria,
the vineyards of Campania. The final stanza, though very compressed, has dignity and truth.

Metre: Alcaic.

1. **quid . . .**: the temple was vowed during the war with Sex. Pompeius
and completed after Actium. It stood near Octavian's own house
and had porticoes adjacent, together with Greek and Latin libraries;
cf. *epist.* 1. 3. 17, 2. 1. 216 f., 2. 2. 94, Suet. *Aug.* 29. 3 'templum
Apollinis in ea parte Palatinae domus excitavit, quam fulmine ictam
desiderari a deo haruspices pronuntiarant; addidit porticus cum
bibliotheca Latina Graecaque, quo loco iam senior saepe etiam
senatum habuit decuriasque iudicum recognovit'. As Octavian
wanted the space (Vell. 2. 81. 3), it was useful that the god did too.

For a detailed description of the temple cf. S. B. Platner and T. Ashby, *A Topographical Dictionary of Ancient Rome*, 1929, pp. 16 ff., J. Gagé, *Apollon romain*, 1955, pp. 522 f., Enk on Prop. 2. 31, E. Nash, *Pictorial Dictionary of Ancient Rome* 1, 1961, pp. 31 f. The archaeological and the literary evidence for its site are in some conflict; for recent discussion cf. J. H. Bishop, *CQ* N.s. 6, 1956, 187 ff., 11, 1961, 127 ff., O. Richmond, ibid. 8, 1958, 180 ff.

Inside the temple stood an Apollo by Scopas, a Latona by Cephisodotus, and a Diana by Timotheus (Prop. 2. 31. 16 f., Plin. *nat.* 36. 25, 24, 32, P. E. Arias, *Skopas*, 1952, pp. 101 f., G. E. Rizzo, *La base di Augusto*, Naples, 1933, pp. 51 ff.). The group may be represented on an altar base from Sorrento, showing Apollo as *citharoedus* (cf. Gagé, op. cit., p. 533 and Plate VI a). Outside there seems to have been another statue of Apollo *citharoedus* (Prop. 2. 31. 5 f., Gagé, op. cit., pp. 535 f.). This probably stood in the attached portico of the Danaids (cf. H. Last, *JRS* 43, 1953, 27 ff.).

dedicatum: for the application of the word to the god rather than the temple, cf. Cic. *dom.* 110, *nat. deor.* 2. 61 'ut Fides, ut Mens, quas in Capitolio dedicatas videmus', Liv. 5. 52. 10 'Iuno regina ... dedicata est', Ov. *fast.* 6. 637 f. 'te quoque magnifica, Concordia, dedicat aede / Livia'. Here the participle implies that the temple has just been dedicated.

P. Veyne, loc. cit., argues that the poem has nothing to do with the temple of Apollo; *dedicatum* refers simply to a private offering. It may be admitted that nothing specific is said about a temple; but in the given historical context, when other poets were describing the dedication, the allusion would be clear. Veyne wrongly sees a difficulty in the use of *dedicare Apollinem* in the sense of *dedicare aedem Apollinis*; he misses the significance of the Meditrinalia; he destroys the contrast between the pomposity of the *vates* on a public occasion and the simplicity of his private prayer.

poscit: 'prays', cf. 1. 32. 1 n. The word is not here deliberative in sense, 'What is he to pray for?', but means 'What does he pray for?'; cf. *epist.* 1. 18. 106.

2. vates: for the word cf. 1. 1. 35 n. The oldest Greek poets spoke of themselves as inspired by the Muses, and this idea soon produced the picture of the poet as priest or προφήτης of the Muses or Apollo; cf. Alcman 30 with Aristides 28. 53 K., Theogn. 769 Μουσέων θεράποντα καὶ ἄγγελον, Pind. fr. 94a. 5 f. μάντις ὡς τελέσσω / ἱεραπόλος, *pae.* 6. 6 ἀοίδιμον Πιερίδων προφάταν, fr. 150 μαντεύεο, Μοῖσα, προφατεύσω δ' ἐγώ, Pl. *Ion* 534 e, Theoc. 16. 29, 17. 115, 22. 116 f., Virg. *georg.* 2. 476, Hor. *carm.* 3. 1. 3, 4. 9. 28, Prop. 3. 1. 3, 4. 6. 1, Ov. *am.* 3. 9. 17 f., Kroll 24 ff.

patera: the flat dish used in libation; cf. Macr. *sat.* 5. 21. 4 'patera enim, ut et ipsum nomen indicio est, planum ac patens est'.

novum: Horace is thinking of the ceremonies of the Meditrinalia, which took place on 11 Oct., two days after the dedication of Apollo's temple. We are told that at this festival, which closed the vintage, there were solemn libations of new and old wine. As these were believed to bring health, Horace is already pointing to the prayer of the last stanza; cf. Varro, *ling.* 6. 21 'Octobri mense Meditrinalia dies dictus a medendo, quod Flaccus flamen Martialis dicebat hoc die solitum vinum ⟨novum⟩ et vetus libari et degustari medicamenti causa; quod facere solent etiam nunc multi cum dicunt: "novum vetus vinum bibo, novo veteri morbo medeor" ', Paul. Fest. 110. 21 ff. L. (= 123. 15 f. M.). There is perhaps a similar allusion in Juv. 10. 248 ff. 'felix nimirum . . . qui . . . novum totiens mustum bibit'. For the Meditrinalia see further *RE* 15. 106 f., F. Bömer, *RhM* 90, 1941, 51 ff.

3. fundens: the word is technical; cf. Serv. *Aen.* 6. 244 'fundere est supina manu libare, quod fit in sacris supernis; vergere autem est conversa in sinistram partem manu ita fundere ut patera convertatur, quod in infernis sacris fit'. The prayer with libation is a simple one, not involving a complicated or expensive *votum*; cf. Pers. 2. 3 'funde merum genio; non tu prece poscis emaci . . .'.

liquorem: cf. Lucr. 5. 14 f. 'liquoris / vitigeni laticem', Tib. 2. 1. 45 'aurea tunc pressos pedibus dedit uva liquores', Petron. 133 v. 16 'spumabat pateris hornus liquor'. The abstract removes the secular associations of wine from the sacral libation.

4. Sardiniae: the island was settled by the pastoral god Aristaeus, a testimony to its fruitfulness (Paus. 10. 17. 3, ps.-Arist. *mirab.* 838ᵇ22 ff., Sil. 12. 365 ff.). The plains were unhealthy but very fertile; cf. Str. 5. 2. 7, Mela 2. 123, Sil. 12. 375 'cetera propensae Cereris nutrita favore'.

Sardinia supplied corn to the Carthaginians in 396 B.C. (Diod. Sic. 14. 63. 4, 14. 77. 6), and after the Roman conquest to the armies of Rome (Liv. 25. 22. 5). For its importance in the first century B.C. cf. Cic. *Manil.* 34 (Sicily, Africa, and Sardinia are) 'tria frumentaria subsidia rei publicae', *epist.* 1. 9. 9, Flor. *epit.* 2. 13. 22 'Siciliam et Sardiniam, annonae pignera', App. *civ.* 2. 40. 161, Varro, *rust.* 2 praef. 3, Val. Max. 7. 6. 1 'Siciliamque et Sardiniam, benignissimas urbis nostrae nutrices'. This support of the *annona* continued to the last ages of the empire. Prudentius denies that the removal of the altar of Victory affected it (*c. Symm.* 2. 942 f.); cf. Salvian. *gub.* 6. 68 (on the Vandal inroads) 'eversis Sardinia ac Sicilia, id est fiscalibus horreis, atque abcisis velut vitalibus venis'.

segetes: 'cornland'; this sense is the commoner one in Republican Latin. The sense 'crop', more normal later, has commended to some editors the interpolation 'opimas Sardiniae segetes feracis'.

5. aestuosae: cf. 1. 22. 5 n. Calabria (in ancient times the heel of Italy, not the toe as now) is both hot and dry; cf. on the neighbouring Apulia 3. 30. 11 'pauper aquae Daunus', *epod.* 3. 16 'siticulosae Apuliae'.

grata . . . armenta: *armenta* normally refers to cattle or horses; cf. Serv. *georg.* 3. 49 'armenta autem sunt equorum et boum . . ., greges vero capellarum et ovium sunt. . . . haec tamen, armenta et greges, sciendum quia plerumque confundit auctoritas' (the second remark is not borne out by our extant texts). In a description of the blessings of wealth, cattle are perhaps more impressive than other animals; cf. Bacch. fr. 21. 1 f. οὐ βοῶν πάρεστι σώματ', οὔτε χρυσός, / οὔτε πορφύρεοι τάπητες.

Two objections have been made to the text. In the first place, it is said, *grata* and *aestuosae* do not stand in the right relation to each other; one expects the noun to refer to something that is particularly welcome in the heat of the day. Hence Campbell proposed *palmeta*, though there are no specific references elsewhere to Calabrian palmgroves. We do hear of the *pineta Galaesi* in Prop. 2. 34. 67 and Stat. *silv.* 2. 2. 111 (*vineta* codd., edd.); but *pineta* is too remote from the manuscripts, and not specifically enough a sign of wealth. Heinze is probably right in defending *aestuosae* . . . *grata* as an oxymoron; he cites Strabo's statement that Calabria was παραδόξως . . . ἀστεία, especially because ἀνυδροτέρα . . . οὖσα εὔβοτος οὐδὲν ἧττον καὶ εὔδενδρος ὁρᾶται (6. 3. 5).

Secondly it is objected that Calabria is not typically associated with cattle. Yet see Virg. *georg.* 2. 195 ff. 'sin armenta magis studium vitulosque tueri, / aut ovium fetum aut urentis culta capellas, / saltus et saturi petito longinqua Tarenti, / et qualem infelix amisit Mantua campum', Luc. 9. 185 'calidi . . . buceta Matini' (cited by ps.-Acro on our passage), Val. Fl. 3. 582 'emicuit Calabris taurus . . . saeptis'. Admittedly the area was most famous for its sheep, the so-called *Graecum pecus*; cf. Colum. 7. 4. 1, Plin. *nat.* 8. 190. Hence Münch and Peerlkamp conjectured *Graia*. But *armenta* does not at all naturally refer to sheep, and the poetical word *Graius* seems too grand to apply to them; moreover, the extra proper name spoils the relation between *non opimae Sardiniae segetes feracis* and *non aestuosae grata Calabriae armenta*.

6. non aurum . . .: gold and ivory are often mentioned together as ornaments for a luxurious town-house; in particular they are deprecated, as here, by moralists who praise the simple life. Cf. 2. 18.

1 f. 'non ebur nec aureum / mea renidet in domo lacunar', Bacch. fr. 20B. 13 χρυσῷ δ' ἐλέφαντι τε μαρμαίρουσιν οἶκοι, Cic. *parad*. 13 'marmoreis tectis, ebore et auro fulgentibus', Prop. 3. 2. 12 'camera auratas inter eburna trabes', Petron. 135. 8 'non Indum fulgebat ebur, quod inhaeserat auro', Luc. 10. 113–19 (of Cleopatra's palace), Dio Chrys. 13. 34 τό τε ἀργύριον καὶ τὸ χρυσίον καὶ τὰ ἐλεφάντινα σκεύη . . . καὶ ξύμπαντα ἁπλῶς τὰ νῦν ἐν τῇ πόλει τίμια καὶ περιμάχητα, Muson. fr. 20 p. 110. 3 Hense κλῖναι μὲν ἐλεφάντιναι καὶ ἀργυραῖ, ἔνιαι δὲ χρυσαῖ, ps.-Lucian, *cyn*. 9 τῶν δὲ χρυσορόφων οἰκιῶν οὐδέν τι μᾶλλον σκεπουσῶν, τῶν δὲ ἐκπωμάτων τῶν ἀργυρῶν οὐκ ὠφελούντων τὸν πότον οὐδὲ τῶν χρυσῶν, οὐδ' αὖ τῶν ἐλεφαντίνων κλινῶν τὸν ὕπνον ἡδίω παρεχομένων, Clem. Alex. *paed*. 2. 3. 35, below, 10 n.

Indicum: the epithet applies both to *aurum* and *ebur*; cf. Soph. *Ant*. 1038 f. τὸν Ἰνδικὸν χρυσόν. In Hdt. 3. 102. 2, Call. 2. p. 118 Pf., Prop. 3. 13. 5 we hear of Indian ants who dug gold from their burrows; there were also more conventional ways of getting gold in India (cf. Plin. *nat*. 33. 66 'aurum invenitur . . . fluminum ramentis, ut in . . . Gange Indiae').

Indian ivory was said to be by now the only one with pieces of any size; cf. Plin. *nat*. 8. 7 'rara amplitudo iam dentium praeterquam ex India reperitur, cetera in nostro orbe cessere luxuriae', Catull. 64. 48 'Indo . . . dente politum (pulvinar)', Virg. *georg*. 1. 57, *RE* 5. 2358.

7. Liris: the Liris rises in the Apennines near Lake Fucinus, flows south through the Marsian territory and Latium, and enters the sea at Minturnae. In its upper course it is still called the Liri, lower down the Garigliano. As the latter it is the boundary between Latium and Campania, with the *ager Falernus* on its left bank and Mons Massicus near by. Pliny is lyrical in his account of the district (*nat*. 3. 59 f.): 'hinc felix illa Campania est, ab hoc sinu incipiunt vitiferi colles et temulentia nobilis suco per omnes terras incluto atque, ut veteres dixere, summum Liberi patris cum Cerere certamen. hinc Setini et Caecubi protenduntur agri, his iunguntur Falerni, Caleni, dein consurgunt Massici Gaurani Surrentinique montes'. In this part of its course the river meanders lazily through vineyards; this area, where it is crossed by the via Appia, was the one best known to most of Horace's readers.

The Liris is a favourite with literary men. The charming preludes of Cicero's *de legibus* describe its beauties at Arpinum (1. 14, 2. 6, and fr. 5). For references in the poets cf. 3. 17. 7 f., Luc. 2. 424, Sil. 4. 438 ff. 'Liris . . . qui fronte quieta / dissimulat cursum ac, nullo mutabilis imbri, / perstringit tacitas gemmanti gurgite ripas', 8. 399 f. 'Fibreno miscentem flumina Lirim / sulpureum tacitisque vadis ad litora lapsum'.

8. mordet: Horace is imitating Call. *ep.* 44. 3 f. πολλάκι λήθει / τοῖχον ὑποτρώγων ἡσύχιος ποταμός; cf. also Lucr. 5. 256 'ripas radentia flumina rodunt', Ov. *ars* 1. 620 'ut pendens liquida ripa subestur (Axelson, *subetur* vel sim. codd.) aqua', Luc. 2. 425 'radensque Salerni / tesca Siler', *Aetna* 112 f. 'seu lympha perenni / edit humum limo', Claud. 1. 259 f. 'terens querceta Maricae / Liris', Serv. *Aen.* 8. 63 'stringentem ripas: radentem, imminuentem; nam hoc est Tiberini fluminis proprium, adeo ut ab antiquis Rumon dictus sit, quasi ripas ruminans et exedens'. ὑποξύω is similarly used in Dionys. *perieg.* 61, 385, Marianus, *anth. P.* 9. 669. 9 f. ἐνθάδε καὶ ποταμὸς λασίην παραμείβεται ὄχθην, / πέζαν ὑποξύων αὐτοφύτοιο νάπης.

taciturnus: cf. Virg. *Aen.* 8. 87 'tacita refluens ita substitit unda', Tib. 1. 7. 13 f. 'Cydne, ... tacitis qui leniter undis / caeruleus placidis per vada serpis aquis', Isaiah 8. 6 'The waters of Shiloah that go softly', and the Byzantine proverb σιγηροῦ ποταμοῦ τὰ βάθη γύρευε (K. Krumbacher, *Mittelgriechische Sprichwörter*, 1893, pp. 128, 223 f.). Horace's *taciturnus*, like Callimachus's ἡσύχιος, ascribes a human disposition to the river, and says more than *tacitus*; cf. 3. 29. 23 f. 'caretque / ripa vagis taciturna ventis'. So in 2. 8. 10 f. 'toto taciturna noctis / signa cum caelo', the stars make no response to complaints of Barine's perjury; cf. Prop. 1. 18. 1 'haec certe deserta loca et taciturna querenti' (the *loca* will not repeat the laments).

9. premant ...: for a similar figure (which, however, makes a different point) cf. Macedonius, *anth. P.* 11. 59. 4 ff. ἄλλοισιν μελέτω Τριπτολέμοιο γέρα κτλ., Paul. Sil. ibid. 11. 60. 3 f. σιτοδόκῳ δ᾽ ἄγραυλος ἀνὴρ βαρύμοχθος ἰάλλοι / γαστρὶ μελαμπέπλου μητέρα Φερσεφόνης.

premant ... falce: cf. Virg. *georg.* 1. 156 f. 'ruris opaci / falce premes umbram', Ov. *met.* 14. 629 f. 'qua (falce) ... luxuriem premit et spatiantia passim / bracchia compescit', Plut. *aud. poet.* 15 f ὅπου ... ὑλομανεῖ τὸ μυθῶδες αὐτῆς καὶ θεατρικόν, ἐπιλαμβανόμενοι κολούωμεν καὶ πιέζωμεν. In the epodes Horace uses the more prosaic 'inutilisque falce ramos amputans' (2. 13). The *falx vinitoria* with its admirable many-purpose blade is described by Colum. 4. 25 and illustrated in D.–S. 2. 969.

Calena: for the wine of Cales cf. 1. 20. 9 n. For the use of the geographical epithet cf. 1. 20. 9 f. 'prelo domitam Caleno / ... uvam' (a fairly close parallel), 3. 6. 38 f. 'Sabellis docta ligonibus / versare glaebas', Catull. 17. 19 'Liguri ... suppernata securi'. If this reading is correct the implicit object of *dedit* ('that they may do so') is to be inferred from the main clause, and *vitem* is governed by *premant*. 'The vine' without qualification cannot be the gift of fortune in this context.

The lemma of Porphyrio reads *Calenam*, which has been accepted by many editors; *dedit* can now govern *vitem*, which in some ways seems more natural. Yet the parallels for *Calena* are so convincing that it is unlikely to be a corruption; it is artificial of Bentley to draw a distinction between a Calene knife, which can be taken somewhere else, and a Calene press, which cannot. It might also be argued against *Calenam* that *falce* in this position without an adjective is curiously isolated and pointless; Virgil's *falce premes* (cited above) gives a much more natural word order.

10. et: for the postponement cf. *Thes.l.L.* 5. 2. 897. 52 ff. There is no certain example before Virgil and Horace; cf. Austin on Virg. *Aen.* 4. 33.

The variant *ut* is accepted by some editors, including Bentley and Klingner; a new idea is thus introduced, that the farmer prunes his vines simply in order to provide a luxury for the trader. But it is undesirable to banish the trader to a subordinate clause: the man who runs risks in order to import luxuries from afar makes an excellent contrast with Horace, who has no trouble in collecting good things that lie ready to hand. The farmer and the trader are in fact in the same situation: just as the trader runs risks for his rewards, so the farmer works hard with the pruning hook for his. For the familiar parallel between farmer and merchant and Horace's preference for a life different from either's one may compare 1. 1. 11–22.

aureis: cf. Philo, *somn.* 2. 61 τί δὲ ἀργυρῶν καὶ χρυσῶν κυλίκων ἄφθονον πλῆθος κατασκευάζεσθαι (ἔδει), εἰ μὴ διὰ τὸν φρυαττόμενον μεγάλα τῦφον καὶ τὴν ἐπ' αἰώρας φορουμένην κενὴν δόξαν;, Muson. fr. 20 p. 111. 1 ff. Hense (earthenware cups) τό τε δίψος σβεννύειν παραπλησίως πέφυκε τοῖς χρυσοῖς, καὶ τὸν ἐγχεόμενον αὐτοῖς οἶνον οὐ λυμαίνεται, ὀσμὴν δέ γε ἡδίω τῶν χρυσῶν παρέχεται καὶ τῶν ἀργυρῶν, above, 6 n.

11. exsiccet: the verb elsewhere has as its object the vessel that is drained; cf. Q. Cic. *epist.* 16. 26. 2 '(lagonae) furtim essent exsiccatae', Sen. *epist.* 58. 32 'qui amphoram exsiccat et faecem quoque exsorbet'. The opposite enallage, *potare pocula* or *cados* (cf. πίνειν δέπας) is more frequent; cf. 3. 15. 16.

culillis: only here and in *ars* 434. Porphyrio says 'proprie autem culilae calices sunt quidam fictiles, quibus pontifices virginesque Vestales in sacris utuntur'. The word may be connected with the archaic *culigna*, κυλίχνη (cf. Alcaeus 346. 2 κὰδ δ' ἄερρε κυλίχναις μεγάλαις, 322, Athen. 481 a).

12. Syra . . . merce: for instance, purple, pepper, and unguents, as Porphyrio suggests. *merce* is unexpected after *mercator*; cf. 1. 29. 16 n.

For the use of the gentile name *Syra* instead of the adjective cf. Mart. 4. 46. 9. Horace uses *Medus, Hiberus, Thynus, Bithynus* as well as the common *Italus*. For Greek parallels cf. Soph. *OC* 314 Θεσσαλίς, fr. 176 P. (= 178 N.) Λάκων (Hedylus, *anth. P.* 6. 292. 1), fr. 272 P. (= 250 N.) Ἀρκάς, Nic. *ther.* 45 Θρήισσα.

L. Müller objected that the importation of Syrian merchandise did not involve entering the Atlantic, and proposed the pointless *sua*. But for the variety of illustration cf. 1. 7. 10 n. The merchandise is Syrian because that is the richest and most exotic, the sea the Atlantic because that is the most dangerous.

reparata: 'got in due return for'; the *re-* is like ἀπο- in ἀποδίδοσθαι, cf. ἀπαιτεῖν, *reposcere.* Cf. Alfenus, *dig.* 15. 3. 16 'iusserat eos (boves) venire et his nummis ... alios reparari. servus boves vendiderat, alios redemerat', Scaev. *dig.* 45. 1. 122. 1 'non reparasset merces' (after 'aliis mercibus emptis').

13. dis carus: θεοφιλής. Horace here makes a sarcastic application of a common idea; cf. Hes. *op.* 120 ἀφνειοὶ μήλοισι, φίλοι μακάρεσσι θεοῖσι (and often elsewhere), Antiphilus, *anth. P.* 10. 17. 5 f. κεῖθεν δ᾽, εἰ Φοίβῳ μεμελήμεθα πάντες ἀοιδοί, / πλεύσομαι εὐαεῖ θαρσαλέως Ζεφύρῳ.

quippe: elsewhere in Horace only at *serm.* 1. 2. 4. Here, like ἅτε, it takes a participle, as *utpote* does in *serm.* 1. 5. 94; cf. K.–S. 1. 791 Anm. 7.

14. Atlanticum: cf. Arist. *protr.* B 53 Düring χρημάτων μὲν ἕνεκα πλεῖν ἐφ᾽ Ἡρακλέους στήλας καὶ πολλάκις κινδυνεύειν.

15. me ...: for praise of vegetarian food in Horace cf. *serm.* 1. 6. 114 f., *epist.* 1. 5. 2, and Alfius in *epod.* 2. 54 ff. 'non attagen Ionicus / iucundior quam lecta de pinguissimis / oliva ramis arborum / aut herba lapathi prata amantis et gravi / malvae salubres corpori'. In the country Horace, like Baucis and Philemon, added a piece of pork (*serm.* 2. 6. 63 f.).

The motif occurs in earlier poetry; cf. Alcman 17. 4 ff. ἔτνεος, οἷον ὁ παμφάγος Ἀλκμὰν / ἠράσθη ... / οὔτι γὰρ †οὐ τετυμμένον† ἔσθει, / ἀλλὰ τὰ κοινὰ γάρ, ὥσπερ ὁ δᾶμος, / ζατεύει, Eur. fr. 714, 892–3, *Phoen.* 554, Philemon fr. 92 K., Lucil. 1235 'o lapathe, ut iactare, nec es satis cognitus qui sis!' Hellenistic poets were particularly fond of stories in which the people of the archaic age hospitably welcomed gods or heroes to their simple fare; this was the theme of Callimachus's *Hecale* and of Eratosthenes's *Erigone*, and is reflected in extant litera-ture in Ovid's story of Baucis and Philemon (*met.* 8. 629 ff.). Cf. particularly Diodorus com. fr. 2. 5 ff. K., Call. frr. 248–52, Eratosthenes fr. 34 Powell, Ov. *fast.* 4. 545 f., *paneg. Mess.* 9 ff., Apollod. 2. 5. 1 with Frazer's note on Molorchus, Nonnus 17. 37 ff., M. Pohlenz, *Die hellenistische Poesie und die Philosophie, Charites für F. Leo*, 1911, pp. 76 ff., Vischer 126 ff.

The philosophers vied with each other in commending the charms of a bread-and-water diet. Cf. Crates's hymn to Eutelia (2), Chrysipp. 3. 177 ff. von A., Teles, p. 41. 3 f. Hense (speaking of Crates) ἠρκεῖτο τρίβωνι μάζῃ καὶ λαχανίοις, Diog. Laert. (on Epicurus) 10. 11, 131, 132, Philodemus, *anth. P*. 9. 412. 1 ff. ἤδη καὶ ῥόδον ἐστι, καὶ ἀκμάζων ἐρέβινθος, / καὶ καυλοὶ κράμβης, Σώσυλε, πρωτοτόμου, / καὶ μαίνη †ζαλαγεῦσα, καὶ ἀρτιπαγὴς ἀλίτυρος, / καὶ θρικάδων οὔλων ἀβροφυῆ πέταλα (clearly referring to an Epicurean *hortulus*). The Epicureans were generally agreed to have outdone their opponents; cf. Cic. *Tusc*. 5. 89 'ipse (Epicurus) quam parvo est contentus! nemo de tenui victu plura dixit', Hier. *adv. Iovin*. 2. 11 'Epicurus voluptatis assertor omnes libros suos replevit holeribus et pomis, et vilibus cibis dicit esse vivendum, quia carnes et exquisitae epulae . . . maiorem . . . poenam habeant in inquirendo quam voluptatem in abutendo'.

pascunt: this clause gives the factual basis for the following prayer. The sequence of thought is, 'Let others live luxuriously; as I need only a simple diet, grant me the following prayer' (1. 7. 10 n.). *pascunt* implies not just 'I eat', but 'I eat my fill'; it suggests that Horace's nourishment is adequate and satisfying.

Tanaquil Faber, followed by Bentley, suggested *pascant*. It is true that after 'Let others do such and such' one often finds a wish for the author (see Bentley's parallels). But here this wish is in fact expressed in the last stanza, to which the present sentence is essentially subordinate; *pascant* would make its relation to what follows very obscure.

olivae . . . : for olives as a simple food cf. *serm*. 2. 2. 45 f., for mallows Hes. *op*. 41 ὅσον ἐν μαλάχῃ τε καὶ ἀσφοδέλῳ μέγ᾽ ὄνειαρ, Ar. *Plut*. 543 f., *RE* 14. 922 ff. *leves* means *non gravantes*, 'easily digestible', and seems to apply to all three plants; cf. *epod*. 2. 57 f. 'gravi / malvae salubres corpori', Cels. 2. 20, 2. 24. 1 f. Cicero complains of diarrhoea brought on by a vegetarian dinner-party (*epist*. 7. 26. 2 'ita ego, qui me ostreis et murenis facile abstinebam, a beta et a malva deceptus sum').

17. frui: emphatic, 'to make good use of'; cf. Lucian, *anth. P*. 10. 41. 3 f. τόνδε πολυκτέανον καὶ πλούσιον ἔστι δίκαιον / · κλήζειν, ὃς χρῆσθαι τοῖς ἀγαθοῖς δύναται.

Horace's prayer has poetic as well as philosophical antecedents; cf. Theogn. 1155 f. οὐκ ἔραμαι πλουτεῖν οὐδ᾽ εὔχομαι, ἀλλά μοι εἴη / ζῆν ἀπὸ τῶν ὀλίγων μηδὲν ἔχοντι κακόν (anon. *anth. P*. 10. 113), Crates 1. 3 f. χόρτον ἐμῇ συνεχῶς δότε γαστέρι, ἥτε μοι αἰεὶ / χωρὶς δουλοσύνης λιτὸν ἔθηκε βίον, Call. fr. 346 (clearly from the *Hecale*) γαστέρι μοῦνον ἔχοιμι κακῆς ἀλκτήρια λιμοῦ, Leonidas, *anth. P*. 7. 736, Tib. 1. 1. 5 f.

paratis: often misinterpreted; the meaning is not *quae paravi* but *quae in promptu sunt* (G. Carlsson, *Philologus* 90, 1935, 391 f., Veyne, loc. cit., 947 ff.). This is a commonplace of philosophic (especially Epicurean) thought; cf. Epicurus, fr. 469 χάρις τῇ μακαρίᾳ φύσει ὅτι τὰ ἀναγκαῖα ἐποίησεν εὐπόριστα, τὰ δὲ δυσπόριστα οὐκ ἀναγκαῖα, Diog. Laert. 10. 130, 144, 148, Teles, p. 7. 4 f. Hense ἢ οὐ μεσταὶ μὲν αἱ ὁδοὶ λαχάνων, πλήρεις δὲ αἱ κρῆναι ὕδατος;, Lucr. 6. 9 f. 'ad victum quae flagitat usus / omnia iam ferme mortalibus esse parata', Cic. *fin.* 1. 45, 2. 90, 91, Hor. *serm.* 2. 3. 166 f., *epist.* 1. 12. 7 f. 'si forte in medio positorum abstemius herbis / vivis et urtica', Sen. *epist.* 4. 10, 90. 18 'ad parata nati sumus: nos omnia nobis difficilia facilium fastidio fecimus', Petron. *anth. Lat.* 694. 1 ff. 'omnia quae miseras possunt finire querellas, / in promptu voluit candidus esse deus. / vile olus et duris haerentia mora rubetis / pugnantis stomachi composuere famem'.

et valido mihi . . .: it was conventional in prayers to ask for health of mind and body; cf. Petron. 61. 1 'omnes bonam mentem bonamque valetudinem sibi optarunt', 88. 8 'ne bonam quidem mentem aut bonam valetudinem petunt', Sen. *epist.* 10. 4 'roga bonam mentem, bonam valetudinem animi, deinde tunc corporis', Juv. 10. 356 'orandum est ut sit mens sana in corpore sano'. For instances of similar phrases cf. *certamen Hom. et Hes.* 167 φρένες ἐσθλαὶ σώμασιν ἀνδρῶν, Pl. *Gorg.* 479 b ὑγιοῦς σώματος . . . ὑγιεῖ ψυχῇ, Isoc. *panath.* 7 τῆς περὶ τὸ σῶμα καὶ τὴν ψυχὴν ὑγιείας, Epicurus, *epist.* 3. 128 ἐπὶ τὴν τοῦ σώματος ὑγίειαν καὶ τὴν τῆς ψυχῆς ἀταραξίαν, ἐπεὶ τοῦτο τοῦ μακαρίως ζῆν ἐστι τέλος.

18. **Latoe**: according to the common practice, Horace turns to the god at the end of his poem. The grandiose ἐπίκλησις belongs to the world of Greek poetry rather than of Roman religion. For the Doric form, which is particularly 'poetical', cf. Mnasalcas, *anth. P.* 6. 128. 2, Ov. *met.* 11. 196; *Letous* and *Letoius* are more common.

et precor: the reading of the paradosis is *at precor*. It would have to be translated 'Grant me a wise enjoyment both in full bodily strength (but only if my mind is also unimpaired) and in old age grant me a life neither contemptible nor unpoetic'. The restrictive parenthesis might seem to be supported by Sen. *epist.* 10. 4 (cited on 17 above). But on this interpretation *valido* has to mean 'when I am young and strong', whereas the parallels show that the prayer for a healthy body was central in such contexts, and not merely incidental. Moreover, the anacoluthon is awkward; *et valido* would lead us to expect *et seni*, but the further development of the latter phrase throws the whole sentence off balance. Finally it might be argued that a restrictive parenthesis would require *sed* rather than *at* (so Housman, cited below).

Lambinus's *et precor* solves all difficulties very simply. Yet scholars have been tempted to look for an explanation that accounts for *at*. Housman championed *adprecor*, which is found in Paris. 7972 (cf. 4. 15. 28 'rite deos prius adprecati'); the word is used intransitively at Apul. *met.* 6. 3. 4. He interprets 'adprecor, Latoe, dones mihi frui paratis et valido integra cum mente senectam degere nec turpem nec cithara carentem' (*PCPhS* 114, 1919, 22). Yet this leaves the structure seriously unsymmetrical: the first prayer is finished within two words (*frui paratis*), the second takes up the rest of the sentence.

integra cum mente: the prayer is for a mind unimpaired by either vice or insanity. For the former sense cf. Cic. *Font.* 32 'mentes tam castae, tam integrae', *Mil.* 61 'pura mente atque integra', for the latter Scaev. *dig.* 28. 3. 20 'integra mente et valetudine'; cf. *Thes.l.L.* 7. 1. 2074. 53 ff., 2075. 30 ff. *bona mens* (*RE* 15. 937), the more usual object of prayer, refers more obviously to moral health.

19. nec. . . nec: καὶ οὔτε . . . οὔτε; cf. K.–S. 2. 46. 1(a).

turpem: cf. Mimnermus 5. 2 f. τὸ δ᾽ ἀργαλεὸν καὶ ἄμορφον / γῆρας, Virg. *georg.* 3. 96, Sil. 15. 651, Juv. 10. 191 f. 'deformem et taetrum ante omnia vultum / dissimilemque sui'.

senectam: the prayer for old age was standard (Juv. 10. 188 'da spatium vitae, multos da Iuppiter annos'). Horace makes some necessary provisos; cf. Synes. *hymn.* 7(8). 15 ff. λιπαρὸν δὲ φέροις ἔτος / εἰς γήραος ἀδονὰν / ἐρίτιμον ἀέξων / πινυτὰν σὺν ὑγείᾳ (see also on *cithara* below). He rejects Maecenas's attitude 'vita dum superest bene est' (cf. Sen. *epist.* 101. 10–15).

Age came early to the ancients, and may not have seemed remote to Horace, who was almost 37 at the dramatic date of this poem. In the same year of his life Philodemus wrote of his white hairs and begged the Muses to put a full stop to his youthful μανία (*anth. P.* 11. 41).

20. cithara carentem: the phrase recalls Greek negative compounds. So Aeschylus calls war ἀκίθαρις (*suppl.* 681) and the song of the Erinyes ἀφόρμικτος (*Eum.* 332), while Sophocles in his brooding chorus on old age speaks of the time Ἄιδος ὅτε μοῖρ᾽ ἀνυμέναιος / ἄλυρος ἄχορος ἀναπέφηνε, / θάνατος ἐς τελευτάν (*OC* 1221 ff.).

Horace's prayer is also a Greek one; cf. Theogn. 791 f. τερποίμην φόρμιγγι καὶ ὀρχηθμῷ καὶ ἀοιδῇ, / καὶ μετὰ τῶν ἀγαθῶν ἐσθλὸν ἔχοιμι νόον, Eur. *HF* 676 (after a lament on the horrors of old age) μὴ ζῴην μετ᾽ ἀμουσίας, fr. 369. 1 ff. κείσθω δόρυ μοι μίτον ἀμφιπλέκειν ἀράχναις, / μετὰ δ᾽ ἡσυχίας πολιῷ γήρᾳ συνοικοίην· / ἀείδοιμι δὲ στεφάνοις κάρα πολιὸν στεφανώσας. Posidippus at the end of his address to the Muses makes a personal prayer that in old age he may be eloquent as well as sturdy, ἀσκίπων ἐν ποσσὶ καὶ ὀρθοεπὴς ἀν᾽ ὅμιλον (24; for text and discussion cf. H. Lloyd-Jones, *JHS* 83, 1963, 75 ff.). In a similar spirit the ageing Callimachus in his famous prologue to the *Aetia* assures himself that the Muses will not desert him (37 f.):

Μοῦσαι γὰρ ὅσους ἴδον ὄθματι παῖδας / μὴ λοξῷ, πολιοὺς οὐκ ἀπέθεντο φίλους.

32. POSCIMVS SI QVID

[P. Ferrarino, *Athenaeum* 13, 1935, 219 ff.; Fraenkel 168 ff.; R. Reitzenstein, *Aufsätze*, pp. 23 ff.]

1–4. *Lyre, if ever thou didst help me in the past, sing a Latin song,* 5–12 *thou that wert first played by Alcaeus of Lesbos, who though brave in war wrote verses on wine and love.* 13–16. *Thou that art healing balm after trouble, accept the salutations of a devotee.*

This poem is addressed to the lyre. For such invocations cf. 3. 11. 7 f. (to the *testudo*) 'dic modos Lyde quibus obstinatas / applicet aures', *h.Merc.* 31 χαῖρε, φυὴν ἐρόεσσα, χοροίτυπε, δαιτὸς ἑταίρη, Sappho 118 ἄγι ... χέλυ δῖα ... φωνάεσσα, Theogn. 761 φόρμιγξ δ᾽ αὖ φθέγγοιθ᾽ ἱερὸν μέλος ἠδὲ καὶ αὐλός, Pind. *P.* 1. 1 χρυσέα φόρμιγξ, Bacch. fr. 20 B. 1 ff. ὦ βάρβιτε μηκέτι πάσσαλον φυλάσσων ... δεῦρ᾽ ἐς ἐμὰς χέρας. Of course Horace did not literally play an Aeolian lyre any more than Gray (cf. Fraenkel 403 f.). The lyre stands for the type of lyric poetry originated by Alcaeus and now practised by Horace.

The ode is set in the form of a hymn: see the notes on 1 *poscimus* and *si quid*, 2 *tecum*, 3 *age dic*, 5 *Lesbio* ... , 13 *o* and *decus*, 15 *salve*, 16 *rite*. Horace beseeches the lyre to utter a poem, and some editors tried to identify this work: 1. 12, 1. 35, 3. 1–6, even the *Carmen Saeculare* were among their fantastic guesses. The right answer is 1. 32: the poem does not introduce another, but simply refers to itself (cf. above, p. 254).

Our ode is not humorous like the pseudo-prayer to the wine-jar (3. 21). On the other hand it should not be treated too solemnly: the contrast between form and substance is too great. Horace professes to regard his poem as a trifle (see note on 2 *lusimus*); he by-passes Alcaeus's political poetry, and emphasizes the soothing power of the lyre both for Alcaeus and himself. He undoubtedly admired the Greek lyric poets, but his admiration was probably more restrained and realistic than that of a post-Romantic Hellenist. The ode is an agreeable trifle, but it has not enough content for greatness.

Metre: Sapphic.

1. **poscimus**: 'I pray' (the verb is etymologically connected with
preces); cf. 1. 31. 1, *epist*. 2. 1. 134 'poscit opem chorus', Virg. *Aen*.
1. 666 'supplex tua numina posco', Norden on Virg. *Aen*. 6. 45. For
similar entreaties at the beginning of a poem cf. Pind. *O*. 12. 1 f.
λίσσομαι παῖ Ζηνὸς Ἐλευθερίου / ʽἹμέραν εὐρυσθενέʼ ἀμφιπόλει, σώτειρα
Τύχα, *P*. 12. 1 ff. αἰτέω σε φιλάγλαε . . . δέξαι στεφάνωμα τόδʼ, *N*. 3. 1 ff.
ὦ πότνια Μοῖσα, μᾶτερ ἁμετέρα, λίσσομαι / . . . ἵκεο Δωρίδα νᾶσον Αἴγιναν.
It is noteworthy that in these passages, as in our own, the verb of
entreaty is followed by an imperative; add Sappho 1. 2 f. λίσσομαί
σε / μή μʼ ἄσαισι . . . δάμνα, Pind. *P*. 1. 71 λίσσομαι νεῦσον Κρονίων,
K. Ziegler, *De precationum apud Graecos formis quaestiones selectae*,
Diss. Vratislav. 1905, pp. 39 ff., Appel 156 ff.

The variant *poscimur* is also well attested in the manuscripts; it
was the reading of the ancient commentators and is adopted by
many modern editors. It is supposed to mean 'I am summoned',
'I am invited to play a tune'. See Pind. *I*. 8. 5 f. αἰτέομαι χρυσέαν
καλέσαι / Μοῖσαν, Ov. *met*. 2. 143 f. 'non est mora libera nobis: /
poscimur', 4. 274 'poscitur Alcathoe', 5. 333 'poscimur Aonides',
fast. 4. 721 'nox abiit oriturque Aurora; Parilia poscor'.

poscimus is certainly right. It suits alike the prayer-formula *si quid*
(see next note) and λίσσομαι in the Greek parallels; this cannot be
due to palaeographic accident. On the other hand *poscimur* is intolerably abrupt; the poem has to make a fresh start after the first
word.

si quid . . .: such clauses in prayers give the reason (expressed
with becoming diffidence) why the god should help the suppliant.
See Hom. *Il*. 1. 39 ff. Σμινθεῦ, εἴ ποτέ τοι χαριέντʼ ἐπὶ νηὸν ἔρεψα / . . .
τόδε μοι κρήηνον ἐέλδωρ, C. Ausfeld, *Jahrb. für class. Phil*. Suppl. 28,
1903, 526, Appel 150 f. Often as here he is asked to help because he
has done so before; cf. Hom. *Il*. 5. 116 f. εἴ ποτέ μοι καὶ πατρὶ φίλα
φρονέουσα παρέστης / . . . νῦν αὖτʼ ἐμὲ φῖλαι, Ἀθήνη, 16. 236 f., Sappho
1. 5 ff. ἀλλὰ τυίδʼ ἔλθʼ αἴ ποτα κἀτέρωτα / τὰς ἔμας αὔδας ἀίοισα πήλοι /
ἔκλυες, Pind. *I*. 6. 42 ff., Soph. *OT* 164 ff., Ar. *Thesm*. 1157 ff., Catull.
34. 22 ff. 'Romulique / antique ut solita es bona / sospites ope gentem'
(the conjecture *Ancique* ignores the pattern), Stat. *Ach*.1. 8 f., Aristides,
or. 43. 1 K. καὶ ὥσπερ ἔσωσας εὐμενῶς καὶ προσοῦ τὰ χαριστήρια τῷ τε
λόγῳ ἐπάρκεσον . . . For the Christian formula 'libera sicut liberasti' with
its Jewish parallels cf. A. Baumstark, *Comparative Liturgy* (English
edition), 1958, p. 73, E. Werner, *The Sacred Bridge*, 1959, pp. 248 f.

vacui: 'in leisure moment'; cf. *serm*. 2. 3. 10 'si vacuum tepido
cepisset villula tecto'. *sub umbra* and *lusimus* underline Horace's
self-depreciation. He is hinting at the *umbratilis vita* of the poet; cf.
epist. 2. 2. 78, Mart. 9. 84. 3 'haec ego Pieria ludebam tutus in umbra',
P. L. Smith, *Phoenix* 19, 1965, 298 ff.

2. lusimus: *ludere*, like παίζειν, is often used of writing light verse; the noun is παίγνιον, in Latin *ludicrum* or *ludus* or *lusus* (Porph. on our passage 'sic poetae fere verecunde carmina sua lusus vocant'). *ludere* is used especially of love-poetry (4. 9. 9 'si quid olim lusit Anacreon', cf. Laevius's *Erotopaegnia*); also of epigram, etc. (Catull. 50. 2 'multum lusimus in meis tabellis'), of satire (*serm.* 1. 10. 37 'haec ego ludo'), of pastoral (Virg. *georg.* 4. 564 'carmina qui lusi pastorum'), indeed of almost any kind of verse outside epic and tragedy (cf. Pind. *O.* 1. 16 f. οἷα παίζομεν φίλαν / ἄνδρες ἀμφὶ θαμὰ τράπεζαν). See further Wagenvoort 30 ff., V. Buchheit, *Studien zum Corpus Priapeorum*, 1962, pp. 29 f.

tecum: cf. Virg. *ecl.* 8. 21 'incipe Maenalios mecum, mea tibia, versus'. Yet in our passage *tecum* seems also to belong to the world of prayer, and to suggest 'with thy help'; cf. Pind. *O.* 14. 5 f. σὺν γὰρ ὕμμιν τὰ τερπνὰ καὶ / τὰ γλυκέ' ἄνεται πάντα βροτοῖς, Theoc. 7. 12 ἐσθλὸν σὺν Μοίσαισι Κυδωνικὸν εὕρομες ἄνδρα, Ariphron 813. 6 ff. ἢ εἴ τις ἄλλα θεόθεν ἀνθρώποισι τέρψις ἢ πόνων / ἀμπνοὰ πέφανται / μετὰ σεῖο, μάκαιρ' Ὑγίεια, / τέθαλε καὶ λάμπει Χαρίτων ὀάροις (for the common σὺν θεῷ see Barrett on Eur. *Hipp.* 169, Gow on Machon 9. 77). Contrast *sine te* in prayers and hymns (1. 26. 9 n.).

quod et . . . .: 'to last till this year' (to be taken with *quid*). Horace continues to speak modestly of his *lusus*; of course he really thinks that it will last very much longer. Cf. Call. fr. 7. 14 ἵνα μοι] πουλὺ μένωσιν ἔτος, Cinna fr. 14 'saecula permaneat nostri Dictynna Catonis', Catull. 1. 10 'plus uno maneat perenne saeclo'.

Bentley took the clause with *carmen* ('a song to last for the ensuing year'); for the use of *hunc* cf. Cic. *Sest.* 20 'habebit senatus in hunc annum quem sequatur'. He saw a contrast between Horace's past trifles and the true Latin poem which he is now writing. But his interpretation goes against the natural run of the sentence (Fraenkel 171 ff.). Nor does it suit the prayer-formula 'help me now even as you have helped me before'. It is quite a different thing to say 'You helped me on a trivial poem before, so utter a grand one now'.

3. vivat: cf. 4. 9. 11 f. 'vivuntque commissi calores / Aeoliae fidibus puellae', *epist.* 1. 19. 2, Liv. 39. 40. 7, Stat. *silv.* 4. 6. 26 f., Pind. *N.* 4. 6 ῥῆμα δ' ἐργμάτων χρονιώτερον βιοτεύει, Call. *ep.* 2. 5 αἱ δὲ τεαὶ ζώουσιν ἀηδόνες.

age dic: cf. 3. 4. 1 f. 'descende caelo et dic age tibia / regina longum Calliope melos'.

Latinum: contrasted with *Lesbio*. It is a long way from Lesbos to Latium, and one does not normally associate the Greek βάρβιτος with an Italian *carmen*, but Horace claims to be writing Roman poetry in the Greek manner: he is the 'Romanae fidicen lyrae'

(4. 3. 23). The poem is addressed not to Horace's private lyre but to 'the lyre', i.e. the instrument first used by Alcaeus. 'The lyre' in this sense has played many tunes before, almost always for Greek poets; there is no suggestion that Horace's previous poems were not 'Latina carmina'.

Some editors wish *Latinum carmen* to mean 'a truly Roman poem', one that is grander than Horace's previous trifles; cf. Pers. 6. 3 f. 'mire opifex . . . marem strepitum fidis intendisse Latinae'. But the present poem (which is all that *carmen* can refer to) is not particularly grand. Moreover, the prayer-formula requires that the *Latinum carmen* should not be any more pretentious than the trifles which have gone before (see note on 2 *quod et* . . .).

4. barbite: a kind of lyre, whose exact characteristics are uncertain (*RE* 3. 4 f., D.–S. 3. 1450, W. D. Anderson, *Ethos and Education in Greek Music*, 1966, pp. 4 ff.). The word was barbarian (Str. 10. 3. 17), but was used by Sappho and Anacreon (Athen. 182 f.), Pindar and Bacchylides, and in the *Anacreontea*. It appears in Horace elsewhere (1. 1. 34, 3. 26. 4), and in Statius and Claudian, but was never fully naturalized in Latin. Dionysius of Halicarnassus comments (*ant. Rom.* 7. 72. 5) παρὰ μὲν ῞Ελλησιν ἐκλέλοιπεν ἡ χρῆσις ἐπ᾽ ἐμοῦ, πάτριος οὖσα· παρὰ δὲ ῾Ρωμαίοις ἐν ἁπάσαις φυλάττεται ταῖς ἀρχαίαις θυηπολίαις.

5. Lesbio . . .: Fraenkel points out that it is a common practice in prayers and hymns to give the birth and childhood of the god (1. 10. 1 n.).

primum: Horace is not saying that Alcaeus was the inventor of the lyre (that was Terpander), but that he was the first to write a particular kind of lyric poetry. It may seem strange that our ode, which attributes so much to Alcaeus, should be written in Sapphics; but it should be observed that Alcaeus also used this metre.

modulate: passive; cf. *ars* 263 'immodulata poemata', Porph. on *serm.* 1. 2 'carmina eius (Horatii) parum scite modulata esse dicebat (Tigellius Hermogenes)', *Thes.l.L.* 8. 1246. 15 ff. So 1. 1. 25 *detestata*, *epod.* 16. 8 *abominatus*, K.–S. 1. 111.

civi: Horace alludes obliquely to the στασιωτικά, in which Alcaeus attacked the regimes of Myrsilus and Pittacus; cf. 2. 13. 31 'pugnas et exactos tyrannos', 4. 9. 7 f. 'Alcaei minaces . . . Camenae', Page, *Sappho and Alcaeus*, pp. 149 ff. Horace suggests that Alcaeus was a champion of constitutional government against tyranny; cf. anon. *anth. P.* 9. 184. 7 f. καὶ ξίφος Ἀλκαίοιο, τὸ πολλάκις αἷμα τυράννων / ἔσπεισεν πάτρης θέσμια ῥυόμενον, Quint. *inst.* 10. 1. 63 'Alcaeus in parte operis aureo plectro merito donatur qua tyrannos insectatus multum etiam moribus confert'.

6. ferox bello: 'although brave in war'; cf. Athen. 627 a Ἀλκαῖος . . .
πρότερα τῶν κατὰ ποιητικὴν τὰ κατὰ τὴν ἀνδρείαν τίθεται, μᾶλλον τοῦ
δέοντος πολεμικὸς γενόμενος. Apart from civil wars Alcaeus fought
against the Athenians in the Troad (Hdt. 5. 95, Str. 13. 1. 38).
Horace is drawing a contrast between Alcaeus's virile temperament and the sensuous character of some of his poetry; cf. Cic.
Tusc. 4. 71 'fortis vir in sua republica cognitus quae de iuvenum
amore scribit Alcaeus!', Quint. *inst.* 10. 1. 63 'sed et lusit et in amores
descendit, maioribus tamen aptior', Athen. 687 d καὶ ὁ ἀνδρειότατος
δέ, προσέτι δὲ καὶ πολεμικὸς ποιητὴς Ἀλκαῖος ἔφη· κὰδ δὲ χευάτω μύρον
ἆδυ κὰτ τὼ / στήθεος ἄμμι. Alcaeus was a fiery warrior and a bold
sailor (this second element is characteristically not spelled out);
yet in the intervals of battle and storm he sang of love and wine.

7. religarat: 'had tied up'; cf. *serm.* 1. 5. 19, Ov. *met.* 14. 248, Luc.
7. 860 f., Kroll on Catull. 64. 174. Horace suggests that Alcaeus had
sought refuge on a wind-swept shore, and was ready to start again
at a moment's notice.

udo: in the tideless Mediterranean wet sand suggests that there
has been a storm.

8. navim: as well as writing about the ship of state (above, p. 179)
Alcaeus seems to have written about a real ship, or at any rate
Horace thought that he did. Cf. 2. 13. 26 ff. 'et te sonantem plenius
aureo, / Alcaee, plectro dura navis, / dura fugae mala, dura belli'; as
navis there is co-ordinate with *fugae* and *belli* it can hardly refer
simply to politics (which include exile and war).

9. Liberum: in his hymn to Hephaestus Alcaeus seems to have referred to Dionysus: cf. 349 c εἰς τὼν δυοκαιδέκων (Page, *Sappho and
Alcaeus*, pp. 259 f.). But here Horace is rather thinking of the convivial poems; cf. 346. 3 f. οἶνον γὰρ Σεμέλας καὶ Δίος υἶος λαθικάδεον /
ἀνθρώποισιν ἔδωκ'. More general praises of wine are also relevant;
cf. Athen. 430 a κατὰ γὰρ πᾶσαν ὥραν καὶ πᾶσαν περίστασιν πίνων ὁ
ποιητὴς οὗτος εὑρίσκεται.

Musas: Peerlkamp said that one would expect *nymphas*, but the
Muses are often found in Bacchus's company. Cf. Solon 20 ἔργα δὲ
Κυπρογενοῦς νῦν μοι φίλα καὶ Διονύσου / καὶ Μουσέων ἃ τίθησ' ἀνδράσιν
εὐφροσύνας, anon. *anth.* P. 5. 135. 3, Antip. Sid. ibid. 7. 27. 9 f.,
Ov. *am.* 1. 3. 11 f., *ars* 3. 348, Marc. Argent. *anth.* P. 10. 18. 1 f.

10. semper haerentem puerum: *Cupidinem* (which does not fit the
metre). For mention of Eros in Alcaeus see 327 δεινότατον θέων /
⟨τὸν⟩ γέννατ' εὐπέδιλλος Ἶρις / χρυσοκόμα Ζεφύρῳ μίγεισα (Page, *Sappho
and Alcaeus*, pp. 269 ff.), 296 (ibid. p. 299). But Horace's language

here is not derived from archaic poetry; it suggests the sentimental child of Hellenistic art and literature. So 1. 2. 34, 1. 30. 5.

11. Lycum: for the loves of Alcaeus see Cic. *Tusc.* 4. 71 (quoted above, 6 n.), *nat. deor.* 1. 79 'naevus in articulo pueri delectat Alcaeum', schol. Pind. *I.* 2. 1b ταῦτα δὲ τείνει καὶ εἰς τοὺς περὶ Ἀλκαῖον καὶ Ἴβυκον καὶ Ἀνακρέοντα, καὶ εἴ τινες τῶν πρὸ αὐτοῦ δοκοῦσι περὶ τὰ παιδικὰ ἠσχολῆσθαι. None of the surviving fragments refer to such attachments, except perhaps 368 κέλομαί τινα τὸν χαρίεντα Μένωνα κάλεσσαι / αἰ χρῆ συμποσίας ἐπόνασιν ἔμοιγε γένεσθαι. In the margin of the obscure fragment 71 there is a comment τὸν Ἀλκαίου ἐρώμενον (Page, *Sappho and Alcaeus*, p. 295). The scholiast on Pind. *O.* 11. 15a reads καὶ Ἀλκαῖος· οὐκ ἐγὼ Λύκον ἐν Μούσαις ἀλέγω. However, recent editors plausibly identify this fragment with Alcman 1. 2 οὐκ ἐγὼ]ν Λύκαισον ἐν καμοῦσιν ἀλέγω.

nigris oculis: ἰοβλέφαρος. Cf. *ars* 37, *Anacreontea* 16. 3 ff. (on Bathyllus) λιπαρὰς κόμας ποίησον, / τὰ μὲν ἔνδοθεν μελαίνας, / τὰ δ᾽ ἐς ἄκρον ἡλιώσας· / . . . μέλαν ὄμμα γοργὸν ἔστω, Varro, *Men.* 375 'oculi suppaetuli nigellis pupulis liquidam hilaritatem significantes animi', Catull. 43. 2.

nigroque: the first syllable of this word is short by nature, but in serious poetry can be lengthened by position; here within the one line Horace gives both possible scansions. This was a licence of Greek poetry which in Hellenistic and Roman times became an affectation. Cf. Soph. *OC* 883 ἆρ᾽ οὐχ ὕβρις τάδ᾽; ὕβρις, [Emped.] fr. 157 ἄκρον ἰατρὸν Ἄκρων᾽ Ἀκραγαντῖνον πατρὸς Ἄκρου / κρύπτει κρημνὸς ἄκρος πατρίδος ἀκροτάτης, Virg. *Aen.* 2. 663, Ov. *met.* 13. 607. For this and similar variations see Jebb on Soph. *Ant.* 1310 f., Gow on Theoc. 6. 19, Headlam on Herodas 7. 115, Munro on Lucr. 4. 1259, Friedrich on Catull. 64. 37, Austin on Virg. *Aen.* 4. 159, E. Zinn, *Der Wortakzent in den lyrischen Versen des Horaz*, 1940, 1. 69 f., 72.

13. o: the exclamation gives an elevated note appropriate to prayers; cf. 1. 30. 1, 1. 35. 1, 3. 21. 1. Horace addresses the lyre with three grand ἐπικλήσεις (the tricolon is quite characteristic of the style). Such an accumulation of attributes was a regular feature of hymns (Norden, *Agnostos Theos*, p. 167); for a similar pattern cf., for instance, Julian, *or.* 5. 179 d ὦ θεῶν καὶ ἀνθρώπων μῆτερ, ὦ τοῦ μεγάλου σύνθωκε καὶ σύνθρονε Διός, ὦ πηγὴ τῶν νοερῶν θεῶν.

decus: the similarity to *decorum* above is hardly noticeable. The word is used naturally in hymns; cf. *carm. saec.* 2, Lucr. 3. 3, Virg. *Aen.* 8. 301, *culex* 11, Sen. *Herc. f.* 592, *Oed.* 405.

Phoebi: cf. Pind. *P.* 1. 1 f. χρυσέα φόρμιγξ, Ἀπόλλωνος καὶ ἰοπλοκά-μων / σύνδικον Μοισᾶν κτέανον.

dapibus: cf. 3. 11. 5 f. '(testudo) nunc et / divitum mensis et amica templis'. We have here a scene from archaic Greece, transferred by the poets to Olympus. Cf. Hom. *Il.* 1. 602 f. (θεοὶ) δαίνυντ' οὐδέ τι θυμὸς ἐδεύετο δαιτὸς ἐίσης, | οὐ μὲν φόρμιγγος περικαλλέος, ἦν ἔχ' Ἀπόλλων, *Od.* 8. 99, 17. 271, *h.Merc.* 31 (Hermes addressing the χέλυς) δαιτὸς ἑταίρη.

14. testudo: χέλυς (D.–S. 3. 1439, 5. 157, Pease on Cic. *div.* 2. 133). The tortoise's shell was still used in the Roman period in the manufacture of lyres; cf. Paus. 8. 54. 7 παρέχεται δὲ τὸ Παρθένιον καὶ ἐς λύρας ποίησιν χελώνας ἐπιτηδειοτάτας, Ambr. *Iob* 4. 36 'testudo enim dum vivit luto mergitur; ubi mortua fuerit, tegmen eius aptatur in usum canendi et piae gratiam disciplinae, ut septem vocum discrimina numeris modulantibus obloquatur'.

15. lenimen: this is the first occurrence of the word in Latin, and it may even be a coinage of Horace's own. Formations in *-men* are more grandiloquent than those in *-mentum*; cf. Löfstedt, *Syntactica* 2. 297, J.Perrot, *Les Dérivés latins en -men et -mentum,* 1961, pp. 104 ff.

For the theme cf. 3. 4. 39 f. 'finire quaerentem labores | Pierio recreatis antro' (of the Muses and Augustus), Pind. *I.* 8. 1 λύτρον εὔδοξον . . . καμάτων (of the κῶμος), Theoc. 22. 221 λιγεῶν μειλίγματα Μουσέων, *Orph. Arg.* 89 ἐπαρήγονα μόχθων (of the lyre), Stat. *Ach.* 1. 185 ff., *anth. Lat.* 887 'Pan tibi, Phoebe tibi, lenimen dulce laborum, | otia dum terimus, carmina mille damus' (see also next note).

medicumque: Lachmann's emendation (proposed almost without argument on Lucr. 5. 311) for *mihi cumque* of the manuscripts and Porphyrio. For the curative properties of poetry cf. Pind. *N.* 4. 1 f. ἄριστος εὐφροσύνα πόνων κεκριμένων | ἰατρός, Soph. *Ichn.* 317 καὶ τοῦτο λύπης ἔστ' ἄκεστρον καὶ παραψυκτήριον, Diod. Sic. 1. 49. 3 ἑξῆς δ' ὑπάρχειν τὴν ἱερὰν βιβλιοθήκην ἐφ' ἧς ἐπιγεγράφθαι Ψυχῆς ἰατρεῖον, Ov. *trist.* 4. 10. 118 'tu (Musa) requies, tu medicina venis', 5. 1. 33 f. 'tot mala pertulimus quorum medicina quiesque | nulla nisi in studio est Pieridumque mora', Val. Fl. 4. 87 'medicabile carmen', Clem. Alex. *protr.* 1. 2. 4 γλυκύ τι καὶ ἀληθινὸν φάρμακον πένθους (Reinkens: πειθοῦς codd.) ἐγκέκραται τῷ ἄσματι, Paul. Nol. *epist.* 4. 1 'litteras . . . quas . . . ut animae meae medicas et altrices . . . teneo', Mart. Cap. 9. 926 'perturbationibus animorum corporeisque morbis medicabile crebrius carmen insonui', Abelard, *planctus David super Saul et Jonatha* 1 ff. 'dolorum solatium, / laborum remedium, / mea michi cythara . . .', John Oldham, *Ode on St. Cecilia's day* 'Music's the cordial of a troubled breast . . .'. For the collocation with *laborum* cf. Tert. *anim.* 43. 7 'somnum . . . pacatorem operum, medicum laborum'.

It is objected that *medicumque* is prosaic, especially after the grandiose *lenimen.* Yet the word is much more poetic than 'medical' or 'medicinal'; it is used by Virgil, *georg.* 3. 455 'medicas adhibere manus', *Aen.* 12. 402. The Greek poets use ἄκος and φάρμακον metaphorically, notably in conjunction with words like πόνων; cf. Pind. *N.* 3. 17 f. καματωδέων δὲ πλαγᾶν ἄκος ὑγιηρὸν ἐν βαθυπεδίῳ Νεμέᾳ τὸ καλλίνικον φέρει, Eur. *Ba.* 283 (of wine) οὐδ᾽ ἔστ᾽ ἄλλο φάρμακον πόνων. *medicum* need not be intolerably repetitive after *lenimen*: the soothing power of poetry is looked at from two different points of view, and it is described as both pleasurable and beneficial to health.

It is also objected that *mihi* of the manuscripts is necessary for the sense. But the pronoun is not required here any more than in such passages as Plaut. *Stich.* 585 'salvo salve Gelasime', Virg. *Aen.* 9. 525 'vos o Calliope, precor, adspirate canenti'. Strictly Horace's phrase means 'accept the salutations of one who calls'; it is a little more modest than if *mihi* were expressed. Williams [below] objects that Horace has not mentioned himself since the first two lines, and that there he uses the plural. Yet it is quite clear who is calling.

It is also urged that the genuineness of *mihi* is protected by the common locution χαῖρέ μοι. Fraenkel, p. 169, cites the end of the hymn to Asclepius χαῖρέ μοι ὦ Παιάν . . . (p. 138 Powell); so in Latin Virg. *Aen.* 11. 97 'salve aeternum mihi, maxime Palla'. But in our passage, after the long vocative, *mihi* seems to begin a new colon; it means not μοι but ἐμοί. Now ἐμοὶ χαῖρε would be difficult to parallel; at Eur. *Hec.* 426 the correct reading is presumably χαῖρ᾽ ὦ τεκοῦσα, χαῖρε, Κασσάνδρα τέ μοι (not τ᾽ ἐμοί).

It may finally be objected that a pause after *medicumque* comes at the wrong place in the line. It is indeed unusual; yet cf. *carm. saec.* 35 f. 'siderum regina bicornis, audi / Luna puellas'. However one solves the crux in our passage, it seems fairly probable that the last colon begins at *salve*.

cumque is accepted by many scholars (cf. H.–Sz. 200). The word is supposed to mean *quandoque*, 'at any time', and is generally taken with *vocanti*; but the hyperbaton gives too much emphasis to a word essentially enclitic, and it is also awkward to have *vocanti* modified by two adverbs (*cumque* as well as *rite*). Editors quote Lucr. 2. 114 f. 'contemplator enim cum solis lumina cumque / inserti fundunt radii per opaca domorum'; but *cum . . . cumque* is much easier than plain *cumque*. No help can be derived from the corruptions of Lucr. 5. 311 f. *cumque* also appears in late Latin as a conjunction meaning 'whenever'; see *Inscr. Christianae urbis Romae, nova series*, 2. 4119. 9 f. 'cuius in arbitrio caelum terramque reliquit / pandere vel potius claudere cumque velit' (seventh century).

Some scholars argue that the indefinite *cumque* must be kept because it suits the hymnal character of the poem. Certainly it was common in hymns and prayers to add an indefinite 'blanket' clause to allow for the possibility that the god had been wrongly addressed; cf. Apul. *met.* 11. 2 (to Isis) 'regina caeli, sive tu Ceres ... seu tu caelestis Venus ... seu Phoebi soror ... seu Proserpina ... quoquo nomine, quoquo ritu, quaqua facie te fas est invocare', Norden, *Agnostos Theos*, pp. 144 ff., Appel 76 ff., Fraenkel 170. But an indefinite 'whensoever' is out of place here (see Müller and Heinze). Horace is paying his devotions at the moment, by the act of writing this particular ode; he is not talking about a future series of poems. This argument is crucial, and has never been answered.

Other interpretations of *cumque* also involve difficulties. Fraenkel (170) suggests that the word may mean *utcumque*; he interprets 'in whatever manner, provided it is done *rite*'. This gets rid of the difficulty mentioned above. Yet the 'how' element in *utcumque* depends entirely on the *ut*; once this has gone, *cumque* could hardly mean 'howsoever'.

G. W. Williams has proposed *quōque* for *cumque* (*CR* N.S. 8, 1958, 208 ff.); he translates 'as I call on you in each and every style'. He interprets *quoque* as *quocumque* or *quoquo*; for this archaic use of *quisque* cf. such passages as Plaut. *capt.* 798 'dentilegos omnis mortalis faciam, quemque offendero'. Secondly, he takes *rite* as an ablative, which it must have been by origin; he cites Stat. *Theb.* 11. 285 'rite nefasto'. For the whole phrase he compares *quoquo ritu* in Apuleius (quoted above). Yet in our ode the translation 'style' is ambiguous; if Horace were referring to the different ἐπι-κλήσεις of the god above mentioned, the natural Latin for that would be not *rite* but *nomine*. Williams points out admirably that Horace avoids *horror archaicus* in his poetry; but his arguments could be used, even if with diminished force, against *quoque* as well as *cumque*. The fact must be faced that Horace did not like early Latin so much as he ought to have done.

T. Kinsey has written a useful article arguing against previous theories (*RhM* 110, 1967, 353 ff.). He himself takes *cumque* with *salve* and interprets 'ever be hale'. This certainly gives a more natural word-order than the usual interpretations of *cumque*. Yet one still has reservations about the position of unemphatic *mihi*; the obscure archaism still jars (even if the desired meaning is accepted); and a reference to the god's future state of health does not seem in point.

salve: χαῖρε occurs near the end of most Homeric hymns and all of Callimachus's, to mention no others. There is no point in trying to distinguish the sense 'welcome' from the sense 'good-bye'; the word means the same alike at the beginning and the end.

16. rite: the ancient Romans set excessive store on the scrupulous observance of conventional forms. The Protestant north cannot understand a system where a sneeze might spoil a sacrifice and a slip of the tongue invalidate a contract. But the Romans were legalistic traditionalists whose religion was based not on believing but on performing, not on dogma but on rite. It was no worse for that.

33. ALBI, NE DOLEAS

[A. Cartault, *RPh* 30, 1906, 210 ff.; J. de Decker, *RPh.* 63, 1937, 30 ff.; J. P. Postgate, *AJPh* 33, 1912, 450 ff.; K. Quinn, *Latin Explorations*, 1963, pp. 154 ff.; B. L. Ullman, *AJPh* 33, 1912, 149 ff., 456 ff.]

1–4. *Albius, let me urge you to stop writing elegies about Glycera's bad faith.* 5–8. *Lycoris loves Cyrus, Cyrus Pholoe, while Pholoe has no time for Cyrus; this is the kind of sport Venus enjoys.* 9–12. *I myself have rejected a better match for love of Myrtale, a freedwoman and a bad-tempered one.*

There can be no reasonable doubt that this ode is addressed to the elegiac poet Albius Tibullus (cf. Schanz–Hosius 2. 181). Horace's Albius wrote plaintive elegies (1 ff.); and though Tibullus's own elegies do not reveal his *nomen*, he is called Albius Tibullus in the manuscripts of his poems, in the ancient biography (derived from Suetonius), by the grammarian Diomedes (*gramm.* 1. 484. 26), and by Porphyrio and ps.-Acro on our passage. Horace also wrote an epistle to a poet called Albius (1. 4); in the absence of any means of discrimination, it would be unreasonable to assume that he is a different person from the recipient of the ode. The epistle, like the ode, is teasing in tone; when Horace says that Albius will surpass the *opuscula* of Cassius Parmensis, the tyrannicide, he clearly did not expect his remarks to be taken as a serious compliment. Albius is handsome and rich (6 f. 'di tibi formam, / di tibi divitias dederunt'); this coheres with the information of the *vita* ('eques R. . . . in-signis forma cultuque corporis observabilis'). It might be argued by an obstinate critic that all this information about Tibullus's *nomen*, fortune, and good looks is simply derived from a false identification with Horace's Albius; yet *eques Romanus* supplies an additional fact that seems to come from other sources.

In this ode Horace professes to console Tibullus for the treachery of his imaginary Glycera. He bases his consolation, in accordance with the laws of the genre, on the general experience of mankind, at least as it is portrayed in the poets. Already Sappho had suggested the imperfect correlation of lovers' emotions (1. 21 ff.):

καὶ γὰρ αἰ φεύγει ταχέως διώξει,
αἰ δὲ δῶρα μὴ δέκετ' ἀλλὰ δώσει,
αἰ δὲ μὴ φίλει ταχέως φιλήσει
κωὖκ ἐθέλοισα.

Here Knox's conjecture κωὖ σε θέλοισαν is supported by the later
development of the commonplace (cf. Page, *Sappho and Alcaeus*,
pp. 11, 14 f.). A less sophisticated Attic scolion ruefully pointed out
the attractions of the acorn on the other side of the fence (*PMG* 904):

ἁ ὖς τὰν βάλανον τὰν μὲν ἔχει, τὰν δ' ἔραται λαβεῖν·
κἀγὼ παῖδα καλὴν τὴν μὲν ἔχω, τὴν δ' ἔραμαι λαβεῖν.

Moschus, in the manner of pastoral, took this simple piece of proverbial wisdom, and elaborated it into an ingenious but implausible
chain of loves (6):

ἤρατο Πὰν Ἀχῶς τᾶς γείτονος, ἤρατο δ' Ἀχὼ
σκιρτατᾶ Σατύρω, Σάτυρος δ' ἐπεμήνατο Λύδᾳ.
ὡς Ἀχὼ τὸν Πᾶνα, τόσον Σάτυρος φλέγεν Ἀχὼ
καὶ Λύδα Σατυρίσκον· Ἔρως δ' ἐσμύχετ' ἀμοιβά.
ὅσσον γὰρ τήνων τις ἐμίσεε τὸν φιλέοντα
τόσσον ὁμῶς φιλέων ἠχθαίρετο, πάσχε δ' ἃ ποίει.
ταῦτα λέγω πᾶσιν τὰ διδάγματα τοῖς ἀνεράστοις·
στέργετε τὼς φιλέοντας, ἵν' ἢν φιλέητε φιλῆσθε.

Horace himself gives a hint of this theme in the fourth book (4. 11.
21 ff.): 'Telephum, quem tu petis, occupavit / non tuae sortis
iuvenem puella / dives et lasciva tenetque grata / compede vinctum'.

The pursuit of love provoked other reflections of a more general
kind. Pindar sententiously explains Coronis's preference for a mortal
over Apollo (*P.* 3. 19 f. ἀλλά τοι / ἤρατο τῶν ἀπεόντων· οἷα καὶ πολλοὶ
πάθον); for Xenophon too it is already a truism that love dislikes
what it can have (*Hier.* 1. 30 οὐ γὰρ τῶν ἑτοίμων ἥδεται ⟨ὁ⟩ ἔρως
ἐφιέμενος, ἀλλὰ τῶν ἐλπιζομένων). Callimachus suggests that the lover
enjoys the pleasure of the chase and scorns a sitting target (*ep.*
31. 5 f.):

χοὖμὸς ἔρως τοιόσδε· τὰ μὲν φεύγοντα διώκειν
οἶδε, τὰ δ' ἐν μέσσῳ κείμενα παρπέτεται.

Theocritus uses similar terms to describe Galatea's coquetry (6. 17
καὶ φεύγει φιλέοντα καὶ οὐ φιλέοντα διώκει; see Gow's note). For this
topic in Latin poetry cf. Ov. *am.* 2. 9. 9 'venator sequitur fugientia,
capta relinquit', 2. 19. 36 'quod sequitur fugio; quod fugit, ipse
sequor', F. Leo, *Plautinische Forschungen*, ed. 2, 1912, p. 156. For
similar expressions, from an opposite point of view, cf. Theoc. 11. 75
τί τὸν φεύγοντα διώκεις; (with Gow's note), Catull. 8. 10 'nec quae

fugit sectare'. Even in the sixth century Macedonius echoes the old theme, playing like Horace on the unsuitability of the girl's name (*anth. P.* 5. 247):

Παρμενὶς οὐκ ἔργῳ· τὸ μὲν οὔνομα καλὸν ἀκούσας
ᾠσάμην· σὺ δέ μοι πικροτέρη θανάτου·
καὶ φεύγεις φιλέοντα, καὶ οὐ φιλέοντα διώκεις,
ὄφρα πάλιν κεῖνον καὶ φιλέοντα φύγῃς.

(Later ages regarded such inconsistency as characteristic of women; cf. Castiglione, *Il Cortegiano* 3. 41 sub fin. 'le donne che son pregate sempre negano di compiacer chi le prega; e quelle che non son pregate, pregano altrui'.)

On the other hand, an endless quest for the unattainable did not suit more realistic poets. Hesiod had already provided them with a motto (fr. 61 νήπιος ὅς τις ἑτοῖμα λιπὼν ἀνέτοιμα διώκει). In a similar spirit Philodemus recommended a limitation of aims: a girl might be agreeable enough even if she had a dusky complexion (*anth. P.* 5. 121), charged only a modest fee (5. 126), and did not know the poems of Sappho (5. 132). Horace himself specifically rejects the Callimachean view of love as a pursuit, and recommends, like Philodemus, a *parabilis Venus* (*serm.* I. 2. 105 ff.). But whereas in the satire Horace is cynically preaching on the pointlessness of adultery, here his criticism is not moral but literary: Tibullus's poems are too plaintive in tone, go on too long, and have nothing to do with the prosaic attachments of real life. The poem derives its humour from being expressed in the elegists' own terms, with a rival and a breach of faith, a Lycoris (5 n.) and a Pholoe (7 n.), an artificial series of loves, a trite ἀδύνατον (7 n.), a yoke and a chain. Best of all, Horace claims that his own liaison with a bad-tempered freedwoman is not due to any lack of eligible candidates, but is simply another instance of Venus's predilection for ill-matched unions. Horace's best love poems are those in which he is making fun of himself or of somebody else; here he does both, with exquisite economy and lightness of touch. Within its brief compass, this ode is one of his most pointed and charming poems.

Metre: Second Asclepiad.

1. **ne doleas:** this form of prohibition, as well as being more collo-quial, is perhaps less peremptory than *ne dolueris* (see the discussion in S. A. Handford, *The Latin Subjunctive*, 1947, pp. 43–8). Some see here a preparatory final clause ('to prevent your grieving, let me tell you that . . .'). Sometimes in this construction the admonition of the *ne* clause is followed by *exempla* in the main clause; one may note

especially 2. 4. 1 ff. 'ne sit ancillae tibi amor pudori, / Xanthia
Phoceu, prius insolentem / serva Briseis niveo colore / movit Achillem'. But though that passage seems superficially similar to our own,
in fact in the present poem the *exempla* are not conventional enough
to carry so much weight. To put the whole first stanza in a subordinate clause would obscure the humour of 3 f., and three-quarters
of the poem would be over by the time the period came to an end.

plus nimio: cf. 1. 18. 15 n. The phrase is felt with both *doleas* and
memor; excessive preoccupation with Glycera breeds excess of grief.

2. immitis Glycerae: the oxymoron indicates that Glycera, for all
her promising name, is only γλυκύπικρος. *immitis*, like πικρός, can
be used both of a harsh temper and of an acrid flavour. Of course
one expects a beloved to be *mitis* or kind; cf. Tib. 1. 4. 53 f. 'tum
tibi mitis erit, rapias tum cara licebit / oscula'.

Glycerae: cf. 1. 19. 5 n. No elegies to Glycera occur among Tibullus's
poems. The name has been taken to conceal the already pseudony-
mous Nemesis or Delia; others imagine that Tibullus destroyed these
unsatisfactory poems, or hunt out relics of them in the *Corpus
Tibullianum*. Such attempts misconceive the nature of these quasi-
biographical references in Horace; but the bibliography on Glycera
will no doubt continue to extend itself fruitlessly.

miserabiles: 'piteous'; the word suggests alike 'querulous' and
'contemptible' (for the active sense cf. *Thes.l.L.* 8. 1110. 73 ff.). The
ancients frequently derived the name of elegy from ἔλεος, and took
lament to be its primary function (*RE* 5. 2263 ff., K. J. Dover, *Fondation Hardt, Entretiens* 10, 1963, pp. 187 ff.); cf. 2. 9. 9 f. (to the elegist
Valgius) 'tu semper urges flebilibus modis / Mysten ademptum',
ars 75 f. 'versibus impariter iunctis querimonia primum / . . . inclusa
est', Dom. Mars. *carm.* fr. 7. 3 (on Tibullus's death) 'ne foret aut
elegis molles qui fleret amores', Ov. *epist.* 15. 7, *am.* 3. 9. 3 'flebilis indignos, Elegeia, solve capillos', *Thes.l.L.* 5. 2. 339. 29 ff., 77 ff.
Tibullus himself claims (1. 5. 37 f.) 'saepe ego temptavi curas de-
pellere vino : / at dolor in lacrimas verterat omne merum'.

3. decantes: the preposition hints that the whimpering has gone on
ad nauseam; cf. *Thes.l.L.* 5. 1. 118. 14 ff.

cur . . .: 'asking why . . .' The indirect question is more querulous
than *quod* or *quia*; cf. *epist.* 1. 8. 9 f., Cic. *Att.* 3. 13. 2 'quod me saepe
accusas, cur hunc meum casum tam graviter feram', Fronto, p. 18. 8 f.
N. (= p. 14. 6 f. van den Hout) 'ut illud queri possim, cur me nondum
ames tantum', *Thes.l.L.* 4. 1451. 30 ff.

iunior: cf. 3. 6. 25 'mox iuniores quaerit adulteros'. The word is
also found at *epist.* 1. 17. 16, 2. 1. 44, but nowhere else in classical
poetry; cf. Axelson 104.

The Rival is one of the stock figures of Roman love poetry, and is not always a specific individual. Catullus's jealousies were real enough; but we cannot judge Gallus's portrayal of his supplanter (cf. Virg. *ecl.* 10. 46 ff.). Certainly Propertius's praetor is shadowy and derivative (1. 8, 2. 16); even more so are the Rivals of *epod.* 15, Prop. 2. 9, 2. 21, 3. 8, Tib. 1. 5.

4. laesa . . . fide: Tibullus laments the infidelity of Delia in 1. 5 and 1. 6, and of Nemesis in 2. 6. The elegists' conception of love as a *foedus* (1. 13. 17 n.) naturally led to complaints of breach of faith.

praeniteat: Tibullus says that his rival was a richer man (1. 5. 47 f., Grassmann 40); no elegiac poet would readily have admitted inferiority in looks. Horace is teasing his more elegant friend (above, p. 368).

5. insignem . . .: the ancients thought that the distance between eyebrows and hair should not be too great; cf. Porph. *ad loc.* 'frons arte minor pulchriorem facit mulierem', Petron. 126. 15 'frons minima et quae radices capillorum retro flexerat', Lucian, *am.* 40 περίεργοι μὲν αἱ μέχρι τῶν ὀφρύων ἐφειλκυσμέναι κόμαι βραχὺ τῷ μετώπῳ τὸ μεταίχμιον ἀφιᾶσι, Arnob. *nat.* 2. 41 'idcirco (deus) animas misit ut divini ponderis et gravitatis oblitae . . . imminuerent frontes limbis . . .?' The taste is well illustrated in ancient painting; cf. the beautiful head of a girl in the National Museum at Naples (A. Maiuri, *Roman Painting*, 1953, p. 100).

In men also an *angusta frons* was admired, being more obviously a sign of youth; cf. *epist.* 1. 7. 26, Stat. *silv.* 2. 1. 43, Mart. 4. 42. 9. A man with too high a brow was called a *fronto*.

Lycorida: the name was made famous by the elegies of Cornelius Gallus, who used it as a synonym for his mistress, the actress Cytheris. Elsewhere it is hardly found; cf. Pape–Benseler 827. It is presumably associated with Apollo (cf. Λυκώρεια), like *Cynthia* and *Delia*.

6. Cyri: for the provenance of the name cf. 1. 17. 25 n. Heinze suggests that the choice of a barbarian name emphasizes the man's brutality, as does the comparison with a wolf.

torret: ὀπτᾷ, 'scorches'; the word vividly reinforces the common image of the fires of love. Cf. Sappho 38 ὄπταις ἄμμε, Soph. fr. 433. 2 f. N. (= 474. 2 f. P.) ἀστραπήν τιν' ὀμμάτων ἔχει, / ᾗ θάλπεται μὲν αὐτὸς ἐξοπτᾷ δ' ἐμέ, Call. *ep.* 43. 5 ὤπτηται μέγα δή τι, Theoc. 7. 55 with Gow's note, Meleager, *anth. P.* 12. 92. 7 f. ὀπτᾶσθ' ἐν κάλλει, τύφεσθ' ὑποκαόμενοι νῦν, / ἄκρος ἐπὶ ψυχῆς ἐστι μάγειρος Ἔρως, Prop. 3. 6. 39 'me quoque consimili impositum torrerier igni' (Palmier, *torquerier* codd.), 3. 24. 13, Ov. *am.* 3. 2. 40, W. R. Smyth, *CQ* 43, 1949, 122 ff.

7. Pholoen: the name, which is not attested outside poetry, is used elsewhere of a girl unwilling to be loved; cf. *carm.* 2. 5. 17 'Pholoe fugax', Tib. 1. 8 (Pholoe is cruel to Marathus), Stat. *silv.* 2. 3. 10 (Pholoe runs away from Pan). Properly Pholoe was a mountain on the borders of Elis and Arcadia (*RE* 20. 513 ff.), which may have been particularly associated with ruggedness (cf. Luc. 6. 388 'aspera te Pholoes frangentem, Monyche, saxa'). It looks as if some Hellenistic poet had used the name in an erotic context (perhaps as in Statius) of a nymph who was 'scopulis surdior'.

sed prius . . .: unnatural unions are standard examples of τὸ ἀδύνατον (1. 29. 10 n.); cf. *epod.* 16. 30 ff. 'novaque monstra iunxerit libidine / mirus amor, iuvet ut tigris subsidere cervis, / adulteretur et columba miluo', Ar. *pax* 1076 πρίν κεν λύκος οἶν ὑμεναιοῖ, Virg. *ecl.* 8. 27 'iungentur iam grypes equis'. For other forms of ἀδύνατα (and similar figures) involving wolves cf. *epod.* 15. 7 ff. '(iurabas) dum pecori lupus et nautis infestus Orion / turbaret hibernum mare / . . . fore hunc amorem mutuum', Virg. *ecl.* 8. 52, *dirae* 4, *corp. paroem. gr.* 1. 269. 11 (the proverb λύκος ὄιν ποιμαίνει is applied to τὸ ἀδύνατον, cf. ibid. 2. 627. 17 ff.), 1. 17. 5 n. Call. *fr.* 202. 70 might also be relevant if we were certain what it said.

Apulis: for Apulian wolves cf. 1. 22. 14 n. Horace gives the standard figure a touch of vividness by the reference to his native land; cf. 1. 29. 12.

9. turpi: in view of *imparis formas* in 10 this probably refers to physical ugliness rather than social inferiority. Heinze plausibly suggests that Lycoris is beautiful and amorous, Cyrus ugly and amorous, Pholoe beautiful and cold.

adultero: cf. 1. 25. 9 n.

10. sic visum: a pompous remark suited to higher styles of poetry; cf. Hom. *Il.* 2. 116 οὕτω που Διὶ μέλλει . . . φίλον εἶναι, Virg. *Aen.* 2. 428 'dis aliter visum', 3. 1 f. Servius on the last passage observes with unaccustomed cynicism that the will of god is invoked to explain things that mortals do not understand: 'quotiescumque . . . ratio . . . non apparet, *sic visum* interponitur, ut Horatius "sic visum Veneri", cum amorem ostenderet non esse pulchritudinis.'

imparis: cf. 4. 11. 31 'disparem vites', *epod.* 15. 14, Prop. 1. 1. 32, 1. 5. 2 'et sine nos cursu quo sumus ire pares'.

11. iuga: in both Greek and Latin the image of the yoke is frequently applied to marriage (cf. A. La Penna, *Maia* 4, 1951, 206); in the Greek tragedians we find ζευγνύναι, σύζυγος, and ἄζυξ quite often used in this connection (cf. the Latin *coniugium*). For pictures of the ancient double yoke, which well render its oppressive character, cf. A. von

Salis, *Corolla L. Curtius*, 1937, Taf. 60. Here Horace is alluding more specifically to the idea of the well-matched pair, which is used both in erotic and in other contexts; cf. 1. 35. 28, 2. 5. 1 ff. 'nondum subacta ferre iugum valet / cervice, nondum munia comparis / aequare', Theoc. 12. 15 ἀλλήλους δ' ἐφίλησαν ἴσῳ ζύγῳ (with Gow's note), Prop. 3. 25. 8 'tu bene conveniens non sinis ire iugum', Ov. *epist.* 9. 29 f., Stat. *silv.* 5. 3. 159 f., Mart. 4. 13. 8, Plin. *epist.* 3. 9. 8, Julian, *or.* 8. 244 c φιληθεὶς τὸ λεγόμενον ἴσῳ ζύγῳ.

In our passage the metaphor of the yoke is imprecise, as the love of one party is not reciprocated, even unequally. It is more serious that *iungi* is used differently in the previous sentence; there it is suggested that Pholoe and Cyrus will never be joined, here they are joined, though under an unequal yoke.

aenea: cf. 3. 9. 18 'diductosque iugo cogit aeneo (Venus)'. In real life yokes were of course made of wood, not bronze; brazen yokes belong to legend, and were used by Jason to tame Aeetes's fire-breathing bulls (Ap. Rhod. 3. 1284, 1308, cf. Val. Fl. 7. 595 f. 'cogitque trementes / sub iuga aena toros').

12. saevo . . . cum ioco: for the oxymoron cf. 3. 29. 49 'Fortuna saevo laeta negotio', Claud. 18. 24 f. 'quaenam ista iocandi / saevitia?' For the idea that the sufferings of lovers are a sport for Aphrodite and Eros cf. 3. 27. 66 ff., Soph. *Ant.* 800 ἄμαχος γὰρ ἐμπαίζει θεὸς Ἀφροδίτα, Moschus 1. 11 (Ἔρως) ἄγρια παίσδων.

13. ipsum me: with amusing solemnity Horace cites himself as a clinching example; cf. 1. 16. 22 n., 1. 22. 9 n.

melior . . . Venus: Horace pretends that the high-class courtesans of elegy pursued him too; for this use of *Venus* as 'mistress' cf. 1. 27. 14, Plaut. *Curc.* 192 'tun meam Venerem vituperas?', fr. inc. 27 'Venus ventura est nostra', Lucr. 4. 1185 'nec Veneres nostras hoc fallit', Virg. *ecl.* 3. 68 'parta meae Veneri sunt munera'.

peteret: cf. 4. 11. 21, Sall. *Cat.* 25. 3 'lubido sic adcensa, ut saepius peteret viros quam peteretur', Prop. 2. 20. 27 'cum te tam multi peterent, tu me una petisti'.

14. compede: Greek poets show women wishing to be the slaves of their lovers or represent themselves as enslaved by Eros; cf. Eur. fr. 132 (from the *Andromeda*) ἄγου δέ μ', ὦ ξέν', εἴτε πρόσπολον θέλεις / εἴτ' ἄλοχον εἴτε δμωίδ', anon. p. 178. 28 Powell ζηλῶ δουλεύειν (54 f.), anon. *anth. P.* 5. 100. 1 λάτρις Ἔρωτος, anon. ibid. 12. 160. 2 χαλεπῆς δεσμὸν ἀλυκτοπέδης. In the classical period they express horror at Hercules's enslavement to Omphale (cf. Soph. *Tr.* 252 f. with Jebb's note). On the other hand Roman and later Greek writers regard such paradoxical enslavement as a commonplace (cf. Men. *mis.* 3).

Catullus already twice calls Lesbia *domina* (68. 68, 156) and once *era* (68. 136), and the former term is frequent in the elegists. For more elaborate developments of the theme cf. Tib. 1. 1. 55 'me retinent vinctum formosae vincla puellae', 1. 6. 37 f., 2. 3. 79 f. 'ducite: ad imperium dominae sulcabimus agros : / non ego me vinclis verberibusque nego', 2. 4. 1 ff., Prop. 1. 5. 19 f., 1. 12. 18, Ov. *am.* 1. 2. 17 f., Diod. Sic. 2. 5. 2 (of Semiramis) συνέβαινε τὸν ἄνδρα τελέως ὑπ' αὐτῆς δεδουλῶσθαι, Aristaenetus 2. 2 δοῦλόν με θέλεις ἔχειν; ὡς ἐθελόδουλον ἔχε, Rufinus, *anth. P.* 5. 22, Paul. Sil. ibid. 5. 230, F. O. Copley, *Servitium amoris in the Roman elegists*, *TAPhA* 78, 1947, 285 ff., A. La Penna, *Maia* 4, 1951, 187 ff., Lilja 76 ff.

compedes is particularly used of the fetters of slaves (*Thes.l.L.* 3. 2059. 81 ff.) ; its use here cleverly points the paradox of enslavement to a *libertina*. For the oxymoron with *grata* cf. 4. 11. 23 f., Prop. 2. 20. 20 'posset servitium mite tenere tuum'. The use of the singular for the plural is poetic ; cf. Porph. ad loc. 'adtendendum autem compedem singulari numero eum dixisse, quod non facile veteres', *Thes.l.L.* 3. 2059. 18 ff.

Myrtale: as Bentley pointed out, Myrtale is a name that belongs to real life, unlike those of the previous stanzas; though found as the name of a courtesan in Herodas 1. 89, 2. 65, Aristaenetus 1. 3 ad fin., Mart. 5. 4, it also occurs in inscriptions, and was often borne by freedwomen (cf. Pape–Benseler 963). For similar names (derived from the myrtle's association with Aphrodite) cf. Headlam on Herodas 1. 89.

The main incision comes after *Myrtale*, not, as editors suppose, after *libertina*.

15. libertina: cf. *epod.* 14. 15 f. 'me libertina neque uno / contenta Phryne macerat', *serm.* 1. 2. 47 f.

acrior: 'tempestuous', cf. Plaut. *asin.* 134 'nam mare haud est mare, vos mare acerrumum'. Myrtale is a scold, and like the sea she goes on and on. Cf. Shakespeare, *Taming of the Shrew*, I. ii. 72 f. 'Were she as rough As are the swelling Adriatic seas', Victor Hugo, *A propos d'Horace*, 'Tu courtisais ta belle esclave quelquefois Myrtale aux blonds cheveux, qui s'irrite et se cabre Comme la mer creusant les golfes de Calabre'.

Hadriae: cf. 1. 16. 4 n.

16. curvantis: cf. Virg. *Aen.* 3. 533 'portus ab euroo fluctu curvatus in arcum', Sen. *epist.* 89. 21 'ubicumque in aliquem sinum litus curvabitur', Luc. 8. 178 'Scythiae curvantem litora pontum', Avien. *ora* 394 'extrinsecus curvat sinus', *Thes.l.L.* 4. 1548. 26 ff., A. Müller, *ALL* 3, 1886, 123. Horace is not referring to the continuous action of the encroaching sea ; he simply means that as a matter of geographical

E e

fact the coastline is curved (cf. Sen. *epist.* 55. 2 '(litus) inter Cumas et Servili Vatiae villam curvatur').

34. PARCVS DEORVM CVLTOR

[A. Delatte, *AC* 4, 1935, 293 ff.; Fraenkel 253 ff.; W. Jaeger, *Hermes* 48, 1913, 442 ff.; La Penna 49 ff.] *Fredrickesmeyer, TAPA 116 (1976) 155 ff*

1–5. *I am compelled to recant my Epicureanism.* 5–12. *I have experienced a miracle, thunder from a clear sky.* 12–16. *I must believe in the power of God, that is, of Fortune, who produces sudden and violent alterations in human affairs.*

Horace's initial impulse may have come from Archilochus 74 (cf. H. Hommel, *Theologia Viatorum* 1, 1949, 127 ff.):

> Χρημάτων ἄελπτον οὐδέν ἐστιν οὐδ' ἀπώμοτον
> οὐδὲ θαυμάσιον, ἐπειδὴ Ζεὺς πατὴρ Ὀλυμπίων
> ἐκ μεσημβρίης ἔθηκε νύκτ' ἀποκρύψας φάος
> ἡλίου λάμποντος. ὑγρὸν δ' ἦλθ' ἐπ' ἀνθρώπους δέος.
> ἐκ δὲ τοῦ καὶ πιστὰ πάντα κἀπίελπτα γίγνεται
> ἀνδράσιν . . .

But what he has to say is considerably more complicated. A bolt from the blue was even more portentous than an eclipse; cf. Hom. *Od.* 20. 113 f. ἦ μεγάλ' ἐβρόντησας ἀπ' οὐρανοῦ ἀστερόεντος, / οὐδέ ποθι νέφος ἐστί· τέρας νύ τεῳ τόδε φαίνεις, Ov. *fast.* 3. 369 f. 'ter tonuit sine nube deus, tria fulgura misit. / credite dicenti; mira sed acta loquor', Delatte, loc. cit., pp. 303 f., Pease on Cic. *div.* 1. 18 and p. 591.

Historians and poets solemnly record examples of the phenomenon in Horace's own age. It was one of the prodigies that marked 63 B.C. as a year of destiny (Cic. *poet.* 11. 23 f. T., Plin. *nat.* 2. 137); various incidents in the civil wars were similarly distinguished (Virg. *georg.* 1. 487 f., Luc. 1. 530 ff., Suet. *Aug.* 95). The augural discipline explained that the prodigy portended a revolution in public affairs; cf. Serv. auct. *Aen.* 2. 693, 9. 627, Ioh. Lyd. *ostent.* 45. Many ancients who should have known better accepted lightning from a clear sky as a meteorological fact. It was thought to presage storms (Plin. *nat.* 18. 354), and a 'scientific' explanation was excogitated for it; cf. Sen. *nat.* 2. 18 (attributed to Anaximander) 'quare et sereno tonat? quia tunc quoque per quassum et scissum aera spiritus prosilit', 1. 1. 15. See further Delatte, loc. cit., pp. 293 ff.

One school raised its voice in protest against this consensus of opinion. To the Epicureans the phenomenon was as incredible as to modern meteorologists, and so thoroughly rejected that it could be used in a *reductio ad absurdum*; cf. Lucr. 6. 400 ff. 'denique cur nunquam caelo iacit undique puro / Iuppiter in terras fulmen sonitusque profundit? / an simul ac nubes successere, ipse in eas tum / descendit, prope ut hinc teli determinet ictus?' Lucretius in fact attached so much importance to a rationalistic explanation even of ordinary thunder and lightning that he deals with it early in Book 6, violating the natural order of his exposition; cf. P. Boyancé, *Lucrèce et l'Épicurisme*, 1963, pp. 265 f.

So when faced with the miracle of thunder from a clear sky, Horace claims to renounce the Epicureanism of his unregenerate youth (cf. *serm.* 1. 5. 101 ff. 'namque deos didici securum agere aevum / nec si quid miri faciat natura, deos id / tristis ex alto caeli demittere tecto'). Of course we must not take the recantation seriously, as many scholars have done; the humour of the first line and the mock-heroics of the two central stanzas exclude such a view. Dryden comments more justly, 'Let his Dutch commentators say what they will, his philosophy was Epicurean; and he made use of Gods and Providence only to serve a turn in poetry'; similarly, Dr. Johnson remarked of our poem, 'Sir, he was not in earnest: this was merely poetical' (see the discussion in Fraenkel 254 ff.). Yet the poem is by no means frivolous or trivial; Horace has the rare gift of being amusing and serious at once.

The serious point of the ode only emerges in the last stanza; it is the inexplicability, the violence, and the suddenness of Fortune's action on human life that have been symbolized by the lightning in a clear sky. Our poem thus ends with the deity who is the subject of the next. There is no need to press too much the relation between them; the present ode, as well as being subtler, and better poetry, is much less concerned to elaborate a picture of Fortune.

It seems strange to the modern mind that Horace should equate *deus* and *Fortuna*; some commentators indeed deny that he does make the equation. But Greek gods were always capricious and irresponsible by the grim standards of an inflexible Jehovah. Tyche represents such success and failure as do not result from calculation. In origin at least, she was not a symbol of blind chance, but of divine power operating inscrutably. More of Pindar's twelfth Olympian is relevant to Horace's poem than is usually realized. There Tyche is σώτειρα and Zeus's daughter (13 n.), and so, on Pindar's assumptions, is an ultimately rational power; but calculation about the future is blind, and men pass suddenly, for no reason that they can understand, from success to disaster and back again. In a more sophisticated age, the same elements of inscrutability and presumed rationality appear in the Stoic definition of τύχη as αἴτιον ἄδηλον ἀνθρωπίνῳ λογισμῷ. The balance was not easy to hold, however, and Tyche often tended to become a capricious deity overruling divine providence. The density of Horace's picture here results from his uniting these two traditions to show a figure in whom is concentrated the power to frustrate expectation.

People have also been surprised to find that Horace emphasizes the power of Fortune after rejecting Epicureanism; Epicurus after all by his doctrine of swerving atoms recognized an element of randomness in the world. But though Epicurus needed 'randomness' for purposes of his own (i.e. to explain the coalescence of atoms and the freedom of the will), most of his system is rigidly mechanical. He says of τύχη that it is neither a goddess nor the uncertain cause of all things (*epist.* 3. 134); chance does not give good and evil to men, though it gives opportunities for good and evil. Moreover, chance has little effect on the good man; cf. *sent.* 144 βραχέα σοφῷ τύχη παρεμπίπτει, τὰ δὲ μέγιστα καὶ κυριώτατα ὁ λογισμὸς διῴκησε κατὰ τὸν συνεχῆ χρόνον τοῦ βίου. (See further the clear-headed discussion by J. Masson, *Lucretius, Epicurean and poet* 2, 1909, pp. 62 ff.) Of course Epicurus recognised that the unforeseen plays a considerable part in life; cf. *epist.* 3. 131 πρὸς τὴν τύχην ἀφόβους, 133 τὴν τύχην ἄστατον ὁρᾶν, Lucr. 3. 1085 f. 'posteraque in dubiost fortunam quam vehat aetas, / quidve ferat nobis casus quive exitus instet', and more surprisingly, 5. 107 'quod procul a nobis flectat fortuna gubernans' (cf. Bailey's commentary, p. 1755). But Horace in his present mood goes further (though his thought is blurred by the conventionalism of his imagery); he sees fortune not merely as an unpredictable concatenation of causes, but as itself a disruptive agent introducing chaos into the pattern of things. And to speak of τύχη in such a poetical and non-scientific way is profoundly un-Epicurean.

The feeling that the ode is not consistent may be partly due to its very great shift of tone. In the first part Horace provides ironic self-mockery, slightly in the manner of the Lalage ode; in the last stanza he reveals his serious conviction that success in life is to be ascribed not merely to sagacity or virtue, but to the roll of a ball or the turn of a wheel. He shows here in fact a range of style that has sometimes disconcerted his critics. For instance, 'nubila dividens / plerumque' is sometimes called inelegant; but the prosaic and anxious exactitude of the Epicurean scientist (7 n.) has ironical point. Again, the hyperbolical description of the effects of Horace's thunderclap is censured as tumid. Yet the mock sublime of these lines with their high-sounding mythology provides a background for and an easy transition to the real sublimity of the last stanza.

Few poets could compass the change from the easy personalities of the first lines to the grandeur of the last with such economy and grace.

Metre: Alcaic.

1. **parcus**: 'niggardly'; cf. Stat. *Theb.* 12. 487 f. 'parca superstitio: non turea flamma nec altus / accipitur sanguis'. The word is not merely synonymous with *infrequens* (for that sense cf. 1. 25. 1 n., Tac. *dial.* 41. 7 'tam raro et tam parce' with Gudeman's note). At this point in his poem Horace has no motive to waste words by saying things twice.

Horace was not an atheist (that would have been eccentric in the ancient world); he simply did not believe that the gods intervened in human affairs. So as they had nothing to offer him, he wasted little time or money on them; for a similar attitude from a different motive cf. Suet. *Tib.* 69.

cultor: the word at this period is rare and grandiloquent; cf. Cic. *Tusc.* 1. 69 'hominem . . . ipsum quasi contemplatorem caeli ac deorum cultorem', Virg. *Aen.* 11. 788. Here it is used with astringent humour.

2. **insanientis . . . sapientiae**: as *sapientia* is the word for philosophy as well as for wisdom, it lends itself to this kind of oxymoron; cf. Eur. *Ba.* 395 τὸ σοφὸν δ' οὐ σοφία, Clem. Alex. *protr.* 5. 64. 3 (of the philosophers) ἄθεοι μὲν δὴ καὶ οὗτοι, σοφίᾳ τινὶ ἀσόφῳ τὴν ὕλην προσ-κυνήσαντες, Greg. Naz. *contra Iulian.* 1. 3. The paradox is sustained by *consultus erro*.

sapientiae consultus: the *consultus* is the expert to whom other people bring their problems. The phrase is modelled on *iuris consultus*, where the genitive is analogical with that in *iuris peritus*. Cf. also Cic. *Phil.* 9. 10 'nec . . . magis iuris consultus quam iustitiae fuit', Liv. 10. 22. 7 'iuris atque eloquentiae consultos', schol. Pers. 5. 90 'legis', *vir. ill.* 72. 2 'eloquentiae'.

3. **erro**: Horace turns the Epicureans' discourteous phrase against themselves; cf. Lucr. 2. 9 f. 'despicere unde queas alios passimque videre / errare atque viam palantis quaerere vitae'.

4. **vela**: here of philosophy, cf. *catal.* 5. 8 f. 'nos ad beatos vela mittimus portus / magni petentes docta dicta Sironis' (so of poetry 4. 15. 3 f. 'ne parva Tyrrhenum per aequor / vela darem'). The phrase is used in its literal sense in Virg. *Aen.* 3. 686 'dare lintea retro'.

5. **relectos**: 'retraced', Heinsius's emendation of the manuscripts' *relictos*. Bentley supplied many closely similar instances of *relegere*

viam, iter, vestigia, etc.; cf. especially Virg. *Aen.* 3. 690 (in the same
context as the passage cited in the previous note) 'relegens errata
retrorsus / litora', Prud. *apoth.* 1003 'perque atavos cursum relegente
vetustos', Paul. Nol. *carm.* 19. 600 ff. (an author well versed in
Horace) 'diximus ut fugiens non fugerit, utque redactis / passibus
emensos sua per vestigia cursus / in cassum totiens volvente rele-
gerit orso'. Here the word is proleptic: when Horace has gone over
his *cursus* again they will be *relecti*; cf. Virg. *Aen.* 5. 500 'validis
flexos incurvant viribus arcus'. The pleonasm is thought by some
distasteful; yet Virgil and Paulinus are just as repetitive. For effective *abundantia* in Horace cf. 1. 17. 14 ff., 2. 5. 10 ff.

   The conjecture is supported not merely by the frequency of *relegere* in similar contexts, but by the difficulty of *relictos*. The phrase
iterare cursus relictos could not mean 'to pick up the right course
from the point where I left it and go on from there'; that does not
suit *iterare*. Nor could it mean 'to repeat in reverse direction my
former course from piety to doubt'; that does not explain *relictos*.
One might more reasonably interpret 'having gone back to the beginning, to repeat the course from which I deviated'. But this makes
the metaphor very obscure. Is the *cursus* the voyage of spiritual
life, from the innocent piety of childhood to the mature wisdom of
the middle-aged man? But there is no reason why Horace should
not rejoin the straight course at the point where he left it; why
should he have to go right back to the beginning? Such an idea
may make religious sense, but it has nothing to do with the present
poem; ancient philosophers would be merely puzzled at the Christian commendation of the 'faith of a little child'. In this poem of
recantation, *cursus* is naturally the path between piety and doubt,
and *iterare* implies a repetition in the reverse direction.

   namque . . .: cf. 1. 22. 9 n. Both these clauses describe a personal
experience that justifies a preceding statement, and both act as the
pivot of the whole poem.

   Diespiter: the old nominative, generally replaced by the vocative
Iuppiter (cf. 3. 2. 29). The form is here archaic and dignified. Arnobius
uses it with malicious intent when deflating the pretensions of the
pagan god (*nat.* 2. 70 *bis*, 4. 20, 5. 3, 5. 20).

   6. nubila: emphatic, contrasted with *per purum* below; cf. 3. 29. 43 ff.

   7. plerumque: ὡς ἐπὶ τὸ πολύ; the tone is scientific. Lucretius is the
only poet who uses the word at all frequently (20 times); it is not
found in Catullus, Tibullus, Propertius, Seneca, Lucan, or Silius, and
in Virgil only at *georg.* 1. 300; it occurs three times in Horace's odes
and three times in Ovid. Cf. Axelson 106.

   For the word's late position cf. *epist.* 2. 2. 83 f. 'statua taciturnius exit / plerumque, et risu populum quatit', Lucr. 5. 1131 f. 'invidia quoniam, ceu fulmine, summa vaporant / plerumque, et quae sunt aliis magis edita cumque'. Here as often Horace puts the emphatic word at the end of its clause and beginning a new line.

tonantis . . .: in popular belief, thunder was the rumbling of Zeus's car over Olympus; cf. Porph. ad loc., 1. 12. 58. Leopardi imitates our passage, *l'Ultimo Canto di Saffo* 11 ff. 'quando il carro, Grande carro di Giove a noi sul capo Tonando, il tenebroso aere divide'. To mimic thunder, Salmoneus used 'aere et cornipedum pulsu . . . equorum' (Virg. *Aen.* 6. 591). Pindar, with characteristic boldness, makes the thunder the actual chariot and horses (*O.* 4. 1 ἐλατὴρ ὑπέρτατε βροντᾶς ἀκαμαντόποδος, Ζεῦ).

8. volucrem: 'winged', as the gods' chariots often are; cf. Eur. fr. 779. 6 πτεροφόρων ὀχημάτων, Pl. *Phaedr.* 246 e Ζεὺς ἐλαύνων πτηνὸν ἅρμα, Ov. *trist.* 3. 8. 15 f., Apul. *mund.* 38 'deus . . . curru volucri superfertur', Prob. Virg. *georg.* 1. 19 of Triptolemus's car. Cf. Sen. *Med.* 1025 'aliti', Val. Fl. 5. 611 'alipedi' (Sil. 7. 700), Arnob. *nat.* 3. 30 'pinnatos', Marvell, *To his Coy Mistress*, 'But at my back I alwaies hear Time's wingèd charriot hurrying near'.

Elsewhere in Horace *volucer* means 'swift as a bird', not 'winged'; for *volucer currus* in this sense cf. Virg. *Aen.* 10. 440, Claud. *rapt. Pros.* 2. 247, Prud. *c. Symm.* 2. 55. Wilamowitz here took *volucrem* to apply properly to *equos* and *tonantis* to *currum* and commented on the boldness of this poetic hypallage (on Eur. *HF* 883, pp. 198 f.). But his difficulty is illusory.

9. quo . . .: the stanza is like a compact version of a long and re-petitive passage of the *Theogony* (839 ff.), on Zeus's conquest of Typhon: σκληρὸν δ᾿ ἐβρόντησε καὶ ὄβριμον, ἀμφὶ δὲ γαῖα / σμερδαλέον κονάβησε καὶ οὐρανὸς εὐρὺς ὕπερθε / πόντος τ᾿ Ὠκεανοῦ τε ῥοαὶ καὶ τάρταρα γαίης. / . . . ἐπεστονάχιζε δὲ γαῖα· / καῦμα δ᾿ ὑπ᾿ ἀμφοτέρων κάτεχεν ἰοειδέα πόντον / . . . ἔζεε δὲ χθὼν πᾶσα καὶ οὐρανὸς ἠδὲ θάλασσα / . . . τρέε δ᾿ Ἅιδης, ἐνέροισι καταφθιμένοισιν ἀνάσσων, / Τιτῆνές θ᾿ ὑποταρτάριοι, Κρόνον ἀμφὶς ἐόντες. See also Catull. 64. 205 f., Sil. 5. 384 ff., Pope, *Rape of the Lock* 5. 49 ff. 'Jove's thunder roars, heav'n trembles all around, Blue Neptune storms, the bellowing deeps resound: Earth shakes her nodding tow'rs, the ground gives way, And the pale ghosts start at the flash of day!'

bruta: 'heavy', 'unresponsive' (Paul. Fest. 28. 23 L. = 31. 15 M. 'brutum antiqui gravem dicebant'). In this, its literal sense, the word is particularly associated with the earth and things of which earth is the main element; cf. Apul. *Socr.* 4 p. 126 'immortalibus animis, . . . brutis et obnoxiis corporibus', 9 p. 140 '(corpora) neque tam bruta quam terrea neque tam levia quam aetheria', Orient. *comm.*

1. 45 'brutum terreno est pondere corpus'. In the present context
it is appropriate because it suggests that even the unresponsive
earth was shaken (cf. Sen. *Thy.* 1020 'immota tellus, pondus ignavum
iaces?'). It also makes an elegant contrast with *vaga*; cf. the balance
of *terram inertem* and *mare ventosum* in 3. 4. 45 f.

vaga: a conventional epithet of rivers; cf. Prop. 2. 19. 30, 3. 11. 51,
dirae 67, Petron. 122 v. 132 f. The use in 1. 2. 18 is different.

flumina: Horace strangely includes rivers, though they do not
lend themselves to such violent commotion. Yet for their importance
in the scheme of things cf. Hes. *th.* 108 f. ὡς τὰ πρῶτα θεοὶ καὶ γαῖα
γένοντο / καὶ ποταμοὶ καὶ πόντος ἀπείριτος, Eur. *HF* 1296 f. with
Wilamowitz's note, Theoc. 17. 91 f. θάλασσα δὲ πᾶσα καὶ αἶα / καὶ
ποταμοὶ κελάδοντες with Gow's note, Lucr. 2. 940, 4. 458 'caelum mare
flumina montis', Liv. 29. 27. 2, Apul. *met.* 4. 33. 2 'quod tremit ipse
Iovis quo numina terrificantur / fluminaque horrescunt et Stygiae
tenebrae'.

10. **Styx . . .**: Styx is a waterfall in NE. Arcadia, of such sublimity
and remoteness that it early became a focus of religious feeling.
Already in Homer the river of Styx was located in the underworld,
and Hesiod (*th.* 775 ff.) mentions the nymph Styx immediately after
Cerberus. Taenarus (Cape Matapan, at the S. point of Laconia) had
a sacred cave, also supposed to be the entrance to the underworld;
cf. Pind. *P.* 4. 43 f. πὰρ χθόνιον / Ἄιδα στόμα, Ταίναρον εἰς ἱερὰν . . .
ἐλθών, Eur. *HF* 23 f. Ταινάρου διὰ στόμα / βέβηκ' ἐς Ἅιδου, Virg. *georg.*
4. 465 'Taenarias . . . fauces, alta atria Ditis', *RE* 4 A. 457 ff. Either
name can be used to indicate the whole of the underworld, not merely
its entrance. The name of Avernus, the Italian entrance to the underworld, is even more commonly used in this extended sense.

invisi: 'hated'; for its use in contexts of death cf. 2. 14. 23 'invisas
cupressos', Virg. *Aen.* 8. 244 f. 'regna . . . pallida, dis invisa', Sen.
Herc. f. 664 'Ditis invisi domus'. The sentiment is like that of Hom.
Il. 8. 368 στυγεροῦ Ἀίδαο, 20. 64 f. οἰκία . . . τά τε στυγέουσι θεοί περ,
Hes. *th.* 775 f. στυγερὴ θεὸς ἀθανάτοισι, / δεινὴ Στύξ. Classical poets
when in heroic mood had no opinion of the consolations of life after
death.

11. **Atlanteus . . . finis**: the grandiloquent phrase is modelled on
Greek poetry; cf. Eur. *Hipp.* 3 f. ὅσοι τε Πόντου τερμόνων τ' Ἀτλαν-
τικῶν / ναίουσιν εἴσω, 746 f. σεμνὸν τέρμονα κυρῶν / οὐρανοῦ, τὸν
Ἄτλας ἔχει, 1053 πέραν γε Πόντου καὶ τόπων Ἀτλαντικῶν, *HF* 234 f.
Ἀτλαντικῶν πέραν / φεύγειν ὅρων.

Ancient poets and geographers applied the name Atlas not to
the whole range between the Atlantic and the Syrtes but only to its
western portion (sometimes confusing it with the southern Pillar

of Hercules); cf. Virg. *Aen.* 4. 480 ff. 'Oceani finem iuxta solemque cadentem / ultimus Aethiopum locus est, ubi maximus Atlas / axem umero torquet', Luc. 1. 555 'Hesperiam Calpen summumque... Atlanta', 4. 671 ff. 'regna / cardine ab occiduo vicinus Gadibus Atlans / terminat', Sil. 1. 200 f., J. O. Thomson, *History of Ancient Geography*, 1948, pp. 259 ff.

Horace mentions Atlas here partly because it is at the ends of the earth, partly because it suggests fixity (like the Rock of Gibraltar); cf. Virg. *Aen.* 4. 247 'Atlantis duri caelum qui vertice fulcit', Sil. 9. 319 f. 'vellere sede / si coeptet Calpen impacto gurgite pontus'. The idea of a god shaking a mountain is not included in the Hesiodic passage imitated in the rest of the stanza. Cf. rather Hom. *Il.* 1. 530 μέγαν δ᾽ ἐλέλιξεν "Ολυμπον, Hes. *th.* 678 ff. δεινὸν δὲ περίαχε πόντος ἀπείρων, / γῆ δὲ μέγ᾽ ἐσμαράγησεν, ἐπέστενε δ᾽ οὐρανὸς εὐρὺς / σειόμενος, πεδόθεν δὲ τινάσσετο μακρὸς "Ολυμπος / ῥιπῇ ὑπ᾽ ἀθανάτων, ἔνοσις δ᾽ ἵκανε βαρεῖα / Τάρταρον ἠερόεντα ποδῶν, h. *Hom.* 27. 6 ff. τρομέει δὲ κάρηνα / ὑψηλῶν ὀρέων... φρίσσει δέ τε γαῖα / πόντος τ᾽ ἰχθυόεις, 28. 9 ff. μέγας δ᾽ ἐλελίζετ᾽ "Ολυμπος, / ... ἀμφὶ δὲ γαῖα / σμερδαλέον ἰάχησεν, ἐκινήθη δ᾽ ἄρα πόντος, Sil. 12. 657 f. 'intonat ipse / quod tremat et Rhodope Taurusque et Pindus et Atlas'.

L. Müller suggested that Horace was referring to the Atlantic Ocean, the boundary of the world (cf. Virg. loc. cit. 'Oceani finem'). This view might seem to derive support from the mention of the sea in the passages quoted above; yet Sil. 12. 657 f. is even more telling on the other side. *concutitur* is also more appropriate to a solid boundary mark. Moreover, the Euripidean passages cited above refer clearly to the Pillars; it would be characteristic of Horace to substitute a singular for Euripides's plurals, and thus to allude to a more up-to-date geographical theory, which made Atlas, rather than the Pillars, the boundary of the continental world.

12. **concutitur**: the historic present is epic and grand; for its use in a relative clause cf. K.–G. 1. 134, K.–S. 1. 119. It is less likely that the tense indicates that the effect of the event still continued in the poet's mind.

valet ...: the gods have power to produce revolutions in human affairs; cf. Hom. *Od.* 16. 211 f. ῥηίδιον δὲ θεοῖσι, τοὶ οὐρανὸν εὐρὺν ἔχουσιν / ἠμὲν κυδῆναι θνητὸν βροτὸν ἠδὲ κακῶσαι. Closer to our passage is the formulation of Hes. *op.* 6 ῥεῖα δ᾽ ἀρίζηλον μινύθει καὶ ἄδηλον ἀέξει. The sentiment became a commonplace; cf. Archil. 58 πολλάκις μὲν ἐκ κακῶν / ἄνδρας ὀρθοῦσιν μελαίνῃ κειμένους ἐπὶ χθονί, / πολλάκις δ᾽ ἀνατρέπουσι καὶ μάλ᾽ εὖ βεβηκότας / ὑπτίους κλίνουσ᾽, Pind. *P.* 2. 51 f. (θεὸς) ὑψιφρόνων τιν᾽ ἔκαμψε βροτῶν, / ἑτέροισι δὲ κῦδος ἀγήραον παρέδωκ᾽ (cf. 8. 6 ff.), Democritus fr. 30, Eur. *Tro.* 612 f., fr. 716. 3 f.,

Hel. 711 ff., *Heracl.* 613 ff., *trag. adesp.* 482, *gnom. Vat.* 553 Sternbach Χίλων Αἰσώπου πυθομένου τί εἴη ποιῶν ὁ Ζεὺς εἶπε· Τὰ μὲν ὑψηλὰ ταπεινοῖ, τὰ δὲ ταπεινὰ ὑψοῖ. The commonplace is exploited for comic effect in Ar. *Lys.* 772 f. τὰ δ' ὑπέρτερα νέρτερα θήσει / Ζεὺς ὑψιβρεμέτης.
— Ἐπάνω κατακεισόμεθ' ἡμεῖς;

Jehovah behaves in a similar way, though in his case the emphasis is naturally on the justice of the effect, not the caprice of the action; cf. *1 Sam.* 2. 7 f. 'The Lord maketh poor, and maketh rich: he bringeth low and lifteth up. He raiseth up the poor out of the dust, and lifteth up the beggar from the dunghill, to set them among princes, and to make them inherit the throne of glory', *ps.* 147. 6 'The Lord lifteth up the meek: he casteth the wicked down to the ground', *Sirach* 10. 14 'The Lord has cast down the thrones of rulers, and has seated the lowly in their place', *euang. Luc.* 1. 52 f. καθεῖλεν δυνάστας ἀπὸ θρόνων καὶ ὕψωσεν ταπεινούς, πεινῶντας ἐνέπλησεν ἀγαθῶν καὶ πλουτοῦντας ἐξαπέστειλεν κενούς.

Fortune first appears as the agent of revolution in Pind. *O.* 12, cf. especially 10 ff. πολλὰ δ' ἀνθρώποις παρὰ γνώμαν ἔπεσεν, / ἔμπαλιν μὲν τέρψιος, οἱ δ' ἀνιαραῖς / ἀντικύρσαντες ζάλαις ἐσλὸν βαθὺ πήματος ἐν μικρῷ πεδάμειψαν χρόνῳ. Later examples are Philemon fr. 111 K. ἅπαντα νικᾷ καὶ μεταστρέφει τύχη, ps.-Plut. *Apoll.* 103 f. (citing Men. fr. 740 Körte and other passages), Lucian, *Nigrin.* 20, Palladas, *anth. P.* 10. 80, Agathias, ibid. 9. 442. 4 ff., anon. ibid. 9. 530, Q. Smyrn. 13. 474 f., anon. *GLP* 99. 4 ff. The idea finds embodiment in the figure of fortune's wheel; cf. D. M. Robinson, *CPh* 41, 1946, 207 ff.

This revolutionary Fortuna is found in Latin already in Enn. *ann.* 312 f. 'mortalem summum Fortuna repente / reddidit e summo regno ut ⟨famul inf⟩imus esset', and probably in Varro, *Men.* 1 'ita sublimis speribus / iactato homines, at volitantis altos nitens trudito' (cf. H. Haffter, *Glotta* 23, 1935, 259); see also Otto 142. Rhetoricians of the empire were particularly moved by Fortune's power to bring men down to professorships; cf. Juv. 7. 197 f. 'si Fortuna volet, fies de rhetore consul; / si volet haec eadem, fiet de consule rhetor', Plin. *epist.* 4. 11. 1 f. 'praetorius hic modo inter eloquentissimos causarum actores habebatur; nunc eo decidit, ut exsul de senatore, rhetor de oratore fieret. itaque ipse in praefatione dixit dolenter et graviter: "Quos tibi, Fortuna, ludos facis? facis enim ex senatoribus professores, ex professoribus senatores."'

ima summis: Horace's description of Fortune's action suggests the conventional complaint of Roman constitutionalists against radical innovators; cf. Cic. *leg.* 3. 19 (the *tribunicia potestas*) 'omnia infima summis paria fecit, turbavit, miscuit', Vell. 2. 2. 3 (Ti. Gracchus) 'summa imis miscuit', Liv. 32. 7. 10, Curt. 8. 8. 8, Rut. Nam. 2. 44, Löfstedt, *Syntactica* 2. 348 f. Similar expressions are applied to

no: these imply leveling, but H. states reversal

Fortune by Sall. *Cat.* 10. 1 'saevire fortuna et miscere omnia coepit',
Tac. *hist.* 4. 47. 3 'instabilis fortunae summaque et ima miscentis',
Boeth. *cons.* 2. 2 'rotam volubili orbe versamus, infima summis
summa infimis mutare gaudemus'.

13. insignem attenuat: ἀρίζηλον μινύθει.
deus: the non-specific word, placed between *Diespiter* and *Fortuna*,
shows their essential identity. Similar associations are found in
Hom. *Il.* 15. 117 μοῖρα Διός, 19. 87 Ζεὺς καὶ Μοῖρα καὶ ἠεροφοῖτις
'Ερινύς, *Od.* 11. 292 θεοῦ ... μοῖρα. In Pind. *O.* 12. 1 Tyche is Zeus's
daughter (as the Fortuna of Praeneste was Jupiter's, *ILS* 3684,
3685). Fate and Zeus were identified by the Stoics; cf. Cleanthes
fr. 2. 1 Powell ἄγου δέ μ', ὦ Ζεῦ, καὶ σύ γ' ἡ πεπρωμένη, Plut. *Stoic.*
repugn. 1050 a ἡ κοινὴ φύσις καὶ ὁ κοινὸς τῆς φύσεως λόγος εἱμαρμένη
καὶ πρόνοια καὶ Ζεύς ἐστιν. Fortune is added in Sen. *ben.* 4. 7. 1 ff.:
God can be called by as many names as he has powers, Juppiter
Tonans being one; he concludes (8. 3) 'sic nunc naturam voca, fatum,
fortunam: omnia eiusdem dei nomina sunt varie utentis sua pote-
state'. Cf. ps.-Dio Chrys. 64. 8, where Fortune, Nemesis, Hope,
Destiny, Themis, Zeus, and a number of other deities are equated.

14. obscura: the generalizing neuter plural belongs to the world of
γνῶμαι; cf. Soph. *Ai.* 647 (χρόνος) φύει τ' ἄδηλα καὶ φανέντα κρύπτεται.
hinc: for the thought cf. 3. 29. 49 ff.
apicem: properly the olive-wood peak that rose from the crown
of the caps worn by Roman priests; cf. D.-S. 2. 1167-9. Horace is
thinking of Tarquinius Priscus; cf. Cic. *leg.* 1. 4 'ab aquila Tarquinio
apicem impositum', Liv. 1. 34. 8 'ibi ei carpento sedenti cum uxore
aquila suspensis demissa leviter alis pilleum aufert, superque car-
pentum cum magno clangore volitans rursus velut ministerio divini-
tus missa capiti apte reponit', Dion. Hal. *ant. Rom.* 3. 47. 3. He
conflates with this story of the eagle a reference to Fortune crowning
and uncrowning kings; cf. Plut. *fort. Alex.* 326 e (Alexander to Fortune) Δαρεῖος ἦν σὸν ἔργον ... καὶ Σαρδανάπαλλος, ᾧ τὸ διάδημα τῆς
βασιλείας πορφύραν ξαίνοντι περιέθηκας, Dio 63. 5. 2 (Tiridates on his
coronation by Nero) σὺ γάρ μοι καὶ Μοῖρα καὶ Τύχη. It is relevant
that *apex* can be used of the mitre of eastern kings; cf. 3. 21. 20
'regum apices'. We should perhaps think of convulsions in the Parthian kingdom (cf. p. xxxii).
rapax: 'snatching' like a Harpy; cf. Sen. *Med.* 219 f. 'rapida Fortuna ac levis / praecepsque regno eripuit, exilio dedit'.

15. stridore acuto: the phrase indicates a shrill scream, like that of
a bird (cf. Aesch. *Ag.* 56 f. οἰωνόθροον / γόον ὀξυβόαν). So Sen. *dial.*
6. 7. 2 'aves cum stridore magno inanes nidos circumfremuerunt',

Liv. 1. 34. 8 (cited on 14) 'cum magno clangore' (cf. Serv. *Aen.* 3. 226 'acyrologia est, si clangorem dixit alarum sonitum'). Others interpret of the beating of wings; cf. 3. 29. 53 f. 'si celeres quatit / pennas' (of Fortuna), Virg. *Aen.* 1. 397 'stridentibus alis'. But then *acuto* would be an inappropriate adjective.

16. sustulit: both this and *posuisse* are best regarded as instantaneous perfects; Fortune's action is so quick that it is over before one can describe it (cf. Virg. *Aen.* 1. 82 ff. 'venti . . . ruunt et terras turbine perflant. / incubuere mari').

posuisse gaudet: the phrase is not a mere periphrasis, but has edge and point: Fortune takes pleasure in capricious change; cf. Men. fr. 630. 1 Körte ὦ μεταβολαῖς χαίρουσα παντοίαις Τύχη, Boeth. *cons.* 2. 2 (cited on 12 above). Usually disaster pleases her best; cf. 3. 29. 49 'saevo laeta negotio', Sen. *nat.* 3 praef. 7 'gaudet laetis tristia substituere, utique miscere'.

35. O DIVA

[W. H. Alexander, *Classical Essays presented to James A. Kleist*, Saint Louis, 1946, pp. 13 ff.; J. D. P. Bolton, *CQ* N.S. 17, 1967, 451 ff.; R. de Coster, *AC* 19, 1950, 65 ff.; Fraenkel 251 ff.; W. Jaeger, *Hermes* 48, 1913, 442 ff.; A. Ker, *PCPhS* 190, 1964, 42 ff.; L. A. Mackay, *CR* 43, 1929, 10 ff.]

1–4. Goddess of Anzio, you can raise the lowly and overthrow the great. 5–16. All men and every nation pray to you. 17–28. Necessity is your lictor, and Hope and Good Faith attend you loyally. 29–40. Preserve Caesar and the armies now raised against Britain and the East. We have fought civil wars too long; refashion our swords for use against distant enemies.

Hymns to Fortune had ample precedents in Greek poetry. Pindar in his Twelfth Olympian emphasizes, like Horace here, the goddess's power to save (σώτειρα) and her influence over sea and land (6 n.); for remains of a lost poem see frr. 38–41. One may note also two hymns of the Hellenistic period, *PMG* 1019 and *GLP* 99; in the latter, as in Horace's ode, the goddess is associated with Necessity (cf. 8 f. πότερόν σε κλήζωμεν Κλωθὼ κελαιν[άν], / ἢ τὰν ταχύποτμον Ἀνάγκαν;). There are indeed many stereotyped elements in our poem; *o* (1. 32. 13 n.), *diva* (1 n.), the relative clause (p. 127), the mention of the cult-place (1. 30. 1 n.), the statement of the goddess's powers (2–16) the anaphora of *te* (1. 10. 9 n.), the list of divine attendants (17 n.).

In the last three stanzas the ode develops from a hymn to a prayer; for parallels in Greek hymns and in Horace cf. 4. 6. 27, Pasquali 171 ff.

The Fortuna of our poem is not merely the capricious power posited by an enlightened Hellenism to account for the unpredictability of the world. Such a view of her nature is not quite absent; in the first and fourth stanzas she is, like Tyche, the agent of change and political revolution. Yet in general the goddess is here both more serious and more Roman, and her companions are such estimable abstractions as Faith, Hope, and Necessity. The Romans thought of Fortuna as sustaining a nation, a family, or an individual (23 n.), and Fortuna in this poem is a stern but beneficent power. Like the *Fortuna populi Romani* worshipped in Republican times, she is the personification of good success.

There were a number of cults of Fortuna in Latium, and one of the most notable was at Antium. Strictly speaking there were two Fortunae in the cult; they appear on coins of the gens Rustia (which came from Antium), one wearing a helmet, the other a diadem (cf. Mattingly 1. 1 f., plate 1. 2 = H. Mattingly and E. A. Sydenham, *Roman Imperial Coinage* 1, 1923, p. 69, plate 1. 1; see also Latte, plate 7). The goddesses were oracular (Mart. 5. 1. 3, Suet. *Cal.* 57. 3, Macr. *sat.* 1. 23. 13). The shrine had profited from lending Octavian money during the Perusine war (App. *civ.* 5. 24. 97), and continued to do well under the Empire (cf. ps.-Acro 'aput Antium autem est Fortunae templum famosissimum, multorum etiam principum donis ornatum; unde etiam civitas Fortunae ipsius tutela dicta est', Roscher 1. 1546 f., Wissowa 259, de Coster, loc. cit.).

The poem is generally assigned to about 27 or 26 B.C., and this was our own original view. Yet there are some metrical reasons for believing it to be considerably earlier (above, pp. xxviii f.); it is there suggested that, though nothing is certain, 35 B.C. is a date at least worth considering. Bolton, loc. cit., thinks that the war for whose happy outcome Horace is praying is the Actium campaign, and takes *iturum* in 29 to be final in sense ('so that he may in future go ...'). But it is hard to believe in a prayer that makes no mention of the real peril impending and concentrates instead on a hypothetical result of its own fulfilment. The laments about civil war are not really suited to the heated patriotism of the Actium period; the pacifism of Augustan poets is most conspicuous after their own side had already won.

It is an interesting circumstance that in 19 B.C., on Augustus's return from Syria, an altar was dedicated to Fortuna Redux (cf. *res gest.* 11). This is portrayed on the reverse of Rustius's coin (see above), which is plausibly assigned to the same year. The altar was situated not at Antium but at the *porta Capena*; but the goddess was represented like one of the Fortunae of Antium, that is, as an Amazon with one breast uncovered. In Imperial times Roman emperors offered vows there before going to the wars (Roscher 1. 1525 ff., *RE* 7. 37 ff.). Our poem is of course too early to refer to this cult. Yet it is significant that Horace asks Fortuna to protect Caesar in his expeditions (29 ff.); the attitudes that produced the cult of Fortuna Redux were already being fostered (perhaps previously by Julius Caesar, as Dr. Weinstock suggests to us).

Horace was imitated by Gray in his *Hymn to Adversity* (as already pointed out by Johnson in his *Lives of the Poets*). Adversity is addressed in ancient hymnal style as 'Daughter of Jove, relentless Power'. She carries equipment as difficult to visualize as Fortuna's, an iron scourge and adamantine chain (17 *Necessitas* n.). She makes 'purple tyrants vainly groan'; cf. 12 'purpurei metuunt tyranni'. 'The summer Friend, the flatt'ring Foe' disperse at her frown (cf. 25 ff.). And she is attended by a dignified cortège, Wisdom, Melancholy, Charity, Justice, and Pity. Gray's ode in turn influenced other English poems of the eighteenth and nineteenth centuries, notably Wordsworth's *Ode to Duty*. See further K. Schlüter, *Die englische Ode*, Bonn, 1964.

Horace's ode, though ambitious, is inferior to his general level. His account of the mutability of Fortune is less compressed and vivid than that of the previous poem. The list of Necessity's instruments is very detailed but makes little appeal to the eye; the passage earned the just censure of Lessing (17 n.). The next stanza is scandalously confused (24 n.). The end of the poem is the best part of it; yet in spite of the vigour of the rhetoric, its political thought is negligible. Horace treated the same subject better elsewhere, in the ode to Pollio (2. 1).

Metre: Alcaic.

1. **diva**: a goddess is often addressed as *dea* or *diva*. A god, on the other hand, must be called by his name or title (except that, very rarely, *dive* occurs in poetry). See Löfstedt, *Syntactica* 1². 94 ff.

gratum: to the goddess herself; cf. 1. 30. 2, Theoc. 1. 126, 15. 100 δέσποιν' ἃ Γολγώς τε καὶ 'Ιδάλιον ἐφίλησας, Virg. *Aen.* 3. 73 f. 'gratissima tellus / Nereidum matri', Ov. *met.* 10. 230, Sil. 13. 345 f., *Orph. h.* 49. 6 ἣ Τμωλὸς τέρπει σε. Of course Antium was a pleasant place (Cic. *Att.* 4. 8. 1 'nihil quietius, nihil alsius, nihil amoenius'); but Horace is not simply thinking of its appeal to men.

Antium: Anzio, the scene of a fierce battle in 1944, now a favourite bathing-place on the Latin coast south of Rome. Cicero gives an agreeable account of life there: hardly anyone knew Vatinius, and he could count the waves in peace (*Att.* 2. 6). It seems soon to have become more fashionable; cf. Str. 5. 3. 5 νυνὶ . . . ἀνεῖται τοῖς ἡγεμόσιν εἰς σχολὴν καὶ ἄνεσιν τῶν πολιτικῶν, ὅτε λάβοιεν καιρόν, καὶ διὰ τοῦτο κατῳκοδόμηνται πολυτελεῖς οἰκήσεις ἐν τῇ πόλει συχναὶ πρὸς τὰς ἐπιδημίας.

2. praesens: a religious word; the gods of the ancient world had a limited sphere of influence, and had to be present before they could be effective (cf. 3. 5. 2 f. 'praesens divus habebitur / Augustus', Petron. 17. 5 'utique nostra regio tam praesentibus plena est numinibus ut facilius possis deum quam hominem invenire', *ps.* 46. 1 'God is our refuge and strength, a very present help in trouble'). The addition of the infinitive *tollere* is an instance of the common Horatian brachylogy (cf. 1. 1. 8 n.). As *praesens* normally suggests beneficent purposes, its conjunction with *vertere* is sardonic.

imo . . .: Horace is clearly thinking of Servius Tullius, the slave's son who became king of Rome; he was believed to have founded many of the Fortuna cults. Cf. Plut. *fort. Rom.* 323 a ἄλλαι τε μυρίαι Τύχης τιμαὶ καὶ ἐπικλήσεις, ὧν τὰς πλείστας Σερούιος κατέστησεν, εἰδὼς ὅτι μεγάλη ῥοπή, μᾶλλον δ' ὅλον ἡ Τύχη παρὰ πάντ' ἐστὶ τὰ τῶν ἀνθρώπων πράγματα, καὶ μάλιστά γ' αὐτοῦ δι' εὐτυχίαν ἐξ αἰχμαλώτου καὶ πολεμίου γένους εἰς βασιλείαν προαχθέντος, Manil. 4. 66 f. (in a list of examples of the power of fortune) 'capto sanguine regem /Romanis positum', Juv. 7. 199 ff. 'Ventidius quid enim? quid Tullius? anne aliud quam / sidus et occulti miranda potentia fati? / servis regna dabunt, captivis fata triumphum'. For other expressions of the commonplace cf. [Dio Chrys.] 64. 19 τίς ἄν ποτε ἤλπισεν Ἰνδῶν ἄρξειν κουρέα, Λυδῶν βασιλεύσειν ποιμένα, τῆς Ἀσίας ἡγεμονεύσειν γυναῖκα;, Amm. 14. 11. 30 'haec fortuna mutabilis et inconstans fecit Agathoclem Siculum ex figulo regem, et Dionysium, gentium quondam terrorem, Corinthi litterario ludo praefecit' (see the whole passage), above, 1. 34. 12 n.

3. mortale corpus: the phrase incisively underlines the powerlessness of man compared with the potent goddess; cf. Sen. *nat.* 6. 2. 3 'iam intellegetis nugatoria esse nos et imbecilla corpora, fluida, non magna molitione perdenda'.

4. vertere: the word sometimes simply means 'exchange'; cf. *ars* 226 'vertere seria ludo', Ov. *met.* 4. 45, 10. 157. But here we need a stronger sense, more like that of *evertere*.

funeribus triumphos: so the two sons of Aemilius Paullus died at his supreme moment of felicity, within a few days of his triumph over Perses (Liv. 45. 40. 6 'sed non Perses tantum per illos dies documentum humanorum casuum fuit . . . sed etiam victor Paullus,

auro purpuraque fulgens'). See also *cons. Liv.* 27 f. 'funera pro sacris
tibi sunt ducenda triumphis / et tumulus Drusum pro Iovis arce
manet'.

5. ambit: 'seeks your support'; the word suggests the ingratiating
blandishments of a canvasser or office-seeker. It is sometimes used
imprecisely, as here, with a singular object; cf. Tac. *hist.* 4. 11. 2
'ille unus ambiri, coli'.

6. ruris: dependent on *dominam* (Wolf, partly following Markland).
The word is commonly supposed to depend on *colonus*, but would
then be quite otiose; objective genitives with *colonus* are all of
a much more specific kind (e.g. Mart. 10. 78. 5 'auriferae . . . terrae'
or, as often in the *Digest*, 'praediorum fisci', cf. *Thes.l.L.* 3. 1708.
81 ff.). For other strange instances of hyperbaton cf. *epod.* 5. 19 f.
'et uncta turpis ova ranae sanguine / plumamque nocturnae strigis',
Hom. *Il.* 22. 189 ὡς δ' ὅτε νεβρὸν ὄρεσφι κύων ἐλάφοιο δίηται, 23. 152 f.
ἐν χερσὶ κόμην ἑτάροιο φίλοιο / θῆκεν, Liv. 30. 3. 3 'castra in conspectu
Hasdrubalis erant', 39. 8. 5 'additae voluptates religioni vini et
epularum', Manil. 2. 60 'canam tacita naturae mente potentem',
Housman on Manil. 5. 568, K.–G. 2. 601, H.–Sz. 692.

Fraenkel, retracting an earlier view, rejects this interpretation;
he argues that the ambiguity would be unparalleled for the mature
poet of the *Odes*. Yet for another unusual hyperbaton cf. *epist.*
1. 19. 28 'temperat Archilochi musam pede mascula Sappho' (where
pede probably goes with *Archilochi*); there Fraenkel finds the construction unparalleled for the *Epistles* and *Satires*, and hence has to
interpret it in an unconvincing way (pp. 342 ff.). Fraenkel also says
that in our passage the hyperbaton would disrupt the archaic prayer-
formula *te . . . te*; but though Horace exploits such formulas, he
does not necessarily aim at a complete reproduction of the sacral
style. It should be recognized that hyperbata are mannerisms of
sophisticated Roman poetry that the reader who is intent on the
sense is expected to pick up. However, Housman, who interprets
our passage correctly, goes too far when he says, 'every Roman
child felt in the marrow of his bones that *ruris* depended on *dominam*' (*CR* 16, 1902, 445).

colonus: a tenant farmer, who owns no land of his own; cf. *serm.*
2. 2. 115 'fortem mercede colonum'. *pauper* suggests frugality rather
than squalor; cf. 2. 14. 12, *CIL* 9. 5659 'colonus pauper fuit aequo
animo'.

aequoris: Fortuna is supreme both by sea and land; cf. Pind.
O. 12. 3 ff. τὶν γὰρ ἐν πόντῳ κυβερνῶνται θοαὶ / νᾶες, ἐν χέρσῳ δὲ λαιψηροὶ
πόλεμοι / κἀγοραὶ βουλαφόροι, Dio Chrys. 63. 2 τύχης γοῦν ἐν θαλάττῃ
γενομένης εὐπλοεῖ ναῦς, καὶ ἐν ἀέρι φανείσης εὐτυχεῖ γεωργός. Horace's

passage is the first unambiguous Roman reference to Fortuna as mistress of the sea. In part at least it is clearly influenced by Pindar, loc. cit., but it may be something more than that.

In art Fortuna is often shown with both a cornucopia and a rudder; the first attested instance is a coin of 44 B.C. (E. A. Sydenham, *The Coinage of the Roman Republic*, 1952, p. 179). The rudder may originally have symbolized Fortune's power of government; cf. Pind. fr. 40 τύχη . . . δίδυμον στρέφοισα πηδάλιον (which probably does not refer to a specifically nautical τύχη), Dio Chrys. 63. 7 τὸ δὲ πηδάλιον δηλοῖ ὅτι κυβερνᾷ τὸν τῶν ἀνθρώπων βίον ἡ τύχη. But Fortuna is sometimes represented with a prow as well as a rudder; she must have come to be thought of as having special associations with the sea (Roscher 1. 1507). So it looks as if Horace's allusion is more than a conventional polarism.

Dr. Weinstock suggests to us that Horace's words may also contain a more contemporary reference. Three altars have been found at Antium dedicated to Neptune, Tranquillitas, and the Winds (*ILS* 3277, 3278, 3279). It is known that Octavian dedicated such altars in 36 B.C., when sailing from Puteoli against Sextus Pompeius (App. *civ.* 5. 98. 406). It would have been very natural if at the same time the Fortuna of Antium also had been given a maritime aspect.

7. Bithyna . . . Carpathium: the epithets give a decorative particularity to the general statement; cf. 1. 1. 13 ff., 1. 7. 10 n., 1. 31. 12 n. Bithynia was a forested country, famous for ship-building; cf. 1. 14. 11, Xen. *an.* 6. 4. 4 ξύλα δὲ πολλὰ μὲν καὶ ἄλλα, πάνυ δὲ πολλὰ καὶ καλὰ ναυπηγήσιμα ἐπ’ αὐτῇ τῇ θαλάττῃ, Theophr. *hist. plant.* 4. 5. 5, Catull. 4. 11 ff., Str. 12. 3. 12, Plin. *nat.* 16. 197, Arrian, *peripl.* 5. 2. The Carpathian sea between Rhodes and Crete was notoriously dangerous; cf. Mayor on Juv. 14. 278.

lacessit: 'challenges', 'provokes', because sailing shows contempt for nature's laws; cf. 1. 3. 23 f., Luc. 3. 193 'inde lacessitum primo mare'.

9. te . . . : in this stanza Horace continues on the extent of Fortune's power. It extends from Latium (where the goddess of Antium belongs) to the barbarian races on the borders of the Roman empire; this points forward to the expeditions of 29 ff. For the universality of Fortune's influence cf. Plin. *nat.* 2. 22 'toto quippe mundo et omnibus locis omnibusque horis omnium vocibus Fortuna sola invocatur ac nominatur', Roscher 1. 1529.

Dacus: cf. p. xxxiii. For the singular see 1. 19. 12 n.; for the change of number to *Scythae* cf. K.–S. 1. 68.

profugi: cf. 4. 14. 42 ff. 'te profugus Scythes / miratur'. Horace seems to be referring to the well-known Russian stratagem of

F f

retreating before an invader (cf. Porph. 'quod scilicet etiam fugiendo
proeliarentur') ; *profugi* therefore makes a contrast with *asper*, which
refers to a different sort of behaviour in war. Cf. Hdt. 4. 126 f., Pl.
Lach. 191 a ὥσπερ που καὶ Σκύθαι λέγονται οὐχ ἧττον φεύγοντες ἢ
διώκοντες μάχεσθαι, Ov. *Pont.* 1. 2. 83 ff., Luc. 6. 50 'refugi . . . Parthi'.
Most editors interpret *profugi* as νομάδες, but it is hard to see how
the word can bear that meaning.

Scythae: here as elsewhere probably used of the trans-Danubian
peoples; cf. 1. 19. 10, 3. 8. 23, *carm. saec.* 55.

10. urbesque gentesque: πόλεις τε καὶ ἔθνη, city-states and barbarian
races, two of the forms of society recognized in the ancient world;
the third, βασιλεία, appears in the next line. For the contrast between
the *exterae nationes* and the cities of the Roman and Hellenistic
world see 1. 2. 5 n. For Fortune as the protector of cities cf. Pind.
fr. 39 Τύχα φερέπολις.

11. matres: cf. 1. 1. 24 f.; a mother's τειχοσκοπία is described in 3. 2. 7.
Horace may have remembered Atossa's part in the *Persae* of Aeschylus. Cf. also *judg.* 5. 28 'The mother of Sisera looked out at a window,
and cried through the lattice, Why is his chariot so long in coming?
why tarry the wheels of his chariots?'

12. purpurei: more trenchant than *purpurati*. Cf. Ov. *met.* 7. 103,
trist. 4. 2. 47 f. '(Caesar) veheris / purpureus populi rite per ora tui',
Pers. 3. 41, Lucian, *Tim.* 20 πορφυροῖ καὶ χρυσόχειρες περιέρχονται,
Sidon. *carm.* 2. 96 f. 'purpureos Fortuna viros cum murice semper /
prosequitur', Tasso, *Ger. Lib.* 7. 52 'Qual con le chiome sanguinose
orrende Splender cometa suol per l'aria adusta, Che i regni muta
e i fèri morbi adduce, A i purpurei tiranni infausta luce' (cf. *Lettere*
22 '*Purpurei tiranni, Povero ciel*, son miei capricci; ma però prima
che miei, furon d'Orazio l'uno, l'altro di Dante').

metuunt: normally tyrants are feared.

13. iniurioso: a strong word (= ὑβριστικῷ); *iniuria* is an act of
violence. For *pede* cf. Aesch. *Pers.* 163 f. μὴ μέγας πλοῦτος κονίσας
οὖδας ἀντρέψῃ ποδὶ / ὄλβον. But Samson more sensibly used his arms
for the purpose (*judg.* 16. 29).

ne . . .: the fear expressed in this clause is felt only by the *tyranni*,
not by the other subjects of *metuunt*; cf. 2. 8. 21 ff.

14. stantem columnam: ὀρθοστάτην, the pillar that props the edifice
of society, but is itself vulnerable; cf. Pind. *O.* 2. 81 f. ὃς "Εκτορ'
ἔσφαλε Τροίας / ἄμαχον ἀστραβῆ κίονα, Archil. (?) 16. 1 f. ὑψηλοὺς
Μεγάτιμον Ἀριστοφόωντά τε Νάξου / κίονας, Aesch. *Ag.* 897 f. (the
king is) ὑψηλῆς στέγης / στῦλον ποδήρη, Enn. *ann.* 348 'regni versatum

summam venere columnam'. For a similar use of *columen* cf. 2. 17. 4, Plaut. *Epid.* 189 'senati qui columen cluent', Tubero, *hist.* 12 'hinc in millesimum annum eorum columine civitas continebitur', F. Leo, *Ausgewählte kleine Schriften*, 1960, 1. 29, *Thes.l.L.* 3. 1736. 65 ff. Addison, in his *Dialogues upon the Usefulness of Antient Medals*, 1726, pp. 46 ff., pointed out that Securitas, Pax, and Felicitas are shown leaning on pillars; cf. the indexes of types in Mattingly.

frequens: often used of the *populus* (*Thes.l.L.* 6. 1. 1298. 5 ff.); the word suggests a seditious assembly rather than a seething mob. Bentley's *fremens* is at first sight attractive; cf. Virg. *Aen.* 11. 453 'arma manu trepidi poscunt, fremit arma iuventus', Stat. *Theb.* 6. 618 'Arcades arma fremunt', 3. 593 'bella animis, bella ore fremunt', Sidon. *carm.* 7. 260 f. 'arma, / arma fremit'. But the frequency of *fremere* in these contexts seems due to Virgil's bold use of it as directly governing *arma* (cf. E. Fraenkel, *Beobachtungen zu Aristophanes*, 1962, p. 32 n. 4).

15. ad arma: the normal call 'to arms!'; cf. Caes. *civ.* 1. 69. 4 'conclamatur ad arma atque omnes . . . exeunt', Liv. 6. 28. 3. The duplication of the expression is stereotyped; cf. Aesch. fr. 140 ὅπλων ὅπλων δεῖ, Virg. *Aen.* 2. 668 'arma, viri, ferte arma', 7. 460, Ov. *met.* 11. 377 f. 'arma, / arma capessamus', 12. 241 'omnes uno ore arma, arma loquuntur', Sil. 4. 98, 11. 133, 12. 168 f., Stat. *Theb.* 7. 135, Tac. *ann.* 1. 59. 2, Tasso, *Ger. Lib.* 12. 44 'onde la guarda / a l'arme, a l'arme, in alto suon raddoppia', Pope, *Rape of the Lock* 5. 37 ' "To arms! to arms!" the fierce Virago cries', Ogilvie on Liv. 3. 15. 6, W. Schulze, *Kleine Schriften*, ed. 2, 1966, pp. 163 f., Fraenkel, op. cit. [above, 14], pp. 31 f.

17. anteit: Horace goes on to describe Fortune's divine attendants (cf. 1. 30. 5 ff. for those of Venus, 3. 21. 21 ff. for those of the deified wine jar). But here there is no cluster of gay and laughing companions. *anteit* suggests a grim squad of Roman lictors, carrying the fearsome symbols of *imperium*, subservient to their arrogant master and implacable to everyone else; cf. Cic. *leg. agr.* 2. 93, *rep.* 2. 31 'ut sibi duodecim lictores cum fascibus anteire liceret', Liv. 24. 44. 10.

saeva: cf. 3. 24. 6 'dira Necessitas', Hom. *Od.* 10. 273 κρατερή . . . ἀνάγκη, Parm. fr. 8. 30 f. χοὔτως ἔμπεδον αὖθι μένει· κρατερὴ γὰρ Ἀνάγκη / πείρατος ἐν δεσμοῖσιν ἔχει, τό μιν ἀμφὶς ἐέργει, Eur. *Hel.* 514 δεινῆς ἀνάγκης.

The variant *serva* is more difficult. It may seem a striking idea that Necessity, which rules everything else, is slave to Fortune. Yet this perhaps emphasizes the power of Fortune too extravagantly; it should be remembered that the Roman poets did not strain for too much originality in their adjectives. It is probably irrelevant

that slaves could not be lictors at this date, and that they would
normally walk behind their masters; in a metaphor of this kind
such sociological detail is hardly a decisive objection.

Necessitas: Ἀνάγκη (Roscher 3. 70 ff.). Necessity is somewhat differently personified in contexts referring to death (1. 3. 32, 3. 1. 14,
3. 24. 5 f.). She is actually identified with Fortune in the Greek hymn
quoted above (p. 386). For the idea of Fortune's unalterability cf.
Philemon fr. 10. 2 ff. K. μετὰ τῶν σωμάτων / ἡμῶν, ὅταν γινώμεθ᾽,
εὐθὺς χὴ τύχη / προσγίνεθ᾽ ἡμῖν συγγενὴς τῷ σώματι, / κοὐκ ἔστιν
ἕτερον παρ᾽ ἑτέρου λαβεῖν τύχην, IG² 12. 5. 302. 7 ἀλλὰ Τύχης οὐκ ἔστι
φυγεῖν ἀμετάτροπα δῶρα. One may also compare the adamantine
spindle of Necessity in Pl. *rep.* 616 c and the adamantine shuttles of
the Μοῖραι in *PMG* 1018(a). 3.

Lessing (*Laokoon*, c. 10, note at end) complained that in the
following lines Necessity has too many attributes; he continues 'the
passage is one of the coldest in Horace. . . . The passage is unpleasing
. . . because the attributes . . . are peculiarly addressed to the eyes;
and if we attempt to acquire by the ear conceptions that would
naturally be conveyed through the eyes, a greater effort is required,
while the ideas themselves are incapable of the same distinctness'.

18. clavos: for nails and bolts as emblems of fixity cf. 3. 24. 5 ff. 'si
figit adamantinos / summis verticibus dira Necessitas / clavos, non
animum metu, / non mortis laqueis expedies caput', Pind. *P.* 4. 71
τίς δὲ κίνδυνος κρατεροῖς ἀδάμαντος δῆσεν ἅλοις;, Aesch. *supp.* 440 f.
πᾶσ᾽ ἔστ᾽ ἀνάγκη, καὶ γεγόμφωται σκάφος / στρέβλαισι ναυτικαῖσιν ὡς
προσηγμένον, 944 f. τῶνδ᾽ ἐφήλωται τορῶς / γόμφος διάμπαξ, ὡς
μένειν ἀραρότως, Plaut. *asin.* 156 'fixus hic apud nos est animus tuos
clavo Cupidinis'. Note especially the proverbial phrase in Cic. *Verr.*
5. 53 'ut hoc beneficium, quemadmodum dicitur, trabali clavo
figeret', Petron. 75. 7 'quod semel destinavi clavo trabali (Scheffer,
tabulari codd.) fixum est', Arnob. *nat.* 2. 13 'ne velut trabalibus
clavis affixi corporibus haereatis'. See also Webster, *White Divel*
1. 2. 153 'tis fixt with nayles of dyamonds to inevitable necessitie'
(with Lucas's note). These passages are sufficient to refute the old
notion (seen, for instance, in Lessing and in Gray) that Horace is
referring in this stanza to instruments of torture or violence.

Roman *clavi* could be half a yard long; anybody who has seen
some of the nails recovered by Sir Ian Richmond from Inchtuthil
(12 tons of them) will understand why Necessity is so equipped.

It may conceivably be relevant that symbolical nails were fixed
in the temple of Nortia, the Etruscan goddess identified by Juvenal
with Fortune, perhaps as a tally of the years; cf. Liv. 7. 3. 7, Paul.
Fest. 49. 7 ff. L. (= 56. 10 f. M.). There is a representation of Nortia

with a nail on a mirror from Perugia (Roscher 3. 457, illustrated in Smith's *Dictionary of Classical Antiquities* 1. 453).

trabalis: suitable for fastening beams. Elsewhere the word means 'as big as a beam'; cf. Enn. *ann.* 589 *telo* (Virg. *Aen.* 12. 294, Val. Fl. 8. 301, Amm. 16. 12. 53), Stat. *Theb.* 4. 6 f. *hastam*, Claud. *rapt. Pros.* 2. 172 f. *sceptro*, 17. 318 f. *vecte.*

cuneos . . .: *cunei* are dowels used to hold together blocks of stone; cf. Cic. *Tim.* 47 'crebris quasi cuneolis liquefactis' (translating Pl. *Tim.* 43 a πυκνοῖς γόμφοις συντήκοντες), *Tusc.* 2. 23 'cuneos' (referring to Aesch. *Pr.* 64 ἀδαμαντίνου . . . σφηνός). See also D. S. Robertson, *A Handbook of Greek and Roman Architecture*, ed. 2, 1943, p. 42 'The blocks in the same course were connected by metal clamps [cf. *uncus* n.], those in different courses by metal dowels, both usually of wrought iron, and molten lead was used to secure both clamps and dowels in position', Blümner, *Technologie* 2. 307 f., 3. 95 ff., R. Martin, *Manuel d'architecture grecque* 1, 1965, pp. 238 ff.

The nature of the *cunei* strongly recommends Campbell's conjecture *aenos*, which also has the merit of giving all the implements a balancing adjective. For bronze dowels cf. Blümner, *Technologie* 3. 96 n. 2, Martin, op. cit. p. 280 n. 2. If *aena* is right, one can only say that the pictorial quality of the stanza is impaired; cf. Athen. 604 b οὐδ' (ἀρέσκει σοι) ὁ ποιητής, ἔφη, ὁ λέγων χρυσοκόμαν Ἀπόλλωνα· χρυσέας γὰρ εἰ ἐποίησεν ὁ ζωγράφος τὰς τοῦ θεοῦ κόμας, καὶ μὴ μελαίνας, χεῖρον ἂν ἦν τὸ ζωγράφημα, Lessing, above, 17 n.

20. uncus: a clamp used to hold a facing of cut stone to a core of cheaper stone or brick. Vitruvius calls it *ansa* (2. 8. 4), and says that if it and lead are used the work will be 'sine vitio sempiternum'. The structure that Necessitas rears is designed to last.

plumbum: cf. Eur. *Andr.* 266 f. καὶ γὰρ εἰ πέριξ σ' ἔχοι / τηκτὸς μόλυβδος, ἐξαναστήσω σ' ἐγώ, Blümner, *Technologie* 3. 96 ff. O. Keller (*Epilegomena zu Horaz*, 1879, p. 22) points out that we should not think of the lead as liquid when it is being carried by Necessity; he compares the dedication of 'lucida funalia' at 3. 26. 6 f.

21. Spes . . .: both Spes and Fides are coupled with Fortuna in Roman cult (Roscher 1. 1538 ff.). Cf. *ILS* 3770 (Capua 110 B.C.) 'mag. Spei Fidei Fortunae mur[um] faciundu coiravere', *reg. urb.* p. 11. 1 'templa duo nova Spei et Fortunae', *ILS* 3688 'simulacra duo Spei corolitica' (dedicated to Fortuna Primigenia at Praeneste), 3687, *carm. epig.* 409. 8 (cf. 1498. 1, 2139. 1) 'Spes et Fortuna, valete'. We also hear of an altar of Τύχη Εὔελπις in the Vicus Longus (Plut. *fort. Rom.* 323 a, *quaest. Rom.* 281 e). The only Greek instances of the association are late, and presumably influenced by Roman practice; cf. [Dio Chrys.] 64. 8 ὠνόμασται . . . τὸ . . . ἄδηλον (τῆς Τύχης) Ἐλπίς,

Macedonius, *anth. P.* 10. 70. 1 f. Τύχης παίζουσιν ἑταῖραι / Ἐλπίδες,
anon. ibid. 9. 134. 1 Ἐλπὶς καὶ σὺ Τύχη, μέγα χαίρετε.

rara: it is not the goddess Fides who is *rara*, but rather the
quality that she represents; cf. 1. 18. 16 n. Horace's theme is developed by Sen. *Herc. O.* 600 ff. 'nunc quoque casum quemcumque
times / fidas comites accipe fatis; / nam rara fides / ubi iam melior
fortuna ruit', Mart. 10. 78. 2, Auson. 12. 3.

Fides: for the conjunction of Fides with Fortuna cf. *ILS* 3770
(quoted above), *carm. epig.* 2065 n. '[T]utela Her[c]ules Fides Fortuna'. A coin of Vespasian's shows a goddess with patera and
cornucopia and the inscription *Fides Fortuna* (Mattingly 2. 216).

22. velata panno: 'with her hand wrapped in a cloth'. The goddess
is given the *pannus* of her priests; cf. Liv. 1. 21. 4 '(in the cult of
Fides, Numa) flamines . . . iussit manu . . . ad digitos usque involuta
rem divinam facere, significantes fidem tutandam sedemque eius
etiam in dexteris sacratam esse', Serv. *Aen.* 1. 292, P. Boyancé in
Hommages à Jean Bayet (ed. M. Renard and R. Schilling), 1964,
pp. 101 ff. *velare* need not apply to the head; cf. Plaut. *Amph.* 257
'velatis manibus', Virg. *Aen.* 7. 154 'ramis velatos Palladis' of sup-
pliants carrying olive branches in their hands (11. 101), Ov. *met.*
11. 279.

nec comitem abnegat: 'and does not refuse to play the comrade'.
The phrase seems to be modelled on such expressions as *agere civem*,
and to have a different shade of meaning from Lygd. 6. 10 'neve
neget quisquam me duce se comitem', Val. Fl. 3. 694 f. 'an sese
comitem tam tristibus actis / abneget'. One may compare Ov. *ars*
1. 127 'comitemque negarat', Hor. *epist.* 1. 18. 2 'professus amicum',
Virg. *Aen.* 2. 591 'confessa deam' (see Austin's note), Luc. 1. 131
'dedidicit . . . ducem', Löfstedt, *Syntactica* 1². 244 ff., K.-S. 1. 93,
H.-Sz. 751.

23. mutata . . . veste: 'in mourning', cf. Petron. 124 v. 252 f. 'huic
comes it submissa Fides et crine soluto / Iustitia ac maerens lacera
Concordia palla'. The Fortune of the house shares the suffering of
the great man; cf. *epist.* 2. 1. 191 'trahitur manibus regum fortuna
retortis'. Fortune in such passages is not a capricious and independent deity; in Roman cult different families had their own
separate *Fortuna* (cf. *Fortuna Crassiana, Fortuna Claudiae Iustae*).
Fortune in this sense is often associated with the *genius*; cf. *ILS*
2013, 3656, 3657 'genio loci, Fortun. reduci, Romae aetern. et fato
bono'.

24. inimica: this word introduces the most extraordinary confusion.
⸮ ⟶ Up to this point Horace suggests that the Fortuna of the family

shares the disaster that befalls the man. But *inimica linquis* gives a totally different picture: Fortune is now a deity independent of the house, who has gone off and left the great man in the lurch (cf. Stat. *Theb.* 2. 311 ff. 'respiciens descisse deos trepidoque tumultu / dilapsos comites, nudum latus omne, fugamque / Fortunae', Plut. *fort. Rom.* 320 a καὶ ἡ τύχη σου καθ᾽ ἑαυτήν ἐστι μεγάλη κολακεύει δὲ τήν τούτου· ἐὰν μὴ μακρὰν ᾖς, οἰχήσεται μεταβᾶσα πρὸς αὐτόν). In such contexts the faithful friend ought to be praised precisely because he does *not* accompany Fortune; cf. Ov. *Pont.* 2. 3. 55 f. 'indignum . . . ducis / te fieri comitem stantis in orbe deae', 1. 9. 15 f. 'adfuit ille mihi, cum me pars magna reliquit, / Maxime, Fortunae nec fuit ipse comes', 4. 10. 74.

For Horace's sake one would be glad to believe that the text is corrupt. Bentley considered *inimica vertis*; one could then imagine the true friends as staying in the ruined house, as opposed to the false friends who fly. But *comitem* strongly supports a verb of motion like *linquis*, and the inconsistency of *inimica* with *mutata veste* still remains. Peerlkamp proposed *sed comitem abnegat* (Fides refuses to go off with Fortune). But then *mutata veste* has to be applied not to Fortune, but to *potentis domos*, and this is not an obvious way of reading the sentence. Moreover, it seems more natural to praise Fides for accompanying the deity she escorts than for a refusal to accompany her. Campbell suggested *manicata* ('in chains') for *inimica*; one would sooner try *lacrimosa* or something of the kind. Then we should have to assume that the great man is going into exile accompanied by his true friends.

Ker, loc. cit., tries another line of approach, which had already been adumbrated in various forms by ps.-Acro, Mackay, Alexander, de Coster, and by Housman in lectures. According to this theory there is no real difference in emphasis between this stanza and the next: Fides deserts the great man and goes off with Fortuna; *at* (21) is a lively continuative particle rather than an adversative; Horace simply passes from the allegorical to the actual, from irony to realism. But this is all very implausible. Surely there is a contrast between *rara* and *volgus*, *Fides* and *infidum*, *nec comitem abnegat* and *retro . . . cedit*.

25. meretrix: an unpoetical word, used 9 times in the *Satires* and *Epistles*, but only here in the *Odes*. However, it is found seven times in Ovid.

26. diffugiunt . . .: for the commonplace cf. Theogn. 643 f. πολλοὶ πὰρ κρητῆρι φίλοι γίγνονται ἑταῖροι, / ἐν δὲ σπουδαίῳ πρήγματι παυρότεροι (with van Groningen's note), Pind. *I.* 2. 11 "χρήματα χρήματ᾽ ἀνήρ" ὃς φᾶ κτεάνων ἅμα λειφθεὶς καὶ φίλων, Soph. (?) fr. 667 N. (= 733 P.)

ἀνδρὸς κακῶς πράσσοντος ἐκποδὼν φίλοι (Pearson cites numerous instances from Euripides and Ovid), Sirach 6. 10 καὶ ἔστι φίλος
κοινωνὸς τραπεζῶν καὶ οὐ μὴ παραμείνῃ ἐν ἡμέρᾳ θλίψεώς σου, Petron.
38. 13 'ubi semel res inclinata est, amici de medio', 80. 9, Lucian,
anth. P. 10. 35. 3 f., Agathias, ibid. 10. 64, Milton, Samson Agonistes
191 ff. 'In prosperous days They swarm, but in adverse withdraw their
head, Not to be found, though sought', Otto 22, S. G. P. Small, YClS
12, 1951, 116 f.

27. cum faece siccatis: the friends stayed so long as there was anything at all to be had. The phrase is humorously bizarre; normally
one drank as far as the lees, not lees and all (cf. 3. 15. 16 'poti . . .
faece tenus cadi', Archil. 5A. 8 ἄγρει δ᾽ οἶνον ἐρυθρὸν ἀπὸ τρυγός,
Otto 130 f.). For a similar point cf. Sen. epist. 58. 32.

28. ferre iugum pariter: the par iugum is the yoke borne in common
by two beasts of burden; cf. Plin. epist. 3. 9. 8 'uterque pari iugo
non pro se sed pro causa niteretur', 1. 33. 11 n. For the use of the
metaphor to refer to shared sufferings cf. Herodas 6. 12 with Headlam's note.

The infinitive with dolosi is unusually bold even for Horace; the
meaning must be 'too treacherous to bear a share of the yoke'.
L. Müller conjectured defugiunt for diffugiunt, and took the infinitive to depend on the verb (cf. 1. 1. 34). But then defugiunt . . .
dolosi has to be regarded as a single indivisible colon, and the phrase
is too long for that. Moreover, diffugiunt is very convincing in this
context and is supported by parallels.

29. serves: cf. Pind. O. 12. 2 σώτειρα Τύχα, Aesch. Ag. 664 Τύχη δὲ
σωτὴρ ναῦν θέλουσ᾽ ἐφέζετο, ILS 3656 'Fortunae conservatrici'. On
the Monumentum Ancyranum Τύχη σωτήριος is the translation of
Fortuna redux.

ultimos: cf. 4. 14. 47 f., Catull. 11. 11 f., 29. 4, Virg. ecl. 1. 66, Pease
on Cic. nat. deor. 2. 88.

30. Britannos: Julius Caesar had imposed tribute on the peoples of
south-east Britain, and hence they could be regarded as rebels
(C. E. Stevens in Aspects of Archaeology, Essays presented to O. G. S.
Crawford, 1951, pp. 332 ff.). Dio mentions plans by Augustus to
conquer the island in 34, 27, and 26 B.C. (49. 38. 2, 53. 22. 5, 53. 25. 2);
he is supported by the literary evidence of the period (A. Momigliano,
JRS 40, 1950, 39 f.). The poets cannot have misinterpreted the in-
tentions of the regime (Brunt, cited p. xxxi).

recens: the older armies had been discharged at the end of the
previous civil war; the word is compatible with a date either in
35 or 27.

31. **examen**: for warriors compared with bees cf. Aesch. *Pers.* 126 ff. πᾶς γὰρ ἱππηλάτας / καὶ πεδοστιβῆς λεὼς / σμῆνος ὡς ἐκλέλοιπεν μελισ/σᾶν σὺν ὀρχάμῳ στρατοῦ, *paneg. Lat.* 2(12). 32. 3 'omnes Scythiae nationes tantis examinibus confluebant'; for bees compared with warriors cf. Varro, *rust.* 3. 16. 30 'consonant vehementer, proinde ut milites faciunt cum castra movent', Virg. *georg.* 4. 21 f. 'cum prima novi ducent examina reges / vere suo ludetque favis emissa iuventus'. It should be remembered that *examen* is derived from *exigo*, and sometimes keeps a flavour of its etymology.

32. **partibus**: of place as 3. 3. 39. More often a genitive is added (3. 24. 37 f. *mundi*, 1. 15. 30) or implied (3. 3. 55 where *mundi* is to be supplied from *mundo* in 53). The sense later became more frequent, cf. μέρη. See Löfstedt, *Syntactica* 2. 440 f., *Late Latin*, p. 113.

Oceano . . . rubro: not just the Red Sea (*sinus Arabicus*), but the totality of the Red Sea, Persian Gulf, and Arabian Sea. *Oceanus* is used not merely of the Atlantic, but of all the circumfluous Ocean.

34. **fratrumque**: 'we are sorry at what we have done to our brothers'; the word is not strictly co-ordinate with the other genitives, but the allusive economy is intended to suggest strong emotion.

Horace's most splendid and imaginative expression of horror at fratricidal war is in *epod.* 7. 17 ff. where the murder of Remus is the symbol of Roman destiny: 'sic est: acerba fata Romanos agunt / scelusque fraternae necis, / ut immerentis fluxit in terram Remi / sacer nepotibus cruor'. Cf. also Virg. *georg.* 2. 510 'gaudent perfusi sanguine fratrum', Luc. 2. 148 ff. Two poems in the *anthologia Latina* (462, 463) deal with a Maevius who at Actium killed his brother without recognizing him and then committed suicide with his brother's sword; cf. especially 462. 9 f. 'fratribus heu fratres, patribus concurrere natos / impia sors belli fataque saeva iubent'. See further P. Jal, *La Guerre civile à Rome*, 1963, pp. 393 ff., Wagenvoort 169 ff.

quid . . .: after his prayers Horace gives his reason for uttering it; for a similar sentiment and technique cf. Virg. *georg.* 1. 500 ff. 'hunc saltem everso iuvenem succurrere saeclo / ne prohibete. satis iam pridem sanguine nostro / Laomedonteae luimus periuria Troiae' (F. Jacoby, *Hermes* 56, 1921, 47 n. 1 = *Kleine philologische Schriften*, 1961, 2. 48 n. 52). Horace moves deftly from vague hints (*quid refugimus?*) to a more explicit statement (*quibus pepercit aris?*). He shows great rhetorical skill in varying the form of his questions and distributing them at various places in the stanza.

dura . . . aetas: cf. *epod.* 16. 9 '(Romam) impia perdemus devoti sanguinis aetas'. Horace may have in mind the impieties of Hesiod's age of iron (*op.* 182 ff.).

35. intactum: for *tangere* of venturing on something forbidden cf.
1. 3. 24, Plb. 7. 13. 6 ἅπτεσθαι τῶν μεγίστων ἀσεβημάτων, Sen. *Thy.*
221 f. 'quid enim reliquit crimine intactum aut ubi / sceleri pepercit?'

nefasti: supplies the genitive of the indeclinable *nefas*; it is so
first used by Horace. Cf. Virg. *Aen.* 1. 543 'deos memores fandi atque
nefandi'.

36. unde: 'from what ...?'

37. metu deorum: εὐσέβεια and good, whereas *timor deorum* is δεισι-
δαιμονία and bad; cf. *serm.* 2. 3. 295 'quone malo mentem concussa?
timore deorum' (Orelli). For the thought cf. Cic. *nat. deor.* 1. 86 'tot
milia latrocinantur morte proposita, alii omnia quae possunt fana
compilant. credo, aut illos mortis timor terret aut hos religionis'.

continuit: *abstinere* is very much commoner with *manum* or
manus (see *Thes.l.L.* 1. 195. 10 ff.), but *continuit* has point: they did
not even check their hands, much less 'keep their hands off'.

quibus pepercit aris: cf. App. *civ.* 4. 62. 268, 4. 64. 274, 4. 73. 311 for
Cassius's exactions of public and sacred funds from Laodicea, Tarsus,
and Rhodes, 5. 24. 97 for Octavian's from the Capitoline temple
and from those of Antium, Lanuvium, Nemi, and Tibur. Yet the
violation of altars was hardly the most conspicuous of the horrors
of the civil war. The sweep of Horace's rhetoric has betrayed him
into some falsity of tone.

39. diffingas: 'reforge' (= *refabrices* according to Porphyrio). Shar-
pening is not enough; complete refashioning is needed. The word
only occurs in Horace (3. 29. 48). For the idea cf. Virg. *Aen.* 7. 636
'recoquunt patrios fornacibus ensis', Sil. 4. 15 'revocantque novas
fornace bipennes'. Fortune is a smith also in Aesch. *cho.* 647 προ-
χαλκεύει δ' Αἶσα φασγανουργός.

retusum: the swords are blunt with excessive use (cf. Luc. 6. 161
'iugulisque retundite ferrum', Sil.16. 105 'hebetataque tela'). *recusum*,
'rehammered', supported by Lambinus and others, is ingenious, but
the word is nowhere attested and is awkward after *incude*. Bentley's
recoctum (proleptic) would vigorously reinforce the point of *nova*
and *diffingas*; but change is unnecessary.

in: for the diversion of troubles on to other people cf. 1. 21. 13 n.
For the feeling that foreign wars are better than civil ones cf. 1. 2. 22,
51.

40. Massagetas: a Scythian tribe living to the east of the Caspian
(*RE* 14. 2123 ff., E. H. Minns, *Scythians and Greeks*, 1913, pp. 111 f.).
Like the Geloni of 2. 9. 23 they belong to the world of Herodotus,
and have nothing to do with Horace or his time. Here the name is
an exaggerated way of saying 'Parthia and regions yet more remote'.

36. ET TVRE ET FIDIBVS IVVAT

1–9. *Numida's safe return from Spain must be celebrated; he is dearer to none than to his old friend Lamia. 10–20. There will be wine and dancing and flowers, and Numida will be embraced by Damalis.*

The recipient of this poem is totally unknown. He is described by Porphyrio as Pomponius Numida, and in many manuscripts as Numida Plotius; these identifications may be reckless. Verrall thought he was a fictitious character, whose name meant 'nomad' or 'wanderer' (*Studies Literary and Historical in the Odes of Horace*, 1884, p. 130); however, the link with the real-life Lamia rules out this view. He may have served in Augustus's Spanish campaign of 27–25, or conceivably with Lamia's father in 24 (4 n.); yet any return from abroad would justify such a poem. Porphyrio asserts that he had been serving in Mauretania; this unimportant information is unlikely to come from independent sources, and is probably an inane inference from the name 'Numida'.

Numida is very undistinguished compared with the other male protagonists of Book I. Horace says nothing of his own friendship for the man, and it may be significant that the poem is not addressed to him. It is not even suggested that Horace is giving the party himself; *iuvat* (1) is carefully impersonal, and the negative imperatives of 10–16 are equally non-committal. On the other hand Horace goes out of his way to emphasize Numida's friendship for Lamia, and implies that Lamia had superior status (8 *rege*). Lamia is the son of an important family, which receives poems from Horace elsewhere (for him and his father see above, p. 301). Perhaps he is the real recipient of the ode. He may indeed have commissioned it.

It was a well-established Roman custom to give a *cena adventicia* in honour of a friend's safe return; cf. Plaut. *Bacch.* 94 'ego sorori meae cenam hodie dare volo viaticam', 186 f., *curc.* 561 f. 'salvos quom advenis / in Epidaurum, hic hodie apud me—numquam delinges salem', *Epid.* 7 f., *most.* 1004 ff., *Poen.* 1151, *Stich.* 470 f., 512 f., Cic. *Att.* 4. 5. 4 'viaticam Crassipes praeripit' (*viaticam* Shackleton Bailey, *viaticum* codd.), Juv. 12. 14 f., Suet. *Vit.* 13. 2 'famosissima super ceteras fuit cena data ei adventicia a fratre, in qua duo milia lectissimorum piscium, septem avium apposita traduntur', Plut. *quaest. conv.* 727 b ὑποδεκτικὸν ὡς Ῥωμαῖοι καλοῦσι . . . δεῖπνον. Such dinners were naturally preceded by a sacrifice *ex voto* (2 n.). The satirist might emphasize the victim, which gave promise of a good meal (*epist.* 1. 3. 36, Juv. 12. 2–14). The lyric poet obeys the law of his genre and concentrates on the symposium (cf. 2. 7

in honour of Pompeius's return, 3. 14 of Augustus's, Theoc. 7. 65,
Mart. 8. 45, 11. 36). Eating played an important part in Roman
social life, but not in Horace's odes.

The poem deals with the conventional literary theme of pre-
parations for a party; cf. 4. 11, *epist.* 1. 5, Plaut. *Pseud.* 162 ff.,
below, pp. 421 f. The traditional elements of a symposium are included: wine, dancing, flowers, girls. These were obviously features of
real parties alike in the Greek and the Roman world; cf. Ar. *Ach.*
1091 στέφανοι μύρον τραγήμαθ' αἱ πόρναι πάρα, Catull. 13. 3 ff. 'si tecum
attuleris bonam atque magnam / cenam, non sine candida puella / et
vino et sale et omnibus cachinnis', Liv. 39. 6. 8 (187 B.C.) 'tunc
psaltriae sambucistriaeque et convivalia ludorum oblectamenta
addita epulis'. Yet Horace shows less than his usual skill in handling
his theme: there are no evocative Roman details, the metre is somewhat jejune, and the list of directions perfunctory (1–2 *et* . . . *et*, 11–16
neu . . . *neu* . . .). Perhaps Horace could think of nothing much to say
about Numida.

Metre: Fourth Asclepiad.

1. **fidibus:** not merely a convention of Greek poetry; the lyre was
played at some Roman sacrifices as an alternative to the pipe. Cf.
Porph. ad loc. 'fidicines hodieque Romae ad sacrificia adhiberi sicut
tibicines nemo est qui nesciat', Plaut. *Epid.* 500 f. 'ut fidibus can-
tarem seni / dum rem divinam faceret', *RE* 6. 2286. When Clodius
attended the ceremonies of the Bona Dea he was disguised as a
ψάλτρια (Plut. *Cic.* 28. 1).

2. **placare:** gods are potentially hostile. Cf. 3. 23. 3, *serm.* 2. 3. 206,
Juv. 12. 89 f. 'hic nostrum placabo Iovem, Laribusque paternis / tura
dabo'.

debito: due *ex voto*; cf. 2. 7. 17, 4. 2. 54, *epist.* 1. 3. 36 'pascitur in
vestrum reditum votiva iuvenca', Ov. *am.* 2. 11. 46, Juv. 12. 2, Sen.
ben. 3. 27. 1 'Rufus vir ordinis senatorii inter cenam optaverat ne
Caesar salvus rediret ex ea peregrinatione quam parabat; et ad-
iecerat idem omnes et tauros et vitulos optare'.

4. **Hesperia:** 'the western land', here Spain, though elsewhere Italy
(1. 28. 26 n.); the meaning in each case is determined by the speaker's
point of view. Servius gives too precise a ruling: 'aut enim Hesperiam solam dicis et significas Italiam aut addis *ultimam* et significas Hispaniam' (*Aen.* 1. 530). It would likewise be prosaic to take
ultima here as a specific reference to Hispania Ulterior. It may
in fact be relevant that L. Aelius Lamia, apparently the father of
the Lamia here, was left in charge of Hispania Citerior on Augustus's

departure in 24 B.C. (p. 301). This prompts the suggestion that Numida had been serving with him. But it may be objected that in that case his friend and contemporary, the younger Lamia, ought to have been in Spain as well.

6. **nulli:** for the phrasing cf. 1. 24. 10.

dividit: cf. Sen. *Thy.* 1023 'fruere, osculare; divide amplexus tribus'. In our passage the word suits *sodalibus* better than *Lamiae*.

oscula: cf. Catull. 9. 6 ff. 'visam te incolumem audiamque Hiberum / narrantem loca facta nationes, / ut mos est tuus, adplicansque collum / iucundum os oculosque suaviabor', Q. Cic. *epist.* 16. 27. 2 (to Tiro) 'ego vos a.d. iii Kal. videbo tuosque oculos . . . dissaviabor'.

8. **non alio rege:** Porphyrio rightly refers this to Lamia himself, who seems to have been the hero of Numida's boyhood. Some editors see an allusion to the children's games where the leader was called *rex* (*epist.* 1. 1. 59, Hdt. 1. 114, Pl. *Theaet.* 146 a, Procop. *anecd.* 14. 14) ; but Horace must be thinking of a more serious and permanent relationship. Some suppose that the *rex* was the schoolmaster of Numida and Lamia; but *non alio* does not mean the same as *eodem*, and cannot refer to some third party hitherto unmentioned.

9. **mutatae . . . togae:** the *toga virilis* was assumed about the age of 15, often at the *Liberalia* (17 March).

10. **Cressa . . . nota:** a 'Cretan mark' is poetic diction for a 'white chalk-mark'; cf. Catull. 107. 6 'o lucem candidiore nota'. *creta* was falsely connected with *Creta*; cf. Isid. *orig.* 16. 1. 6 'creta ab insula Creta ubi melior est'.

The 'candida nota' was no doubt by origin a primitive way of marking a calendar. However, the ancients connected the expression with an alleged custom of the Thracians: if a day was happy they put a white pebble in an urn, if unhappy a black one; they could thus accurately compute the felicity of their lives (Plin. *nat.* 7. 131, Otto 64 f.). Phylarchus tells a similar story about the Scythians (*FGrH* 81 F 83), and Porphyrio explains our passage by applying the legend to the Cretans. But here a specific reference to *white* marks is required (as Bentley was the first to point out). One should distinguish references to a 'white day' (Pearson on Soph. fr. 6, Pfeiffer on Call. fr. 178. 2).

11. **neu . . . amphorae:** 'let there be no stint in bringing out the amphora'. One may compare the title of one of Varro's Menippean Satires, *est modus matulae*. A standard amphora contained nearly seven gallons, so there would be no shortage of supplies. *amphorae* is probably genitive, balancing *pedum*; cf. Cic. *Tusc.* 4. 82 'sit iam huius disputationis modus'.

12. Salium: an adjective, = *Saliarem*; cf. 4. 1. 28, Fest. 439 L.
(= 329 M.) 'Salias virgines'. The Salii were priests of Mars, who had
charge of the *ancilia* or sacred shields; their name was derived from
salire, and they were especially famed for their ritual dance (Liv.
1. 20. 4, Ov. *fast.* 3. 387 ff.). This singular exhibition could be observed
even in Horace's day; we are told that Appius Claudius (probably
the consul of 38 B.C.) prided himself on excelling his colleagues
(Macr. *sat.* 3. 14. 4).

Horace's expression is curiously ambiguous; at first sight it seems
to imply that the Salii kept their feet still. In fact *neu sit requies
pedum* means *et sit concitatio pedum*; so at Virg. *Aen.* 2. 94 *nec tacui
demens* means *et clamavi demens*.

13–16. The sequence of these lines causes some doubt. Among other
possibilities, Peerlkamp proposed that 13–14 should be placed after
15–16. On this hypothesis the two references to Damalis are brought
together, and (what matters more) the unimportant flowers are
given less emphasis. There is something to be said for this proposal;
though in an ode which shows signs of imperfection one cannot be
certain.

13. multi . . . meri: πολύοινος; cf. Cic. *epist.* 9. 26. 3 'non multi cibi
hospitem accipies, sed multi ioci', Ov. *met.* 14. 252 'nimiique Elpenora
vini'. For drinking by women at symposia cf. Phalaecus, *epig.*
1. 3 f. Gow–Page (on Cleo) ἴσα δὲ πίνειν / οὔτις οἱ ἀνθρώπων ἤρισεν
οὐδαμά πω, Hedylus, *epig.* 3. 1 Gow–Page ἡ διαπινομένη Καλλίστιον
ἀνδράσι, anon. *anth.* P. 7. 329, Catull. 27. 4, Tib. 1. 9. 59 f., Prop. 2. 33.
25 ff., 4. 8. 30 'sobria grata parum; cum bibit, omne decet', Sen.
epist. 95. 21 'non minus pervigilant, non minus potant, et oleo et
mero viros provocant', Ael. *var. hist.* 2. 41 εἰ δὲ χρὴ καὶ γυναικῶν
μνημονεῦσαι ἄτοπον μὲν γυνὴ φιλοπότις, καὶ πολυπότις ἔτι πλέον. εἰρήσθω
δ' οὖν καὶ περὶ τούτων. Κλεώ φασιν ἐς ἅμιλλαν ἰοῦσα οὐ γυναιξὶ μόναις
ἀλλὰ καὶ τοῖς ἀνδράσι τοῖς συμπόταις δεινοτάτη πιεῖν ἦν, καὶ ἐκράτει
πάντων, αἴσχιστόν γε τοῦτο φερομένη τὸ νικητήριον, ὥς γε ἐμοὶ κριτῇ.

Damalis: the word means literally 'a heifer'. The name is found
surprisingly often in Latin inscriptions (*Thes.l.L.* Onom. 3. 23. 1 ff.);
it was borne, for instance, by a woman so obviously respectable as
the sempstress of the Empress Livia (*CIL* 6. 4029 'Damalis Liviae
sarcinatrix dat Alexandro viro suo ollam'). But the Damalis of this
poem is clearly a *hetaera*.

It is not clear why Horace should say 'Let heavy-drinking Damalis
fail to defeat Bassus'. Even if Bassus is also a heavy drinker (see
below), one would naturally expect the man to defeat the woman.
neu vincat would, it is true, be consistent with a prolonged and evenly
balanced contest (cf. διαπινομένη above). Even so, the transmitted

reading seems to divert our attention a little too much from the spectacular Damalis to the unimportant Bassus.

Ps.-Acro interpreted 'Let Damalis compete in drinking with Numida, her new lover, and no longer with Bassus'; but *neu vincat* ought to suggest not the transference of the contest from one pair to another, but great abundance of drink (so *neu modus . . . sit* above, *neu desint* below). Peerlkamp proposed *nec* for *neu*, and took the negative closely with *multi*: 'let Damalis, a woman of not much wine, defeat Bassus'. But this makes Damalis's normal behaviour impossibly demure. Campbell suggested that *Damalis* in 13 has displaced a man's name (e.g. *Marius*); but it is uneconomical to introduce two characters who serve no further purpose. One might suggest reading *Damalin* and *Bassus*; yet this spoils the elegant variation *Damalis . . . Damalin . . . Damalis*. The text would make sense if one emended *neu* (12) to *et* (accepting Peerlkamp's transposition); yet one is reluctant to give up a single *neu*.

14. Bassum: Propertius addressed a poem to a Bassus (1. 4. 1), probably the writer of *iambi* mentioned by Ovid (*trist.* 4. 10. 47 f.). But Horace may not be referring to a real person; perhaps the name is chosen because it resembles 'Bassareus' (1. 18. 11 n.). Bassus may be the type-name for a heavy drinker in Martial 6. 69: 'non miror quod potat aquam tua Bassa, Catulle; / miror quod Bassi filia potat aquam' (in the second line there is a variant *Bassae*).

vincat: cf. Sen. *epist.* 83. 24 'quae gloria est capere multum? cum penes te palma fuerit et propinationes tuas strati somno ac vomitantes recusaverint, cum superstes toti convivio fueris, cum omnes viceris virtute magnifica et nemo vini tam capax fuerit, vinceris a dolio'.

amystide: a συνεχὴς πόσις (as Hesychius describes it) or sconce; this custom was associated with the hard-drinking barbarians of the north. The word is derived from ἀμυστί, 'without closing the lips'. See also Anacreon 356a. 1 ff. ἄγε δὴ φέρ' ἡμὶν ὦ παῖ / κελέβην ὅκως / ἄμυστιν / προπίω . . . , Eur. *Cycl.* 417, *Rhes.* 419, Call. fr. 178. 11 f. καὶ γὰρ ὁ Θρηικίην μὲν ἀπέστυγε χανδὸν ἄμυστιν / οἰνοποτεῖν, ὀλίγῳ δ' ἥδετο κισσυβίῳ, Sidon. *epist.* (*carm.* 22) 5.

15. rosae: flower-petals were scattered at a symposium; cf. 3. 19. 22, 3. 29. 3, Prop. 4. 8. 40 (of a castanet-girl) 'facilis spargi munda sine arte rosa', Mayor on Juv. 11. 122.

16. apium: σέλινον or celery (the English word is ultimately derived from the Greek); the ancient plant was unblanched and bitter in taste. *apium* is often translated 'parsley', but this was probably *petroselinum* (from which the English word is derived). For a full and interesting discussion cf. A. C. Andrews, *CPh* 44, 1949, 91 ff.; add *RE* 6. 252 ff., J. André, *Lexique des termes de botanique en latin*, 1956, p. 35.

Celery was often used at symposia for garlands; cf. 4. 11. 3, Anacreon 410 ἐπὶ δ᾽ ὀφρύσιν σελίνων στεφανίσκους / θέμενοι θάλειαν ἑορτὴν ἀγάγωμεν / Διονύσῳ, Theoc. 3. 21 ff., Virg. *ecl.* 6. 68. The plant is *vivax* because it does not wither quickly; cf. Theoc. 13. 42 θάλλοντα σέλινα, Nic. *ther.* 649 ἀειφύλλοιο σελίνου.

breve lilium: the lily, unlike celery, is short-lived; cf. 2. 3. 13 f., Val. Fl. 6. 492 f. 'lilia . . . quis vita brevis totusque parumper / floret honor, fuscis et iam notus imminet alis'.

17. **putris**: languishing not with wine, as Porphyrio thinks, but with love; cf. Pers. 5. 58 'in Venerem putris', Ibycus 287. 2 τακέρ᾽ ὄμμασι δερκόμενος, Eubulus fr. 104. 7 K., Lucian, *amor.* 14, Apul. *met.* 3. 14. 5, Agathias, *anth. P.* 5. 287. 8 ὄμματι θρυπτομένῳ, Rohde, *Roman*³, p. 159 n. 2, Russell on Longinus 4. 4, West on Hes. *th.* 910.

18. **deponent oculos**: cf. Xen. *symp.* 1. 9 Αὐτολύκου τὸ κάλλος πάντων εἷλκε τὰς ὄψεις πρὸς αὐτόν. *defigent* would have been more normal, but *deponent* reinforces the languishing effect of *putris*.

19. **adultero**: ablative; Numida is hinted at.

20. **lascivis**: *libere vagantibus*. The word is artfully chosen; it suits the girl even more than the ivy. For the simile cf. *epod.* 15. 5, Eur. *Hec.* 398 ὁποῖα κισσὸς δρυὸς ὅπως τῆσδ᾽ ἕξομαι, Eubulus fr. 104. 1 ff. K. ὦ μάκαρ ἥτις . . . συνίλλεται . . . / ἡδύτατον περὶ νυμφίον εὔτριχα / κίσσος ὅπως καλάμῳ περιφύεται, Catull. 61. 33 ff., 61. 102 ff., Stat.*silv.*5. 1. 48 f., Claud. 14. 18 ff., Paul. Sil. *anth. P.* 5. 255. 13 f. ῥεῖά τις ἡμερίδος στελέχη δύο σύμπλοκα λύσει / στρεπτά, πολυχρονίῳ πλέγματι συμφυέα, Rohde, *Roman*³, p. 168 n. 2, Shakespeare, *Midsummer Night's Dream* IV. 1. 44 f. (Titania to Bottom) 'The female ivy so Enrings the barky fingers of the elm'.

ambitiosior: 'more embracing'. The long word with its startling literalness rounds off an indifferent poem magnificently. For a similar usage cf. Plin. *nat.* 5. 71 '(Iordanes) amnis . . . ambitiosus'. See also *ars* 447 f. 'ambitiosa recidet / ornamenta'; in view of *recidet* there must be a suggestion of the twining tendril.

37. NVNC EST BIBENDVM

[I. Becher, *Das Bild der Kleopatra in der griechischen und lateinischen Literatur*, 1966; S. Commager, *Phoenix* 12, 1958, 47 ff.; Fraenkel 158 ff.; J. Gwyn Griffiths, *Journal of Egyptian Archaeology* 47, 1961, 113; E. Groag, *Klio* 14,

1914–15, 57 ff.; H. U. Instinsky, *Hermes* 82, 1954, 126 ff.; La Penna 54 ff.; J. V. Luce, *CQ* N.S. 13, 1963, 251 ff.; M. L. Paladini, *Latomus* 17, 1958, 240 ff.; Pasquali 38 ff.; F. Wurzel, *Der Krieg gegen Antonius und Kleopatra in der Darstellung der augusteischen Dichter*, Diss. Heidelberg, 1941.]

1–4. *Now at last we can celebrate.* 5–12. *It was wrong to do so while Cleopatra in her madness was plotting Rome's ruin.* 12–21. *She was brought to her senses by defeat at Actium and the pursuit by Octavian, who sought to enchain her.* 21–32. *But she preferred a nobler death: she did not shrink from battle or try to escape, but killed herself with snakes rather than submit to a Roman triumph.*

This poem celebrates the suicide of Cleopatra in 30 B.C. She was descended from Alexander's marshal Ptolemy (Soter), who on the death of his master (323 B.C.) carved a kingdom for himself in Egypt. The house was therefore Macedonian by blood, but it adopted some traditional Egyptian customs, ruler-worship among others. In 52 B.C. Cleopatra succeeded her father, Ptolemy Auletes, who is much mentioned in the correspondence of Cicero; she shared the throne in turn with two younger brothers, to whom she was nominally married. She supported Julius Caesar in the Bellum Alexandrinum of 48–47, and followed him to Rome in 46; she claimed, rightly or wrongly, that Caesarion was their child (for the evidence see J. P. V. D. Balsdon, *CR* N.S. 10, 1960, 69 ff.). After the Ides of March she returned to the East, and in 41 met Antony at Tarsus. Their liaison was interrupted by his marriage to Octavia in 40, but was revived in 37. In the succeeding years they lived together in imperial magnificence at Alexandria.

The compact between Antony and Octavian expired on the last day of 33 B.C., and the long-predicted confrontation ensued. Though he now held no constitutional position Octavian dominated the senate with his armed bodyguard, and the new consuls fled to Antony together with three hundred senators. The civil conflict had begun, but it was not recognized as such: instead war was declared on Cleopatra with antique formality. By a brilliant manœuvre, which had some precedents in Roman history, Antony was not treated as a principal; he was simply deemed to have adhered to the nation's enemies (Dio 50. 6. 1). Horace does not even mention Antony, thereby obfuscating what the war was about. Cf. Dio 51. 19. 5 (describing the celebrations at the end of the campaign) τὸν γὰρ Ἀντώνιον καὶ τοὺς ἄλλους Ῥωμαίους τοὺς σὺν ἐκείνῳ νικηθέντας οὔτε πρότερον οὔτε τότε, ὡς καὶ ἑορτάζειν σφᾶς ἐπ' αὐτοῖς δέον, ὠνόμασαν.

'Huc mundi coiere manus': the dynasts clashed off Actium, on the west coast of Greece, on 2 September 31 B.C. The conflicting ships

were numbered in hundreds; vast armies supported them on shore.
It is impossible now to disentangle the tactics (cf. W. W. Tarn, *JRS*
21, 1931, 173 ff., more plausibly J. Kromayer, *Hermes* 68, 1933, 361 ff.,
G. W. Richardson, *JRS* 27, 1937, 153 ff.). The poets found Actium a
profitable subject; see *epod.* 9, Virg. *Aen.* 8. 675 ff., Prop. 3. 11 and
4. 6, [Rabirius], *Bellum Actiacum* (A. Baehrens, *poet. Lat. min.* 1
pp. 212 ff., edited most recently by G. Garuti, 1958), anon. *GLP* 113,
Paladini, loc. cit., Wurzel, loc. cit. Propertius wrote a very poetical
account (4. 6. 26 'armorum et radiis picta tremebat aqua'), but Horace
avoids such picturesque colouring. Both Virgil and Propertius mention remarkable celestial phenomena, such as have been observed
at many battles from the Milvian Bridge to Mons; but Horace
has nothing to say even about Actian Apollo. Romantic miracles
would not suit his realistic and political treatment.

It is left to other writers to describe the sensation when Cleopatra
fled, soon to be followed by Antony. The possibility of a break-out
must have been contemplated; it is significant that Antony took on
board not only sails but also his war-chest. Yet in a civil war it is
unwise to abandon an army that is still in being (Plut. *Ant.* 68. 2),
and it seems possible that Cleopatra moved too soon. Horace's
ninth epode preserves, or rather recaptures, the incredulity of the
victors: Antony's fleet has taken refuge in port, his army is largely
intact, he himself has vanished on the high seas. In our poem, which
is not primarily about Actium, he compresses all this to a single
inaccurate line, 'vix una sospes navis ab ignibus'. In fact Cleopatra
escaped with 60 ships, and Antony with others; moreover, the effect
of the fire-ships, not mentioned in the epode or in Plutarch, is
greatly exaggerated (so Virg. *Aen.* 8. 694 f., Dio 50. 34). Octavian's
own dispatch shows that the casualties were not unduly heavy, and
that most of Antony's fleet surrendered intact; cf. Plut. *Ant.* 68. 1
καὶ νεκροὶ μὲν οὐ πλείους ἐγένοντο πεντακισχιλίων, ἑάλωσαν δὲ τριακόσιοι
νῆες, ὡς αὐτὸς ἀνέγραψε Καῖσαρ. For the preservation of some ships
cf. Tac. *ann.* 4. 5. 1, Philippus, *anth. P.* 6. 236, J. Gagé, *Actiaca*,
MEFR 53, 1936, 41 ff.

Next Horace describes the pursuit. Octavian was dependent entirely on oars (Dio 50. 33. 5 τοὺς γὰρ φεύγοντας ἅτε καὶ ἄνευ ἱστίων ὄντες
καὶ πρὸς τὴν ναυμαχίαν μόνην παρεσκευασμένοι οὐκ ἐπεδίωξαν). He sent
a few ships ahead, which captured two of Antony's ships (Plut. *Ant.*
67. 2 f.), but inevitably abandoned the chase. Obviously he did not
pursue in person, and *remis adurgens* (17) is distinctly misleading;
so Flor. *epit.* 2. 21. 8 (presumably based on Livy) 'sed instare vestigiis
Caesar'. Horace's simile of the hawk and the doves lacks both truth
and humanity. Contrast Plutarch's picture of Antony sitting in the
prow with his head in his hands (67. 1), or Virgil's subtle description

of the Nile-God receiving the defeated fleet in the secluded reaches
of the Delta (*Aen.* 8. 711 ff.):

> contra autem magno maerentem corpore Nilum
> pandentemque sinus et tota veste vocantem
> caeruleum in gremium latebrosaque flumina victos.

Virgil's poetry has a whole dimension that Horace's lacks.

Octavian returned to Italy to suppress sedition (Dio 51. 4. 3–6),
and later wintered in Samos; but Horace runs together the pursuit
from Actium and the war in Egypt. Antony and Cleopatra sought
peace terms, and Octavian offered Cleopatra her kingdom if she
killed Antony (Dio 51. 6. 6, Plut. *Ant.* 73. 1). Finally, after an ineffective campaign, Alexandria capitulated on the first of August 30 B.C.;
Horace may exaggerate Cleopatra's resistance and her determination
not to run away (23 n.). Antony's suicide marks the end of the war,
but Horace must not speak of Antony. Cleopatra tried to kill herself
first by a dagger, then by hunger-strike; but by threatening her children Octavian compelled her to desist (Plut. *Ant.* 78–82). Octavian
even interviewed her personally (Flor. *epit.* 2. 21 'pulchritudo infra
pudicitiam principis fuit'). But when she was ordered to leave for
Rome in three days (Plut. *Ant.* 84. 1) she apparently killed herself.

Octavian claimed, and the world believed, that he wished to see
Cleopatra paraded at his triumph. Such a petty spectacle would
gratify his partisans, but great statesmen are surely capable of
larger views. Cleopatra was completely untrustworthy, she knew
too much, and she occupied the throne of Egypt. Obviously she had
to die. But the strangling of Caesar's mistress in the Tullianum might
seem superfluous even to Roman consciences; perhaps there were
better ways. There is no need to assume that Cleopatra was murdered, though the possibility cannot be excluded (the death of her
servants Iras and Charmion was certainly opportune). But it seems
that no excessive precautions were taken to prevent her suicide (in
similar circumstances Aemilius Paullus gave Perses a broad hint;
cf. Plut. *Paul.* 34. 2). Of course one cannot be sure that the official
story was false; all one can say is that Octavian could calculate his
interests better than most men. See further E. Groag, loc. cit., E.
Herrmann, *PhW* 51, 1931, 1100.

The story of the snakes is supported by a wealth of unsubstantial
evidence. Suetonius says *putabatur* (*Aug.* 17. 4), Plutarch shows
equally unaccustomed caution: λέγεται ... φάσκουσιν ... τὸ δ' ἀληθὲς
οὐδεὶς οἶδεν ... The trail of the snakes was detected only on the
beach, and the marks on Cleopatra's arm were very faint (*Ant.*
86. 1–3; cf. Str. 17. 1. 10, Dio 51. 14. 1, Ael. *hist. anim.* 9. 61); the
testimony of the doctor Olympus is more substantial (*Ant.* 82. 2),

but even that is not completely reliable. Snake-bite has been thought an implausibly unpleasant method of suicide, but Cleopatra's asps were Egyptian cobras, which are painless; cf. Nicander, *ther.* 187 ff. with Gow's note, Galen, *ther.* 941 (14. 237 K.), Luc. 9. 816 f. 'nulloque dolore / testatus morsus', Plut. *Ant.* 71. 4, *RE* 2 A. 524 ff., Becher, op. cit., pp. 152 f. If there is any truth in the story about Cleopatra's death it might have had religious significance (cf. Prop. 3. 11. 53 'sacris . . . colubris', T. Hopfner, *Fontes historiae religionis Aegyptiacae*, 1922–5, s.v. *serpens*, Pease on Cic. *nat. deor.* 3. 47). Snakes were associated alike with Isis (Roscher 2. 533 ff., Becher, op. cit., pp. 157 f.), and with Egyptian kings; and it has even been suggested that their bite brought apotheosis (W. Spiegelberg, *Ägypt. Mit. Sitzungsb. Münch.* 1925, 3 ff., quoting Joseph. *contra Apionem* 2. 7. 86 '(the Egyptians honour asps) quando eos qui ab istis mordentur . . . felices et deo dignos arbitrantur'). Yet this method of killing was used both for murdering enemies (Cic. *Rab. Post.* 23), and the execution of criminals (Galen, loc. cit., [Rabirius] 36–51). Besides, a Ptolemy was a god already, and needed no adventitious aids to immortality (Griffiths, loc. cit.).

The tale of Cleopatra's barbaric death was a godsend to Octavian's propaganda; it provided the perfect confirmation of his own assessment. At the triumph the queen's image was accompanied by snakes (Plut. *Ant.* 86. 3); Propertius can dutifully claim 'bracchia spectavi sacris admorsa colubris' (3. 11. 53). The account is accepted by Virgil, *Aen.* 8. 697: 'necdum etiam geminos a tergo respicit angues'. Likewise pseudo–Rabirius's poem describes the sufferings of Cleopatra's victims as she tested various poisons. The story was almost too good to be true. Perhaps it was not true.

But whatever one thinks of its historical accuracy, Horace's ode is a magnificent piece of rhetoric. The tone is political and Roman throughout. There is no languorous death-scene; the snakes are horrible and scaly to the touch; Cleopatra dies from pride and not for love. Horace uses precise and prosaic words like *privata, deduci, triumpho*. The magnanimity of 'non humilis mulier' suits the attitudes affected by the victor; cf. Plut. *Ant.* 86. 4 Καῖσαρ δὲ καίπερ ἀχθεσθεὶς ἐπὶ τῇ τελευτῇ τῆς γυναικός, ἐθαύμασε τὴν εὐγένειαν αὐτῆς, Dio 51. 14. 6 ἐκεινὴν μὲν καὶ ἐθαύμασε καὶ ἠλέησεν. Less attention is paid to Horace's gibes (*dementis, ebria, furorem, lymphatam, fatale monstrum, contaminato cum grege turpium morbo virorum*); these also have links with history, as they reflect the virulent propaganda campaign waged between Octavian and Antony (K. Scott, *MAAR* 11, 1933, 7 ff., H. Bardon, *La Littérature latine inconnue* 1, 1952, pp. 287 ff.). Even in the latter half of the poem, which alone has any magnanimity, Cleopatra commits suicide only to cheat the *carnifex*;

the crucial word *generosius* (21) is usually misunderstood. The distortion of history is perhaps almost as great as in the romantic picture. Shakespeare, following Plutarch, drew a character in depth, gay, calculating, sensuous, and untrustworthy. Horace writes as an orator: he expresses one viewpoint with astonishing power, but he does not increase our understanding of the way things happen. Cleopatra was 39 when she died, and an ugly and vindictive woman (for the numismatic evidence cf. A. B. Brett, *AJA* 41, 1937, 452 ff.); but she did not captivate two great men simply by strategic resources and political acumen.

Metre: Alcaic.

1. **nunc est bibendum**: the poem begins with an imitation (in the same metre) of Alcaeus 332 νῦν χρῆ μεθύσθην καί τινα πὲρ βίαν / πώνην, ἐπεὶ δὴ κάτθανε Μύρσιλος (πὲρ Lobel: πρὸς cod.). The educated reader, who knows the Greek original, will understand that the tyrant is dead.

Several Augustan poems describe symposia in honour of political events; the literary convention is obvious, the element of reality may be negligible. Horace's ninth epode, written immediately after Actium, finishes with an uninhibited carousal. Propertius's poem on the anniversary of the battle ends with the patriotic vow 'sic noctem patera, sic ducam carmine donec / iniciat radios in mea vina dies' (4. 6. 85 f.). Our ode avoids such frivolity, the celebrations are communal and Roman (note *Saliaribus* and *pulvinar*), and they soon give place to graver themes.

libero: 'unfettered', referring alike to the nimbleness of the dance and to Rome's freedom from Cleopatra's chains. For the transferred epithet cf. 3. 5. 22 'tergo . . . libero', Aesch. *Ag.* 328 f. ἐξ ἐλευθέρου / δέρης, Eumelus, *PMG* 696. 2 ἐλεύθερα σάμβαλ' ἔχοισα, 1. 4. 13 n.

2. **pulsanda tellus**: characteristic of an uninhibited celebration; cf. Epict. 3. 24. 8 (if somebody returns from a journey) ὀρχώμεθα καὶ κροτῶμεν ὡς τὰ παιδία, above, 1. 4. 7 n. But though stamping the ground may have been natural in rustic festivities, one must not imagine that Roman gentlemen behaved this way.

Saliaribus . . . dapibus: after his Greek opening Horace strikes a Roman note here and in *pulvinar*. The Salii were famous for their magnificent dinners; cf. Fest. 439 L. (= 329 M.) 'Salios quibus per omnis dies ubicumque manent quia amplae ponuntur cenae, si quae aliae magnae sunt, Saliares appellantur', Cic. *Att.* 5. 9. 1 'epulati essemus Saliarem in modum', Suet. *Claud.* 33. 1 'ictusque nidore prandii quod in proxima Martis aede Saliis apparabatur, deserto

tribunali ascendit ad sacerdotes unaque decubuit', Otto 306. The
Roman priestly colleges were exclusive clubs whose members made
no profession of asceticism; cf. 2. 14. 28 'pontificum potiore cenis'.
Macrobius preserves the menu of such a dinner held about 70 B.C.
(sat. 3. 13. 2); it is too long to quote here.

3. pulvinar: at the so-called *lectisternium* feasts were placed beside
couches on which were laid images of the gods. For such offerings
on occasions of national rejoicing cf. Cic. *Cat.* 3. 23, *res gest.* 9. 2,
RE 12. 1108 ff., Latte 242 ff., Ogilvie on Liv. 5. 13. 6. For the celebrations after the death of Cleopatra cf. Dio 51. 19. 5 καὶ προσεψηφίσαντο
τῷ Καίσαρι καὶ στεφάνους καὶ ἱερομηνίας πολλάς (i.e. *supplicationem
multorum dierum*). A public holiday was held in succeeding years
on August 1; cf. *fasti Amiternini, inscr. Ital.* 13. 2. 25 'feriae ex s.c.
q(uod) e(o) d(ie) imp. Caesar divi f. rempublic. tristissim[o] periculo
liberat'.

4. tempus erat: more urbane than *tempus est*; cf. Liv. 8. 5. 3, Ov. *am.*
2. 9. 24, 3. 1. 23, *trist.* 4. 8. 25, Sen. *Med.* 111, Mart. 4. 33. 4. Some
editors explain 'it has been time all along', and cite Ar. *eccl.* 877
τί ποθ' ἄνδρες οὐχ ἥκουσιν; ὥρα δ' ἦν πάλαι. But even if the imperfect
was temporal in origin, it cannot have seemed so to Horace; such
an interpretation does not suit *nunc* (one would expect *iam*), and
blurs the point of *antehac* in the next stanza.

  sodales: Horace is imitating the ὦ φίλοι of archaic Greece; cf. *epod.*
13. 3 f. 'rapiamus, amici, / occasionem de die' (where Housman's
Amici is clearly wrong).

5. antehac: Horace professed to drink Caecuban immediately after
the battle of Actium (*epod.* 9. 36); but as the symposia in both places
are purely literary, the inconsistency is easily explained.

  nefas: during the second Punic War a certain Fulvius was detected
wearing a rose-garland for a party, and was incarcerated by the
senate for the duration of hostilities (Plin. *nat.* 21. 8).

  Caecubum: regarded by some connoisseurs as the best wine of all
(1. 20. 9 n.). It came from Fundi in the reassuring countryside of
Latium, quite unlike Cleopatra's vile Mareotic (14).

6. cellis avitis: cf. Tib. 1. 10. 48, Ov. *ars* 2. 695.

  Capitolio: the site of the temple of Jupiter Optimus Maximus,
and therefore the most sacred place in Rome. Cleopatra had threatened
to dispense justice there, or so at least it was believed; cf. Dio 50. 5. 4
ὥστ' αὐτὴν καὶ τῶν Ῥωμαίων ἄρξειν ἐλπίσαι τήν τε εὐχὴν τὴν μεγίστην,
ὁπότε τι ὀμνύοι, ποιεῖσθαι τὸ ἐν τῷ Καπιτωλίῳ δικάσαι. See also Prop.
3. 11. 45 f. 'foedaque Tarpeio conopia tendere saxo, / iura dare et

statuas inter et arma Mari', Ov. *met.* 15. 827 f. 'frustraque erit illa
minata / servitura suo Capitolia nostra Canopo', Manil. 1. 918 'atque
ipsa Isiaco certarunt fulmina sistro', Luc. 10. 63, *anth. Lat.* 462. 4.

7. regina: Cleopatra is nowhere named in Augustan poetry; she is
called *regina* or *mulier* or *illa*. For *regina* cf. Cic. *Att.* 14. 8. 1, 14. 20. 2,
15. 15. 2 'reginam odi', Virg. *Aen.* 8. 696, 707, Prop. 3. 11. 39 'incesti
meretrix regina Canopi'. When Virgil in the decade after Cleopatra's
death described Dido as *regina*, readers may have noticed a parallel.
Here *regina* is effectively juxtaposed with *Capitolio*; a *rex* was
hateful to the Romans, and it was even worse to be enslaved to a
woman. Cf. *epod.* 9. 12 'emancipatus feminae', Prop. 3. 11. 49 'si
mulier patienda fuit', 3. 11. 58, 4. 6. 57, *eleg. in Maecen.* 53 f. 'hic modo
miles erat ne posset femina Romam / dotalem stupri turpis habere
sui', Manil. 1. 917, Dio 50. 24. 7 γυναικὶ ἀντ᾽ ἀνδρὸς δουλεύοντες.

dementis: we are in the world of political invective; Cicero often
attributes madness to his enemies. The adjective is defensible, if
Horace is saying that to destroy Rome would be a mad act. Yet one
expects him to say 'To think that one can destroy Rome is a sign of
madness'; if that is what he means, the transference of *dementis* to
ruinas is irrational. There is a little to be said for Arthur Palmer's
dementer (*Hermathena* 60, 1942, 98).

8. funus: often used by Cicero of national catastrophe; cf. *prov. cons.*
45 'casum illum meum funus esse reipublicae'.

imperio: cf. Flor. *epit.* 2. 21. 2 'hinc mulier Aegyptia ab ebrio
imperatore pretium libidinum Romanum imperium petit; et pro-
misit Antonius', Val. Max. 5. 2. 1 (on Coriolanus) 'funus ac tenebras
Romano imperio minitantem'.

9. contaminato . . .: cf. *epod.* 9. 13 f. '(Romanus) spadonibus / servire
rugosis potest'; the present passage may be higher in style, but
scarcely in subject-matter. For other allusions to immorality at
Cleopatra's court cf. Prop. 3. 11. 30 'et famulos inter femina trita
suos', Sen. *epist.* 87. 16 'Chelidon, unus ex Cleopatrae mollibus',
Luc. 10. 60 'Romano non casta malo', Suid. 4. 797 (λέγεται Χελίδων)
καὶ ὁ Κλεοπάτρας κίναιδος. In the ancient world Egypt had a low
moral reputation (Str. 17. 1. 11, Mart. 4. 42. 4).

grege: derogatory, as often (cf. ἀγέλη). So Mart. 3. 91. 2 'semiviro
Cybeles cum grege', Tac. *ann.* 15. 37. 8 '(Nero) uni ex illo contamina-
torum grege . . . in modum sollemnium coniugiorum denupsisset',
Suet. *Tit.* 7. 1 'exoletorum et spadonum greges'.

10. morbo: the word refers to sexual perversion; cf. Catull. 57. 6
'morbosi pariter, gemelli utrique', Sen. *epist.* 83. 20 'impudicus morbum
profitetur ac publicat', *priap.* 46. 2, Juv. 2. 17, Call. *ep.* 46. 6 τὰν

φιλόπαιδα νόσον, Lucian, am. 21 τῆς οὐδὲ ῥηθῆναι δυναμένης εὐπρεπῶς νόσου, Thes.l.L. 8. 1481. 54 ff.

virorum: the word is presumably ironical and refers to the eunuchs at Cleopatra's court (such as Mardian). For the position of eunuchs in the ancient world cf. RE Suppl. 3. 453 f., H. Herter, RLAC 4. 620 ff., M. K. Hopkins, PCPhS 189, 1963, 62 ff.

Bentley found awkwardness in the irony after so much direct offensiveness; he proposed opprobriorum for morbo virorum. Dr. Shackleton Bailey tentatively suggests a comma after turpium; he translates 'her crew of foul creatures, men only in vice' (Proceedings of Leeds Philosophical Society, vol. 10, part 3, p. 113). One would sooner dispense with the comma and explain 'foul men-only-in-perversion'; yet this may be thought more difficult than the conventional interpretation (by which morbo is taken with turpium).

10. impotens: ἀκρατής; Cleopatra had none of the self-control which the Romans so much admired. The following infinitive is a characteristic Horatian brachylogy.

12. ebria: cf. Dem. 4. 49 οἶμαι ... ἐκεῖνον μεθύειν τῷ μεγέθει τῶν πεπραγμένων, Sidon. epist. 5. 7. 4 'novis opibus ebrii'. Horace also hints at the literal meaning of the word. Antony's drunkenness was notorious, and he was forced to write an apologia 'de ebrietate sua' (Sen. epist. 83. 25, Plin. nat. 14. 148, K. Scott, CPh 24, 1929, 133 ff.). For similar aspersions on Cleopatra cf. Prop. 3. 11. 55 f. ' "non hoc, Roma, fui tanto tibi cive verenda" / dixit et assiduo lingua sepulta mero' (the drunkard queen is driven to a realization of facts just as in line 15 of our poem), Plut. Ant. 29. 1 συνεκύβευε καὶ συνέπινε. Strabo says of Octavian, reflecting contemporary propaganda, τὴν Αἴγυπτον ἔπαυσε παροινουμένην (17. 1. 11).

There may also be relevance in a Greek epigram attributed to Asclepiades or Antipater of Thessalonica; this refers to an amethyst engraved with the figure of Μέθη, and set in a ring belonging to a Queen Cleopatra (anth. P. 9. 752 εἰμὶ Μέθη τὸ γλύμμα σοφῆς χερός, ἐν δ' ἀμεθύστῳ / γέγλυμμαι· τέχνης δ' ἡ λίθος ἀλλοτρίη. / ἀλλὰ Κλεοπάτρης ἱερὸν κτέαρ· ἐν γὰρ ἀνάσσης / χειρὶ θεὸν νήφειν καὶ μεθύουσαν ἔδει). Tarn thinks that this poem refers to μέθη νηφάλιος or the divine joy of life (CAH 10. 38 f., H. Lewy, Sobria Ebrietas, Zeitschrift Neutest. Wiss. 1929, Beih. 9); in that case stories of Cleopatra's drunkenness might be a wilful misinterpretation of this symbol. However, his theory is very speculative, partly because of uncertainty about the poem's date; Gow thinks on grounds of style that the third-century Asclepiades is a more likely author than the first-century Antipater (Gow–Page 2. 148), while Cichorius refers the poem to Cleopatra Selene, the great Cleopatra's daughter (Römische Studien, 1922, pp. 331 f.). Tarn also sees a counter-blast to these stories about Cleopatra's drunkenness in *orac. Sib.* 3. 356 ff. ὦ χλιδανὴ ζάχρυσε Λατινίδος ἔκγονε 'Ρώμη, / παρθένε, πολλάκι σοῖσι πολυμνήστοισι γάμοισιν / οἰνωθεῖσα . . . (*JRS* 22, 1932, 138).

13. **vix una sospes . . .**: 'the almost total destruction of her fleet'; for the *ab urbe condita* construction cf. 1. 15. 33 f., 2. 4. 10 ff., 3. 10. 15, 4. 11. 25, K.–S. 1. 770, H.–Sz. 393 f.

14. **mentemque . . .**: for the absence of the normal caesura after the fifth syllable cf. p. xli. Some scholars explain the irregularity by the ode's early date, but a dizzy effect may be intended.

lymphatam: 'ex ebrietate vesanam' (Porphyrio); as the word suggests *lympha*, the combination with *Mareotico* produces an oxymoron. *lymphatus* normally refers to irrational panic terror (cf. νυμφόληπτος, πανικόν, Sen. *epist.* 13. 9 'nulli itaque tam perniciosi . . . quam lymphatici metus sunt'); see Gruppe 2. 829 n. 2, Roscher 3. 514 f., Pease on Cic. *div.* 1. 80.

Mareotico: Alexandria is built on a strip of land between Lake Mareotis (Mariut) and the sea (*RE* 14. 1676 f.). The lake dried up in the Middle Ages, but was flooded again during Abercrombie's operations in 1801. The area produced the most famous wine in Egypt; cf. Virg. *georg.* 2. 91 'sunt et Mareotides albae', Str. 17. 1. 14 εὐοινία τέ ἐστι περὶ τοὺς τόπους ὥστε καὶ διαχεῖσθαι (*diffundi*) πρὸς παλαίωσιν τὸν Μαρεώτην οἶνον. Horace tries to give the drink a sinister sound; cf. Gratt. 312 f. (on luxury) 'haec illa est Pharios quae fregit noxia reges, / dum servata cavis potant Mareotica gemmis'. In fact it was a light wine; cf. Athen. 33 d–e ὁ γινόμενος οἶνος κάλλιστος· λευκός τε γὰρ καὶ ἡδύς, εὔπνους, εὐανάδοτος, λεπτός, κεφαλῆς οὐ καθικνούμενος, διουρητικός (it was not strong enough for Cleopatra to offer to Caesar; cf. Luc. 10. 161 ff.). For another reference see *Pap. Fayûm* 134 (a private letter of the 4th century A.D.) ἐὰν . . . καὶ καλὸν Μαρεωτικὸν δυν[ήσε]ι μοι σειρῶσαι. Of course the tenets of Islam are different from those of the Hellenistic world; and viticulture in Egypt is now confined to districts with a predominantly Greek or Coptic population.

Perhaps Shakespeare vaguely remembered this passage; see *Antony and Cleopatra* v. ii. 280 f. 'now no more The juice of Egypt's grape shall moist this lip'. Nothing is said in Plutarch about specifically Egyptian wine.

15. **veros:** 'justified'; cf. Luc. 1. 469 'vana quoque ad veros accessit fama timores'.

17. **accipiter velut . . .**: the simile is a piece of epic convention. Cf. Hom. *Il.* 22. 139 ff., ἠΰτε κίρκος ὄρεσφιν, ἐλαφρότατος πετεηνῶν, /

ῥηιδίως οἴμησε μετὰ τρήρωνα πέλειαν· / ἡ δέ θ' ὕπαιθα φοβεῖται, ὁ δ'
ἐγγύθεν ὀξὺ λεληκὼς / τάρφε' ἐπαίσσει, Aesch. supp. 223 f., Pr. 856 ff.,
Eur. Andr. 1140 f., Ap. Rhod. 4. 485 f., Lucr. 3. 751 f., Virg. Aen.
11. 721 f. 'quam facile accipiter saxo sacer ales ab alto / consequitur
pinnis sublimem in nube columbam', Ov. fast. 2. 90 (with Bömer's
note), Sil. 4. 105 ff., Thes.l.L. 3. 1731. 57 ff., D'Arcy W. Thompson,
Glossary of Greek Birds, 1936, pp. 227 f.

18. molles: cf. τρήρωνα above, Juv. 3. 202 'molles ubi reddunt ova
columbae'. The pre-Christian world realistically associated doves
with cowardice rather than innocence; cf. 4. 4. 31 f., Varro, rust.
3. 7. 4 'nihil . . . timidius columba', Otto 88.

citus: the ancients hunted for the most part on foot, running
behind their dogs. Cf., for instance, epist. 1. 18. 51, Varro, Men. 294, 296
(Meleagri), Phaedr. app. 28. 9 'venator citus', Nemes. cyn. 2, 49
'totisque citi discurrimus arvis'.

In our context citus has caused some doubts, but they are probably
unjustified. In the first place, the word occurs in the next stanza; yet
for such repetitions cf. 1. 29. 16 n. Secondly, Octavian took eleven
months to catch up with his prey; yet one must not demand historical
precision from a patriotic poet. Thirdly, it can be argued that when
there was snow about (cf. nivalis) ancient huntsmen normally dis-
pensed with dogs (Xen. cyn. 8. 1–2, Opp. cyn. 1. 454 ff., Arr. cyn.
14. 5 f.). Yet for the use of dogs in such circumstances cf. epod. 6. 5 ff.
'nam qualis aut Molossus aut fulvus Lacon, / amica vis pastoribus, /
agam per altas aure sublata nivis / quaecumque praecedet fera'.

Wyngaarden proposed canis (see Burges's note on Aesch. Eum.
229), Peerlkamp premit, Palmer catus (Hermathena 60, 1942, 98). This
last adjective is appropriate to a stalker; it is not normally used in
the higher forms of poetry, yet see 3. 12. 10 f. 'catus idem per apertum
fugientis agitato / grege cervos iaculari'. On the other hand citus is
much better suited to the epic tone of the passage. Possibly the word
is to be taken with accipiter as well as with venator (and mollis with
leporem as well as with columbas).

20. Haemoniae: properly an area of Thessaly, but used by the
Alexandrian and Roman poets as a name for Thessaly in general
(RE 7. 2219 f.). The Thessalian snow is conventional; cf. Stat. Ach.
1. 476 f. 'quis enim Haemoniis sub vallibus alter / creverit, effossa
reptans nive?'

catenis: at a triumph the chief prisoners were led in chains; cf.
epod. 7. 7 f., epist. 2. 1. 191, Cic. Pis. 60 'vincti ante currum duces',
Prop. 2. 1. 33, Stat. silv. 3. 2. 120 'Actias Ausonias fugit Cleopatra
catenas'.

21. fatale: here 'bringing doom' rather than 'sent by the fates'. This must be the meaning of 3. 3. 19 (on Paris) 'fatalis incestusque iudex'; cf. Cic. *Pis.* 9 (on Clodius) 'a fatali portento prodigioque reipublicae', Luc. 10. 59 (on Cleopatra) 'Latii feralis Erinys'.

monstrum: a *monstrum* is a thing which *monet* (cf. *claustrum, lustrum*, etc.), i.e. a portent or something outside the norm of nature. Unlike 'monster' the word does not immediately suggest a wild animal, but such a meaning is no doubt present here; Octavian like some ancient hero cleared the world of a foul beast. *monstrum* was a common word in Latin invective; cf. Cic. *Pis.* fr. 1 'ut hoc portentum huius loci, monstrum urbis, prodigium civitatis viderem', Flor. *epit.* 2. 21. 3 'monstrum illud' (of Cleopatra), I. Opelt, *Die lateinischen Schimpfwörter*, 1965, s.v.

Yet the word may have a special point as applied to Cleopatra. Her father Ptolemy XI Neos Dionysus (Auletes) was married to his sister, Cleopatra V Tryphaena; she died between 7 August 69 and 25 February 68 (*RE* 11. 749). The famous Cleopatra was 39 at the time of her death in August 30; therefore she was probably the daughter of Cleopatra V. The only other possibility is that she was illegitimate and later legitimized (*RE* 11. 750); but this is nowhere suggested. If the famous Cleopatra was the offspring of a brother–sister union, a Roman would certainly regard her as a *monstrum*. One is only surprised that if this was the case it is not pointed out somewhere more explicitly.

quae . . .: *constructio ad sensum*; cf. Cic. *Verr.* 2. 79, K.-S. 1. 27. At this point Horace ends his invective and in three magnificent stanzas, which make the poem, describes Cleopatra's death. Note the complication of the period: there is not a really strong pause throughout the ode. Kiessling suggests that Horace had not yet gained full control over his medium, Pasquali speaks of 'immaturità giovenile . . . nella composizione e nel periodare troppo complicato', Campbell criticizes 'this long trailing sprawling invertebrate sentence'. These objections are astonishing. One should rather admire Horace's virtuosity in building so elaborate a structure in so difficult a metre with such power and precision (cf. 4. 4. 1 ff.).

generosius: editors explain that to perish was nobler than to be led in chains; cf. Dio 51. 13. 2 μυρίων θανάτων χαλεπώτερον. Yet the Latin naturally means that Cleopatra wanted a nobler death than at the hands of the executioner, the normal end of a Roman triumph; cf. Liv. 26. 13. 15 'neque vinctus per urbem Romanam triumphi spectaculum trahar, ut deinde †in carcerem† aut ad palum deligatus, lacerato virgis tergo, cervicem securi Romanae subiciam', Joseph. *bell. J.* 7. 5. 6 ἦν γὰρ παλαιὸν πάτριον περιμένειν μέχρι ἂν τὸν τοῦ στρατηγοῦ τῶν πολεμίων θάνατον ἀπαγγείλῃ τις. The sentimental and

unpolitical shrink from the notion that Octavian might have destroyed Cleopatra; yet he killed Caesarion and Antyllus (the young
son of Antony and Fulvia). In any case it is quite clear what the
Augustan poets expected; cf. Prop. 4. 6. 63 ff.: 'illa petit Nilum
cumba male nixa fugaci, / hoc unum, iusso non moritura die. / di
melius! quantus mulier foret una triumphus, / ductus erat per quas
ante Iugurtha vias'.

22. muliebriter: cf. Vell. 2. 87. 1 '(Cleopatra) expers muliebris metus
spiritum reddidit', Shakespeare, *Ant.* v. ii. 237 f. 'My resolution's
placed and I have nothing Of woman in me'.

23. expavit ensem: Horace is talking of events before the capture
of Alexandria (line 25); so the sword belongs to Octavian's invading
army, and has nothing to do with Cleopatra's attempt at suicide
(Plut. *Ant.* 79. 2).

nec latentis . . .: Cleopatra in fact thought of hauling her fleet
over the Suez isthmus to the Red Sea; however, she desisted when
the Arabs from Petra burned some of her ships (Plut. *Ant.* 69. 2 f.,
cf. Dio 51. 7. 1). Antony contemplated a voyage to Spain (Dio
51. 6. 3, Flor. *epit.* 2. 21. 9 'praeparata in Oceanum fuga'); but Cleopatra was said to have caused his ships to desert (Dio 51. 10. 4).

24. reparavit: literally 'took in exchange', and hence 'reached'. The
decisive parallel is a pastiche of grand verse in *carm. epig.* 258
'Silvano sacr., M. Vicirius Rufus v(otum) s(olvit) / quod licuit
Iunianos reparare penates'. *reparare* seems to be modelled on
ἀμείβειν or ἀλλάσσειν (so 2. 16. 19 *mutamus*). Cf. Aesch. *Th.* 304 f.
ποῖον δ᾽ ἀμείψεσθε γαίας πέδον / τᾶσδ᾽ ἄρειον, Pind. *P.* 5. 37 f. Κρισαῖον
λόφον / ἄμειψεν ἐν κοιλόπεδον νάπος, Eur. *Hec.* 482 f. ἀλλάξασ᾽ Ἅιδα
θαλάμους, Antip. Sid. *anth. P.* 9. 567. 7 Ἰταλίην ἤμειψεν. The English
expression 'to repair' is irrelevant; it is derived from French *repairer*,
late Latin *repatriare*.

25. ausa: 'enduring to' (τλᾶσα); as often the word refers to καρτερία
rather than to boldness. *et* means 'even' (in 26 it means 'and').

iacentem . . . regiam: 'the royal city prostrate in defeat'; cf. Sen.
Tro. 54 'regni iacentis', *Thes.l.L.* 7. 1. 26. 48 ff. *regiam* seems to refer
to the royal area of Alexandria (cf. the Imperial City of Pekin). This
occupied a square mile, perhaps a quarter or third of the whole
city; cf. Str. 17. 1. 8, Plin. *nat.* 5. 62. Sometimes *regia* means 'capital
city' (*epist* 1. 11. 2 'Croesi regia Sardes', Plin. *nat.* 5. 20 'Caesarea . . .
Iubae regia'); but the Ptolemies' 'capital' was the royal city rather
than Alexandria as a whole. The word here can hardly have its
usual sense of 'palace'; in that case *iacentem* would suggest that the
building had literally collapsed.

26. voltu sereno: Cleopatra concealed her intention of suicide, to which this clause naturally leads; cf. Plut. *Ant.* 83. 5 τούτοις ὁ Καῖσαρ ἤδετο παντάπασιν αὐτὴν φιλοψυχεῖν οἰόμενος, Dio 51. 13. 3 ἐπεὶ δ᾽ οὐδὲν ἐπέραινε, μεταγιγνώσκειν τε ἐπλάσατο . . . καὶ ἑκουσία τε πλεύσεσθαι ἔλεγε. Such equanimity was commended by the philosophers; cf. Cic. *Tusc.* 3. 31 (on the *voltus semper idem* and *frons tranquilla et serena* of Socrates), Pease on Virg. *Aen.* 4. 477.

fortis et . . . : a characteristic Horatian construction; cf. 1. 1. 8 n., Stat. *silv.* 3. 2. 126 'fortis et Eoas iaculo damnare sagittas'. Old editors punctuate after *fortis*; the correction, which is obvious once it is pointed out, was already made in the 15th century.

asperas: the word partly means 'fierce'; cf. 1.'23. 9 'tigris ut aspera', 1. 35. 9, 3. 2. 10. But here in combination with *tractare* there is a clear suggestion that snakes are rough to the touch (which is not in fact the case). Cf. Nic. *ther.* 157 f. αὐαλέῃσιν ἐπιφρικτὴν φολίδεσσιν / ἀσπίδα φοινήεσσαν.

27. serpentes: Horace speaks of plural snakes like Virg. *Aen.* 8. 697, Prop. 3. 11. 53, Flor. *epit.* 2. 21. 11; only one asp is mentioned by Plutarch (*Ant.* 85–6) and Dio 51. 14. 1. The double snake was a royal symbol in Egypt (Griffiths, op. cit., pp. 116 ff.). No doubt the image of Cleopatra at Octavian's triumph was portrayed with two snakes (Prop. loc. cit.).

atrum: both 'black' and 'deadly'; cf. *epod.* 17. 31 f. 'atro delibutus Hercules / Nessi cruore', Ap. Rhod. 4. 1508 μελάγχιμον ἰόν, Nic. *ther.* 243, 327, Virg. *georg.* 2. 130, Ov. *epist.* 9. 115, Sil. 3. 312, André 48 ff.

28. corpore: according to Propertius, Galen, Plutarch, and Dio the snake bit Cleopatra in the arm. Peerlkamp recorded *pectore*, which suits some ancient accounts; cf. Fulg. *aet. mund.* p. 176 'Aegyptiacam superatam reginam lactandas praebere mammas serpentibus persuasit', Ponnanus, *anth. Lat.* 274. 2 f. 'nam vivere serpens / creditur et morsu gaudens dare fata papillae', *corp. paroem. gr.* 1. 126, Walter of Châtillon 209. 518 b Migne 'lactandasque dedit hydris Cleopatra papillas', Shakespeare, *Ant.* v. ii. 309 f. 'Dost thou not see my baby at my breast That sucks the nurse asleep?' Horace is more realistic.

29. deliberata: normally *deliberare* means 'to deliberate on', but sometimes as here 'to decide on'; cf. Turp. *com.* 180 'certum ac deliberatum est me illis obsequi', Afran. *com.* 274. But the word means more than *decernere*; it suggests that the decision has been taken after weighing the pros and cons (cf. Plin. *epist.* 1. 22. 10 'deliberare vero et causas eius [sc. mortis] expendere . . . ingentis est

animi'). For similar phrases cf. Luc. 4. 533 f. 'stabat devota iuventus /
damnata iam luce ferox', Sen. *Ag.* 210, Stat. *Theb.* 12. 760.

ferocior: Horace is not contrasting Cleopatra's spirit with her
timidity at Actium: rather he is saying that her innate *ferocia* is now
increased.

30. Liburnis: fast galleys used first by the Liburnian tribe in the
coastal waters at the north of the Adriatic (Lucian, *am.* 6, App.
Illyr. 3. 7). Both sides presumably had them at Actium, but Octavian
made greater use of them: the little ships which destroyed Antony's
galleons played an important part in the legend of the battle (Dio
50. 18. 4 f.). See further *epod.* 1. 1, Prop. 3. 11. 44 '(Cleopatra dared)
baridos et contis rostra Liburna sequi', Veg. *mil.* 4. 33. At the battle
Octavian cruised in one of these ships, and afterwards they were used
in the pursuit (Plut. *Ant.* 67. 2). See further C. Torr, *Ancient ships*,
1894, pp. 16 f., R. C. Anderson, *Oared fighting ships*, 1962, pp. 31 ff.

31. privata: no longer a queen. For Cleopatra's attitude cf. Galen,
ther. 940 (14. 235 K.) ἑλομένη μᾶλλον ἔτι βασίλισσα οὖσα ἐξ ἀνθρώπων
γενέσθαι ἤπερ ἰδιώτης Ῥωμαίοις φανῆναι, Dio 51. 11. 2 ἔν τε τῷ ὀνόματι
καὶ ἐν τῷ σχήματι αὐτῆς (τῆς δυναστείας) ἀποθανεῖν ἢ ἰδιωτεύσασα ζῆν
ᾑρεῖτο. According to Plutarch (*Ant.* 85. 3) she died κεκοσμημένη
βασιλικῶς; cf. the death-scene in Shakespeare ('Give me my robe,
put on my crown').

deduci: to be taken to Rome for the triumph; therefore *triumpho*
must mean more or less *ad triumphum*. In such a context *deducere*
can only have this meaning; cf. Liv. 28. 32. 7 'quos secum in patriam
ad meritum triumphum deducere velit', *Thes.l.L.* 5. 1. 274. 51 ff. It
cannot mean 'to be led in the triumph'; for this plain *duci* is the *vox
propria*. The fact that Horace names the ships and not the soldiers
confirms that he is here talking of the voyage from Alexandria to
Rome.

32. non humilis: with the pride of a Lagid; cf. Plut. *Ant.* 85. 4
πρέποντα τῇ τοσούτων ἀπογόνῳ βασιλέων, comp. *Dem. et Ant.* 1. 3
γυναικὸς ὑπερβαλομένης δυνάμει καὶ λαμπρότητι πάντας πλὴν Ἀρσάκου
τοὺς καθ' αὑτὴν βασιλεῖς, Dio 51. 15. 4 περιφρονήσει θρασείᾳ χρησαμένη.

triumpho: the poem of triumph suitably ends with this Roman
word. For Cleopatra's attitude cf. Porph. ad loc. 'nam et Titus Livius
refert illam cum de industria ab Augusto in captivitate indulgentius
tractaretur identidem dicere solitam fuisse οὐ θριαμβεύσομαι'; so
Shakespeare, *Ant.* IV. xv. 23 ff. 'not th' imperious show Of the full-
fortuned Caesar ever shall Be broocht with me'. For similar remarks
cf. Liv. 26. 13. 15 [21 *generosius* n.], Sen. *Tro.* 150 ff. In fact
Cleopatra's effigy was carried in the triumph (Prop. 3. 11. 53 f.), and

her young children Alexander Helios and Cleopatra Selene, later
the wife of Juba (1. 22. 15 n.), were marched through the streets of
Rome. Cf. Augustus's proud boast (res gest. 4. 3) 'in triumphis meis
ducti sunt ante currum meum reges aut regum liberi novem'.

38. PERSICOS ODI

[Fraenkel 297 ff.; G. L. Hendrickson, *AJPh* 39, 1918, 32 ff.; Pasquali 324 f.;
R. Reitzenstein, *Aufsätze*, pp. 15 f.]

1–8. *I do not care for elaborate accessories when I drink. A plain
myrtle wreath suits both my slave boy and myself.*

The address to an attendant slave was a common and natural
device in Greek sympotic lyric and epigram. The theme can already
be found in Anacreon:

Ἄγε δὴ φέρ' ἡμίν, ὦ παῖ,
κελέβην . . .   (356)

Φέρ' ὕδωρ, φέρ' οἶνον, ὦ παῖ, φέρε ⟨δ'⟩ ἀνθεμόεντας ἡμὶν
στεφάνους ἔνεικον.   (396)

Pseudo-Aristotle quotes a scolion in memory of Cedon, who had
attacked the Peisistratids (*Ath. pol.* 20. 5):

Ἔγχει καὶ Κήδωνι, διάκονε, μηδ' ἐπιλήθου,
εἰ χρὴ τοῖς ἀγαθοῖς ἀνδράσιν οἰνοχοεῖν.

The formula was taken over by later poets, who wrote for a literary
public rather than for a symposium. Cf. Catull. 27. 1 f. 'minister
vetuli puer Falerni, / inger mi calices amariores', Hor. *carm.* 2. 11.
18 ff., Mart. 9. 93. 1 'addere quid cessas, puer, immortale Falernum?',
14. 170. 2, Marc. Argent. *anth.* P. 5. 110. 2 ἕνα μοι, λάτρι, δίδου κύαθον.
Sometimes the master tells the slave to do some shopping. This
element can be found in the comic poet Ephippus, where a master
asks for simple food (fr. 15 K.):

A. Ἀλλ' ἀγόρασον εὐτελῶς·
ἅπαν γὰρ ἱκανόν ἐστι. B. φράζε δή ποτε.
A. μὴ πολυτελῶς ἀλλὰ καθαρείως. ὅ τι ἂν ᾖ,
ὁσίας ἕνεκ'. ἀρκεῖ τευθίδια, σηπίδια . . .
B. ὡς μικρολόγος εἶ. A. σὺ δέ γε λίαν πολυτελής.

See also Antiphanes fr. 68 K. The theme was taken over into
Hellenistic epigram, where a small speech is sometimes put into the

master's mouth; there is a group of such poems at *anth. P.* 5. 181–5, one of them by Asclepiades (185):

> Εἰς ἀγόραν βαδίσας, Δημήτριε, τρεῖς παρ' Ἀμύντου
> γλαυκίσκους αἴτει καὶ δέκα φυκίδια·
> καὶ κυφὰς καρῖδας (ἀριθμήσει δέ σοι αὐτός)
> εἴκοσι καὶ τέτορας δεῦρο λαβὼν ἄπιθι.
> καὶ παρὰ Θαυβορίου ῥοδίνους ἐξ πρόσλαβε ...
> καὶ Τρυφερὰν ταχέως ἐν παρόδῳ κάλεσον.

Cf. also the couplet of Philodemus (*anth. P.* 11. 35. 5 f.):

> †ᾠὸν καὶ στεφάνους καὶ σάμβαλα καὶ μύρον ἡμῖν
> λάμβανε, καὶ δεκάτης εὐθὺ θέλω παράγειν.

In our poem the shopping motif is much attenuated; in the earlier lyric manner Horace is concerned about wine and garlands rather than *frutta di mare*. Somewhat similar, though more specific, is 3. 14. 17 ff. 'i pete unguentum, puer, et coronas ...'.

Horace must also have known many other epigrams, not addressed to slaves, which praised simplicity at the symposium. Reitzenstein mentions Nicaenetus's picnic poem (cf. p. 215, Giangrande, *Fond. Hardt* 15, 146). He also cites Philodemus (*anth. P.* 11. 34):

> Λευκοΐνους πάλι δὴ καὶ ψάλματα, καὶ πάλι Χίους
> οἴνους, καὶ πάλι δὴ σμύρναν ἔχειν Συρίην,
> καὶ πάλι κωμάζειν, καὶ ἔχειν πάλι διψάδα πόρνην
> οὐκ ἐθέλω· μισῶ ταῦτα τὰ πρὸς μανίην.
> ἀλλά με ναρκίσσοις ἀναδήσατε, καὶ πλαγιαύλων
> γεύσατε, καὶ κροκίνοις χρίσατε γυῖα μύροις,
> καὶ Μυτιληναίῳ τὸν πνεύμονα τέγξατε Βάκχῳ,
> καὶ συζεύξατέ μοι φωλάδα παρθενικήν.

This poem is more complex than Horace's, but some features are obviously similar.

Horace's ode has been the victim of symbolical interpretation. Pasquali, loc. cit., finds in it not merely an affirmation of Epicurean simplicity but a declaration of interest in the poetry of love and wine—'Mirto e vite, amore e convito improntano di sè tutta la poesia di Orazio ... il commensale che siede coronato di mirto e beve, è il lirico erotico e simposiaco.' Such an interpretation turns the little ode into a puzzle poem. It is true that the myrtle Horace chooses belongs to Venus; but so do the roses and the *philyra* that he rejects (cf. Cornutus, *nat. deor.* 24 τῶν γε μὴν φυτῶν ἡ μὲν μυρσίνη διὰ τὴν εὐωδίαν Ἀφροδίτης εἶναι διείληπται, ἡ δὲ φιλύρα διά τε τοὔνομα ... καὶ ἐπεὶ πρὸς τὰς στεφάνων πλοκὰς εἰώθασιν αὐτῇ μάλιστα χρῆσθαι). A poet who sets out to allegorize should allegorize less cryptically than this.

It is plainness, not association with Venus, that here commends the myrtle crown.

Fraenkel finds a different form of symbolism: Horace is showing that he approves of simplicity in literary style. It would be a poor argument against this view to suggest that Horace's style is in fact very complex. But it is relevant that nothing in the poem suggests that he is talking of style; and the closest Greek parallels are clearly talking of life. On Fraenkel's own principles we should never read into a poem anything that is derived from sources extraneous to the text; he himself points out that the Horatian ode had no title to help its elucidation. One wonders whether mere position in the book can give a poem a meaning it would not otherwise have possessed. Simplicity of life, more than simplicity of style, is a true Horatian ideal; the equally prominent poem at the beginning of book 3 is devoted almost entirely to the theme.

But the position of the ode has undoubted relevance; its elegant simplicity makes an effective contrast with the grand manner of 1. 37, and gives an agreeable and characteristic ending to the book. Such irony invites misunderstanding. Voltaire (as reported by Macleane) dismissed the poem with contempt; Macleane himself thought it 'only a good imitation of Anacreon'; L. Müller, with remarkable precision, numbered it among Horace's three least important productions (together with 3. 22 and *serm*. 1. 7). Sometimes it was felt that Horace could not have rounded off the book with so slight a poem; two odes must surely have been lost, to make the number up to forty. An obliging versifier filled the gap and enabled Horace to end, in many early nineteenth-century editions, with an address to his book:

> Te Roma cautum territat ardua:
> depone vanos invidiae metus;
> urbisque, fidens dignitati,
> per plateas animosus aude (v.l. *audi*).

But perhaps Horace was right to stop where he did.

Metre: Sapphic.

1. Persicos: Persian luxury was proverbial; cf. Xen. *Cyr.* 8. 8. 15 ἀλλὰ μὴν καὶ θρυπτικώτεροι πολὺ νῦν ἢ ἐπὶ Κύρου εἰσί, Nep. *Paus.* 3. 2 'epulabatur more Persarum luxuriosius quam qui aderant pati possent', Val. Max. 9. 1 ext. 3, Plut. *fort. Alex.* 342 a, *corp. paroem. gr.* 2. 38 Μηδικὴ τράπεζα· ἐπὶ τῶν εὐπόρων, Athen. 144–5 (citing passages from the historians).

Horace's rejection of Eastern splendours echoes a traditional

H h

theme; cf. Archil. 22 οὔ μοι τὰ Γύγεω τοῦ πολυχρύσου μέλει, anon. *anth. P.* 11. 3. 1 ff. ἤθελον ἂν πλουτεῖν, ὡς πλούσιος ἦν ποτε Κροῖσος, | καὶ βασιλεὺς εἶναι τῆς μεγάλης Ἀσίης· | ἀλλὰ ... τὴν Ἀσίην πωλῶ πρὸς μύρα καὶ στεφάνους, *Anacreontea* 7. 1 ff. οὔ μοι μέλει τὰ Γύγεω, | τῶν Σαρ-δίων τυράννου | ... ἐμοὶ μέλει μύροισιν | καταβρέχειν ὑπήνην· | ἐμοὶ μέλει ῥόδοισιν | καταστρέφειν κάρηνα. In real life the recalcitrant Cn. Piso made good use of the old commonplace; cf. Tac. *ann.* 2. 57. 5 'vox quoque eius audita est in convivio, cum apud regem Nabataeorum coronae aureae magno pondere Caesari et Agrippinae, leves Pisoni et ceteris offerrentur, principis Romani, non Parthi regis filio eas epulas dari; abiecitque simul coronam et multa in luxum addidit'.

odi: 'I reject'; the verb is not appreciably stronger than *displicent* in 2; cf. 3. 19. 21 f. 'parcentis ego dexteras / odi: sparge rosas', *epist.* 1. 14. 11, 2. 1. 101, Prop. 3. 8. 27 'odi ego quae nunquam pungunt suspiria somnos'. There is a similar use of μισῶ in Greek; cf. Eur. fr. 886, 905 μισῶ σοφιστὴν ὅστις οὐχ αὑτῷ σοφός, Call. *epig.* 28. 1 ff. ἐχθαίρω τὸ ποίημα τὸ κυκλικόν, οὐδὲ κελεύθῳ | χαίρω, τίς πολλοὺς ὧδε καὶ ὧδε φέρει· | μισέω καὶ περίφοιτον ἐρώμενον, οὐδ᾽ ἀπὸ κρήνης | πίνω· σικ-χαίνω πάντα τὰ δημόσια. For a movement of thought similar to Horace's cf. Strato, *anth. P.* 12. 200. 1 ff. μισῶ δυσπερίληπτα φιλήματα ... καὶ μὴν καὶ τὸν ... εὐθὺ θέλοντα ... οὐ πάνυ δή τι θέλω· | ἀλλὰ τὸν ἐκ τούτων ἀμφοῖν μέσον. Two Greek examples are particularly relevant as they occur in contexts expressing contempt for wealth; cf. Philodemus, p. 422 above, Parmenio, *anth. P.* 9. 43 ἀρκεῖ μοι χλαίνης λιτὸν σκέπας, οὐδὲ τραπέζαις | δουλεύσω, Μουσέων ἄνθεα βοσκόμενος. | μισῶ πλοῦτον ἄνουν, κολάκων τροφόν, οὐδὲ παρ᾽ ὀφρὺν | στήσομαι· οἶδ᾽ ὀλίγης δαιτὸς ἐλευθερίην.

puer: ὦ παῖ. The word would suit a slave of any age; yet a gar-landed wine-server is presumably a boy.

2. philyra: bast, the fine conductive membrane between the bark and cambium of the lime; it was once widely used for string and mats. In antiquity it served to bind or stitch together complicated garlands of flowers; cf. Plin. *nat.* 16. 65 'philyrae, coronarum lem-niscis celebres antiquorum honore', 21. 11 'eoque luxuria processit ut non esset gratia nisi mero folio (petals) sutilibus', Mart. 9. 90. 6, 9. 93. 5, Cornutus, p. 422 above, Gow–Page 2. 646, D.–S. 1. 1523. According to Pliny, all such ποικιλία was initiated by the garland-maker Glycera, who was eager to provide her lover, the painter Pausias, with new pictorial subjects (*nat.* 21. 4).

3. mitte sectari: for this form of prohibition cf. *epod.* 13. 7 'cetera mitte loqui', Plaut. *Persa* 207 'mitte male loqui', Ter. *Andr.* 873, 904, Lucr. 6. 1056, Ov. *met.* 3. 614, Val. Max. 7. 2 ext. 2. Our phrase is imitated in Symm. *epist.* 4. 28. 1 'omitte sectari per naturam faciliora'.

quo locorum: *quo loci* is a common locution even when there is no marked idea of 'place whither'; cf. Cic. *div.* 2. 135 'quo illa loci nasceretur', *Att.* 7. 16. 3, 8. 10, H.–Sz. 652. The plural may be more stylized; yet Plautus uses *postid locorum* (*Cas.* 120, *Poen.* 144, *truc.* 661) as well as *postidea loci* (*cist.* 784, *Stich.* 758). Horace has *ubicumque locorum* at *epist.* 1. 3. 34. For further examples see K.–S. 1. 430.

4. sera: in high summer or a little later, according to the place; the time is the same as that suggested by *sub arta vite bibentem*. The rose in Italy was normally a spring flower and died off in the heat of summer; cf. 2. 3. 13 ff., Theophr. *hist. plant.* 6. 8. 2 τὸ δὲ ῥόδον ... τελευταῖον μὲν φαίνεται, πρῶτον δ' ἀπολείπει τῶν ἐαρινῶν· ὀλιγοχρονία γὰρ ἡ ἄνθησις, Cic. *Verr.* 5. 27 'cum rosam viderat tum incipere ver arbitrabatur', Colum. 12. 28. 3 'per ver, florente rosa'. Yet Horace still promised Maecenas roses in the dog-days (3. 29. 3), and there was a late and much prized variety at Praeneste (Plin. *nat.* 21. 16, 21. 20).

Some wrongly see in our passage an instance of the common theme of winter roses, an extravagance admired by court-poets and deplored by moralists; cf. Crinagoras, *anth. P.* 6. 345. 1 f. εἴαρος ἤνθει μὲν τὸ πρὶν ῥόδα, νῦν δ' ἐνὶ μέσσῳ / χείματι πορφυρέας ἐσχάσαμεν κάλυκας, Sen. *epist.* 122. 8 'non vivunt contra naturam qui hieme concupiscunt rosam ...?', Plin. *nat.* 21. 19, Mart. 4. 22. 5 f., 4. 29. 3 f., 6. 80, 13. 127, Lucian, *Nigrin.* 31, *paneg.* 3(11). 11. 3, 2(12). 14. 1, Athen. 196 d, V. Hehn, *Kulturpflanzen und Haustiere*, 1911, p. 257, Shakespeare, *Love's Labour's Lost* 1. i. 104 ff. 'Why should I joy in an abortive birth? At Christmas I no more desire a rose Than wish a snow in May's new-fangled earth; But like of each thing that in season grows'. But such roses are described as early, not late. Horace is rejecting a much simpler and more natural luxury.

5. simplici: myrtle and myrtle only; the word keeps its literal meaning of 'singlefold'. Myrtle was sometimes intertwined with other leaves or with flowers; cf. 3. 4. 18 f. (myrtle and laurel), 3. 23. 15 f. (myrtle and rosemary), Athen. 678 d Φιλίτας δ' ἐν τοῖς Ἀτάκτοις ὑποθυμίδα Λεσβίους φησὶ καλεῖν μυρσίνης κλῶνα, περὶ ὃν πλέκειν ἴα καὶ ἄλλα ἄνθη. For a preference similar to Horace's cf. Eubulus fr. 99 K. Α. στεφάνους ἴσως βούλεσθε· πότερ' ἐρπυλλίνους / ἢ μυρτίνους ἢ τῶν †διηνθηθμένων; / Β. τῶν μυρτίνων βουλόμεθα τουτωνί· σὺ δὲ / τά γ' ἄλλα πώλει πάντα πλὴν τῶν μυρτίνων.

myrto: one of the commonest plants; for its appearance at a symposium cf. 2. 7. 23 ff., Philoxenus, *PMG* 836 a. 5 ff. εἶτ' ἔφερε στέφανον / λεπτᾶς ἀπὸ μυρτίδος εὐ/γνήτων κλαδέων δισύναπτον. The myrtle wreath was said to dispel the fumes of wine (Philonides ap. Athen. 675 e). For a picture see E. Abbe, *The Plants of Virgil's Georgics*, 1965, p. 146.

nihil adlabores sedulus curo: 'you needn't exert yourself to add anything'. To intertwine the myrtle with flowers would be a work of supererogation; this point is brought out by the prefix *ad*. The verb is attested elsewhere only at *epod.* 8. 20 and Tert. *patient.* 13. 1; neither passage is relevant.

The negative element in *nihil* is to be taken with *curo* and the accusative element with *adlabores*; cf. *carm. saec.* 11 f. 'possis nihil urbe Roma / visere maius', Cic. *epist.* 2. 8. 1 'ne illa quidem curo mihi scribas' (a passage that shares with ours the rather rare omission of *ut* after *curo*). When combined with a negative *curo* means 'I do not want', or strictly speaking 'I am not interested'; cf. Lucil. 593 'Persium non curo legere, Laelium Decumum volo'. The attitude of urbane unconcern suits the mood of the poem.

Bentley took the *nihil* entirely with *adlabores*; as a result, he felt that the sentence showed too much concern for the slave ('mirum ni Saturnalia tunc agebantur et servi dominis imperabant'). He therefore proposed *cura*, 'see to it'; cf. *serm.* 2. 6. 38 'imprimat his cura Maecenas signa tabellis'. But this may not be the place for blunt orders, 'I positively forbid you to procure fancy garlands'. Rather Horace is saying, with a characteristic shrug, 'You needn't bother'.

Fraenkel takes *nihil* entirely with *curo*, and *nihil curo* is certainly a natural turn of phrase. But here the hyperbaton puts too much emphasis on *nihil*; Fraenkel cites 2. 20. 5 ff. and 4. 6. 13 ff., but there strong emphasis is appropriate. And if *nihil* is to be taken with *curo*, the relation of *adlabores* to *myrto* becomes more difficult.

6. sedulus: to be taken with *adlabores*; the word refers to the officiousness of an over-zealous servant (cf. Porph. 'sedulus ... id est officiosus'). Some join the word with *curo*; thus L. J. D. Richardson (*Hermathena* 59, 1942, 129 ff.) paraphrases 'I am no fusspot and don't want you to add any extra elaboration'. One sees the attraction of placing a slight break at the end of the line after *adlabores*; this is no doubt one of the reasons why *curo* has been suspected. Yet *sedulus* suits an assiduous servant better than a pernickety master (a distinction obscured by the English 'fuss'); it reinforces *adlabores* admirably, whereas with the idiomatic *curo* it simply gets in the way.

7. dedecet: when combined with a negative this verb suggests positive elegance (cf. 2. 12. 17 'quam nec ferre pedem dedecuit choris'). No doubt Horace means us to think of the slave as a good-looking boy; he adds characteristically that he can still wear myrtle with some style himself.

arta vite: 'my shady pergola'; cf. Porph. 'artam vitem spissam ac per hoc umbrosam accipe', 3. 12. 11 f. 'celer arto latitantem / fruticeto excipere aprum', Caes. *Gall.* 7. 18. 3 'carros . . . in artiores silvas abdiderunt', Sen. *Oed.* 277, Tac. *Agr.* 37. 4 'artiora . . . rariores silvas'. Such bowers of vines were and remain popular in Mediterranean lands; cf. Gow on Theoc. 15. 119, *copa* 8 'triclia umbrosis frigida harundinibus', Plin. *nat.* 14. 11 'una vitis Romae in Liviae porticibus subdiales inambulationes umbrosis pergulis opacat', Colum. 11. 2. 32, Plin. *epist.* 5. 6. 36 with Sherwin-White's note, D.–S. 4. 392 f. Others think that the epithet means 'narrow' and reinforces the affectation of ἀφέλεια; but a pergola is not so luxurious an object that Horace need emphasize that he had only a little one.

INDEX NOMINVM

INDEX VERBORVM

INDEX RERVM